A Speaking Aristocracy

A Speaking Aristocracy

Transforming Public Discourse
in Eighteenth-Century Connecticut

Christopher Grasso

Published for the Omohundro Institute

of Early American History and Culture,

Williamsburg, Virginia, by the

University of North Carolina Press,

Chapel Hill and London

The Omohundro Institute
of Early American History and
Culture is sponsored jointly by
the College of William and Mary
and the Colonial Williamsburg
Foundation.

On November 15, 1996, the
Institute adopted the present
name in honor of a bequest from
Malvern H. Omohundro, Jr.

Manufactured in the
United States of America
Library of Congress
Cataloging-in-Publication Data
Grasso, Christopher.
A speaking aristocracy : transforming
public discourse in eighteenth-century
Connecticut / Christopher Grasso.
 p. cm.
Includes bibliographical references and
index.
ISBN 0-8078-2471-2 (alk. paper). —
ISBN 0-8078-4772-0 (pbk. : alk. paper)
 1. Connecticut—Intellectual life—18th
century. 2. Discourse analysis—Social
aspects—Connecticut—History—18th
century. 3. Rhetoric—Social aspects—
Connecticut—History—18th century.
4. Elite (Social sciences)—Connecticut—
History—18th century. 5. Intellectuals—
Connecticut—History—18th century.
I. Omohundro Institute of Early American
History & Culture. II. Title.
F97.G73   1999
306'.09746'09033—dc21   98-35945
                                      CIP

03 02 01 00 99   5 4 3 2 1

To the Memory of My Parents

and Charlotte F. Wing

ACKNOWLEDGMENTS

I would like to thank the following archives and libraries for permission to quote from unpublished materials: Beinecke Rare Book and Manuscript Library at Yale University, Connecticut Historical Society, Connecticut State Library, Detroit Public Library, Jones Library, Inc., Amherst, Mass., Massachusetts Historical Society, New Haven Colony Historical Society, Sterling Memorial Library at Yale University. I also wish to thank the American Antiquarian Society, Beinecke Rare Book and Manuscript Library, Yale University Library, and the Yale Art Gallery for permission to reproduce illustrations. I am also grateful for permission to reprint material that was first published as "The Experimental Philosophy of Farming: Jared Eliot and the Cultivation of Connecticut," *William and Mary Quarterly*, 3d Ser., L (1993), 502–528; "Print, Poetry, and Politics: John Trumbull and the Transformation of Public Discourse in Revolutionary America," *Early American Literature*, XXX (1995), 5–31; and "Misrepresentations Corrected: Jonathan Edwards and the Regulation of Religious Discourse," in Stephen J. Stein, ed., *Jonathan Edwards's Writings: Text, Context, Interpretation* (Bloomington, Ind., 1996), 19–38.

For financial support, I would like to thank the Charlotte W. Newcombe Foundation, which awarded me a Doctoral Dissertation Fellowship in 1990–1991, and the Pew Foundation, for a Fellowship in Religion and American History, 1994–1995. Harry Stout deserves mention here, too, for all the paying jobs, big and small, that he dug up for me in graduate school and for making my research trips back to Yale possible. Thanks to Skip and Sue Stout for welcoming me into their home.

Thanks to the staffs at the following institutions: Connecticut State Library, Connecticut Historical Society, Massachusetts Historical Society, St. Olaf College Library, New Haven Colony Historical Society, Yale University's Divinity, Law, and Forestry Libraries, Sterling Memorial Library (Manuscripts and Archives), and the Beinecke Rare Book and Manuscript Library. Thanks to John B. Hench of the American Antiquarian Society for the list of Connecticut imprints. I am grateful for the long-distance research assistance from Gail Moreau and Andrew Lewis, and for help with the graphs from Matt Ober.

Many teachers, colleagues, and friends have encouraged me along the way: Kate Umphlett, Jerry Berenty, Mark Heidmann, Leanne Smith, Bryan Wolf, and Frank Turner; my friends associated with the Works of Jonathan Edwards; my colleagues at St. Olaf College. I am grateful to the following people for reading and commenting upon portions of this work or the dissertation that preceded it: John Agnew, Patricia Bonomi, Steve Bullock, Jim Farrell, Steve Grossbart,

David Jaffee, Michael McGiffert, Ken Minkema, Jonathan Sassi, Barry Shain, Tamara Plakins Thorton, John F. Wilson, the University of Minnesota's Colonial History Workshop, and the anonymous referees of *Early American Literature, William and Mary Quarterly,* and the Omohundro Institute of Early American History and Culture. Special thanks to Fredrika Teute, for the extensive, carefully detailed, and thought-provoking commentary upon my drafts; to Virginia Chew, for meticulous copyediting of a difficult manuscript; to James Horn, for helpful suggestions in the later stages of revision; and to Kathryn Burdette, Kevin Butterfield, Robert Nelson, Sharon M. Sauder, and Robert Shaposka, for help checking citations.

The necessarily formulaic language of an Acknowledgments page makes it hard to express my appreciation to the following people. To Scott Casper, for the friendship, help, and encouragement since the early days of graduate school. To my Yale mentors Jon Butler and Harry Stout, who, in my first graduate seminars, "converted" me to the discipline of history, the colonial period, and the study of religion and since then have continued to support me in ways too numerous to mention. This book is dedicated to the memory of other mentors. Mrs. Charlotte F. Wing, by opening her library and her home to the college kid who cut her lawn, changed a life. My parents would not have guessed that the son more interested in the gym than the library would have chosen an academic life. But they were my finest teachers.

To Janet, Anna, and Daniel Grasso, I owe everything else.

CONTENTS

ILLUSTRATIONS

A Speaking Aristocracy

Introduction

The wave of religious enthusiasm that had swept through New England, the Connecticut minister declared, "loudly threatens a subversion to all peaceable Order in a Government" and casts "barefac'd Contempt . . . upon Authority both Civil and Ecclesiastical." This warning came from the Reverend Isaac Stiles, addressing a New Haven freemen's meeting on April 11, 1743. Preaching from a scriptural passage condemning hypocrisy, Stiles argued that the "New Lights" running after itinerant preachers and calling for change in local government were out to destroy the colony's Standing Order of godly magistrates and learned ministers. The civil rulers, as election day preachers liked to say, were God's vicegerents on earth; the clergymen, in the famous words of a seventeenth-century Connecticut minister, liked to see themselves as "a speaking *Aristocracy* in the face of a silent *Democracy*." Together, magistrate and minister were to lead God's People in New England. For Stiles, the challenge to the speaking aristocracy and to the state power supporting it shook the very walls of New England's Jerusalem.[1]

In the summer of 1799, another New Haven orator ridiculed new enthusiasms and complained that citizens were turning their backs on the lessons of New England's past and "the old-fashioned meeting house." But David Daggett was not a minister. He was a lawyer delivering an address on July

1. Isaac Stiles, *A Looking-Glass for Changelings: A Seasonable Caveat against Meddling with Them That Are Given to Change* . . . (New London, Conn., 1743), 21 (Stiles expressed similar sentiments in his election sermon, *A Prospect of the City of Jerusalem, in It's Spiritual Building, Beauty, and Glory* [New London, Conn., 1742]); Samuel Stone, quoted in Cotton Mather, *Magnalia Christi Americana; or, The Ecclesiastical History of New-England, from Its First Planting in the Year 1620, unto the Year of Our Lord, 1698* (1702; reprint, Hartford, Conn., 1820), I, 395; and see David D. Hall, *The Faithful Shepherd: A History of the New England Ministry in the Seventeenth Century* (Chapel Hill, N.C., 1972), 114. By "speaking aristocracy," I mean the domination of the few over the production of formal public speech and writing. This speaking aristocracy is a subset of the social elite, comprising primarily clergymen in the first half of the century and clergymen and other educated white males in the second half of the century.

Fourth; the text he "opened" was, not from Scripture, but from *Gulliver's Travels*. National politics rather than ecclesiastical schism divided the citizenry: the righteous party of "Washington, Adams and Ellsworth" stood against the "Cosmopolites," "Jacobins," and "Democrats." Magazines and newspapers rather than "Old Light" and "New Light" preaching styles were the badges of party affiliation: "The *Connecticut Journal,* the *Connecticut Courant,* or the *Centinel*" denounced what was printed in "the Aurora, the Argus and the *Bee.*" Daggett's speech, like Stiles's, rallied New England to its traditions. But the speaker, occasion, literary rhetoric, political message, and prominence given to the local press all reveal how many of those traditions had changed.[2]

A *Speaking Aristocracy* explores the ways that learned men tried to shape the broader culture of eighteenth-century New England as the style, content, and social matrix of intellectual life and public communications evolved. College-educated men like Stiles and Daggett helped to transform public speaking and writing. Even as they argued to preserve moral order and protect the status of men like themselves, they raised questions about the very nature of public persuasion. Who could speak or write with authority? What knowledge had the most social value? How might ideas best be communicated to the public? New answers to these questions, in turn, redefined the character of New England's intellectual elite. As cultural authority was reconstituted in the Revolutionary era, knowledge reconceived in the age of Enlightenment, and the means of communication radically altered by the proliferation of print, speakers and writers began to describe themselves and their world in new ways. To ground these sweeping changes in a local context and in individual experience, this book focuses on the intellectual culture of Yale College and the world of public speech, writing, and print in eighteenth-century Connecticut.

In the first half of the century, assumptions about social legitimacy, personal authority, and religious calling regulated who could speak or write to a general audience and anticipate its attention and respect. There was no aristocracy in the Old World sense, and in fact there was less difference between the elite gentleman and the common laborer in Connecticut than in most other places in the British world. But this was still a hierarchical society, and public speaking and writing was not the province of everyone. In the 1740s, Old Light antirevivalist Isaac Stiles wholeheartedly agreed with New Light opponent Jonathan Edwards's contention that a "common" person should not address "a multitude" as "a public teacher." Those who did so "clothe[d] themselves" with the

2. David Daggett, *Sun-Beams May Be Extracted from Cucumbers, but the Process Is Tedious; An Oration, Pronounced on the Fourth of July, 1799* ... (New Haven, Conn., 1799), 15–16, 18, 27.

authority proper to a minister. Even on matters unrelated to religious instruction, to address the public was to assume an authoritative voice usually reserved for the elite. Men of wealth, family connections, and military experience could command attention when they spoke at town meetings; their sons, who displayed their logic, Latin, and elocution at college commencements, showed by their speaking and writing that they were distinguished from their neighbors and prepared to be leaders in church and state. Those among the educated elite who were licensed to preach joined an order of men specifically charged to address the public. Ministers were the primary public speakers and writers in every colonial New England town's little aristocracy of elite men. The clergy's sermons were the only frequent and regular form of public communication. The specter of the illiterate lay preacher during the "Great Awakening" of the early 1740s challenged traditional assumptions about public speech and cultural authority, and it focused debate upon the role of higher learning in a religious society. Still, when the dust settled and the revival fervor cooled, the college-educated clergy continued to dominate public speech and writing through the pulpit and the press.[3]

3. Jonathan Edwards, *Some Thoughts concerning the Present Revival . . .* (1742), in Edwards, *The Great Awakening . . .* , ed. C. C. Goen, in Perry Miller et al., eds., *The Works of Jonathan Edwards,* IV (New Haven, Conn., 1972), 484, 486: "The common people in exhorting one another ought not to clothe themselves with the like authority . . . proper for ministers. . . . May a man be said to set himself up as a public teacher, when he in a set speech, of design, directs himself to a multitude, either in a meeting house or elsewhere, as looking that they should compose themselves to attend to what he has to say." See also Harry S. Stout, *The New England Soul: Preaching and Religious Culture in Colonial New England* (New York, 1986), 3. Jackson Turner Main, in *Society and Economy in Colonial Connecticut* (Princeton, N.J., 1985), describes colonial Connecticut as a relatively open society: "The people of Connecticut thus differed greatly in status at any given moment," but "the level of inequality of wealth and status did not increase and the names of men at the top rotated" (374, 381). Using the term "aristocracy" to refer to such a society, as the anonymous author of *The Security of the Rights of Citizens in the State of Connecticut Considered* (Hartford, Conn., 1792) acknowledged, could lead to some confusion without clarifying the difference between a "natural" aristocracy ("government of the best or better part") and an "artificial" aristocracy ("heredity nobility") (41n, 48n). Actually, in Connecticut, both "natural" and "artificial" characteristics (merit and family) mattered. On "aristocracy" in early America, see also Gordon S. Wood, *The Radicalism of the American Revolution* (New York, 1992), 24–42. Jane Neill Kamensky, "Governing the Tongue: Speech and Society in Early New England" (Ph.D. diss., Yale University, 1993), shows how gender, race, status, and age all rigorously determined who could speak publicly in seventeenth-century New England. Pierre Bourdieu argues that we need to look to the "complicitous silence" that keeps such an order in place. Such an analysis would discover presuppositions about gender, race, and class common to early modern Western culture generally rather than reveal much about the

After midcentury, however, newspapers, essays, and eventually lay orations began to compete with sermons for public attention, introducing new rhetorical strategies to persuade or instruct an audience. Political ideologies stressing citizen virtue and civil liberty reformulated the language of public debate. Lawyers challenged the clergy's dominance in intellectual life. Learned men with the Enlightenment's faith in progress and practical knowledge encouraged a scientific attitude. Writers in the Revolutionary era cultivated literary sensibility by publishing satirical verse and epic poetry.

In the early Republic, as the proliferation of newspapers and libraries inculcated new habits of reading and learning among mechanics and farmers, leaders of the Federalist-Congregational Standing Order focused upon the subversive potential as well as the persuasive power of the printed and spoken word. At the end of the century, Connecticut's dominant Federalists tried to tighten the bonds between the churches, the learned vocations, and New England's republican society, while Democratic-Republicans challenged such connections. Educated men on both sides, speaking and writing to instruct the public, now had to compete with other voices and address multiple audiences. Public speech and writing, understood in the early eighteenth century as the words of the authoritative few *to* the people, came to be understood by many in the Revolutionary era as the civic conversation *of* the people. Neither ministerial training nor a liberal education necessarily gave a speaker or writer a license to either instruct or express the sentiments of what had come to be called the "public mind." Yet political and religious dissenters to the Standing Order continued to complain that the state was still dominated by a speaking aristocracy intent upon silencing the voices of democracy.

The changes in both the content and form of public writing and speaking were connected to the reconstruction of the social role of the learned man and the realignment of those institutions—church, state, and college—sustaining the elite. These changes reveal reorientations of values, reconfigurations of ideas about God and man, self and society, religion and politics, knowledge and power. Old literary forms and rhetorical strategies evolved, and new ones appeared. New media developed, fundamentally altering the system of communications for an increasingly complex society and economy. A new politics emerged, based on the consent of an informed citizenry and upheld by the institutionalization of reasoned debate and the dissemination of knowledge to

---

give-and-take of debate within a particular community of speakers and writers. See Bourdieu, "Structures, Habitus, Power: Basis for a Theory of Symbolic Power," in Nicholas B. Dirks, Geoff Eley, and Sherry B. Ortner, eds., *Culture / Power / History: A Reader in Contemporary Social Theory* (Princeton, N.J., 1994), 155–199.

a vastly expanded "public." To study the eighteenth-century transformation of public speaking and writing—to explore the shifting determinations of who spoke or wrote, what they said, and how their messages were conveyed—is to confront many of the major themes that have interested historians of eighteenth-century America: the impacts of the Awakening, the Enlightenment, and the Revolution; the variously described processes of Anglicization, Americanization, democratization, and modernization; the complex relationships between piety and intellect, Protestantism and republican ideology, Puritans and Yankees.

Despite the many rich layers of scholarship devoted to these themes, the very force and apparent coherence of bold, unifying narratives have often obscured the complexity and contingency of the past. Some writers compress a century of cultural change under the rubric of "Revolution" or "Great Awakening." Others turn polemical labels like "Old Light" and "New Light" into reified categories that caricature the complex relationships between religion and politics. An important concept like the national covenant, discussed in Chapter 1, can be turned into a remarkably rigid, homogeneous formula at any given moment and then conveniently stretched to include almost any casual reference linking America and God. Authors with an eye on social history can be too eager to anticipate the *mentalité* of the market economy. Religious historians tend to read the eighteenth century as a transition from Puritanism to antebellum revivalism. For literary historians, the period often becomes a ramshackle bridge between Puritan typology and the American Renaissance.

This study tries to avoid such distortions of emphasis by placing eighteenth-century concerns and conceptual categories ahead of modern paradigms. It examines a variety of printed and manuscript sources, including sermons, essays, speeches, letters, journals, newspaper articles, and poems. These sources are approached as speech and writing emerging from a context of previous discussion embedded (at least initially) in a particular social environment and participating in a larger dialogue created by other speakers and writers. An election sermon, for example, should not be reduced to a formulaic utterance ritually delivered as part of the election day pomp and circumstance. The sermon's content may or may not have much apparent relevance to the pressing social problems of the day. But the preacher's performance is produced from a tradition of New England election sermons, and only by seeing it against the range of rhetorical variation within the genre can we determine how a particular speaker was using or breaking conventions for his own purposes. We may be far more used to seeing how a satiric poem plays upon the conventions of poetic satire, and in this case it might be more illuminating to pay attention to the immediate social context—to ask questions about the cultural work a thoroughly conventional poem may be performing for an intended audience at a particular time.

The term "discourse" in the book's subtitle deserves more attention here, because it refers to both the subject of this book and the evidence upon which it is based. "Discourse" refers to a category of sources that includes a wide range of writings. The term also implies how those writings will be approached: to read sources as discourse, Terry Eagleton has written, is to see speaking and writing as "forms of *activity* inseparable from the wider social relations between writers and readers, orators and audiences, and largely unintelligible outside the social purposes and conditions in which they were embedded." Eighteenth-century writers used the word "discourse" in reference to anything from an informal discussion to the printed texts of sermons and formal orations. That range is illustrated by a quotation from Elisha Paine, who went to the Reverend James Cogswell in 1745 to complain about a sermon. "I am come on purpose to discourse with you concerning your Sermon," Paine reportedly said. "The whole Discourse [the sermon] was nothing but Trifling; it was spending Time to prove what both Sides allowed to be true, like a young Attorney at the Bar." Eighteenth-century usage supports the modern inclination to conceive of discourse as a category that includes speech as well as writing, formal as well as informal language, the public performance as well as the private exchange.[4]

A study of discourse, therefore, may include the oral and written, the formal and informal, the public and private, but it should not obscure these im-

---

4. Terry Eagleton, *Literary Theory: An Introduction* (Minneapolis, Minn., 1983), 206; Elisha Paine, quoted in James Cogswell's sworn testimony, signed Oct. 9, 1744, in *A Letter from the Associated Ministers of the County of Windham, [Connecticut], to the People in the Several Societies in Said County* (Boston, 1745), 7. Despite a shared inclination to study "discourse," the books and articles across the academic disciplines that have been devoted to the topic define it in very different ways. See Teun A. Van Dijk, ed., *Handbook of Discourse Analysis*, I, *Disciplines of Discourse* (London, 1985); Michael Stubbs, *Discourse Analysis: The Sociolinguistic Analysis of Natural Language* (Chicago, 1983); Jonathan Potter and Margaret Wetherell, *Discourse and Social Psychology: Beyond Attitudes and Behaviour* (London, 1987); Hayden White, *Tropics of Discourse: Essays in Cultural Criticism* (Baltimore, 1978); White, *The Content of the Form: Narrative Discourse and Historical Representation* (Baltimore, 1987); Robert Wuthnow, *Meaning and Moral Order: Explorations in Cultural Analysis* (Berkeley, Calif., 1987); Wuthnow, *Communities of Discourse: Ideology and Social Structure in the Reformation, the Enlightenment, and European Socialism* (Cambridge, Mass., 1989); Michel Foucault, *The Order of Things: An Archaeology of the Human Sciences* (New York, 1971). J.G.A. Pocock discusses the history of political thought (or discourse) as written by the "Cambridge School" in *Virtue, Commerce, and History: Essays on Political Thought and History, Chiefly in the Eighteenth Century* (Cambridge, 1985), chap. 1.

portant distinctions. Theoretically broadening the field of investigation to include speech and unpublished writing as well as print does not alter the nature of the evidence. Students of New England's religious culture have stacks of sermons to read and plenty of pulpit messages to decode but far less information about how those messages were received and understood by the people in the pews. At first glance, Elisha Paine's 1745 discourse (discussion) about the Reverend James Cogswell's discourse (sermon), which counters the minister's exposition of doctrine with the rough speech of obstinate lay religiosity, seems to supply that missing response. But this conversation was recorded in—and is only available to us as—published writing. Furthermore, Paine's speech was paraphrased by Cogswell in a formal complaint against his religious opponents. The testimony was printed by the county ministerial association for distribution to the members of local churches. That Paine was a self-trained lawyer turned Separatist exhorter, that he compared Cogswell's preaching to courtroom argumentation, that he challenged the minister both privately and publicly and prompted Cogswell to respond through the mechanisms of the association and through publication—all these issues are worth pursuing if we want to understand the Paine-Cogswell exchange and, more important, the culture in which it is embedded. The student of discourse, in this case, would have to keep in mind that the informal conversation was mediated by the formal publication, the layman's speech by the minister's writing.[5]

A Speaking Aristocracy focuses primarily, but not exclusively, upon *public* discourse. In general, this means speech or writing explicitly or implicitly addressed to what Edwards had simply called the "multitude." Public discourse makes claims on the attention of its broadly defined audience by purporting to address general concerns. This definition is merely a rule of thumb. The ways that writers and speakers define and address the "public" vary with context

5. As commentators often note, some versions of modern discourse analysis in many ways resemble the ancient discipline of rhetoric. Classical, medieval, and early modern rhetorical theory approached writing and speaking as verbal actions within particular social situations, as concrete performances of writers and orators trying to persuade or instruct audiences. See James S. Baumlin, "Introduction: Positioning *Ethos* in Historical and Contemporary Theory," in Baumlin and Tita French Baumlin, eds., *Ethos: New Essays in Rhetorical and Critical Theory* (Dallas, Tex., 1994), xi–xxvii; John Bender and David E. Wellbery, "Rhetoricality: On the Modernist Return of Rhetoric," in Bender and Wellbery, eds., *The Ends of Rhetoric: History, Theory, Practice* (Stanford, Calif., 1990), 3–39; Eagleton, *Literary Theory*, 206; Teun A. Van Dijk, "Introduction: Discourse Analysis as a New Cross-Discipline," in Van Dijk, ed., *Handbook of Discourse Analysis,* I, *Disciplines of Discourse,* 1; Robert J. Connors, Lisa S. Ede, and Andrea A. Lunsford, eds., *Essays on Classical Rhetoric and Modern Discourse* (Carbondale, Ill., 1984); S. M. Halloran, "On the End of Rhetoric, Classical and Modern," *College English,* XXXVI (1975), 621–631.

and change over time and can only be described in relation to other kinds of speech and writing. Chapter 3, for example, explores the significantly different versions of Yale president Thomas Clap's argument to preserve the college as a religious seminary: an uncirculated manuscript draft, a published essay, and the manuscript text of a speech delivered to the General Assembly. Chapter 5 discusses the relationships between Ezra Stiles's private journals, scholarly correspondence, and preaching. Chapter 8 looks at how, in a tense political climate, private correspondence and speech could be recategorized as public by an unintended audience (those who overhear a private exchange or intercept a private letter and then feel justified in publicizing it). How members of the listening and reading public were affected by an essay or sermon remains a question that will be answered here, not by speculations about a broadly shared mentalité, but by examining those unrepresentative few who responded verbally: the readers and auditors who in turn became speakers and writers.[6]

Because discourse is so often reduced to a reflection of other interests, it is important to see ideological and rhetorical variation occurring *despite* similarities in educational background, social status, religious persuasion, and parochial sympathies. Although the discussion in *A Speaking Aristocracy* rests on a considerable volume and variety of eighteenth-century sources, it draws these sources primarily from an admittedly narrow band of characters: Connecticut men—many of them clergymen—who were associated with Yale College as either teachers or students. The sample is limited partly by design and partly by the facts of publication and public speaking in the eighteenth century. The primary producers of public speech and writing in southern New England were educated Anglo-American males.[7]

Two lines of inquiry—what might be called the social history of print and the cultural history of discourse—can help illuminate how public speaking and

6. See Pocock, *Virtue, Commerce, and History*, 18. On public and private, see Lawrence E. Klein, "Gender and the Public / Private Distinction in the Eighteenth Century: Some Questions about Evidence and Analytic Procedure," *Eighteenth-Century Studies*, XXIX (1995), 97–109.

7. The focus on Yale men delineates what can be called a "community of cultural production." They, of course, were not the only ones shaping public discourse. Public speech and writing could also be found in popular protests, petition drives, and parades and more informally in taverns, coffeehouses, and in the streets. Formal writings and speeches reacted to and were created within this larger sphere of dialogue. Elite writers tried to reach a public far more inclusive than the learned culture they encountered at college, although it is true that even this broader sense of audience usually excluded, outside a religious context, women, poor white men, and men of color. A generation ago, an investigation of these characters would have been labeled as another exposition of "The New England Mind." Perry Miller's major explications of the New England mind are *The New England Mind: The*

writing in Connecticut changed over the course of the eighteenth century. In 1700, information was scarce and books were expensive. Print was a far less important form of communication than personal exchanges, and the topics of public knowledge and discussion were relatively limited. Public news from outside the village was usually disseminated hierarchically, from state proclamations to colonial subjects, from pulpits to congregations, from networks of elite gentlemen to the general populace—when, that is, the elite deemed public instruction appropriate. Nonelites, though mostly literate, tended to use literacy in their daily business and private devotions and not as an opening onto high culture or the affairs of a wider world. By 1800, however, information was abundant and diverse. Printed pamphlets, newspapers, and books had become more important to the families of merchants, farmers, and artisans. People got their information from plural sources and embraced the idea that the survival of a republic depended upon an informed citizenry.[8]

Seventeenth Century (Cambridge, Mass., 1939), *The New England Mind: From Colony to Province* (Cambridge, Mass., 1953), and *Errand into the Wilderness* (Cambridge, Mass., 1956). Late-eighteenth-century writers, not just mid-twentieth-century historians like Perry Miller, spoke of a "public mind" that could be discerned in the writings of the period (see Chapter 7). At its worst, the conception of a public mind can homogenize learned culture and negate the distinction between the intellectuals' latticework of ideas and a supposedly pervasive worldview. For summaries of the long debate of Miller's ideas and those of his critics, see James Hoopes, "Art as History: Perry Miller's *New England Mind,*" 3–25, and the responses by David D. Hall, P.M.G. Harris, Margaret Sobczak, and Joyce Appleby, in *American Quarterly*, XXXIV (1982), 25–48; George Selement, "The Meeting of Elite and Popular Minds at Cambridge, New England, 1638–1645," and the responses by David D. Hall and Darrett B. Rutman, in *William and Mary Quarterly*, 3d Ser., XXXXI (1984), 32–61.

8. Richard D. Brown, *Knowledge Is Power: The Diffusion of Information in Early America, 1700–1865* (New York, 1989); see also Brown, *The Strength of a People: The Idea of an Informed Citizenry in America, 1650–1870* (Chapel Hill, N.C., 1996). The social history of print and the cultural history of discourse emerged in the 1970s as historians reapproached the relationship between elite and popular minds by pursuing something of a methodological middle way between social and intellectual history. See David D. Hall, "The World of Print and Collective Mentality in Seventeenth-Century New England," in John Higham and Paul K. Conkin, eds., *New Directions in American Intellectual History* (Baltimore, 1979), 170; see also Hall, "The Uses of Literacy in New England, 1600–1850," in William L. Joyce et al., eds., *Printing and Society in Early America* (Worcester, Mass., 1983), 1–47; Hall and John B. Hench, eds., *Needs and Opportunities in the History of the Book: America, 1639–1876* (Worcester, Mass., 1987); Hall, "On Common Ground: The Coherence of American Puritan Studies," *WMQ,* 3d Ser., XLIV (1987), 193–229; Hall, *Worlds of Wonder, Days of Judgment: Popular Religious Belief in Early New England* (New York, 1989); Robert Darnton, "What Is the History of Books?" in Cathy N. Davidson, ed., *Reading in America: Literature and Social History* (Baltimore, 1989), 27–52. Thomas Bender, however, in "The Cultures of Intellectual Life: The City and the Professions," in Higham and Conkin, eds., *New Directions in American Intel-*

This transformation cannot be seen as merely the inevitable cultural response to an abundance of print produced by a developing economy; it involved a new consciousness *about* print and public dialogue. Michael Warner has shown how the language of republican political culture constituted—and was constituted by—a whole new set of ground rules for public discourse. Print, instead of merely capturing the authoritative voice of a minister or projecting the power of the state, created an open, impersonal forum for discussion, criticism, and debate by "the public"—that is, by white male propertyholders who, no matter what their occupation and wealth, conceived of themselves no longer as silent, deferential subjects in a status hierarchy but as disinterested, virtuous republican citizens. The increased abundance, accessibility, and importance of print that Richard D. Brown has described is therefore intimately related to the new modes of discourse—and new modes of consciousness—of a new sovereign people.[9]

---

lectual History, 181–195, did not think following the French history-of-the-book approach and hunting for quantitative data on book distribution was the most fruitful way to reconnect intellectual and social history. Bender turned attention toward the social matrix of intellectual life and the changing structures of discourse shaping how writers, speakers, and their audiences shared ideas. See also Bender, *Intellect and Public Life: Essays on the Social History of Academic Intellectuals in the United States* (Baltimore, 1993).

9. See Michael Warner, *Letters of the Republic: Publication and the Public Sphere in Eighteenth-Century America* (Cambridge, Mass., 1990), which applies and modifies the theoretical model developed by Jürgen Habermas in *The Structural Transformation of the Public Sphere: An Inquiry into a Category of Bourgeois Society,* trans. Thomas Burger (Cambridge, Mass., 1989). See also Terry Eagleton, *The Function of Criticism: From "The Spectator" to Post-Structuralism* (London, 1984); Craig Calhoun, ed., *Habermas and the Public Sphere* (Cambridge, Mass., 1992); Anthony J. La Vopa, "Conceiving a Public: Ideas and Society in Eighteenth-Century Europe," *Journal of Modern History,* LXIV (1992), 79–116; La Vopa, "Herders' *Publikum:* Language, Print, and Sociability in Eighteenth-Century Germany," *Eighteenth-Century Studies,* XXIX (1995), 5–24; Dena Goodman, "Public Sphere and Private Life: Toward a Synthesis of Current Historiographical Approaches to the Old Regime," *History and Theory,* XXXI (1992), 1–20; Goodman, "Introduction: The Public and the Nation," *Eighteenth-Century Studies,* XXIX (1995), 1– 4; Nancy Fraser, "Rethinking the Public Sphere: A Contribution to the Critique of Actually Existing Democracy," in Bruce Robbins, ed., *The Phantom Public Sphere* (Minneapolis, Minn., 1993), 2–26; Margaret C. Jacob, "The Mental Landscape of the Public Sphere: A European Perspective," *Eighteenth-Century Studies,* XXVIII (1994), 95–113; Kathleen Wilson, "Citizenship, Empire, and Modernity in the English Provinces, c. 1720–1790," ibid., XXIX (1995), 69–96. Habermas's work on the public sphere has been criticized as being too idealized—not attentive enough to social structure and power relations, especially when contrasted to the work of Michel Foucault or Pierre Bourdieu. See, especially, Bourdieu, *Language and Symbolic Power,* ed. John B. Thompson, trans. Gino Raymond and Matthew Adamson (Cambridge, Mass., 1991); Dennis K. Mumby, "Two Discourses on Communication, Power, and the Subject: Jürgen Habermas and

Some of the changes that Brown and Warner discuss can be glimpsed in the record of 3,500 eighteenth-century Connecticut imprints. Most obvious is the tremendous growth in the numbers of imprints published, a growth curve that roughly resembles that of eighteenth-century America generally (see Appendix, Figures 19 and 20). The shift from the limited, authoritarian, institutional print early in the century to the growing abundance and diversity after the Revolution is also apparent and can be illustrated by comparing the Connecticut imprints from two years, 1728 and 1798. Typical of the first few decades of Connecticut printing, the 1728 list contains only a handful of imprints: a dozen pages of the colony's laws, a broadside of theses to be defended at Yale College's public commencement, an essay approved by a county ministerial association promoting regular singing in church, and 4 sermons—2 for funerals, 1 on a recent earthquake, and 1 to the General Assembly. In 1798, Connecticut presses produced 164 imprints. Church, state, and college are still well represented by sermons (25 of them and 3 volumes of collected sermons), government laws and proclamations, and the college broadside describing commencement exercises. The list also includes 10 secular orations (8 delivered on July Fourth). It contains the proceedings of the General Assembly, the congressional journal, 2 volumes of Connecticut court reports, and a handbook for justices of the peace. Pamphlets cover state politics, national politics, religious conversion, ecclesiastical controversy, land speculation, atheism, dancing, etiquette, yellow fever, and cheese making. There are books of prophecies, maxims, music, and astrology; there are textbooks, primers, almanacs, a cookbook, and 2 volumes on female education. The reader interested in verse could find clever stanzas promoting newspapers, satirical political verse, religious poems, and poetry for women. The aficionado of ecclesiastical dispute could turn to dissertations on (or against) Baptism, Presbyterianism, and Episcopalianism. Connecticut presses also issued an autobiography (Benjamin Franklin), a biography (Ezra Stiles), and a book of memoirs (George Whitefield) as well as a slave narrative, a narrative on Freemasons, a history of the Algerine captives, juvenile tales and stories, and three novels.

Publication data, like broad generalizations about structural change, can help depict the transformations of public discourse in broad strokes. But the "big picture" cannot tell us much about the eighteenth-century writer's very human struggle to articulate and persuade. *A Speaking Aristocracy* looks at how these changes were effected and experienced by people in the midst of them. It

Michel Foucault," in George Levine, ed., *Constructions of the Self* (New Brunswick, N.J., 1992), 81–104; and Habermas et al., "Concluding Remarks," in Calhoun, ed., *Habermas and the Public Sphere,* 462–479.

employs case studies of individual writers and particular public debates to show, first, how publications and speeches shaped—and were shaped in—their cultural and rhetorical contexts, second, how participation in public discourse helped constitute the social role of the learned man, and, third, how ideas about moral order these speakers and writers described changed over time. Part I, "Meaning and Moral Order," examines different ways writers depicted—and tried to regulate—moral order: the first chapter discusses covenant discourse through the colonial era, the second, the call by Jonathan Edwards and later Connecticut's Joseph Bellamy for a "purer" church after the Awakening, and, the third, Yale president Thomas Clap's legalistic efforts to secure orthodoxy. Part II, "Cultivation and Enlightenment," looks at how the new learning could reconstruct community and refashion the learned man's sense of self. Chapter 4 features the agricultural reform efforts of Jared Eliot, a clergyman and physician from Killingworth, and Chapter 5, the scholarship and preaching of Ezra Stiles. Part III, "Revolution and Steady Habits," focuses upon the relationships between politics, religion, literature, and publication in the last decades of the century. The sixth chapter centers on Revolutionary satirist John Trumbull, and the seventh on the poet and political preacher Timothy Dwight. Chapter 8 is about the links between new modes of public discourse (like secular orations and partisan newspaper commentary) and the new politics of post-Revolutionary Connecticut.

Four late-century writers illustrate some of the different ways contemporaries interpreted the changes that they witnessed. In 1787, David Daggett described for his July Fourth audience the world the Revolution had transformed:

> This state, and many others, were under a most perfect aristocracy.—The name we truly disowned, yet quietly submitted to a government essentially aristocratic.—
>
> The minister, with two or three principal characters were supreme in each town.—Hence the body of the clergy, with a few families of distinction, between whom there was ever a most intimate connection, in effect, ruled the whole state. The loss of this happy influence of the clergy, in this country, is deeply to be regretted, and is to be ascribed to two causes—the increase of knowledge, and growing opposition to religion.—Knowledge has induced the laity to think and act for themselves, and an opposition to religion has curtailed the power of its supporters.

Daggett's claim that clergymen and a few elite families ruled colonial Connecticut certainly caricatures pre-Revolutionary clerical power and elite control. Although some towns were dominated by three or four leading families, power and authority were more contested in larger towns and more diffuse in recently settled villages. The local pastor usually did form close ties with leading families, but he was not always the mouthpiece for their interests (or they the agents for his), and sometimes he got caught between contending factions. Moreover, Connecticut's democracy was hardly unthinking and never as silent as the ministerial elite might have wished. The unlettered and unwashed laity were quite capable of thinking and acting for themselves, as shown by their participation in numerous church schisms. Still, like any good caricature, Daggett's sketch exaggerates features of a recognizable figure. Although the clergy did not necessarily dictate thought and action, they did monopolize the formal means of public expression. They were indeed a speaking (and writing) aristocracy—a special order within the social and political elite Daggett describes, authorized by God, their congregations, and the state to articulate the normative ideas and values of their society. It was the loss of this monopoly rather than Daggett's alleged "growing opposition to religion" that led to their diminished (but still substantial) influence as arbiters of politics, education, literature, and manners after the Revolution. American Independence, as Daggett went on to say, had indeed opened the public stage to ambitious men eager to develop their talents and contribute to the progress of the arts and sciences, agriculture and commerce, jurisprudence and civil policy. The influence of the clerical speaking aristocracy was curtailed as public discussion drew upon an increasingly diverse array of sources beyond holy writ and men in other professions rose in status and learned to court public favor.[10]

Another orator, T. William Johnson, delivering a Phi Beta Kappa address in 1793, implied that the clerical speaking aristocracy had been replaced by an open, vibrant public sphere that might resemble the ideal of Immanuel Kant or Jürgen Habermas. Along with universal suffrage and frequent elections, this new arena of public discussion could be the basis of an egalitarian democracy: "The contests between the opposite opinions of men, in a free state, are sufficient to give the political element a salutary agitation. The eager desire to know the situation of public affairs, and to discuss the conduct of those, to whom they are intrusted, discovers vivacity and health. This engagedness and activity is the preservation of political union, though, to a superficial observer, when contrasted with the gloomy silence of despotism, it may have the appearance

---

10. David Daggett, *An Oration, Pronounced in the Brick Meeting-House, in the City of New-Haven, on the Fourth of July, A.D. 1787* (New Haven, Conn., [1787]), 6. On elite power in New England towns, see, especially, Edward M. Cook, Jr., *The Fathers of the Towns: Leadership and Community Structure in Eighteenth-Century New England* (Baltimore, 1976).

of confusion." Democracy was not—could not be—silent. The Revolution had created a political system that had opened the door to the kind of ballot-box and soapbox egalitarianism that Johnson envisioned; the explosion of print and public discussion that he witnessed might even have made this future seem likely and welcome—welcome, that is, before the caustic partisanship of the later 1790s made the contest of opinion seem much less "salutary."[11]

Walter Brewster, a shoemaker writing political essays from 1791 to 1794, however, found this supposedly open public forum fenced off by old habits and prejudices that kept all but the educated elite silent and subservient. He began writing with high hopes. This was a new age, when mechanics could write to the newspaper and intelligently discuss policy and politics. It was true that "the public mind is opposed to correction, and tenacious of its own established maxims" and that it was a difficult task to make people think for themselves. "General opinion is a stubborn thing," but a writer could break through the public's customary prejudices by appealing to the individual reader's reason. Enlightenment optimism and the new accessibility of public discourse, Brewster believed as he began his series of essays, could give men who worked with their hands a public voice and allow them to contribute—intellectually, not just physically—to the commonweal. But he soon despaired. The elite men who continued to dominate politics and public discussion only mocked or ignored him, and the laboring class did not listen: "There is scarce an old woman who knows not a sentence I have written, but exclaims, What! a man bred up to mechanical employment pretends to have common sense, and to write on the great and mysterious subjects of taxation and government! O folly." The public's deference to the speaking aristocracy proved to be an "insurmountable barrier" to his efforts at reasonable persuasion.[12]

Republican orator Abraham Bishop in 1800 was even more critical. A reconstituted "aristocracy," he charged, had created military, commercial, financial, and political systems that kept nine-tenths of the population under the yoke of the upper tenth. The majority was kept silent and docile by a "political delusion" manufactured by the artful discourse of learned men—mostly lawyers and clergymen—who in essays, orations, and sermons subtly persuaded the common people to adopt opinions and habits that perpetuated their oppression. "These great men . . . are the *best informed* men in society. They are

---

11. T. William Johnson, Phi Beta Kappa Oration, Sept. 12, 1793, Yale University Phi Beta Kappa Records, YRG 40-A-11, Manuscripts and Archives, Yale University Library, New Haven, Conn.

12. [Walter Brewster], "The Mechanick on Taxation, No. 1," *Norwich Packet* (Conn.), Apr. 4, 1792, No. 4, Apr. 16, 1792, No. 6, Sept. 13, 1792.

well versed in languages and history and political science, and are able to say *more* and argue *better* on the wrong side of the question than the people are on either side of it." A hegemony argument, we might say, and there is more to it than an opposition writer's frustration with the entrenched power of Connecticut's Federalist-Congregational Standing Order. Older patterns of power and authority might have been altered, as Daggett had argued. But the fierce contest among elites for power not only energized but polarized the public, stripping down some of the potentially rich diversity that Johnson envisioned and making it even less likely that voices like Brewster's would be heard.[13]

All four of these writers—Daggett, Johnson, Brewster, and Bishop—distort and exaggerate the power of public speaking and writing and of the people who controlled it or participated in it. Yet each conveys a partial truth about Connecticut's—and America's—cultural transformation. The pulpit no longer had the same broad authority it had in Puritan times. A dynamic public sphere had been created where the discourse *of*—not just *to*—the public was an essential component of political life. A social and intellectual elite, however, still dominated public discussion and debate and worked with increased energy to silence popular dissent. Living in neither a Puritan aristocracy nor a Yankee democracy, Connecticut speakers and writers at the end of the eighteenth century struggled to understand and give their own meaning to both New England tradition and Revolutionary change.

13. Abraham Bishop, *Connecticut Republicanism: An Oration on the Extent and Power of Political Delusion* . . . ([New Haven, Conn.?], 1800), 27. On hegemony, see Raymond Williams, *Marxism and Literature* (Oxford, 1977); and T. J. Jackson Lears, "The Concept of Cultural Hegemony: Problems and Possibilities," *American Historical Review,* XC (1985), 567–593. Working from the concept first developed by Antonio Gramsci, Williams and Lears both stress that hegemony is not just an ideology manufactured by the ruling class but a cluster of values that penetrates to the level of "common sense" and the habits of daily life for other classes as well. Abraham Bishop's *Oration Delivered in Wallingford* . . . (New Haven, Conn., 1801), described the common man in New England as shackled by an "invisible slavery," blind to his own oppression by the ruling class: "He has a master to every power and faculty, to every thought and opinion and on every subject" ([iii]).

PART 1

Meaning and Moral Order

Eighteenth-century speakers and writers often honored the memory of the first planters who established the colony of Connecticut and the charter that framed its civil institutions. Settlers from Massachusetts seacoast towns, orators recalled, had braved a howling wilderness in the 1630s, crushing Indian resistance and clearing the land. The Restoration charter of 1662 annexed the New Haven colony and consolidated a representative government that would be praised in the decades to follow as a rock of stability.

From the beginning of the eighteenth century through the end of the colonial period, Connecticut society expanded, and its institutions differentiated. Larger towns, like New London and New Haven along the coast or Middletown and Hartford along the Connecticut River, became more commercial, and social relationships within them became more complex. The colony's population grew from about thirty thousand in 1700 to more than two hundred thousand in 1780. Most of those people were farmers, many of them producing surpluses of grain and livestock for external markets by 1740. By the middle of the century, good land had become scarcer and more expensive, and increasing numbers of people migrated west and north. The West Indian trade expanded dramatically after 1750, and midcentury merchants also tried, with less success, to bypass Boston and New York and establish direct trade with Europe. After 1760, some businessmen began showing more interest in manufacturing.[1]

Despite this growth and change, some historians have considered colonial Connecticut's nickname as "the land of steady habits" appropriate. Without significant immigration, the colony's white population was not divided by ethnic and broad cultural differences; without a royal governor it remained more distant from imperial concerns and metropolitan manners; without the development of a central city or dominant port, the differences between small farm towns and the largest trading towns did not amount to a stark contrast between rural and urban life. Frequent elections and participatory, decentralized government lessened the distance between the rulers and the ruled. Despite rapid

1. The major studies of society and economy in colonial Connecticut are Oscar Zeichner, *Connecticut's Years of Controversy, 1750–1776* (Chapel Hill, N.C., 1949); Gaspare John Saladino, "The Economic Revolution in Late Eighteenth Century Connecticut" (Ph.D. diss., University of Wisconsin, 1964); Richard L. Bushman, *From Puritan to Yankee: Character and the Social Order, 1690–1765* (Cambridge, Mass., 1967); Bruce C. Daniels, *The Connecticut Town: Growth and Development, 1635–1790* (Middletown, Conn., 1979), population figures on 47; Jackson Turner Main, *Society and Economy in Colonial Connecticut* (Princeton, N.J., 1985), population figures on 13.

population growth and the expansion of trade, colonial Connecticut in the eighteenth century remained a place where the richest attained only moderate wealth, a broad middling class lived frugally but comfortably, and the poor had a better chance than in most places to improve their lot.[2]

What meaning did people find in the social structures that historians have sketched? What moral compass did the colonists use to guide them in a shifting economic environment? Historians who emphasize change and those who stress continuity share premises (usually implicit) about the relationship between social experience and cultural expression. Those who stress social stability and the continuing rhythms of agricultural life tend to highlight the perpetuation of traditional, communal values. Others, who describe dramatic changes wrought by a diversifying economy and the penetration of the market, have connected these forces to the erosion of communal sensibility and the emergence of an individualism more suited to a complex, modern society. Another line of interpretation similarly focuses upon the dislocations caused by the new market economy but explains these changes as the impetus for new forms of communalism. In each of these cases, it is assumed that particular ideologies or cultural forms are associated with particular social configurations through some kind of logical or psychological fitness. Belief systems and worldviews are thought to have implicit social and political logics that flourish in and help sustain certain social orders—evangelicalism and democracy or capitalism, for example, can be described as having "isomorphic" structures. More often the link between ideology and social reality is assumed to occur in the minds of the historical actors themselves: entrepreneurs adopt Lockean language to legitimate and rationalize their activity; sectarians join together in the comforts of Christian communalism as an antidote to the alienation and uncertainty produced by a capitalist economy.[3]

Although such sociological and social-psychological generalizations might help create narratives of broad social and cultural transformation through the centuries of Western history, they are less useful when examining specific times, places, and people. More closely examining the ideas said to be linked in iso-

2. Main, *Society and Economy in Colonial Connecticut*, 369. One cannot simply say, however, that Connecticut was a democratic, egalitarian society. Its participatory government was characterized by the electorate's deference to a small pool of leaders. The difference between rich and poor, though narrower than in other colonies, was still real and meaningful.

3. The discussion in this paragraph and the next two draws in large measure from Robert Wuthnow, *Meaning and Moral Order: Explorations in Cultural Analysis* (Berkeley, Calif., 1987). For an example of an argument about isomorphic structures, focused on a later period, see George M. Thomas, *Revivalism and Cultural Change: Christianity, Nation Building, and the Market in the Nineteenth-Century United States* (Chicago, 1989).

morphic structures, the intellectual historian finds that the concepts often do not mesh so well after all—that the relationship between Christian and civic virtue, for example, or civil and religious liberty might as easily be antagonistic as symbiotic. The biographer finds that the historical actors joining churches, leading movements, or spouting political opinions were not necessarily aware of the kinds of connections and correspondences that later interpreters posit. The individuals in the past also do not seem as apt to construct holistic world-views that coherently integrate religious, political, economic, and social ideas and behaviors; instead, people are drawn to ideas, beliefs, and practices that are often logically inconsistent if not paradoxical. In addition, the literary, religious, and cultural historians find that the materials they examine resist being reduced to mere vehicles of calculated self-interest or mystifications conjured in reaction to social anxiety.[4]

As the historical sociologist Robert Wuthnow has argued, changes in the social environment do not necessarily produce new ideologies. But when change of any sort provokes discourse about moral order—public discussion about how people ought to understand their own self-interest, their relation to their society, and their lives under the gaze of God—the door is opened for new ideas. Perhaps the perception of change merely prompts speakers and writers to reiterate traditional ideas and values, like the famous Puritan jeremiad, which repeatedly invoked the past to castigate a backsliding people. But even ritual incantations of traditional forms and ideas can take on new meaning, or at least be given a new emphasis, in a new context. Once expressed, an altered vision of moral order, or an innovative prescription for how society might achieve or sustain it, will only be perpetuated if, for whatever varied reasons and mixed motivations, some people find that it makes sense. In order to gain force as an alternative ideology, a cluster of new ideas or a new configuration of themes needs to be institutionalized—incorporated into rituals or proclaimed by the state or other organizations that regularly repeat the particular understanding of moral order in public speech and print.[5]

---

4. A good example of the ways that similar religious doctrines can have very different social and political implications in different contexts is Mary Fulbrook's *Piety and Politics: Religion and the Rise of Absolutism in England, Württemberg, and Prussia* (Cambridge, 1983).

5. Wuthnow, *Meaning and Moral Order,* 150: "Changes in the [social] environment may not affect ideologies directly, but if these changes alter the moral order, then ideologies will almost certainly be affected. What this [population ecology] conception provides is an alternative to purely subjective or social psychological conceptions of ideology. Rather than positing individual moods as the link between ideology and social structure, moral order is posited as the mediating connection. From this perspective ideologies do not arise primarily from anxieties or feelings of dislocation or other psychological needs attributed to the

When eighteenth-century New Englanders talked about moral order, the discussions never ranged very far from the public institutions designed to perpetuate it: the state, the churches, and the college founded to supply future leaders for both church and state. The first three chapters examine models of moral order embedded in these institutions and in the relationships between them: the doctrine of the "public covenant," often voiced by election day preachers through the colonial period, the call for a "purer" church made by Jonathan Edwards and his followers after the revivals of the 1740s, and the legalistic enforcement of "orthodoxy" by Thomas Clap, the president of Yale College from 1740 to 1766.

The public covenant integrated a sense of corporate identity under God, the obligations of subjects to the commonweal, and the moral authority of church and state. Its gradual deemphasis as a dominant paradigm of moral order does not signal the culture's transition from communalism to individualism. The public covenant became one formulation among others in an increasingly diverse vocabulary of identity, morality, and order. The post-Awakening debates of the 1740s weakened the covenant as a legitimation of church and state authority. The ecclesiastical disputes and French wars of the 1750s and 1760s rendered it increasingly ambiguous as a marker of broad public community. After midcentury, whig political idioms tended to supplant the public covenant as a guide to citizenship, even in clerical discourse.

The Edwardsean call for stricter requirements for church membership was an attempt to recognize institutionally the vital piety that had seemed to be in such evidence during the religious revivals of the early 1740s. But it was also a reaction to the collapse of the revival movement and an effort to restore clerical discipline over the laity. Neither a sectarian withdrawal from society nor a civil religionist's embrace of contemporary culture, the Edwardsean post-Awakening effort at ecclesiastical reform emphasized the authority of parish ministers within the established churches to regulate the meaning of religious language, and thus the boundaries of religious community. Edwardseans and their opponents engaged in arguments about the meanings of words in public religious life and about whether the speaking aristocracy of ministers or the laypersons professing their faith had the authority to define them.

Thomas Clap's efforts to legislate orthodoxy and legally secure the autonomy of Yale College were in part a reaction to the failure of the state and the individual churches to quash heterodoxy and disorder. Like the election day

---

individual. They arise instead from changes in the moral order—in public definitions of moral obligations—that make room for or necessitate new efforts to dramatize the nature of social relations."

clergymen who preached about the public covenant, and like the Edwardseans trying to tighten clerical control over the language of the church, Clap thought he could preserve moral order by controlling religious language. But he believed that neither election day rituals nor local pastors catechizing their flocks in the true meaning of public professions were enough to preserve the true faith. The clergymen themselves had to be properly trained and regulated, and the language of orthodoxy needed to be more formally institutionalized and firmly secured by the rule of law. The controversies Clap was involved in, therefore, also shed light on the reconception of the place of the law within intellectual life and the larger social order. Even before the 1770s, when Yale started to produce more graduates who became lawyers than ministers, a rapidly developing legal culture encouraged college-educated speakers and writers to draw their public arguments from legal textbooks rather than the Scriptures. Clap's own arguments for Yale as a "religious society," which were filled with legal references and citations of precedent, acknowledged the importance of the law as an intellectual discipline outside strictly clerical concerns. By contrast, the student rebellion of 1766 that forced Clap from office demonstrated the limits of his legal rhetoric. In the era of the Stamp Act riots, Clap saw his legal arguments defeated by public protest and the ritual violence of the crowd.

CHAPTER 1

The Power of the Public Covenant

Shortly before he became governor of Connecticut in 1784, Matthew Griswold took pen in hand and laboriously copied an election sermon first written and preached by Gurdon Saltonstall in 1697. Saltonstall wrote in the wake of the Glorious Revolution, as Connecticut shook off the trauma of royal tyranny under Sir Edmund Andros's regime and adjusted to its place in the new British empire; Griswold rewrote after the American Revolution, as Connecticut once again celebrated the preservation of liberty and looked toward the future within the united states of America. What kept Griswold at his desk, scrawling through more than 125 manuscript pages, copying a document that, after all, existed in print? Was Griswold paying homage to—or seeking guidance from—the past? Saltonstall himself had been called from the pulpit to occupy the governor's chair from 1707 to 1724. His administration secured passage of the Saybrook Platform in 1708, which would be Connecticut's "ecclesiastical constitution" for three-quarters of a century. Saltonstall also helped establish the colony's first printing press, which printed the Platform as well as the annual laws, proclamations, and election sermons at government expense. The Saltonstall sermon that Griswold copied, along with the text of the Platform itself and the county declarations and election sermons surrounding its ratification, printing, and distribution (1709–1714), voiced the shibboleths of Puritan public discourse: We are "a people who God hath by special favor taken to be his own Peculiar"; he brought our fathers to this wilderness to enjoy his Word; he "set New-England as a seal upon his heart." But now clearly the Lord "hath a Controversy with us," for "We are risen up a Generation that have in a great Measure forgot the Errand of our fathers." The times are corrupt, we degenerate, and an angry God has justly punished us for our sins with long droughts and early frosts, with "sickness and the sword." But if we humble ourselves before the Lord, "better mutually watch over each other," and turn from our wicked ways, there is hope. As Saltonstall wrote and Griswold rewrote, "If we are true to this Interest and Cause of God and walk in the Covenant of the Lord God of our fathers it shall be well with us."[1]

Griswold's administration of one of the new united states, still operating under the old colonial charter, began with a revision of colonial laws that silently dropped the Saybrook Platform's statements about church discipline and orthodox belief but left in place the tax support for the clergymen. Griswold's terms in office, like Saltonstall's, began with election day festivities that brought ministers and magistrates together to consult with one another, dine together, and hear the election sermon that was still printed and distributed by the government throughout Connecticut. The post-Revolutionary governor, like the colonial minister-magistrate, would hear his fellow citizens likened to God's covenant people Israel. He, too, would hear warnings about declension, calls for repentance and reformation, and hopeful prayers for the future. But he would also hear differences in biblical interpretation and political argument, changes in substance as well as style. So, as Griswold copied Saltonstall's sermon, rewriting the language of the past in a post-Revolutionary age, which passages seemed like quaint relics of a bygone era? And which seemed as powerful and relevant at the end of the eighteenth century as they might have been at the beginning?

Writers in the Reformed tradition, especially within English Puritanism, borrowed covenant terminology from the Scriptures and used it as a device for theological integration and—most prominently in New England—to encourage social cohesion. The public covenant was a powerful, biblically grounded conception of a people's collective relationship to God and moral bonds among

---

1. Matthew Griswold, MS copy of Gurdon Saltonstall, *A Sermon Preached before the General Assembly of the Colony of Connecticut* . . . (Boston, 1697), Griswold Collection of Connecticut Election Sermons, vol. IX, Beinecke Rare Book and Manuscript Library, Yale University, New Haven, Conn. (hereafter cited as Beinecke Library), 82–87 (quotations on 86–87), 94 (pagination refers to Griswold's copy); Stephen Buckingham, *The Unreasonableness and Danger of a Peoples Renouncing Their Subjection to God* (New London, Conn., 1711), 19; Samuel Whitman, *Practical Godliness the Way to Prosperity* (New London, Conn., 1714), 30; New Haven County Council Declaration, Branford, Apr. 13, 1709, in Williston Walker, *The Creeds and Platforms of Congregationalism* (1893; reprint, Boston, 1960), 512; and the preface to *A Confession of Faith* . . . (the Saybrook Platform) (New London, Conn., 1710), in Walker, *Creeds and Platforms*, 517–520. Thomas Short was the colony's first printer in 1709, but he died shortly after printing the colony's first book (the Saybrook Platform) in 1710. Timothy Green was then established as the government's printer. See J. Hammond Trumbull and Charles J. Hoadly, eds., *The Public Records of the Colony of Connecticut*, 15 vols. (Hartford, Conn., 1850–1890), V, 192, 477. For the larger political context of the Platform, see Richard R. Johnson, *Adjustment to Empire: The New England Colonies, 1675–1715* (Rutgers, N.J., 1981), 364–421.

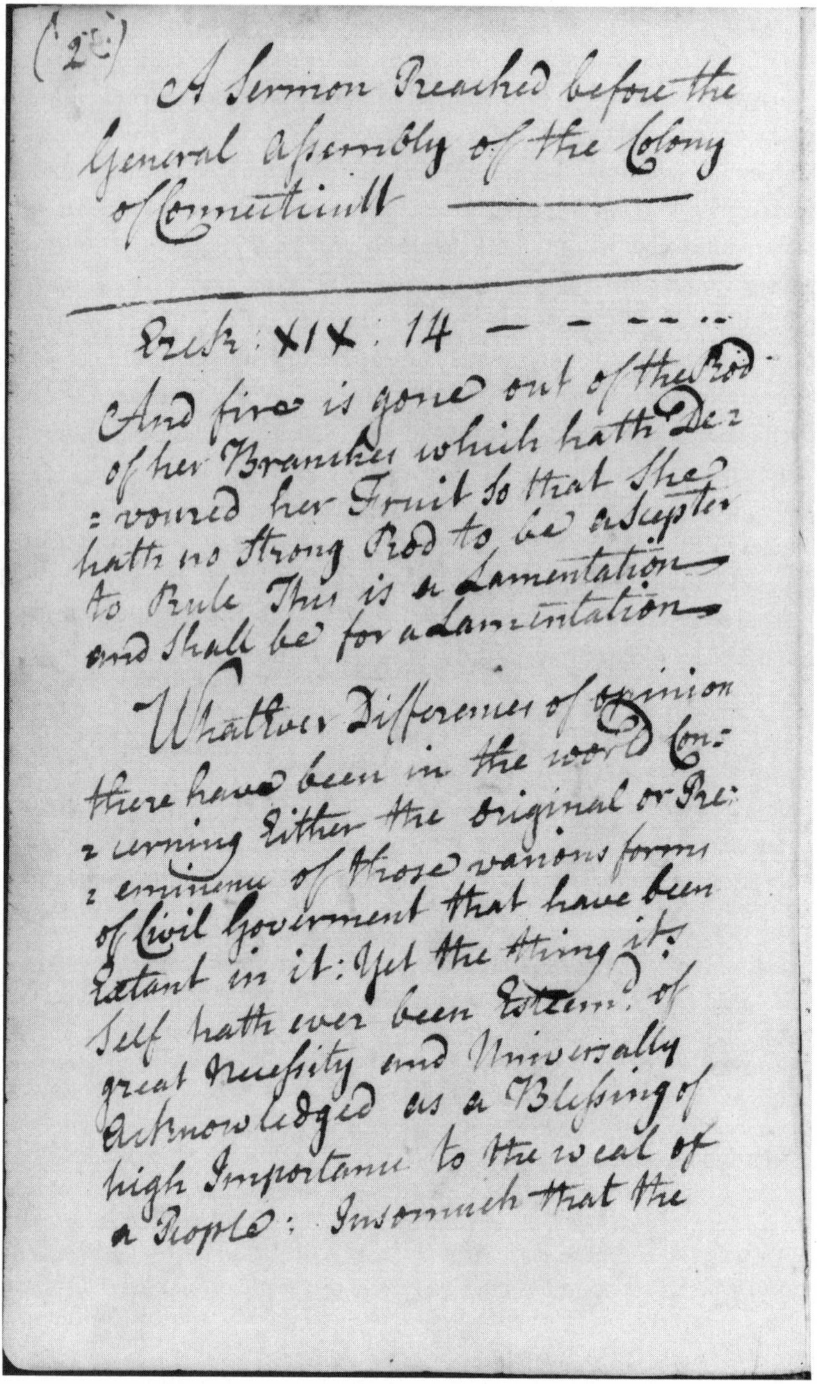

(2)

*A Sermon Preached before the
General Assembly of the Colony
of Connecticut* —

Ezek: XIX: 14 — - - - - -

And fire is gone out of the Rod
of her Branches which hath De=
=voured her Fruit so that she
hath no strong Rod to be a Scepter
to Rule This is a Lamentation
and shall be for a Lamentation

Whatever Differences of opinion
there have been in the world Con=
=cerning Either the original or Pre=
=eminence of those various forms
of Civil Government that have been
Extant in it: Yet the thing it=
self hath ever been Esteem'd of
great Necessity and Universally
Acknowledged as a Blessing of
high Importance to the weal of
a People: Insomuch that the

Figure 1. Matthew Griswold's MS copy (c. 1783) of Gurdon Saltonstall, *A Sermon Preached before the General Assembly of the Colony of Connecticut . . .* (Boston, 1697), first page. Courtesy, Beinecke Rare Book and Manuscript Library, Yale University, New Haven, Conn.

themselves. Seventeenth-century New England ministers and magistrates described their relationships to God, church, and society at large as a series of related covenants, compacts binding the parties involved by solemn promise or mutual moral obligation.[2]

The central theological doctrine concerned the Covenant of Grace. As a young Connecticut theology student named Elisha Williams explained in a 1713 manuscript treatise, the first article of this covenant, summed up in John 3:36, grants eternal life only to those individuals who believe in the Son. The saving faith fulfilling the condition of the covenant is a gift given to only the elect. The public or national covenant—the concern of this chapter—operated by a different logic. Williams's treatise referred to the public covenant as both the second article of the Covenant of Grace and as a separate but related covenant.[3]

2. Although disagreeing over the extent to which covenant theology was the marrow of Puritan divinity, no historians deny that the fast, thanksgiving, and election day invocation of the public covenant was an important staple of Puritan public discourse. See Perry Miller, *The New England Mind: The Seventeenth Century* (Cambridge, Mass., 1939); Peter Y. De Jong, *The Covenant Idea in New England Theology, 1620–1847* (Grand Rapids, Mich., 1945); John S. Coolidge, *The Pauline Renaissance in England: Puritanism and the Bible* (New York, 1970); J. Wayne Baker, *Heinrich Bullinger and the Covenant: The Other Reformed Tradition* (Athens, Ohio, 1980); Michael McGiffert, "Grace and Works: The Rise and Division of Covenant Divinity in Elizabethan Puritanism," *Harvard Theological Review*, LXXV (1982), 463–502; McGiffert, "From Moses to Adam: The Making of the Covenant of Works," *Sixteenth-Century Journal*, XIX (1988), 131–155; David Zaret, *The Heavenly Contract: Ideology and Organization in Pre-Revolutionary Puritanism* (Chicago, 1985); John Von Rohr, *The Covenant of Grace in Puritan Thought* (Atlanta, Ga., 1986); Theodore Dwight Bozeman, *To Live Ancient Lives: The Primitivist Dimension in Puritanism* (Chapel Hill, N.C., 1988); David A. Weir, *The Origins of the Federal Theology in Sixteenth-Century Reformation Thought* (Oxford, 1990), with an appendix containing an extensive bibliography of secondary works. Richard Niebuhr's often-cited "The Idea of Covenant and American Democracy," *Church History*, XXIII (1954), 126–135, ultimately suggests that the term "covenant" can be applied to any relationship defined by moral commitment rather than the mere "mutual advantage" entailed by the covenant's bastard child, the contract. This definition would be too broad for most eighteenth-century preachers.

3. Elisha Williams, "The Doctrine of the Publick Covenant between God and His People," 1713, Beinecke Library. The fullest account of Williams's life is in Glenn Weaver, "Elisha Williams: The Versatile Puritan," Connecticut Historical Society, *Bulletin*, LIII (Hartford, Conn., 1988), 119–233. The standard account is in Clifford K. Shipton, *Biographical Sketches of Those Who Attended Harvard College in the Classes 1701–1712*, Sibley's Harvard Graduates, V (Boston, 1937), 588–598. See also Francis Parsons, "Elisha Williams: Minister, Soldier, President of Yale," New Haven Colony Historical Society, *Papers*, VII (New Haven, Conn., 1908), 188–217. As Weaver notes, Shipton and other modern biographers must rely on the appendix added to James Lockwood's funeral sermon, *Man Mortal: God Everlasting . . .* (New Haven, Conn., 1756). Weaver identifies the author of that appendix as Thomas Clap

The public covenant joined God and whole societies rather than God and individuals. The condition or obligation on the human side did not require saving grace, but only obedience to God's moral law. A people or nation, Williams like many others before him explained, had no eternal existence and was therefore rewarded and punished in this world rather than the next, just as Israel was saved at the Red Sea and chastised in the wilderness. As many commentators have pointed out, these two covenants—or two branches of the one Covenant of Grace—amounted to an unstable combination of Jehovah's Old Testament tribal compact with the chosen people Israel and the New Testament's promise of salvation through Christ. Linking the eternal fate of the soul to the historical experience of the community, further complicated by church covenants that looked both to this world and the next, the covenantal system tried to connect—even as it made distinctions between—personal faith and sociopolitical practice.[4]

Although agreeing that covenant ideas were important to seventeenth-century preaching, historians have disagreed widely over the persistence and ideological significance of the public covenant in the eighteenth century. The dissolution or perpetuation of covenant discourse is often held up as the key to the religious meaning of the Revolution, the mythic basis of American character, or the transformation of a premodern to a modern worldview. Interpreters who see an eighteenth-century paradigm shift from covenant discourse to something else point to unmistakable changes in religious and political sensibility, but they also have to ignore or explain away later appearances of covenant language. Perry Miller in "From the Covenant to the Revival," for example, argued that, by the end of the eighteenth-century, clergymen "really had no way of holding the entire nation responsible for the observance of a covenant with heaven." A few pages later, he acknowledged that jeremiads "continued to be a staple in evangelical preaching" well past the 1830s, but "only as a species of utilitarian exhortation"—that is, covenant preaching lacked "the sting" it had in the past because it was devoid of "any living sense

---

(123 n. 18). For a comprehensive study of the family culture from which Williams emerged, see Kevin Michael Sweeney, "River Gods and Related Minor Deities: The Williams Family and the Connecticut River Valley, 1637–1790" (Ph.D. diss., Yale University, 1986). Historians following Perry Miller usually have spoken about two different but related covenants; Theodore Dwight Bozeman, in "Federal Theology and the 'National Covenant': An Elizabethan Presbyterian Case Study," *Church History*, LXI (1992), 394–407, argued that there was one covenant with a "bipolar thrust."

4. See David M. Scobey, "Revising the Errand: New England's Ways and the Puritan Sense of the Past," *William and Mary Quarterly*, 3d Ser., XLI (1984), 3–31.

of a specific bond between the nation and God." On the other hand, those who argue, like Sacvan Bercovitch, that the jeremiad never lost its sting or that the covenant conception remained central to America's political mythology fail to adequately explain how this ideological consensus could be perpetuated in radically different theological and social contexts.[5]

How, then, can we determine what happened to covenant discourse in the eighteenth century? One method simply looks to see whether the early language is repeated later. Indeed, some studies fasten on the mere repetition of key phrases—covenant, errand, New Israel—as evidence of ideological continuity. But that will not do. Miller, as we have seen, sensibly suggests that language can be repeated without the same meaning or impact. Bercovitch just as sensibly supposes that, even without the same words functioning as cues for a specific theological justification, the same logic—or, perhaps, the same rhetorical experience—can bear the same ideological freight (we are special; we have failed and deserve our suffering; if we recommit ourselves and change our ways, all will be well). Determining whether or not the living sense, implicit logic, taken-for-granted myth, or presupposed worldview is stable or changing by reading between the lines, however, can lead to interpretive anarchy,

---

5. Perry Miller, "From the Covenant to the Revival," in Miller, *Nature's Nation* (Cambridge, Mass., 1967), 110, 115. T. H. Breen, in *The Character of the Good Ruler: A Study of Puritan Political Ideas in New England, 1630–1730* (New York, 1970), argued that covenant terminology ceased to be effective by the early 1700s. Perry Miller, especially in *Jonathan Edwards* (1949; reprint, Amherst, Mass., 1981), pointed to the revivals of the early 1740s as a major break from the corporate covenant. However, in "From the Covenant to the Revival," Miller argued that covenant preaching was the central mechanism of social cohesion through the American Revolution. Mark A. Noll, "Jonathan Edwards and the Transition from Clerical to Political Leadership in New England's Intellectual History," paper presented at the conference, "The Writings of Jonathan Edwards: Text and Context, Text and Interpretation," Bloomington, Ind., June 2–4, 1994, argued for a dramatic shift away from covenant language between 1745 and 1755. Sacvan Bercovitch's *American Jeremiad* (Madison, Wis., 1978) showed the jeremiad (the three-part rhetorical form based upon the covenant) wriggling free from its covenantal moorings during the Revolutionary period to shape the public discourse of American national identity. Harry S. Stout, "The Puritans and Edwards," in Stout and Nathan O. Hatch, eds., *Jonathan Edwards and the American Experience* (New York, 1988), concluded that the national covenant remained in place as the primary source of corporate identity at least through the end of the eighteenth century. Other studies claim that the covenant had a prominent role in American religious nationalism through the Civil War. See, for example, Drew Gilpin Faust, *The Creation of Confederate Nationalism: Ideology and Identity in the Civil War South* (Baton Rouge, La., 1988); and Mitchell Snay, *Gospel of Disunion: Religion and Separatism in the Antebellum South* (New York, 1993).

where ideas float free from both textual evidence and historical context. What is needed is a more discriminating approach to the biblical doctrines, sermon forms, and scriptural themes so often blurred in studies of myth and civil religion.[6]

Although not the only way preachers linked religion and politics in public discourse, the public covenant was, to be sure, a remarkably integrative doctrine. It explained God's superintendence of the community, defined New England's corporate identity in biblical terms, legitimated the church's and the state's close moral supervision of society, and connected the subject's social and political obligations to his or her local involvement with the church and personal relationship with Christ. But the propositions it contained were neither unique to covenant preaching nor necessarily bound together. The doctrine of the public covenant contains or implies three main propositions: God punishes and rewards corporate morality; New England or America has a special status among nations; church and state must cooperate closely to maintain moral order under the covenant. Each of these three propositions could be made without any necessary linkage to the covenant, and each had a different trajectory through the eighteenth century. The way that God rewards and punishes corporate bodies—the logic behind the rhetoric of the jeremiad—did not have to be grounded in a special covenant relation between Jehovah and a new Israel. An alternate explanation, which became increasingly common before midcentury and predominant afterward, described the pattern of God's universal moral law, his providential treatment of any and all nations. The notion of New England's (or later America's) special status as a chosen nation, which served as a counterpoint to the providential universalism just described, was often a variant of, but not an essential aspect of, the national covenant. The idea waxed and waned through the eighteenth century, but in general historians have overemphasized it. Although the loose analogy to Israel was a commonplace, by 1760 the theological assertion that New England was an elect nation with its own covenant was not. The proposition about the close cooperation between church and state's being necessary to maintain the moral order demanded by God's covenant was successfully attacked after the Awak-

6. Mythic themes are discussed in Conrad Cherry, ed., *God's New Israel: Religious Interpretations of American Destiny* (Englewood Cliffs, N.J., 1971); and Ernest Lee Tuveson, *Redeemer Nation: The Idea of America's Millennial Role* (Chicago, 1968). The civil religion hypothesis, applied to the colonial period, is best represented by Catherine L. Albanese, *Sons of the Fathers: The Civil Religion of the American Revolution* (Philadelphia, 1976). For a sound critique of civil religion, see John F. Wilson, *Public Religion in American Culture* (Philadelphia, 1979).

ening. If not destroyed by post-Awakening argument, the public covenant certainly lost a good deal of its political sting.[7]

By the American Revolution, the public covenant had been superseded as an explanation of God's rule by a more universally administered providence. It had become increasingly awkward as a depiction of corporate identity. Who was in the covenant? New England? Great Britain, too? The thirteen colonies? It was no longer effectively used to legitimate moral regulations and the union of church and state.

Just as the religious and political language of moral order during the first half of the century should not be described as merely the lingering of a monolithic Puritan idiom, neither is the discourse of the latter half of the century accurately depicted by a new synthesis, whether created by an evangelical millennialism thrust forward during the Awakening or by a civil religion emerging during the Anglo-French wars or the Revolution. The striking thing about the period between the 1750s and the early 1780s is the increasingly diverse ways writers linked religion and politics. One line of argument emphasized the details of secular politics and the affairs of state; another minimized the affairs of state and focused on the progress of the church in Christ's work of Redemption. The themes of sacred liberty and Christian virtue allowed writers to conflate scriptural themes with whig thought and classical republicanism.

Eighteenth-century election sermons might seem to be an odd place to look for this diversity and dynamic change. Delivered as part of the annual election day ritual by prominent ministers chosen by the governor and General Assembly, election sermons almost always eschewed innovation. Preachers explained that they stood in the election day pulpit, not to instruct, but to remind the audience of what was already known. Some even apologized when time constraints prevented them from going through the entire list of usual themes. Election preachers might touch upon particular policies and issues in their conclusions, but the body of their sermons dwelled upon the general values at the crossroads of religion and politics. They drew from familiar references—the Bible, New England history, praise for the British constitution. They articulated what they hoped was a consensus and then challenged a community to live up to these fundamental values as sacred duties. The ritual that brought ministers and magistrates together, its institution as an annual occasion tying

---

7. A fourth proposition: people in a covenanted nation have a special status whether they are personally church members or not. The relationship between the national covenant and church membership will be discussed in Chapter 2.

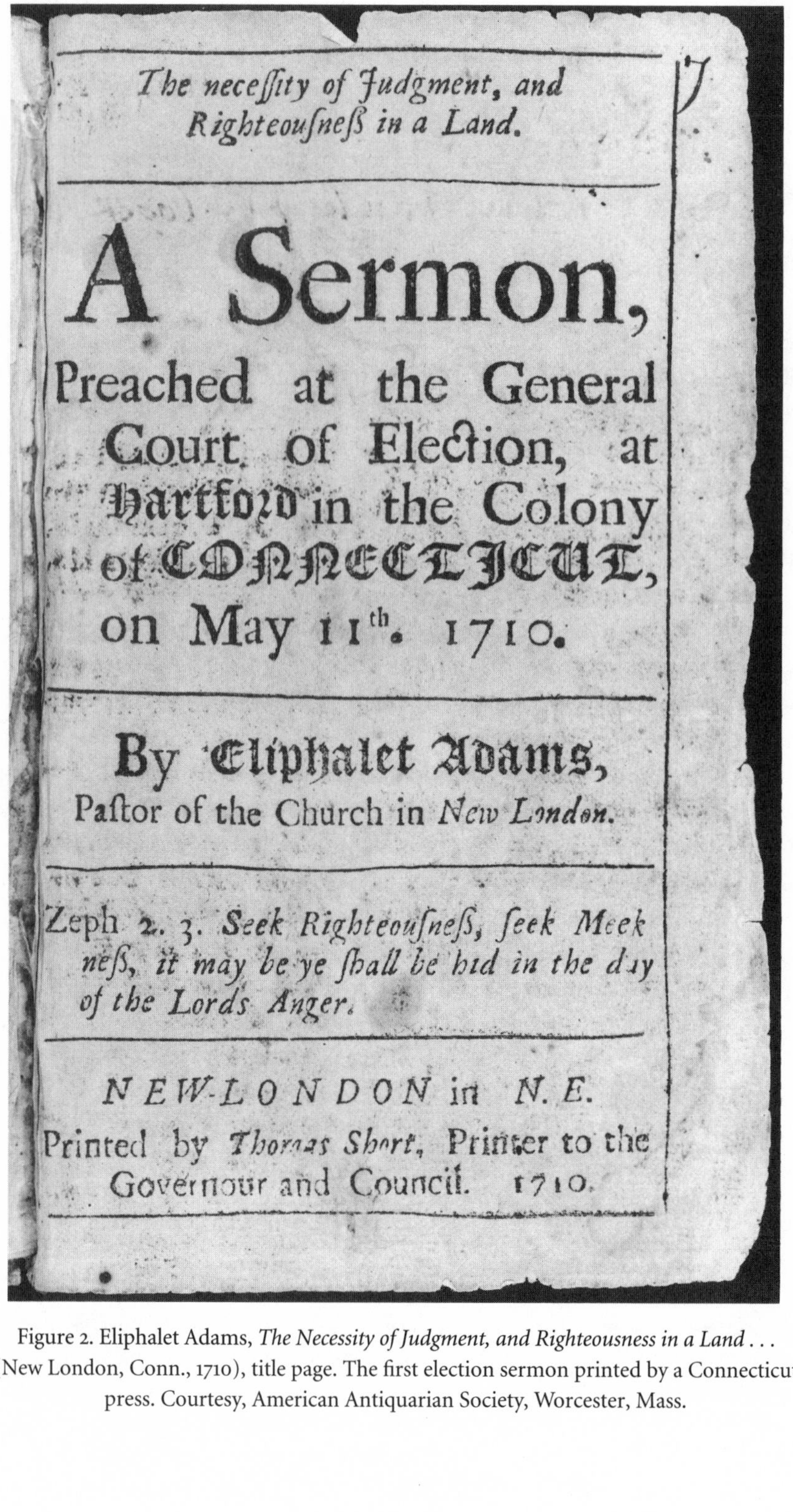

The necessity of Judgment, and Righteousness in a Land.

A Sermon,

Preached at the General Court of Election, at 𝕳𝖆𝖗𝖙𝖋𝖔𝖗𝖉 in the Colony of 𝕮𝕺𝕹𝕹𝕰𝕮𝕿𝕵𝕮𝖀𝕿, on May 11th. 1710.

By 𝕰𝖑𝖎𝖕𝖍𝖆𝖑𝖊𝖙 𝕬𝖉𝖆𝖒𝖘,

Paſtor of the Church in *New London.*

Zeph 2. 3. *Seek Righteouſneſs, seek Meekneſs, it may be ye ſhall be hid in the day of the Lords Anger.*

N E W-L O N D O N in *N. E.*
Printed by *Thomas Short,* Printer to the Governour and Council. 1710.

Figure 2. Eliphalet Adams, *The Necessity of Judgment, and Righteousness in a Land . . .* (New London, Conn., 1710), title page. The first election sermon printed by a Connecticut press. Courtesy, American Antiquarian Society, Worcester, Mass.

the present to the past, and the sermon itself all expressed the interrelatedness of (and divine sanction for) civil and ecclesiastical power.[8]

The distribution of the printed sermons to the colony's Assembly members and ministers was yet another symbolic expression of power and authority. It reflected what Richard D. Brown has described as the hierarchic diffusion of knowledge in early America: "This approach, which relied on networks of gentlemen, . . . was simply part of a political outlook that recognized the elite as the active, initiating element in the body politic—that is, as leaders—and the general population as followers. . . . If the [election day] message was to reach the general public at all, it was only through the medium of town leaders who might, if they chose, read the sermon aloud in a private prayer meeting, a tavern, or in a meetinghouse." The sermons were also advertised for purchase, singly and collected in bound volumes, and other ministers sometimes preached election day sermons to their local congregations, sermons that remained unpublished but could draw upon the printed texts. Along with other occasional sermons that could have a political cast—especially fast, thanksgiving, and militia sermons—and despite their intent to ritually reproduce traditional values and beliefs, election sermons show how new ideas could be absorbed and domesticated by being grounded in tradition and how old ideas, by emphasis or context, could serve new functions.[9]

8. The first systematic analysis of New England election sermons, Alice M. Baldwin's still valuable *New England Clergy and the American Revolution* (Durham, N.C., 1928), speaks of seventeenth- and eighteenth-century election sermons as a relatively undifferentiated whole. The best studies are the introduction to A. W. Plumstead, ed., *The Wall and the Garden: Selected Massachusetts Election Sermons, 1670–1775* (Minneapolis, Minn., 1968), although the tone, emphasis, and timing of change is different for Connecticut sermons; Martha Louise Counts, "The Political Views of the Eighteenth Century New England Clergy as Expressed in Their Election Sermons" (Ph.D. diss., Columbia University, 1956); and Jonathan Douglas Sassi, "To Envision a Godly Society: The Public Christianity of the Southern New England Clergy (Congregationalism)" (Ph.D. diss., University of California, Los Angeles, 1996).

9. Richard D. Brown, *Knowledge Is Power: The Diffusion of Information in Early America, 1700–1865* (New York, 1989), 33. Baldwin, *New England Clergy*, 5–6, 6n–7n, discusses the dissemination of election sermons and their influence. One of printer Timothy Green's advertisements is in Moses Dickinson, *A Sermon Preached before the General Assembly of the Colony of Connecticut* . . . (New London, Conn., 1755), 58. Every annual election sermon from 1710 to 1800 was published, except for the years 1729, 1735, 1739, 1743, and 1782 (see Appendix 2). Elisha Williams preached to the fall session of the General Assembly in 1727, published as *Divine Grace Illustrious, in the Salvation of Sinners* (New London, Conn., 1728). In "Elisha Williams," Conn. Hist. Soc., *Bull.*, LIII (1988), 154, Weaver notes that the legislators ordered "an unusually large edition of 700 copies" but that sales were "disappointingly small." I make no claims about how the content of these sermons, by their repetition and

Election sermons contain more rhetorical and ideological variation than descriptions of the covenant as a consensual myth suggest. They did reaffirm the idea that God looked upon New Englanders as members of a single corporate body and that he was involved in their collective historical experience. But the lessons about New England's corporate identity and the logic of God's involvement could vary with regard to three themes. A clergyman who considered New England an elect nation might argue that God had given New England a special commission, a peculiar errand in redemptive history, and thus had raised it above all other Christian nations. A minister emphasizing universal providence, on the other hand, would show how God's moral government of New England exemplified his universal rule of conduct toward all nations and peoples. Between the extremes of providential universalism and New England exceptionalism, a preacher adhering more closely to "Deuteronomic covenantalism" would hold that God treats New England and other Protestant nations equally but distinct from the heathen and apostate world, just as he distinguished the Jewish nation from the Gentile world before the coming of Christabel.[10]

All three versions of God's relationship to New England were voiced in Connecticut election sermons between 1700 and 1740. The vision of New England as an elect nation, a covenant people on a special errand for God, had been developed to its fullest in the second-generation jeremiads of the 1660s through the 1680s, when Indians destroyed towns on the frontier during King Philip's War and the restored monarchy first reined in and then, under the brief Andros regime, took over the colonial governments. As Sacvan Bercovitch has shown, the Puritan errand was an especially powerful fusion of providential

---

diffusion, were internalized by the public consciousness; they will be taken as a particular kind of state-sanctioned clerical discourse.

10. A preacher's emphasis upon New England's unique errand, or upon its status as simply one of the Protestant nations in covenant, or upon its place as merely one of many corporate bodies under God's universal providence, was often a rhetorical choice, not necessarily the marker of a rigid doctrinal distinction. A minister could talk about New England's errand on one occasion and universal providence the next. Still, these choices described New England identity and God's rule over the moral world in different ways, and change in emphasis over time suggests altered understandings and shifts in values.

history (the rise and fall of nations in the cycles of time) and redemptive history (the progress of the church and the gathering of the elect to eternal life). The idea of the special errand persisted beyond the era of Indian raids, the threat to New England's charters, and the expeditions against French Canada into the second quarter of the eighteenth century. The later sermons, though, lacked the sense of immediacy, the sense of God speaking directly to New England through the Scriptures, that one finds in the earlier jeremiads.[11]

By the 1730s, with Connecticut troubled by currency problems and land disputes rather than French and Indian wars or royal threats to its chartered privileges, Eliphalet Adams was giving the impression that New England's errand had become a tale told too often. What had been a powerful reinforcement of corporate identity against external dangers was slowly falling from fashion in the election day pulpit as a stale rhetorical device. Adams tried to defend its use. Preachers in decades past, he wrote, "would Expatiate largely upon and often refresh the Memories of the People therewith." Adams endorsed their repetition by likening them to the "Divine Writers," who in biblical book after book return to "the Story of God's dealing with the *People of Israel* . . . till some might be ready to think that it was worn threadbare and become quite impertinent." Adams suggested another reprint of past election sermons so "that we might know at least, what sense of things the faithful servants of the Lord had in those times." Four years later, printer Timothy Green advertised a three-volume set, but, by this time, the election sermon had already become some-

11. Connecticut's first published election sermon, by John Norton, described New England as *Sion the Out-cast Healed of Her Wounds* (Boston, 1661). Samuel Wakeman's New England, in *Sound Repentance* (Boston, 1685), was no longer the "Out-cast" but was still distinguished from England within a larger parallel to Old Testament history: "*Israel* was Gods peculiar People of all the world, so *Judah* was the best part of *Israel,* and *Jerusalem* the chief place of *Judah: Jerusalem* then was God's special peculiar People." God's "special peculiar People" in his seventeenth-century New England Jerusalem did not just apply Old Testament teachings to contemporary situations when the circumstances seemed similar. God applied the Word to *them,* as immediately and directly as he did to his first chosen people. "Jerusalem was, New-England is, they were, you are Gods own, Gods Covenant People," Wakeman argued from Jer. 6:8 (6, 18). No eighteenth-century election day preacher would approach the exegetical effort of Samuel Hooker in *Righteousness Rained from Heaven* . . . (Cambridge, Mass., 1677) or Samuel Wakeman in 1685. For eighteenth-century Connecticut sermons that stressed New England's errand, see Buckingham, *The Unreasonableness and Danger;* William Burnham, *God's Providence in Placing Men in Their Respective Stations and Conditions* . . . (New London, Conn., 1722); Thomas Buckingham, *Moses and Aaron; God's Favour to His Chosen People, in Leading Them by the Ministry of Civil and Ecclesiastical Rulers* . . . (New London, Conn., 1729), preached 1728.

thing of an inbred generic form, with preachers quoting and referring to little else besides previous election sermons.[12]

Not all sermons arrogantly declared the region's chosen status, however, sugarcoating the public covenant with pretensions of exceptionalism. The idea that Christian peoples and nations were in covenant with God and were subject to God's temporal rewards and punishments according to their obedience was embedded in Reformed tradition. As Theodore Dwight Bozeman has argued, this "Deuteronomic covenant" (which Bercovitch dismissed as a "European" interpretation) shaped the New England founders' understanding of their experience more than any exclusive mission for world Redemption. This interpretation, which gives New England a more modest role within international Protestantism, can be found both before and after the great New England jeremiads of the late seventeenth century.[13]

Writing within the Deuteronomic tradition, Elisha Williams, the theology student who wrote a twelve-chapter treatise, "The Doctrine of the Publick Covenant," in 1713, argued that New England was in covenant with God only as part of Great Britain. Deut. 5:2 showed that God had a public covenant with Israel. He then asserted that all "professing gentile Nations are also in relation to God as Israel was" (Eph. 2:14, describing Christ's breaking down the walls separating the Jews from other people). Christian nations are grafted onto the tree of Abraham, and so "the promises and Threatenings that were propounded To the people of Israel are propounded To us also." Each "distinct professing Kingdom and commonwealth" has its own separate (though identical) covenant with God: Great Britain has one, Geneva another, and so on. Although there is a single "catholic" visible church in the world, "an aggregate body comprehending all the professors of the True Religion," this universal church is not "one Political Body under one Government." No single temporal institution had the power to punish sins and correct errors in each particular part of the whole church. God's public covenants, therefore, are tied to each body politic, with each having its own separate tally sheet of divine punishments and rewards. As Williams explained, the public sins of Christians in one nation could not be held against Christians living in another: "If the Church of Geneva Carry corruptly That dont make us Guilty in New England." Colonies

12. Eliphalet Adams, *A Discourse Shewing That So Long as There Is Any Prospect of a Sinful People's Yielding Good Fruit Hereafter, There Is Hope That They May Be Spared . . .* (New London, Conn., 1734), 45, preached 1733; see also 26–27.

13. Bozeman, *To Live Ancient Lives*, 151–152, notes that the Puritan national covenant remained in the "magisterial mainstream" of Reformed tradition and contrasts it with the Lutheran conception of the church as a small community of believers within a larger community defined by the civil state.

or provinces, though, no matter how distant, shared in the blessings and punishments meted out to the mother country. It is true, Williams argued, that particular cities or colonies may receive special blessings for their holiness or that people in New England were "more abundantly Guilty of our own Iniquities than the kingdom of England is." But New England did not have its *own* covenant, because God covenants with the whole body politic, not with individual towns, counties, or provinces.[14]

Williams's 1713 treatise, like an increasing number of election sermons after it, lacked the New England chauvinism that marked errand sermons and Cotton Mather's *Magnalia Christi Americana* (1702). It was the product of a time when young, ambitious scholars like Williams were growing up, not as Zion's outcasts, but with closer ties to British commerce and culture. Williams himself, a young Harvard graduate living in Wethersfield, Connecticut, was not cultivating a New England mind; he aspired to leadership, but not as a peculiarly American Nehemiah like the old leaders Mather eulogized. Williams, like many of the young preachers, considered himself an English Christian in a New World province, and his God shared his cultural priorities.[15]

Deuteronomic covenantalism did not raise a single Christian nation above others who embraced Christianity, but it did distinguish between "professing people" and others in the world. As Elisha Williams assumed in his 1713 treatise, God deals "in a more steady way . . . with a professing People according To the Tenour of the covenant," whereas toward "heathenish nations" he acts more arbitrarily. Yet the apparent capriciousness of God's dealings outside his covenant did not sit well with those who were being drawn to the more rational vision of Isaac Newton's God and universal law. Timothy Cutler, who became Yale rector in 1719, argued two years earlier that God did not deal with the Jews any differently than with other nations—it was only that others failed to perceive the steady hand of Providence behind second causes.[16]

14. Williams, "Publick Covenant," 2, 3, 6.

15. Cotton Mather, *Magnalia Christi Americana; or, The Ecclesiastical History of New-England, from Its First Planting in the Year 1620, unto the Year of Our Lord, 1698* (1702; reprint, Hartford, Conn., 1820). Sacvan Bercovitch used Mather's work to discuss the origins of American identity in *The Puritan Origins of the American Self* (New Haven, Conn., 1975). The public covenant was an effective device in both errand and Deuteronomic sermons, not because it entangled a sovereign God in the chains of legalism, binding him to obligations toward his covenant people, but because it incorporated a shared catastrophe like a crop failure into a courtroom drama and brought a guilty people to the bar. See Eleazar Williams, *An Essay to Prove That When God Once Enters upon a Controversie, with His Professing People; He Will Manage and Issue It . . .* (New London, Conn., 1723).

16. Williams, "Publick Covenant," 2–3 (see also his manuscript sermon on Amos 7:2, dated Sept. 27, 1724, Beinecke Library); Timothy Cutler, *The Firm Union of a People Repre-*

Other clergymen who adhered to New England Congregationalism, and even some who continued to dust off the Puritan errand for special occasions, were beginning to emphasize God's disinterested, universal providence rather than Jehovah's decrees as monarch of his covenanted Israel. They professed their fathers' Calvinism and did not want to tinker with the church polity they inherited but admired the cosmic order and regularity being depicted by the new natural science and the cosmopolitan sensibility of the early British Enlightenment. Their key text was Prov. 14:34: "Righteousness Exalteth a nation; but Sin is a Reproach to any People." The verse substitutes timeless truth for the historical narrative of old and new Israel and a universally applicable law for the exclusive covenant relation. God no longer acts like a plaintiff bringing an accused people to court, as in Eleazar Williams's forensic analogy of 1723, but as the all-wise, omnipresent disposer of all things, as Jacob Heminway explained in 1740. James Lockwood spelled out what would become the preferred argument of both Boston rationalists and New Divinity moral government theologians after 1750. God nowhere confines or limits himself to deal with other nations and kingdoms as he did with his people Israel, Lockwood wrote. In other words, there was no scriptural justification for saying that a modern commonwealth has a public covenant with God, a special and peculiar relationship, just as Israel had. But God's promises and threats to Israel "may justly be applicable to other Nations, and civil Combinations of men," because "the same glorious Being, who was the God of *Israel* and their king, is the moral Governor of all mankind." Since all civil communities are "Creatures of Time," Lockwood reasoned, "God will manifest the Holiness of his Nature, and the

---

sented . . . (New London, Conn., 1717), 29–30. Cutler is an extreme case of what scholars have termed the "anglicization" of early-eighteenth-century colonial culture: he not only turned from New England's old-fashioned habits of mind and adopted the latest British thought but also abandoned the faith of his fathers for the Anglican way. Cutler had been corrupted by the recently acquired latitudinarian and rationalist writings that he and four other ministers and two tutors had explored in Yale's library. In 1722, he dramatically renounced Congregationalism and his chair at Yale to take orders in the Church of England. Elisha Williams replaced Cutler as Yale rector.

On anglicization, see John M. Murrin, "Anglicizing an American Colony: The Transformation of Provincial Massachusetts" (Ph.D. diss., Yale University, 1966); and Harry S. Stout, *New England Soul: Preaching and Religious Culture in Colonial New England* (New York, 1986), chap. 7. The Dummer collection refers to the eight hundred books (including works by Newton, John Locke, Edmond Halley, and Richard Steele) that Jeremiah Dummer collected for Yale in England (the first shipment of nine boxes arrived in Boston in September 1714). The stories of Yale's Dummer collection and the "Great Apostasy" of 1722 are well told in Richard Warch, *School of the Prophets: Yale College, 1701–1740* (New Haven, Conn., 1973), 99–118.

Equity of his Government" to them all. God's blessings and judgments are universally rendered according to the obedience and religious virtue of all peoples and nations.[17]

Despite their important differences, sermons discussing New England's special errand, its Deuteronomic covenant, or simply its place within God's providential economy all provided a logic that coordinated God's judgments with corporate morality. All were clear on one essential point: God gazed upon a people not just as a collection of individuals but as a public body bearing corporate guilt. A people must humble itself before God and offer repentance and reformation or thanks and praise in order to forestall judgments and continue mercies. Such conceptions of corporate responsibility, no matter how formulated or qualified, must have been psychologically powerful to a people used to interpreting experience through the twin prisms of biblical narrative and popular supernaturalism. Yet for a more historically specific and contextualized understanding of the covenant's power, we need to see how the idea supported specific policies at particular times. We need to examine, in other words, how covenant discourse supported, or failed to support, ideological innovation or a sudden shift in political or social power. For this, the passage of the Saybrook Platform in 1708, the post-Awakening debates of the 1740s and 1750s, and a look at a figure prominent in the story of both events, Elisha Williams, are illustrative.[18]

17. Whitman, *Practical Godliness*, 1; Williams, *An Essay to Prove That When God Once Enters upon a Controversie;* Jacob Heminway, *The Favour of God the Best Security of a People and a Concern to Please Him Urged . . .* (New London, Conn., 1740), 13–20; James Lockwood, *Religion the Highest Interest of a Civil Community, and the Surest Means of Its Prosperity . . .* (New London, Conn., 1754), 9–10. Benjamin Colton, *The Danger of Apostasie . . .* (New London, Conn., 1738), preached 1737, illustrates that the difference between the "providentialist" and "covenantalist" positions, especially before midcentury, was often one of emphasis and attitude rather than doctrine. Colton discussed New England's covenant but then went on to stress the immutability of God and the "reasonableness" of obeying God's moral laws because they promote a people's temporal welfare. For a discussion of the early Enlightenment among Massachusetts clergymen, see John Corrigan, *The Prism of Piety: Catholick Congregational Clergy at the Beginning of the Enlightenment* (New York, 1991). A. W. Plumstead detected a shift in tone and ideas toward the eighteenth-century Enlightenment occurring in the Massachusetts election sermons of the 1730s; see *The Wall and the Garden,* 4, 19, 223. See also Michael P. Winship, *Seers of God: Puritan Providentialism in the Restoration and Early Enlightenment* (Baltimore, 1996). On the New Divinity, see Mark Valeri, "The New Divinity and the American Revolution," *WMQ,* 3d Ser., XLVI (1989), 741–769; and Valeri, *Law and Providence in Joseph Bellamy's New England: The Origins of the New Divinity in Revolutionary America* (New York, 1994).

18. On popular supernaturalism, see David D. Hall, *Worlds of Wonder, Days of Judgment: Popular Religious Belief in Early New England* (New York, 1989).

Not by coincidence did Connecticut, in the first dozen years of the eighteenth century, establish a college to train its future ministers and magistrates, pass the Saybrook Platform, and set up a printing press for the regular publication of laws, proclamations, and election sermons. All were efforts by overlapping groups of clergymen and civic leaders to institutionalize religious orthodoxy, enforce moral order, and project the power of the state against what was perceived as the moral declension of an expanding colonial society. After the crown forced Connecticut to tolerate religious dissenters in 1708, Governor Gurdon Saltonstall urged the General Assembly to reform and strengthen the colony's ecclesiastical structure just as his friend and predecessor, Fitz-John Winthrop, had supported legislative, judicial, and financial reform at the beginning of the century and had worked to centralize authority and strengthen the hand of the executive. The Saybrook Platform consisted of a "Confession of Faith," a statement of agreement between Congregationalists and Presbyterians, and fifteen articles, devised at Saybrook, "for the Better Regulation of the Administration of Church Discipline." Of interest here is the language in the preface used to justify the Saybrook resolves. Directed toward two audiences— "Brethren in this Colony" and "Brethren" across the Atlantic—the text waffles between exalting New England's "Peculiar" and "distinguishing Glory" and acknowledging that New England's success is but one "Among the Memorable Providences relating to our *English Nation* in the last *Century*." The preface reminds readers that the New England forefathers were "by a Divine Impulse" led to follow the Lord into "a vast and howling Wilderness" for the sake of "*Religion, and the Liberty of their Consciences*." Echoing the errand sermons, it states "That *the Lord was with them,* to a Wonder preserving supporting protecting and animating them." Yet the preface admits that, if the crown's current policy of toleration had been in effect in 1630, New England's fathers would never have left their native land in the first place.[19]

19. The quoted phrase is from the Saybrook Platform, printed in Walker, *Creeds and Platforms,* 503. Eight of the twelve Saybrook ministers were also Yale trustees. The seventy-nine-page "Confession of Faith," like the Boston Declaration of 1680, only slightly modified the Savoy Declaration of 1658; the "Heads of Agreement" was a twenty-page text from an aborted English attempt to unify Presbyterians and Congregationalists in 1691. For good discussions of the Platform, see ibid., chap. 15; and M. Louise Greene, *The Development of Religious Liberty in Connecticut* (Boston, 1905), chaps. 5–7.

The Saybrook divines and the Connecticut General Assembly under Governor Saltonstall's leadership then employed a familiar logic to justify the need for a state-sanctioned profession of faith and a state-enforced system of church discipline and regulation. Inhabitants of Connecticut colony are "part of that Body" upon which God has showered mercies and wonders "from the Beginning of our Fathers settling this country until now." God's Word teaches "that the practical piety and Serious Religion of our progenitors is exemplary and for our Imitation, and will reflect confounding shame on us, if we prove Degenerate." We and our children must not forget the designs of our fathers; we cannot exchange "the Interest of Religion . . . for a Temporal Interest without the Fowlest Degeneracy and most Inexcusable Defection." The text goes on to list the "solemn Rebukes of Providence"—drought, military defeat, and sickness—proving that Connecticut must be straying from the path of righteousness because God was obviously punishing it. These distressing conditions "*cannot successfully be Improved but by a self humbling Consideration of our Ways and a thorough Repentance of all that is amiss.*" The Assembly bill calling for stricter ecclesiastical discipline and bidding for greater ministerial power was justified as a sacred duty demanded by an angry God.[20]

The Saybrook Platform and Elisha Williams's "Doctrine of the Publick Covenant" were written amid the great challenges to the Congregational way in the early eighteenth century. Massachusetts ministers, led by Increase and Cotton Mather, tried but failed to formalize ministerial associations and give them some authority over local congregations. John Wise of Ipswich wrote against these "Presbyterian" innovations in *The Churches Quarrel Espoused* in 1713, and his more famous "rationalist" defense of congregational polity would appear in 1717. Williams followed the lead of his father, William Williams of Hatfield, and of his step-grandfather, Solomon Stoddard, who had broached the idea of a presbyterial national church in 1700. With the help of covenant logic, the innovators wanted to tighten moral discipline and strengthen the hand of the learned clergy by empowering them in new associations and synods. The institutional basis of the "New England Way," which had been the civil establishment of congregational churches composed of visible saints, was being questioned, revised, and, by some, discarded.[21]

20. *A Confession of Faith* (New London, Conn., 1710), in Walker, *Creeds and Platforms,* 517, 520. Unlike Saltonstall's election sermon in 1697 and Thomas Buckingham's in 1711, the preface does not use the word "covenant" to describe New England's corporate relationship with God.

21. Walker, *Creeds and Platforms,* chap. 15; John Wise, *The Churches Quarrel Espoused . . .* (New York, 1713). See also Miller, *From Colony to Province,* chap. 16, "The Failure of Centralization"; and Richard L. Bushman, *From Puritan to Yankee: Character and Social Order*

Elisha Williams's 1713 manuscript treatise, written during his first few months of residence in Connecticut and almost certainly circulated among his intellectual friends and mentors, follows Stoddard's *Instituted Churches* and is in essence an argument to move the colony even further away from Congregationalism than the Saybrook Platform had taken it. The argument builds toward the grand Stoddardean "Inference" of its final chapter: "If there be an Publick Covenant between God and a Professing people there must of Necessity be Some Ecclesiasticall power Over Every Congregation." Many, like John Wise, still looked upon particular congregations "as So many Little Spiritual Kingdoms." But if the whole country is in covenant, it needs an ecclesiastical government working together with the civil government to oversee the moral order of the whole. A national synod would unite "the severall Congregations that are Integral parts of it," just as the civil government unites the towns of the realm into a single society.[22]

---

in Connecticut, 1690–1765 (Cambridge, Mass., 1967), 150–155. On John Wise, see Breen, *The Character of the Good Ruler*, 251. On William Williams, see Sweeney, "River Gods," 160–180. On the Mathers, see Robert Middlekauff, *The Mathers: Three Generations of Puritan Intellectuals, 1596–1728* (New York, 1971), chap. 12. On Solomon Stoddard, see Stoddard, *The Doctrine of Instituted Churches Explained and Proved from the Word of God* (London, 1700); and Ralph J. Coffman, *Solomon Stoddard* (Boston, 1978). Although some historians describe the period from the new Massachusetts charter in 1691 to Cotton Mather's death in 1728 as the epitaph of Puritanism, others hail it as a time when the Puritan errand was placed upon new foundations and secured as a legacy for the American future. As Cotton's father Increase wavered between reading New England's churches and New England society as a whole as the type of Israel, Cotton moved from church polity and institutional arrangements to ecumenical piety and practical moralism as the basis of Christian union. Sacvan Bercovitch's *The Puritan Origins of the American Self* focused on Cotton Mather's *Magnalia Christi Americana*. For a reading of seventeenth-century jeremiads less as consensual myth and more as partisan political documents, see Stephen Foster, *The Long Argument: English Puritanism and the Shaping of New England Culture, 1570–1700* (Chapel Hill, N.C., 1991).

22. Williams, "Publick Covenant," 27. The inference about the circulation of this treatise is based upon the appearance of the manuscript: impeccable penmanship, page numbering, contents page, chapter headings, and so on. Williams's Wethersfield mentors were the Reverend Stephen Mix and a Dr. Burnham (Weaver, "Elisha Williams," Conn. Hist. Soc., *Bull.*, LIII [1988], 128). Williams was preparing for his master's degree, which Harvard conferred upon him in 1714. Grandfather Stoddard's ideas were more congenial in Connecticut than in Massachusetts (Coffman, *Solomon Stoddard,* 127). That is not to say Stoddardeanism swept the colony. Robert G. Pope, *The Half-Way Covenant: Church Membership in Puritan New England* (Princeton, N.J., 1969), chaps. 3, 9, shows how open communion and the move away from congregational polity by some churches predated Stoddard's arguments. Paul R. Lucas, in *Valley of Discord: Church and Society along the Connecticut River, 1636–1725* (Hanover, N.H., 1976), 169–188, described the general resistance to "Stoddardean" open com-

This was Stoddard's conception of the "Instituted Church." It denied the validity of the Congregationalist's church covenant, which held that God covenanted with local members of one particular church only. When Christians controlled civil government, Stoddard argued, they baptized their children into a national church. The public covenant was a national church covenant. All people in such a nation are under the "External" aspect of the Covenant of Grace; they are "the Visible People of God," and all but the openly scandalous among them have the right and duty to attend all the ordinances of public worship. Civil and ecclesiastical institutions govern together, maintain moral order, and try to ensure that the people keep their covenant with God.[23]

For Williams and Stoddard, moral order did not depend upon Christian love, or upon the balance of power between saints and sinners, but upon the "natural" and "legal" powers all shared as moral agents within the external covenant. Williams argued that the "Visible People of God" did indeed consist of two kinds of people: "Godly men Who Labour Under a great darkness Weakness and Infirmity[,] and Carnall men Who are Under the power [of] their Corruptions." Both had the power to perform external obedience; both were obliged to learn their duty, reform their lives, and submit to discipline. Elisha Williams defined public sins by sharply distinguishing between the internal (faith) and the external (obedience). The saving faith and eternal salva-

---

munion. Samuel Harrison Rankin, Jr., noted in "Conservatism and the Problem of Change in the Congregational Churches of Connecticut, 1660–1760" (Ph.D. diss., Kent State University, 1971), 42–44, that at least five churches had moved toward some kind of comprehensive parish by 1708. James P. Walsh, in "The Pure Church in Eighteenth-Century Connecticut" (Ph.D. diss., Columbia University, 1967), 44, argued that open communion was a common but not the predominant practice in Connecticut between 1700 and 1740.

23. Solomon Stoddard, *The Inexcusableness of Neglecting the Worship of God, under a Pretence of Being in an Unconverted Condition* (Boston, 1708), 23. See chap. 3 in Coffman, *Solomon Stoddard,* for a discussion of "how far apart Stoddardean church government was from the Cambridge Platform" (109). Coffman argues that "Stoddard's 1700 treatise was not merely a rejection of Congregational polity or latitudinarian theology, it was a rejection of the magisterial Reformation" (108). Although Stoddard and Williams would give the magistrate less power over ecclesiastical affairs, their covenant idea was not unlike that of Heinrich Bullinger (1504–1575), as described by J. Wayne Baker in *Heinrich Bullinger and the Covenant:* "As in Israel, the conditions of the covenant applied to society as a whole, since the inclusive visible church was coterminus with civil society. The same people of God formed both the church and the commonwealth. . . . Bullinger did not view the commonwealth in terms of church and state but rather as the people of God gathered together in a Christian society based on the covenant. The church did not exist within society; it was society. Both magistrate and pastor played their roles within the same sphere, whether it was called church or commonwealth. It was the Christian community" (107, 110).

tion of individuals, the subject of the "first article" of the Covenant of Grace, "dont Depend on the Carriage of the Country [in] which they dwell." Belief in Jesus Christ and love to God, on the other hand, are not part of the public covenant, since "there is no power In any Country To see that such a Covenant be kept." "The Country can neither make men believe nor punish them for their secret Unbelief." Only "Visible Sincerity is Required In Order To the blessings of the outward Covenant." Some sins, therefore, may stain the soul but do no harm to the community: "There be many sins Committed in a Land, that are not the sins of the Land."[24]

There would be, however, no national synod, no stronger Saybrook Platform. The Platform relocated sovereignty from individual congregations to the newly created county consociations. Although county representatives in Hartford and New London embraced it, and in Fairfield County "ministers interpreted the Platform to give them even greater powers than were intended by the framers," New Haven County "clung to the tradition of strict Congregationalism" and "preferred to read Presbyterianism out of the Platform." In many parishes in Connecticut, a conservative laity stiffly resisted the Platform's presbyterianism. These differing sentiments and varying interpretations of the Platform did not become a major issue until the Awakening, when factionalism and ecclesiastical strife on the local level became incorporated into colony-wide—and intercolonial—debate. In the meantime, the power of Saybrook's consociational system was more theoretical than real. Covenant rhetoric had been used to support the Platform, but the Platform was not able to ensure that Connecticut lived up to the covenant's moral obligations.[25]

Although not all preachers distinguished as sharply as Williams did between internal faith and external obedience, or between private and public sins, their sermons early in the century did stress open and public sins like drunkenness and sabbath breaking and called for discipline and obedience. Yet by the 1720s and 1730s, Connecticut clergymen began moving away from institutional in-

24. Williams, "Publick Covenant," 7–9, 21. On the moral order's dependence upon the balance of saints and sinners, compare James Fitch, *An Holy Connexion; or, A True Agreement between Jehovahs Being a Wall of Fire to His People, and the Glory in the Midst Thereof* (Cambridge, Mass., 1674), 12. Fitch had pondered "the two nations," the saints and sinners, stirring in the womb of the commonwealth and wondered which would prevail. On the distinction between public and private guilt, see Nathanael Chauncey, *Honouring God the True Way to Honour* (New London, Conn., 1719), 46, who listed "three things that will raise a Sin to be a Publick Guilt, viz. Common Practice, Publick Establishment and Connivance, and General Insensibleness."

25. Bushman, *From Puritan to Yankee*, 151. See also Walker, *Creeds and Platforms*, 508–513, and Rankin, "Conservatism and the Problem of Change," 254.

novation or calls for a stronger, presbyterial discipline as solutions to the problem of moral declension and focused more upon the spiritual revitalization of the institutions they already had. Yale's "Great Apostasy" in 1722—the conversion of Rector Timothy Cutler and his group to Anglicanism—was a stunning blow to Connecticut's Standing Order of godly magistrates and Congregational ministers. The defection caused many clergymen to look beyond questions of church order and discipline to worry about theological complacency and spiritual lethargy. As they did so, they moved in the opposite direction from Williams's 1713 treatise: not toward sharpening the logical distinctions between internal and external, public and private, personal salvation and corporate well-being, but to further blurring those distinctions rhetorically.[26]

Any flirtation with doctrines that rewarded good works and praised natural powers—the Arminian path that Congregationalists associated with Anglicanism—troubled Calvinists. Sunday after Sunday ministers preached that, without inner grace, good works counted for nothing. As Elisha Williams himself told Connecticut's General Assembly in 1727, "The best we do in the matter of our Salvation should be accounted by us, as menstruous Rags." On public occasions like fast, thanksgiving, or election days, however, the same ministers in the same pulpits taught their congregations that good deeds made God smile upon the land and make its people prosperous. Some continued to distinguish carefully between the different logics behind the internal and external aspects of the Covenant of Grace or relied on the different rhetorical occasions to help separate a weekday message to the people at large from a Sabbath sermon to individuals. But in the ritual complaints about declension that issued from the election day pulpit after the mid-1720s, those distinctions were more often lost as preachers spoke about the necessity of God's spiritual presence in public life.[27]

26. Williams realized that, even in an ideal situation, civil and ecclesiastical government could only do so much. Some sins are public but not within the reach of civil or ecclesiastical punishment: "Neglect of Charity" and "Unsavory discourses" may bring a blight upon the land; so may parents who overindulge their children and creditors who are too lenient with debtors (Williams, "Publick Covenant," 12). See also Jonathan Marsh, *An Essay, to Prove the Through* [sic] *Reformation of a Sinning People Is Not to Be Expected . . .* (New London, Conn., 1721), 15. On the effect of the Great Apostasy at Yale in 1722, see Warch, *School of the Prophets,* 282.

27. Williams, *Divine Grace Illustrious,* 37. On the rhetorical separation of Sabbath from occasional preaching, see Stout, *New England Soul,* 13–31. The five points of Calvinism (total depravity, unconditional election, limited atonement, irresistible grace, perseverance of the saints) can be contrasted to the five points of Arminianism: first, people are not totally depraved—they have some ability to choose God and grace; second, God elected some on the basis of his foreknowledge of what their free choice would be; third, atonement was of-

For Williams in 1713, God in the administration of his public covenant was not the searcher of hearts. A person's secret sins were not imputed to the whole community; nor did moral obedience have to proceed from a regenerated heart. Though not stated as baldly as in Williams's treatise, this premise also seemed to inform many of the early-eighteenth-century sermons. But a decade after Williams wrote, his uncle Eleazar Williams spoke of the "secret departure of heart from God," contributing to God's anger toward his people. William Russel in 1730 reemphasized that obedience and moral behavior must spring from an inner love to God through Christ. "Grace is not Hereditary," he preached. No covenant obliges God to keep a generation of hypocrites from total apostasy.[28]

Believing that traditional calls for external obedience were being answered by a complacent formalism, many preachers began using every pulpit opportunity to take aim at the inner recesses of their auditors' souls. That was especially true for those Connecticut Valley "awakening" preachers of the Stoddard-Williams clan, like Elisha, who preached Calvinism and conversion to the General Assembly in 1727, and his kinsman Timothy Edwards, whose 1732 election sermon brushed political theory aside to expound upon the doctrine that "All the Living must surely Die and go to Judgment." In 1740, four months before English itinerant George Whitefield arrived in New England to ignite the religious revivals known as the "Great Awakening," Jacob Heminway flatly asserted that there was only one way for a people to please God: they must believe in his Son, and, for that, people—individually—"must be Converted, Renewed and Sanctified by the Grace of God." In the midst of the Awakening, Elisha's half-brother Solomon Williams exhorted his congregation to be holy first, and then public virtue and temporal prosperity would follow. "It's not enough to keep up a shew of Religion and Vertue," but an awakened people must "labour to be truly Renew'd and Sanctified."[29]

---

fered to everyone, and it was the responsibility of every individual to repent; fourth, God's grace could be resisted by the hardened sinner; fifth (according to some Arminians), some saints could fall from grace. See Weir, *Origins of the Federal Theology*, 20.

28. Williams, *An Essay to Prove That When God Once Enters upon a Controversie*, 11, a statement that would not have been at all unusual for a seventeenth-century Puritan; William Russel, *The Decay of Love to God in Churches, Offensive and Dangerous . . .* (New London, Conn., 1731), 14.

29. Williams, *Divine Grace Illustrious;* Timothy Edwards, *All the Living Must Surely Die, and Go to Judgment* (New London, Conn., 1732); Heminway, *The Favour of God the Best Security,* 11–12; Solomon Williams, *A Firm and Immovable Courage to Obey God, and an Inflexible Observation of the Laws of Religion, the Highest Wisdom and Certain Happiness of Rulers* (New London, Conn., 1741), 43. See also Sweeney, "River Gods," 208. Other manuscript sermons from the Beinecke collection that demonstrate Elisha Williams's evangelical Calvin-

The religious revivals of the early 1740s further accentuated what had been a continuing concern about the presence of God's Spirit in political experience and public life. Most preachers focused on the immanence of the divine in guiding the good ruler and shaping his character. Solomon Williams argued that, without "a special and gracious Assistance of [God's] Spirit and Providence," even "the greatest Politician" would fail in his efforts to do good. Williams believed, as Gurdon Saltonstall had written at the end of the previous century, that "the Purest Politicks are but Insipid Trash Unless they have this Seasoning" of godliness. Solomon Williams played down the tenet that God was present with civil rulers by virtue of their office rather than as an extension of their personal piety. "Governours and Magistrates are Entitled to our Respect and Reverence, because they have the Image of God put upon them," Williams conceded. But he quickly added that, "if this be nothing but an Outward and Visible Image in their Authority and Power, . . . the Respect paid them on this account, will like the Image it self, be for the most part but an Outward shew." Williams's argument parallels the debate over the danger of an unconverted ministry that raged in the 1740s. Gilbert Tennent had thundered that, whatever the dignities of the office, an unregenerate minister could no more effectively preach the new birth than a dead man could father a child.[30]

---

ism during this period are the following: Sermon on Eph. 2:4–5, Hartford, 1722 (sovereign grace); Sermon on Matt. 5:19, March 1723 (the smallest sins punished by the greatest severity); Sermon on Rom. 7:9, Sept. 22, 1723 (true conviction of sin requires spiritual power); Sermon on Col. 3:2, July 17, 1724 (necessity of the new birth); Sermon on Luke 18:11–12, May 30, 1725 (not trusting our own righteousness). Revival preaching, rather than church government or sacramentalism, was Stoddard's main focus in the last two decades of his life, and his teachings on evangelical preaching and conversion had a considerable impact on the next generation. See Coffman, *Solomon Stoddard*, chap. 4; and Thomas A. Schafer, "Solomon Stoddard and the Theology of the Revival," in Stuart C. Henry, ed., *A Miscellany of American Christianity: Essays in Honor of H. Shelton Smith* (Durham, N.C., 1963), 328–361.

30. Williams, *A Firm and Immovable Courage*, 27–29, 35; Gurdon Saltonstall's remark is from *A Sermon Preached*, Griswold transcript, 34. Williams could not simply join Jonathan Marsh in *God's Fatherly Care of His Covenant Children* . . . (New London, Conn., 1737), preached 1736, and Benjamin Colton in *The Danger of Apostasie*, preached 1737, and urge magistrates to imitate God's paternal care or Christ in his kingly office. He also suggested an alternative to considering the divine image as merely a royal seal legitimating authority. Williams's language lacks the Neoplatonic luster, but not the intention, of James Fitch's sermon of two generations before. Fitch spoke in 1674 of a people having the glory of God in the midst of them, "not only Glory set before them as a copy, [pat]tern, and Example, as the Rule is the Idea or Example of *Euprax[ie* or] *Well-acting*" but the transforming image shining from God's Word and ordinances. Such a people would have magistrates who "shine with pious policy, religi[ous righteous]ness, and holy carriage"; see Fitch, *An Holy Connexion*, 7–8.

Most agreed that, whether the civil magistrate bore the external image of God because of the office the ruler occupied or had been spiritually reborn in the image of Christ, the people were duty-bound to submit to the magistrate's lawful exercise of civil power. Those clerics who continued to argue that the subject's obedience needed only to spring from the instructed conscience rather than from a regenerated heart, however, were forced into a difficult position by the Awakening. They had taught that, although the magistrate and the minister were supposed to walk arm in arm like Moses and Aaron to lead the people, the minister was the one in charge of cultivating a conscientious citizenry. William Worthington exhorted his ministerial brethren to "endeavour that their people be well Affected and Obedient to the Civil Magistrate." "Mens Consciences must be convinced of the great Sin of reviling the Gods." But during the Awakening, when some parishioners stopped listening to—or openly defied—their pastors, some clerics were ready to turn back to the Saybrook Platform and employ the coercive arm of the state. If the ministers' powers of persuasion could no longer move people to support good government, they reasoned, government would have to move to support the ministry.[31]

POST-AWAKENING DEBATE:
FROM COVENANT TO CONTRACT AND CONSCIENCE

Thus, what is often described as a single current of public discourse actually contained important variations that could exalt New England's exclusive mission, subordinate New England to Britain's role within a phalanx of covenanted Protestant nations, or describe local experience as part of God's universal moral government. Covenant discourse early in the century supported a specific reconfiguration of civil and ecclesiastical power but by the 1730s was being replaced by other rhetorical weapons against moral malaise. Perhaps the story of a monolithic ideological consensus shattered by the Great Awakening is more dramatic, but it is also less accurate.[32]

References to covenants, errands, and providence made up a vocabulary that New Englanders used to argue about their corporate identity and their relationship to God; it was a language that at one time could support and define

31. William Worthington, *The Duty of Rulers and Teachers in Unitedly Leading God's People . . .* (New London, Conn., 1744), 20.

32. As we will see in the next chapter, the Awakening and its aftermath launched a debate over the meaning of covenanting and local church membership that altered the way people thought about Christian community and corporate identity. Here the focus will be on the political saliency of discourse about the public covenant.

important political strategies and at another time could be set aside. One might think that, when the Saybrook Platform was debated after the Awakening, the covenant rhetoric used to justify it initially would return. But covenant discourse, although still familiar in other contexts, soon ceased to function effectively as political rhetoric.

The General Assembly passed the Act for Regulating Abuses and Correcting Disorders in Ecclesiastical Affairs in May 1742. The act, citing the Saybrook Platform as "the ecclesiastical constitution established by the laws of this government," stipulated that someone who preached in a parish without an express invitation "by the settled minister or the major part of the church" would be heavily fined, imprisoned, or banished. The 1742 act, therefore, rested on the Platform just as the Platform rested on the covenant. But supporters of the legislation could not so easily argue that the provision, like the Platform itself, was needed simply to restore moral order under the obligations of the covenant. Under the covenant, church and state were joined in the same moral enterprise. As Gurdon Saltonstall wrote in 1697, "God hath Design'd the Civil Government of his People to Concenter with Ecclesiastical administrations and (tho by Different Medicines) they are both Leveld at the same End[:] the maintaining of piety and Promoting of a Covenant walk with him." Although antirevival preachers in the 1740s might agree in substance, they described the relationship between church and state differently. Both Isaac Stiles and William Worthington, for example, described the church (not society at large) as a public body under siege; civil authority was not "concentered" with the church but should act like a protective wall or hedge around it.[33]

For all their bluster, the Old Light election sermons after 1741 were frank confessions of clerical impotence. The Spirit seems to have withdrawn from our preaching, Isaac Stiles complained, and our people "turn *away their Ears from the Truth,* and are turned *unto Fables:* [they] Come not to *the Law and to the Testimony,* and thence neither speak nor act according to this Word."

33. The Saltonstall quotation is from *A Sermon Preached,* Griswold transcript, 84. The 1742 act is reprinted in Stephen Nissenbaum, ed., *The Great Awakening at Yale College* (Belmont, Calif., 1972), 136–139; and in Richard L. Bushman, ed., *The Great Awakening: Documents on the Revival of Religion, 1740–1745* (New York, 1970), 58–60. A Connecticut minister who preached uninvited outside his own parish would lose his tax-supported salary, and a Connecticut layman who preached or exhorted without such permission would be fined one hundred pounds. The act also stipulated that any "stranger" or "foreigner" to the colony, ordained or not, who preached without local approval would be escorted out of the colony "as a vagrant person." On the politics of the passage of the 1742 law, see Bushman, *From Puritan to Yankee,* 185–187; and Rankin, "Conservatism and the Problem of Change," 219–255. Many local officials refused to make arrests and prosecutions, so the law was only sporadically enforced.

For years, election day ministers had called themselves the watchmen on the walls of Jerusalem. But in 1742, Stiles handed that title over to the magistracy. Magistrates were not just lookouts but also the builders of the wall, and Stiles urged that, while they built it with one hand, the other should hold a sword. The clergy had no power of coercion, no sword to wield. The minister's "most awful weapons" were "the winning, endearing methods of Persuasion," and these were being "degraded and spurn'd at by sinners" and accounted "but *as stubble, straw and rotten wood.*" Stiles spoke to the session of the Assembly that would pass the 1742 act. Two years later, William Worthington was still applauding the measure. He thanked the "true Patriots" in the General Assembly for rescuing the established ministry: "We had strangely lost our influence upon the Affections and Consciences of many of our people; when God encouraged Your Honors to become zealous for himself." After all, he argued, "the Church as a Politick Body, hath her temporal Interests," and civil authority must protect them. "Who don't see the necessity of the Magistrate's interposing, Sword in hand, to protect the Church against such Impious Outrage" and "to prevent arbitrary and Unministerial Intrusions." Against any who break "the Civil Hedge" set around his church, "God expects that the sword be drawn." The church authority could not suppress the enthusiasts, so if the magistrates did not step in, who would stop the Moravians, Papists, and Mahometans that might pour in through the breach?[34]

Opponents of the 1742 act moved debate even further away from covenant themes. In 1744, three decades after writing "The Doctrine of the Publick Covenant," Elisha Williams published *The Essential Rights and Liberties of Protestants,* a response to Connecticut's "Anti-Itinerancy" legislation and one of the most forceful arguments for religious liberty to be published in New England before midcentury. Williams represented Wethersfield in the General Assembly during the Awakening and opposed the 1742 law. In 1743, he was dropped from his positions as Hartford County justice of the peace and assistant judge of the Connecticut Superior Court in a general purge of justices who seemed to be working too hard to "prevent the ill effects" of the act, thereby subverting its punitive purpose. Williams's *Essential Rights,* signed by "Philalethes" of "Eleutheropolis," March 30, 1744, was printed in Boston and purported to be "a Letter from a Gentleman in *Massachusetts Bay* to his friend in *Connecticut*" in response to the 1742 law. The sixty-six-page essay began with a discussion of

34. Isaac Stiles, *A Prospect of the City of Jerusalem, in It's Spiritual Building, Beauty, and Glory* (New London, Conn., 1742), 23, 52; Worthington, *The Duty of Rulers and Teachers,* 10, 17–18, 22–24, 30, 36. Samuel Hall, *The Legislatures Right, Charge, and Duty in respect of Religion . . .* (New London, Conn., 1746), 19, continued Stiles's lament.

the origins and ends of civil government. By following "the celebrated *Lock*" rather than the Old Testament, and reasoning from the state of nature rather than God's public covenant, Williams proceeded to delineate the inalienable rights of the people and the limitations on civil power. *Essential Rights* did not merely reassert the individual responsibilities or voluntary aspects of the public covenant; it sidestepped covenant discourse altogether, building upon the rights individuals carried with them from the state of nature, rights unaffected by any civil or corporate relations they might enter.[35]

In the heat of post-Awakening debate, *Essential Rights* helped alter the rhetorical forms and conceptual categories in which discussions about church and state, individual faith and corporate morality were cast. Dissenting Congregationalists, known as "Separates" or "Separatists," would use this pamphlet along with works by John Locke, John Wise, and Jonathan Edwards to combat the Standing Order for years. *Essential Rights* declared that the 1742 law and the Saybrook Platform were invalid, reminding readers that Connecticut's charter stipulated that no colony laws could be contrary to the laws of England. It denied the implicit premise of so much covenant discourse: that a people under God must strive to maintain unity of faith and a uniformity of religious practice. Its historical benchmark was, not New England's founding, but England's Toleration Act; its supporting texts were, not New England election sermons, but John Locke on government and toleration; its central theme was, not covenant order under God, but liberty of conscience in Christ.[36]

The differences between *Essential Rights* and Williams's treatise on the "Publick Covenant" are startling. Williams's 1713 argument did not need to be concerned with the origins and ends of government as such, but with the nature

35. [Elisha Williams], *The Essential Rights and Liberties of Protestants; a Seasonable Plea for the Liberty of Conscience, and the Right of Private Judgment, in Matters of Religion, without any Controul from Human Authority* . . . (Boston, 1744), 4. There has been some question about the authorship of this pamphlet. Modern scholars have followed the judgment of Clifford K. Shipton in 1935, who noted that all the evidence points to Williams, including a copy of the pamphlet at Harvard with the eighteenth-century inscription "E——a W——ms." See Shipton, *Biographical Sketches*, V, 593n; and Weaver, "Elisha Williams," Conn. Hist. Soc., *Bull.*, LIII (1988), 82. Edmund Morgan reprinted 1–9, 38–51, and 60–65 under Elisha Williams's name in *Puritan Political Ideas, 1558–1794* (Indianapolis, Ind., 1965), 267–304. Sweeney, in "River Gods," 440–441, added further proof, pointing to a note in Jonathan Edwards's Account Book about loaning out "Rector Wms Seasonable Plea." The quotation about justices' preventing the ill effects of the act is from [Thomas Clap?], Appendix, in Lockwood, *Man Mortal*, viii–ix, Williams's funeral sermon.

36. On the Separatists' use of Williams's *Essential Rights*, see William G. McLoughlin, *New England Dissent, 1630–1833: The Baptists and the Separation of Church and State*, 2 vols. (Cambridge, Mass., 1971) I, 405, 25n.

A feafonable P L E A

F O R

The Liberty of Confcience,

A N D

The Right of private Judgment,

In Matters of R E L I G I O N,

Without any Controul from *human Authority.*

Being a L E T T E R,

From a Gentleman in the *Maffachufetts-Bay* to his Friend in *Connecticut.*

W H E R E I N

Some Thoughts on the Origin, End, and Extent of the *Civil Power,* with brief Confiderations on feveral late Laws in *Connecticut,* are humbly offered.

By a *Lover of* TRUTH *and* LIBERTY. *E Elisha Williams ?*

Matth. xxii. 21.---- *Render unto* Cæfar *the Things which are* Cæfar's; *and unto* GOD, *the Things that are* GOD's.

" If our Purfes be *Cæfar's,* our Confciences are GOD's : ---
" and if *Cæfar's* Commands interfere with GOD's, we
" muft *obey* GOD *rather than* Men.--- HENRY on the Place.

B O S T O N : Printed and Sold by S. KNEELAND and T. GREEN in Queenftreet. 1 7 4 4.

and necessity of government within a corporate body already in covenant with God. In the earlier work, the public covenant, and not the state of nature, had been the ground of civil power. In the 1744 essay, Williams argued that the only "rational Inducement" for men willingly to leave the state of nature and unite together under a government is to promote their own good and better secure what belongs to them. In doing so, they give up only those natural liberties and powers necessary to preserve their rights of person and property within the community. "Hence then the Fountain and Original of all civil Power is from the People, and is certainly instituted for their Sakes; or in other Words . . . *The great End of civil Government, is the Preservation of their Persons, their Liberties and Estates, or their Property.*" [37]

The youth who had written on the public covenant had gone on to study law. According to the account appended to his funeral sermon, Williams had "endeavored to make himself thoroughly acquainted with the Constitution of the *English* Government, Privileges and Laws; and drank in . . . a Love of *British* Privileges, as well as of the Rights and Liberties of Conscience." A serious illness in his mid-twenties had brought Williams near to the grave but nearer to Christ, and in 1721 he became an ordained minister, and then Yale's rector, rather than a practicing lawyer. He told friends that, even as he had buried two sons and a daughter between November 1740 and October 1741, he had been filled with a sense of God's sovereignty, goodness, and wisdom. During the Awakening, he strongly supported the revivals and felt that even the wild itinerant James Davenport, though tinged with enthusiasm, might do some good. In 1744, Judge Elisha Williams, who set Israel's covenant aside to show the body politic rising from the state of nature, was both more learned and more deeply pious than the scholar of 1713. [38]

As either biography or history of political rhetoric, this is not simply a story of secularization, the metamorphosis of God's covenant into the social contract. The standard argument between 1713 and 1744 had been that civil government was a sovereign gift to creatures who were both naturally sociable and yet sinfully self-interested. The particular forms of government might vary among nations, but the ultimate end was the glory of God. Positing a "state of nature" between Eden and civil society does not in itself deny that government is a divine gift; it just changes the manner by which that gift was bestowed. More important than the use of the state of nature is the way Williams's 1744 essay lifts political discourse outside of the sacred circle of divine origins and ends. Williams would not have denied that the *ultimate* origin and aim of gov-

37. [Williams], *Essential Rights,* 4.
38. Appendix, in Lockwood, *Man Mortal,* ii, vii.

ernment was God's glory, but these considerations, rather than grounding his entire discussion in the manner of a covenant sermon, are irrelevant to his argument.[39]

In contrast, Jared Eliot, the first election day preacher to consider the state of nature at any length, had tried to give the theory scriptural sanction in 1738. Eliot, a cleric-physician from Killingworth, first noted that, whereas some called the state of nature a groundless fiction, "a great Writer" (Locke) had convincingly argued that "Government is before Hystory and Records, and therefore Governments are ignorant of their own Original." Besides, Eliot continued, the Scriptures give an "exact account" of that state in Gen. 16:12, with the reference to Ishmael, a wild man with his hand against every man and every man's hand against him. Williams and Eliot both cited Matt. 22:21 on their title pages but had very different ideas about what the Christian who has left the state of nature and entered civil society must "render unto Caesar." Eliot argued that, whatever the form of government and however it was established over a particular people, Christians are called to "submit yourselves to every ordinance of men for the Lord's sake" (1 Pet. 2:13–14). Subjects must pay their taxes, obey civil laws conscientiously, and honor their civil "parents" in accord with the fifth commandment. Williams glossed Matt. 22:21 with a comment by Matthew Henry: "If our Purses be *Caesar's*, our Consciences are God's—and if *Caesar's* Commands interfere with God's, we must *obey* God *rather than Men*." Conscience, for Williams, is no longer just that which secures the obedience of individuals under God's covenant; it has replaced the covenant as the foundation of moral order.[40]

Conscience for Williams in 1713 had been a secret interior space. Here consciousness reflected upon itself and apprehended the soul's own saving faith or "secret unbelief"; here the inner witness spoke God's law and passed sentence upon the person's thoughts and acts. This inner witness had important, though mostly passive, political and public functions. In 1744, Williams emphasized

39. For a discussion of the instrumental and ultimate ends of government, see Samuel Estabrook, *A Sermon Shewing that the Peace and Quietness of a People Is a Main Part of the Work of Civil Rulers*... (New London, Conn., 1718), 3–6.

40. Jared Eliot, *Give Caesar His Due; or, The Obligations that Subjects Are Under to Their Civil Rulers* (New London, Conn., 1738), 27. Like the public covenant preachers, Eliot grafted the modern body politic onto the tree of Abraham, but to Ishmael's branch of the family rather than Isaac's. The state of nature for Eliot could encompass both the hermit Nebuchadnezzar's grazing like an ox (Dan. 4:33) and the rudimentary social organization of a clan of thieves (Job 30:3–6) or a wild Arab tribe. But it was a nasty, brutish, miserable condition and hardly the Lockean prepolitical social order that Williams assumes. Williams cites only "Henry," probably referring to Matthew Henry (1662–1714), *Exposition of the Old and New Testaments*... (London, 1715).

conscience as the source of private judgment, directing the subject's choices and actions in the world. The subject not only judges himself but judges *for* himself and must be allowed to follow the dictates of his conscience. In the language of the faculty psychology of the day, conscience was a function of the understanding that Williams now bound closer to the will; a person's conscience not only assesses moral fitness but determines *to do* what he or she sees fit.[41]

In civil society, individuals transfer power to the whole community and are bound to acts of the majority as the will of the whole. But in religious matters, "where Conscience and Men's eternal Interests are concerned," they cannot. "This *Right* of *judging every one for himself in matters of Religion* results from the Nature of Man, and is so inseparably connected therewith, that a Man can no more part with it than he can with his *Power of Thinking*." Williams maintained that "No Action is a religious Action without the Understanding and Choice in the Agent." The unregenerate may not have an experiential knowledge of Christ or an affecting sense of his "satisfying sweetness," but each man has "a Freedom of Will and Liberty of Acting" that "is grounded on his having Reason." This "Freedom of Will" is not the Arminian conception that Jonathan Edwards would dissect. Williams was not arguing from the premise of an indifferent understanding's freedom from any divinely predetermined inclination of the soul. The free will he described was, not some essentially autonomous moral agency, but "a *Freedom* from any *superior Power on Earth*, and not being under the Will or legislative Authority of *Man*, and having only the *Law of Nature* (or in other Words, of its MAKER) for his Rule." Nor was Williams trying to open the door to radical subjectivism. *"This natural Freedom* is not a Liberty for every one to do what he pleases without any Regard to any *Law*; for a *rational* Creature cannot but be made under a *Law* from its MAKER." [42]

41. Conscience was drawn into the public sphere in two ways: by explicit oaths and as the implicit ground of civic virtue. Oaths and vows bound men and women to their word and their word to their conscience. The freemen who annually voted magistrates into office, for example, committed themselves by a solemn oath to God to vote from the dictates of their conscience. Oath breaking put the individual's soul *and* the body public at risk. Once elected, rulers could not pry into the secrets of a subject's conscience, but they could point to Rom. 13:5 and call for obedience "not only for wrath, but also for conscience sake"—that is, not only external compliance out of fear of punishment or shame but out of a sincerely felt moral obligation. See also Keith Thomas, "Cases of Conscience in Seventeenth-Century England," and Patricia Crawford, "Public Duty, Conscience, and Women in Early Modern England," in John Morrill, Paul Slack, and Daniel Woolf, eds., *Public Duty and Private Conscience in Seventeenth-Century England: Essays Presented to G. E. Aylmer* (Oxford, 1993), 29–56, 57–76.

42. [Williams], *Essential Rights*, 2–3, 8, 49. See also Elisha Williams, MS sermon on Canticles 1:7, July 1743, Beinecke Library, for the "satisfying sweetness" of Christ's manifesta-

As Williams had argued, the right of private judgment in matters of religious belief and practice was essential to Protestants. The Reformers had shouted to Rome that God's Word alone was the rule to judge by and that everyone had the right and duty to read the Scriptures and decide religious questions for oneself. In establishing their godly commonwealth, however, Puritan leaders had embraced the qualification expressed by William Ames: the liberty of conscience is granted only to the conscience rightly informed from Scripture properly interpreted. For the proper interpretation, the individual must be edified by the learned and godly men within the community of saints. These gifted searchers of the Word, Williams himself maintained, could assemble in synods to address questions of broad public concern. Writing in 1713, he had qualified his call for synodical authority by granting that synods and individuals alike were bound to the Word: "All Persons must Go by Their own Light and Synods by their Light." In *Essential Rights*, he was more insistent about the rights that could not be surrendered to synods or other bodies of men attempting to safeguard orthodoxy. The detestable 1742 law, after all, had been suggested by a clerical assembly. In giving that counsel, Williams wrote, the learned ministers had urged the state to usurp the power of Christ as "the *Lord* of *Conscience*." [43]

---

tions of love to the soul, also described as the "peculiar fruits of his Love that strangers do not intermeddle with." The doctrine of an early, undated MS sermon fragment in the Beinecke collection is "That All Naturall Men Voluntarily Elect Their Own Eternall Ruin," to which is added in a later hand "(Men Naturally are Chusing The Means that bring Destruction upon them)." Williams had argued against the idea of the soul's "indifferency" in *Divine Grace Illustrious*, 17–18. God's regeneration is a positive act that does not leave the soul in equilibrium, though this act is still not inconsistent with freedom of the will. Williams speaks unequivocally of free grace: "If any Thing of ours be the Cause, Motive, or ground of Salvation, then it is not wholly of Grace; And if it be wholly of Grace, then all of Self is wholly Excluded. . . . Grace, can have no Partner" (36). Williams again preached on God's sovereignty, man's helplessness, and the divine and supernatural "frame of Holiness, which is inwrought in our souls by the spirit of God in regeneration"; see MS sermon on Rom. 8:7, March 1746, Beinecke Library. Perry Miller, in *Jonathan Edwards*, is far from correct when he paints all the Williamses as closet Arminians. As Sweeney in "River Gods" notes, Edwards himself "could not recognize the sincerity and depth of his clerical opponents' views nor acknowledge their intellectual commitment" (455). On Willams's Calvinism, see also Patricia J. Tracy, *Jonathan Edwards, Pastor: Religion and Society in Eighteenth-Century Northampton* (New York, 1979), 184–185; and Warch, *School of the Prophets*, 180–182.

43. On Ames's qualification, see Edmund S. Morgan, *Roger Williams: The Church and the State* (New York, 1967), 132–133. See Williams, "Publick Covenant," 31; [Williams], *Essential Rights*, 12. As Keith Thomas explained in "Cases of Conscience in Seventeenth-Century England," in Morrill, Slack, and Woolf, eds., *Public Duty and Private Conscience*, 30–31, conscience in the older understanding was a person's knowledge of right and wrong applied to a particular case—a knowledge based on natural reason and God's Word. Conscience, there-

Williams insisted that, in civil society, rational beings do not give up their right of free speech or their rights to read the books and hear the preachers of their choice. They may assemble to worship God as Anglicans, Presbyterians, Congregationalists, Baptists, or Quakers. Individual churches may consociate and form advisory synods if they wish and then may later withdraw from those societies as they see fit. A number of Christians, following the dictates of their conscience, may withdraw from a church and form a separate worshiping assembly. The state must protect all these rights, not infringe upon them. Allowing the state to step in and settle "ecclesiastical disorders" is tantamount to letting the state determine what such a disorder is, clearing the way for tyranny over the rights of conscience.

Essential Rights helped redefine the entire debate about religious liberty, state power, and moral order. It provided a rationale for church separation and civil disobedience that could not be dismissed as the mad prattling of an enthusiast or the harangue of an "illiterate" exhorter. Six weeks after Williams had sent his essay to the Boston press, William Worthington preached Connecticut's election sermon and noted that some were denying the magistrate's right to legislate about ecclesiastical affairs, "as if every man had a good right to follow his Conscience how dreadfully soever it Errs." On the contrary, Worthington declared, God has given laws that circumscribe conscience without infringing any natural rights. The statutes God gave Israel, for example, can be justly applied to the modern state because they are consistent with God's perfection and human nature.[44]

Worthington also addressed the issue of itinerant preaching and the invocation of natural rights. "We of late, often hear of the Natural Right of a Person or People, to hear whom they please." But it was wrong, he argued, to appeal to natural rights in an affair that was a matter of divine institution, civil compact, or some mixture of the two. Charles Chauncy had elaborated upon the idea of the pastoral relation as a civil contract in *Seasonable Thoughts* (1743) and countered the calls to liberty with a defense of property rights. Citing 1 Cor. 3:21–22, he argued that Christians have a right to hear all ministers in the same way that they have a right to all things. Despite the apostle's words, "All Things are your's," private property is not destroyed and all things are not held in common. "*Particular* Men have their *own* Wives, and *particular* Women their *own*

---

fore, was thought to have an objective basis, and since Calvinists distrusted the power of a natural moral law engraved upon the hearts of all men they stressed God's Word. It was a sin to act against conscience, but it was also a sin to act according to an erroneous conscience, so lay men and women were encouraged to consult clerical experts.

44. Worthington, *The Duties of Rulers and Teachers*, 11–12.

Husbands; this Man has his *own* House or Field, and so has *that:* Nor can they invade one another's Property without sinning against GOD." People may have a right to (or "Propriety in") any particular thing or minister, but "only in Subordination to *prior* Rights." The fundamental issue for Chauncy and Worthington was, not the individual's liberty to choose his minister, analogous to his right in a state of nature to "all things," but the contractual relation between particular churches and pastors, where each has stated rights with respect to the other. Itinerants who break in upon these rights and subvert church order interfere with a divine institution *and* a civil contract. If magistrates should not meddle with divine institutions, they certainly must uphold contracts. Instead of countering the appeal to natural rights with an argument about covenant duties—that is, instead of contending that the revivalists' anarchic liberty was leading to public sins that would be punished by a covenant God—Old Lights responded with an argument about property rights that only fueled resentment of Standing Order ministers as petty autocrats trying to reign over parish fiefdoms. Cynical opponents would conclude that the antirevivalists were less concerned about who preached in their parishes than about who paid the pastor.[45]

Although Williams was not the only one arguing for liberty of conscience, his pamphlet seems to be the one that set the agenda for public debate. A New Light like Philemon Robbins found Williams's arguments useful as he made his case for congregational autonomy, and Separatist Ebenezer Frothingham recommended Williams's pamphlet along with Locke's *Letter concerning Toleration*. The Reverend Jonathan Todd, responding to an anonymous writer who in 1747 had echoed the argument for a congregation's "Right of Private Judgment in matters of Religion" as an "unalienable Right," denounced *Essential Rights* by name as a "sophistical Pamphlet" designed to encourage *"lawless Liberty."* Samuel Hall's 1746 election sermon reads like a point-by-point rebuttal of *Essential Rights*. Hall began by erasing the brackets Williams had placed around political argument, and he restored the discussion of the origins and ends of government to "that which is Divine and Eternal." Although the legislature derives its authority "immediately" from the people through election, its power

---

45. Ibid., 11; Charles Chauncy, *Seasonable Thoughts on the State of Religion in New England . . .* (Boston, 1743), 63–64. [Elihu Hall], *The Present Way of the Country in Maintaining the Gospel Ministry by a Publick Rate or Tax, Is Lawful, Equitable, and Agreeable to the Gospel* (New London, Conn., 1749), 26–27, in answering those who challenged the tax-supported ministry, clearly explained what sort of covenant was at issue: "Such covenanting between Ministers and people, is a meer Civil and Moral thing, and therefore as lawfully Transacted as any other civil temporal Covenant whatsoever." It was simply "a civil contract."

is from God "originally." Furthermore, Hall contended, God directly invests it with the additional power of the sword and "a Jurisdiction extending over Life," which no man transfers to civil society because no man has it to begin with. The end of any governmental action or law is, not the protection of liberty and property, but obedience to God. Williams had complained that Paul's injunction to the Romans to "obey the powers that be" had been "wrecked and tortured" by apologists for arbitrary power and civil tyranny. Respect the powers that be *of God,* he urged; when civil magistrates step outside of their duty to protect the civil interests of the people, the power of God fails them and the obligation to obey them disappears. Hall answered that "the Sentence of Judgment by the Legislature is God's Sentence." To the descendants of colonists who had sheltered the regicides, Hall preached something very near to unlimited submission.[46]

Williams envisioned a reasonable world where consciences awakened to the ideals of the Reformation, where the state was becalmed under the Act of Toleration, and where Protestant churches were formed by voluntary association. Hall returned to the arena of power politics. The "sad experience" of Protestant states, he argued, had shown that firm establishment, and not just tolera-

46. Philemon Robbins, *A Plain Narrative of the Proceedings of the Reverend Association and Consociation of New-Haven County, against the Reverend Mr. Robbins of Branford* (Boston, 1747); Ebenezer Frothingham, *A Key to Unlock the Door, That Leads in, to Take a Fair View of the Religious Constitution, Established by Law, in the Colony of Connecticut . . .* ([New Haven, Conn.], 1767), 192–193; John Locke, *A Letter concerning Toleration . . .* (London, 1689). Benjamin Pomeroy, New Light pastor of Hebron, also owned a copy (Baldwin, *New England Clergy,* 65, 3n). The petitions against the 1742 law submitted to the General Assembly by associations of ministers also pointed to natural rights, liberty of conscience, the Act of Toleration, and the violation of church covenants. See Ecclesiastical Papers, VII, nos. 261, 262a, 263a, 265, 267, 268, Connecticut State Library, Hartford, discussed and excerpted in Baldwin, *New England Clergy,* 60–61. The quoted phrases on private judgment as an unalienable right are from "Remarks by Another Hand; in a Letter to a Friend," in Robbins, *A Plain Narrative,* 40. Jonathan Todd, in *A Defence of the Doings of the Reverend Consociation and Association of New-Haven County, respecting Mr. Philemon Robbins . . .* [New London, Conn., 1748], 100, 104–105, suspected that these remarks were written by the same man who wrote *Essential Rights.* The quotations from Hall are from *The Legislatures Right, Charge, and Duty,* 5–6, 8, 11. See also 8: "God will have our Obedience approved in indifferent Things, as well as necessary; and both are charged upon the Consciences of men by the Apostle." Three decades earlier, Hall had been a tutor with young Elisha at the Wethersfield branch of the college and then an assistant to Solomon Stoddard from 1718 to 1721. He might have guessed the identity of "Philalethes." Jonathan Mayhew's famous *Discourse concerning Unlimited Submission and Non-Resistance to the Higher Powers . . .* was published four years later (Boston, 1750). The quotation from Elisha Williams is from his commentary on Rom. 13:1 in *Essential Rights,* 26.

tion, was necessary to keep sectarians away from each other's throats. Religion was and always would be the magistrate's business because of a necessary chain of dependencies: "Society cannot subsist without Government, Government cannot subsist without Peace, Peace cannot subsist without Honesty, and Honesty cannot subsist without Godliness." The stability of the commonwealth could not be left to the whims of private judgment. According to Hall, "Many are ready to say of the Magistrate, Let him take care of my Safety and my Rights, I will take care of my manners and my Religion." But alas, he wrote, human nature is too depraved for such liberty. With the strongest plea for the state's coercive power to issue from the election day pulpit in four decades, Hall argued that men may be forced to be virtuous: "What is begun in Force, may end in Choice; What is begun in Fear, may end in Love." He pointed to the biblical image of Manasseh in chains and fetters, brought to know that the Lord was God. But even if force did not lead to choice and love, "men could be brought to be visibly or externally Good and vertuous." Williams would have recognized the reasoning and remembered his own emphasis years earlier on the visible and the external as the moral domain of the public covenant.[47]

But after the Awakening, Williams had attempted to clear away the exegetical rubbish lying in the way of political understanding. He tried to reconstruct civil and ecclesiastical polity from the inalienable rights of conscience. He used rational arguments and secular language (along with proof texts mostly from the New rather than the Old Testament) to clear away a private, unmolested space for individuals, families, and congregations to enjoy the religion of the heart. His strategic use of political theory was not new to the ebbs and flows of public argument in New England: when John Wise had set aside his Bible and employed Country Party rhetoric in 1717, he still had spoken in a language New England learned culture understood. But after the Awakening, the language of secular political argument gained a reception and an authority it never had before, and it was used much more persistently to address the fundamental questions of moral order. For some, it was simply a new idiom to help reinforce old arguments in a rhetorical world still shaped by religious symbols; for others, like Williams, it helped to separate the realms of church and state, public and private.[48]

47. Hall, *The Legislatures Right, Charge, and Duty,* 15, 19, 20. The reference to Manasseh is from 2 Chron. 33:11–13.

48. Williams's use of rationalist arguments for pietistic ends, therefore, does not fit the categories of Ellis Sandoz, *A Government of Laws: Political Theory, Religion, and the American Founding* (Baton Rouge, La., 1990), 123, and William G. McLoughlin, "The Balkcom Case (1782) and the Pietistic Theory of Separation of Church and State," *WMQ,* 3d Ser.,

In the late 1740s, other Connecticut Calvinists tried to move toward reconciliation rather than prolong the rancor of post-Awakening debate. In 1747, Elisha Williams was chosen to serve on a committee to revise the colony's laws. When issued in 1750, the revision had dropped the 1742 law and restored the Toleration Act that had been repealed in 1743. Nathanael Eells's conciliatory 1748 election sermon borrowed from both sides of the debate. Eells encapsulated the argument for the rights of conscience but warned against the "multitudes that please themselves with the [thoughts] of being saved" and yet "refuse to be governed by the Laws of Christ" or stay humbly in the social stations Providence assigned them. Eells, who had preached Awakening sermons in New London in 1741 and yet had been smeared by itinerant revivalists as a hireling preacher, was more concerned in 1748 with the depressed state of the clergy as a whole owing to the depreciation of currency. Jonathan Todd resumed a harsher tone the following year, but in 1750 Noah Hobart returned to Eells's themes and tried to balance rights and liberties with civil government's duty to support virtue and suppress vice. Like a covenant preacher, Hobart argued that "Sin . . . brings public Guilt; public Guilt deserves public Judgments," and God will punish a wicked community. Yet, for Hobart, civil government was not "concentered" with ecclesiastical government as it was for Gurdon Saltonstall in 1697; nor was it a protective wall around the church, as it was for supporters of the 1742 law. For Hobart, as for Elisha Williams, civil government existed to protect the rights and liberties of individuals.[49]

ELISHA WILLIAMS AS MORAL PURITAN AND PIOUS YANKEE

The movement from covenant to conscience as the foundation of moral order and the focus of debates about state power and religious authority has been seen by some historians as a symptom of broader social and economic transformation. Changes in public discourse are said to reflect eighteenth-century New England's increasingly heterogeneous society and its expanding and di-

XXIV (1967), 267–283, who sharply distinguish between the "pietistic" and "deistic" theories of the separation of church and state, contrasting James Madison's abstract legalism to Isaac Backus's reliance on Scripture and faith. On John Wise, see Breen, *The Character of the Good Ruler*, 252.

49. Nathanael Eells, *The Wise Ruler a Loyal Subject* (New London, Conn., 1748), 28, and see 32–39; Jonathan Todd, *Civil Rulers the Ministers of God, for Good to Men . . .* (New London, Conn., 1749); Noah Hobart, *Civil Government the Foundation of Social Happiness . . .* (New London, Conn., 1751), 18, preached 1750.

versifying economy. Public discourse is also said to herald the emergence of new character types, new conceptions of personal identity emerging out of new social and economic experience. Williams's own passage from "the Publick Covenant" to "Private Judgment" helps clarify what some historians have called the transition from Puritan to Yankee. Taken together, do *Essential Rights* and Williams's public life after the Awakening illustrate the Yankee character? Lockean theories, Richard Bushman argued, "affirmed that men formed the civilized state in pursuit of naked self-interest" and supported Williams's interest in an "economic expansion [that] had generated vital new concerns having to do more with trade and agriculture than with morality." Perry Miller was even blunter, linking the commercial and the theological interests of the whole Williams clan by calling them crypto-Arminian self-worshipers as well as "grafters and land-grabbers." But to understand Williams, the operative word might be "family" rather than "self"; to understand *Essential Rights,* we need to look more to its place within public discourse than to its prefigurations of economic man.[50]

Until his death in 1755, Williams lived very comfortably as a merchant and farmer in Wethersfield. He had been a pastor, a judge, Yale rector, speaker of the house, and a Connecticut militia colonel. The man, like his private letters, coupled piety and commerce, the business of this world and the next; he could be read in different ways. In 1749, Williams had been named as one of the colony's agents to London. Connecticut had petitioned Parliament to be reimbursed for military expenses; Williams, a speculator in soldiers' wages, had paid off his troops and expected a handsome profit when Parliament acted. As he prepared for his voyage, he started making elaborate plans to extend his success as an inland trader to the transatlantic market. Dr. Philip Dodderidge, a leading nonconformist minister who met Williams in England, noted Williams's "ardent sence of religion" and called him "one of the most valuable men

50. Bushman, *From Puritan to Yankee,* 277, 278. As Bushman defined it, the Yankee character combined a "passionate independence" with "avarice and shrewdness," the individualism of nascent capitalists with "a hidden yearning for God" (287). Bushman links Williams's 1744 defense of an individual's pre-political rights to two major forces corroding the Puritan covenant community: economic liberalism and the democratizing, individualizing aspect of revivalism. The Yankee was New England's version of Liberal Man, a character some historians saw being created by complex social and economic processes they labeled "modernization." For a review and powerful critique of the "modernization thesis," see Kenneth A. Lockridge, "The American Revolution, Modernization, and Man: A Critique," in Richard Maxwell Brown and Don E. Fehrenbacher, eds., *Tradition, Conflict, and Modernization: Perspectives on the American Revolution* (New York, 1977), 103–119. Miller discussed the Williamses in *Jonathan Edwards,* esp. 250.

upon earth." Ezra Stiles called him "a Man of Splendor"; Charles Chauncy, perhaps remembering Williams's wealth and political ambitions, thought him too often motivated by self-interest.[51]

Correlations between a religious ethic and the spirit of commerce can be found, not in any drift toward Arminian notions of an unfettered free will, but by returning to Williams's ecclesiology. The merchant's interest in commerce and the minister's sacramentalism intersect at Williams's doctrine of private judgment. Although the dimensions of his character should not be reduced to projections of a philosophical principle, there are more than just verbal similarities between Williams's views of religious and commercial practice. He had spelled out the analogy in 1724: "The [church] ordinances are sometimes Resembled To a Market where there is plenty of all Things needfull To be obtained" from "Christ the fountain of Grace." If he remained a firm believer in Stoddardean "open communion," Elisha would, like his brother Solomon and the Windham County Consociation, "admit all that make an outward, visible and solemn Profession of Faith, not contradicted by their visible Life and Conversation." True saints could enjoy the "peculiar fruits" of Christ's love, whereas carnal men, content with the outward forms of religion, "Naturally are Chusing the means that bring Destruction upon them." The pastor, like the merchant, opened his doors and displayed his wares; it was then up to the "consumers" to choose wisely.[52]

51. Glenn Weaver, *Jonathan Trumbull: Connecticut's Merchant Magistrate (1710–1785)* (Hartford, Conn., 1955), 39–40; Weaver, "Elisha Williams," Conn. Hist. Soc., *Bull.*, LIII (1988), 192–195. With their own vessel and some contacts with London merchants, Williams and his partners hoped to bypass Boston importers and establish a lucrative trading network that would include Ireland, Nova Scotia, and the West Indies. Before setting sail, Williams also conferred with his brother Solomon in Lebanon, Connecticut, about responding to the controversy that was driving Jonathan Edwards from his Northampton pulpit. Members of Edwards's Northampton congregation had asked Elisha to write against Edwards's position, but Elisha left that responsibility, along with some preliminary notes, with Solomon. See Sweeney, "River Gods," chap. 5, esp. 439–442. Dodderidge is quoted in Shipton, *Biographical Sketches*, V, 596; Ezra Stiles, *The Literary Diary of Ezra Stiles, D.D., L.L.D. President of Yale College*, 3 vols., ed. Franklin Bowditch Dexter (New York, 1901), II, 336; Charles Chauncy to Ezra Stiles, 1768, cited in Dexter, *Biographical Sketches of the Graduates of Yale College with the Annals of the College History*, 6 vols. (New York, 1885–1912), I, 665. Chauncy described this "undue regard to self" as a Williams "family foible."

52. The "market" quotation is from Elisha Williams, MS conference sermon on 1 Cor. 11:2, Beinecke Library. Just as a person praying should consider what his soul needs, "so when he is Going to hear the word, he should consider what word he most needs, whether Instruction, awakening, Conviction or Comfort . . . so when he comes to [the Lord's supper] he should consider what he especially wants—whether he needs Grace to be Implanted

For Elisha Williams in 1713, the Lord's Supper had also been a communal ritual that confirmed the public covenant: it was a seal to the second article of the Covenant of Grace as well as the first. But in *Essential Rights,* he speaks only of the *"Gospel Charter"* in which Christ "has granted the Privilege of attending on him in the *Ordinances* he has instituted." In a society that happily tolerates the diverse practices of "the several Denominations in the State," church ordinances could no longer have a broad civil function. Christ's marketplace was considerably larger, and choices, though privately determined, were more public and more diverse. Men will form and follow different judgments about religion just as they do about *"Wit* or *Poetry, Trade,* or *Husbandry,"* Williams wrote. Private judgments, like private property, expressed the character of the man in the public sphere.[53]

However, the idea of corporate morality had not dissolved completely into a free market of individuals pursuing the dictates of their consciences. Self and family, church ordinances and property, all still could be integrated in the rhetoric of the Stoddardean church. In 1736, Elisha's father William had addressed the "covenant people" of Hatfield, Massachusetts—not beneath the rubric of one political body under one government, but as the children of Abraham, an extended family with an inheritance that had to be personally "owned" and then transmitted to the next generation. "Hopes of *Profit* set the whole World at Work," the elder Williams preached, and God's ways were the surest path toward both spiritual and temporal prosperity. But he warned "Private spirits" who would "inclose Religion to themselves" that the pious road to spiritual as well as worldly profit was not just a journey of the self: "You are concern'd to preserve *civil Liberties* and *Properties* to your children, but it is a Thing of far greater Importance to *transmit Religion* to them." In 1759, Elisha's half-brother Solomon Williams would talk in similar terms about God's covenant relation

---

or Increased." Attending church ordinances, each person privately determines whether he needs to have "his joy in Christ more Raised[,] To have his mind more enlightened to see and admire Christ, [or] his heart more Enlarged in obedience to him." The language about open communion is from *The Result of a Council of the Consociated Churches of the County of Windham* ... (Boston, 1747), 14. Solomon Williams signed this report. Solomon Stoddard had argued that it was not for the Christian community to separate apparent saints from morally sincere sinners. He did not restrict the Lord's Supper to those who could testify to a conversion experience but considered it a converting as well as a "sealing" ordinance. Like prayer and preaching, it was a divinely appointed medium to communicate grace in all its particular operations in or upon the soul. Quotations from Elisha Williams on personal choice are from Elisha Williams, MS sermon on Canticles 1:7, July 1743, and Williams, undated MS fragment, both in the Beinecke Library.

53. Williams, "Publick Covenant," 22; [Williams], *Essential Rights,* 34, 42.

to his church as a legacy that needed to be transmitted to the next generation of British Americans.[54]

In his later years, Elisha Williams's greatest moral concern was, not about the encroachment upon individual rights, but about "the woful Relaxation of *Family-Discipline* and Government," as his friend James Lockwood recalled in 1755. Families like the extensive kin network of the Williamses of Massachusetts and Connecticut had become the self-appointed guardians of liberty, property, and evangelical piety. Conscientious heads of households were now the bulwarks of moral order in an expanded religious marketplace, and the community was encouraged to trust them and the invisible hand of Providence to guide individual moral choices for the good of the whole. As an analysis of property relations in Williams's Wethersfield concludes, to posit the sudden rise of an ideology of competitive, self-interested individuals "is to foreshorten history."[55]

In 1713, Williams's doctrine of the public covenant had joined two aspects of God's governance over men in the world: the Father's care of nations and peoples and the Son's presence in the hearts of the redeemed. It knit together church and state, piety and politics, in a single moral discourse. In 1744, the Williams brothers began unraveling that rhetoric and suggested that two distinct arguments could be put in its place for discussing the relationship between church and state. Solomon Williams's collection of sermons entitled *Christ, the King and Witness of Truth* is the pietistic counterpart to Elisha's political argument. Christ's kingdom is spiritual, not worldly, Solomon insists. A

54. William Williams, *The Duty and Interest of a People, among Whom Religion Has Been Planted, to Continue Stedfast and Sincere in the Profession and Practice of It, from Generation to Generation* (Boston, 1736), 41, 57, 79; Solomon Williams, *The Relations of God's People to Him*... (New London, Conn., 1760). See also William Williams, *An Essay to Prove the Interest of the Children of Believers in the Covenant, and the Obligations of Both Parents and Children, Arising from Thence* (Boston, 1727); and William Williams, *The Great Concern of Christians, and Especially of Ministers, to Preserve the Doctrine of Christ in It's Purity* (Boston, 1723).

55. Lockwood, *Man Mortal*, 39; Toby L. Ditz, *Property and Kinship: Inheritance in Early Connecticut, 1750–1820* (Princeton, N.J., 1986), esp. 163–172 (quotation on 172). Ditz's discussion relates inheritance strategies in Connecticut to Revolutionary-era ideology and complements Sweeney's study of Williams's family culture. Elisha's will tried to "control filial behavior" by tying his son's ownership of the home lot to continued residence with Elisha's widow (109). "Williams used Lockean logic to argue that the [1742 anti-itinerancy] legislation illegitimately encroached on 'natural liberty.'... But Lockean logic did not produce any malaise about prolonged tutelage with respect to parental property.... As corrosive as a Lockean argument could sometimes be in the public sphere, it was no threat to the internal domestic organization of even the more patriarchal households of American freemen" (109–110).

person can become one of Christ's subjects only by free choice, and can so choose only if regenerated. "The Constitutions of Civil Governments [are] entirely of a different Nature and Design," he wrote. "The Laws of earthly Kingdoms respect the Estates and Properties of Men, their Lives and Limbs . . . but the Laws of Christ reach all the inward Motions and Actings of the Heart." The Williams brothers never denounced the doctrine of the public covenant itself, only the inferences about civil and ecclesiastical power that so many (like Elisha in 1713) had drawn from it. Indeed, Solomon used covenant language again in his thanksgiving sermon for the fall of Quebec in 1759. By that time, however, writers were finding other ways to talk about the relationship between religion and public life.[56]

The public covenant had always been a compound of Old Testament national election and New Testament congregational covenant; it tried to combine the medieval church's notion of a comprehensive Christendom with the Reformation's exclusive gathering of saints; it blended God's providential rule over the rise and fall of nations with his special care for the redemptive work of the church as it progressed through time toward the last days. Williams's 1713 argument had leaned toward the Old Testament and supported the power and authority of church and state to maintain moral order demanded by the covenant. After the Awakening, he leaned the other way, toward a defense of the rights of conscience and the private practice of religion, and an increasing number of writers leaned with him. The 1742 law had shown many besides the Williamses that the state needed to be distanced from religious life, and that distance substantially diminished the power of the public covenant as the theological foundation of social order.

LINKING THE SACRED AND THE PROFANE, 1750–1785

So how can we assess the fate of covenant discourse in the eighteenth century? It was not a monolithic consensual myth before 1740, and it did not vanish from the scene after 1750. After midcentury, covenant language was used less for society at large and applied more exclusively to the church (though cove-

56. Solomon Williams, *Christ, the King and Witness of Truth, and the Nature, Excellency, and Extent of His Kingdom, as Founded in Truth, and Only Promoted by It* (Boston, 1744), 65, 75, 80. The focus on Christ's kingdom would be developed into a Christocentric politics that ignored Old Testament covenantalism completely. For another early example, see Timothy Woodbridge's Connecticut election sermon for 1727, *Jesus Christ Doth Actually Reign on the Earth . . .* (New London, Conn., 1727).

nant ideas were challenged and redefined in that context as well). Many clergymen stopped speaking about God's making national covenants with contemporary kingdoms or commonwealths, and yet, on special public occasions, some still addressed "God's People" in New England and spoke of their "Covenant God." The covenant they mentioned, however, usually in a passing phrase as part of the exhortative rather than exegetical portion of their sermons, is in most cases more accurately understood as God's covenant promise to all Christian churches, including those in New England, rather than God's public covenant with New England society at large. That did not mean the body politic was exempt from God's corporate judgments. The national covenant might have dropped from the political vocabulary of Christian gentlemen like Elisha Williams, but state fasting and thanksgiving proclamations along with occasional sermons from the 1750s through the 1780s continued to remind Connecticut's citizens that God, in his providential rule and moral government of the universe, still punished public sins.[57]

Covenant language did not disappear; it lost its power to legitimate church-state coercion in the name of moral order. Elisha Williams and others who argued against the 1742 law shifted the scriptural grounds of the debate from the Old Testament to the New and the historical grounds from New England's heritage to the English subject's inheritance under the Toleration Act. Anglicans, on the other hand, poisoned the coercive party's arguments for magisterial power by agreeing wholeheartedly with them; but Anglicans vested that power

57. George Beckwith rejoiced that earthquakes in 1755 had devastated "popish, and mahometan Countries" but had only rumbled a warning to God's Covenant People. Peter Raynolds explained instead that God follows a single rule in his dealings with nations and had bestowed favors on their land because the "truly Godly" had kept it from sinking as low as other parts of the world. See Beckwith, *That People a Safe, and Happy People, Who Have God for, and among Them* . . . (New London, Conn., 1756), 62, 62n–63n; Raynolds, *The Kingdom Is the Lord's; or, God the Supreme Ruler and Governour of the World* . . . (New London, Conn., 1757), 37. On providential rule, see, for example, Lockwood, *Religion the Highest Interest of a Civil Community;* and Samuel Sherwood, *A Sermon, Containing, Scriptural Instructions to Civil Rulers, and All Free-Born Subjects* . . . (New Haven, Conn., 1774), in Ellis Sandoz, ed., *Political Sermons of the American Founding Era, 1730–1805* (Indianapolis, Ind., 1991), 373–407. Ashbel Woodbridge, in *A Sermon Delivered before the General Assembly of the Colony of Connecticut, on the Anniversary Election at Hartford, May 14, 1752* (New London, Conn., 1752), had singled out a particular public sin, a sin arising from a lapse in family government and a peculiar form of property: the fornication of unmarried and often unbaptized slaves (35–37). No doubt Elisha Williams catechized his six slaves and acknowledged their liberty of conscience, even as he wrote out his final bequests and willed them to his children "to be at [their] Absolute Dispose" (Elisha Williams, Will, July 16, 1755, Beinecke Library).

in the crown and Parliament and called for the Connecticut establishment of the Church of England rather than the Saybrook Platform. That shifted the Congregationalist-Anglican debate toward political and constitutional questions about the relationship between the colonies and the mother country. Old Lights themselves seemed to surrender the hope for consensus and uniformity under the covenant by arguing on the basis of majority rights and contractual obligations. In the 1750s and 1760s, when in some counties antirevivalists became the minority even in the ecclesiastical associations, Old Lights too raised the cry of "liberty of conscience" against New Light persecution. The plea for liberty of conscience was not the intellectual property of New Light libertarians opposing Old Light spokesmen of order and authority; it was a polemical weapon that the 1742 law helped reintroduce into public debate in Connecticut. The authoritarian "we" of covenant rhetoric was a fiction that could no longer be used to cover the fractious midcentury debates.[58]

Yet some New England ministers would still find covenant language serviceable in an imperial context during the wars with France, a struggle that at times seemed to threaten the very existence of British America and tested every premise of New England's collective identity. Some preachers were confident that a covenant people could vanquish papist idolaters and their heathen accomplices; others lost faith in the New England people at large and hoped that God would bring victory for the sake of the godly. Rhode Island's William Vinal simply expanded the outer boundaries of New England's national covenant to include all of British America. Vinal's sermon on Braddock's defeat em-

---

58. On the Anglican debate, see J[ohn] Wetmore, "A Prefatory Address to the Gentlemen of America," in [Edward Weston], *The Englishman Directed in the Choice of His Religion* (Boston, 1748), 5–31. Weston's arguments must have sounded familiar to Connecticut Old Lights: How can there be unity in the church if everyone follows his fancy and none submit to public order? "But who is to be the Judge of this Order and Decency? Is every private person fit to Judge what is to be done in the House of God?" (64). Wetmore cites John Cotton's writings on the covenant, the Saybrook Platform, and the 1742 Anti-Itinerancy Act as evidence that New England Congregationalists affirmed that the civil magistrate could legislate in religious affairs. Once one acknowledges "the Authority of King and Parliament" as "the supreme Magistracy of this Nation," the establishment of the Anglican Church in New England follows as a logical conclusion (25–30). Beginning in the 1750s, it was the Old Lights who argued for private judgment and essential rights against proposals for orthodoxy tests. See, for example, William Hart, *A Few Remarks upon the Ordination of the Rev'd Mr. James Dana . . .* (New Haven, Conn., 1759); and Bushman, *From Puritan to Yankee*, 217–219. Anglican Samuel Johnson also blasted Yale for infringing upon its students' liberty of conscience. For Johnson's criticisms, see Louis Leonard Tucker, *Puritan Protagonist: President Thomas Clap of Yale College* (Chapel Hill, N.C., 1962), 178–183.

MEANING AND MORAL ORDER

ployed the traditional "errand" rhetoric of New England as "God's peculiar People," but then simply noted that "by New-England, some understand all the British Colonies in North America; others only a Part." Vinal asserted that, under the eyes of both God and man, "All the *British* Colonies consider'd *collectively* and *politically*, are *one Body*." [59]

There were other ways, though, to talk about the religious meaning of the Anglo-French wars. Solomon Williams did not begin his 1755 discourse on the war by invoking covenant logic or casting the struggle as a holy war with apocalyptic significance. Instead he argued from the just war tradition. Not because of a special status assumed a priori, but because their cause was just, British Americans could march forward under God's banner with the hope that he would decide the controversy in their favor. When Quebec fell, Williams returned to covenant language and chose the text for his thanksgiving sermon carefully. In Exod. 15:2, Moses and the Israelites sing God's praises just after pharaoh's army had been drowned in the Red Sea. "God had not yet explicitly taken them into Covenant with himself, as he did a little after this at *Mount Sinai,*" Williams explained. But the Israelites could look back to the covenant God had made with their fathers, Abraham, Isaac, and Jacob, and the promises extending to their seed. This generation of Israelites, then, prefigured bap-

59. Whereas Samuel Webster was confident that God would not forsake the New England Israel that he had planted in the American Canaan, Timothy Harrington considered the extinction of American Protestantism a distinct possibility. Though Samuel Checkley preached that God honored and strengthened his externally covenanted people when they marched off to war, Samuel Wigglesworth, Thomas Pollen, and John Ballantine warned that having once been God's favorite People meant nothing. John Cotton followed the prophet Zephaniah, who called for all the Jews to repent, yet, "having little Expectation of prevailing with them in general, he turn[ed] his Speech to the faithful Ones." Old and New England had been blessed with prosperity solely for the sake of the godly, not for some external covenant, he argued. Perhaps it was time for the saints to be wafted to heaven, Cotton preached, and for the rest of New England to be destroyed. See Samuel Webster, *Soldiers and Others, Directed and Encouraged, When Going on a Just and Important, tho' Difficult, Enterprize against Their Enemies . . .* (Boston, 1756); Samuel Checkley, *The Duty of God's People When Engaged in War* (Boston, 1755); Samuel Wigglesworth, *God's Promise to an Obedient People, of Victory over Their Enemies . . .* (Boston, 1755); Thomas Pollen, *A Sermon Preached in Trinity Church, Newport, Rhode-Island . . . upon Occasion of the Embarkation of Some of the Colony's Troops, in Order to Go against the Enemy* (Newport, R.I., 1755); John Ballantine, *The Importance of God's Presence with an Army Going against the Enemy; and the Grounds on Which It May Be Expected . . .* (Boston, 1756); John Cotton, *God's Call to His People;— Shewing Their Duty and Safety, in Days of General Calamity* (Boston, 1757), 9. The quotations from William Vinal are from *A Sermon on the Accursed Thing That Hinders Success and Victory in War . . .* (Newport, R.I., 1755), 15n, 20.

tized but unconverted Christians: they lived under the *promises* of their fathers' covenant and had to engage those promises by honoring God and preparing "an habitation" for him. Williams applied this text "to *New-England,* and the rest of the *British subjects* in America." You too, he told his congregation, had pious and holy fathers in covenant. You too have been saved from your enemies. As a vast British empire in America opened for settlement, "every *English American*" ought to prepare his soul as God's habitation and resolve to cleave to God as the New England forefathers had. Williams also joined many others in calling for the country as a whole to prepare a habitation for Christ's church on the frontier by sending missionaries to Christianize the Indians.[60]

The covenant relation depicted in Williams's 1759 thanksgiving sermon is ambiguous, as it is in other sermons during the French wars. Was the covenant in question a covenant with the nation or with the church? Did the sermon declare that English Americans were now in a covenant with God, or did it merely set out the obligations the rising generation was under according to the covenant made by their New England fathers, a covenant that they had not yet made their own? If theologically ambiguous, Williams was rhetorically successful in combining a persuasive appeal aimed at baptized but unconverted congregants with a dawning vision of the westward course of Anglo-American civilization. Many ministers (like Solomon and Elisha Williams) had abandoned the use of covenant language as a warrant for the exercise of state power in religious affairs; others went further and spoke of the covenant only in reference

60. Just war arguments had been recently given fresh currency after Gilbert Tennent's debates with the Quakers over Christian pacifism. See Gilbert Tennent, *The Late Association for Defense, Encourag'd; or, The Lawfulness of a Defensive War* (Philadelphia, [1748]); Tennent, *The Late Association for Defense, Farther Encourag'd...* (Philadelphia, [1748]); Tennent, *The Late Association for Defense ... in a Reply to Some Exceptions against War in a Late Composure, Intituled, The Doctrine of Christianity, as Held by the People Called Quakers, Vindicated* (Philadelphia, 1748). On preaching, the just war tradition, and the American Revolution, see Melvin B. Endy, Jr., "Just War, Holy War, and Millennialism in Revolutionary America," *WMQ,* 3d Ser., XLII (1985), 3–25. See Williams, *The Relations of God's People to Him,* 10–11: "Tho' God did not call our fathers in that extraordinary Manner, as he did *Abraham,* nor promise them *New-England,* or *North America,* as he promised *Canaan* to *Abraham* and his seed. Yet he offer'd our fathers the Call of the Gospel, and the Privileges of the Covenant of Grace through Jesus Christ, and by his Grace he persuaded them to accept this Offer. So they became his People, and he became their God as truly, and really, as if this had been transacted by an immediate Call from Heaven." Cf. Eli Forbes, *God the Strength and Salvation of His People...* (Boston, 1761), a sermon preached the following year on the same text (Exod. 15:2). Neither Forbes nor David Hall's *Israel's Triumph...* (Boston, 1761), on Exod. 15:1, focused on *how* the colonies "resemble" the tribes of Israel, as Williams does.

to the church and not when addressing broad public concerns. Some preachers, however, like Solomon Williams, recast the rhetoric to fit new situations.[61]

The public covenant persisted into the Revolutionary period too, but not as the dominant motif. In 1775, Connecticut's General Association of Congregationalist churches commented on the "melancholly state of public affairs" and called both church members and "others" to repentance under the public covenant. A General Association call for a fast in 1780, however, instructed the people to acknowledge their God "in that relation, in which they respectively stand." Rather than a people's single, unifying relationship to God under the public covenant, the declaration was careful to distinguish three "relations": full church members, people who had only been baptized, and those who were distinguished from heathens only by living in a place where the gospel was preached.[62]

Not every mention of a "covenant" that does appear in the political sermons of this period is a reference to the myth of New England as City on a Hill or America as Redeemer Nation. In some cases, the assertion found in the sources that "We are a Covenant people" is nothing more than saying, "We are Christians," or "We are under the teachings of the Gospel," as opposed to heathens or anti-Christian papists, and has nothing at all to do with pretensions of national election for England, New England, or America, a typological relation between a modern nation and Israel, or any elevation of Christians in one country over Christians in others. References to God's helping George Washington win a battle can be (and were) explained by just war arguments and

61. Hopeful expansiveness is a component of what Nathan O. Hatch has termed the "civil millennialism" of this period; see Hatch, *The Sacred Cause of Liberty: Republican Thought and the Millennium in Revolutionary New England* (New Haven, Conn., 1977), chap. 1.

62. Congregational Churches in Connecticut, General Association, *The Records of the General Association of the Colony of Connecticut; Begun June 20th, 1738; Ending June 19, 1799* (Hartford, Conn., 1888), 85, 106. Cyprian Strong, pastor of the First Church in Chatham, described New England as an apparently covenanted New Israel in a sermon probably preached in 1775, but later in the century he preached an election sermon arguing that no people had been especially chosen since the Jews and that God administered the affairs of all nations in precisely the same way. See Strong, *God's Care of the New-England Colonies . . .* (Hartford, Conn., [1777]), which seems to have been preached before the first shots were fired in 1775; and Strong, *The Kingdom Is the Lord's . . .* (Hartford, Conn., 1799). On Dec. 11, 1783, for the thanksgiving celebration of the peace with Great Britain, Massachusetts Presbyterian John Murray preached *Jerubbaal; or, Tyranny's Grove Destroyed, and the Altar of Liberty Finished . . .* (Newburyport, Mass., 1784), which explicitly invokes the public covenant. This is the only postwar covenant sermon cited by Jonathan Sassi's "To Envision a Godly Society."

providence and do not necessarily imply a covenant relation. Millennialist accounts explaining how Revolutionary events were directly related to the outpouring of the sixth or seventh vial mentioned in Revelation can do so without at all sacralizing the American nation-state or granting all Americans a peculiar status in God's eyes (the church in America is not the same as America as church, or, in other words, as a privileged body of believers).[63]

North Haven pastor Benjamin Trumbull's unpublished sermons reveal how the ambiguities of covenant discourse make it easy to confuse discussions that refer to a public covenant between God and a whole people or nation and a more exclusive church covenant offered to everyone but actually encompassing only the converted full members of the church. In some sermons, Trumbull spoke interchangeably about God's dealings with churches and communities, nations and peoples, New England and America; he described a people in general taking hold of the covenant or a whole nation enjoying covenant privileges. But then he would go on to argue that no one could enter into a covenant with God except through a true, heartfelt belief in Christ, that the phrase "God's people" referred only to the regenerate, that nations meant nothing, and all was done to prosper the church of the saints. People did not participate in the covenant Trumbull described because they were citizens of a Christian nation; they were party to the covenant only if they had been born again and professed a personal faith.[64]

63. Joseph Huntington, *God Ruling the Nations for the Most Glorious End . . .* (Hartford, Conn., 1784), for example, defined God's "covenant people" as "the church, the people of God in every age," scattered through the nations of the earth (18). Certainly, the comparison to Israel was everywhere, but what was the nature of that comparison? Ezra Stiles in his famous 1783 election sermon, *The United States Elevated to Glory and Honor . . .* (New Haven, Conn., 1783), spoke loosely of "God's American Israel," but he did not mean that America was under the mantle of a national covenant. He explained the difference between moral law and a covenant relation. Moral law is in force "without any reference to the consent of the governed." On the other hand, "in the case of Israel [God] condescended to a mutual covenant," which the people of Israel voluntarily engaged. Stiles then described Israel as unique in the history of the world as God's peculiarly chosen people. When Stiles turned to America, he did not say, "And we have a covenant too." He wrote, "I have assumed the [biblical] text only as introduction to a discourse upon the political welfare of God's American Israel; and as allusively prophetic of the future prosperity and splendor of the United States" (5–7). When he listed the reasons why Americans might expect the flourishing of their Republic, he mentioned nothing about its covenantal status. For more on Stiles and covenant preaching, see Chapter 5.

64. See the following manuscript sermons in the Benjamin Trumbull Papers, Manuscripts and Archives, Yale University Library, New Haven, Conn.: Sermon No. 1219, 1220, Jan. 20, 1776 (on the fall of General Montgomery and the defeat of his army at Quebec), 1249,

It is not accurate to depict the Puritan national covenant as the central paradigm of the Revolutionary clergy's public discourse about moral order. But neither is it accurate to replace this old synthesis with a new one. Studies that focus exclusively upon a rhetoric of evangelical liberty rooted in the Awakening, a "civil millennialism" formulated during the Anglo-French wars, or a republican religion accommodating radical whig thought after the Stamp Act crisis emphasize some themes at the expense of others, overly homogenizing the clergy's political-religious expression.

After midcentury, the themes of what we might call "providential politics" and "redemptive history" moved through public discussion as different ways to understand God's relationship to human societies. We have seen how the rhetoric of universal providence emerged alongside Deuteronomic and errand sermons early in the century; after midcentury, universal providence became the most common explanation of God's involvement with kingdoms and nations. The key text was still Prov. 14:34: "Righteousness exalteth a nation: but sin is a reproach to any people." But whatever Old Testament text they preached from, ministers emphasized the *difference* between the original context—Jehovah's speaking to his covenant people Israel—and the contemporary situation. Even in a thanksgiving sermon celebrating American Independence Thomas Brockway reminded his congregation that the events they had experienced differed significantly from Israel's victory over Canaan because "England came not against the covenant people of the Lord." "We had no such national covenant to plead, as had the Jews." God's instructions to Israel were taken as general maxims that could be freely applied to any nation.[65]

1250, written June 19, 1776, delivered Feb. 16, 24, 1777, 1277, 1278, May 4, 1777, 1279–1284, June 8, 15, 1777, 1340, 1341, Sept. 27, 1778, 1925, Nov. 1, 1787, 2180, circa 1795–1796. Trumbull also seems to have preached yearly at the Freemen's meeting, but he focused on themes like the character of the good ruler and the necessity of religion to government rather than the public covenant.

65. Thomas Brockway, *America Saved; or, Divine Glory Displayed in the Late War with Great Britain* . . . (Hartford, Conn., [1784]), 7. Peter Raynolds, *The Kingdom Is the Lord's; or, God the Supreme Ruler and Governour of the World* . . . (New London, Conn., 1757), explained that "God has a *Two fold Kingdom* in the World.—The *Kingdom of his Power, or Providence:* And the *Kingdom of his Grace*" (10). My distinction between "providential" and "redemptive" is *not* the difference between Christian teleology and a cyclical classical republicanism stressing the turning wheel of *Fortuna*. "Providential" and "redemptive" are both Christian interpretations. A providential interpretation reminds the reader or listener that temporal events like the rise and fall of nations, the coming of revolutions, victory or defeat in battles (right down to weather conditions and the mood of the soldiers) are not dependent upon chance or fortune but are directed by the hand of God for his purposes.

In sermons from the 1750s through the 1780s that stressed universal providence, the proposition that the prevalence of vice among a people created a suffering and miserable society revealed, not Jehovah's chastisements, but principles rooted in moral phenomena just as gravitation and attraction were fixed principles of the physical universe. Some ministers, like Moses Mather in 1775, would even describe providence as a synonym for nature: "It is with states as it is with men, they have their infancy, their manhood and their decline: Nature hath its course in all, and never works in vain; when a people are ripe for any change, means wont be wanting to effect it. For what providence hath done and is doing for us, we must learn, what is our duty to do; for we may only follow, where nature leads, and in this is infinite safety."[66]

In the explosion of political debate from the Stamp Act crisis in 1765 through the Revolutionary period, preachers positing universal providence focused intently upon the "second causes" of temporal happiness and misery, whereas the unchanging rules of providence moved further into the background. That is, one hears less of God's specific and active interpositions into the affairs of society and more about the struggle of men among themselves, less about sin, judgment, and mercies and more about charters, constitutions, and natural rights. Clergymen argued that "the great, and primary end of civil government, (subordinate to GOD's glory) is the good of mankind, or the public interest," giving God's glory a quick parenthetical nod and then elaborating on the ways civil government served or betrayed the public interest. In *Scriptural Instructions to Civil Rulers* (1774), Samuel Sherwood went so far as to argue that, if the king and ministry destroyed Connecticut's royal charter, the noxious effects would be so severe that even God in his providence would be unable to make

---

These purposes may still appear hidden to us, but certainly the event must be part of God's larger plan for human history (although the writer or orator does not pause to speculate about the specifics of this plan). Sermons emphasizing redemptive history are keyed much more specifically to Christ's temporal work of Redemption, saying of a particular event or occurrence not just that God directed it but how it fits into the linear sequence of events from Adam's Fall to the millennium. Providential readings primarily assert divine agency behind temporal events; redemptive readings explicate divine intentions according to a continuation of the sacred narrative.

66. [Moses Mather], *America's Appeal to the Impartial World* (Hartford, Conn., 1775), in Sandoz, ed., *Political Sermons*, 439–492 (quotation on 488–489). See also Sherwood, *Scriptural Instructions to Civil Rulers*, ibid., 373–407; Enoch Huntington, *The Happy Effects of Union and the Fatal Tendency of Divisions* . . . (Hartford, Conn., 1776); Benjamin Trumbull, *God Is to Be Praised for the Glory of His Majesty, and for His Mighty Works* . . . (New Haven, Conn., 1784); and the election sermons for 1754, 1755, 1762, 1766, 1770, 1771, 1774, 1775, 1779, 1781, 1785, and 1787 (citations in Appendix 2).

the people secure and happy without suspending the laws of nature and performing "immediate miracles."[67]

If God's hand becomes less visible in these political sermons, in the Christocentric sermons of redemptive history it is secular politics and the affairs of state that wither into relative insignificance. Often infused with the millennial fervor that historians have found so prevalent in the second half of the eighteenth century, these Christocentric sermons reduce the civil state to a mere appendage of the church militant; secular affairs become little more than marginalia to the central story of Christ's work of Redemption and the progress of his church in the world. In the late 1760s, Edward Eells and Eliphalet Williams demonstrated that Jesus Christ himself was the "immediate fountain of the magistrate's power." Rather than the covenant preacher's Jehovah or the universal providence sermon's Creator, it was Christ who created, sustained, and regulated civil governments, the movements of profane history, and all the affairs of the temporal world. Izrahiah Wetmore told the Connecticut General Assembly in 1773 that worldly statesmen and politicians had it backward: they considered Christianity "a little inferior Object" used to strengthen and improve civil government. But in fact, Wetmore argued, "Civil Government is kept up and supported in the Methods of Providence, chiefly and principally as a Mean to promote the Church of Christ." In Christ's plan of Redemption, the affairs of nations and states were but "mean, and trifling things."[68]

One of the most famous redemptive sermons is *The Church's Flight into the Wilderness* by Samuel Sherwood, pastor of a church in Weston, Connecticut.

67. Samuel Lockwood, *Civil Rulers an Ordinance of God, for Good to Mankind . . .* (New London, Conn., 1774), 10; Sherwood, *Scriptural Instructions to Civil Rulers*, in Sandoz, ed., *Political Sermons*, 398. Counts, "The Political Views of the Eighteenth Century New England Clergy," 138, also found a shift in emphasis toward the temporal aims of government in this period.

68. Edward Eells, *Christ, the Foundation of the Salvation of Sinners, and of Civil and Ecclesiastical Government* (Hartford, Conn., [1767]), 18; Eliphalet Williams, *A Sermon Preached in the Audience of the General Assembly of the Colony of Connecticut* (Hartford, Conn., 1769) (the quotation is from Williams's doctrine, but Eells uses similar language); Izrahiah Wetmore, *A Sermon Preached before the Honorable General Assembly of the Colony of Connecticut . . .* ([New London, Conn.], 1773), 11–12, 16. See also Levi Hart, *Liberty Described and Recommended . . .* (Hartford, Conn., 1775), in Charles S. Hyneman and Donald S. Lutz, eds., *American Political Writing during the Founding Era, 1760–1805*, 2 vols. (Indianapolis, Ind., 1983), I, 305–317; Huntington, *The Happy Effects of Union;* Joseph Huntington, *God Ruling the Nations for the Most Glorious End . . .* (Hartford, Conn., 1784); Brockway, *America Saved;* Rozel Cook, *A Sermon Delivered at New-London, North-Parish . . .* (New London, Conn., 1784); Ammi R. Robbins, *The Empires and Dominions of This World Made Subservient to the Kingdom of Christ . . .* (Hartford, Conn., 1789).

Preached from Rev. 12:14–17 on January 17, 1776, the sermon is notable for the way it ties the American struggle to scriptural prophecy, concluding: "We have incontestible evidence, that God Almighty, with all the powers of heaven, are on our side. Great numbers of angels, no doubt, are encamping round our coast, for our defence and protection." Sherwood wrote with his gaze fixed upon the Second Coming but had no intention of providing timetables or predictions. He argued that the scriptural prophecies could be applied to the Church of Christ in every age as it struggled against the forces of Antichrist and that each of these "parallel" struggles may be "types and figures" of the final decisive battles of the Apocalypse. He did not, however, anoint the Continental colonies as a redeemer nation, proclaim Americans as the new chosen people, or sacralize the civil state. America is simply the place—the particular "quarter of the globe"—where the church (like Revelation's "woman in the wilderness") escaped and might flourish into the Latter Days. Secular powers, like the material riches drawn from the continent itself, could help nourish and protect the church, but the kingdoms of the world would all be dissolved when Christ began his millennial reign on earth.[69]

It is a mistake to try to crudely divide providential and redemptive preachers according to putative party affiliations—New Light versus Old, Arminian versus Calvinist, liberal versus conservative. Writers like Samuel Sherwood could speak in both idioms. The challenge was—absent the integrating function of the public covenant—getting the two idioms to intersect. How was politics, with its increasingly technical disputes over natural liberties, legal statutes, royal charters, and constitutional rights, still connected in vital ways to the work of the church? On the other hand, how could the minister preaching about the work of Redemption promote an active engagement in civic affairs if the church was all that really mattered and states and nations might be ready to dissolve in the millennial dawn? No longer relying upon covenant discourse, preachers from the 1750s through the 1780s found other ways to relate—if not

69. Samuel Sherwood, *The Church's Flight into the Wilderness . . .* (New York, 1776), in Sandoz, ed., *Political Sermons*, 504, 507, 508, 513–514, 522, 525, 532n. Just war theory holds that God actively helps the party in a conflict whose cause is just, without imputing any special status to the party itself. Sherwood went beyond that and wrote that Americans were engaged in a *sacred* cause—an *international* struggle for civil and religious liberty. The moment Americans, or anyone else, embrace this cause, they are doing God's work and furthering the cause of his church. But the only people, or institution, or corporate body that retains any special or redemptive or sacred status is Christians and the church, not Americans and the United States. For a discussion of Sherwood's argument, see Stephen J. Stein, "An Apocalyptic Rationale for the American Revolution," *Early American Literature*, IX (1975), 211–225.

fuse—religion and politics, Redemption and providence, the sacred and the profane.

One way preachers yoked contemporary events to the sacred was simply to speak loosely and figuratively about the present with scriptural language, establishing a rhetorical if not a theological connection. Preachers could perpetuate the stock phrases of Puritan public discourse and the habit of identifying New England (or America) with Israel even if the doctrinal basis for that relationship no longer existed. A sermon could begin by explaining that God's moral government was quite different before the Christian era, assert that no nations were in covenant with God as Israel had been, and disclaim any divinely instituted typological relationship between the events described in the sacred text and those occurring outside the meetinghouse windows; a sermon could do all of that and then go on to refer to the New England "Israel" enjoying the American "Canaan" or struggling to be freed from the British "Pharaoh." During the Revolution, that was often more than mere rhetorical embellishment. John Devotion and Nicholas Street in 1777 and David Avery in 1778 so thoroughly interwove biblical history and descriptions of contemporary events that any doctrinal distinctions were overwhelmed; juxtaposed with sacred stories and narrated with King James cadences, local experience and the latest news could be elevated to cosmic importance as powerfully as in any seventeenth-century errand sermon. Sometimes, however, the borrowed scriptural language or extended analogies can seem quite forced. Joseph Huntington sounded the redemptive theme in 1784, arguing the doctrine that God divided and regulated the nations of the world according to the interests of his true church, his covenanted Christians scattered throughout many kingdoms and states. But in the final "improvement" section of the sermon, Huntington lists the similarities between Israel and the United States: their Canaan was fertile, and so is our Columbia; they had a population of about three million, and do so we; they had a Sanhedrin of thirteen tribes, we have a Congress of thirteen states; "their government was theocratical; so for substance is our free elective government, according to that old maxim, *vox populi vox dei.*" [70]

70. John Devotion, *The Duty and Interest of a People to Sanctify the Lord of Hosts* . . . (Hartford, Conn., 1777); Nicholas Street, *The American States Acting over the Part of the Children of Israel* . . . (New Haven, Conn., 1777); David Avery, *The Lord Is to Be Praised for the Triumph of His Power* . . . (Norwich, Conn., 1778). Bernard Bailyn offered a similar reading of "a wonderfully obscure Connecticut parson," Stephen Johnson of Lyme, Connecticut, in "Religion and Revolution: Three Biographical Sketches," *Perspectives in American History,* IV (1970), 85–169 (quotation on 86), republished in Bailyn, *Faces of Revolution: Personalities and Themes in the Struggle for American Independence* (New York, 1990), 104–149 (quo-

Preachers also tried to integrate religion and politics through the theme of "sacred liberty." Paeans to liberty entered political sermons in the late 1750s, as the war with France heightened the contrast between Catholic tyranny and the New Englanders' own chartered privileges and constitutional freedoms. Liberty was celebrated as a more expansive principle than Elisha Williams's freedom from restraints on the rights of conscience. Liberty, James Lockwood wrote, is "the Nurse of Arts and Sciences, the Parent of Diligence and Industry, the Procurer of Wealth and Riches, and needful to the unmolested Profession and Practice of Christianity it self: it adds Chearfulness, Ease and Alacrity to the Mind—Sweetens and endears the Social Life, and heightens the Relish of all the common Enjoyments of Time." It became for some, in short, the fundamental defining principle of Protestant civilization. Clergymen hurriedly melded the religious liberty of conscience, the ecclesiastical liberty of the church, the civil liberty of the Protestant state, and the spiritual liberty from sin through Christ. Vestigial traces of old errand sermons appeared as the New England founders, though admittedly lacking enough of the modern spirit of toleration, were hailed as champions of liberty. With language that resembled the calls for an outpouring of God's Spirit in the 1730s, preachers in the 1760s and 1770s hoped for a heightened "public spirit" in defense of the sacred cause of liberty. In 1776, Samuel Sherwood directly connected the outpouring of grace to the inflamed passion for liberty: those who shared the sentiment for liberty and joined the cause for its defense were, at least for the moment, doing God's work, whether they were New England Baptists, Southern Episcopalians, or Europeans cheering from across the Atlantic. Two years later, David Avery saw signs that the Revolutionary struggle for liberty was beginning to spark a religious revival. Just as in the 1740s, however, there were others who cautioned that not everything about the public's awakened enthusiasm bespoke a Christian spirit: "Would to God," Chauncey Whittelsey preached in 1778, "that the animation of piety was as strong and universal, as the passion for liberty."[71]

tation on 105). In a 1766 fast sermon on the Stamp Act, Johnson conflated biblical history and secular sources by drawing from Samuel Shuckford, *The Sacred and Prophane History of the World Connected . . .* (London, 1728). The result, Bailyn argued, was, not "a single sustained identification of images," as in a typological interpretation, but "a shifting series of overlays—of individuals, events, and statements—the net impact of which is an unspecified yet comprehensive portrayal of seventeenth- and eighteenth-century problems in biblical terms" (145–146). The quotation from Joseph Huntington is in *God Ruling the Nations,* 24.

71. James Lockwood, *The Worth and Excellence of Civil Freedom and Liberty Illustrated, and a Public Spirit and the Love of Our Country Recommended . . .* (New London, Conn., 1759), 24–25; Hart, *Liberty Described and Recommended,* in Hyneman and Lutz, eds., *American Political Writing,* 305–317; Sherwood, *The Church's Flight into the Wilderness,* in San-

Historians have often written about the important role of New England's ministerial "black regiment" during the Revolution; although the political writers of the day might logically persuade the people with their reasoned arguments for independence, some have argued, the preacher's passionate rhetoric stoked the emotional fires for the cause of liberty. Some preachers, however, wished they could direct some of the zeal for liberty toward more specifically religious purposes. In 1777, Jeremiah Day urged Connecticut congregations in North Preston, East Greenwich, and Kent to be good soldiers for Jesus Christ (2 Tim. 2:3). "Whilst the Statesman and the Patriot in this critical Day are exciting the Force of their Eloquence to rouse the country to Arms— to inflame their zeal in the Public Cause and awaken every Passion in the Human Breast for Liberty . . . it becomes the Minister of the Gospel to animate the soldiers of Jesus Christ to Zeal and Fidelity in their master's service." Day seemed almost envious of the rhetorical power of political polemicists like Thomas Paine: "You have read the American Crisis, Every Sentence penetrates your Hearts, inkindles the Fire of Patriotism and makes you impatient to rush forth in the Defence of your native land. . . . A kind of Enthusiasm seizes you." Day admitted to feeling this enthusiasm himself, and called for Christians in their daily battle against sin to imitate the zealous soldiers marching off to war.[72]

The most prevalent and perhaps most important way that preachers attempted to connect the sacred calling of religion to the profane world of politics in the second half of the eighteenth century was through discussions of Christian virtue. In the 1750s and 1760s, traditional treatments of the character of the good ruler (and the subject's duty to obey him) continued. But in other political sermons, the distance between ruler and ruled began to be reduced by

---

doz, ed., *Political Sermons*, 496, 513; Avery, *The Lord Is to Be Praised*, 44; Chauncey Whittelsey, *The Importance of Religion in the Civil Ruler, Considered* . . . (New Haven, Conn., 1778), 16. Abraham Keteltas, who had to flee to Connecticut when the British occupied his home on Long Island in 1776, described America's sacred cause as part of an international movement in *God Arising and Pleading His People's Cause* . . . (Newburyport, Mass., 1777), in Sandoz, ed., *Political Sermons*, 579–605. On the themes of sacred liberty, see also Connecticut election sermons for 1764, 1766, and 1772 (citations in Appendix 2); Sherwood, *Scriptural Instructions to Civil Rulers*, in Sandoz, ed., *Political Sermons*, 373–407; Hart, *Liberty Described and Recommended*, in Hyneman and Lutz, eds., *American Political Writing*, I, 305–317; Huntington, *The Happy Effects of Union*. For a discussion of how New Englanders reinterpreted their past through the lens of sacred liberty, see Hatch, *The Sacred Cause of Liberty*, 44–54.

72. Jeremiah Day, MS sermon on 2 Tim. 2:3, preached Jan. 12, Apr. 4, May 6, Oct. 5, 1777, Day Family Papers, Manuscripts and Archives, Yale University Library.

a broadly shared "faithful patriotism." Noah Hobart in 1750 extolled the civic virtues of "the righteous." In Hobart's sermon, the righteous are pious, upstanding citizens who follow their conscience but do not use liberty "as a Cloak of Maliciousness." They refuse to join the mudslinging of factional politics, worry about the taste for luxury impoverishing the community, and are ever watchful for corruption. In the early 1760s, other clergymen argued that "public spiritedness" was an essential virtue for men in every station but disagreed over the relationship between self-interest and disinterested service to the public, patriotism and a Christian's benevolence to mankind. In 1759, James Lockwood had looked at Paul, not as a Jew, a Christian, or an apostle, but as a Roman, in order to discuss civil liberty and praise Roman virtue. But admiration for Rome and Greece raised another question for political preachers from the 1760s through the 1780s: How could heathen notions of civic virtue be suitable for a Christian republic?[73]

"Virtue" was everywhere in the political talk and writing of the 1770s, though historians have disagreed about what it all meant. Montesquieu's popular *Spirit of the Laws* insisted that virtue was the motivating principle of a republic and distinguished three general kinds of virtue: Christian, political, and moral. These virtues roughly correspond to the three areas of thought that different historians have placed at the center of Revolutionary ideology: Reformed Protestantism, classical republicanism, and British (especially Scottish) moral philosophy. Although there has been much argument about opposing "paradigms," Revolutionary writers and speakers often borrowed from different traditions as they tried to rouse their audiences to patriotic virtue. The relationships between different (and often logically if not rhetorically incongruous)

---

73. Hobart, *Civil Government*, 14, 30. On the relationship of ruler and ruled, Benjamin Throop showed civil power flowing downward from God and the king, and Stephen White warned people not to be merely good subjects but to obey for conscience' sake God's vicegerents on earth. But Ashbel Woodbridge described the rulers and ruled in a "mutual Relation," and Joseph Fish noted that "all Ranks of men" joined in "repairing the walls of Jerusalem." See Woodbridge, *A Sermon Preached before the General Assembly*, 9; Joseph Fish, *Christ Jesus the Physician, and His Blood the Balm, Recommended for the Healing of a Diseased People . . .* (New London, Conn., 1760), 41; Benjamin Throop, *Religion and Loyalty, the Duty and Glory of a People . . .* (New London, Conn., 1758), 9; Stephen White, *Civil Rulers Gods by Office, and the Duties of Such Considered and Enforced . . .* (New London, Conn., 1763), 9, 37. On patriotism, see election sermons for 1749 and 1750 (citations in Appendix 2). On Paul as a Roman, see Lockwood, *The Worth and Excellence of Civil Freedom*. The relationship of Christian and heathen virtue to politics will be discussed at greater length in Chapter 7. Election sermons addressing this theme before 1790 include those for 1764, 1775, 1780, and 1787 (citations in Appendix 2).

strains of virtue politics are sometimes hard to discern. The larger interpretative difficulty, though, has been to gauge the relationship between any of them and what has been called the Lockean tradition, which stresses individual rights and interests and deemphasizes the political function of public virtue of any sort. The eclectic combination of arguments and idioms is especially apparent in the hectic 1770s, as a British resistance movement turned into civil war and then a revolution creating a *novus ordo saeclorum*.[74]

Jeremiah Day's sermonic appropriation of Thomas Paine's "Crisis Number 1" in 1777 shows how different meanings of virtue, public spirit, and common interest fused into a powerfully charged exhortation. In Day's sermon, Paine's essay joins Paul's Second Epistle to Timothy to help the congregation both understand and feel what it meant to be "a good soldier of Jesus Christ." Paine's famous first line—"These are the times that try men's souls"—as well as his subsequent references to God's unlimited sovereignty and providential care of a virtuous people—established familiar reference points for New England congregations schooled by countless jeremiads. Both Paine and Day called the true patriot/Christian to action: "Throw not the burden of the day upon Providence," Paine wrote, "but *'show your faith by your works,'* that God may bless you." Although essays like Paine's "awaken up every Passion in the Human Breast for Liberty," Day preached, and encourage all to "exert themselves according to their Abilities for the salvation of their Bleeding Country," Day was trying to "animate" those who heard him to serve under Christ's banner with "Zeal and fidelity." Paine's text also rings with (and Day's more faintly echoes) the language of republican virtue: self-sacrificing devotion to the public good, duty and firmness, perseverance and fortitude, "a manly and martial spirit." "The Crisis" contrasts the "hope and virtue" true patriots showed in the face of "common danger" to the tory's "servile, slavish, self-interested fear." Paine illustrated this contemptible self-interest with an anecdote about a man at an Amboy tavern who, while holding the hand of his pretty little child, wished for peace in his own day, even if such a peace would only condemn the

74. Charles Secondat, Baron de Montesquieu, *The Spirit of the Laws* (1748; reprint, New York, 1949), bk. III, 19–28, esp. 23n, bk. V, esp. 40–47. James T. Kloppenberg, in "The Virtues of Liberalism: Christianity, Republicanism, and Ethics in Early Modern Political Discourse," *Journal of American History*, LXXIV (1987–1988), 9–33, connected Montesquieu's three categories to the traditions of religious, republican, and Scottish common sense philosophy. He pointed out that "not only were those conceptions of virtue not clearly compatible . . . there were inconsistencies within each of the three traditions as well" (19). See also Ruth H. Bloch, "The Gendered Meanings of Virtue in Revolutionary America," *Signs: Journal of Women in Culture and Society*, XIII (1987), 37–59.

next generation to worse strife and bloodshed. For Paine, however, as for most New England preachers like Day (and unlike some recent characterizations of republicanism), when liberty was threatened, there was no stark separation between private and public virtue or between legitimate private interest and the common good. "If we reason to the root of things," Paine argued, resisting the individual villain when he threatens one's life, liberty, or property and resisting the tyrant with his army threatening murder, slavery, and robbery were morally identical acts.[75]

The language of virtuous feeling that both Paine and Day used suggests an influence other than classical republicanism, the Puritan jeremiad, or the revivalist preacher's talk of religious affections and Christian union. As in *Common Sense*, Paine in "The Crisis" appealed to the natural capacity that all human beings have and to the judgments of conscience, which speak nature's moral law: "The heart that feels not now is dead. . . . He whose heart is firm, and whose conscience approves his conduct, will pursue his principles to the death." Like the Scottish moral philosophers, Paine wedded passion to universal moral principle and considered modern virtue superior to Greek and Roman patriotism on precisely this point. Paine's sense of virtue reflected the modern, more humanized, domesticated virtue of eighteenth-century commercial society more than the republican virtue of the Spartan army camp. Day, like Paine, appealed to the emotional experience of his audience and referred to his own; his discussion of the "Fire of Patriotism" also seems to spring

75. Jeremiah Day, MS sermon on 2 Tim. 2:3; Thomas Paine, "The Crisis Number I," (1776), in Paine, *Political Writings*, ed. Bruce Kuklick (Cambridge, 1989), 39–48 (quotations on 41, 43, 44, 46). Michael P. Zuckert, in *Natural Rights and the New Republicanism* (Princeton, N.J., 1994), 155–158, contends that Gordon S. Wood, *The Creation of the American Republic, 1776–1787* (Chapel Hill, N.C., 1969), stressed a notion of public virtue that "obliterated the individual" (Wood, *Creation*, 61). Isaac Kramnick, in *Republicanism and Bourgeois Radicalism: Political Ideology in Late Eighteenth-Century England and America* (Ithaca, N.Y., 1990), also tends to dichotomize public and private virtue to stress the latter in opposition to classical republican conceptions (see 196, 248–250, 273–278). J.G.A. Pocock's understanding of republicanism, or what he called "civic humanism," in *The Machiavellian Moment: Florentine Political Thought and the Atlantic Republican Tradition* (Princeton, N.J., 1975), centered on the Aristotelian idea of the *zoon politikon*, the idea that human fulfillment depends upon political participation. Paul A. Rahe, in *Republics Ancient and Modern: Classical Republicanism and the American Revolution* (Chapel Hill, N.C., 1992), however, argued that few in eighteenth-century America or Britain endorsed such an idea (570). See also Zuckert, *Natural Rights*, 159–164; Lance Banning, "Some Second Thoughts on Virtue and the Course of Revolutionary Thinking," in Terence Ball and J.G.A. Pocock, eds., *Conceptual Change and the Constitution* (Lawrence, Kans., 1988), 194–212; Ann Fairfax Withington, *Toward a More Perfect Union: Virtue and the Formation of American Republics* (New York, 1991).

from a common moral sense rather than from the gracious affections bestowed upon the regenerate.[76]

Defining the specifically Christian character of public virtue became especially important in Connecticut after the war ended and the 1784 revision of laws dropped the Saybrook Platform, as forces both in the state and outside it pushed for full disestablishment. The Saybrook Platform had authorized state enforcement of orthodox belief and church discipline, warranted by the perceived need for unity, uniformity, and moral order under the covenant. The revised ecclesiastical constitution under Governor Griswold's administration was justified in its continued tax support for the church, according to the election day preachers, because the church was uniquely able to cultivate a virtuous citizenry. Although a powerful conception, the nature of public virtue—like the nature of liberty, the relationship of the commonwealth to Israel, or the role of the Revolution in the coming millennium—was a topic of continued discussion and debate. Even more than the doctrine of the public covenant, the idea of public virtue was a slippery concept that was defined and used in different ways. That was true even on election days, when the gathered dignitaries of Connecticut's Standing Order expected to hear, not innovative argumentation, but a ritual repetition of traditional values.

Perhaps Governor Griswold, though, who had copied over Saltonstall's 1697 sermon, was especially sensitive to the importance of ritual and rhetorical tradition. By reinscribing Saltonstall's text, Governor Griswold might have been trying to preserve sacred meaning and civil authority in a society where words and meanings were increasingly volatile. By proclaiming state fast and thanksgiving days in language that echoed the speech of his Puritan predecessors

76. Paine, "The Crisis Number I," in Paine, *Political Writings*, ed. Kuklick, 46. On Paine's opinion of Greece and Rome, see A. Owen Aldridge, *Thomas Paine's American Ideology* (Newark, N.J., 1984), 243; on his affinity to (but probably not firsthand knowledge of) the British moral philosophy of the 3d earl of Shaftesbury and Francis Hutcheson, see 62, 274. On the "modern" virtue influenced by sentiment and Scottish common sense philosophy, see Ronald Hamowy, "Jefferson and the Scottish Enlightenment: A Critique of Garry Wills's *Inventing America: Jefferson's Declaration of Independence*," *WMQ*, 3d Ser., XXXVI (1979), 503–523; Jay Fliegelman, *Prodigals and Pilgrims: The American Revolution against Patriarchy, 1750–1800* (Cambridge, 1982), 9–35; Fliegelman, *Declaring Independence: Jefferson, Natural Language, and the Culture of Performance* (Stanford, Calif., 1993), 44–54; Rahe, *Republics Ancient and Modern*, 254–334; Richard B. Sher and Jeffrey R. Smitten, eds., *Scotland and America in the Age of the Enlightenment* (Princeton, N.J., 1990), introduction and pt. 2; Gordon S. Wood, "Afterword," in Milton M. Klein, Richard D. Brown, and John B. Hench, eds., *The Republican Synthesis Revisited: Essays in Honor of George Athan Billias* (Worcester, Mass., 1992), 143–162; Wood, *The Radicalism of the American Revolution* (New York, 1992), 213–225.

more than the election sermons by his ministerial contemporaries did, Connecticut's post-Revolutionary governor might have been trying to embody the Puritan godly magistrate even as the letter of the law changed the relationship between church and state.[77]

After rewriting Saltonstall's 1697 sermon, perhaps Griswold heard more than other magistrates and ministers as he listened to the political sermons of the 1780s. He certainly would have noticed a change in style. Old Puritan sermons bristling with scriptural citations and demonstrating that God was speaking directly to New England had been replaced, for the most part, by reasoned essays on religious and political themes that might toss in references to William Shakespeare, John Milton, Cicero, and Virgil. Griswold would have heard mention of God's "covenant people," though almost always in reference to the church, and one preacher would make it clear that America "had no such national covenant to plead, as had the Jews: for it is but a scattered few, in this vast continent, that can claim even the visibility of a covenant relation to God." The logic of the jeremiad was still repeated because most continued to assume that God still punished public sins, although more than one preacher would question even this. Another clergyman, writing essays in the *New-Haven Gazette* in 1786, criticized elements of the customary election sermon "as a blind perpetuation of ancestral bad taste." In the political sermons of the 1780s, Griswold could still hear or read the lofty character of the good ruler described and the citizen's obedience demanded; but he could also encounter, against the usual assertions that only the wise few could master the necessary intricacies of law and statecraft, the argument that there was nothing essential to political wisdom that was not easily comprehended by common sense and conscience.[78]

77. Gov. Matthew A. Griswold's thanksgiving day *Proclamation* (New London, Conn., 1785) hardly differs from those of his predecessors, going back to Saltonstall. Griswold encouraged the population to give thanks not just for the fruits of the earth but also because of the "signal Deliverances granted to the Inhabitants of this Land" and because "it hath pleased the Most High, who ruleth over the Kingdoms of Men, to give us an equal Rank among the Sovereign nations of the Earth, with the full Enjoyment of our Constitutional Rights, Civil and Religious Liberties and Privileges, in Peace and Tranquility." Although he referred to "all Denominations" rather than a single professing people, he did not hide behind the deistic platitudes of an inoffensive civil religion: he called for prayers for the advance of the Redeemer's kingdom so the divine perfection of "Jesus Christ, our Lord and saviour" could be displayed throughout the world. The language of the state proclamations had changed less than the sermons that expounded upon them.

78. Thomas Brockway said America had no covenant in *America Saved,* 7; Stiles, in *United States Elevated to Glory and Honor,* and Samuel Wales, in *The Dangers of Our National Prosperity; and the Way to Avoid Them . . .* (Hartford, Conn., 1785), questioned the relation between behavior and blessings; Timothy Dwight's essay series entitled "The Friend,"

The biggest difference between Saltonstall's sermon and the political sermons of Griswold's era can be found in Saltonstall's claim that God designed church and state to be "concentered" and aimed at the same end: maintaining piety and "Promoting a Covenant walk with [God]." An election day preacher in 1787 would admit that "the immediate ends of the magistracy and ministry are different." Over the course of the eighteenth century, the idea of the public covenant was superseded as a way to understand God's rule over human societies by a more universally administered providence, shoved aside as an explanation of the citizen's social and political obligations by a political language about social contracts and civic virtue, and stigmatized as an instrument of state coercion by an outmoded policy—Saltonstall's Saybrook policy that had sought to impose unity of belief, uniformity of practice, and social control over an increasingly heterogeneous society. The idea of a public or national covenant was also weakened by ecclesiastical arguments over the nature of covenanting. However Connecticut ministers tried to redefine the relationship between religion and politics in the early years of the Republic, the public covenant would never again have the power to join church and state at the heart of the public body the way that the ministry and the magistracy had been combined in the person of the Reverend Governor Gurdon Saltonstall.[79]

New-Haven Gazette, and the Connecticut Magazine, Mar. 23, 1786 – Oct. 4, 1787, criticized the usual practice of addressing—and praising—the officeholders at the end of the sermon; Enoch Huntington's *Political Wisdom; or, Honesty the Best Policy . . .* (Middletown, Conn., 1786), denied that the elite monopolized the subject.

79. Saltonstall, *A Sermon Preached,* Griswold transcript, 84; Elizur Goodrich, *The Principles of Civil Union and Happiness . . .* (Hartford, Conn., 1787), in Sandoz, ed., *Political Sermons,* 933. A superficial similarity of phrasing in longer excerpts from Goodrich's and Saltonstall's sermons might lead one to falsely conclude that the two were actually saying the same thing. The key distinction is between immediate and ultimate aims. For Saltonstall, civil and ecclesiastical government have the same immediate end: to maintain piety day by day and promote a covenant walk with God, though the medicines (means) are different. For Goodrich, civil government aims at establishing peace and order in this world—more limited goals, good in themselves. Peace and order, in turn, provide the stability the church needs to do its work. In this way, civil government is instrumentally and ultimately, but not immediately, related to the specific work of the church. A similar distinction between immediate and ultimate aims can be found in Moses Dickinson's 1755 election sermon, *A Sermon Preached before the General Assembly.*

CHAPTER 2

Only a Great Awakening

Jonathan Edwards and the Regulation of

Religious Discourse

The Awakening, it seemed, was over. Jonathan Edwards wrote to Scotland in 1743, mourning the "manifold sinful errors by which we have grieved and quenched the Spirit of God" in New England. "You have heard great things from New England of late," Edwards wrote to James Robe. "But now we have not such joyful news to send you; the clouds have lately thickened, and our hemisphere is now much darkened with them." If the Awakening itself had raised Edwards's hopes for the coming millennium, its passing would prompt an attempt to redefine Christian community—an enormously influential effort that depended upon controlling the language a religious people used to understand itself. But in the spring of 1743, Edwards's letters to Scotland were as much lamentations over the withdrawal of God's Spirit as outlines for religious reform. He told William McCulloch: "God is now going and returning to his place. . . . I hope God will show us our errors, and teach us wisdom by his present withdrawings: now in the day of adversity we have time and cause to consider, and begin now to have the opportunity to see the consequences of our conduct." Beneath darkening skies, New England clergymen like Edwards looked back over the previous three years and sought to understand their meaning.[1]

We are still considering the consequences of the "Great Awakening," a term

---

1. Jonathan Edwards to James Robe, May 12, 1743, Edwards to the Reverend William McCulloch, May 12, 1743, in Edwards, *The Great Awakening . . .*, ed. C. C. Goen, in Perry Miller et al., eds., *The Works of Jonathan Edwards*, IV (New Haven, Conn., 1972), 536, 540.

historians use "to describe a unique wave of intercolonial religious revivals that peaked throughout many of the colonies in the years 1740–1742." This chapter focuses on three overlapping phases, each characterized by different uses of public discourse. The initial phase—the Awakening proper—was marked by the powerful, dramatic preaching of George Whitefield and the itinerants who followed in his wake. It also produced Whitefield's published journal, other revival narratives, printed conversionist sermons, public letters, and newspaper accounts describing events that helped constitute an intercolonial—and, indeed, transatlantic—phenomenon. The second phase, beginning in 1742, is one of ideological division: the emergence of New Light and Old Light positions in polemical sermons, treatises, and testimonies that either actively supported the revival movement against an engaged opposition or denounced it by refuting the claims of its promoters. It is inaccurate, however, to describe the New Light–Old Light division as a stable, coherent ideological polarity that remained in place through the Revolution and beyond. Polarized argument over the revivals created a rhetorical framework through which other local and regional political and religious disagreements could be expressed. Although the New Light and Old Light labels remained in Connecticut politics through the 1760s, the connection to the revival movement became increasingly obscure.[2]

The experience of the Awakening and the ideological division that followed it led to a third phase of institutional formation and reformation, beginning with antirevival legislation (1742–1743) and the first illegal church separations (1744–1745). Again, it should be stressed that institutional developments (new laws, churches, school charters, communication networks, and ecclesiastical reforms) arose from far more than the Awakening or the Old Light–New Light division; they were also consequences of other complex social and cultural forces. Historians have traced New Light church schisms and the growth of the Separate Congregational and Baptist movements in New England. Others have described how the patterns of correspondence and itinerant preaching that were prominent during the revivals became regularized as evangelical net-

2. H[arry] S. Stout, "Great Awakening," in Daniel G. Reid, ed., *Dictionary of Christianity in America* (Downers Grove, Ill., 1990), 494–496. Compare this minimalist description to the interpretive definition found in another reference work: "The Great Awakening was America's first mass religious revival, an intercolonial, interdenominational, multiethnic movement of popular piety, especially among the Calvinist churches, during the second quarter of the eighteenth century" (Stephen A. Marini, "The Great Awakening," in Charles H. Lippy and Peter W. Williams, eds., *Encyclopedia of the American Religious Experience: Studies of Traditions and Movements*, 3 vols. [New York, 1988], II, 775–798 [quotation on 775]).

works, perpetuating a sense of participation in new religious translocal communities. Most New England churchgoers, however, remained within tax-supported Congregational churches and continued to think of them as their primary religious communities and institutions. That does not mean the Standing Order churches were immune from the drive for post-Awakening institutional reform. One such reform effort, begun by Jonathan Edwards in 1749, shunned separatism and tried to mediate between Old and New Light extremes while working to redefine the nature of New England's Congregational Church and its terms of Christian communion. The Edwardsean campaign against "lax" standards of church admission lost Edwards his parish in the early 1750s, but, reenergized in Connecticut during the 1760s, the movement for a "purer" church would be largely successful by the end of the century.[3]

Distinguishing these three phases preserves a sense of the novelty and dramatic impact of the Awakening without exaggerating it as a transformative watershed or paradigm shift in American history. We can see the ideological division between Old and New Lights as a polemical context in which writers reexamined questions about religious community and authority, rather than as the breakdown of the Puritan mind or the origin of the later split between Unitarian and evangelical Protestants. The final sections of the chapter examine how some of those writers after the Awakening tried to reform or preserve what was perhaps their single most important institution: the local Congregational Church. Tracing the Edwardsean attempts to regulate public religious discourse at the parish level returns us to the covenant language of community, but this time from a local perspective. Edwardsean "New Divinity" arguments about the church also demonstrate how a (clerical) speaking aristocracy tried to control public discourse even as it helped to transform it.

3. On Separatists, see C. C. Goen, *Revivalism and Separatism in New England, 1740–1800: Strict Congregationalists and Separate Baptists in the Great Awakening* (1962; reprint, Middletown, Conn., 1987); William G. McLoughlin, *New England Dissent: The Baptists and the Separation of Church and State, 1630–1833*, 2 vols. (Cambridge, Mass., 1971). On evangelical networks, see Timothy D. Hall, *Contested Boundaries: Itinerancy and the Reshaping of the Colonial American Religious World* (Durham, N.C., 1994); Susan O'Brien, "A Transatlantic Community of Saints: The Great Awakening and the First Evangelical Network, 1735–1755," *American Historical Review*, XCI (1986), 811–832. According to James Patrick Walsh, "The Pure Church in Eighteenth-Century Connecticut" (Ph.D. diss., Columbia University, 1967), 44, 218, in 1740 nearly half of the churches in Connecticut practiced the kind of "open communion" that Edwards would come to argue against. By 1770, stricter churches outnumbered open ones three to two; by 1800, four to one. Of the thirteen new churches formed after 1770, all were strict. See also David D. Hall, "Editor's Introduction," in Jonathan Edwards, *Ecclesiastical Writings*, ed. Hall, in Miller et al., eds., *Works of Jonathan Edwards*, XII (New Haven, Conn., 1994), 86.

Historians have borrowed the phrase "Great Awakening" from eighteenth-century religious language. "Awakening" was a word ministers applied to a sudden onset or renewal of religious excitement and concern in their flocks. Prodded by a clergyman's preaching, by prayer groups among the laity, or by extraordinary events like epidemics or earthquakes, people would be shaken from the dull rhythms of daily routine to confront their ultimate concerns and anxiously ponder the state of their souls: "What must I do to be saved?" Perhaps such a period of intense concern would only briefly revive piety in a congregation, increase church membership, or reform the morals of a community, but the lack of any long-term impact does not deny the psychological and social reality of the phenomenon itself. Many churches and communities in New England had long experienced occasional awakenings, periodic revivals, or "seasons of grace." The Awakening of the 1740s differed from previous local or regional episodes because of the sheer numbers of people involved throughout New England and the middle colonies. It also differed because of itinerant revivalists like the Anglican preacher George Whitefield, who stirred up audiences in Britain and British America and convinced the awakened that they were participating in a great intercolonial, transatlantic event with sacred significance.[4]

The events of the early 1740s did not completely bewilder New England ministers and shatter their conceptual world, but neither did the experiences of those years immediately fit into preconceived categories marked "revival" or "enthusiasm," "outpouring of grace" or "Satanic delusion." The phenomenon of the Awakening was first and foremost a set of signs to be interpreted. The public interpreters were, not armchair philosophers, editorializing pundits, or squabbling academics, but men who felt it was their sacred charge to explain the will of God to their fellow men and women. They believed that divine and demonic spirits were busy in the human world, and discerning the traces of spiritual activity was serious business. They sought the essence of the Awakening as a spiritual phenomenon. We can see it emerge and evolve as a topic of public commentary, first in the efforts to interpret events and then in the struggle to empower one interpretation over others as the true reading.

News of George Whitefield's dramatic preaching in the middle colonies had been covered by the Boston newspapers in the summer of 1740. The charis-

4. See Appendix 3, "A Note on the Historiography of the Great Awakening."

matic evangelist himself landed at Newport, Rhode Island, on September 14, 1740, and launched a forty-five-day tour of Massachusetts and Connecticut. He delivered 175 sermons to thousands of New Englanders, preaching without notes in a powerfully direct and dramatic manner calculated to touch the hearts and ignite the religious passions of his audience. He left towns and villages buzzing with excitement and the talk of emotional religious experience. In the dialectic of event and exegesis that began with Whitefield's tour, Boston presses produced nearly all of the publications for New England's Awakening, but Connecticut, which still had only one printing press, was the site of some of the more dramatic and memorable episodes. Whitefield's visit to Middletown in 1740, so vividly described by Nathan Cole, prompted farmers from the surrounding countryside to run from their fields, race their horses, and row their boats down to the shores of the Connecticut River to see Whitefield mount the scaffold like a latter-day apostle and preach the new birth. In Enfield a year later, Jonathan Edwards preached *Sinners in the Hands of an Angry God,* one of the most famous sermons in American history, and employed such powerful imagery that members of the congregation moaned and shrieked in despair. The most notorious incident of New England's Awakening, however, and a key event for observers trying to determine where the Awakening would lead, was revivalist James Davenport's book burning on a New London street on March 6, 1743. Observers like Boston minister Charles Chauncy collected reports of such incidents and assessed their spiritual import. Clergymen who participated more directly in the movement, like Connecticut's Jonathan Parsons, published narratives that chronicled events and revealed more of how their interpretations developed as the movement progressed.[5]

Parsons, a minister in Lyme, Connecticut, recalled that the excitement had begun when accounts of Whitefield's revivals reached the parish in the fall of 1740: "Our People were more generally rous'd up to bethink themselves, and to converse about Religion." Worried about the "surprising Effects" that Whitefield's preaching seemed to have, Parsons rode to New Haven to hear him and spoke with many who had been in the midst of the great crowds who hung upon the itinerant's every word. After Whitefield left New England, Parsons "heard of a very great Concern upon the Minds of many People at *Hartford*." He wrote letters and then visited several "*judicious* and *prudent*" gentlemen to

5. On the dramatic effect of Whitefield's preaching, see Michael J. Crawford, "Notes and Documents: The Spiritual Travels of Nathan Cole," *William and Mary Quarterly,* 3d Ser., XXXIII (1976), 89–126; Harry S. Stout, *The Divine Dramatist: George Whitefield and the Rise of Modern Evangelicalism* (Grand Rapids, Mich., 1991), 113–132; and Stout, *The New England Soul: Preaching and Religious Culture in Colonial New England* (New York, 1986), 189–195.

see if they believed that they were witnessing an outpouring of God's Spirit. Convinced that people were not just swooning over fiery preachers but were being truly awakened, Parsons decided in late March of 1741 to "sound an alarm" to his own "drowsy, careless People."[6]

Parsons preached, and his people began to weep, sigh, and sob. Many told him afterward "that they never had such an awaken'd Sense of the Danger of putting off the grand Concern of their Souls to a future season before." Gilbert Tennent, a New Jersey Presbyterian following in Whitefield's wake, arrived the next month, and many more "dated their first Awakenings" from his second sermon from the West Parish pulpit. Suddenly Parsons's soul-searching sermons were in great demand: "Before it was the Cry of their Hearts, *'When will the Sermon be over, and the Sabbath be ended';* but now the Minister always left off too soon, and the Time between Sermons was too long." Many asked for regular lectures to supplement Sunday preaching, and their invigorated pastor responded with a weekly public lecture "to several Hundreds" and "several private ones in various Parts of the Parish." He was even asked for a special sermon on election day, customarily in Lyme a time of "Feasting, Musick, Dancing, Gaming," and other worldly pursuits. Young people frequently came to Parsons for advice and formed several religious societies for prayer and Bible study. "Whenever they fell into Companies, the great Salvation was the subject of their Conversation." Public discussion was intensely concentrated upon religion.[7]

For many historians, applying the term "awakening" to what Parsons described would automatically imply a radical and irreversible transformation, whether spiritual or cultural. But mid-eighteenth-century clergymen like Parsons understood the term differently. In discussions of religious experience, "awakening" almost always applied to behaviors that manifested the "external" action of the Holy Spirit, rather than the "indwelling" work necessary for conversion itself. Jonathan Dickinson, a Yale graduate who had become a leading New Jersey Presbyterian, made this distinction with particular clarity in *The Witness of the Spirit,* a sermon published in Boston in 1740. No arguments persuade unconverted sinners, he wrote, "until the Spirit of God opens their Eyes,

---

6. Jonathan Parsons, "Account of the Revival of Religion at Lyme West Parish in Connecticut," in Thomas Prince, Jr., ed., *The Christian History, Containing Accounts of the Revival and Propagation of Religion in Great Britain, America . . . ,* II (Boston, 1745), 125–126. This periodical was published weekly from March 1743 through February 1745 and was collected in annual volumes in 1744 and 1745. Parson's account began in the issue for Saturday, June 9, 1744 (no. 67), II, 118–120, and continued in the next six issues (nos. 68–73), II, 121–162.

7. Ibid., 133–136.

sets their Danger in View, and awakens them out of this stupid and dead state." These "awak'ning Influences of the blessed Spirit" begin but do not necessarily continue or complete a good work within them and are "no certain Evidence of a sanctifying Change." Jonathan Edwards agreed: "The awakening and convincing influences of the Spirit of God," he wrote in *A Treatise concerning Religious Affections,* may still be quenched by the corrupt heart and are not necessarily followed by the great change of nature wrought by infused grace.[8]

This understanding of "awakening" was shared by most who would be called Old Lights as well. Preachers of "heart religion" like Dickinson and Edwards have been portrayed as being separated from "rationalists" like Charles Chauncy by "a veritable chasm" because of "irreconcilable differences between their respective views of man." Chauncy did argue that much being called the work of the Spirit actually arose from the people's frenzied imaginations, which could "awaken" their natural "Powers" and prompt them to exert themselves "with a sort of *extatic* violence." But he also spoke of the Holy Spirit's awakening influences upon the sinner: "I doubt not, but the *divine* SPIRIT often accompanies the *preached Word,* so as that, by *his Influence,* Sinners are awakened to a Sense *of Sin,* and filled with *deep Distress* of Soul." Awakened sinners are in "a critical state" but should not rest until their hearts are regenerated and their lives committed to Christ. Although Chauncy and Edwards argued from different psychological and epistemological premises, they argued within a

8. Jonathan Dickinson, *The Witness of the Spirit . . .* (Boston, 1740), 6, 7, 9. Dickinson denies that even the most zealous preacher could, without the Spirit's action, "awaken these dead Men to such a lively lasting Concern about their Souls." See Dickinson, *A Display of God's Special Grace . . .* (Boston, 1742), 30; Jonathan Edwards, *A Treatise concerning Religious Affections . . .* (1746), ed. John E. Smith, in Miller et al., eds., *Works of Jonathan Edwards,* II (New Haven, Conn., 1959), 157. Joseph Tracy, in *The Great Awakening: A History of the Revival of Religion in the Time of Edwards and Whitefield* (Boston, 1842), defined his study of "The Great Awakening" as the history of a "great idea [that] was then extensively at work, breaking up established and venerated habits of thought, feeling and action, and producing a revolution in the minds of men, and thus in the very structure of society" (viii–xiii, quotation on viii). This "idea" was itself a description of radical change within individual experience: it was the idea of conversion, the "new birth." William G. McLoughlin, in *Revivals, Awakenings, and Reform: An Essay on Religion and Social Change in America, 1607–1977* (Chicago, 1977), xiii, distinguished between revivals, which "alter the lives of individuals," and awakenings, which "alter the world view of a whole people or culture." His discussions of the "new birth" fall under the narrower category of Protestant revivalism, whereas "awakenings . . . are periods of cultural revitalization that begin in a general crisis of beliefs and values and extend over a period of a generation or so, during which time a profound reorientation in beliefs and values takes place." For both McLoughlin and Tracy, the label "awakening" did not introduce a topic of investigation. Instead, it summarized a thesis.

theological framework that distinguished between the awakening and the converting work of the Holy Spirit.[9]

An awakened sinner is not necessarily born again, and an awakened community is not necessarily transformed. "Awakening" when applied to a corporate body did not refer directly to an outbreak of conversions or to a dramatic rise in church membership. The clergy usually used the term to denote a time of "religious commotions," a general preoccupation with "soul concerns," and an extraordinary excitement and intensity among the laity with regard to matters of religion. For the pastors themselves, it was a time of expectation and redoubled efforts. They hoped for conversions, but the rising tide of religious interest and spiritual fervor was enough reason to give thanks for the outpouring of God's grace.[10]

After Whitefield had left New England in 1740, many local ministers like Jonathan Parsons of Lyme labored to become instruments of both awakening and conversion in their congregations. These supporters of the revivals soon concluded that they were witnessing more than just the external operations of the Spirit. They described the awakening of sinners but also the awakened being converted and those who were already visible saints being "quicken[ed]" in their religious affections and "comfort[ed]" in their faith. There was a danger, however, in being too presumptuous about the indwelling work of the Spirit, especially when addressing colleagues who were not yet convinced that there

9. C. C. Goen, "Editor's Introduction," in Edwards, *The Great Awakening*, ed. Goen, in Miller et al., eds., *Works of Jonathan Edwards*, IV, 83. See also Alan Heimert and Perry Miller, "Introduction," in Heimert and Miller, eds., *The Great Awakening: Documents Illustrating the Crisis and Its Consequences* (Indianapolis, Ind., 1967), xxxix: "The great divide that we call the Awakening," Miller writes, "forced both American parties, whether proponents or opponents, to shift the focus of analysis to the nature of man." Heimert, extending Miller's argument, claims that "the central conflict of the Awakening was not theological but one of opposing theories of the human psychology" (xxxix). But the move from theology and ecclesiology to psychology, however gratifying to our modern interest in the human psyche, may shift too much attention away from what contemporaries were arguing about: the work of the Spirit. The quotations from Charles Chauncy are in *Enthusiasm Described and Caution'd Against* (Boston, 1742), 6; Chauncy, *Seasonable Thoughts on the State of Religion in New England, a Treatise in Five Parts* (1743), ed. Richard Warch (New York, 1975), 99; Chauncy, *The Out-Pouring of the Holy Ghost* (Boston, 1742), 14.

10. See the remarks made in October 1740, published as *Invitations to the Reverend Mr. George Whitefield, from the Eastern Consociation of the County of Fairfield* (Boston, 1745). Thomas Foxcroft would again make this general point in 1747: "Nay, be it but an unusual Season of *Conviction* and *Awakening* of Sinners, which is the Work of the *Spirit*, and above the Power of Men and Means . . . [it] claim[s] our Notice and Remembrance." See Foxcroft, *A Seasonable Memento for New Year's Day* (Boston, 1747), 55.

was such an effusive outpouring. In May 1741, Solomon Williams's Connecticut election sermon noted the "great and uncommon Concern" about eternal salvation "awakened in the minds of many of our People, and hopes that the Spirit of God will be more and more poured out upon the Land." Williams hoped that the clergy's "Zeal and Fervour will not be Restrain'd by a fear that this Work is not of God." Certainly men ought to be concerned about their eternal salvation, he argued. "And when they are Awakened to mind this as the One Thing Needful, and in Earnest to get a Saving Knowledge of Christ, and determined to know nothing Else. . . . Can we doubt whether God is Mercifully carrying on his Work in their Souls?"[11]

Jonathan Edwards, too, tried to be cautious. Instead of describing "Surprizing" conversions in his 1741 Yale address, Edwards discussed "that uncommon Operation that has lately appeared on the Minds of many of the People of this Land." He argued: "Whether persons' convictions, and the alteration in their dispositions and affections, be in a degree and manner that is saving, is beside the present question. If there be such effects. . . . it is nevertheless a sign of the influence of the Spirit of God." Rather than rest their case on a premature tally of "hopeful conversions," the promoters pointed to the multitudes that were awakened. In New Hampshire, John Blunt added 50 to communion but could say that "the *Awakening* in Months past was almost universal." Eleazar Wheelock thought that only 4 or 5 were converted in Voluntown, but great numbers cried out and trembled when he preached. Boston's John Webb added 102 to full church membership in 1741, yet he had counseled more than 1,000 with "soul concerns" in just three months.[12]

At the very least, the supporters proclaimed, this was a great and general

11. Jonathan Edwards, "The State of Religion at Northampton in the County of Hampshire, about a Hundred Miles Westward of Boston," in Edwards, *Great Awakening,* ed. Goen, in Miller et al., eds., *Works of Jonathan Edwards,* IV, 547 (orig. publ. in Prince, ed., *Christian History,* I, 367–381 [nos. 46–48, Jan. 14, 21, 28, 1743/44]); Solomon Williams, *A Firm and Immovable Courage to Obey God, and an Inflexible Obervation of the Laws of Religion, the Highest Wisdom and Certain Happiness of Rulers* (New London, Conn., 1741), 40, 41.

12. Edwards described the earlier revivals as "Surprizing" in *A Faithful Narrative of the Surprizing Work of God in the Conversion of Many Hundred Souls in Northampton and the Neighboring Villages* (1737) and the "uncommon Operation" in Jonathan Edwards, *The Distinguishing Marks of a Work of the Spirit of God Applied to that Uncommon Operation . . .* (1741), both in Edwards, *The Great Awakening,* ed. Goen, in Miller et al., eds., *Works of Jonathan Edwards,* IV, 128, 214, 263 (extended quotation); John Blunt, quoted in Prince, ed., *Christian History,* I (August 20, 1743), 199; Eleazar Wheelock, *Extracts from the Private Journal of the Rev. Eleazar Wheelock,* in Tracy, *The Great Awakening,* 201. John Webb's information was reported to Thomas Prince by Benjamin Colman, quoted in Tracy, *The Great Awakening,* 117, 119–120.

Awakening. "That there has been a great religious Commotion in the World in our present Day, is so evident, that it cannot be deny'd," Samuel Finley declared. When Finley's sermon was first printed in 1741, most were still willing to grant that at least the awakening influences of the Holy Spirit seemed to be at work in those "Commotions." Even as Charles Chauncy began pointing out abuses, he still referred to 1740 as an "awakened year." Harvard president Edward Holyoke, who would sign a scathing testimony against Whitefield in 1744, gave a convention sermon in 1741 that praised the work of God and the labors of Whitefield and Tennent: "Many, no doubt, have been savingly converted from the Error of their Ways, many more have been convicted, and all have been in some Measure rouzed from their Lethargy." The following May, Chauncy could still write: "A concern, I am sensible, has been generally awaken'd in the minds of people, in one place and another. . . . And we ought to be thankful for what of the SPIRIT, we have reason to hope there is among us."[13]

Those more skeptical about the predominant source of the Awakening had been willing to wait and see what the "issue" of all the excitement would be. But, after watching churches split, "converts" fall into trances, and "illiterate" lay exhorters preach like men possessed, they had seen enough. On June 15, 1742, Connecticut's General Association of ministers, a body created by the Saybrook Platform, had declared itself of the opinion that "the God of all grace has been mercifully pleased to Remember and visit his people by Stiring up Great Numbers among us to a concern for their Souls, and to be asking the way to Zion with their faces thitherward." The convention of Connecticut ministers thereby acknowledged the work of God but then focused instead upon the efforts of "the great Enemy of Souls" who was "very busy" trying to destroy

13. Samuel Finley, *Christ Triumphing, and Satan Raging* (Philadelphia, 1741), 23 (reprinted, Boston, 1742, 18). As Edwin Scott Gaustad noted, "Before 1743 the Great Awakening had by nearly all been regarded as at least in part a divine operation." See Gaustad, *The Great Awakening in New England* (New York, 1957), 69; Charles Chauncy, *The New Creature Describ'd, and Consider'd as the Sure Characteristick of a Man's Being* (Boston, 1741), quoted in Edward M. Griffin, *Old Brick: Charles Chauncy of Boston, 1705–1787* (Minneapolis, Minn., 1980), 55; Edward Holyoke, *The Duty of Ministers of the Gospel to Guard against the Pharisaism and Sadducism, of the Present Day* (Boston, 1741), 23. In 1745, Holyoke retracted both his judgment that many had been savingly converted and his high opinion of Whitefield and Tennent: "How was I deluded by Show and Appearance. . . . Whatever Good was done, hath been prodigiously over balanced by the Evil"; see Edward Wigglesworth, *A Letter to the Reverend Mr. George Whitefield . . . ; to Which Is Added, the Reverend President's Answer to the Things Charg'd upon Him . . .* (Boston, 1745), 4 of the *President's Answer*. See Chauncy, *The Out-Pouring of the Holy Ghost*, 43. See also the anonymous *Wonderful Narrative; or, A Faithful Account of the French Prophets . . .* (Boston, 1742), which Chauncy had a hand in and helped to publish.

that work. The Association denounced those who followed "impulses and impressions made on the mind as tho' they were immediate Revelations" from God. The convention's ministers declared that lay preaching contradicted the gospel order and vowed to give "no countenance" to those who brought discord to the Church of Christ. The clergymen approved of the steps that the civil authorities had taken twelve days earlier: the magistrates had ordered the arrest of traveling revivalist James Davenport under Connecticut's new Anti-Itinerancy Act and expelled him from the colony.[14]

The convention's prefatory acknowledgment was one of the last attempts to preserve the thin veneer of clerical consensus, and taken as a whole the record of the convention's discussion makes the transition from the first phase—the Awakening proper—to the second phase of ideological division. The language of the Awakening—the nonjudgmental reports of "religious commotions," the discussions of "soul concerns," the tentative interpretations of the external work of the Holy Spirit—was being replaced.

IDEOLOGICAL DIVISION

The Awakening had been dominated by a single question: "What must I do to be saved?" The Awakening ended as factions formed that proclaimed different answers. Critics like John Caldwell decided that there was nothing extraordinary about the concern and that the commotions were directly attributable to enthusiasm, a deluded condition in which dreams, impulses, and other mental states were falsely attributed to God. The awakenings being reported, he argued bluntly, were "More like a bodily Distemper, than a religious Conviction," and the so-called conversions were "Epileptick-like Fits." Those concerned with the salvation of their souls, he suggested, needed to distance themselves from this madness. Supporters of the revivals, however, began focusing less on the merely awakened and emphasized the more sudden, even cataclysmic conversion experiences that had become more common since Whitefield's tours. Nathanael Leonard of Plymouth wrote that, after Andrew Croswell's preaching on February 13, 1742, "conversions were so open and public, that we seemed to see souls, dead in trespasses and sins, revive and stand up monuments of divine grace." Edwards noted, too, that "conversions were frequently wrought more sensibly and visibly . . . and the progress of the Spirit of God in convic-

14. Congregational Churches in Connecticut, General Association, *The Records of the General Association of the Colony of Connecticut; Begun June 20th, 1738; Ending June 19, 1799* (Hartford, Conn., 1888), 11–13 (entry for June 15, 1742).

MEANING AND MORAL ORDER

tion, from step to step, more apparent; and the transition from one state to another more sensible and plain; so that it might, in many instances, be as it were seen by bystanders." Promoting the work of the Redeemer meant promoting the revivals, which by 1742 seemed, to some, to be more clearly the means, not just of awakening, but of saving grace.[15]

When interpreters of the religious excitement had to choose between acknowledging conversions and diagnosing insanity, attributing "the Work" to either God or the devil, public discourse became polemical controversy. Daniel Wadsworth, pastor of Hartford's First Church, noted in his diary as early as the fall of 1741 that "the great awakening etc. seems to be degenerating into strife and faction." Edwards wrote that the differences between two "parties" had "long been growing more and more visible." In 1742, Boston presses printed some sermons from a skirmish begun the previous fall. The Reverend John Caldwell of New Londonderry had risen from the congregation after a sermon by the Reverend David MacGregore called *The Spirit of the Present Day Tried* and had challenged the preacher to a public debate. MacGregore declined, and both ran off to printers to hurl arguments at one another and to use 1 John 4:1, a verse encouraging the effort to distinguish between true and false spirits and cautioning about false prophets, for their own purposes. Isaac Stiles's Con-

15. John Caldwell, *An Impartial Trial of the Spirit Operating in This Part of the World . . .* (Boston, 1742), 22, 23–24. Caldwell made up his mind about the Awakening, he wrote, after about six months (20). The Harvard faculty, in *The Testimony of the President, Professors, Tutors, and Hebrew Instructor of Harvard College in Cambridge, against the Reverend Mr. George Whitefield, and His Conduct* (Boston, 1744), 4, defined an "enthusisast" as "one that acts, either according to Dreams, or some sudden Impulses and Impressions upon his Mind, which he fondly imagines to be from the Spirit of God, perswading and inclining him thereby to such and such Actions, tho' he hath no Proof that such Perswasions or Impressions are from the holy Spirit." For a general study, see David S. Lovejoy, *Religious Enthusiasm in the New World: Heresy to Revolution* (Cambridge, Mass., 1985). Peter Thacher, in Prince, ed., *Christian History*, II, 89, in Tracy, *The Great Awakening*, 174, described the previous norm for conversions: of the two hundred or so awakened in his Middleborough congregation during the third week of November 1741, "Most of them tarried long in the birth," and "it was some days, and weeks, and months, before they were brought sensibly to close with Christ." John Sergeant illustrates the continuing skepticism of some to these cataclysmic conversions: "In the *General,* I believe, it will hold for a true Observation, that by how much the more *sudden* a supposed *Conversion* is, by so much the more Reason there is *to doubt* of the Genuineness of it." See Sergeant, *The Causes and Danger of Delusions in the Affairs of Religion . . .* (Boston, 1743), 27. Nathanael Leonard described Andrew Crosswell's preaching in Prince, ed., *Christian History*, II, 313, in Tracy, *The Great Awakening*, 161; Jonathan Edwards wrote about quick, visible conversions to the Reverend Thomas Prince, in Edwards, *The Great Awakening*, ed. Goen, in Miller et al., eds., *Works of Jonathan Edwards*, IV, 549.

necticut election sermon in May 1742 did not just caution against enthusiasm; it refuted Edwards's 1741 Yale sermon, *The Distinguishing Marks of the Work of the Spirit of God,* and condemned New Lights as subversives. Whatever arguments and invectives New England writers could not invent on their own, they could borrow from the well-developed pamphlet battles in the other colonies: the exchanges between Whitefield and South Carolina Anglican Alexander Garden, for example, or the clashes between New Side and Old Side Presbyterians in the middle colonies.[16]

New England was further polarized by the public demonstrations of the wild Long Island itinerant James Davenport and his followers. Davenport had lost his wits long before he almost lost his pants to a pile of idolatrous clothing intended for a bonfire on a New London pier on March 7, 1743. That had been the judgment, at least, of learned magistrates and ministers in Hartford and Boston, who had him arrested the previous year for slander and disturbing the peace. A scion of New Haven's founding family and a graduate of Yale College at the age of sixteen, Davenport began his career as an itinerant revivalist after the successful tours of Whitefield and Tennent. But, whereas Whitefield and Tennent had left pulpits to preach to thousands in open fields, Davenport had led his followers from the fields to sing hymns through the streets. Davenport presented himself, not just as a preacher, but as a man sent on a mission by the Lord. Stirrings of the Holy Spirit helped him expose and denounce the sinful, unconverted hearts of the local ministers who opposed him. It was not until he had cast books of divinity to the flames in a public bonfire in New London on March 6 and had heaped up articles of clothing to be burnt as vain idols the next day that Davenport himself felt God's Spirit leave him. Was God's Spirit withdrawing from New England, too, as Edwards wrote in his letters to Scot-

16. Daniel Wadsworth, Diary, quoted in Samuel Harrison Rankin, Jr., "Conservatism and the Problem of Change in the Congregational Churches of Connecticut, 1660–1760" (Ph.D. diss., Kent State University, 1971), 220; Edwards to James Robe, in Edwards, *The Great Awakening,* ed. Goen, in Miller et al., eds., *Works of Jonathan Edwards,* IV, 536. On the Caldwell-MacGregore exchange, see the preface to Caldwell, *Impartial Trial of the Spirit;* and the preface and appendix to David MacGregore, *The Spirit of the Present Day Tried . . . ,* 2d ed. (Boston, 1742). See Isaac Stiles, *A Prospect of the City of Jerusalem, in It's Spiritual Building, Beauty, and Glory* (New London, Conn., 1742). On the relationship between Edwards and Isaac Stiles, see Edmund S. Morgan, *The Gentle Puritan: A Life of Ezra Stiles, 1727–1795* (New Haven, Conn., 1962), chap. 2. Stiles's sermon was not, however, "the first public attack on the Great Awakening in New England" (41). On Whitefield and Garden, see Heimert and Miller, "Introduction," in Heimert and Miller, eds., *The Great Awakening,* xxxv–xxxvi. John Caldwell, who preached one of the earliest New England antirevival sermons, claimed in *An Impartial Trial of the Spirit* that he had not seen Garden's attack on Whitefield.

land? Did the excesses of Davenport and his followers show that Satan was trying to discredit the Awakening? Or was the incident a fitting symbol for three
years of fervor characterized by far more pathological enthusiasm than grace?
Was Davenport—the Yale man burning religious books, the preacher tearing
off his breeches—a suitable emblem of the New England mind gone mad?[17]

In 1743, Edwards saw a wall being raised between the promoters and opposers of the revivals, a wall built in part from the broadsides, pamphlets, and
books that continued to pour from the presses. The controversy developed significantly even in the short weeks between Davenport's New London bonfire
and the *Boston Weekly Post-Boy* article that reported it on March 28. An anonymous pamphlet entitled *The Late Religious Commotions in New England Considered*, published in Boston, again challenged Edwards's *Distinguishing Marks*.
The first issue of Thomas Prince, Jr.'s *Christian History, Containing Accounts of
the Revival and Propagation of Religion in Great Britain and America* appeared.
On March 25, the *Boston Weekly News-Letter* published the tables of contents
to announce Edwards's *Some Thoughts concerning the Revival* and Charles
Chauncy's forthcoming *Seasonable Thoughts on the State of Religion in New
England*, the Awakening's two major treatises. "Some call it a Time of great
Reformation at this Day; others, a Time of great Delusion and Giddiness,"
Nathanael Eells lamented. "Thus we are divided and broken." The Awakening
had been sparked by powerful orators who linked local communities as they
traveled from town to village; the subsequent controversy over the effects of
that Awakening were marked by an unprecedented flurry of print, as clergymen sought to proclaim their authoritative judgments beyond the confines of
their local congregations to a broader audience. Promoters and opponents of
the revivals each claimed a larger sphere of publicity and authority. The controversy was not just the expression of different interpretative opinions; it was
a struggle over which reading of recent events would be legitimized and enforced by the powers of church and state.[18]

17. *Boston Weekly Post-Boy*, Mar. 28, 1743, in Richard L. Bushman, ed., *The Great Awakening: Documents on the Revival of Religion, 1740–1745* (New York, 1970), 51–53; Extract from
New London court records, Mar. 31, 1743, in J. M. Bumsted, ed., *The Great Awakening: The
Beginnings of Evangelical Pietism in America* (Waltham, Mass., 1970), 91–92; James Davenport, *The Reverend Mr. Davenport's Confession and Retractions* (Boston, 1744). See Harry S.
Stout and Peter Onuf, "James Davenport and the Great Awakening in New London," *Journal of American History*, LXX (1983–1984), 556–578; and Onuf, "New Lights in New London: A Group Portrait of the Separatists," *WMQ*, 3d Ser., XXXVII (1980), 627–643.

18. Jonathan Edwards, *Some Thoughts concerning the Present Revival . . .* (1742), in Edwards, *The Great Awakening*, ed. Goen, in Miller et al., eds., *Works of Jonathan Edwards*, IV,
289–530; Nathanael Eells, *Religion Is the Life of God's People . . .* (Boston, 1743). Edwards's ref-

The published testimonies of two ministerial assemblies in May and July 1743 made it clear that the time had come for the clergy to pass judgment upon what they called the "essence" of "the Work." In May, Massachusetts ministers met at their annual convention in Boston and subsequently published a testimony "against several Errors in Doctrine and Disorders in Practice, which have of late obtained in various Parts of the Land." [19] But unlike the New London convention's declaration of 1742, the Boston document did not begin with what Benjamin Prescott called "so full and enlarged a Testimony for a glorious Work of divine Grace." The majority at the May convention suggested that enthusiasts and Antinomians like Davenport were not merely sinful "appendage[s]" to what had been, in essence, a glorious work of God; they were becoming the rule of rather than the exception to the general state of religion in New England. Outmaneuvered and outvoted at the May conference, supporters of the revivals issued a call five days later in the *Boston Gazette* for a second meeting and a second "conjunct testimony." These men wanted to ensure that the public would not mistake the May 25 testimony as the judgment of the New England clergy as a whole. After all, perhaps no more than thirty-eight ministers, or about a fifth of the Massachusetts clergy, had voted for the first testimony; the July Assembly brought together sixty-eight ministers, and fifty-six more sent letters of attestation from four colonies. This second gathering, although it denounced the same disorders, read the signs of the times differently. [20]

---

erence to a wall separating the two parties is in Edwards to James Robe, May 12, 1743, in Edwards, *The Great Awakening*, ed. Goen, in Miller et al., eds., *Works of Jonathan Edwards*, IV, 535–538 (reference on 536).

19. *The Testimony of the Pastors of the Churches in the Province of Massachusetts Bay, in New England, at Their Annual Convention in Boston, May 25, 1743* . . . , in Tracy, *The Great Awakening*, 287.

20. Ibid.; Benjamin Prescott, *A Letter to the Reverend Mr. Joshua Gee* . . . (Boston, 1743), 24. Davenport's *Confession and Retractions* described his methods as "great Blemishes to the Work of God" and distinguished "the *Appendage* from the *Substance*" (4, 7). Benjamin Colman pressed for a stronger condemnation in *A Letter from the Reverend Dr. Colman of Boston, to the Reverend Mr. Williams of Lebanon* (Boston, 1744). Davenport then asked that his confession be changed, stating that his actions were not "appendage[s]" to "*the Work*" but "*were no Parts of it, but of a different and contrary Nature and Tendency.*" See Solomon Williams and Eleazar Wheelock, *Two Letters from the Reverend Mr. Williams and Wheelock of Lebanon, to the Rev. Mr. Davenport* . . . *with a Letter from Mr. Davenport* (Boston, 1744), 30–31. *An Impartial Examination of Mr. Davenport's Retractions* [Boston, 1744], however, had no patience with these distinctions and argued that "the *Work* is plainly proved *not of* GOD but *of Men*, because 'tis come to Nothing" (8). See also *The Testimony and Advice of an Assembly of Pastors of Churches in New England, at a Meeting in Boston, July 7, 1743* . . . , in Tracy, *The Great Awakening*, 294–301 (quotation on 294). Tracy also reprints the notice for the second convention, which appeared in the *Boston Gazette*, May 31, 1743 (294–295). See

Ministers could no longer be content to thank God for true revivals where they found them and to condemn particular errors when they appeared. In an increasingly polarized debate, partisans on both sides saw prudence as an evasion of sacred obligations. For more than a century, New England ministers had played the part of "watchmen upon the walls of Jerusalem," sounding the alarm at the sight of enemies both outside and inside the city on the hill. According to the May testimony, 1743 was the time to sound another general alarm; according to the July testimony, it was time for the watchmen to "sound the trumpet of praise" and announce that "the King of Zion cometh." As the period of Awakening ended, New Lights and Old Lights struggled to shape the "official" understanding of how God's Spirit had worked through New England for the redemption of mankind.[21]

The ministers were not alone in this effort. The two testimonies were followed in September by *The Testimony and Advice of a Number of Laymen respecting Religion, and the Teachers of It; Addres'd to the Pastors of New-England.* Whereas the two ministerial testimonies "give contradictory Accounts of the State of Religion in these Parts, show the great Prevalence of a Party Spirit, and have a tendency to perplex the minds of the weak and unstable," these anonymous laymen felt it was their duty to step forward and testify to the truth. This testimony blamed the recent madness on Whitefield, Tennent, and local Cal-

---

also Joshua Gee, *A Letter to the Reverend Mr. Nathanael Eells, Moderator of the Late Convention of Pastors in Boston* . . . (Boston, 1743); John Hancock, *An Expostulatory and Pacifick Letter, by Way of Reply to the Revd Mr. Gee's Letter of Remarks, on the Printed Testimony of the Late Convention of Pastors in Boston* . . . (Boston, 1743); Benjamin Prescott, *A Letter to the Reverend Mr. Joshua Gee* . . . (Boston, 1743); J. F., *Remarks on the Reverend Mr. Joshua Gee's Letter to the Reverend Mr. Nathanael Eells, Moderator of the Late Convention* [Boston, 1744].

21. *Testimony and Advice of an Assembly of Pastors* . . . *July 7, 1743,* in Tracy, *The Great Awakening,* 296. Compare New Haven's Isaac Stiles in *A Looking-Glass for Changelings* . . . (New London, Conn., 1743), 31: "For my part, I think it's high time to blow the Trumpet in Zion, to sound an Alarm in God's Holy Mountain, and bear the most publick Testimony and Remonstrance against that horrid and insufferable Contempt that is cast upon Authority both Civil and Ecclesiastical." Nathanael Eells had urged that ministers evaluate the revivals with a case-by-case approach in *Religion Is the Life of God's People,* 20. George Beckwith in Lyme also had denounced the errors and sinful conduct of religious zealots but never doubted that the great concern about religion was really from the Spirit. He complained that "to Consider all together in a Lump" was unfair: "No doubt every one ought to stand or fall by his own personal Conduct, and not be condemned meerly because he is a favourer of this or that Party." Beckwith, *Spiritual Judgments the Most Awful, and Dreadful Judgments* . . . *September, 1743* (New London, Conn., 1744), 52n–54n. John Sergeant of Stockbridge had tried to chart a middle course by urging those who looked upon the revivals from the outside to "Let the Awakenings of others *awaken* you" but warned that sinners could be deluded every step of the way. See Sergeant, *The Causes and Danger of Delusions,* 36.

vinist zealots but warned clergymen on both sides of the issue "to put off all lordly and assuming airs" and to remember that when they preached they were not the only learned men in the room: "Consider, That there are among the Laity those who are well acquainted with and have taken great Pains to understand the true Sense of the Holy-Scriptures, and are competent Judges of Reason and good Argument." Connecticut's Jonathan Parsons was singled out for even harsher treatment by an anonymous Boston layman, who called the visiting preacher a wheedling, arrogant rabble-rouser, sneered at his *awkward Similie's* and *Affectation of polite Writing,*" and warned him not to "talk saucily of his Betters." When the Awakening began, preachers were thrust to the center of attention, but the danger now was an anticlerical backlash. And both sides knew it. As Chauncy (of all people) warned in 1744, the continual bickering among a divided clergy exposed the whole ministry to contempt.[22]

But how long did these divisions last? Edwards worked to distance himself from the "spiritually proud" Separatists who had withdrawn from their Old Light churches, and by 1747 he sounded remarkably like the Chauncy of 1741. None could deny, he wrote, "that there have been great awakenings of late." Yet he acknowledged the "great diversity of opinions about the issue" of them and added his voice to those who insisted that the awakenings "have not issued well, but have ended in enthusiasm and delusion." In 1750, the assessment of Edwards's Connecticut disciple Joseph Bellamy was similar:

> It has doubtless appeared as a thing strange and dark to so many pious persons, and occasioned not a little perplexity of mind, to observe what has come to pass in *New England* since the year 1740.—That there should be so general an outpouring of the spirit—so many hundreds and thousands awakened all over the country, and such an almost universal external reformation, and so many receive the word with joy; and yet, after all, things come to be as they now are: so many fallen away to carnal security, and so many turned enthusiasts and heretics, . . . and a flood of *Arminianism* and immorality, ready to deluge the land.

The early 1740s had not marked New England's regeneration after all. It had been only a Great Awakening.[23]

22. *The Testimony and Advice of a Number of Laymen respecting Religion, and the Teachers of It; Addres'd to the Pastors of New-England* (Boston, 1743), 1, 9; *Mr. Parsons Corrected . . .* ([Boston], 1743), 14–15; Charles Chauncy, *Ministers Cautioned against the Occasions of Contempt* (Boston, 1744), 11–12, 43–45.

23. Jonathan Edwards, *An Humble Attempt to Promote Explicit Agreement and Visible Union of God's People in Extraordinary People . . .* (1747), in Edwards, *Apocalyptic Writings,* ed. Stephen J. Stein, in Miller et al., eds., *Works of Jonathan Edwards,* V (New Haven, Conn.,

To doubt that the Awakening was either the key to the American Revolution or the origin of American democracy is not to argue that it completely lacked social and political ramifications; to avoid characterizing it as the death of Puritanism or the birth of evangelicalism is not to say that it left religious life unchanged. The Awakening affected individuals and communities, local and colonial institutions. It challenged notions of religious authority and corporate life and left its mark upon public discourse in several ways, including the introduction of a new style of popular persuasive speech. Yet in Connecticut, the legacy of the Awakening would be carried in large measure, not by radical architects of a new order, but by those who tried to revivify the old one and resuscitate the orthodox faith.[24]

In Connecticut, the Awakening touched thousands of lives, changing some forever. Some people, like the young Ezra Stiles in New Haven, realized that they would never be able to find God and truth in the mindless emotionalism they saw in the revivals; for others, it was as if they were hearing the gospel and seeing the world for the first time. In Norwich, Isaac Backus was converted in 1741 and went on to become a leader and historian of the Baptist Church in New England. In Montville, a young Mohegan named Samson Occom, who had rejected the efforts of previous white missionaries, was converted and inspired to learn to read; he was eventually ordained and gained fame touring England and Scotland as an Indian preacher. Nathan Cole, who had raced to see Whitefield preach at Middletown, began his spiritual autobiography years later with a sentiment that could have been seconded by many others: "I was born Feb 15th 1711 and born again octo 1741."[25]

1977), 363, 364; Joseph Bellamy, *True Religion Delineated; or, Experimental Religion . . .* , in Heimert and Miller, eds., *The Great Awakening,* 552. See also Jonathan Edwards, *The Life of David Brainerd* (1749), ed. Norman Pettit, in Miller et al., eds., *Works of Jonathan Edwards,* VII (New Haven, Conn., 1985), 153. Edwards, Bellamy, and many others in New England continued to hope that the Awakening, though fleeting, was a prelude to a much greater outpouring of grace.

24. On the revivalist's popular rhetorical style, see Harry S. Stout, "Religion, Communications, and the Ideological Origins of the American Revolution," *WMQ,* 3d Ser., XXXIV (1977), 519–541. This style will be discussed at greater length in connection with the pulpit rhetoric of Ezra Stiles in Chapter 5.

25. Isaac Backus, *The Diary of Isaac Backus,* 3 vols., ed. William G. McLoughlin (Providence, R.I., 1979), I, [3]. On Occom, see W. DeLoss Love, *Samson Occom and the Christian*

Many people stepped forward to commit themselves to a church, although one historian's estimate that 6–10 percent of Connecticut's population either joined a church, progressed from halfway to full membership, or renewed a profession of faith during the Awakening can only be a guess. Church adherence certainly rose sharply in the early 1740s. Contemporaries commented especially upon the number of young people and males who were brought into the church. One statistical study of church admissions, based on church records from eastern Connecticut, argues that a younger conversion age and a larger proportion of males was the usual admission pattern during local congregational revivals before and after the 1740s, suggesting that the Awakening was a normal, periodic harvest of the local population at risk. Unlike previous local revivals, however, the Awakening linked the individual's personal, deeply felt experience to a pervasive and highly charged religious climate that transcended the local.[26]

Some of the people who were deeply moved by the revivals abandoned churches that they now considered to be cold and lifeless and sought to create new communities of the faithful. Empowered by their personal experience of the Spirit's work upon their hearts, they denied the legitimacy of laws binding them to their local congregation and its appointed minister. The result was an unprecedented number of ecclesiastical schisms in New England. The religious fervor of the early 1740s did not suddenly tear the social fabric of peaceable Puritan communities, however; it often fueled long-standing local struggles over how much to pay the minister, where to build the new meetinghouse, or whether to allow the outlying village to have its own church. Disgruntled factions illegally separated from their churches and formed new congregations. There were 19 separations in Connecticut and 13 in Massachusetts between 1742 and 1745, rising to 40 and 37, respectively, by 1750. By the end of 1754, the height of the Separatist movement, these separations had led to the

Indians of New England (Boston, 1899); Harold Blodgett, *Samson Occom* (Dartmouth, N.H., 1935); Leon Burr Richardson, ed., *An Indian Preacher in England . . .* (Hanover, N.H., 1933); and Margaret Connell Szasz, "Samson Occom: Mohegan as Spiritual Intermediary," in Szasz, ed., *Between Indian and White Worlds: The Cultural Broker* (Norman, Okla., 1994), 61–84. The Cole quotation is from Crawford, "The Spiritual Travels of Nathan Cole," *WMQ*, 3d Ser., XXXIII (1976), 92 (quotation).

26. The 6–10 percent estimate is in Rankin, "Conservatism and the Problem of Change," 211. Gaustad discussed the difficulties in assessing the number of "new births" and church admissions in *The Great Awakening in New England*, 103–104. On the Awakening as a normal harvest, see Stephen Grossbart, "Seeking the Divine Favor: Conversion and Church Admission in Eastern Connecticut, 1711–1832," *WMQ*, 3d Ser., XLVI (1989), 696–740.

formation of 35 dissenting "Strict Congregational" churches in Connecticut and 51 in Massachusetts. Growth in the established Congregational churches more than offset these gains, however: Connecticut added 38 new church societies in the 1740s and 1750s, and New England as a whole gained more than 150. Furthermore, many of the dissenting congregations formed in the aftermath of the Awakening were dissolving by the 1760s, their congregants rejoining the established churches, becoming Baptists, or leaving the colony altogether. Not long after midcentury, the Standing Order had come to be more concerned about the rising number of Anglicans than about the Separatists. Post-Awakening schisms had not destroyed the Standing Order, but they did signal to the "land of steady habits" that the threat of pluralism and the problem of dissent would not go away. The tension between the Standing Order of tax-supported Congregationalists and the dissenting denominations, however, cannot be interpreted as the institutional perpetuation of the Old Light–New Light division, since many pro-revival ministers—like the New Divinity Edwardseans—stayed within the established Congregational Church.[27]

If not mirrored by ecclesiastical reality, the Old Light–New Light division has nevertheless been portrayed as a lasting cultural legacy of the Awakening. Just as historians have found Edwards's 1742 suggestion that the millennium might be dawning in New England more stirring than his pessimistic assessment of the Awakening in 1747, his 1743 description of two great parties with "a wall between them up to heaven" has provided a more provocative model for post-Awakening clerical opinion and intellectual life than the more complicated position he expressed during the communion controversy in 1750. Edwards's claim that "true virtue or holiness has its seat chiefly in the heart, rather than the head" is often contrasted to Chauncy's comment that "an enlightened

27. J. M. Bumsted, "Revivalism and Separatism in New England: The First Society of Norwich, Connecticut, as a Case Study," *WMQ*, 3d Ser., XXIV (1967), 588–612; Stout, *New England Soul*, 208; Bruce C. Daniels, *The Connecticut Town: Growth and Development, 1635–1790* (Middletown, Conn., 1979), 97; Gaustad, *The Great Awakening in New England*, 114. For the number of Strict Congregational churches established, I have used the estimates in McLoughlin, *New England Dissent*, I, 346–347n, rather than the chart in Goen, *Revivalism and Separatism in New England*, 300–327, which includes Old Light and Episcopal separations. McLoughlin "also located thirteen Separate groups in Massachusetts and twenty-four in Connecticut which conducted worship in barns or private homes but which apparently never organized as churches or installed pastors." Although Congregationalism would remain the established and tax-supported denomination in Connecticut until the new state constitution of 1818, dissenters made up 20 percent of the population by the census of 1790, and, of 307 church societies existing in that year, 58 were Anglican, 30 Baptist, 14 Strict Congregational, and 2 Quaker (Daniels, *The Connecticut Town*, 104).

Mind, not raised Affections, ought always to be the Guide of those who call themselves Men." In this interpretation, the forces of eighteenth-century Pietism and the Enlightenment pull apart the Puritan synthesis of piety and intellect. By the century's end, the Awakening's dual legacy for American religiousness clearly emerges in the cool negations of a cerebral, enlightened Christianity and the convulsive barking of frontier revivalism. In the more rarefied realm of theology, this reading of intellectual bifurcation conveniently locates the origins of Boston Unitarianism in Chauncy's side of the argument and the roots of nineteenth-century Trinitarian Calvinism in Edwards's defense.[28]

This bipolar model of post-Awakening thought, however, becomes less compelling when examining particular developments between 1740 and 1800 in their immediate social and political context. The Old Light–New Light division can be particularly misleading when applied to Connecticut. The terms were used in the religious polemics of the 1740s and the political polemics of the 1760s. "Old Lights" in Connecticut, however, are not the same as Massachusetts "Old Lights," usually characterized as Boston "liberals" straying from Calvinist orthodoxy toward a supposedly softer, more humanistic Arminianism. In Connecticut, they were, for the most part, conservative Calvinists trying to preserve church order and political power. "New Light" was a derogatory title they gave rather indiscriminately to "enthusiastic" Separates and Baptists, to pro-revival but anti-Separatist Edwardseans, and to old antagonists centered in the eastern counties who, they said, used ecclesiastical disorder to further political aims. Yet, although New Lights had demanded religious freedom and decried Old Light institutional tyranny in the 1740s, the tables had turned by 1760, with Old Lights crying for liberty and New Lights trying to build institutions to maintain church order. That Yale president Thomas Clap could be considered a ringleader of the Old Lights in 1745 and of the New Lights in 1760 without modifying any of his principles should suggest caution in using the labels. "Old Light" and "New Light," like "liberal" and "conservative," have limited analytical uses beyond the level of broad generalization and partisan name-calling. It has been suggested that the fine philosophical distinctions drawn in Massachusetts became smudged by political animosities in Con-

28. Edwards to James Robe, May 12, 1743, in Edwards, *The Great Awakening*, ed. Goen, in Miller et al., eds., *Works of Jonathan Edwards*, IV, 536; Edwards and Chauncy, quoted in Richard Warch, "Introduction," in Chauncy, *Seasonable Thoughts*, ed. Warch, 5w. Gaustad, in *The Great Awakening in New England*, wrote of the contending forces of Enlightenment and Pietism, but Alan Heimert's liberals and Edwardseans, in *Religion and the American Mind: From the Great Awakening to the Revolution* (Cambridge, Mass., 1966), more neatly translate into quasi-political parties.

necticut and that Connecticut simply lacked the intellectual caliber to conduct a pamphlet war on a high level of theological abstraction, bickering instead over issues of social control. But in fact Connecticut demonstrates that theologies, ecclesiologies, political positions, and cultural attitudes do not necessarily cohere in nicely standardized worldviews. The fault lines from the Awakening did not so neatly divide culture.[29]

Some historians have argued that the two-party model does not adequately represent the positions taken by clergymen in any of the colonies even during the early 1740s. They try to define a third faction, a forgotten middle-of-the-road group that would become more influential than either Old Lights or New Lights between 1745 and the Revolution. Other studies have rightly emphasized the broad common ground of a ministry united against external attacks by the mid-1740s. New England's Cape Breton expedition in 1745 and the subsequent wars with France became considerably more important than arguments about the merits of Whitefield. Defending the sacred cause of religious liberties against French papists, New England's Congregational clergy also united against the encroachments of the Church of England and its rumored plan for an American bishop. In Connecticut, the middle ground was occupied not so much by a third party or a broad consensus as by a struggle over the meaning of New England tradition in the name of Calvinist orthodoxy. Connecticut "Old Lights" or "Old Calvinists," "Moderates," "New Lights," and "New Divinity" Edwardseans all tried to stake their claim to the territory between the Anglicans and the Baptists, or between Arminianism and enthusiasm, as they repaired the institutional and intellectual foundation beneath the true religion their fathers had left them. This foundation was shaken by the Awakening and threatened by the ideological divisiveness that had followed it.[30]

29. Richard L. Bushman, *From Puritan to Yankee: Character and the Social Order in Connecticut, 1690–1765* (Cambridge, Mass., 1967), 216–219. On Thomas Clap, see below, Chapter 3. The Connecticut focus on social control is discussed by Stephen Nissenbaum, "Introduction," in Nissenbaum, ed., *The Great Awakening at Yale College* (Belmont, Calif., 1972), 3.

30. J. M. Bumsted and John E. Van de Wetering, in *What Must I Do to Be Saved? The Great Awakening in Colonial America* (Hinsdale, Ill., 1976), 97, finds three shifting factions: radicals, moderates, and the Old Light antirevivalists. David Harlan, in *The Clergy and the Great Awakening in New England* (Ann Arbor, Mich., 1980), argues for the importance of "Regular Lights," a "middle-of-the-road group" of Old Calvinists that was actually much larger and more influential than either the crypto-Arminian Old Lights in Boston or the hyper-Calvinist Edwardseans and revivalists. Both studies are sensitive to the problem of defining lasting parties emerging from the Awakening. Leigh Eric Schmidt describes four parties in "'A Second and Glorious Reformation': The New Light Extremism of Andrew Croswell," *WMQ*, 3d Ser., XLIII (1986), 222–223, 243. John L. Brooke, in *The Heart of the Commonwealth: Society and Political Culture in Worcester County, Massachusetts, 1713–1861*

But as New England Congregational ministers who stayed within the established order pondered the consequences of the Awakening in the latter 1740s and the 1750s, their thoughts were as likely to turn to their own congregations as to society at large. How were they to rekindle religious affections without reigniting destructive passions and religious enthusiasm? How were they to strengthen moral order and Christian discipline without infringing upon the rights of conscience or merely perpetuating the dry customs of a so-called covenant people? How could ministers reassert pastoral authority over flocks that had proved dangerously receptive to indiscriminate itinerant preaching and lay testimonies about visions and trances? An increasing number of pro-revival clergymen and divinity students turned to the theologian of the revivals, Jonathan Edwards, for answers, even as his own flock turned away.

MISREPRESENTATIONS CORRECTED:
EDWARDS AND THE COMMUNION CONTROVERSY

"The great Thing which I have scrupled," Jonathan Edwards declared in the preface to his *Farewell Sermon* (1751), was that, when people came to be admitted to communion, they publicly assented only to a "Form of Words . . . without pretending thereby to mean any such Thing as an hearty Consent to the Terms of the Gospel-Covenant." By common custom and established principle, a public profession of faith in Northampton had come to rest on a "*diverse Use*" of words and signs. "People have in Effect agreed among themselves," he complained in *An Humble Inquiry,* that persons who use the words need not intend their proper meaning "and that others need not understand them so." Professing Christianity and owning the church covenant had become empty formalities for many young couples who wanted to have their babies baptized. He also argued that, when families in Northampton and inhabitants in New

---

(Cambridge, Mass., 1989), 67–70, writes that the Awakening pushed people toward ideological extremes "while it defined a mediating middle ground" characterized by "a reemersion in traditional institutions, infused with the transcendent purposes of the evangelical cause." He concluded that "rather than a symptom of rebellion, the early orthodox revivals brought a submission to traditional, deferential, corporate unity and harmony." A good discussion of the post-Awakening theological spectrum is in Allen C. Guelzo, *Edwards on the Will: A Century of Theological Debate* (Middletown, Conn, 1989). On Congregational opposition to the Anglicans and the French, see Carl Bridenbaugh, *Mitre and Sceptre: Transatlantic Faiths, Ideas, Personalities, and Politics, 1689–1775* (New York, 1962); Nathan O. Hatch, *The Sacred Cause of Liberty: Republican Thought and the Millennium in Revolutionary New England* (New Haven, Conn., 1977); Stout, *New England Soul,* 233–255.

England called themselves "Christians," they merely flattered themselves with a name while growing fat off the land and resting content with the hollow forms of faith. After the Awakening, Edwards asserted his authority as preacher of the Word and teacher of words to bring practice and profession closer to the gospel truth. He tried to discipline his congregation by policing the meanings of words, sacramental symbols, and other signs within Northampton.[31]

The communion controversy in Northampton and Edwards's subsequent dismissal is a familiar story in the annals of American religious history. In February 1749, Edwards told his congregation that he could no longer abide by the lax standards of church membership that Northampton had followed under the long tenure of Edwards's grandfather Solomon Stoddard, who had become pastor in 1672. The shocked and enraged parishioners quickly concluded that, under Edwards's new scheme, only those people who could demonstrate to the satisfaction of the autocratic pastor that they had been born again would become church members and be able to have their children baptized as Christians. After sixteen months of bitter wrangling, Edwards was dismissed from his pastorate. He was prescient when he wrote that the controversy would "be very famous" and "long remembered." The tale of the great theologian's being rejected by his own flock belongs, according to Perry Miller, "to the symbolism of America." Miller told the story as the triumph of the merchant ethic over Christian virtue. Other scholars, looking more closely at Northampton than at American cultural archetypes, have tried to reveal the personal, social, and political tensions woven through the town's debate over church polity and practice. Less attention has been given to the published arguments the controversy generated. But the rhetoric of the communion controversy reveals the ways that communal cohesiveness and corporate identity were rooted in a public religious vocabulary; it shows questions arising about how public language was meaningful and who had the authority to regulate those meanings.[32]

31. Jonathan Edwards, *A Farewel-Sermon . . .* (Boston, 1751), iii; Edwards, *An Humble Inquiry into the Rules of the Word of God, concerning the Qualifications Requisite to a Compleat Standing and Full Communion in the Visible Christian Church* (Boston, 1749), 15–16: "And therefore whatever some of these Words and Signs may *in themselves* most properly and naturally import or signify, they entirely cease to be Significations of any such Thing among People accustomed to understand and use them otherwise."

32. Jonathan Edwards, "Narrative of the Communion Controversy," in Edwards, *Ecclesiastical Writings*, ed. Hall, in Miller et al., eds., *Works of Jonathan Edwards*, XII, 569; Perry Miller, *Jonathan Edwards* (1949; reprint, Amherst, Mass., 1981), 211. On Edwards in Northampton, see Patricia J. Tracy, *Jonathan Edwards, Pastor: Religion and Society in Eighteenth-Century Northampton* (New York, 1979); Gregory H. Nobles, *Divisions throughout the Whole: Politics and Society in Hampshire County, Massachusetts, 1740–1775* (Cambridge, Mass.,

Edwards attempted to regulate public religious discourse—to control the meaning of signs *in* a community and to redefine the language *of* Christian community. First, he insisted that the minister, not the parishioners, set the terms of debate. Second, he sought to clear away the ambiguity and confusion arising from a diverse use of signs, some of which can be found in his own earlier preaching. Third, Edwards's definition of "visible sainthood" involved spelling out not just *what* this term should mean but also *how* terms should signify meaning. His disagreements with his cousin Solomon Williams and the Separatist position articulated by Ebenezer Frothingham reveal how each writer's position was based upon different epistemologies and different conceptions of signification. Williams, writing from Lebanon, Connecticut, for the Stoddardean opposition, attacked Edwards's scriptural argument for restricted communion and his epistemological explanation of Christian profession. Frothingham, a Middletown, Connecticut, Separatist, embraced Edwards's stricter view of the church as a gathered communion of saints but found his arguments mystifying and contradictory.[33]

Fourth and finally, Edwards wanted to restrict the rhetorical uses of flattering titles like "God's Covenant People" for all nominally Christian New Englanders, even when such language could be doctrinally justified. This last goal is related to a post-Awakening rhetorical strategy that sought to accent the difference between nature and grace and is connected to the question of Edwards and the national covenant. Clerical rhetoric during the Seven Years' War (including Edwards's own) once again exploited the systematic equivocations at the heart of New England's interlocking covenants, but in the 1760s Bellamy, Edwards's New Divinity disciple in Connecticut, resumed the effort to dispel

---

1983). For an overview of the basic theological issues and a summary of some of the initial arguments on both sides, see David D. Hall, "Editor's Introduction," in Edwards, *Ecclesiastical Writings,* ed. Hall, in Miller et al., eds., *Works of Jonathan Edwards,* XII, 1–90. In 1768, New York Presbyterian Jacob Green considered using the terms "Stoddardian" and "Edwardian" to label the opposing parties in the continuing controversy over the church, since Stoddard and Edwards were "the two most noted Men in our Part of the World, who have writ on opposite Sides of the Question." See Green, *An Inquiry into the Constitution and Discipline of the Jewish Church . . .* (New York, 1768), [iii].

33. Solomon Williams, *The True State of the Question concerning the Qualifications Necessary to Lawful Communion in the Christian Sacraments . . .* (Boston, 1751); Ebenezer Frothingham, *The Articles of Faith and Practice, with the Covenant, That Is Confessed by the Separate Churches of Christ in General in This Land; Also a Discourse, Holding Forth the Great Privileges of the Church of Jesus Christ . . .* (Newport, R.I., 1750). Hereafter, references to the "Discourse" following the "Articles" and "Covenant" will be referred to as Frothingham's *Discourse.*

ambiguity and reassert clerical authority. Bellamy's debates on the Half-Way Covenant would dramatize once again how the battle for the meaning of signs could become a contest over who could regulate public religious discourse.

More than a sacramental controversy, therefore, the dispute Edwards set in motion after the Awakening in an effort to reform the church made New Englanders question what it meant to call themselves "God's People." The issue involves broader questions of rhetorical emphasis as much as the narrower points of ecclesiastical doctrine, and understanding that rhetoric is essential to finding Edwards's place between his Puritan predecessors and the New Divinity theologians who followed him. The language of corporate identity changed in Edwards's preaching, as it would change throughout mid-eighteenth-century New England. Arguments articulated during and after the communion controversy help reveal what Edwards perpetuated and what he discarded in the image of New England as "God's New Israel" as well as what he contributed to the myth of America as a "Redeemer Nation." But more important, because their efforts affected how local congregations and individual congregants understood themselves and their place in the church, Edwardseans helped redefine the language that constituted Christian community.[34]

Like his cousin Elisha Williams, who had written *The Essential Rights and Liberties of Protestants* in 1744, Edwards would grant people the liberty of conscience. But he knew that a collection of individuals following the dictates of their private judgments did not make a community. He believed that the church's public rituals should not be a marketplace for people to come and choose what they need or want, but a communal expression of a single commonly understood idea. Yet the value of religious words and signs in New England seemed to depreciate as fast as the public bills of credit.[35]

34. Mark A. Noll has discussed the social, economic, and cultural conditions that might have made mid-eighteenth-century New England less receptive to the rhetoric of the national covenant in Noll, "Jonathan Edwards and the Transition from Clerical to Political Leadership in New England's Intellectual History," paper presented at the conference "Writings of Jonathan Edwards: Text and Context, Text and Interpretation," Bloomington, Indiana, June 2–4, 1994.

35. The debate in the marketplace forms an interesting parallel. Magistrates attacked the problem of currency depreciation by first authorizing a fixed value to the bills of credit and then securing individual compliance by requiring personal oaths. Both the 1748 recall of Old Tenor bills in Massachusetts and the excise tax proposed to resupply the treasury in 1754 required oaths. But mandatory oath taking only recast an economic problem as a moral one, for opponents claimed that now the solemn oaths themselves were being devalued by overuse. See *A Letter to the Freeholders and Other Inhabitants of the Massachusetts-Bay . . .* (Boston, 1749); Cornelius Agrippa, *Appendix to Massachusetts in Agony* ([Boston], 1751); and *An*

Edwards did not want to change what people said, but what they meant. He would be content with a simple statement, similar to those already used by candidates for church membership: "I hope, I do truly find a Heart to give myself wholly to God, according to the Tenor of that Covenant of Grace which was seal'd in my Baptism, and to walk in a way of that Obedience to all the Commandments of God, which the Covenant of Grace requires, as long as I shall live." But what did these words mean? In Northampton after the Awakening, Edwards complained, they still meant some indeterminate degree of a common faith and moral sincerity short of true godliness. A candidate, awakened but unconverted, could utter these words to express that she wanted to obey God's commandments and that she hoped someday to have a "heart"— that is, a predominant inclination—to give herself wholly to the Lord. The candidate should be professing, Edwards argued, that she believes she *presently* finds such a heart within herself, and hopes she is right. In Edwards's scheme, people with merely awakened consciences but not true religious affections need not apply; their so-called desire to obey God did not flow from their heart's love of God, but merely from their natural fear of hell.[36]

The Northampton parish interpreted Edwards's break from local church practices as a bid for ministerial power over the congregation, and they were right. But it was not, as some murmured, that he wanted to set himself up as the exclusive judge of other people's religious experiences; he continued to maintain that even the most experienced eye could be deceived in such matters. Nor did he claim the sole right to measure a candidate's behavior against her profession, for, when a minister did so, he acted publicly and only as an officer of the whole church. But Edwards did insist "that it belonged to me as

---

Address to the Freeholders and Inhabitants of the Massachusetts-Bay in New England (Boston, 1751). Seven pamphlets on the excise tax in 1754 argue about the oath, but see, especially, *The Good of the Community Impartially Considered . . .* (Boston, 1754), 42–43. In Connecticut, currency problems are discussed in the election sermons for 1747, 1748, 1749, and 1751 (citations in Appendix II); and also in [Roger Sherman], *A Caveat against Injustice; or, An Enquiry into the Evil Consequences of a Fluctuating Medium of Exchange . . .* (New York, 1752). Sherman argues against the idea that bills receive value through common use rather than by statute. On the devaluation of oaths, see Moses Dickinson, *A Sermon Preached before the General Assembly of the Colony of Connecticut . . .* (New London, Conn., 1755), 43–49. See also Dickinson, *The Nature and Importance of Oaths and Juries* (New York, 1747). Like the New England magistrates, Edwards fixed the value of signs, demanded personal oaths, and met with resistance.

36. For the simple statement of faith, see Jonathan Edwards, "Letter to Peter Clark," May 7, 1750, quoted in Edwards, *Misrepresentations Corrected, and Truth Vindicated* (Boston, 1752), 9.

a Pastor, before a Profession was accepted, to have full Liberty to instruct the Candidate in the Meaning of the Terms of it, and in the Nature of the Things proposed to be professed." [37]

Edwards's bid to control the meaning of the terms of Christian profession quickly became a power struggle played out in contests pitting different forms of speech and writing against each other: preaching and speeches at committee meetings, gossip and private correspondence, printed treatises and published sermons. As soon as he notified the church about his change of mind in early 1749, rumors spread. People in the town and outside it quickly jumped to conclusions about Edwards and his new position. Some called him an ecclesiastical tyrant; others thought he had become a Separatist who wanted to set up a pure church of the regenerated only. Again and again, through the long months of increasingly bitter controversy, Edwards asked the committee of the church if it would consent to let him preach on the issue and explain himself. Again and again they refused, arguing that delivering his opinions from the pulpit would only factionalize the town. They agreed to let him print his argument instead, and in March and April 1749 he hurriedly composed *An Humble Inquiry*, which would be published in Boston in July and distributed in Northampton in August. Edwards wondered whether print rather than preaching might be the more desirable way to get his message out anyway. The townspeople had become so overwrought that even if he did preach they would not be able to hear him: "There would be no opportunity to be heard with any tolerable degree of calmness and attention before what I was writing on the subject was published." As he would argue that fall, "Hearing in a high degree of fermentation of mind . . . is no fair hearing." The printed word, he seemed to believe, would be received with the appropriate calm, rational attention, whereas his speech from the pulpit might only provoke emotions that would block the comprehension—and fair assessment—of his arguments. [38]

As he wrote *An Humble Inquiry*, he also realized that he had to address a broader audience outside the confines of Northampton. He expressed candid concern about the damage to his reputation, as New England by the spring of 1749 was already "full of Noise, Misrepresentations, and many Censures concerning this Affair." It was therefore necessary, he argued, to defend himself through the press "before the Country" even before he made his case to his

37. Edwards, *Farewel-Sermon*, vi.

38. Edwards, "Narrative of Communion Controversy," in Edwards, *Ecclesiastical Writings*, ed. Hall, in Miller et al., eds., *Works of Jonathan Edwards*, XII, 510, 568. Edwards believed he had the authority to preach on the topic but thought it would be disruptive if he did so without the consent of the church committee.

"own People." Later in the controversy, he explained to a ministerial council that, because of his own and Northampton's reputation in the Christian world, established through his publications about revivals in the mid-1730s and the Awakening of the early 1740s, the controversy would "produce an extensive and great effect—as great, and on some accounts much greater, on places at a distance than on places that are near. . . . The result of the final council will undoubtedly be published to the world, and will be regarded with deep attention by many, not only in New England, but the other provinces of North America, as well as by some perhaps in England and Scotland." The controversy, he knew, would send shock waves through the different (though overlapping) publics addressed by local speech, correspondence networks, and print.[39]

To Northampton, Edwards insisted that the controversy could not move forward until his people read or heard what he had to say. But when Colonel Timothy Dwight returned from Boston and distributed twenty copies of *An Humble Inquiry* in August, the townspeople "showed an utter aversion to reading it," Edwards complained, some saying "that they would not even let the book come into their houses." By November 1749, he was arguing that his parishioners "have never given me an opportunity to state the reasons of my opinion, even in private conversation." If preaching was forbidden and his printed words were ignored, though, perhaps private discussion was the only way that communication between the pastor and his people could take place. After a group of consulted ministers counseled the town to stop the public meetings about the controversy and urged the pastor and his people to converse freely and privately about their differences, the precinct meeting created a seven-member committee to talk to Edwards. Edwards declined. That was not his idea of free and private conversation; even though the whole town would not be present for the discussion, the meeting was clearly arranged "to be a debate or discourse managed in behalf of the whole." The proposal was, in other words, public discourse disguised as a private chat—public discourse on the committee's terms.[40]

Edwards pressed again to preach, although by December 1749 he knew his dismissal was all but inevitable. "There is a great multitude of them, many

39. Edwards, "Author's Preface," *Humble Inquiry,* iv; Edwards, "Narrative of Communion Controversy," in Edwards, *Ecclesiastical Writings,* ed. Hall, in Miller et al., eds., *Works of Jonathan Edwards,* XII, 550.

40. Edwards, "Narrative of Communion Controversy," in Edwards, *Ecclesiastical Writings,* ed. Hall, in Miller et al., eds., *Works of Jonathan Edwards,* XII, 561; see 575 on the proposed meeting with the committee. The "precinct" was another term for "parish," the civil body in charge of ecclesiastical issues, encompassing every male taxpayer (513n).

mouths to reproach me, and they are very much abroad in various parts in New England, and I have only my own single voice to defend myself with." He argued to a church council that he needed the opportunity to address the whole congregation, not just the town's "leading men." He asserted his right to be heard by those who, even in ideal circumstances, could not be expected to read and understand his *Humble Inquiry,* especially Northampton's youth, "both male and female." A parish committee proposed that he could preach if he was immediately followed in the pulpit by a minister preaching on the opposite side of the question, and they told Edwards that he would have to supply the opposing speaker a legible copy of his sermon in advance. Edwards agreed, as long as he too could have an advance copy of his opponent's sermon, but nothing came of the plan. And Edwards was still worried that his parishioners would not listen to any words he uttered from the pulpit on the subject. Their agitated state of mind was abundantly clear from their own public and private speech: "It is manifest, not only from the customary conversation of the people in private houses, but from the whole tenor of their public proceedings: from the methods which have been taken, from the measures adopted, from the proceedings of church meetings and precinct meetings and their committee, from the speeches which have been publicly made and the acts which have been publicly done." He urged a council of neighboring ministers to find ways to calm the people and convince them that it was his right to preach and the people's duty to listen.[41]

Through 1749 and into the spring of 1750, town and church meetings dragged on, bogged down by protracted legalistic debates in which a young lawyer named Joseph Hawley made a name for himself as a speaker for the anti-Edwards majority. While the town's leaders refused to read Edwards's book or hear him preach, they were busy trying to get other ministers to preach and publish against him. They wanted not just "many mouths" raised against Edwards but an authoritative voice to answer him from God's pulpit and a clerical author to engage and defeat their pastor's arguments in the larger public arena created by print. The Reverend Peter Clark of Salem Village was initially approached to answer Edwards in the press, though the task eventually fell to Connecticut's Solomon Williams. In February 1750, Edwards finally announced that he would offer a series of weekday lectures explaining his position, although another vote passed in a precinct meeting asking him not to do so. The lectures on Ezek. 44:9, delivered from February 15 to March 22, 1750, were "thinly attended" by his own people; more than half the congrega-

41. Ibid., XII, 544, 562, 566, 570.

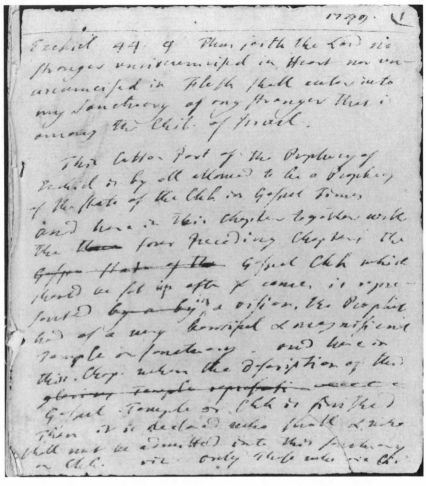

Figure 4. Jonathan Edwards, MS Sermon on Ezek. 44:9 (booklet). Delivered
Feb. 15–Mar. 22, 1750. The original size is approximately 10 × 11 centimeters,
which would have fitted in the palm of Edwards's hand. Courtesy, Beinecke Rare Book
and Manuscript Library, Yale University, New Haven, Conn.

tion were "strangers" in town for the meeting of the county court. Most of
Northampton's parishioners continued to avoid their pastor's words.[42]

Those who came and listened heard Edwards make his arguments by establishing what basic terms like "professing" Christianity, "owning" the covenant,
and "visible" sainthood should mean. His demand for "a higher sense" of these

42. Ibid., XII, 544, 598. The legalistic debates were over the jurisdiction of the county
clerical association, the status and relevance of the Cambridge Platform, the propriety of debating in the precinct meeting rather than the church, and other procedural disputes.

MEANING AND MORAL ORDER

terms was part of an effort to stem the erosion of meaning that had continued under his own ministry, as scriptural words and phrases had been applied like rhetorical tags to a variety of circumstances. He was not just renouncing the doctrine of his grandfather and predecessor Solomon Stoddard, who had allowed striving sinners to the Lord's Table in the hope that they might be converted there. He was also renouncing the rhetorical imprecision of his own earlier preaching, which had moved among the various senses in which the covenant was offered and owned and had acknowledged the different degrees of Christian profession. Scattered in the pews among the curious strangers, Northampton parishioners who had heard Edwards preach for the past two decades were in a better position to understand where his "new sentiments" had come from.[43]

Edwards had for years told his congregation that they were a covenant people. He had explained back in 1737 that a covenant people could be recognized as such because it has access to the Scriptures, it visibly takes hold of the covenant in its profession, and it receives special mercies and judgments from God. But all covenanted nations were not equally favored. Edwards's fast and thanksgiving sermons, from a very early effort in the late 1720s to some of his laments during the French wars through the 1740s, described how the English nation had been raised above all other covenanted peoples to enjoy the peculiar blessings of religious liberty. God had distinguished "the Land" (New England) even above the rest of the nation; whereas England was overrun with deists and skeptics, New England had trained Protestant preachers and churches in every village. New England, Edwards wrote, more closely paralleled God's covenant people Israel as "perhaps no People now on the face of the Earth." Every community where the Word was preached and acknowledged could call itself a "covenant people" or a "professing society." But Edwards explained that God distinguished a community as a covenant people, not just

43. Jonathan Edwards, MS sermon on Ezek. 44:9 (booklet 1), delivered Feb. 15–Mar. 22, 1750, Beinecke Rare Book and Manuscript Library, Yale University, New Haven, Conn. (hereafter cited as Beinecke Library). All manuscript sermons cited hereafter are from the Beinecke collection. Manuscript leaves have been numbered by modern editors. For a brief discussion of this sermon, see Hall, "Editor's Introduction," in Edwards, *Ecclesiastical Writings,* ed. Hall, in Miller et al., eds., *Works of Jonathan Edwards,* XII, 88. In a November 1746 lecture to young people, Edwards had tried to explain the various senses and different degrees behind a commonly used title like "God's Children." Spoken to the people of Israel in Isa. 1:2, the words could also denote all mankind, since man was created in God's image, or refer to all who have been raised in "the House of God" among Christians. In a higher sense, the term could be limited to the saints, those "acknowledged as true born Children and not bastards" in God's family.

by revealing the gospel light to them, but by, in greater or lesser degrees, pouring out his Spirit among them and blessing their religious efforts. Similarly, the community's profession in response to God's offer and blessings had varying degrees. A people made "a higher profession" when they acknowledged a greater degree of God's presence or mercies or "when there is a far Greater Number among them that do make a Profession of special Experiences and of Extraordinary Light."[44]

A year after Northampton's 1735 revival, Edwards had delivered a remarkable sermon that raised the town above all New England "as a city set on a hill." He was not just a preacher tailoring a timeworn simile to his own locale. The religious excitement and "surprising conversions" in Northampton manifested an outpouring of the Spirit that had to that point surpassed any local revival in living memory. New England's "fashionable divinity" had in recent times rejected the work of vital godliness "as whimsey and enthusiasm," he had preached, and "the Country has in a Great Measure forgot the language . . . of such Powerfull works of God's Spirit." The eyes of New England were therefore upon Northampton; "The country in General was probably never so filled with talk of any work of such nature." Not just in New England but also "in new york . . . the Jerseys . . . upon Long Island . . . the Highlands on Hudson's River," and even in London eyes were turning toward God's People in Northampton. The town now had to honor its high profession with godly practice, for the stakes had been raised: "It seems so to be ordered in Providence at Present that not only our own Credit and the Credit of the Late work of God amongst us but the Credit of all vital Religion and the Power of Godliness on the Land depends very much on the behaviour of the People in this Town." Northampton's high profession of heartfelt Christianity in 1735 and 1736 (and Edwards's own reputation as the revival's publicist and interpreter) is what continued to make the town such a focus of attention during the communion controversy of 1750.[45]

The "high profession" that Edwards had discussed in 1736 referred to those reports of religious experiences spread abroad, most notably by Edwards himself, first in a letter that Boston's Benjamin Colman summarized for his London correspondents, and then in the famous *Faithful Narrative*. In 1737, Edwards urged that the townspeople's profession become more formal and ex-

44. Jonathan Edwards, MS fast sermon on 2 Chron. 23:16, March 1737, 3r–4v, 13r; MS sermon on Matt. 5:14, July 1736, 4v. See also MS sermon fragment C, ca. 1727. By "religious efforts," I am referring to the instituted "means of grace," that is, prayer, preaching, and public worship.

45. Jonathan Edwards, MS sermon on Matt. 5:14, July 1736, 14v, 18r, 20r, and see also 15r.

plicit in a reaffirmation of their obligations under the Covenant of Grace. As the town's new church building was raised, he called for a "Joint Resolution" made by the civil magistrate and the ministers of the gospel, "the Leading men amongst a People and those that are Led by them," the rich and the poor, the old and the young. Like the high priest Jehoiada in Second Chronicles, Edwards called his people to bind themselves to God and to one another under God's covenant. He urged them to make their identity as God's People manifest in clear words and plain practices in their business and public affairs.[46]

At the height of the Awakening in March 1742, Edwards had again called the people of Northampton to commit themselves to be God's People. This time it was no mere public resolution; he asked every person in the congregation over fourteen years old to stand up, solemnly own the covenant, and vow to seek and serve God. Each congregant was to swear adherence to a sixteen-paragraph summary of proper Christian behavior, committing all to Christ and promising to treat neighbors in a spirit of meekness and charity. This was a solemn oath to God, Edwards reminded his people a year later; it was an "extraordinary explicit vow" that was greater than an "ordinary implicit" one in that it called upon God to confirm the truth of what was said. "Take heed," Edwards warned, "words are gone out of your mouths and you can not go back." He told backsliders in 1747 that "their own former voice" would witness against them on Judgment Day, "so they will be sentenced out of their own mouths." The words of the oath he had written for his parishioners to speak he now used to chastise them before an angry God.[47]

In 1745 and again in 1747, Edwards had explained that the 1742 covenant was

46. Jonathan Edwards, MS fast sermon on 2 Chron. 23:16, March 1737, 7v, 8v, 9v. Here, Edwards again notes that Northampton has been exceedingly exalted "as a most honourable People in the Esteem and Eye of the world" (17v), and "no Town this day on the Face of the Earth" was more obliged "Jointly and with one Consent to Resolve upon it that we will be the Lords People" (16r). On Edwards's letter to Benjamin Colman, see Goen, "Editor's Introduction," in Edwards, The Great Awakening, ed. Goen, in Miller et al., eds., Works of Jonathan Edwards, IV, 32–46.

47. Edwards included a copy of the 1742 covenant in his Dec. 12, 1743, letter to Thomas Prince, who published it in Christian History, I (Jan. 14, 21, 28, 1744), 367–381, in Edwards, The Great Awakening, ed. Goen, in Miller et al., eds., Works of Jonathan Edwards, IV, 550–554. The sermon Edwards preached for the occasion drew its doctrine from Josh. 24:15–27: "A visible people of God on some occasions are called plainly and publically to renew their covenant with God." Quotations from the 1743 sermon are from MS sermon on Eccles. 5:4–6, October 1743, 12v, 14v. Edwards told his congregation that they could not take back their words by saying that the covenant was forced upon them during "an Extraordinary Time" when their minds were not calm, for the oath is still binding; they could not excuse themselves just because many others were breaking their vows: "So in hell—firebrands [are]

more explicit but "not essentially different" from what parents dedicated their children to in baptism. It was a fuller expression of what people implicitly acknowledged by attending church on the Sabbath and what their actions signified and renewed at the Lord's Table. By 1749, Edwards was arguing that any "implicit" professions such as joining public prayers and keeping the Sabbath only take on meaning if they are rooted in "a declarative explicit covenanting" that all baptized true believers must make upon reaching adulthood. Eating and drinking at the Lord's Supper are only "speaking Signs" that symbolically reiterate a meaning that must already be fixed by the communicant's words.[48]

Not long after these words about what the Lord's Supper ought to mean were published in *An Humble Inquiry*, however, the Lord's Supper in Northampton had come to signify something quite different. Church members, embittered by the controversy, began refusing to join Edwards at the Lord's Table. This, too, Edwards wrote, was a speaking sign: "Besides the reproaches of my people by word of mouth, their public conduct towards me is such as casts a reproach upon me. The whole series of their conduct has this language, uttered too with a loud voice, that I am most insufferably criminal. This is particularly true of their openly refusing, once and again, to receive the sacrament of the Lord's Supper at my hands. It has this look, that I am a scandalous person: this is the language of it; it has this appearance to the world." Even as he claimed the authority to define the words and signs of religious community, the people's language, shouted in a loud voice to the world, drowned out the words he preached and published.[49]

Jonathan Ashley was the clerical voice chosen to answer Edwards's preaching from the Northampton pulpit, but by the time Ashley delivered his rebuttal in February 1751 Edwards was already preaching to the Indians in Stockbridge, having been dismissed by Northampton the previous June. The clergyman who agreed to answer Edwards in print was Solomon Williams, another grandson of the town's venerated former pastor Solomon Stoddard. Edwards responded to Williams's *True State of the Question* (1751) with *Misrepresentations Corrected, and Truth Vindicated* (1752). Both writers were perhaps less concerned with addressing the Northampton parishioners by this point than with the broader audience of the controversy that, as Edwards wrote in his 1752 response, had

bound in bundles" (40v). His warning to backsliders is in MS quarterly lecture on Josh. 24:21–22, August 1747, 5r.

48. Jonathan Edwards, MS sermon on Ps. 111:5, August 1745, 6r; MS quarterly lecture on Josh. 24:21–22, August 1747, 6r; Edwards, *Humble Inquiry*, 16, 76.

49. Edwards, "Narrative of Communion Controversy," in Edwards, *Ecclesiastical Writings*, ed. Hall, in Miller et al., eds., *Works of Jonathan Edwards*, XII, 544.

filled "a great Part of *New-England*, with Noise and Uproar, for about two Years and a half." Although Edwards had recognized from the start that a broader audience would be eager to hear and read about the controversy, he criticized Williams for trying to contribute to the debate from seventy miles away. Edwards contrasted his own intimate knowledge of Northampton's people and of the ways the argument had been played out locally with Williams's clumsy attempt to defend grandfather Stoddard and common church practices by misrepresenting the tenets of everyone involved. In an appendix to *Misrepresentations Corrected*, written as a letter to Northampton but also, of course, to the wider readership of the published debate, Edwards warned about the pernicious effects of Williams's book. Ostensibly a defense of Stoddardean tradition and, more broadly, of New Englanders' Christian status and their rights to have their children baptized, Williams's ill-conceived arguments, Edwards contended, would unwittingly give readers notions that Stoddard himself had "esteemed as of fatal Tendency to the Souls of Men." Northampton had asked Williams to write the book and paid for its publication. It would be natural that the townspeople who had refused to let Edwards's *Humble Inquiry* into their houses would welcome Williams's *True State of the Question*, and Edwards expected that his opponent's book would be "dispers'd in [their] Families, and will be valued, and much made use of by [them] as a Book of great Importance." The danger, Edwards wrote, was that by turning to Williams's text they were turning away from the true doctrines of the Bible.[50]

Solomon Williams argued that Edwards's call for a personal explicit profession as a requirement for admission had no scriptural basis and no precedent in ecclesiastical history. Edwards answered that actions, by themselves, were not properly a profession at all. "The Reason of Mankind teaches them the Need of joining *Words* and *Actions* together in publick Manifestations of the Mind, in Cases of Importance: *Speech* being the great and peculiar Talent, which God has given to Mankind, as the special Means and Instrument of the Manifestation of their Minds one to another." Over the course of Edwards's Northampton preaching, his use of the term "profession" had narrowed, its meaning refined from a vague or implicit acknowledgment of God's gospel offer to the explicit, personal oath of the individual Christian. What Edwards expected people to profess (and not just how they professed) had undergone a similar redefinition. What did it mean to visibly "own" the covenant? Edwards's early position resembled his cousin Solomon's. The candidate must signify his belief that the doctrines of the gospel are true, submit himself to the terms of

50. Edwards, *Misrepresentations Corrected*, 5–6, 167–168.

Christ's covenant, and endeavor to obey all the moral rules of the gospel. No one with this belief and resolve can know for sure that he is not regenerated, and the church must give him the benefit of the doubt.[51]

If Williams and Northampton's parishioners had been able to look through Edwards's private notebooks, they could have detected his "new scruples" about the Stoddardean Lord's Supper and full membership in the visible church appearing as early as 1728. His first corollary to a 1736 notebook entry on the Covenant of Grace was that "the revelation and offer of the gospel is not properly called a covenant till it is consented to," and, as in *An Humble Inquiry* thirteen years later, he compared this consent to a woman's acceptance of an offer of marriage. But his parishioners had not seen his notebooks; they had only heard him preach. And although it is true that some passages in the sermons he preached at Northampton before the controversy broke in 1749 seemed to tighten the requirements for owning the covenant, others had continued to encourage a broader Stoddardean interpretation that his congregation, and their champion in the press Solomon Williams, would have found unobjectionable.[52]

In his 1737 fast sermon on 2 Chron. 23:16, for example, Edwards had told his congregation what was required of them as God's People. It is not just "an acknowledgement of the mouth," a professing of Christ in name only, for owning the covenant while having "an inward prevailing opposition" to God's rule is no real consent to it at all. Owning the covenant is a consent of the understanding, "because they are Convinced of it and see the Reason of it"; it is the consent of the will, because "they dont [just] see that it is so but they are willing it should be so . . . they choose to be the Lords"; it is, in sum, the consent of "the Heart" to God's absolute sovereignty over body and soul. Clearly, only converts could so renounce the world and embrace Christ as a spouse. But this is the same sermon where Edwards also spoke more broadly of the people's consent to the covenant as a public resolution, of at least visibly "taking hold" of the covenant, of "each one contribut[ing] what in him lies towards it that

51. Williams, *True State of the Question,* 20, 60; Edwards, *Misrepresentations Corrected,* 80, 148 (quotation). See also Jonathan Edwards, *The "Miscellanies,"* ed. Thomas A. Schafer, in Miller et al., eds., *Works of Jonathan Edwards,* XIII, no. 338, 413. For passages in Williams's *True State of the Question* related to owning the covenant, see iv, 5, 8, 9, 11, 24, 28, 53, 81, 83, 111, 112, 122, 125, 130, 133, 134.

52. See Edwards, *"Miscellanies,"* ed. Schafer, in Miller et al., eds., *Works of Jonathan Edwards,* XIII, nos. 389, 393, 394; and no. 617 (still unpublished, Jonathan Edwards Papers, Beinecke Library). I am indebted to Kenneth P. Minkema for this reference. Thomas A. Schafer, as cited by Patricia J. Tracy in *Jonathan Edwards, Pastor,* 258, n. 1, points to an important discussion in "Miscellanies" no. 689, written in early 1736.

we may be the Lords People." Could not the unconverted, therefore, in some sense own the covenant as well?[53]

For loyal Stoddardean Solomon Williams, the answer was yes. The unregenerate could own the covenant and be counted among God's People because to do so meant to consent to the terms of Christ's offer. They need not profess saving faith, since the term "belief" in the New Testament can signify "no more than the Assent of the Understanding" or "a Conviction of the Judgment and Conscience, that Jesus was the Messiah, or that the Gospel was true." The unconverted "do enter into Covenant with God, and with all the Earnestness and Sincerity of Soul they possibly can, do engage to keep Covenant." They submit to the rules and ordinances of Christ and vow to obey him to the utmost of their natural and legal—but not gracious—powers.[54]

In *An Humble Inquiry* and in his 1750 pulpit defense of his new position, Edwards made a clean break from both Stoddardeanism and from the ambiguities of his own earlier preaching. "I cant understand that there is any such notion of owning the Covenant any where in the Christian world but in this Corner of it here in New England," he announced. He then looked behind Stoddard to earlier New England customs. "But now the Great part of the Country has forgotten the meaning of their forefathers and have gradually brought in a notion of owning the Covenant of Grace without pretending to profess a compliance." Owning the covenant means not only acknowledging its terms but complying with them, he argued. Christ offers salvation for saving faith; the unconverted who offer only the promise of outward obedience are in no sense parties to the covenant.[55]

But Solomon Williams answered that this notion of covenanting confuses entering a covenant with fulfilling one and destroys the whole concept of visible sainthood. Williams, Edwards, and even Connecticut Separatist Ebenezer Frothingham agreed that only visible saints should be allowed to own the covenant and sit at the Lord's Table—but the three completely disagreed about what the term "visible sainthood" meant. Their definitions reveal the very dif-

53. Edwards, MS fast sermon on 2 Chron. 23:16, 1737, 4v–6v, 22r.

54. Williams, *True State of the Question*, iv, 8–9, 10, 53, 134. According to Bruce Purinton Stark, "Lebanon, Connecticut: A Study of Society and Politics in the Eighteenth Century" (Ph.D. diss., University of Connecticut, 1970), Williams's First Church technically maintained the Half-Way Covenant throughout his pastorate. "Substantial evidence exists, however, that Williams was extremely lenient in his admission policy, and the church must be characterized as Stoddardean. Williams baptized adults without requiring evidence of faith, and was willing to receive all who offered themselves to communion, provided they were of sound knowledge in religion and free from scandal" (107).

55. Edwards, MS sermon on Ezek. 44:9, delivered 1750, 17r, 17v, 18r.

ferent epistemologies that helped shape visions of the church in eighteenth-century New England.

For Williams, visible saints are Christians according to all that is visible: profession of the gospel truth and good behavior. Arguing from Stoddard's skepticism about the ability of men to distinguish the truly gracious from the morally sincere, Williams described visible sainthood as a larger category that included real saints. Not all who are visible saints on earth will turn out to be real saints on Judgment Day, but until then the church has no business trying to search hearts and separate sheep from goats. At the other extreme, Frothingham, the New Light Separatist, maintained that a true Christian could certainly discern the presence of sanctifying grace in someone else. The Holy Spirit makes manifest, or visible, the godliness of saints to each other: "the Beams or Rays of Divine Light shining into the Soul" enlighten the understanding and guide a Christian's judgment of his neighbor. Edwards tried to take the middle ground between Stoddardean uncertainty and Separatist certainty. For him, visibility was neither a category distinct from the real nor a supernatural manifestation of the real, but a sign that referred to the real the way a properly used word refers to the essence of the thing signified.[56]

He contended that there must be a stronger relation between the visible and the real—between what man sees and what God sees—than Stoddardeanism recognized. For both Edwards and the Separatists, the reality at the heart of public worship was the "peculiar love" Christians had for one another. This affection "must have some Apprehension of the Understanding, some Judgment of the Mind, for it's Foundation." Perhaps Williams's lukewarm "benefit of the doubt" could be extended to all moral people who called themselves Christians, but for Edwards the "mind must first Judge some Amiableness in the Object" before affections are bestowed. Edwards wanted something to tip the scales of uncertainty in a positive direction, some sign that gave the church probable grounds for judging a candidate a real saint before calling him a visible saint.[57]

Frothingham represented a category of readers outside Northampton that Edwards had worried about even as he composed An Humble Inquiry in 1749. Edwards knew that his discussion of visible sainthood, so grounded in a nuanced theory about the interpretation of signs, might itself be misinterpreted

56. Ebenezer Frothingham, *Discourse*, 47; see also 37.

57. Edwards, *Humble Inquiry*, 71, 73; Edwards, *Misrepresentations Corrected*, 10. Edwards spoke of the "very *distinguishing* Kind of Affection, that every true Christian *experiences* toward those whom he looks upon as truly *gracious* Persons." Frothingham too builds his church upon a foundation of Christian love. After his conversion, he had been astonished to find that it "far surpass'd the Love of Women" (Frothingham, *Discourse*, 130).

by Separatists as support for their own enthusiastic doctrines. Frothingham recommended Edwards's *Humble Inquiry* as an improvement over Stoddardeanism but complained that Edwards "writes in a misterious Manner, backwards and forwards, about this Visibility." Whereas Stoddard extended charity to all because he could obtain no reliable knowledge about their souls, and Edwards limited visible sainthood because he could gain probable knowledge of grace in others, Frothingham insisted that the church was a communion of real saints who were certain of each other's godliness. If I ask for a sheep, Frothingham wrote, and someone brings me either a sheep or a goat, "is the Sheep visible, or is it not?" The answer was either yes or no, not a degree of probability. "Therefore to have a Thing visible that is requested, amounts to certain Knowledge of the Thing thus presented." What was presented had to be more than "a bare Profession of Godliness" and good behavior, however. Candidates for admission in a Separatist church had to describe their experiences of God's grace upon their hearts and tell the story of their conversion to Christ.[58]

After the Awakening, Edwards had had his fill of people publicly describing their trembling, trances, and visions, and he took great pains to distance himself from Separatist enthusiasm, denouncing those "slanderous" reports that said he "had fallen in with those wild People." The Stoddardean church did not do enough institutionally to recognize conversions, but the Separatist church placed too much emphasis on publicizing personal experience, and it fostered spiritual pride. He argued that the pastor should be the one to decide when a particular conversion narrative might edify the whole congregation. Regular professions should not describe the details of conversion. The candidate's

---

58. Frothingham, *Discourse*, 38, 39. In other passages, he tries to step back from the stark Antinomianism of these statements in three ways. First, he grants that even Separates acknowledge "three sorts of Persons": Christians (certainly known by their spiritual fruits), sinners (as plainly known by their fruits), and "others [who] again have had Convictions, and some Light and Comfort, but we cannot tell whether it be true and genuine, and dare not say whether they be or be no Christians; but must leave it 'till Divine Light and Fruits make manifest what they be, whether Saints or Sinners." Only "to the omniscient God there is but two Sorts of Persons of the human Race . . . which are Saints and Sinners" (131). Second, he declares that the saint's certain discerning or knowledge "is not an immediate Discovery . . . but mediate in an ordinary Way, judging and knowing from the Fruits of special sanctifying Grace, made visible and manifest to the spiritual Understanding, by the Improvement and Practice of the Saints" (47). Third, he argues that, although saints are made certainly visible "to the spiritual Eye of true Christians, if not to the Observations of enlightened Sinners" (44), a saint may be deceived by his "old Eye" of nature (101). That begs the whole question of how the saint knows which eye he is using at a given moment and how he can be certain.

words and deeds, in fact, need not even signify that he was assured of his own conversion. But they did need to signify that he had experienced the essence of Christian piety: believing with his heart, loving God with all his soul, and loving his neighbor as himself. The simple language of the kind of profession Edwards would accept did not describe how the person came to be born again; it referred to the experience of godliness as an unspoken context and necessary precondition for the candidate's appearance before the church. Edwards did not want the focus to be upon the candidate's subjective sensations of fear or joy but upon *"the Supreme holy Beauty, and Comliness of divine Things, as they are in themselves, or in their own Nature"*—a beauty that human signs can only gesture toward.[59]

When Williams read Edwards's discussion of an individual's examination of his own heart prior to profession, he thought that he found the fatal flaw to the whole scheme. If coming to the Lord's Supper without saving grace is a damning sin (as Edwards claimed), how could anything short of certainty about conversion induce a person to come? A man believes the gospel and sincerely desires to do his duty before Christ. But he hesitates. What if this belief and sincerity, which he knows he has, is "no more than moral Sincerity; the Effect of common Grace and Illumination"? Common and saving grace are often hard to distinguish, and all but those wild Separatists acknowledge that assurance is hard to come by. On the other hand, any sane person with a healthy conscience must know whether he is being morally sincere or not. Such an awareness is essential to moral agency and distinguishes the man from his sheep and goats. Therefore, the awakened person who still doubts whether he has saving grace should be allowed to make "such a Profession as he finds he can truly make." Solomon Williams's church, like his half-brother Elisha's politics, rested on the rock of the awakened conscience.[60]

But in the next step, as this morally sincere candidate offers himself to the church, Williams went beyond Stoddard. Williams argued that the church, listening to the candidate's profession of belief and sincerity, must take his words in their highest sense, as a profession of saving grace. Whether the candidate thinks he is converted or not is beside the point, since he may be mistaken either way. The church, "without any metaphysical Speculations, or abstruse Reasonings, upon the Nature of *Visibilities* and *Realities,*" should treat the professor as if he were converted.[61]

59. Edwards, *Farewel-Sermon,* i–ii (see also the preface to the *Humble Inquiry);* Jonathan Edwards, *True Grace, Distinguished from the Experience of Devils* (New York, 1753), 33.

60. Williams, *True State of the Question,* 111.

61. Ibid., 11–14.

Edwards found this more disturbing than anything in the bland rebuttal preached from his former pulpit by Jonathan Ashley of Deerfield in 1751. Ashley welcomed the merely moral to the Lord's Table, but he at least did not then pretend that they were regenerate. After Williams set forth his position as an argument from common sense, Edwards dismantled it with an argument based on three propositions about signification, summed up in a footnote citing Paul in 1 Cor. 14:7 and then Locke's *Essay:* "He that uses Words of any Language without DISTINCT Ideas in his Mind . . . only make a Noise without any Sense or Signification." When a man says he has a king in his room, we do not know if he means George II or a chess piece. If he says he has metal in his pocket, we are not obliged by charity to assume it is gold and not brass. If a professor uses words allowed to signify either moral sincerity or real piety, he makes "no Profession at all of *Gospel Holiness.*" [62]

Like Locke, Edwards knew that language becomes the "common Tye of Society" if the signs a person uses are held in common. Locke distinguished between "ordinary" discourse, in which meanings established by "common" use and "tacit" consent usually served well enough, and "philosophical" discourse, which was more in need of an "Under-Labourer" in "The Commonwealth of Learning" who could point out abuses and demand more precision in the use

---

62. Jonathan Ashley, *An Humble Attempt to Give a Clear Account from Scripture, How the Jewish and Christian Churches Were Constituted . . .* (Boston, 1753), first preached in Northampton, Feb. 10, 1751. The quotation is from Edwards, *Misrepresentations Corrected,* 41–42. The biblical quotation from 1 Cor. 14:7 is as follows: "And even things without life giving sound, whether pipe or harp, except they give a distinction in the sounds, how shall it be known what is piped or harped?" The quotation from Locke is in Edwards's copy of John Locke, *An Essay concerning Human Understanding: In Four Books,* 2 vols., 7th ed. (London, 1716), II, 103. Stephen H. Daniel, in *The Philosophy of Jonathan Edwards: A Study in Divine Semiotics* (Bloomington, Ind., 1994), argues that Edwards draws upon two models of communication: classical-modernist hermeneutics, which always looks for intended meaning behind the sign (in an idea held in the mind of a speaking subject, for example); and Stoic-Renaissance semiotics, where all the world is a divine text, and signs refer only to other signs. According to Daniel, Edwards uses the classical-modernist paradigm to describe the mentality of humankind after the Fall but Stoic-Renaissance semiotics to describe how the elect apprehend the signifying logic informing God's two books (nature and Scripture). The Lord's Supper, according to Edwards, is a sign instituted by Christ that participates in a system of types and images something like the divine semiotics Daniel describes. But saints do not evaluate the profession a candidate brings before them with a special spirit of discerning or privileged understanding of divine semiotics. They do so through the same exercise of rational judgment available to all fallen human beings: a probabilistic determination about whether or not the signs a candidate presents (his profession and behavior) refer to holiness. In Daniel's terms, this operation is performed within the classical-modernist (Lockean) paradigm.

of words. Edwards, too, in his treatises on the will, true virtue, and original sin, tried to reform the vocabulary of the Commonwealth of Learning, aiming especially at points where ordinary and philosophical usage became confused. But before he left Northampton for the Stockbridge settlement where he would write those treatises, he was more immediately concerned with reforming a different community of discourse. He tried to correct the damage that common usage and tacit consent had done to terms like "professing" Christianity, "owing" the covenant, and "visible" sainthood. For Edwards, controlling the terms of public religious discourse was part of following Paul's injunction: "Let all things be done decently and in order" in "all churches of the saints."[63]

THE NEW ENGLISH ISRAEL

Scholars have long appreciated the central place Edwards and his followers gave to the individual's relationship to God in the Covenant of Grace. The public, or national, covenant, however, conspicuously absent from Edwards's published writings, was thought to have been repudiated or replaced by new forms of Christian union achieved through revivalism or concerts of prayer. At any rate, New Divinity ministers, others said, were too caught up with metaphysics and the millennium to be distracted by the mundane social and political concerns that Puritan covenant sermons had so often addressed. Since the 1980s, studies of Edwards's and the New Divinity ministers' manuscript sermons have reassessed the importance of the public covenant in Edwardsean preaching. One contends that the Puritan national covenant was for Edwards an inherited formula and a "taken-for-granted reality" and that neither he nor any other eighteenth-century established minister denied "New England's attendant identity as a special people with a messianic destiny." A second agrees that Edwards preached about the public covenant but argues that he did so as a "pessimistic" critic within the Deuteronomic tradition, not as an endorser of New England's special errand or America's manifest destiny. A third interpretation suggests that Edwards's references to New England's covenant were "somewhat untypical" of his preaching and argues that after 1750 Edwards, Bellamy, and Samuel Hopkins replaced covenantal terminology with the language of moral law and spoke of a God who did not give special treatment to an elect nation but ruled through impartial, "universal moral standards." All

---

63. The phrases from John Locke are from *An Essay concerning Human Understanding* (1689), ed. Peter H. Nidditch (Oxford, 1975), 10, 402, 476, 501; the phrases from Paul are from 1 Cor. 14:33, 40.

three of these studies point toward the need to put Edwards's covenantal preaching in the context of both the Stoddardean church he inherited and the post-Awakening evangelical union he championed. Changes in emphasis and relative importance are revealed only when the national covenant is seen within a larger understanding of Edwards's language of corporate identity—a language that changed as Edwards's focus shifted from Northampton and New England to the revival movement within international Protestantism.[64]

Covenant language was neither taken for granted nor atypical; it was an integral part of Edwards's pulpit discourse of corporate identity before 1750. Certainly, Edwards's early preaching recognized New England's high spiritual privileges, if not with grandiose claims for New England national election. But to castigate Northampton for its spiritual and moral declension after the 1735 revival and the 1740 Awakening, Edwards pointed to the outpourings of the Spirit that they had all so recently witnessed rather than to an "inheritance" from the New England founders or the town's pious forefathers. During the communion controversy, even as Edwards discussed Israel's covenanting in Deuteronomy, he emphasized the *experience* of the people's religious revival rather than the legal *fact* of their covenantal status.[65]

Some historians have contrasted the covenant preaching of Puritan fast-day Jeremiahs with the New Light calls for revival and evangelical union. Covenantal jeremiads, one wrote, had become conservative, backward-looking instru-

64. Perry Miller incorrectly thought that Edwards had outgrown covenant theology altogether, but see Conrad Cherry, *The Theology of Jonathan Edwards: A Reappraisal* (Garden City, N.Y., 1966); and Carl W. Bogue, *Jonathan Edwards and the Covenant of Grace* (Cherry Hill, N.J., 1975). Heimert, *Religion and the American Mind,* 126, argues that the covenant had been replaced. The older view of an apolitical New Divinity can be found in Edmund S. Morgan, "The American Revolution Considered as an Intellectual Movement," in Arthur M. Schlesinger, Jr., and Morton White, eds., *Paths of American Thought* (Boston, 1963), 11–33. Harry S. Stout's "The Puritans and Edwards," in Nathan O. Hatch and Stout, eds., *Jonathan Edwards and the American Experience* (New York, 1988), 142–159, discusses the covenant as a "taken-for-granted reality" and New England's "messianic destiny" (157). Mark Valeri's "The New Divinity and the American Revolution," *WMQ,* 3d Ser., XLVI (1989), 741–769, calls Edwards's references to the covenant "somewhat untypical" (751n) and describes the move to moral law (745); see also Valeri, *Law and Providence in Joseph Bellamy's New England: The Origins of the New Divinity in Revolutionary America* (New York, 1994). Gerald R. McDermott's *One Holy and Happy Society: The Public Theology of Jonathan Edwards* (University Park, Pa., 1992), 17, describes Edwards as a pessimistic Deuteronomic critic.

65. Contrast, for example, William Williams, *The Duty and Interest of a People, among Whom Religion Has Been Planted, to Continue Stedfast and Sincere in the Profession and Practice of It, from Generation to Generation* (Boston, 1736), which was published with Edwards's account of the 1735 Northampton revival.

ments of social control, trying to impose order mechanically through institutional discipline and calls for obedience. New Lights called instead for an "affectionate union" of Christian brethren in Christ, looking ahead to the millennial age. In 1747, Edwards published *An Humble Attempt to Promote Explicit Agreement and Visible Union of God's People* and compared the two forms of public worship. A fast day proclaimed by the civil government of a Christian society and a concert of prayer promoted by private Christians differed only in "circumstances," he argued. The union of Christians in either case depended upon joining for prayer at a fixed time rather than gathering in a single place. Although the precedent Edwards cites for the concert of prayer had been proposed for the national deliverance of Great Britain in 1712, the concert he promoted was to be "an *union* among Christians of distant places," from many different cities, countries, and nations. Although proposed by pro-revival ministers in Scotland and encouraged by private praying societies that had sprung up during the Awakening, Edwards offered the plan as an attempt to heal the divisions the Awakening had spawned. Nevertheless, the concert, which people joined voluntarily—much more than New England's public covenant, which fell to them because of where they lived—matched the transatlantic vision and personal appeal of midcentury Protestant revivalism.[66]

Edwards in the 1740s also reordered the relationship between the national covenant and the Covenant of Grace. Seventeenth-century Congregationalists spoke of the Covenant of Grace for individual saints, church covenants for those who professed to be saints (and, in some sense, for their children), and the national covenant for a whole people who acknowledged Christianity as the established religion. Although all these covenants, technically, were branches of a single Covenant of Grace, rhetorically preachers stressed the different aspects of God's covenanting when applied to individuals, churches, and public societies. Northampton's Solomon Stoddard had, in effect, blurred these distinctions, speaking instead of the internal (individual) and external (corporate) aspects or articles of the Covenant of Grace and placing public worship and especially the Lord's Supper as the central ritual of God's covenant in all

66. Edwards, *Humble Attempt,* in Edwards, *Apocalyptic Writings,* ed. Stein, in Miller et al., eds., *Works of Jonathan Edwards,* V, 372–373, 428 (differing in circumstances), 430, and also 317, 360–361, 371 (a union in time of Christians from many places), 434 (to heal divisions). Heimert, in *Religion and the American Mind,* 95, 97, 100, 120, 157, 402, 425, 470, contrasts the covenantal jeremiad to the concert of prayer. He claims that "the crucial premises of Calvinist rhetoric [of union] were disclosed in Edwards' argument for a concert of prayer" (115). See also Perry Miller, "From the Covenant to the Revival," in Miller, *Nature's Nation* (Cambridge, Mass., 1967), 90–120.

its manifestations. Stoddard's model was the Old Testament "Jewish church," rather than the early Christian congregations that were set up before Christianity had been instituted as a national religion. Edwards separated what Stoddardean practice had joined: the local community of the faithful from the nation that called itself Christian.[67]

When Edwards first defended his position on church membership before his congregation in 1750, he closed his argument by quickly dismissing any objections arising from a comparison to Israel's covenanting in the Old Testament. But the senses in which the Jews—and, like them, New Englanders—were "God's People" would loom larger in subsequent debates. Like Stoddard, Solomon Williams spoke of people's keeping the external, public covenant by their natural powers and keeping the internal covenant by saving grace. Edwards argued that outward covenanting must express an inward covenanting or it signifies nothing. Yet, did not Edwards himself preach that God makes a public covenant with a professing people, a covenant that does not require true piety but only religion and virtue in outward exercise and things visible? True, Edwards had explained that this public or national covenant was one that God made with whole societies and not with particular persons; but then, are not particular persons, as members of society and in respect to things external and temporal, in covenant, just as the Jews were? The Jews, Williams wrote, gracious and moral alike, covenanted with their God and "were alike called *the People of God, A chosen Generation, a royal Priesthood, an holy Nation, a peculiar People.*"[68]

67. See, for example, Solomon Stoddard, *An Appeal to the Learned* . . . (Boston, 1709), 55, 68–69, 82. Like Stoddard, Congregationalists recognized that their individual, church, and national covenants were in fact merely the different aspects of the single Covenant of Grace. But their practice as well as their rhetoric often emphasized the differences between inhabitants in New England, members of particular churches, and saints qualified to attend the Lord's Supper. See Samuel Willard, *Covenant-Keeping the Way to Blessedness* . . . (Boston, 1682), esp. 26–28, 68–74, 96–101. It is a mistake to assume that the individual and corporate aspects of covenanting created radically distinct covenants with incommensurate aims and logics, but one may err at the other extreme by arguing that the "boundaries between self and society" were always blurred by the "bipolar thrust" of a single unified doctrine (Theodore Dwight Bozeman, "Federal Theology and the 'National Covenant': An Elizabethan Presbyterian Case Study," *Church History*, LXI [1992], 394–407 [quotations on 403]).

68. Williams, *True State of the Question*, 9; on 129, Williams quotes a passage from Stoddard's *Appeal to the Learned*, 84, and then amplifies it with his own remarks, 129–130. Technically, Williams acknowledged only a single Covenant of Grace that was exhibited in two ways: internally to those who are converted and externally to those who profess and enjoy church ordinances (23). Edwards dismissed the comparison to Israel in MS sermon on

Edwards argued "that such Appellations as God's *People,* God's *Israel,* and some other like Phrases, are used and applied in Scripture with considerable *Diversity* of Intention." There were appendages to Abraham's Covenant of Grace, promises to his family and bloodline that ceased with the gospel dispensation. Sometimes "God's People" referred to all Jews in this carnal aspect of the covenant, which did not literally apply to Christians. But Williams dismissed that as more blather about names and words. Christians are in covenant just as the Jews were, he contended. He transcribed a long quotation from Thomas Blake's 1653 treatise on federal theology. All Christian Gentiles are grafted onto the root of Abraham, so God's promise extends to them and their seed—meaning that all the children of Christian parents are born into a state of "Federal Holiness" and are (at least externally) in the covenant with their parents.[69]

Edwards at first seemed to concede the narrow doctrinal point to Williams and his "great author" Blake, though he in no way surrendered the larger issue. He turned to "the Ambiguity of the Phrase, *Being in Covenant*" and noted that it "signifies two distinct Things: either (1.) *Being under the Obligations* [and] *Bonds of the Covenant;* or (2.) *A being conformed to the Covenant, and complying with the Terms of it.*" Many ungodly Jews and New Englanders can be said to be some of God's Covenant People in the first, weaker sense of that expression, he admitted. But—and here Edwards reduced Williams's federal theology to an empty husk—being people under obligations of the covenant is hardly a special privilege, for "So are all Mankind" in covenant in this sense. Unconverted New Englanders are "God's Covenant People" in no greater sense than are *"Mahometans,* or *Heathens."*[70]

Thus, Williams's "external covenant" seemed to be extended as the moral law of all mankind, and the title "God's People" became an empty phrase on

---

Ezek. 44:9, delivered 1750, 20r. Hypocrites though many of the Jews were, he argued, they still promised to abide by the covenant with all their heart and soul. For Edwards's argument that outward covenanting must express an inward covenanting, see Edwards, *Misrepresentations Corrected,* 89. On the public covenant made with whole societies, see Edwards, MS sermon on Lev. 26:3–13, Feb. 28, 1745; and MS sermon on Josh. 7:12, "Fast on the Occasion of the War with France," June 28, 1744, and March 1755. Moses Mather argued in 1772, referring to Edwards's published writings, that "when the late President *Edwards* wrote upon this controversy, he kept this general [external] dispensation of the covenant of grace, out of both his own, and his reader's view; and predicated his arguments only upon the covenant of grace, taken in its most limited tenor." See Moses Mather, *A Brief View of the Manner in Which the Controversy about Terms of Communion in the Visible Church Has Been Conducted, in the Present Day* (New Haven, Conn., 1772), 6.

69. Edwards, *Humble Inquiry,* 84; Williams, *True State of the Question,* 89.

70. Edwards, *Misrepresentations Corrected,* 137, 151, 152.

the lips of the ungodly. Williams was horrified. Edwards's scheme denied morally sincere New Englanders under "the good Impressions of Convictions and Awakenings" their place alongside the truly godly; it classed them with the heathens and would perplex their tender consciences. But that was precisely Edwards's point. Awakened sinners "are very ready to flatter themselves that they are willing to accept of Christ," Edwards asserted, but they need to be driven to their knees. They need to see that they have not "the least Spark of Love to God." Devils are even more convinced of the truth of the gospel; sinners roasting in hell have their consciences far more awakened than they ever had in this world. Edwards warned that Williams's book might lead people to suppose that the Christless could be friends to Christ, when actually they were enemies who bore greater guilt than the heathens who had neither Bibles nor preachers.[71]

Although the unregenerate living in a Christian nation could call themselves "God's People" in a very weak sense, Edwards wanted to strip them of their titles. "Now why is it looked upon so dreadful, to have great Numbers going without the *Name* and honourable *Badge* of Christianity[?]" Too many are "contented with the *Sign,* exclusive of the *Thing* signified!" They overvalue common grace and moral sincerity. "This, I can't but think, naturally tends to sooth and flatter the Pride of vain Man."[72]

Here lies the crux of Edwards's post-Awakening rhetorical strategy, which his New Divinity followers would accentuate and develop. Names and "Appellations" that flattered graceless men, even if there was some scriptural precedent for their use, were to be applied with great care or avoided. The verbal badges of Christianity must conform to doctrine and cut through the rhetorical fog obscuring the chasm between nature and grace. Edwards tried to sift through the ambiguities of being "in" or "under" the covenant; later, Edward-

---

71. Williams, *True State of the Question,* 133; Edwards, *Misrepresentations Corrected,* 168–171 (quotation on 168–169). See also Edwards, *True Grace Distinguished from the Experience of Devils;* Edwards, *The Nature of True Virtue,* chap. 5, along with editor Paul Ramsey's discussion of the development of Edwards's concept of natural conscience in "Appendix II: Jonathan Edwards on Moral Sense, and the Sentimentalists," both in Edwards, *Ethical Writings,* ed. Ramsey, in Miller et al., eds., *Works of Jonathan Edwards,* VIII (New Haven, Conn., 1989), 589–599, 689–705. Like the Pharisees of Christ's day, nominal Christians were at once closest to the kingdom of God and farthest from it. They enjoy the greatest of God's blessings, yet, by so misimproving their privileges, they become more vile than heathens. Instead of taking pride in being members of God's privileged people, they should be confronting their own sin in fear and trembling. Nathaniel Appleton discusses this close-and-yet-far relationship in *Some Unregenerate Persons Not So Far from the Kingdom of God as Others . . .* (Boston, 1763). Appleton, however, unlike Edwards, argues that someone with a good understanding of doctrine *is* closer to the kingdom.

72. Edwards, *Humble Inquiry,* 128–129.

seans like Nathanael Emmons simply defined a "covenant" as a mutual contract requiring the personal consent of all parties and declared all other uses of the term, even in Scripture, to be figurative. "If faith is the condition of the covenant of grace," Emmons wrote as he carried the argument into the 1790s, "there can be no medium between being completely in and completely out of it."[73]

It would seem that historians' arguments about the importance of the national covenant for Edwards might be more suited to Edwards before the communion controversy. Other interpretations stressing God's impartial moral government of nations or emphasizing Edwards's focus on the "affectionate union" of Christians within the international visible church might be more appropriate for the later Edwards. But there are problems with this conclusion. Edwards's shift toward moral law terminology can be seen in his private notebooks, implied in some of his sketchy outlines to sermons preached to the Stockbridge Indians, and inferred, perhaps, from his endorsement of Bellamy's *True Religion Delineated* in 1750. In the 1750s, however, Edwards again preached several sermons written in the 1740s or earlier. In 1755, he explained that "God in a national Covenant promises prosperity to External duties." In 1754 and again in 1757, he described the great difference between these externally covenanted "People of God" and others: though under the same moral law, God's People receive more special favors and mercies. How could he give such titles to those he so strenuously argued did not deserve them—to those inhabitants of a nation who did not *experience* union through *religious* affections? How could he now hand out the badges of Christianity?[74]

73. Nathanael Emmons, *A Dissertation on the Scriptural Qualifications for Admission and Access to the Christian Sacraments: Comprising Some Strictures on Dr. Hemmenway's Discourse concerning the Church* (Worcester, Mass., 1793), 45. See also Emmons, *A Candid Reply to the Reverend Dr. Hemmenway's Remarks . . .* (Worcester, Mass., 1795). Emmons studied under John Smalley, who in turn had been Joseph Bellamy's student. I am referring to the preachers' explicit emphasis upon the differences between nature and grace, the godly and the ungodly, not to the bifurcated psychological response described by Stephen R. Yarbrough and John C. Adams, *Delightful Conviction: Jonathan Edwards and the Rhetoric of Conversion* (Westport, Conn., 1993). For commentary upon the latter, see Christopher Grasso, "Images and Shadows of Jonathan Edwards," *American Literary History*, VIII (1996), 683–698. The best study of Edwards's sermon rhetoric is Wilson H. Kimnach, "General Introduction to the Sermons: Jonathan Edwards' Art of Prophesying," in Edwards, *Sermons and Discourses, 1720–1723*, ed. Kimnach, in Miller et al., eds., *Works of Jonathan Edwards*, X (New Haven, Conn., 1992), 1–258.

74. On moral law terminology, see Edwards, "Miscellanies" no. 1338, probably written after 1755 (see Ramsey, "Appendix II," in Edwards, *Ethical Writings*, ed. Ramsey, in Miller

One answer lies in the difference between doctrine and rhetorical strategy. After careful study of the Scriptures, Edwards had determined what God's will was with regard to admitting people to full communion in the church. He sacrificed his pulpit to this doctrine. He never completely abandoned the idea of a national covenant, although he argued that it could be neither sealed by church ordinances nor inflated with pretensions of unique national election. He had strongly objected to the diverse use of signs that had become a local habit and to the common custom that gave distinguishing names and titles to the whole body public. But correcting those who abused the idea of a national covenant or obscured the distinguishing marks of godliness became less important when faced, not by hypocrites sitting at the Lord's Table, but by French and Indian minions of Antichrist who threatened to wipe Protestant churches off the continent. The rhetorical context had changed, not his doctrinal commitments.

It is not that Edwards, having moved to the Stockbridge frontier, had decided that a little flattering exhortation might help rouse the militia. Just the opposite: he blamed General Edward Braddock's defeat in 1755 upon those who had trusted their own power rather than committing all to God's hands. Still, he called the soldiers who marched off to war "God's People," and did so because they fought *for* Christ's church (though many of them might not have been fully *in* Christ's church) against its openly professed enemies. They were God's covenant people in this weaker sense because they lived in a land of family Bibles and learned preachers who *offered* the covenant, rather than in a nation of priestly inquisitors with Latin Bibles under lock and key.[75]

If, during the communion controversy, it had been Edwards's burden to clarify the ambiguities of New England's covenant discourse for the sake of the church, during the Seven Years' War he would exploit those ambiguities once again as he exhorted the defenders of Protestant civilization in the New World. Just as the sacramental controversy had drawn attention to the language that distinguished (or failed to distinguish) between the church and society at large,

---

et al., eds., *Works of Jonathan Edwards*, VIII, 692); Edwards, MS sermon on Luke 16:19, June 1753. The quotation is from Edwards, MS sermon on Josh. 7:12, "Fast on Occasion of the War with France," June 28, 1744, preached again March 1755. Other references to externally covenanted peoples in the 1750s are Edwards, MS sermon on Exod. 33:19, "Thanksgiving for Victory over the Rebels," August 1746, preached again November 1754; MS sermon on 1 Kings 8:44–45, "Fast for Success in Cape Breton Expedition," Apr. 4, 1745, preached again July 1755; MS thanksgiving sermon on Jer. 51:5, Dec. 5, 1745, preached again November 1757.

75. Cf. William Hobby, *The Happiness of a People, Having God for Their Ally . . . on Occasion of an Expedition Design'd against Canada . . .* (Boston, 1758).

the war weakened that rhetorical boundary line. Edwards, however, did not live to see Quebec fall; the effort to regulate the church's covenant discourse after the war would be carried on by his student and friend in Connecticut, Joseph Bellamy.

THE CONTINUING DIALOGUE

Some preachers during and immediately after the Seven Years' War, like Solomon Williams, recast covenant rhetoric to fit new situations, some of them also voicing, at least for the moment, what Nathan O. Hatch has called "civil millennialism." With the fall of New France arose expansive visions of a new era in which God would spread Anglo-American Christian civilization across the continent. Were all British Americans now "God's People"? In the heady 1760s, Joseph Bellamy returned New England's attention to the local and ecclesiastical dimensions of the question and made another attempt to regulate public religious discourse. He drew from Edwards's experiences in Northampton but also from other recent debates. Although the renewed argument about church membership added few new insights about profession, visibility, or covenants, the pamphlets produced did show a significant shift in rhetorical strategy. The lengthy, densely written, point-by-point polemics were supplemented by dialogues. The dialogue was especially suited to the audiences of "lower capacities" that Bellamy was trying to reach. Edwards's parishioners had refused to read his *Humble Inquiry* and conduct the debate on his terms. Bellamy's dialogues tried to explain the Edwardsean position in a form that mimicked familiar conversation and in language that would be more accessible to those who could not follow the theological and epistemological argumentation of the clerical exchanges.[76]

76. On civil millennialism, see Hatch, *The Sacred Cause of Liberty,* 21–54. Many dialogues were little more than an extension of the question-and-answer technique long favored by Puritan preachers, but some of the midcentury ones edged toward the belletristic by making attempts to delineate character and dramatize awakenings. The dialogue form, Peter Clark explained, "is a Way of writing . . . in a more lively and familiar Manner to discuss Points in Controversy, and which has something in it peculiarly agreable to Mankind, and is more proper to engage the Reader's Attention" (Clark, *A Defence of the Divine Right of Infant-Baptism* [Boston, 1752], 10–11). Clark was defending Jonathan Dickinson's important and often reprinted *A Brief Illustration and Confirmation of the Divine Right of Infant Baptism, in a Plain and Familiar Dialogue between a Minister and One of His Parishioners* (Boston, 1746). In *True Religion Delineated,* Bellamy wrote that he had "labored very much to

Bellamy's *Half-Way Covenant* dialogue in 1769 paired a minister and his parishioner. The "Parishioner" wants to have his baby baptized. He explains that he "owned" the covenant where he had previously lived and had made his profession by the standard formula. He did not intend the words he used to be a profession of saving grace, for he considered himself unconverted, but still claimed his right to baptism as a "half-way" church member. The "Minister" asks him to support this claim from the Scriptures. "I have not studied the point," the Parishioner responds. "I cannot mention any texts of Scripture; but it is the custom where I was born and brought up." The Minister then proceeds to explain how this practice arose after the synod of 1662 and why it is faulty. He informs the Parishioner that making a profession that excludes any reference to the Covenant of Grace is unscriptural and that professing that covenant without inner holiness is a wicked lie before God. Convinced that he cannot get his child baptized until he is converted himself, the Parishioner thanks his Minister and goes off to ponder the state of his soul.[77]

Bellamy's *Half-Way Covenant* dialogue was more than just a concise and accessible application of Edwardsean principles; it was also a lesson in lay-clerical relations and an example of discursive regulation. Bellamy explains that one motive in writing the pamphlet was to portray "the friendly Manner in which dissatisfied Parishioners ought to apply to their Minister, and the kind Reception he ought to give them." Bellamy modeled the kind of conversations that ministers and parishioners ought to be having and the ways that potential lay-

---

adapt myself to the lowest capacities, not meaning to write a book for the learned and polite, but for common people" (in Bellamy, *The Works of Joseph Bellamy, D.D. . . .* , 2 vols. [Boston, 1853], I, 11). Bellamy's first dialogue, *Theron, Paulinus, and Aspasio; or, Letters and Dialogues upon the Nature and Love to God, Faith in Christ, Assurance of a Title to Eternal Life . . .* (Boston, 1759), aimed higher and tried to warn sinners with a "fine," "entertaining," and "charming Pen." Bellamy's later dialogues attempt to engage the polite reader *and* make difficult arguments more accessible to the less learned. *A Dialogue on the Christian Sacraments* (Boston, 1762), long attributed to Bellamy, was more probably written by Edward Billing. See Clifford K. Shipton, *Biographical Sketches of Those Who Attended Harvard College in the Classes 1731–1735*, Sibley's Harvard Graduates, IX (Boston, 1956), 23. See also the discussion in James Patrick Walsh, "The Pure Church in Eighteenth-Century Connecticut" (Ph.D. diss., Columbia University, 1967), 173.

77. Joseph Bellamy, *The Half-Way Covenant; a Dialogue* (New Haven, Conn., 1769), 3. The "half-way" practice allowed the unconverted to baptize their children but still required a profession of faith and repentance or a conversion relation for admission to the Lord's Supper and full church membership. For the development of this practice and its relation to the "declension" of New England Puritanism, see Robert G. Pope, *The Half-Way Covenant: Church Membership in Puritan New England* (Princeton, N.J., 1969).

clerical disputes could be avoided by friendly yet informed discussions. Though employing the conversational, give-and-take format of the dialogue, the work plainly displays a minister's authority to define the meaning of religious terms. The Minister tells the Parishioner what the words in the profession really mean. Alas, the Parishioner laments, "I never knew what I was about, nor considered the import of the words, I publicly gave my consent unto."[78]

Bellamy's 1769 dialogue was quickly answered in dialogues by Nathaniel Taylor and Ebenezer Devotion. Taylor presented arguments for the external aspect of the Covenant of Grace. Bellamy responded by asserting that all the various ways that divines talked about ungracious, external covenanting (including "half-way" church covenants and public or national covenants) were "creatures of the imagination, a mere human device." Devotion continued the exchange between the Minister and the Parishioner with the Parishioner's complaint about how Bellamy had represented him in the first dialogue: "I was uncommonly dull and muddy, in stating my difficulties and supporting my objections." In Devotion's pamphlet, the two characters speak with different voices. The patronizing Minister (now acknowledged to be Bellamy himself) is more pompous and arrogant in his condescension. Devotion's Parishioner says he "would not presume to instruct a gentleman of your cloth and character" but then does so, forcefully.[79]

Rather than meekly succumbing to his learned clergyman's reasoning, Devotion's Parishioner presents his own arguments and claims to be able to support them "as clearly as any theorem is demonstrated in Euclid." He challenges Bellamy's interpretation of Matthew 22, even calling into question the translation of a particular Greek word. The Parishioner concludes that the words of a church covenant no more presuppose saving grace than saying the Lord's Prayer and calls for "a reasonable construction" of the terms that both the converted and the unconverted could profess according to the degree of grace God gives them.[80]

In Bellamy's reply to Devotion, the Minister and the Parishioner meet again and agree that the "half-way" practice is "founded only in ignorance, and the

78. Bellamy, *Half-Way Covenant,* table of contents, 9.

79. [Nathaniel Taylor], *A Second Dialogue, between a Minister and His Parishioner, concerning the Half-Way-Covenant* (Hartford, Conn., 1769); [Ebenezer Devotion], *The Half-Way Covenant, a Dialogue between Joseph Bellamy, D.D., and a Parishioner, Continued by the Parishioner; Correcting Some Errors Contained in the Former Dialogue* (New London, Conn., 1769), 2, 16; Joseph Bellamy, *The Inconsistence of Renouncing the Half-Way-Covenant, and Yet Retaining the Half-Way-Practice; a Dialogue* (New Haven, Conn., [1769]), 9–10.

80. [Devotion], *The Half-Way Covenant,* 7, 8.

mistaken notions of the vulgar" and that the ministers who perpetuate it con-descend to that common ignorance. Bellamy's Parishioner disowns the learn-ing he displayed in Devotion's dialogue and admits to having "one of the most learned and ingenious ministers in the colony" as his patron. The pastor says that he recognized "the voice of the clergy" speaking through the layman's words in Devotion's pamphlet. But the Parishioner makes a brief stand for himself, resisting further instruction from Bellamy's Minister about the mean-ing of his profession. "I'm not so ignorant neither," he protests. "I mean to adopt the words of the covenant in a different sense." This exposes one of the main Edwardsean points about signification: members of a religious commu-nity cannot individually choose to understand the words of public religious language as signifying anything other than a single, commonly understood idea, for this would destroy the real essence of Christian communion and make a church a gathering of Christians in name only.[81]

The next two letters to Bellamy by Devotion's Parishioner and Bellamy's fi-nal dialogue in response get entangled by their rhetorical device, arguing over which one of them could put words in the Parishioner's mouth and over whether or not the Parishioner who spoke in both sets of pamphlets was the same character. This contention about the artifice of the dialogue as a rhetor-ical form is also a battle over the cultural power claimed by the clerical speak-ing aristocracy. Devotion's Parishioner claims that Bellamy's is just a straw man for Bellamy to kick, box, scuffle, squeeze, and force to beg friendship: "You seem very fond of bringing your parishioner to your foot, there to ask your prayers for him." Bellamy charged that when the Parishioner spoke as Devo-tion taught him, the character treated the ministry with contempt. Devotion urged Bellamy not to make the Parishioner "talk quite so silly" while "person-ating of him," because it turned a discussion of sacred things into a farce. "And truly, Dr. the whole dialogue, leaving out your name and titles, might pass for a tolerable satyr upon the cause you espouse."[82]

The struggle over the character of the Parishioner dramatizes the substance of the argument itself and the social context in which it occurred. The debate,

---

81. Joseph Bellamy, *That There Is but One Covenant . . . to Which Is Prefixed, an Answer, to a Dialogue concerning the Half-Way-Covenant, Lately Printed at New London* (New Ha-ven, Conn., 1769), 3–4, 6.

82. [Ebenezer Devotion], *A Letter to the Reverend Joseph Bellamy, D.D., concerning Quali-fications for Christian Communion . . . from the Parishioner* (New Haven, Conn., 1770), 18, 19; [Devotion], *Second Letter, to the Reverend Joseph Bellamy, D.D. . . . from the Parishioner* (New Haven, Conn., 1770), 4–5, 16; Bellamy, *The Controversy Brought to a Point; the Fourth Dialogue between a Minister and His Parishioner* (New Haven, Conn., [1770]), 17.

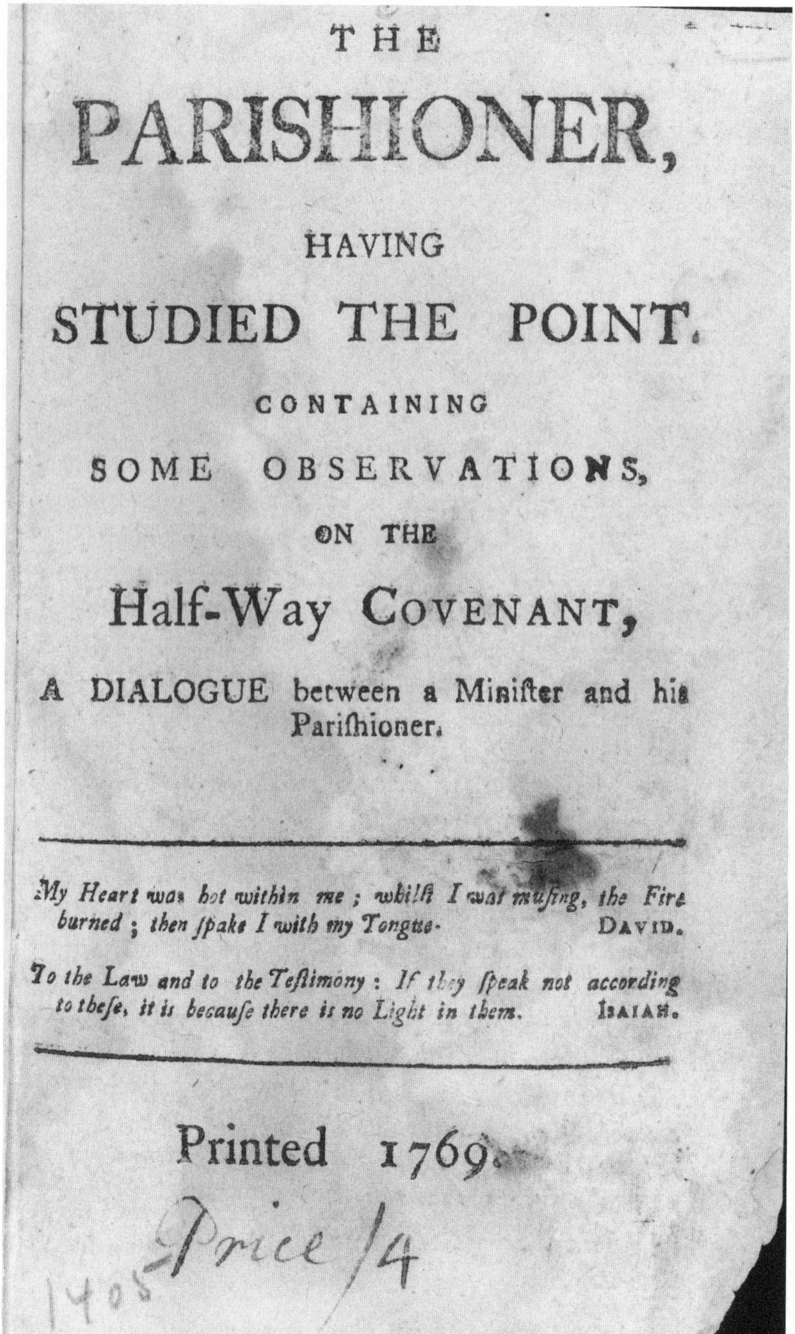

THE

PARISHIONER,

HAVING

STUDIED THE POINT.

CONTAINING

SOME OBSERVATIONS,

ON THE

Half-Way Covenant,

A DIALOGUE between a Minifter and his
Parifhioner.

---

*My Heart was hot within me ; whilft I was mufing, the Fire
burned ; then fpake I with my Tongue·*   DAVID.

*To the Law and to the Teftimony : If they fpeak not according
to thefe, it is becaufe there is no Light in them.*   ISAIAH.

Printed 1769.

Price /4

1405

Figure 5. *The Parishioner, Having Studied the Point, Containing Some Observations,
on the Half-Way Covenant, a Dialogue between a Minister and His Parishioner*
([Hartford, Conn.], 1769), title page. This work is sometimes attributed to the Reverend
Ebenezer Devotion but was almost certainly written by a layman. Courtesy, Beinecke
Rare Book and Manuscript Library, Yale University, New Haven, Conn.

after all, was over who could control the meaning of what real parishioners said. Bellamy's Minister instructs his deferential and ultimately grateful Parishioner in the true meaning of his words. Devotion's Parishioner steps outside of the deferential relationship and insists on applying the common meaning to the words, a meaning broad enough to allow a range of subjective intentions. Although the relation of pastor to parishioner normally forbids it, Devotion's layman explains, he still feels constrained to call upon Bellamy "to review your writings, and retract the errors contain'd in them."[83]

The layman's voice, however, would be heard and not just represented in this controversy over public religious meaning and church reform. Ebenezer Devotion was a minister himself, and thus he, too, was a clerical ventriloquist, putting words in the Parishioner's mouth. Yet, Bellamy's dialogues were answered by another pamphlet, marked as the work of an actual layman by its acid anticlericalism. Here, the Parishioner speaks directly to the Minister, and, though the clergyman is reportedly "impatient" at one point and feeling insulted at another, he remains silent throughout. This Parishioner says he has studied the point to the best of his "poor capacity." He has concluded that the arguments in favor of the morally sincere's being allowed to baptize their children and come to the Lord's Supper should "convince any rational mind that has not suffered [itself] to be implicitly swallowed in the dark abyss of theological mysteries."[84]

Bellamy and Devotion had squabbled over the rules of church admission, but this anonymous Parishioner recognized that Bellamy's unqualified statements also robbed civil society of its public or national covenant with God. Edwards had deemphasized, even denigrated, the national covenant, but, when Bellamy thundered that there was but *one* covenant that God made with man, the Covenant of Grace, and that it demanded nothing less than holiness, he denied the national covenant's existence. For this Parishioner, the national covenant was the foundation of "good order in civil societies." He argued that all Englishmen "have a right to look upon themselves as much in visible covenant with God as ever the Jews had." Ministers who deny this right are infringing upon the religious liberties of the laity. "And are not our religious liberties as valuable as our civil ones?" the Parishioner asked, alluding to the Stamp Act controversy in his "Preface to the Laity." "Why then should we exhaust all our zeal in opposing the appearance of tyranny in civil ministers,

83. [Devotion], *Second Letter, to . . . Bellamy*, 16.
84. *The Parishioner, Having Studied the Point, Containing Some Observations, on the Half-Way Covenant; a Dialogue between a Minister and His Parishioner* ([Hartford, Conn.], 1769), 5, 11, 15–16.

whilst we passively submit to whatever ecclesiasticks think it their interest to tell us is our duty."[85]

After the Awakening, supporters of the revivals had faced an old dilemma with a new urgency. Religious community, they believed, was constituted by a shared public understanding of religious meaning. But how could men and women reborn in the Spirit still be part of the same community, and the same conversation, with the unconverted? New Light Separatist Ebenezer Frothingham said they could not and showed that one of the institutional consequences of the Awakening was the re-formation of the local church as an exclusive gathering of saints who had shared this experience of transforming grace. New Light Stoddardean Solomon Williams argued to preserve a more inclusive sense of Christian community. The status of a person's soul, he wrote, was a question for each individual's awakened conscience, and the answer was known certainly only by God. The semantic disjunction between the subjective meanings a person might privately give to the words of her profession and the public import of those words, giving her "the benefit of the doubt," was a small price to pay to hold together an intergenerational community of morally sincere people who were trying to live Christian lives. The lay Parishioner who wrote against Bellamy in 1769 understood Christian community, and the rights of individuals within it, in more explicitly political terms. He denounced the New Divinity cleric's attempt to dictate the terms of Christian communion as ecclesiastical tyranny, akin to Parliament's encroachment upon English civil liberties in America. The shared understanding that seemed to bind the lay Parishioner's community together was based, not primarily upon grace or conscience, but upon civil and ecclesiastical *rights*.

For Edwardseans, who would become increasingly influential in Connecticut through the second half of the eighteenth century, the key to reforming the church and redefining Christian community was in regulating the language people used to profess their faith and understand their membership in the communion of believers. They argued that the words of public religion could not transparently manifest saving grace, as Separatists seemed to assume; nor should they be sealed off from the subjective realm of conscience, as Williams's plan seemed to entail; nor should they, in the surge of civil religiosity after the fall of Quebec and the prominence of political argument after passage of the Stamp Act, be deflected into the language of law and constitutional rights, as the lay Parishioner implied. Edwards's attempt to regulate religious discourse

85. Ibid., [3], 22.

involved fixing the meaning of particular words used in public professions, controlling how religious signs in general ought to refer to divine realities and signify commonly understood ideas, and placing this regulatory power firmly in the hands of ministers rather than parishioners. His own earlier preaching contained some of the "diverse use" of signs with regard to covenants and profession that he objected to during the communion controversy. His preaching during the Seven Years' War employed the kind of ambiguous terminology for the imperial context that he had condemned in connection with the local church, but followers like Joseph Bellamy abandoned discussions of the public or national covenant and helped erase that ambiguity. They continued his effort to bring moral order to a changing world by controlling the terms of public religion. By asserting the authority to regulate an increasingly diverse use of signs, Edwardseans fueled further antagonisms between laity and clergy. Like Edwards, of course, they believed that they were only trying to correct the ways that discourse had come to misrepresent the Word.[86]

86. On the second and third generations of the Edwardsean New Divinity movement, see Joseph A. Conforti, *Samuel Hopkins and the New Divinity Movement: Calvinism, the Congregational Ministry, and Reform in New England between the Great Awakenings* (Grand Rapids, Mich., 1981); David W. Kling, *A Field of Divine Wonders: The New Divinity and Village Revivals in Northwestern Connecticut, 1792–1822* (University Park, Pa., 1993).

CHAPTER 3

Legalism and Orthodoxy

Thomas Clap and the Transformation

of Legal Culture

In May 1763, President Thomas Clap of Yale College rode from New Haven to Hartford to answer charges leveled against his administration by a group of petitioners to the colony's General Assembly. Three ministers and six laymen had signed the "memorial" complaining of unjust laws, extravagant fines, and the arbitrary rule of the autocratic president. Five other clergymen had written separately, supporting the call for the Assembly to oversee college affairs. Stephen White's election sermon, too, reminded his audience that the college was subordinate to the legislature and called for a committee of visitation. Clap had heard the complaints and the proposed remedies before, but this time they were being formally submitted to the colony's highest court by two of Connecticut's leading lawyers. As he rose to answer, he knew he was arguing for more than his disciplinary policies at Yale. Clap had to defend the college's identity as a religious society raised above all others to protect orthodox Calvinism and Connecticut's moral order.[1]

After Clap's reply, the Assembly refused to act on the memorial. Although the upper house still disagreed with the president about the question of visitation, Clap crowed three years later in his *Annals or History of Yale-College* that

1. Edward Dorr et al., Memorial on Yale College, MS, [1763], Connecticut Archives, "Colleges and Schools," 1st Ser., II, 66a–h, Connecticut State Archives, Connecticut State Library, Hartford; Stephen White, *Civil Rulers Gods by Office, and the Duties of Such Considered and Enforced* . . . (New London, Conn., 1763), 31–32; Thomas Clap, "The Answer of the President and Fellows of Yale College," MS, [1763], Conn. Arch., "Colleges and Schools," 1st Ser., II, 71a–w.

his arguments had probably settled the question of Yale's founding and auton-omy once and for all. Benjamin Trumbull, who might have been an eyewitness to Clap's 1763 defense, wrote years later in praise of the president's masterful le-gal arguments: "In points of law, especially as they respected colleges, he ap-peared to be superior to all the lawyers, so that his antagonists acknowledged that he knew more, and was wiser than all of them." Trumbull added that Clap had shown himself "to be a man of extensive knowledge and real greatness." Clap's modern biographer was less generous, attributing the Yale president's triumph more to the support of political friends in the legislature than to the "display of erudition" that "enveloped the issue in a fog of legalism."[2]

Clap's legalism, however, was more than a smoke screen: for decades it was an integral part of his efforts as a defender of the received faith. The scene of his 1763 speech before the General Assembly—the audience he addressed, the opponents he faced, the language he used, and the principles he defended—illustrates several converging currents in the transformation of law, religion, and society in colonial Connecticut. Clap believed that preserving the mean-ing and purpose of New England meant preserving Calvinist orthodoxy, a goal he thought would be best achieved by making the ecclesiastical identity of Yale College legally and politically secure. His arguments, though in fact based upon willful distortions of the public record, represent the growing rhetorical power of lawyerly language. The campus riots that drove him from the Yale presidency on the heels of the Stamp Act protests in 1766, however, demonstrate the lim-its of that power. If Clap's appeal to what a critic called his "old law books" and "sonorous parade of learning" had persuasive force, so did the popular legal discourse of protest and crowd action. Yale students in the third quarter of the eighteenth century would learn from both.[3]

If eighteenth-century legal history could be written only as the story of law-yers professionalizing, court systems reforming, and jurists reconceptualizing the law's place and function in society, a study of Connecticut would inevita-bly focus upon the post-Revolutionary period. But historians of eighteenth-

2. Thomas Clap, *The Annals or History of Yale-College in New-Haven . . .* (New Haven, Conn., 1766), 76–77; Benjamin Trumbull, *A Complete History of Connecticut, Civil and Ec-clesiastical . . .* , II (1818; reprint, New London, Conn., 1898), 333; Leonard Louis Tucker, *Pu-ritan Protagonist: President Thomas Clap of Yale College* (Chapel Hill, N.C., 1962), 226.

3. [Samuel Whittelsey Dana], *Yale-College Subject to the General Assembly* (New Haven, Conn., 1784), 11, 33. Clap was not a *theological* legalist—one who emphasized Old Testament law over the gospel, or the covenant of works over the Covenant of Grace. By "legalism," I mean his emphasis on, and even exaltation of, explicit rules and formal structures of gov-ernment to resolve disputes.

century American law have broadened and deepened the study of legal culture, asking more questions about what they have called the pre-Revolutionary conditions of the law and the colonial legal *mentalité*. Such studies have focused on both the cultural roots of later institutional developments and the sharp discontinuities between colonial legal culture and the American legal culture shaped in the early Republic. The legal history of the colonial era—before lawyers were solidly established in a respected calling with a self-conscious professional organization, and before the law itself was conceived as "a separated, bounded, distinctive sphere of activity and thought"—requires studies that move more freely between law, moral philosophy, politics, and theology.[4]

Thomas Clap's crusades for law and order dramatized the development of Connecticut's pre-Revolutionary legal culture in two ways. First, Clap's legalistic style signaled the growing power of legal discourse. Between 1740 and 1763, the law became more formal and technical, lawyers more professional, and le-

4. Hendrik Hartog, "Distancing Oneself from the Eighteenth Century: A Commentary on Changing Pictures of American Legal History," in Hartog, ed., *Law in the American Revolution and the Revolution in the Law: A Collection of Review Essays on American Legal History* (New York, 1981), 229–257 (quotation on 242). On professionalization, see Anton-Hermann Chroust, *The Rise of the Legal Profession in America*, I, *The Colonial Experience* (Norman, Okla., 1965); Maxwell Bloomfield, *American Lawyers in a Changing Society, 1776–1876* (Cambridge, Mass., 1976); and Robert A. Ferguson, *Law and Letters in American Culture* (Cambridge, Mass., 1984). On colonial legal history, see John Phillip Reid, *In a Defiant Stance: The Conditions of Law in Massachusetts Bay, the Irish Comparison, and the Coming of the American Revolution* (University Park, Pa., 1977); Reid, *In a Rebellious Spirit: The Argument of Facts, the Liberty Riot, and the Coming of the American Revolution* (University Park, Pa., 1979); Hendrik Hartog, "Losing the World of the Massachusetts Whig," review of Reid's *Defiant Stance*, in Hartog, ed., *Law in the American Revolution*, 143–166; Shannon C. Stimson, *The American Revolution in the Law: Anglo-American Jurisprudence before John Marshall* (London, 1990); Jack P. Greene, "From the Perspective of Law: Context and Legitimacy in the Origins of the American Revolution," *South Atlantic Quarterly*, LXXXV (1986), 56–77. For an overview of developments in legal history, see William E. Nelson and John Phillip Reid, *The Literature of American Legal History* (New York, 1985); and "Forum: Explaining the Law in Early American History—A Symposium," *William and Mary Quarterly*, 3d Ser., L (1993), 3–50. On post-Revolutionary developments in Connecticut: Tapping Reeve, founder of the nationally renown Litchfield Law School, moved to Connecticut in 1772, but did not begin regular lectures on the law until 1782. The Connecticut legislature had called for written court reports in 1784. See Leon P. Lewis, "The Development of a Common Law System in Connecticut," *Connecticut Bar Journal*, XXVII (1953), 419–427; and Everett C. Goodwin, *The Magistracy Rediscovered: Connecticut, 1636–1818* (Ann Arbor, Mich., 1981), 89–94. Zephaniah Swift published his enormously influential and scientific commentary on Connecticut law in *A System of the Laws of the State of Connecticut*, 2 vols. (Windham, Conn., 1795). Swift's was "the first comprehensive treatise on American law of any kind" (Goodwin, *Magistracy Rediscovered*, 95).

galism more prominent in public debate. As churches borrowed the forms and procedures of secular courts for disciplinary proceedings and ministers began citing legal dictionaries in their arguments about the church, Clap bluntly challenged lawyers on what they were beginning to claim as their own ground. But when Clap defended Yale as a seminary, more of its best students were choosing law careers than ever before; when he staked his claim for clergymen as society's intellectual elite and public voice, he borrowed the language of lawyers. The baton of intellectual leadership was being shared, if not passed.

Second, Clap's tactics revealed the developing conflicts among different conceptions of the sources of law and its legitimate use and exploited the fundamental uncertainties plaguing legal and constitutional questions at every level. Arguments about the legal status of a chartered corporation (Yale) within a chartered corporation (Connecticut) invariably raised questions about the applicability of British common and canon law to the colonies, the political relationship of chartered colonies to crown and Parliament, and the limitations of all governmental power by that often-praised but variously defined British constitution. Clap's common law conservatism also exposed the emerging conflict between the "imperial" legal theory that envisioned law as an instrument of state power for the preservation of order and the "local" legal theory that was grounded in local custom and resisted or restrained the exercise of centralized power. Clap's ouster from Yale, like the forced resignation of stamp commissioner Jared Ingersoll, was a ritual expression of that conflict.

Clap was a hard-nosed Calvinist pursuing his own strategy to preserve moral order in post-Awakening New England. His career should be a caveat to religious historians who borrow the ideological reductionism of eighteenth-century polemicists. Mapping the cultural landscape as a battlefield of New Light and Old Light ecclesiastical parties or as a theological chasm between Arminians and Calvinists oversimplifies the relationship between fundamental principles and social practices. As large and important as they were, the differences between Elisha Williams's call for a freer marketplace of religious opinion, the Edwardseans' effort to regulate religious discourse, and Clap's attempt to strengthen the institutional foundations of orthodoxy were differences of style and strategy, not deviations from the fundamental tenets of Calvinist theology. Clap's ultimate failure was a judgment upon his means, not his motives; it signaled a defeat of coercive religious legislation, not the eclipse of a Calvinist worldview.[5]

5. Indeed, Clap spoke very highly of Elisha Williams's piety and orthodoxy, and, even as he argued with Edwards over George Whitefield, he asserted that he and Edwards were in complete agreement theologically.

No matter how often Clap appealed to the authority of written codes and laws, they remained a means to an end: perpetuating the design of New England's founders. For Clap, "design" was a word with vast legal but also epistemological, philosophical, and theological implications. To grasp the design of the founders was to perceive the spirit behind the letter of the law, the motivating force behind every legal instrument shaping the moral order: "true religion" or "orthodoxy." The content of orthodoxy, too, was being contested, but here Clap clung to a faith made certain through personal trials, and he allowed no room for ambiguities. People may disagree about "matters of Governments and Discipline, And all external Order," he wrote, but without agreement "about the great and fundamental Doctrines of the Gospel and the Terms of Salvation[,] there can be no external Harmony." Moral order could not be secured merely by preachers exhorting citizens to righteousness under the public covenant or by parsons trying to regulate religious language and behavior in their parishes. A harmonious moral order had to be grounded in orthodox belief, and orthodoxy had to be defended and enforced by the law.[6]

LAW, ORDER, AND DISCIPLINE

On July 7, 1763, Thomas Clap wrote in a private journal for spiritual reflections for the first time since 1741, ten months after he had come to Yale. "I have not had such a strong and lively Exercise of Grace [nor] made much Progress in it as I ought to have done," he confessed, partly because of "being so Constantly involved in public Business." Much of Clap's energy had been spent trying to manage the "public Business" of religious controversy during a period when the "public" was being redefined and the language in which it conducted its "Business" was changing. Clap's career at Yale reflected and influenced some of those changes. He is perhaps an extreme example of a clergyman who put great stock in the efficacy of written rules and laws to direct reasonable, virtuous action and control the anarchy of the passions. But Clap made his mark, not because he promoted a benign legal rationalism, but because he used the law as a blunt weapon in ecclesiastical power struggles.[7]

6. Thomas Clap, "Thots on the Present State of Religion Occasionally Minuted Down," undated post-1757 MS, Thomas Clap Presidential Papers, Yale Record Group 2-A-5, Manuscripts and Archives, Yale University Library, New Haven, Conn.

7. Thomas Clap, "Memoirs of Some Remarkable Occurrences of Divine Providence towards Me in the Course of My Life, Together with Some Reflections and Observations on Them," MS, 49, Manuscripts and Archives, Yale University Library.

Clap had called for the rationalization of procedures to settle church quarrels and the codification of rules for church disciplinary cases in his first published work, a 1732 ordination sermon. Clap, then a twenty-nine-year-old minister in Windham, Connecticut, complained: "We have few or no *stated or known Rules,* for a minister's Direction. . . . Hence one ecclesiastical judgement is no Precedent for another, the same Methods are not always observed in the same Cases, but Things left fluctuating in Uncertainties." Disputes always arise from the natural differences of opinion among a people, he argued, but if left to the natural passions and arbitrary wills of fallen men churches will split into parties, and the contention will invariably focus on the minister. Scripture and "the fundamental Maxims of Policy and good Government" both dictated "a Necessity of keeping to certain stated Restrictions and Regulations, in all ecclesiastical Procedures."[8]

Clap was not alone in his desire to bring more order to colonial religious society. As one study of colonial Connecticut's legal history has shown, in the second quarter of the eighteenth century "church disciplinary proceedings began to adopt the rhetoric and procedures of secular courts." Writs of summons issued by ministers became identical to those issued by justices of the peace, and church proceedings came to "resemble civil trials in virtually every important respect," their language "mimic[king] common law practice so closely that references to 'prayer' or 'the church' are what seem anomalous." Procedural formalism and legalism in church proceedings echoed continuing developments in the secular legal system. Technical language and the abstract, homogenizing principles of law were replacing the informal procedures of dispute resolution, which had recognized the multilayered personal and social relationships of the parties involved.[9]

Clap became known as a rigorous disciplinarian in his Windham parish, and the Yale trustees expected him to bring the same zeal for ordered govern-

8. Thomas Clap, *The Greatness and Difficulty of the Work of the Ministry: A Sermon Preached at the Ordination of the Reverend Mr. Ephraim Little at Colchester, September 20, 1732* (Boston, 1732), 10, 12.

9. Bruce H. Mann, *Neighbors and Strangers: Law and Community in Early Connecticut* (Chapel Hill, N.C., 1987), 9, 143, 144, 147, and see chap. 3. Cornelia Hughes Dayton, in *Women before the Bar: Gender, Law, and Society in Connecticut, 1639–1789* (Chapel Hill, N.C., 1995), in some passages dates the shift toward English formalism earlier, the late seventeenth century (8, 196), but she generally agrees with Mann and stresses the period after 1720 (44–45, 52, 81, 307). Clap realized that a community was a complex union of people with different interests and "humours," but he argued that its best government made rational inferences and deductions from general principles and translated them into stated methods of procedure. See Clap, *The Greatness and Difficulty,* 20.

ment to the college when they named him rector in the spring of 1740. His "First Business of Special Importance," as he put it, was to compile a new "Body of Laws" for the college, which each student would transcribe in Latin upon admission. He also wrote down "all the Customs of College which had from time to time obtained and been established by Practice[,] which made as large a Volume as the Laws." Rules of conduct, he remarked proudly, were now "more known[,] fixt and Certain and the Government of the College became more uniform and steady and less Arbitrary." As Clap tightened the internal administration of the college, he also sought to shore up its legal status within the colony. A new college charter, drawn up by Clap and passed by the General Assembly in 1745, incorporated the rector and trustees as the more powerful "President and Fellows" of Yale College.[10]

Clap's more immediate concern in the first years of his administration, however, had been with the disorders of the Awakening. Like most everyone else in the colony, Clap had welcomed George Whitefield's first visit in October 1740. But by the end of Gilbert Tennent's week-long, seventeen-sermon assault on New Haven in April 1741, Clap had soured on the Awakening, recoiling from the emotional extravagance and deeply resenting the itinerants' attacks on the learned ministry. Whitefield had felt obliged to tell Harvard and Yale that their "light had become darkness," and Tennent had warned of "modern Pharisees" hiding their dead hearts behind a veneer of scholarship. When, in July, James Davenport denounced New Haven minister Joseph Noyes to his face, calling him "a Wolf in Sheep's Cloathing" and publicly urging Noyes's flock to desert him, Clap took action.[11]

With other brethren of the New Haven church, Clap pushed the first lever on an institutional machine that they hoped would stop the itinerants and return the colony to law and order. They held a meeting in Noyes's house where they questioned Davenport about his conduct and his accusations. Hardly a model of judicial order, the inquest ended in "Noise, Confusion and Conster-

10. Thomas Clap, "Annals of Yale College," MS, 1747, Clap Presidential Papers, Yale Record Group 2-A-5, 46, 48, Manuscripts and Archives, Yale University Library. The new charter was approved by the trustees in 1744, revised by Governor Thomas Fitch, and passed by the General Assembly in 1745.

11. George Whitefield to the Students at Harvard and Yale, July 1741, "Thomas Clap to the *Boston Post-Boy*," Oct. 5, 1741, both in Stephen Nissenbaum, ed., *The Great Awakening at Yale College* (Belmont, Calif., 1972), 25, 113; Gilbert Tennent, *The Danger of an Unconverted Ministry...*, 2d ed. (Philadelphia, 1741; Boston, 1742), in Alan Heimert and Perry Miller, eds., *The Great Awakening: Documents Illustrating the Crisis and Its Consequences* (Indianapolis, Ind., 1967), 86. On Clap's change of attitude, see Tucker, *Puritan Protagonist*, 124–125.

nation," as Davenport suddenly broke into a fifteen-minute prayer for Noyes's unconverted heart. Clap and the New Haven Ministerial Association then petitioned the General Assembly to call a colonywide consociation of churches, allowed under the Saybrook Platform. The Assembly approved, and representatives of the churches met at Guilford in November, voting on a series of resolves drafted by Clap and his New Haven colleagues. Supported by Governor Jonathan Law, the "Guilford Resolves" passed the General Assembly in May 1742 as the Anti-Itinerancy Act. As Clap's biographer concluded, Clap might not have been the architect of all the antirevival legislation, but he certainly was a "prime force" behind its passage.[12]

The General Assembly also took two actions in 1742 that strengthened Clap's hand at Yale and Yale's position in the colony. Many of the teenage boys studying at the college had become too flushed with the excitement of the revivals to heed Clap's calls for deference, discipline, and decorum. In the fall of 1741, he had closed the college hall to itinerants and expelled David Brainerd for insulting a tutor. When students proved incorrigible the following spring, caring more about exhorting and arguing than studying, Clap sent them all home and closed the college. This move prompted the Assembly to call for a special investigative committee, and the committee's report on the college, approved by both houses, recommended funding special instruction "in the true principals of Relegion, according to our confession of faith and Eclesiastic constitution." It further urged the rector and trustees "to use all such proper measures" to keep students from imbibing the errors of "Strangers and foraigners." The Assembly also passed an act that closed down the newly formed "Shepard's Tent" in New London, which had threatened to be an alternative institution for training evangelical ministers, and confined the established ministry to

12. "Thomas Clap to the Boston *Post-Boy*," in Nissenbaum, ed., *The Great Awakening at Yale*, 113–115 (quotation on 115). Events leading up to the Anti-Itinerancy Act are chronicled in New Haven Ministerial Association Memorial to the General Assembly, Oct. 8, 1741, Conn. Arch.; "Ecclesiastic Affairs," VII, 243, Conn. St. Libr.; The General Assembly's Response, and "An Act for Regulating Abuses and Correcting Disorders in Ecclesiastical Affairs," in J. Hammond Trumbull and Charles J. Hoadly, eds., *The Public Records of the Colony of Connecticut*, 15 vols. (Hartford, Conn., 1850–1890), VIII, 438–439, 454–457; Resolution of the New Haven Association, November 1741; "Resolves of the General Consociation, Convened at Guilford, Nov. 24th 1741," Connecticut Historical Society, *Collections*, XI (Hartford, Conn., 1907), 5–10. All of the above documents are reprinted in Nissenbaum, ed., *The Great Awakening at Yale*, 125–139. On Clap as a "prime force," see Tucker, *Puritan Protagonist*, 131. The 1742 act was supplemented by the repeal of the 1708 Toleration Act the following May and further strengthened by the Assembly in October 1743. See Nissenbaum, ed., *The Great Awakening at Yale*, 191–193.

graduates of Yale, Harvard, "or some other allowed foreign protestant college or university." [13]

The expulsion of David Brainerd had earned Clap the resentment of influential men like Jonathan Edwards and Aaron Burr, but the expulsion of John and Ebenezer Cleaveland in 1745 was an even more outrageous "Stretch of Colle[g]e Power," as a complaint in a New York newspaper put it. While on vacation, and with the permission of their parents, the Cleavelands had attended a Separatist meeting in Canterbury, Connecticut. Clap expelled them both for violating the laws of the college, the colony, and the gospel, supposedly telling John privately that "the laws of God and the laws of the College are one." Defending his action in print, Clap declared that Yale would not tolerate subversives, because "the principal End and Design of Erecting this College . . . was, *To Train up a Succession of Learned and Orthodox Ministers.*" Yet, on this principle, Clap would soon become a kind of separatist himself. [14]

From 1746 to 1757, Clap labored to secure funding for a divinity professor, withdraw Yale students from New Haven's First Church, and establish an independent college chapel. He claimed that in doing so he was following the principal design of the college's founders and the colony's forefathers and argued that his separation was a moral, reasonable, and legal act. Clap's former Old Light friends howled at the betrayal and attacked his conversion to "political New Light" as a naked pursuit of "Power, Authority, Influence and Riches in the Country." Although their ad hominem attacks precluded the possibility that he might have had nobler motives, Clap's critics accurately assessed his tactics and aims. He wanted to fix the meaning of words in declarations of orthodoxy and give formal creeds the force of law. He sought to enforce the regulation of orthodoxy in the colony by influencing colonial legislation, creating a more formalized system of ecclesiastical courts, and controlling religious instruction and worship at the college. [15]

13. The General Assembly's Report on Yale, May 1742, in Nissenbaum, ed., *The Great Awakening at Yale*, 164–167; "An Act Relating to, and for the Better Regulating Schools of Learning," in Trumbull and Hoadly, eds., *Public Records of Connecticut*, VIII, 500–502 (in Nissenbaum, ed., *The Great Awakening at Yale*, 183–185).

14. *New-York Weekly Post-Boy*, Mar. 17, 1745, and John Cleaveland, "A Just Narrative of the Proceedings," in Nissenbaum, ed., *The Great Awakening at Yale*, 222, 237; Thomas Clap, *The Judgment of the Rector and Tutors of Yale-College concerning Two of the Students Who Were Expelled; Together with the Reasons of It* (New London, Conn., 1745), 10.

15. [Thomas Darling], *Some Remarks on Mr. President Clap's History and Vindication of the Doctrines, etc., of the New-England Churches* (New Haven, Conn., 1757), 42. Clap began setting money aside for a chair of divinity in 1746, withdrew Yale students from New Haven's First Church and the preaching of Joseph Noyes in 1753, and finally established a sep-

By the 1750s, Clap felt that orthodoxy was much more threatened by the gains Anglicans had made than by the weakening Separatist movement, and Arminian gentility was seducing more Yale graduates than Antinomian enthusiasm. Since many Congregationalists who had looked with favor on the revivals and had opposed the 1742 law shared Clap's desire to make a strong stand for Calvinism against "Arminian corruptions," he formed new alliances. He also saw ecclesiastical power shifting into the hands of younger, moderate New Lights, who were replacing their Old Light elders in the county consociations, and political power in the General Assembly beginning to favor a coalition of interests from strongly New Light counties. He was too much the shrewd politician to let accusations of betrayal stand in his way.[16]

LAW, ORTHODOXY, AND THE ECCLESIASTICAL CONSTITUTION

Legal argument and legalistic rhetoric played a heightened role in midcentury ecclesiastical debates. Disputants increasingly tried to step away from the morass of scriptural exegesis and philosophical posturing and appeal to the law of the land. Clap's words and actions, from his political conversion in the early 1750s through the Stamp Act era in the 1760s, helped draw attention to fundamental questions about the rule of law in religious society and the use of written creeds and constitutions as the basis of social consensus.

Connecticut in the 1750s was not yet in a revolutionary situation, where political struggles can sweep ordinary legal proceedings aside and courts become the focus of fundamental questions about the meaning of law and the power that would determine it. Yet, in two related midcentury disputes, the court-

arate college church in 1757. See Tucker, *Puritan Protagonist,* 184–186; and Ralph H. Gabriel, *Religion and Learning at Yale, the Church of Christ in the College and University, 1757–1957* (New Haven, Conn., 1958). On Clap's trying to rally Calvinists against Arminians, see Clap to Solomon Williams, June 6, 1754, William Williams Papers, Manuscripts and Archives, Yale University Library.

16. On the post-Awakening growth of the Church of England, see Bruce E. Steiner, "Anglican Officeholding in Pre-Revolutionary Connecticut: The Parameters of New England Community," *WMQ,* 3d Ser., XXXI (1974), 369–406. Samuel Harrison Rankin, Jr., "Conservatism and the Problem of Change in the Congregational Churches of Connecticut, 1660–1760" (Ph.D. diss., Kent State University, 1971), 296, argued that, by late 1754, all local associations and consociations had New Light majorities, with the exception of New Haven East and Fairfield West. On the growth of the New Lights as a political party, see William Samuel Johnson to J. Beach, Jan. 4, 1763, Johnson Family Papers, Connecticut Historical Society, Hartford. See also Tucker, *Puritan Protagonist,* 210.

room did become both an actual and a symbolic center for resolving contested claims to legitimacy. The storm over Clap's orthodoxy test at Yale in 1753 and the "Wallingford Controversy" over the ordination of James Dana in 1758 and 1759 reveal the established clergy's legalistic turn. In an apparent reversal of their 1742 positions, Old Lights found themselves arguing for liberty of conscience and congregational autonomy, whereas New Lights were now trying to use the presbyterial apparatus framed by the Saybrook Platform as a mechanism of ecclesiastical control. Clap's former allies wanted to broaden the latitude of interpretation for creeds, whereas he wanted to narrow it; they wanted to narrow interpretation of the powers granted by the Platform, and he wanted to broaden it. They tried to define the ecclesiastical constitution wholly by the written word, yet they refused to allow the written confession—or the writings of Thomas Clap—to define the faith.[17]

Sometimes the appeal to the rule of law in midcentury debate was little more than a rhetorical gesture. New Lights who withdrew from Noyes's New Haven church borrowed the form if not the substance of the law to give their separation the illusion of legitimacy. Invoking law and equity and dropping several legal catchphrases, they appropriated the tone of authoritative legal discourse as they sought the official recognition as an ecclesiastical society that Connecticut law would not allow.[18]

This tactic can be contrasted to the efforts and language of more radical

17. Legal historian Shannon Stimson in *The American Revolution in the Law*, 29, has written: "In revolutionary settings, contests over the locus and legitimacy of law-determining power are eminently political. The question of who controls the legal ground, that is, who gives content and meaning to the law in such situations, transcends the boundaries of legal technicalities as the courtroom becomes an active centre for resolving contested claims of legitimacy within the state." On the shifting positions of Old Lights and New Lights, see Tucker, *Puritan Protagonist*, 210–211. As Tucker notes, by the 1750s those referred to as Old Lights were not as staunchly orthodox as in the 1740s, and the term New Light no longer defined a party of militant revivalists. In any case, not all 1742 Old Lights had supported the Anti-Itinerancy Act, and not all 1742 New Lights chafed at Presbyterianism. Yet, as imprecise and confusing as they are, these labels were used by contemporaries, who also criticized the reversals on the question of the Saybrook Platform by men like Noah Hobart and Jonathan Todd.

18. Bruce Hartling Mann, "Parishes, Law, and Community in Connecticut: 1700–1760" (Ph.D. diss., Yale University, 1977), 193–199. Members of the New Haven New Light ("White Haven") church had to wait seventeen years after the 1742 schism for official recognition. After gaining a majority of New Haven's Congregationalists by 1757, they succeeded in dividing the parish in 1759. The document Mann referred to was signed by sixty-eight men and three women in 1749. Mann notes a similar conflation of legal and ecclesiastical forms in the records of a 1731 deliberation over Guilford's First Church (163–191).

Separatists like Ebenezer Frothingham or the Rogerene Baptist John Bolles, who denied the legitimacy of the colony's interference in ecclesiastical affairs and called its leadership away from their lawbooks and back to their Bibles. "*O New-England! Connecticut! Connecticut!* for the Lord's Sake, consider what Laws are them that confront an infinite God," Frothingham pleaded. Both men argued that Connecticut's ecclesiastical laws, Confession of Faith, and Saybrook Platform had been written in the image of "the Beast" and in the spirit of Antichrist. The established clergy's legalism was hardly surprising in a society where, in Frothingham's opinion, ecclesiastical power was determined by "Money Qualifications," and the system of justice was perverted by the same moneyed interests through the tricks of legal formalism:

> Once more, we enquire whether or no that antient Law Book, called the Bible, is not too, too much laid aside, and not duly consulted by them that are the Law-makers, and by them also that set to judge in the Courts of Common Pleas, as of civil Justice and Equity between Man and Man? And whence is it, that there are such Volumes of Men's crafty Wisdom and human Tradition brought into the Courts of civil Justice, that when an honest Man comes to have Justice done him in the Court, that unless he comes in such a critical Shape and Form, marked out by Men's Traditions, the poor Man is non-suited, and his Case drops through.

Frothingham felt that the Wallingford Controversy of 1758 and 1759 strikingly illustrated the established clergy's infatuation with human laws rather than with the word of God: "Constitution! Constitution! is the all and all with them." But the Wallingford affair, and the Yale controversy that preceded it, were more than spectacles of learned men's contending over what Frothingham called a mere "Shadow." [19]

19. Ebenezer Frothingham, *The Articles of Faith and Practice, with the Covenant, That Is Confessed by the Separate Churches of Christ in General in This Land; Also a Discourse, Holding Forth the Great Privileges of the Church of Jesus Christ . . .* (Newport, R.I., 1750), 252, 256, 259; Frothingham, *A Key to Unlock the Door, That Leads in, to Take a Fair View of the Religious Constitution, Established by Law, in the Colony of Connecticut . . .* ([New Haven, Conn.], 1767), 75–76. In the first publication, Frothingham argued that the same men who had rejected "the late blessed Work of God in the Year 1741–42" and had "made Laws to crush it, and in one sense, crucified it, and buried it" continued to sip from the cup of the Whore of Babylon and were joined by former New Lights who had grown more concerned about their salaries than the cause of Christ (176, 235, 345–346). In *A Key*, Frothingham criticized Connecticut justice again (208–211). He assailed "Money Qualifications" in this later work too (57–68), by which he meant the law qualifying any person with a freehold rated at fifty shillings or forty pounds in the common list to vote for a town's minister. See also John Bolles,

The dispute over the legal enforcement of orthodoxy and the Wallingford Controversy were about the boundaries of acceptable interpretation for empowered texts and about how common practice could expand or contract those boundaries. These issues were first raised in 1753, when Clap had persuaded the Yale Corporation to approve a more explicit creedal statement and "loyalty oath" for all college officers and then used the orthodoxy test against his old ally, New Haven minister Joseph Noyes. Noyes was a Yale fellow and the students' regular preacher; revealing his inadequacies would help justify the establishment of a separate church at Yale. Noyes's supporters saw Clap's move as the latest tactic in the New Light crusade for power, though Clap would have denied any connection to events of the previous decade. During the Awakening, James Davenport had attacked Noyes for his unconverted heart, basing his assessment on hearsay and a feeling Davenport had after speaking with Noyes; Clap pointed to the public record and criticized Noyes's preaching, charging him with heresy and using the 1753 orthodoxy act as legal sanction to call for a hearing before the Yale board. Noyes was able to avoid the inquest, and his supporters managed to get the General Assembly to suspend Yale's annual one-hundred-pound grant. But Clap got his college church.

The antagonisms continued in the Wallingford Controversy in 1758 and 1759 over the ordination of James Dana, which became the most divisive ecclesiastical issue since the Awakening. Although Clap had tried to remain inconspicuous in the affair, his opponents insisted that he was at "the true Source and Spring" of the clerical infighting. The Wallingford dispute threatened the colony's ecclesiastical constitution and launched a political scheme to unseat the governor and several members of the legislature's upper house. It began when a vocal minority of the Wallingford parishioners objected to Dana's Harvard liberalism and questioned his orthodoxy. They called in the New Haven Consociation of Churches, influenced by Clap, to block the ordination. The pro-Dana faction, supported by Noyes and the New Haven Association of ministers, ordained Dana anyway, denying the authority of the Consociation and thus of the Saybrook Platform itself. The lower house of the General Assembly supported the anti-Dana parishioners and passed an act that would incorporate them as a separate society and free them from taxes that paid Dana's salary. But Governor Thomas Fitch and the upper house vetoed the measure.

To Worship God in Spirit, and in Truth, Is to Worship Him in the True Liberty of Conscience That Is in Bondage to No Flesh . . . ([New London, Conn.?], 1756); John Bolles and John Walterhous, *Concerning the Christian Sabbath, Which That Sabbath Commanded to Israel, after They Came out of Egypt, Was a Sign Of* ([New London, Conn.], 1757); [Bolles], *A Relation of The Opposition Which Some Baptist People Met with at Norwich . . .* [n.p., 1761].

Some angry New Haven citizens then tried to get Fitch and other opponents out of office by surreptitiously substituting the names of more suitable candidates on nomination lists. Clap's chief opponent, Killingworth physician Benjamin Gale, intercepted and published a private letter that implicated Clap himself in the scheme.[20]

The flurry of pamphlets these events provoked did occasionally rise above invective to focus discussion on the nature of New England orthodoxy itself. All Protestants agreed that the Bible was the only foundation of faith, Clap wrote in 1755, but "the Question is, in what sense we are to understand it." Clap acknowledged that every person has the right to judge the Scriptures for himself, but every community or body of men also has such a right, and, without "a *joint-declared Consent*" to a specific list of articles of faith, its "Unity is founded upon *Nothing*."[21]

Clap's critics challenged his "Notion of Orthodoxy" rather than his list of Calvinist doctrines and charged that he was trying to legally establish the Confession over the Bible as the rule of faith. No person could be perfectly orthodox any more than perfectly righteous, one pamphlet signed "Catholicus" argued. "Orthodoxy" must signify "a right Belief of the Substance of all the essential and most important Doctrines of the Christian Religion, accompanied with an honest Love to Truth, and a sincere Endeavour to attain a more perfect Knowledge of it." This definition presupposed that people who agreed

20. *A Letter to the Clergy of the Colony of Connecticut, from an Aged Layman of Said Colony* ([New York], 1760), 13; Benjamin Gale, *A Few Breif* [sic] *Remarks on Mr. Graham's Answer; and on His Vindication of Mr. President Clap, Published in the Connecticut Gazette, of October Last*... (New Haven, Conn., 1760). See also Jonathan Todd, *A Reply to the Reverend Mr. Eells's Serious Remarks, upon the Faithfull Narrative*... (New Haven, Conn., 1760), 6–7; William Hart, *Remarks on a Late Pamphlet Wrote by Mr. Hobart, Entitled the Principles of Congregational Churches . . . Considered, and Applied to the Case of the Late Ordination at Wallingford*... (New Haven, Conn., 1760), 46–49.

21. Thomas Clap, *A Brief History and Vindication of the Doctrines Received and Established in the Churches of New-England with a Specimen of the New Scheme of Religion Beginning to Prevail* (New Haven, Conn., 1755), 38, 39, 40, and see also 25. The first of ten resolutions adopted by the Yale fellows in 1753 acknowledged the Old and New Testaments as the only rule of faith. The second resolution declared that the Westminster Confession of Faith, established in Connecticut in the Saybrook Platform of 1708, expressed the true sense and summed up the important doctrines of the Scriptures in common language. Expositions contrary to Westminster should be considered "wrong and erroneous." The third resolution dictated that disputes over the interpretation of particular words and phrases in the Confession should be settled by recourse to the general usage of Protestant divines. See Yale University Corporation Records, I, Nov. 21, 1753, 106–108, typewritten transcript, Manuscripts and Archives, Yale University Library (hereafter cited as Yale Corporation Records).

on the "Substance" of doctrines would often disagree over circumstantials and that knowledge of "right Belief" was progressive. "Catholicus" added that divines continued to disagree over even the fundamentals of Christianity. It was therefore ridiculous to think that a human composition was a fully adequate expression of the true faith. The Confession was a good guide for faith, but it never should be imposed as a religious test or as part of a legal oath.[22]

Clap's opponents refused to fix principles in writing as a legal standard. In an anonymously published pamphlet, Noyes's son-in-law Thomas Darling argued that using the Confession in place of the Scriptures as a test of orthodoxy was like using two slightly different bushel baskets as a standard measure, a practice that even his slave Tom would find absurd. Confessions were the opinions of a single generation of men, both Darling and "Catholicus" argued, not a timeless distillation of essential truth; they were crafted in controversy and often used language that tried to smooth over areas where divines continued to disagree. Darling spent more than 30 of his 125 pages pulling back the curtain history had drawn over synods and assemblies to expose the bitter clerical power struggles behind expressions of orthodox faith. Even Clap himself, Darling charged, had some idiosyncratic opinions about infant damnation and could be considered orthodox on that article only with considerable "Latitude" of interpretation.[23]

Complaints that confessions of faith were fallible human compositions, Clap reasoned, "might be as well urged against Preaching, writing, [or] Con-

22. *A Letter to a Clergyman, in the Colony of Connecticut, from His Friend; in Which the True Notion of Orthodoxy Is Enquired into* (New Haven, Conn., 1757), 6, 10. See also [Benjamin Gale], *A Reply to a Pamphlet, Entitled, The Answer of the Friend in the West, Etc. . . .* ([New London, Conn.], 1755), 31.

23. [Darling], *Some Remarks*, 18, 27. See also *A Letter to a Clergyman*, 18; and William Hart, *Remarks on a Late Pamphlet Wrote by Mr. Hobart.* [Shubael Conant], *A Letter to a Friend Wherin Some Free Thoughts Are Offered on the Subject of the Rev. Mr. Noyes's Proposed Examination* (New Haven, Conn., 1757), tried to show that there was nothing more behind the current cries for orthodoxy than yet another bid for ecclesiastical dominion. "A Set of Narrow-Spirited Bigots" were interpreting every "hairsbreadth" deviation from their sentiments as heresy, he claimed, in order to blacken the reputations of those who held to a more "*moderate catholick Calvinism*" (10). Hart continued the argument with New Divinity minister Joseph Bellamy, who had joined Clap in denouncing such "catholick" and "latitudinarian" sentiments as subversive to the foundation of New England's churches. But by the time Bellamy had written his response to Hart in 1760, the controversy had moved far beyond the Yale Corporation and the attack on Joseph Noyes. See [Hart], *A Letter to Paulinus; Containing an Answer to His Three Questions, Lately Proposed to the Public, in the Connecticut Gazette . . .* (New Haven, Conn., [1760]); [Joseph Bellamy], *A Letter to Scripturista . . .* (New Haven, Conn., 1760).

versation. . . . Would it not be much better for a minister in the Pulpit instead of pretending [to] declare and Explain divine Doctrines in his own Humane Fallible Terms only to read a Chapter in the bible and then he would be sure to say nothing wrong and all the congregation would certainly agree with him." But what meaning of the text would they be agreeing to? His opponents insisted that belief be measured against only the Bible. Why, then, were there so many religious pamphlets, books, and treatises, if meaning was so clear in the scriptural texts themselves? There was so much disagreement over words and phrases in the Bible, in fact, that to declare a belief in a particular biblical phrase without elaborating its meaning by declaring the doctrines and propositions it contained "is to declare nothing at all." [24]

Clap attacked as an open-ended hermeneutical strategy the objection to fixing principles in written declarations. The objection presupposed that "men should be always learning and yet never be able to come to the knowledge of the Truth" and that communities should "continue in a state of Doubt and enquiring to the end of the world." Clap's primary target, the Reverend William Hart, had offered an analogy to judgments rendered in a civil court. What if New Haven judges declared their sense of a law in writing, Hart asked, and decided that in the future their exposition should be taken as the law? Judges were not legislators, and their written interpretations should not replace the written law. Here was a perfect looking glass reflecting the ecclesiastical situation, Hart wrote. Clap welcomed the comparison.[25]

For Clap, the looking glass reflected a common law jurisprudence that defined the very character of the moral order. Recoiling from the implications of an epistemology that rested with *sola scriptura* and the conscience of Everyman, Clap argued for the mature reasoning of learned and pious men as a social necessity. He pointed to what judges on the King's Bench always did: "After mature Deliberation, they wrote down their opinion upon the sense and

24. Thomas Clap, "A Brief History and Vindication of Confessions of Faith," Beinecke Rare Book and Manuscript Library, Yale University, New Haven, Conn. (hereafter cited as Beinecke Library), punctuation added. Clap added that even translating from the Greek and Hebrew introduces the fallible hand of man and inevitably distorts meaning. Clap's opponents admitted that, despite the imperfections and ambiguities of language, it was possible for people to convey their ideas and sentiments to each other and that this was an allowable function for a confession of faith. This essay responded to a pamphlet exchange but remained unpublished after Joseph Bellamy's similar piece (*A Letter to Scripturista*) beat Clap's to the press. Although the sustained argument that I am drawing from here never became public, Clap made his views known in private conversation, as Darling's *Some Remarks* demonstrates.

25. Clap, "Brief History . . . of Confessions of Faith"; [Hart], *Letter to Paulinus*, 18–19.

meaning of the Law[,] not in the very words of the statutes themselves, to help their own memories or as a precedent to themselves and other Courts." Sir Edward Coke's opinions, he added, were usually set down in the margins. If the process of interpretation, deliberation, and judgment and the practice of recording written opinions as precedents suggested flexibility, the phrase "after mature Deliberation" and the apotheosis of Coke indicated the fixity that Clap wanted to emphasize. "After hearing the Point of Law frequently disputed and Mature Consideration thereupon, their Judgments were not altered or likely to be altered by any future Pleadings." This was the state of all mature and stable courts, Clap argued. It also characterized the Westminster Assembly in 1645. From the beginnings of the Reformation to Westminster, he asserted, the Bible had been more intensively studied than at any time before or after, probably until the millennium. Protestants had good reason, therefore, to remain "fixed and unshaken in their Judgments" that the Confession expressed scriptural truth.[26]

Not only must principles be declared and fixed, Clap argued, but they must be legally established for public officers. "The Doctrinal Tests required of [Yale's] officers . . . stands on the same foundation in that respect as the Kingdom itself." Ministers like Noyes or Wallingford's James Dana, who refused to be questioned about their orthodoxy by the communities they were going to lead, claimed more prerogative than the king himself. The king held his crown on the condition that he upheld Protestantism, according to the terms of the Westminster Confession and the Thirty-Nine Articles, which were interwoven and essential parts of the British constitution. This was a fundamental principle in a kingdom ruled by laws and not men; it resisted arbitrary power and promoted unity and peace.[27]

Clap could hardly understand why Hart had introduced the civil court as a looking glass, since Clap saw nothing but his own arguments supported and Hart's overturned in that mirror. It was no careless illustration on Hart's part. His first pro-Dana pamphlet in the Wallingford Controversy might have been clumsy or ostentatious as it tried to appeal to the laws of the nation by peppering an appendix with legal terminology and citations. But Hart's aim was to establish the relationship between common and statutory law—between customary practices and the Saybrook Platform as a written constitution. He argued that consociational power was wholly grounded in and absolutely limited by the language of the Platform. Moreover, it was "a maxim in law and reason"

26. Clap, "Brief History . . . of Confessions of Faith."
27. Ibid.

that the words of an act that grants power be understood "in the most limited and restrained sense."[28]

Both sides in the Wallingford debate searched for the proper constitutional relationship between written law and local traditions. Clap's ally Noah Hobart responded to Hart: "To use the language of the *lawyers,* which these gentlemen seem very fond of, councils had this authority at *common law,* and the *statute* does not take it away." Hobart contended that custom loses its authority only when it contradicts particular legislation. Two laymen also published comments on these questions, one apologizing for publicly addressing the reverend gentlemen of the clergy, the other justifying publication by noting that the Wallingford affair "hath become a general, if not universal concern in the government; and not only affects the church, but also the state." On the interpretation of statutory language, the "Aged Layman" repeated the rule "that Grants of Power shall always be construed in the most limited and restrained, and not in the largest Sense, the Words will bear." The "Platformist" argued that meaning was ordinarily governed by general usage but added that those who lived at the time a law was written usually understood its true intent better than others. The "Platformist" also challenged Hobart on the distinction between custom and statute, arguing that in legal parlance "custom" meant a common practice originating in common consent, not a common practice founded on a prior statute. To be changed, the ecclesiastical constitution would have to be rewritten, not reinterpreted to be more in accord with practices existing prior to and outside it.[29]

28. William Hart, *A Few Remarks upon the Ordination of the Rev'd Mr. James Dana . . .* (New Haven, Conn., 1759), Appendix, vii, ix. "A *caveat* is only entered by one that claims the *avowson,*" Hart wrote; "'Tis a common thing also . . . in a *Quare impedit,* to get out a writ, called, *Ne admittas.*" Hart cites John Godolphin, *Repertorium Canonicum; or, An Abridgement of the Ecclesiastical Laws of This Realm, Consistent with the Temporal . . .* (London, 1678), William Nelson, *The Rights of the Clergy of England* (London, 1715), and Giles Jacob, *A New Law-Dictionary: Containing, the Interpretation and Definitions of Words and Terms Used in the Law . . .* (London, 1729). The quotation about restricted interpretation is in Hart, *Remarks on a Late Pamphlet Wrote by Mr. Hobart,* 18.

29. Noah Hobart, *The Principles of Congregational Churches, Relating to the Constitution and Authority of Ecclesiastical Councils . . .* (New Haven, Conn., 1759), 15, 17, 33. Hobart agreed that the questions were of vastly "great importance, as the *very being* of our ecclesiastical constitution depends on the resolution of them" ([3]). See also *A Letter to the Clergy of the Colony of Connecticut, from an Aged Layman of Said Colony* ([New York], 1760), 4, 19; *A Letter to a Friend, Occasioned by the Unhappy Controversy at Wallingford; by a Layman and Platformist* (New Haven, Conn., 1760), [2]. For the "Aged Layman," the primary question was how to secure a constitutional arrangement where the rights and powers of both clergy

These broad questions about constitutional interpretation were not resolved, of course, but the midcentury disputes did have one immediate practical result: they lengthened the list of Clap's enemies. From the time of Yale's orthodoxy resolutions in 1753 through the Noyes affair, the Wallingford Controversy, and the election of 1759, Clap's political adversaries increased and stepped up their efforts to break his stranglehold on the college. The General Assembly ignored anti-Clap petitions in 1753 and 1757. Even in 1759, only a fourth of the lower house supported a call for visitation, and in 1761 yet another complaint was set aside. In 1763, Clap was challenged again, and his lawyer tried to get the matter dropped on procedural grounds. But when it was clear that Yale's administration would have to offer some defense to the General Assembly, Clap rode to Hartford to speak for himself.[30]

COURTS, LAWYERS, AND LEGITIMACY

The court that received the Yale memorial and the lawyers who submitted it represented the past and the future of Connecticut's legal culture. The court system, burdened by a huge increase in litigation, had been built on the Puritan ideal of the godly magistrate, the patriarch of piety and broad legal wisdom who would pass laws and administer justice. The lawyers, answering an expanding economy's need for more legal expertise, were defining an emerging profession and a new social role for the colony's learned elite. That learned elite, however, was still being educated under Thomas Clap. Challenged for control of the college, Clap in turn challenged his opponents' legal expertise and the authority of the court system itself.[31]

The General Assembly that Clap addressed was both a legislature and a court. The 1662 charter had invested the governor and his council of twelve "assistants" (the upper house) with adjudicative power as an "ombudsman" court of highest authority, and it also served as the colony's highest court of appeal. The "deputies" (representatives of the lower house) shared in passing laws, but only gave their advice to the interpretation and application of those laws once they were on the books. The upper house delegated judicial author-

---

and laity were secured, in the way that the British constitution preserved both the crown's prerogative and the people's liberty.

30. See Tucker, *Puritan Protagonist*, 222–224.

31. According to Bruce Mann, in "Parishes, Law, and Community," 36, the number of cases coming before the New Haven County Court increased eightfold between 1710 and 1753, twice the rate of the population growth.

ity to lower courts that were staffed by judges appointed yearly by the whole Assembly.[32]

This system was under considerable strain by the third quarter of the eighteenth century. As one legal historian has remarked, although appeals from lower courts were strictly limited in 1762, "as late as 1770, the General Assembly still maintained its complete range of authority . . . exercis[ing] unlimited jurisdiction in all matters of adjudic[a]tion, original and on appeal, at law and in equity." A variety of grievances and petitions like the Yale memorial crowded the docket at the Assembly's biannual sessions. In 1774, the Assembly finally referred all equity cases to the superior court to lighten its own load and focus on legislative rather than judicial concerns.[33]

But governing and administering justice still fell to the same small pool of leading men. The legislative and judicial wisdom of the godly magistrate was being spread too thin, despite attempts made to limit appeals and prevent a single judge who was sitting on more than one court from hearing the same case twice. Benjamin Gale, who in 1782 would criticize this multiple office-holding and help spur legislation that took the first real steps toward an independent judiciary, had published similar remarks two decades before in an attack on Thomas Clap's administration of Yale College. Giving all the legislative authority to the same person who is also the principal executive authority is,

32. Everett C. Goodwin, *The Magistracy Rediscovered: Connecticut, 1636–1818* (Ann Arbor, Mich., 1981), 76. I have also relied on William K. Holdsworth, "Law and Society in Colonial Connecticut, 1636–1672" (Ph.D. diss., Claremont Graduate School, 1974). The best overview of the Connecticut court system can be found in John T. Farrell, "Introduction," in Farrell, ed., *The Superior Court Diary of William Samuel Johnson, 1772–1773* . . . (Washington, D.C., 1942), xi–lxv. The superior court was traditionally made up of the deputy governor as chief justice and four assistants. A county court justice and two justices of the quorum constituted each county court, which were also attended by representatives from each town called grandjurors. As Farrell writes, "A County Court resembled in form the General Assembly, the Justices corresponding to an upper house, the Grandjurors corresponding to a lower house," and, like the Assembly, they attended to a variety of judicial *and* administrative matters (xv). The court system was completed by the county probate courts and justices of the peace. Although justices of the peace were the bottom rung of the judicial ladder, their importance should not be minimized, as Jackson Turner Main has argued in *Society and Economy in Colonial Connecticut* (Princeton, N.J., 1985), 323, 329–330. One did not have to be an assistant to be appointed to this office, but 60–70 percent of eighteenth-century justices came from leading families (compared to 42 percent of the ministers, for example).

33. Goodwin, *Magistracy Rediscovered*, 53. Goodwin notes that, in 1770, the Assembly "enacted 15 laws and appointed 590 officers; but as a court of specific adjudication for contests it also acted on 164 cases of contest." On the 1774 act, see Farrell, "Introduction," in Farrell, ed., *Superior Court Diary of William Samuel Johnson,* xix.

Gale wrote in 1759, "a monstrous Absurdity in Politics." The 1763 memorial echoed Gale's complaint and remarked that Clap ended up acting as judge in cases of disobedience against himself as executive authority, and he ruled by laws he had created as the college legislator.[34]

Yet most of the men that Clap faced in 1763 probably still embraced an older ideal: legislation and adjudication were not powers to be kept separate in government; they were simply different activities of the godly magistrate, shaped alike by his broad experience and wisdom. The assemblymen in 1763 had been elected because they were recognized as leaders in their respective communities. Marked by private wealth, family connections, or superior learning, they had become deputies in the lower house or assistants in the upper house only after demonstrating their competence and earning the respect of their fellow townsmen at the local level. A general knowledge of basic legal principles and forms was one of the requirements for service in higher public office. Perhaps only 15 of the 136 men seated in the 1763 Assembly could be called "attorneys," but the law was something of a popular science for the litigious people of eighteenth-century Connecticut. Though not all practicing lawyers, more than 60 percent of the men in the 1763 Assembly had prior experience on the courts or were named to the bench in that year.[35]

34. [Benjamin Gale], *A Letter to a Member of the Lower House* (New Haven, Conn., 1759), 17. Dorr et al., Memorial on Yale College, 6e, echoes this argument. Goodwin, in *Magistracy Rediscovered*, 84, points to [Benjamin Gale], *Brief, Decent, but Free Remarks and Observations on Several Laws Passed by the Honorable Legislature of the State of Connecticut since the Year 1775* (Hartford, Conn., 1782). In that pamphlet, Gale urged that, instead of "loading some with so many places of honor, trust and authority, [that] they can hardly stagger under the weight of them," Connecticut should employ more men and keep the departments of government "separate and distinct" (31). An act was passed in 1784 that prevented members of the General Assembly from sitting on the superior court.

35. Jackson Turner Main, in *Society and Economy in Colonial Connecticut*, 325, and chap. 9, argued that colonial Connecticut's leadership was not dominated by a small number of wealthy families in a static "Standing Order." Closer to Jefferson's vision of a natural aristocracy, 27 percent of the wealthy men in the eighteenth century had self-made fortunes, and at any given time two of five leaders did not belong to important families. Town studies, however, offer evidence of both democratic participation and officeholding by a relatively small elite. See, for example, William F. Willingham, "Deference Democracy and Town Government in Windham, Connecticut, 1755 to 1786," *WMQ*, 3d Ser., XXX (1973), 401–422. On the problem of "deference" in the election of local elites, see Joy B. Gilsdorf and Robert R. Gilsdorf, "Elites and Electorates: Some Plain Truths for Historians of Colonial America," in David D. Hall, John M. Murrin, and Thad W. Tate, eds., *Saints and Revolutionaries: Essays on Early American History* (New York, 1984), 207–244. On the law as a "popular science," see John T. Farrell, "The Administration of Justice in Connecticut about the Middle of the Eighteenth Century" (Ph.D. diss., Yale University, 1937), 153. The judicial experience of the

The men who appeared at the pre-Revolutionary Connecticut bar were a mixed lot. The Puritans of the previous century had been deeply suspicious of lawyers, and the corruptions of the English courts were among the abominations they fled when they emigrated to the New World. "Attorneys in fact"— that is, anyone granted the power of attorney or officially appearing for another in court—were common in Connecticut by the 1660s, but the legal profession would take shape only gradually in the decades before 1776. Traditionally, legal practice had been combined with other occupations. Samuel Darling, father of one of Clap's antagonists, had been a cordwainer when he took the attorney's oath in 1737. Ambrose Whittlesey operated the Saybrook Ferry when he was not arguing a neighbor's case in court. Joseph Adams, who got a degree from Yale in 1740, was a lawyer and innkeeper in New Haven; Peletiah Mills, lacking a degree, held the same two occupations in Windsor. Roger Sherman had been a cobbler, a surveyor, and a merchant as well as a lawyer by the time he moved to New Haven in 1761.[36]

The English distinctions between barristers, who pleaded cases, and attorneys or solicitors, who did other kinds of legal work but might not have had much formal education, never developed in Connecticut. Massachusetts governor Thomas Hutchinson introduced the barrister-solicitor division to that colony in 1762, along with trappings of the English legal profession like robes and wigs. But Connecticut's only legislative effort to limit and in effect professionalize the practice of law was an act passed in 1730 restricting the number of attorneys to eleven. With the repeal of that act in 1731, nothing stood between a man's desire to be a lawyer and his becoming one, other than the ability to draw formal writs and pleas, a simple oath at court, and a client willing to pay his fee.[37]

1763 assemblymen is based on my survey of records in the Conn. Arch., "Civil Officers," 2d Ser., I, Conn. St. Libr.

36. Holdsworth, "Law and Society," 477; Chroust, *Rise of the Legal Profession*, I, *Colonial Experience*, 121–125; Farrell, "The Administration of Justice in Connecticut," 169–194; Farrell, "Introduction," in Farrell, ed., *Superior Court Diary of William Samuel Johnson*, liv–lxiv. It should be noted that Roger Sherman temporarily retired from practice when he moved to New Haven to devote his energies to his expanding business concerns.

37. On changes in Massachusetts, see John M. Murrin, "Anglicizing an American Colony: The Transformation of Provincial Massachusetts" (Ph.D. diss., Yale University, 1966), 231–236. See Trumbull and Hoadly, eds., *The Public Records of the Colony of Connecticut*, for attorneys being recognized as officers of the court in 1708 (V, 48), the 1730 rule limiting the number of lawyers (VII, 279), the repeal of the previous act in 1731 (VII, 358), the passing of an act forbidding sheriffs and deputies from filing writs or giving legal advice (VIII, 458–459). See also Richard B. Morris, "Legalism versus Revolutionary Doctrine in New England," *New England Quarterly*, IV (1931), 199.

Some of Connecticut's citizens recognized the colony's important and influential attorneys even if its legal institutions did not. A committee considering taxes on "posts of honour or profit" for the General Assembly singled out twelve lawyers in 1756 for a ten-pound tax, while suggesting that "Every other sworn Attorney" pay five pounds. But if "an element of professional exclusiveness to the practice of law" becomes discernible by the 1750s, this list still reflects quite a range between men who practiced law as one of many activities and attorneys who devoted most of their energies to legal study and practice. Jedidiah Elderkin, for example, was a wealthy Norwich silk merchant and a busy lawyer who died with only about a dozen legal volumes in his library, whereas Matthew Griswold had more than two hundred and was known as "a good reader of law." [38]

Before 1750, it was not uncommon for a minister, as one of the few learned men in a small town, to help his neighbors in suits at court. Two names on the 1756 list, however, represent a new breed of professional attorney: Jared Ingersoll and William Samuel Johnson—the same two men who presented the memorialists' case against Clap in 1763. Historians have given the title "Father of the Connecticut Bar" to each of them. Both devoted themselves to studying and practicing law, building large libraries, cultivating New York clients, and gaining intercolonial reputations. Johnson, who graduated from Yale in 1744, was the son of Anglican clergyman Samuel Johnson, who had skirmished with Clap over college ecclesiastical policy in 1754. William Johnson studied in New York under Judge William Smith and began practice in Stratford in 1748. His political rise to national prominence had not yet begun in 1763, but by that time he had a thriving practice and the means to place a single order with a London bookseller for forty-four volumes or volume sets. [39]

Jared Ingersoll had graduated under Clap in 1742 and stayed on another year as a Berkeley scholar to pursue his legal studies. The future stamp commissioner was appointed king's attorney for New Haven County in 1751 and the colony's agent to London from 1758 to 1761. While in England, Ingersoll spent his spare time listening to William Pitt's speeches in the House of Commons,

38. Conn. Arch., 1756, "Finance and Currency," 1st Ser., IV, Conn. St. Libr., 104b (this document is also printed in Farrell, "The Administration of Justice in Connecticut," 208–209); Farrell, "The Administration of Justice in Connecticut," 161, 176, 178.

39. Farrell, "The Administration of Justice in Connecticut," 184. Johnson would go on to serve in the colony's upper house in 1766, as colonial agent to London in 1770, and as a superior court justice in 1772. He received an honorary doctorate from Oxford in 1776. A reluctant whig during the Revolution, he nevertheless would achieve prominence as a delegate to the Constitutional Convention and as a United States senator. He also served as president of Columbia College.

observing the advocates in the common law and chancery courts, and angling for a nomination to a proposed vice admiralty court for Connecticut. His friend Johnson wrote to him about the Wallingford Controversy and sent along some pamphlets. Ingersoll was thoroughly disgusted. "You think it a pity I am not at home at this time to gain an intimate Acquaintance with the Ecclesiastical Constitution of my Country, the deep mysteries of which you seem to suppose I am not altogether Master of," he wrote. But he preferred London, where people had better manners than to bother their neighbors about such things. In any case, he considered all the noise about the ecclesiastical constitution "but meer pretext to Cover, what is really at bottom, pride, Envy, malice, insatiable thirst after dominion[,] Superiority and the like." It is likely that Ingersoll, a member of Noyes's church in New Haven and a strong supporter of its pastor, had Thomas Clap in mind.[40]

Benjamin Gale, the author of five anti-Clap pamphlets between 1755 and 1760, was delighted to hear that Ingersoll was joining his crusade in the summer of 1762. "I began the controversy when it was disreputable to oppose one esteemed a man of God," Gale wrote to Ingersoll. "I was alone," he recalled, because others were too intimidated to speak out. Gale's aim all along, he explained, had been "to convince the World that the President was an Assuming, Arbitrary, Designing Man, who under a Cloak of Zeal for Orthodoxy, Designed to govern Church and state and Damn all who would not worship the Beast." Gale thought he had succeeded. "If You now Undertake the Cause, You will engage at a time when it is reputable, and I wish you good success."[41]

Certainly the time was ripe to challenge Clap's characterization of Yale as a Congregational seminary. Only 28 percent of Yale graduates under Clap (1741–1765) became Congregational clergymen: including those who took orders in the Church of England, 280 of about 700 Yale graduates entered the ministry, whereas 79 became physicians, and 75 became lawyers. Yale would not start producing more attorneys than clergymen until after the Revolution, but the number who opted for the bar rather than the pulpit was rising. One study

40. Jared Ingersoll to William Samuel Johnson, [1760], Johnson Family Papers, Conn. Hist. Soc. The standard work on Ingersoll remains Lawrence Henry Gipson's *Jared Ingersoll: A Study of American Loyalism in Relation to British Colonial Government* (New Haven, Conn., 1920). A "Berkeley scholar" was a promising student who pursued his studies at Yale after completing his bachelor's degree; the fellowship was established by a gift from Bishop George Berkeley in 1733 (Brooks Mather Kelly, *Yale: A History* [New Haven, Conn., 1974], 39, 180).

41. Benjamin Gale to Jared Ingersoll, Aug. 9, 1762, MSS #68, Ingersoll Family Collection, the Whitney Library of the New Haven Colony Historical Society, New Haven, Conn. Gale had conferred privately with Ingersoll when he launched his attack in 1755. See Gale to Ingersoll, June 13, 1755, Ingersoll Family Collection.

notes that "beginning with the class of 1748, the number of [Yale and Harvard] graduates who entered the law increased with each three-year period through 1765." Yale alone produced 25 young men who entered the legal profession between 1760 and 1765. Physician Benjamin Gale was not thrilled with the rising number of lawyers either, but it helped prove his point that Yale was, not Clap's *"Monastery,"* but a collegiate school of arts and sciences preparing young men for different professions and broad public service.[42]

To press the issue about the nature of Yale's charter at the very moment when the Susquehanna land controversy was coming to a climax, however, might have been unwise, since both issues could draw unwanted royal attention to the colony's precious "chartered privileges." The Susquehanna Company began with a 1755 memorial to the General Assembly that exploited the sea-to-sea clause in the 1662 charter in order to claim a seventy-mile strip of Pennsylvania for Connecticut. In 1761, Jared Ingersoll had warned the company that his majesty's attorneys considered this a dubious claim; it was based on vague language in an ancient charter drawn up in geographical ignorance. By the spring of 1763, with more than one hundred families ready to start an initial settlement and many more willing to follow, the colony got word of the king's opposition to the plan. Since many of the assemblymen were shareholders, the company held a meeting concurrent with the legislature's May session, where they decided to send an agent to London to press the claim. At the Assembly meeting itself, four Iroquois spokesmen appeared and pre-

---

42. [Gale], *A Reply to . . . the Friend in the West,* contends that Clap's definition of a college is more suited to a monastery (40). See Franklin Bowditch Dexter, *Biographical Sketches of the Graduates of Yale College with the Annals of the College History,* 6 vols. (New York, 1885–1912). Statistics concerning occupation can be found in the back of each volume. Nearly half of the 472 Yale graduates from 1705 to the new charter in 1745 had chosen the ministry, whereas only 30 turned to medicine and 33 to law. For discussions of these figures, see Dexter, "The Founding of Yale College," New Haven Colony Historical Society, *Papers,* III (New Haven, Conn., 1882); and Tucker, *Puritan Protagonist,* 266; Goodwin, *Magistracy Rediscovered,* 67–71. Between 1778 and 1792, Yale graduated 168 men who became lawyers, 129 who chose the ministry, and 57 who became doctors. See Dexter, *Biographical Sketches,* IV, 744; and Goodwin, *Magistracy Rediscovered,* 71–73. The quotation about Yale and Harvard graduates is from John M. Murrin, "The Legal Transformation: The Bench and Bar of Eighteenth-Century Massachusetts," in Stanley N. Katz and John M. Murrin, eds., *Colonial America: Essays in Politics and Social Development,* 3d ed. (New York, 1983), 554. Benjamin Gale complained about "the Multiplicity of Law-Suits in this Government, and Strange Litigious Disposition of its Inhabitants" in *The Present State of the Colony of Connecticut Considered* ([New London, Conn.], 1755), 3. He opposed Clap's "monastery" with his more secular vision of a liberal arts college in all his writings, but especially in *A Reply to . . . the Friend in the West.*

sented formal complaints, and Governor Thomas Fitch, who had vacillated previously, assured them that Connecticut now joined the king in opposition to the settlement.[43]

The Yale controversy was certainly overshadowed by this dispute, but it was not unconnected to it. Benjamin Gale, who like Clap tended to lump his enemies together as a single conspiratorial faction, saw clear links between Clap's orthodoxy campaign and the eastern Connecticut radicalism that over the years had produced paper money schemes, religious separatism, and the land-hungry Susquehanna Company. But Clap himself seems to have viewed the Susquehanna dispute less as an opportunity for coalition building than as a potential crisis in legal and political legitimacy that he could exploit for his own purposes. Yale's charter rested on Connecticut's, a document that the Susquehanna Company had read so carefully and that the antiexpansionists feared would be lost if the king got tired of the tiny colony's swaggering like an independent republic. Yale's identity did not depend upon a charter, Clap had tried to prove, but Connecticut's did: "If ever there should be some Change of Government, in the Plantations in North America," Clap told the Assembly, "the Essential Constitution and Privileges of [the] College, *at least,* would still continue." He said that of course he wished for no such change, but he had considered telling the Hartford legislators, just to twist the knife, that "the principal Seat of the Government over New England" would probably be in New York or Boston.[44]

Clap's opponents had claimed that the legislature had the right to visit and correct abuses at the college and that students had a right to appeal the president's decisions to the legislature, but Clap turned both issues against them. "Do not encourage the students to appeal from my jurisdiction to the governor and council," Clap seemed to threaten, "lest you suggest that I appeal the colony's court decision to king and parliament." "Order a visitation of the college by the assembly and you open the door to visitors from England appear-

43. Edith Anna Bailey, "The Susquehanna Company: First Period," in *Influences toward Radicalism in Connecticut, 1754–1775, Smith College Studies in History,* V (1920), 191–207; Julian P. Boyd, "Introduction," in Boyd, ed., *The Susquehannah Company Papers,* 4 vols. (Wilkes-Barre, Pa., 1930–1933), I, ix–lxxxix; Boyd, *The Susquehanna Company: Connecticut's Experiment in Expansion,* Tercentenary Commission of the State of Connecticut, Committe on Historical Publications, no. 34 (New Haven, Conn., 1935); Richard L. Bushman, *From Puritan to Yankee: Character and the Social Order in Connecticut, 1690–1765* (Cambridge, Mass., 1967), 256–258.

44. Benjamin Gale to Jared Ingersoll, January 1765 [error for 1766], N.H. Col. Hist. Soc., *Papers,* IX (1918), 372; Thomas Clap, "Answer of the President," 71t–u. The quoted phrase about government's being moved to New York or Boston is crossed out in the manuscript.

ing in Connecticut 'with full power in themselves to redress everything in our laws or courts which they might esteem to be abuses.'"[45]

LEGAL ARGUMENT AND RELIGIOUS DESIGN

Clap had developed a common law defense that protected the rights and powers of a local community against both state interference from the outside and demands for broader individual rights within. He presented his argument with the style of a well-read lawyer who had mastered the archive of primary documents and commanded a catalog of legal precedent. His authoritative style masked important inaccuracies, misrepresentations, and deceptions and carried him to victory. Clap had become, however, the hypothetical New Haven judge that William Hart had glimpsed in his looking glass: he had interpreted documents and declared his sense of the law in writing and then tried to substitute his exposition for the law itself.

Representing the memorialists in 1763, Jared Ingersoll charged that the president and fellows of Yale College had "made and published Sundry Laws, Books and ordinances requiring obedience thereto, which . . . are inconsistent with and an infringement of, the natural rights of Englishmen." In particular, the petition he submitted called attention to the college law that prevented a student from prosecuting a suit in a common law court against any other student or officer of the college before the president and fellows could deal with the matter. Another objectionable law seemed to make it a criminal offense "for any Scholar in any Part of the Colony or Elsewhere to attend any Divine worship not approved of by the President." The memorialists also questioned some irregular taxes imposed on students to fund college construction projects and complained that in disciplinary cases Clap acted as legislator, executor, and judge, and students were prevented from defending themselves or appealing his decisions.[46]

Clap's response to the General Assembly pointed out mistakes and misrepresentations made in the memorial and then picked apart the complaints piece by piece. On the matter of disciplinary cases and the students' recourse to the law courts, Clap claimed that his scholars *did* get a chance to speak for themselves and wondered whether the memorialists would rather call in the king's

45. The paraphrase of Clap is in Jurgen Herbst, "From Religion to Politics: Debates and Confrontations over American College Governance in the Mid-Eighteenth Century," *Harvard Educational Review,* XLVI (1976), 419–420.

46. Dorr et al., Memorial on Yale College, 66c–d. The petition seems to be in Ingersoll's handwriting rather than Johnson's.

attorney to draw up indictments and defense lawyers to plead for every campus infraction. Concerning the "building tax," Clap acknowledged that money collected from student fines was put toward completing the new college chapel. But the only *tax* levied for campus construction, he explained, was the occasional three or four shillings to replace an outhouse that had become "rotten" or "unfit for use." Whether this college custom was *"an Infraction upon the Privileges of Englishmen,"* Clap noted sarcastically, hardly seemed an important question for "the wise Determination of this Honourable Assembly."[47]

But the more fundamental issue raised by the memorial, and the one that both houses of the Assembly voted upon, concerned the legal relationship between the college, the colony, and Connecticut's churches. The memorial's list of grievances presupposed that the colony's legislature, acting for the public, had founded the college in 1701 "for the Instruction of youth . . . for publick service in Church and state." Yale had been given a new charter in 1745, but the public—meaning the legislature—retained the sole right of visitation to reform abuses.[48]

Clap's reply summed up the case he had been trying to make since 1754. First, he claimed that the handful of Congregational ministers who had donated books for a collegiate school sometime before 1701 were legally Yale's founders. Second, citing Coke's *Reports,* Thomas Wood's *Institute of the Laws of England,* and Bishop Edward Stillingfleet's *Discourse* in the House of Lords, he argued that, under English common law, the founders of eleemosynary corporations alone had the right of visitation. Third, he asserted that the founders had originally designed, and thus Yale must continue to be, an institution for training orthodox Calvinist ministers. He closed his remarks to the General Assembly in 1763 by charging that both the recent campus unrest and the memorial's veiled attack on Yale's ecclesiastical identity arose from pernicious factions in the colony who were bent on destroying true religion.[49]

Clap had been stressing the founder's design to train an orthodox ministry since he withdrew his students from New Haven's First Church and drafted the orthodoxy act for the Yale Corporation in the fall of 1753. But King's College president Samuel Johnson's complaints in the winter of 1753–1754 about how the new religious policy infringed upon the rights of Yale Anglicans probably pushed Clap toward the explicitly *legal* defense he would develop—and

47. Clap, "Answer of the President," 71r.

48. Dorr et al., Memorial on Yale College, 66a–b.

49. Clap, "Answer of the President," 71c, 71g. Clap cited Sir Edward Coke, *The Reports of Sir Edward Coke . . .* (1600–1615), 2d ed. (London, 1677); Thomas Wood, *An Institute of the Laws of England* (London, 1720); Edward Stillingfleet, *A Discourse concerning the Power of Excommunication in a Christian Church . . .* (London, 1662).

THE

Eccleſiaſtical Conſtitution

O F

COLLEGES.

THE original End, and Deſign of Colleges was to Inſtruct, Educate, and Train up Perſons for the Work of the Miniſtry. The Council of Cabilone, A. D. 813. Decreed, *That the Biſhops ſhould Conſtitute Schools, or* Colleges, *in which the Doctrines of Scripture ſhould be taught, and ſuch may be Educated, of whom it may be deſervedly ſaid, by the Lord,* Ye are the Salt of the Earth ; *and who may teach the People, &c.* Harduini Collectio Conciliorum, Vol. 4. P. 1032. A Houſe with the Appendages, in which Students live, and ſtudy, under the Inſtruction and Government of a Preſident, *&c.* is called a *College.* And if ſuch a Political State is formed, or even deſigned to be formed, it is called a *College in Reputation,*

A 2

fabricate—in the coming years. "Ought not the Catholic Design of the princi-pal Benefactors," Johnson argued, referring to Anglican donors like Bishop George Berkeley, "also in strict justice to be regarded, who in the sense of En-glish Law, are to be reckoned among the Founders?" Johnson also threatened to take his complaint to "the Government at Home," which, he said, would not waste time repealing Clap's law: "They would declare it a nullity in itself; and not only so, but even the [Yale] Corporation that hath enacted it; inasmuch as it seems a Principle in Law *that a Corporation* [Connecticut] *cannot make a Corporation,* nor can one be made without his Majesties Act."[50]

A comparison between a manuscript treatment of the ecclesiastical consti-tution of colleges that Clap wrote sometime in 1754 and his public arguments in 1754 and 1763 shows how his legalistic defense might have developed. Clap began the 1754 manuscript with an extended etymological argument. The word *college,* he wrote, "in the usual and appropriate sense . . . signifies a Company of ministers united for the Education of ministers." The word could be applied by analogy to other companies of men, but it needed some modifier, as in "the college of physicians." He then cited Old Testament examples of "Schools of Prophets" and argued that the "essence" of the Christian college was embod-ied by Christ and the twelve apostles. But his central argument in the unpub-lished manuscript rested on precedents found in ecclesiastical history. The churches created colleges, he insisted, citing a ninth-century decree; civil au-thorities began conveying charters four or five hundred years later merely as a convenience. Civil charters always take for granted "the original Nature and Constitution of a College."[51]

50. Samuel Johnson to Thomas Clap, Feb. 15, 1754, Clap Presidential Papers, YRG 2-A-5. Johnson instructed Clap to "see *Viner* on the Title, *Founders,*" and "under *Titles, Corpora-tion,* and *By Laws.*"

51. Thomas Clap, "The Antient Ecclesiastical Constitution of Colleges," MS (ca. 1753–1757), 3, 14, Beinecke Library. Franklin Bowditch Dexter wrote that this was written "after 1753" and before a second draft, "The Ecclesiastical Constitution of Colleges under the Jew-ish and Christian Dispensations," MS, 1757, Beinecke Library. See Dexter, "Thomas Clap and His Writings," N.H. Col. Hist. Soc., *Papers,* V (1894), 273. But paragraph 12 of the ear-lier MS cites two books that Dexter shows Clap did not have until March 1754 (259n). Gale's 1755 attack on Clap's canon law argument suggests that this manuscript was not written af-ter 1755. That it was copied over in 1757, with a long section on the college of Alexandria that describes the religious asceticism of collegiate life, may indicate that Clap now intended it for internal use at the college. I cannot with any certainty declare that the earlier "Ecclesias-tical Constitution" MS preceded the more legalistic *Religious Constitution of Colleges, Espe-cially of Yale-College in New-Haven in the Colony of Connecticut* (New London, Conn., 1754). But, since it deals with Clap's earlier problem (establishing the college's independence from

The strength of Clap's 1754 published argument, however, rested on common law, not etymology or ecclesiastical history, and references to Scripture were outnumbered by citations of Giles Jacob's *Law Dictionary* and Wood's *Institute of the Laws of England*. Clap's 1763 defense before the General Assembly was an even bolder stand upon common law, perhaps because Clap's opponents had effectively attacked him on other grounds. Benjamin Gale had countered the abbreviated, published version of Clap's etymological argument with definitions of his own and reminded Clap "that Time and Custom, alters the Meaning of Words." Gale also challenged Clap's use of ecclesiastical history. Clap relied on canon law, Gale charged, which was taken "chiefly [from] popish Councils, and Decrees of Popes, [and] is of but little Authority in a Protestant country. . . . The Force of Canon Law, then, will not make a College an Ecclesiastical Body, if the common Law does not." In 1763, Clap challenged all comers, even the formidable legal minds of Ingersoll and Johnson, to argue on the basis of common law. "We stand ready to dispute," he told the Assembly, and presented his case.[52]

Clap's praise of common law was genuine: "The Courts of Common law have been alwaies . . . among the greatest Bulwarks of the english Liberties," he wrote in 1764. He had made the memorialist's lofty appeals to the rights of Englishmen look ridiculous with his comment about the outhouse, but in this 1764 argument with students he attacked a vague natural rights argument with the principles of common law jurisprudence. He denied that students had a "natural right" of appeal, that is, a right "antecedent to positive laws and Constitution" rather than "subsequent to the laws of the Community." It was true that the general rules for any polity were drawn from common sense and the experience of the multitude. But particular rules were refined over time in a course of judgments by wise and disinterested men. "It is this which gives the civil Courts especially the King's bench such a full and almost absolute authority over the nation," he argued. The nation did not depend "upon the Wisdom and Justice of these 3 or four men personally considered but upon the Wisdom and Justice of the law by which they are bound."[53]

---

the churches) and devotes little attention to the problem beginning to take shape in 1754 (the relationship between the college and the civil government), its earlier composition is likely. We may simply have two arguments, written about the same time, addressing the two different aspects of Yale's independence. If so, it is still significant that the more legalistic argument was the one that shaped public debate.

52. Clap, *Religious Constitution of Colleges;* [Gale], *Reply to . . . the Friend in the West,* 43; Clap, "Answer of the President," 71c.

53. Thomas Clap, MS draft of a letter on the right of appeal of students in the college, Feb. 2, 1764, Clap Presidential Papers, YRG 2-A-5.

Clap at Yale would resist legislative intrusion just as Lord Coke had resisted royal prerogative and American whigs would soon resist the long arm of parliamentary sovereignty. His vision of the law also opposed, however, the more radical American perception of the law that elevated the role of juries and the common sense of common men. Deciding important legal questions went beyond stomping one's foot and shouting about the rights of Englishmen. To pass judgment without researching similar cases, Clap wrote, smacks too much of "self-sufficiency." Clap the moral philosopher dismissed postulates about a common "moral sense" because they were inconsistent with natural depravity; Clap the college president opposed any legal epistemology that denied the central place of godly learning.[54]

Common law jurisprudence also fitted Clap's pose of rhetorical authority. As the man who had constant access to Yale's library and cataloged its holdings, he was able to portray himself as the master of the archive. Not only were writers who opposed him cast as scribblers ignorant of the facts and unable to frame legal arguments to organize those facts, but they also could not do the research required to give the discussion historical context. As his former tutors knew, Clap seldom read a book from cover to cover but could pore over fifty volumes researching a particular subject, and he used his citations to good effect. Since the debate was "a Matter of the utmost Consequence to the Religion of Colleges, upon which the Religion of whole Countries very much depends," he wrote in 1755, "I have set myself with the utmost Diligence to enquire into it; and have read all the Authors I could any ways procure upon that Subject." Again, in 1764, he suggested that if his opponent could "hint at any principles in the law of nature and nations which are contrary to those which I have laid down I will search all authors to find them."[55]

Clap's arguments might have won the day in 1763, but they hardly settled questions once and for all, as he had claimed. Only three months after campus protests finally forced his resignation in the summer of 1766, the Assembly asserted its supervisory role, and Benjamin Gale claimed victory. The legend of Clap's triumph, however, would have a longer life. Digging beneath the legend, modern scholars have concluded that "Thomas Clap infused disastrous illu-

54. Ibid. Perhaps Clap, the staunch Calvinist, thought that once again he had caught the scent of pernicious Arminianism. On the radical American perception of the law, see Stimson, *The American Revolution in the Law*.

55. On Clap's research methods, see Ezra Stiles to Chauncey Whittelsey, Jan. 20, 1767, Yale Miscellaneous Manuscripts, Manuscripts and Archives, Yale University Library; [Thomas Clap], *The Answer of the Friend in the West, to a Letter from a Gentleman in the East, Entitled, The Present State of the Colony of Connecticut Considered* (New Haven, Conn., 1755), 8; Clap, letter on the right of appeal, Clap Presidential Papers, YRG 2-A-5.

sions into the study of American Academic government." While invoking a "tradition" and defending Yale as an independent religious institution, Clap was actually redefining the college and breaking from a model of Protestant academic government in place since the Reformation. Connecticut's "collegiate school" had in fact been established as a quasi-public, provincial institution for training leaders in both church and state, not as an autonomous religious seminary. Clap's "reaffirmation" of Yale's independence from the state and its place as a "superior ecclesiastical society" was an innovation.[56]

Other studies have been even more unforgiving of Thomas Clap, historian. Even though Samuel Whittelsey Dana's 1784 tract had effectively challenged the old president's account, Clap's *Annals of Yale College* (1766) had been the received text for Yale historians until investigations late in the nineteenth century began untangling the strands of fact, biased opinion, and falsification. Clap's case rested on his contention that Yale College had been founded by ten ministers who symbolically donated books in Branford sometime before the General Assembly passed its "Act for Liberty to Erect a Collegiate School" in October 1701. A painstaking modern study demonstrates conclusively that Clap "had radically changed his successive stories [about the founding] over the years 1745–66, had knowingly predated some events, had perhaps invented others, in any case had quoted himself without saying so, had inserted his own

56. The quotation about Clap's "disastrous illusions" is in W. H. Cowley, "Thomas Clap and the Founding of Yale," typescript, [1971], 39, Manuscripts and Archives, Yale University Library. This paragraph relies upon Jurgen Herbst, *From Crisis to Crisis: American College Government, 1636–1819* (Cambridge, Mass., 1982), 1–4, 38–47, 64, 66–81, 114–122; and Richard Warch, *School of the Prophets: Yale College, 1701–1740* (New Haven, Conn., 1973). When the idea for a collegiate school was proposed in the late seventeenth century, legal advice was divided. Wethersfield lawyer and physician Gershom Bulkley, citing several acts and statutes of Parliament, argued that an application for a charter had to be directed to the king and Parliament. Others pointed to *Calvin's Case* of 1608, which distinguished between the "realm of England" and the "dominions of the King" and ruled that, in the dominions, acts and statutes like the ones Bulkley cited were not in force unless specifically named or locally adopted (Herbst, *From Crisis to Crisis,* 39). Opinions were divided again during the 1717 controversy over the permanent location of the college. Clap fought for colonial incorporation in 1745, and the charter he helped to draft stated that a supervisory role for the General Assembly came along with its gracious legitimizing act and continued financial support. But in 1763, Clap "reminded his listeners that their status was uncertain" (Herbst, *From Crisis to Crisis,* 119). The relationship between Yale and the legislature would again inflame debate in the next decade, and the struggle over the college's government would continue intermittently until a new charter in 1792 gave seats on the Yale Corporation to the governor, lieutenant governor, and six members of the Council. Yet, the legend of Clap's triumph lived on. George Wilson Pierson, in *The Founding of Yale: The Legend of the Forty Folios* (New Haven, Conn., 1988), discusses the legend in meticulous detail.

prejudicial words in public documents, and had quoted the charters of 1701 and 1745 in ways to misrepresent what they actually said." Dana in the eighteenth century realized that Clap's dates for the founding were remarkably inconsistent; later research has shown how Clap was "progressively doctoring his documents" between 1747, when he wrote a manuscript history of Yale, and 1766, when he published his *Annals*. Clap moved back the book donation from 1702 to 1699 and changed its significance. What had been a series of acts symbolizing the beginnings of a library for a college that did not yet exist became for Clap a dramatic occasion that legally founded the college.[57]

Clap's casuistry, which has proved so vexatious for modern historians, was rooted in his conceptions of himself as legislator-founder and common law judge. Central to both roles was the need to interpret and perpetuate the founders' design. "Design" is a term that appears again and again in Clap's writings, sometimes nearly synonymous with "motive," a general impulse that prompts a person to act, and at other times closer to a more explicit and specific "plan" or "scheme" for carrying out a person's intentions. In brief, Clap took his forefathers' general design (motive) to propagate the faith and twisted it into explicit support for his design (plan or model) of Yale as an independent religious seminary.[58]

Clap saw himself as one who was perpetuating the design of New England's

---

57. Pierson, *The Founding of Yale*, 140. [Dana], *Yale-College Subject to the General Assembly*, pointed to the dating problem (38n). Herbst in *From Crisis to Crisis* and, especially, Cowley in "Thomas Clap" had already exposed most of the problems with Clap's historical argument. Pierson "reluctantly" had to agree with them: "Consciously or unconsciously, Clap repeatedly altered the documents and changed his tune to suit his own needs. His deviations from strict honesty began earlier, came more often, and went further than perhaps even his severest critics have realized" (118). Clap's 1747 manuscript history of Yale puts the Branford donation in 1702, and in 1752 Clap seems to have authorized tutor Ezra Stiles to commemorate Yale's fiftieth anniversary. His *Religious Constitution of Colleges* moved the donation to November 1701, still a month *after* the legislature's act. In 1755, Clap's *Answer of the Friend in the West* (New Haven, 1755), 15, asserted that the ten ministers "were a Company or Society by Compact, a Year or two before they had a Charter" (1699–1700). Pierson agrees with Herbst that Clap "changed history" with this pamphlet. Clap's "decisive" statement would be in the 1763 defense, when the donation is described as a pre-1701 ceremonial act of founding. Cowley dismissed the book donation as Yale's "Donation of Constantine." Pierson pieces together evidence from a variety of sources and concludes that there were several donations of books for a collegiate school in New Haven between 1656 and 1702 that Clap, and subsequent Yale lore, "telescoped" into one dramatic event. See Cowley, "Thomas Clap," 32; and Pierson, *The Founding of Yale*, 251.

58. In the rest of this section, I draw widely from Clap's brief and scattered comments on law, history, and moral philosophy and make an admittedly speculative attempt to interpret the design of Clap's words and actions.

"first Planters." Their original motive, he argued, had been to maintain the purity of doctrine, discipline, and worship and to transmit it to their posterity. In order to maintain purity, they established it by law, most recently and soundly in the Saybrook Platform of 1708. In order to transmit pure religion to posterity, they instituted the means of propagating it by establishing colleges and schools. Just as the Platform's framers in 1708 had continued to build the colony's seventeenth-century religious foundation, and in that sense became founding fathers along with the original colonists, Clap too continued or completed the act of founding. He had maintained pure religion by drafting Yale's 1745 charter and 1753 orthodoxy bylaws. He ensured that orthodoxy would be passed to the next generation by more securely establishing religious instruction at Yale College, the school of the prophets. As Samuel Whittelsey Dana wrote sarcastically in 1784: "The first founders live on in their successors. What a pretty immortality is here! the founders live by succession, always bearing about with them a godly and worthy *will*, that is ever to be religiously executed." [59]

Legislation had been passed and the college church established, but, before 1763, "mature judgment" had not been rendered to settle continuing disputes. Clap was determined to get a decision, either from Connecticut's highest court or from a British chancery court, that supported his interpretation of the point of law concerning eleemosynary corporations and the legal fact of Yale's founding. Again, Clap's own judgment rested on his interpretation of the book donors' design.

He argued that the donors' design to supply the churches with orthodox ministers was evident from their words and actions, just as he had argued in 1745 that George Whitefield's design to destroy New England's ministry had been evident from his. Actions are not truly virtuous or vicious based on how they measure up to ethical rules and laws, Clap wrote in his moral philosophy textbook, but based on the inner motive they proceed from. Of course, he wrote elsewhere, "a Man's Intention can never be directly and absolutely proved, yet his Words or Actions may carry with them such a *strong Presumption* as may prove his Intention in the Law." If an angry man shoots at another man and kills him, "the Law in that Case presumes *Malice,* and that he *design'd* to murder him." The defendant's plea that he was only trying to scare the victim "would signify nothing." Clap had not presumed to read Whitefield's mind but had argued that Whitefield's anticlerical sermons and itinerant preaching would prove malicious intention in a law court despite the itinerant's denials.

59. [Dana], *Yale-College Subject to the General Assembly,* 24.

Clap went even further: he had charged that Whitefield's obvious design was not just to cast opprobrium upon the standing ministry but to replace New England ministers with his own disciples. Similarly, Clap tried to show that the book donation was a ceremony of words and actions that carried with it an "Intention in the Law" not just to promote religion but to do so with a particular "formal Scheme of a College" in mind.[60]

Challenged by Samuel Johnson in 1754 and Benjamin Gale in 1755, Clap had sought a founding that preceded the Assembly's 1701 act, but his problem was that donating books, unlike firing a gun at a man or, to use another of Clap's examples, waving a white flag in battle, was not an instituted sign—it did not, at least, have the legal meaning that he claimed for it. So he embellished the event, misrepresented its immediate purpose, and twisted the language of public documents for his own designs.

How did he carry the day? The question has puzzled modern historians. One suggested that "his audience could not individually have read all of Yale's charters or enabling acts" and perhaps "that counsel for the prosecution, however eminent and able, had not done their homework." Indeed, Clap might have been historically inaccurate, legally unscrupulous, and morally dishonest, but he was rhetorically effective. Clap's success did not puzzle his student Benjamin Trumbull, who wrote that Clap had shown himself to be a learned man whose legal expertise and reasoning was superior to that of the finest attorneys in the colony. As a later commentator wrote, Clap had "grounded himself upon English authorities, in the true style of a well-read lawyer." Perhaps neither Clap nor Gale truly won the public debate of May 1763, but the style of a well-read lawyer did.[61]

60. Thomas Clap, *An Essay on the Nature and Foundation of Moral Virtue and Obligation*... (New Haven, Conn., 1765). Clap's moral philosophy was built on the distinction between merely obeying rules and laws from baser motives, like self-interest and the pursuit of honor, and acting with true virtue out of love for God and a desire to conform to his standard of perfection. See Clap, *The Declaration of the Rector and Tutors of Yale-College in New-Haven, against the Reverend Mr. George Whitefield, His Principles and Designs* . . . (Boston, 1745), 7; Clap, "The Ecclesiastical Constitution of Colleges," MS, 1757, 31.

61. Pierson, *The Founding of Yale*, 139; Trumbull, *History of Connecticut*, II, 333; James Kent, "An Address Delivered at New Haven . . . September 13, 1831," in Pierson, *The Founding of Yale*, 38. Other historians have also pointed to Clap's political friends or his threat to appeal to the crown to explain his success. But Clap's political allies had not been powerful enough to restore Yale's annual grant, and his threat of appeal would not possibly endanger Connecticut's chartered privileges as much as the Susquehanna issue. Most could not match his legal arguments. The few who could, like Ingersoll and Johnson, whose legal expertise was in great demand, might have been too busy to do their homework, as Pierson suggested.

"IT DON'T SIGNIFY TO PARLY":
THE LAWYER'S STYLE AND THE LAW OF THE CROWD

The lawyer's style might have been enough to impress the General Assembly, but the colony's elected leaders were not the only ones influencing the debate about law and legitimacy in Connecticut. In the three years that followed their 1763 confrontation, both Ingersoll and Clap would learn the limits of forensic persuasion.

Jared Ingersoll sailed for England in the fall of 1764 after helping to write Connecticut's cautious protest to Parliament's Stamp Act. While in London, he did what he could to soften the measure but was ultimately swayed by George Grenville's arguments and returned to Connecticut in 1765 as the colony's stamp commissioner. Newspapers promptly printed condemnations of his "treachery," and citizens in four towns hanged him in effigy. As he rode from New Haven to Hartford for a special session of the General Assembly on September 19, he was stopped by a militia of about five hundred "Sons of Liberty" demanding his resignation. He insisted that he could only properly offer his resignation to the duly appointed government, but the crowd contended that *it* expressed the will of the people. Ingersoll spoke privately to the leaders of the band, and almost managed to talk his way out of the situation, but the crowd as a whole seemed to agree with the man who said, "It don't signify to parly . . . you must resign." The crowd did not want any more fancy arguments; it wanted unequivocal action. Ingersoll then tried to draft his own letter of resignation, but they rejected it and made him sign theirs and had him seal it with three cheers for "Liberty and Property" and the toss of his hat into the air. Joined by another five hundred marchers, the Sons of Liberty then escorted Ingersoll to Hartford, surrounded the Assembly building, and had him repeat the cheers and the hat toss.[62]

These events dramatized the hardening divisions between local and imperial conceptions of the law. Ingersoll denied that a mob gathered from Windham and New London counties had any legitimate authority. Parliament was sovereign, and even an unconstitutional act had to be obeyed until repealed; furthermore, the act would be repealed only after humble petitions submitted

---

62. The best account of Ingersoll and the Stamp Act is Gipson's *Jared Ingersoll* (quotation on 182). See also Edmund S. Morgan and Helen M. Morgan, *The Stamp Act Crisis: Prologue to Revolution*, rev. ed. (New York, 1962), chap. 13; and Edmund S. Morgan, ed., *Prologue to Revolution: Sources and Documents on the Stamp Act Crisis, 1764–1766* (New York, 1959), esp. 29–34, 114.

through normal legal channels persuaded the royal authorities to do so. In contrast, the Sons of Liberty saw themselves as acting within a venerable tradition of crowd protest. Distrustful of elite men like Ingersoll who could manipulate language and work the state machinery for their own purposes, they appropriated the power to define the terms of debate and the boundaries of legitimate action. They had resorted to extra-institutional means to redress abuses of customary rights and nullify unconstitutional statutes. For them, the cheers and the hat toss were more than just symbolic gestures in a vigilante street theater. Certainly, the actions signaled Ingersoll's readmittance to the community after an admission of an offense against the body public, just as the mock trial and execution of his effigy had been staged to express general moral outrage. But Ingersoll's ritual actions, from the crowd's perspective, were also performative acts: the statement, the cheers, and the hat toss were legal enactments of Ingersoll's resignation, based on an understanding of law and legitimacy that Ingersoll himself denied. The Stamp Act protests were an alternate public discourse of law and moral rectitude that academic elites like Ingersoll and Clap refused to recognize.[63]

Events at Yale in many ways mirrored the crisis of legitimacy in the colony at large. The incidence of campus vandalism and rioting had been rising for a decade. To show their general displeasure of Clap's policies, students did everything from ringing the bell at odd hours to setting off homemade bombs in the college yard, from scribbling in library books and boycotting classes to poisoning food in the commons and sending the president a note that threatened to "skin old Tom Clap's Hide." In August 1765, as Ingersoll's effigy swung from various gallows and Clap's divinity professor Naphtali Daggett launched

---

63. For interpretations of crowd action and popular uprisings, see E. P. Thompson, "The Moral Economy of the English Crowd in the Eighteenth Century," *Past and Present,* no. 50 (February 1971), 76–136; Pauline Maier, "Popular Uprisings and Civil Authority in Eighteenth-Century America," *WMQ,* 3d Ser., XXVII (1970), 3–35; Richard Maxwell Brown, *Strain of Violence: Historical Studies of American Violence and Vigilantism* (New York, 1975), chap. 2; Dirk Hoerder, *Crowd Action in Revolutionary Massachusetts, 1765–1780* (New York, 1977); Reid, *In a Rebellious Spirit.* Greene, in "From the Perspective of Law," *South Atlantic Quarterly,* LXXXV (1986), 62n, is correct when he notes that Reid's labeling this emerging division as "Whig" and "Tory" law "overemphasizes its partisan character." A whig like John Adams and a tory like Thomas Hutchinson could agree that only in very limited circumstances was crowd action constitutional. Whig leader James Otis argued against the Stamp Act, but on the grounds that it was unadvisable, not unconstitutional. (See Maier, "Popular Uprisings," *WMQ,* 3d Ser., XXVII [1970], 24; and Hoerder, *Crowd Action,* 80, 113, 115, 137). As Reid notes, the whig theory of law was still evolving between 1766 and 1770. The whole idea of constitutionality, and the role of popular action, was undergoing a complex evolution in this period.

a verbal attack against "the Stampman" in the pages of the *Connecticut Courant*, Clap testified in a New Haven superior court against eight Yale students whose riotous assault on Clap's house had shattered several windows and slightly injured the president. By February 1766, as debate raged in New Haven over anti–Stamp Act proposals, a majority of Yale's students petitioned the Yale Corporation, again complaining about Clap's autocratic behavior and demanding the right to appeal his judgments. When the petition was ignored, students stepped up their campaign, destroying college property and terrorizing Clap's tutors. "It don't signify to parly," the students seemed to have decided, and it was time to set the lawyer's rhetoric and tactics aside.[64]

Although Clap's common law defense of Yale against state encroachment resembled Connecticut's resistance to Parliament, within the Yale community Clap was cast as a tyrant, denying students their natural rights of conscience and their constitutional rights of due process. Unable to make any headway with petitions, legal arguments, and the usual institutional procedures, the students followed the Stamp Act protesters' example and tried to establish the fact of Clap's oppression by their extreme reaction to it. The Yale Corporation blamed the insurrection on "the spirit of the times, and the influence of others," rather than Clap's policies. Clap's antagonist Benjamin Gale, who deplored the Stamp Act mobs, would not have "influence[d]" the scholars to borrow their tactics from the Sons of Liberty, but he was pleased with the final result. Clap resigned on July 1, 1766. Two members of the Yale Corporation thought they knew just the man to replace him: Jared Ingersoll. Ingersoll would instead secure a fat royal salary on the Philadelphia vice admiralty court, and Yale would limp along with a president pro tempore until Ezra Stiles took over in 1778.[65]

64. On the campus unrest, see Dexter, *Biographical Sketches*, II, 777–779; and Tucker, *Puritan Protagonist*, chap. 10. The comment about "old Tom Clap's Hide" is quoted in Tucker, *Puritan Protagonist*, 253. Daggett wrote as "Cato," and Ingersoll responded under the name of "Civis." On the court case against the eight students, see Yale Corporation Records, July 31, Sept. 11, 1765, I, 170, 171, Manuscripts and Archives, Yale University Library; Records of the Superior Court, New Haven Session, 1763–1765, XV, New Haven Session, Aug. 27, 1765, Conn. St. Libr., discussed in Gipson, *Jared Ingersoll*, 159–160n, and Tucker, *Puritan Protagonist*, 255–256. On student actions leading to Clap's resignation, see Thomas Clap, "Journal of Scholar's Conduct 1766," MS, Clap Presidential Papers, YRG 2–4-A, Feb. 10–Apr. 5.

65. Yale Corporation Records, Apr. 22, 1766, I, 173. Historians have assumed that Gale was the chief "outside influence" alluded to in the Corporation Records. Gale denounced the "Rage and Folly" of the Sons of Liberty "Babel Convention" of Dec. 25, 1765, in a Jan. 13, 1766, letter to Ingersoll, printed in N.H. Col. Hist. Soc., *Papers*, IX (1918), 372–373. Gipson, *Jared Ingersoll*, 238–239n, citing Franklin Bowditch Dexter, ed., *Extracts from the Itineraries and Other Miscellanies of Ezra Stiles, DD., LL.D., 1755–1794, with a Selection from His Corre-*

Clap died six months after his resignation, but his "torrent of law learning" would remain for another twenty years the reflexive argument of clerical trustees struggling to preserve their exclusive control over higher education in Connecticut. In 1784, Samuel Whittelsey Dana, a young Middletown lawyer, challenged his professional colleagues to do what attorneys Ingersoll and Johnson had failed to do effectively two decades earlier: enter the lists against Clap and defeat him on the ground he had chosen. President Clap, Dana wrote dismissively, was, after all, no lawyer. He had "perverted, misapplied, and tortured" the laws of England "to speak a language which they know not." Reading through Clap's supposedly persuasive arguments, "we find ourselves invaded with such a sonorous parade of learning, and are demanded to surrender our natural faculties of reason and thinking." But, in fact, Dana charged, Clap's case had been "more formidable in sound, than in substance." For Dana, it was as if the legal profession had to vanquish the ghost of an old clerical pettifogger in order to exonerate itself in the eyes of the public:

> We beg the favour of the gentlemen of the law, that they would take the trouble of examining this [clerical] claim of exclusive right [to govern Yale], and see what force there is in all those pompous arguments pretended to be drawn from the principles of the common law . . . to dispel the almost impenetrable darkness, which has so long involved and obscured this subject—to lay open truth to the public eye—to convince the world that there are no such mysterious or magic rules, or maxims, in their profession, as to be able to convert right into wrong, reason into absurdity, and equity into a violation of the obvious principles of justice.[66]

---

spondence (New Haven, Conn., 1916), 5, notes that Elnathan Whitman and Solomon Williams supported an Ingersoll presidency at a meeting of the Yale Corporation in 1766. One can only speculate about how Ingersoll would have changed Yale's character. Certainly, many students would have admired his scholarship and professional style, if not his politics. Differences in ideology and religious inclination did not get in the way of the desire for legal expertise. Stephen Mix Mitchell, for example, a future judge and senator, graduated from Yale in 1763, tutored for three years under Clap, leaned toward the religion of Edwards and Bellamy, and studied law with Ingersoll. Benedict Arnold, leader of the New Haven radicals in the 1760s and 1770s, hired Ingersoll, leader of the New Haven conservatives, as his lawyer. (Gipson, *Jared Ingersoll*, 375, notes a further twist in the Arnold connection: by 1780, loyalist Ingersoll was secretly serving the patriots, while patriot Arnold was secretly serving the loyalists.)

66. "An Aged Laymen," for example, answered a series of twelve essays by "Parnassus" that were harshly critical of Yale (*Connecticut Courant*, Feb. 4–May 27, 1783) by retorting that "Mr. Clap answered for himself, and in the name and behalf of the Corporation; and the complainants were beat, and they, with their lawyer, got nothing but disgrace" ("Ob-

Dana, who graduated from Yale in 1775, and the rising generation of young, ambitious, anticlerical lawyers he represented were part of Clap's legacy. The old president would not have appreciated the irony. By overemphasizing Yale's purpose as a school to train ministers, he provoked others to stress its secular character. In his school of the prophets, students saw the power of legal language and gained practical experience in the arts of challenging entrenched authority. The law courts that had mirrored Clap's image of moral order offered a new professional identity for the educated man, and the printing press he helped establish in New Haven offered a new medium for local debate, as public discourse's center of gravity began to shift from sermons and sola scriptura to a republic of letters dominated by learned lawyers. Clap's crusade to preserve Calvinist orthodoxy at Yale, begun with the Awakening, had ended in a period of new enthusiasms for politics and law.[67]

---

servations upon Parnassus" [cont.], *American Mercury*, Apr. 29, 1783). See [Dana], *Yale-College Subject to the General Assembly*, 10, 11, 41.

67. As John M. Murrin has noted in "The Legal Transformation," in Katz and Murrin, eds., *Colonial America*, 565, "The relationship between the rise of the bar and the Revolution is one of the strangest paradoxes of early American history." Murrin's study of Yale and Harvard graduates who became lawyers concluded that those who graduated before 1765 most likely became tories, and those graduating after that date, whigs (566).

PART 2

Cultivation and Enlightenment

Knowledge itself was reconceived in eighteenth-century New England, and along with it the social role of the learned man. The small group of ministers and Yale tutors discovering the new learning of Locke and Newton in the college library's new collection of books between 1715 and 1722 quickly came to believe that the scholastic and Ramist curriculum they had mastered had been swept into the dustbin. But neither in their minds nor in Connecticut's intellectual life more generally were old ideas and systems so quickly discarded. Yale into the 1740s and 1750s reflected an eclectic mixture of old and new learning in place of what had once been thought a coherent body of knowledge. "The old curriculum of the seven liberal arts was breaking up, and a new one was not yet devised," one student of the period has written. Yale men and other Connecticut thinkers, "like most of the rest of the world, were still groping in the rubble, trying to find some familiar landmarks, and at the same time gazing in admiration at the new structures which more enterprising hands were beginning to raise." But the students and scholars could not just stumble through ancient ruins and admire the new monuments to modern genius for the sheer intellectual thrill of it all; they felt the obligation to turn and face a broader public and make use of what they had learned.[1]

Jared Eliot (1685–1763) and Ezra Stiles (1727–1795) embraced the pursuit of practical knowledge with a passion. Together they shed light on what historians have called the "moderate" Enlightenment in America. Both were ministers, but they did not confine their energies to theology and pastoral work. Eliot was also a physician, and he wrote pamphlets on agricultural reform. Stiles's voluminous private notebooks convey his fascination with science and history and his acute observation of the natural and social world around him. Neither man believed that his religious commitments to New England Congregationalism ought to be a barrier to the free pursuit of knowledge of the empirical world or an active participation in a transatlantic republic of letters.[2]

As New England opened to the new ideas animating the larger European world, it also opened to the increasing shiploads of consumer goods from England. Ships that carried crates of books to Yale also carried clothing, furniture,

1. Edmund S. Morgan, *The Gentle Puritan: A Life of Ezra Stiles, 1727–1795* (New Haven, Conn., 1962), 50–51, 56. See also Joseph J. Ellis, *The New England Mind in Transition: Samuel Johnson of Connecticut, 1696–1772* (New Haven, Conn., 1973), chap. 3; and Richard Warch, *School of the Prophets: Yale College, 1701–1740* (New Haven, Conn., 1973).

2. On the moderate Enlightenment in America, see, especially, Henry F. May, *The Enlightenment in America* (New York, 1976), 3–101.

silverware, and china to colonists who seemed ever more eager and able to buy them. As commerce prospered and European trade expanded, so did the colonial consumption of English styles, customs, habits, and ideas. This refinement of America was marked by the adoption, first by the British American gentry and later by the middling classes, of a modified version of genteel manners and an emphasis upon comfort, leisure, social display, and a cosmopolitan appreciation of the finer things.[3]

Both the genteel, cosmopolitan attitudes toward cultural life and a liberal acceptance of the new learning merged to produce the Anglicization of the colonial American gentry in the eighteenth century. This embrace of Englishness, in broad cultural terms, was translated for some New Englanders into an affinity for the Church of England, which accepted theological positions that emphasized human reason and choice and welcomed investigations in science and philosophy. Eliot, a member of the reading group that had been introduced to the new learning by Yale's Dummer collection of books, veered toward Anglicanism in 1722, but, unlike his friends Samuel Johnson and Yale rector Timothy Cutler, Eliot stayed a Congregationalist. Stiles, too, was tempted by the Church of England when the well-salaried pastorate of cosmopolitan Newport's elegant Trinity Church was offered to him in 1752. He declined and accepted the call to Newport's Congregationalist Second Church in 1755, upon the recommendation of Jared Eliot. Eliot refused to speak ill of Anglicans, even as Anglican-Congregational relations soured considerably in the 1750s. At the time of his death in 1763, he thought the religious and political bigotries dividing British Protestants in both the Old World and the New could be transcended by efforts at general social improvement. For Stiles in Revolutionary New England, however, the Church of England became the emblem of toryism, tyranny, and persecution, and Anglicans became the religious and political nemesis to Stiles's new, self-proclaimed identity as an American Puritan.

Eliot's efforts to promote agricultural reform, most notably his essays on field husbandry (1748–1762), which adapted English agricultural advice for New Englanders, were more than attempts to produce and disseminate practical knowledge about farming. He hoped that a public discussion of experimental husbandry could cultivate harmonious and productive local communities as well as cooperation between Britain and the colonies. Eliot's cultivation of Connecticut, taken in this broader sense, failed because the Stamp Act crisis altered the cultural landscape. After his death, local husbandmen joined to

3. Richard L. Bushman, *The Refinement of America: Persons, Houses, Cities* (New York, 1992). See also the essays in Cary Carson, Ronald Hoffman, and Peter J. Albert, eds., *Of Consuming Interests: The Style of Life in the Eighteenth Century* (Charlottesville, Va., 1994).

oppose British economic policy and bring about political independence, not to promote that policy with an agricultural revolution.

Just as the pursuit of knowledge was transformed by the new learning, the scholarly self and the relationship of the learned man—especially the learned clergyman—to his society was redefined in the Revolutionary era. Ezra Stiles, who would serve as Yale's president from 1778 to 1795, believed that the diffusion of knowledge through the public was essential to America's rising glory. His experiences as a preacher through the Stamp Act protests and the Revolution, however, taught him that America needed zealous Calvinists more than enlightened scholars in its pulpits. The Revolutionary crisis forced him to refashion his public and private identities: the Reverend Mr. Stiles who preached and lectured and the scholarly Ezra who sought the truth about the world and himself. He moved from the eighteenth century's Enlightenment to a self-conscious embrace of the Puritan past and developed a keen sense of the changing relationship between learning and public discourse within a culture struggling to redefine itself.

CHAPTER 4

The Experimental Philosophy of Farming

Jared Eliot and the Cultivation of Connecticut

Connecticut minister and physician Jared Eliot's *Essays upon Field-Husbandry* (1761), the first important agricultural book written in the American colonies, proposed to "set before the Reader the Way of mending our poor Land, and raising Crops." Central to the method of efficient farming Eliot espoused was the drill plow, which enabled one man and a team of oxen to plant more straight rows of seeds in a day than a hundred men could plant by hand. In essays first published between 1748 and 1759, Eliot offered a design for a drill plow that would be cheaper and simpler than the one developed by the English agricultural innovator Jethro Tull, since, Eliot wrote, "the several Parts are all plain Work, open and easy to the Understanding." Interested in cultivating minds as well as land, he matched mechanical improvements of Tull's plow with rhetorical improvements of Tull's language. He complained that "Mr. *Tull* has had but little Regard to the Capacity of his Reader: . . . there being so many Words used by him which common Farmers do not understand." Eliot chose to write in a "plain simple Manner," not only to disseminate "important Truths" to an "Unlearned" audience but also to create a forum where practical knowledge could be freely and clearly communicated among people regardless of status: "I have learned many useful Things from the lowest of the People, not only in Rank, but in Understanding too." [1]

---

1. Jared Eliot, *A Continuation of the Essay upon Field-Husbandry, as It Is, or May Be Ordered in New-England* (New York, 1754), 7, 8, 34. Eliot published six essays on field husbandry between 1748 and 1759, which were collected in Eliot, *Essays upon Field-Husbandry in New-England as It Is or May Be Ordered* (Boston, [1761]) (the title page has a publication date of 1760); the modern reprint of this collection is Eliot, *Essays upon Field Husbandry in New England and Other Papers, 1748–1762*, ed. Harry J. Carman and Rexford G. Tugwell

Eliot's essays reflect the social, intellectual, and ideological transformations that redefined mid-eighteenth-century America. His efforts to produce and disseminate practical knowledge were shaped by broader moral motives and the ideological context of the 1750s. Eliot wanted to unite the transatlantic republic of letters and local farming communities. He hoped that, after the French were defeated in the contest for empire in America, experimental husbandry, the restoration of commerce, and territorial expansion based on the New England model of settlement would combine to promote economic prosperity and moral revitalization. He envisioned Great Britain and its American plantations flourishing under a single moral and economic order that balanced ethics and economics, self-interest and public duty, colonial needs and the empire's greater good.[2]

Eliot (1685–1763), grandson of John Eliot, Puritan missionary to the Indians, and son of a Guilford, Connecticut, minister, graduated from Yale in 1706 and received his master of arts from Harvard in 1709. He was pastor of the Congregational church in Killingworth (now Clinton), Connecticut, from 1707 until his death and was one of Connecticut's leading physicians. He became a Yale trustee in 1730. After turning over his medical practice to his son-in-law in the mid-1740s, he began writing about farming. *An Essay upon Field-Husbandry in New-England as It Is or May Be Ordered* (1748) was the first of six essays to be published in New London, New York, New Haven, and Boston between 1748 and 1759. The first four essays also ran in the *New-York Gazette* from May 14 to June 30, 1753, and the fifth from February 4 to 25, 1754. A collected edition

---

(New York, 1934). See also Eliot, *An Essay on the Invention, or Art of Making Very Good, If Not the Best Iron, from Black Sea Sand* (New York, 1762), 27 (hereafter cited as *Essay on Iron*).

Jethro Tull (1674–1741) had been an undergraduate at Oxford, a student at Gray's Inn, and a young man about town in London before taking over his father's farm. He conducted agricultural experiments and built his first implements between 1699 and 1701. He traveled in Europe from 1713 to 1715, where observations of vineyard cultivation settled him in his principles. Tull gained local fame for growing wheat for thirteen consecutive years without manure. *The New Horse-Houghing Husbandry . . .* (1731), his first effort, was incorporated as chapters 16–20 in *The Horse-Hoing Husbandry; or, An Essay on the Principles of Tillage and Vegetation . . .* (London, 1733), his folio treatise with illustrations and descriptions of his "engines." See T. H. Marshall, "Jethro Tull and the 'New Husbandry' of the Eighteenth Century," *Economic History Review*, II (1929–1930), 41–60. For clarifications of Tull's family background and life, see Norman Hidden, "Jethro Tull I, II, III," *Agricultural History Review*, XXXVII, pt. 1 (1989), 26–35.

2. Norman S. Fiering, "The Transatlantic Republic of Letters: A Note on the Circulation of Learned Periodicals to Early Eighteenth-Century America," *William and Mary Quarterly*, 3d Ser., XXXIII (1976), 642–660; David Jaffee, "The Village Enlightenment in New England, 1760–1820," *WMQ*, 3d Ser., XLVII (1990), 327–346.

printed in Boston in 1761 was followed by *An Essay on the Invention, or Art of Making Very Good, If Not the Best Iron, from Black Sea Sand* (1762), sometimes called the "Seventh Essay."[3]

The intensive agricultural methods that Eliot advocated were not widely adopted in New England until the nineteenth century. His failure to make any great impact upon the practices of his contemporaries has consigned him to the footnotes of agricultural history. One modern scholar dismissed the essays as "an amusingly magpie collection of speculations and observations, typical for that age of intellectual enthusiasm." But both Benjamin Franklin and John Adams recognized Eliot's effort to improve farming practices as an important contribution to the development of the colonies. Moreover, Eliot's essays reveal an ideological purpose, not just intellectual enthusiasm. His lack of immediate influence highlights how rapidly the political and economic climate changed after his death in 1763.[4]

With the drill plow, the essays, and the communications network he briefly established among scholarly farmers, Eliot tried to cultivate colonial society in similar and related ways. The drill plow would enable farmers to till their land more efficiently and encourage them to continue improving the design. It would also demonstrate the new husbandry to farmers mired in tradition. Similarly, the essays would teach readers to think as experimental husbandmen. Eliot wrote at a time when the minister's voice still dominated intellectual life; he died before the Revolutionary crisis shaped the local press into a political forum. But his fifth essay stepped into the future, where the prolifer-

3. Jared Eliot, *An Essay upon Field-Husbandry in New-England as It Is or May Be Ordered* (New London, Conn., 1748). This essay was written in 1747 (dated Dec. 31), and there also seems to have been an edition published in Boston (it is called "The First Essay" in Eliot, *Essays,* ed. Carman and Tugwell). The subsequent essays are *A Continuation of the Essay upon Field-Husbandry, as It Is or May Be Ordered in New England* (New London, Conn., 1749); *A Continuation of the Essay upon Field-Husbandry as It Is, or May Be Ordered in New England* (New London, Conn., 1751); *A Continuation of the Essay upon Field Husbandry, as It Is, or May Be Ordered in New-England* (New York, 1753); *A Continuation of the Essay upon Field-Husbandry, as It Is, or May Be Ordered in New-England* (New York, 1754); *The Sixth Essay on Field-Husbandry, as It Is, or May Be Ordered in New-England* (New Haven, Conn., 1759); and *An Essay on the Invention, or Art of Making Very Good, If Not the Best Iron, from Black Sea Sand* (New York, 1762).

4. On New England agriculture generally, see Howard S. Russell, *A Long, Deep Furrow: Three Centuries of Farming in New England* (1976; reprint, Hanover, N.H., 1982). Clifford K. Shipton dismissed Eliot's husbandry essays in *Biographical Sketches of Those Who Attended Harvard College in the Classes 1701–1712,* Sibley's Harvard Graduates, V (Boston, 1937), 200. As noted below, Benjamin Franklin corresponded with Eliot and distributed his essays, and John Adams's first newspaper essays recommended Eliot's work.

ation of print and the development of an enlightened rhetorical style appealed to the common sense of a broad reading public. Finally, Eliot's efforts opened an agricultural communications network that linked Boston, New Haven, Philadelphia, and London. Through publication and private correspondence, he encouraged the development of agricultural societies, with the hope that farmers who enjoyed reading and writing about agriculture might exchange information with neighborhood husbandmen who were more comfortable with plows than with pamphlets or pens.

Altogether, Eliot's material, literary, and social practices proposed to cultivate a developing colonial society. But if his ideas and rhetoric looked to the future, his vision of society would soon be relegated to the past. His essays subordinated colonial interests to imperial designs, promoting a set of political and economic relationships between the colonies and Britain that many Americans found unworkable after the Stamp Act crisis in 1765. Eliot tried to take advantage of opportunities afforded by an expanding market economy without threatening New England's social structure and without unsettling the political relationship with Britain. His understanding of moral order was based upon the positive virtues of the yeoman freehold, virtues that accommodated private interest and local public service to national obligation; his ideology was not primarily defined by opposition to external corruption and tyranny, which were the perceived threats that galvanized public opinion after his death.

THE DRILL PLOW: THEORY AND PRACTICE

Eliot's introduction of a drill plow to New England in 1754 involved two ironies that illustrate the gulf between agricultural theory and farming practice. The first was that Eliot, a champion of experimentalism, would allow speculative theory to govern practice—and a theory, moreover, that was derived from Aristotelian categories rather than careful observation. The drill plow was not really a plow at all, but a wheeled device, drawn by a team of horses or oxen, that dropped seeds into the soil at regular intervals and depths. It replaced the haphazard method of broadcasting seeds by hand and enabled the farmer to plant seeds in even rows. But the desire for even rows of crops with space between them for plowing or hoeing was created by Tull's theory of crop nutrition, which asserted that increased tilling between rows of grain would greatly increase yield. The second irony was that Eliot, after assuring readers that he had studied the topic carefully, exposed his incomplete knowledge of Tull's designs and of current agricultural debate in England. Citing Tull's treatise showed that he approached farming with a scholarly seriousness, but relying on an early, unrevised edition also revealed him as an isolated provincial. Still, constructing the drill plow was an experiment in itself, and one that symbolized the kind of cooperation between learned men and practical craftsmen that Eliot was trying to encourage.

By discussing Tull's theory of plant nutrition, Eliot placed his work within a context of scientific and philosophical debate. In an appendix to the 1761 edition of the *Essays*, Judge Peter Oliver of Massachusetts noted that "great Disputes" continued about "whether Fire, Air, Earth or Water" was the chief cause of vegetation. Of these four Aristotelian elements, Tull had championed earth as the essential "Pabulum" of plants. He also dismissed the often-discussed Paracelsian "Nitre" and "Salts" as crop nutrients, declaring that they acted only to help break up particles of soil. Although Eliot sometimes seemed to grant a larger role to "nitrous salt[s]," he accepted the basic theoretical premise of crop nutrition behind Tull's "New Husbandry."[5]

Eliot introduced Tullian husbandry as a simple way in which New England's old land could be made new. Since plants ate microscopic particles of earth through their roots, the more soil the roots came in contact with the better the plants would grow. The husbandman's goal, then, was to break up the soil and keep it loose enough for the roots to penetrate. That was achieved either by the traditional practice of manuring the fields (using dung to break up the soil through fermentation, which did not, Tull believed, add nutrients) or by tillage. Tull's bold suggestion was that a new system of increased tillage would enable farmers to do without dung, which carried weed seeds, was always in short supply, and was a substance of "Filth and Nastiness." No need to rotate crops or to leave fields fallow, Tull asserted; all methods of maintaining soil fertility could be reduced to a single system based on efficient tillage. Tull believed that plowing and hoeing had infinite possibilities. Although the number of acres a farmer owned might never increase, the surface area of the soil that could be in contact with roots might be multiplied through tillage; since "Matter is di-

5. [Peter Oliver], "Appendix," in Eliot, *Essays upon Field-Husbandry* ([1761]), [157]–166. The 1934 edition incorrectly attributes the appendix to "John Turner," without explanation. A letter from Oliver dated Dec. 14, 1761 (reprinted in Eliot, *Essays*, ed. Carman and Tugwell, 243–249) and another to Eliot on July 19, 1761 (Beinecke Rare Book and Manuscript Library, Yale University, New Haven, Conn. [hereafter cited as Beinecke Library]) about delays in the publication of the collected essays confirm Oliver's authorship. See also Shipton, *Biographical Sketches*, V, 191–204. Tull discusses the Aristotelian elements in *Horse-Hoing Husbandry*, chap. 3. Eliot discusses nitrous salts in *Continuation of Essay* (1753), 23–24; and *Continuation of Essay* (1754), 18, 20. On the Aristotelian and Paracelsian theories, see G. E. Fussell, *Crop Nutrition: Science and Practice before Liebig* (Lawrence, Kans., 1971).

visible *ad Infinitum,*" by tillage "we can enlarge our Field of Subterranean Pasture without Limitation."[6]

Eliot championed Tullian husbandry at a time when Tull's reputation had dimmed in England. His controversial theories and recommendations had sparked a pamphlet war, but after his death in 1741 Tull was largely forgotten until Henri Duhamel's *Traité de la culture des terres suivant les principes de M. Tull* was introduced to England between 1759 and 1764. Eliot maintained that Tull had "entered deeper into the true Principles of Husbandry" than any other writer he had come across, but he proceeded cautiously because the Tullian system entailed a radical innovation and an apparent waste of farmland (by leaving empty strips of soil between rows of crops). "Before I took any Step or Pace towards this Sort of Tillage," he assured his readers, "I read all I could find upon the Subject with Care, [and] thought and studied on it with Attention."[7]

It is difficult to know which of the "sundry Books on *Husbandry* wrote in *England*" Eliot actually got his hands on. He inherited a library from his immigrant grandfather, who was said to have brought twenty-three barrels of books out of England, and there might have been farming books squeezed in among the tomes of divinity. The nearby Yale library made a few more titles available. But Eliot made specific reference in his *Essays* to only five post-

6. Tull, *Horse-Hoeing Husbandry,* 18, 21. See also Eliot, *Continuation of Essay* (1754), 13–14.

7. Eliot, *Continuation of Essay* (1754), 7, 21. On the reception of Tull, see Marshall, "Jethro Tull," *Econ. Hist. Rev.,* II (1929–1930), 44–59; G. E. Fussell, *More Old English Farming Books: From Tull to the Board of Agriculture, 1731 to 1793* (London, 1950), 1–6; and E. R. Wicker, "A Note on Jethro Tull: Innovator or Crank?" *Agricultural History,* XXXI, no. 2 (1957), 46–48. The Society of Improvers in the Knowledge of Agriculture in Scotland (1723–1746) discussed the Tullian system, as did the Royal Dublin Society for Promoting Husbandry and Manufactures. Stephen Switzer launched a monthly periodical, *Practical Husbandman and Planter . . .* (London, 1733–1774), in order to attack Tull. Francis Home's *Principles of Agriculture and Vegetation,* 2d ed. (London, 1759) dismissed Tull in a single sentence, but [Adam Dickson], in *A Treatise of Agriculture* (Edinburgh, 1762), allotted more space to a refutation only because Tull had pronounced his doctrines with such certitude (Marshall, "Jethro Tull," *Econ. Hist. Rev.,* II [1929–1930], 44). French savant Henri Louis Duhamel du Monceau (1700–1782), called Duhamel, was favorably impressed and wrote his six-volume *Traité de la culture des terres suivant les principes de M. Tull* between 1751 and 1760; John Mills published a "jumbled precis" of the *Traité* entitled *A Practical Treatise of Husbandry . . .* (London, 1759), and Philip Miller's translation of a primer for farmers written by Duhamel (*Eléments de l'Agriculture* [1754]) appeared in 1764. It was Mills's work that created the false opposition between the "New Husbandry" of Tull and the "Old Husbandry" practiced by everyone else, including other innovators and reformers, which set the tone for the renewed controversy in the 1760s and 1770s. See G. E. Fussell, *The Classical Tradition in European Farming* (Rutherford, N.J., 1972), 148, 153.

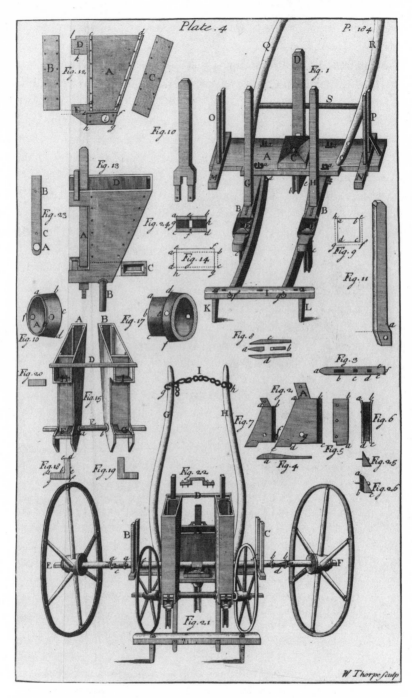

Figure 7. Jethro Tull's Wheat Drill. From *The Horse-Hoing Husbandry; or, An Essay on the Principles of Tillage and Vegetation . . .* (London, 1733), facing p. 184. Courtesy, Beinecke Rare Book and Manuscript Library, Yale University, New Haven, Conn.

classical agricultural writers besides Tull. He also referred to the publications of the Irish and Scottish agricultural societies and to the London Society for the Encouragement of Arts, Manufactures, and Commerce.[8]

We know that Eliot had not seen any revised edition of Tull's treatise when he built his drill plow sometime after 1748. Working from Tull's 1733 prototype, he described the function of the instrument, which was "peculiar to this Husbandry." In order to expose more crop roots to "subterranean pasture," wheat had to be sown in even rows, with enough space between every few rows for "Horse Hoing"—that is, plowing. Eliot wanted to simplify the mechanism that dropped seeds at a regular rate, and he also wanted to add a "Dung Drill" in order to add a small amount of manure to each planting. "Mr. *Tull's* Wheat-Drill," Eliot remarked, describing his improvements, "required two Pair of Wheels: We have two Drills fastened upon a Frame . . . each performing its respective Part of Work at one Movement; and to the Whole but one Pair of Wheels."[9]

8. On John Eliot's library, see Ezra Stiles, "Itineraries," II, 151, Ezra Stiles Papers, Beinecke Library. Samuel Hartlib (ca. 1599–ca. 1670) was especially known for *Samuel Hartlib His Legacie; or, An Enlargement of the Discourse of Husbandry used in Brabant and Flaunders* . . . (London, 1651). Eliot refers to him in *Continuation of Essay* (1749), 21; and *Continuation of Essay* (1751), 9, 17. On John Evelyn (1620–1706), see Blanche Henrey, *British Botanical and Horticultural Literature before 1800* . . . , 3 vols., I (London, 1975), 181. Eliot describes one of Evelyn's experiments in *Continuation of Essay* (1754), 20. Richard Jackson sent Eliot a copy of Philip Miller, *The Gardener's Dictionary* (London, 1731); see Richard Jackson to Jared Eliot, Feb. 10, 1755, Beinecke Library. Eliot calls it a "valuable book" in *Sixth Essay* (1759), 21. William Ellis (ca. 1700–1758), who appeared in Eliot's *Continuation of Essay* (1749), 8, 32, and *Continuation of Essay* (1751), 15, wrote *The Modern Husbandman* . . . (1732) and other works. In his *Continuation of Essay* (1753), 27, Eliot refers to "The Honourable Society for promoting Husbandry and Manufactures in *Ireland*"; he might have seen an article on raising calves sent by the Royal Dublin Society to the editor of *Gentleman's Magazine, and Historical Chronicle*, XX (1750), 14. See Carl Raymond Woodward, *Ploughs and Politicks: Charles Read of New Jersey and His Notes on Agriculture, 1715–1774* (New Brunswick, N.J., 1941), 335n. From Peter Collinson in London, via Franklin in Philadelphia, Eliot received Robert Maxwell, ed., *Select Transactions of the Honourable the Society of Improvers in the Knowledge of Agriculture in Scotland* . . . (Edinburgh, 1743). See Franklin to Eliot, Dec. 10, 1751, in Leonard W. Labaree, ed., *The Papers of Benjamin Franklin*, 33 vols. to date (New Haven, Conn., 1959–), IV, 215; and Eliot, *Continuation of Essay* (1754), 24. Eliot mentions *Transactions of the Society Instituted at London, for the Encouragement of Arts, Manufactures, and Commerce* (1783–1851) in *Sixth Essay* (1759), 4.

9. Eliot, *Continuation of Essay* (1754), 30, 33. In an appendix to *Continuation of Essay* (1749), [36], dated Dec. 31, 1748, Eliot promised future discussion of Tullian husbandry and the drill plow but explained that he had not built a plow yet because the friend he had hoped would help him had become ill. Russell H. Anderson, in "Grain Drills through Thirty-Nine

Eliot's redesign of Tull's plow was a cooperative project that drew upon both the knowledge of a learned divine and the practical ingenuity of a local mechanic. Eliot first sought help from Yale president Thomas Clap's "mathematical Learning, and mechanical Genius." Clap's alterations helped reduce the cost of constructing the drill plow by 75 percent, but, when Eliot actually brought it to the fields, he found that the wheels did not fit his ridges and had to be replaced.

> The next Thing I wanted in order to compass my Design, was a Dung Drill; this is an Invention intirely new, for which there was no Precedent or Model. For this I applied myself to *Benoni Hylliard,* a very ingenious Man of this Town, a Wheel-Wright by Trade. I told him what I wanted, and desired him to make one. At first we could think of no Way but to make it as a distinct Instrument: But at length his Ingenuity led him to set this and the Wheat Drill upon one Frame, so that it became one Instrument.

Clap the college professor had modified an existing design; Hylliard the mechanic invented something new and made sure the whole thing actually worked.[10]

Adding the dung drill to an implement originally designed to make manuring obsolete, Eliot acknowledged, seemed contrary to Tullian precepts. But Eliot's practicality overruled his admiration for Tull's doctrine. New England's climate was harsher than England's, and his own land was low and poor. "I shall have need enough of my Dung-Drill, at least, when I first begin with this kind of Husbandry. I hope that in Time, the Land may be so inriched by Tillage, that this may prove needless." [11]

Tull's theory and Eliot's improved drill plow aroused both enthusiasm and skepticism among American scholar-farmers. Nathan Bowen wrote from Marblehead, Massachusetts, proclaiming his support for drill plows and his belief that "the whole process of Vegitation is as Mechanical and Regular as the movement of your Watch . . . and as Reduceable to Geometrical rules"; but Bowen disagreed with Tull's contention that fertilizers added no nutrients to the soil. Oliver, on the other hand, declared himself "entirely of Mr. Tull's

---

Centuries," *Agri. Hist.,* X (1936), 157–205, notes that drilling seeds was an old idea but that drills were a "plaything" until studied and popularized by Tull (168). Joan Thirsk also discusses Tull's precursors in "Agricultural Innovations and Their Diffusion," chap. 19 in Thirsk, ed., *The Agrarian History of England and Wales,* V, pt. 1, *1640–1750: Regional Farming* (Cambridge, 1985), 581–585.

10. Eliot, *Continuation of Essay* (1754), 31.

11. Ibid., 32.

Mind" and encouraged Eliot to try tillage without manure. William Logan of Pennsylvania asked Eliot if he could get one of the new drill plows built for him and shipped to Philadelphia. Eliot's nephew H. W. Robinson in South Kingston, Rhode Island, who was still hoping Hylliard would make him one in the summer of 1762, spoke of the plow as if it were an essential prerequisite to a program of agricultural reform: "I am truly fond of introducing the Drill Husbandry into this Colony, and could I get the Plough I'm certain I could establish it." [12]

Some readers questioned Eliot's improvements or doubted that drill plows would ever come into general use. Oliver thought that Eliot had "missed the true Construction of Mr. Tull's Drill Plough" because he had worked from Tull's first folio edition (1733) rather than from his later supplements. In the appendix to the third edition, Oliver explained, Tull "condemns his own first four Wheel'd Plough, and has given a Draft of the two Wheel'd one, of which I inclose a Copy." Peter Collinson, writing from London, thought Eliot's drill plow still too complex, too liable to break down, and "So will never become of General Use." He wrote that he never saw Tullian husbandry actually practiced anywhere. Perhaps "Gentlemen and yoemen" might be persuaded to try it, "but the Common Farmers or Husbandmen would not come into It, tho its Advantages was So conspicuous." When Logan finally received his plow, he was disappointed. The dung drill would probably be more trouble than it was worth, he thought, and he did not expect to make much use of the seed drill, "as it is I think one of the Worst pieces of workmanship I Ever Saw put together. . . . I think One Days plowing Would tear it all to pieces." [13]

Oliver published Eliot's six essays as a group with the author's approval in 1761 and asserted that they had needed "no material Corrections," despite apparent problems with the drill plow. He understood that Eliot had never intended to provide flawless designs for machines that would convert New England to some fully realized system of "new husbandry." Eliot had clearly set out his motives in the preface to his first essay, written in 1747. He wanted to contribute what he could to the public fund of useful knowledge, but he wanted

12. William Logan to Eliot, July 25, 1754, Peter Oliver to Eliot, Mar. 31, 1756, Nathan Bowen to Eliot, Aug. 3, 1761, H. W. Robinson to Eliot, July 13, 1762, in Eliot, *Essays,* ed. Carman and Tugwell, 207–209 (quotation on 209), 229, 239, 252.

13. Oliver mentions the third (1751) edition in his Mar. 31, 1756, letter to Eliot, in Eliot, *Essays,* ed. Carman and Tugwell, 238. Tull published "The Supplement" (1735), "Addenda" (1738), and "The Conclusion" (1739). The revised text was republished in 1743, 1751, and 1762. See Peter Collinson to Eliot, Mar. 1, 1754, William Logan to Eliot, Oct. 14, 1755, in Eliot, *Essays,* ed. Carman and Tugwell, 213, 231.

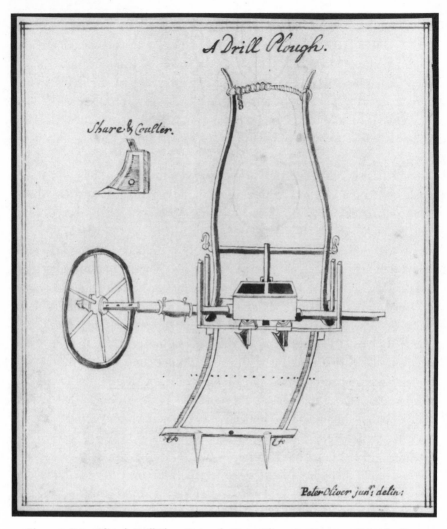

Figure 8. Peter Oliver's Drill Plow. Drawn by Peter Oliver, Jr. Courtesy, Beinecke Rare Book and Manuscript Library, Yale University, New Haven, Conn.

even more to promote husbandry as a respected branch of learning. He hoped "to Excite those who are more Sufficient and more Equal to the Business" and to set their "Pens and Hands" to work. New attitudes, not just new instruments, would improve New England.[14]

14. [Peter Oliver], "Appendix," in Eliot, *Essays upon Field-Husbandry* ([1761]), reprinted in Eliot, *Essays,* ed. Carman and Tugwell, 154. When he urged Eliot at the end of that year to "publish additions to your first Designs," he was calling for more essays, not revisions of the first six. See Peter Oliver to Eliot, Dec. 14, 1761, in Eliot, *Essays,* ed. Carman and Tugwell, 245. The quotation from Eliot is from the "Preface," ibid., 4 (this was originally the preface to the *Essay upon Field-Husbandry* [1748] and to the 1761 collection of essays).

The experimental philosophy of farming that Eliot advocated had both literary and scientific roots. The Baconian spirit had infused the agricultural tracts of Samuel Hartlib in the 1650s and the efforts of the Royal Society's Georgical Committee after the Restoration; combined with the georgic sensibility so popular after John Dryden's translation of Virgil's *Georgics* (1697), Baconian empiricism helped to make scientific husbandry fashionable in England by the mid-eighteenth century. Nonetheless, Eliot believed, husbandry was still a grossly underdeveloped branch of learning even in Great Britain. His own efforts to advance the art and science of farming blended self-conscious observations of personal experience with the selfless pursuit of scientific objectivity. His first four essays ranged loosely over a number of topics: draining swamps, clearing land, using seaweed as compost, and planting English grasses. In each of the four, he shifted between rambling, conversational, first-person reflections to factual, third-person observations and instructions—borrowing, in effect, the style of both the familiar essay à la Montaigne and the experimental essay of Robert Boyle and the Royal Society.[15]

For Eliot's fifth essay, his literary model was closer at hand: the New England sermon. Eliot quoted a passage from Tull, then proceeded through "three Heads":

I. To explain the Doctrine or Principles of Mr. *Tull* in such a Manner as to be open to any common Understanding.

II. To offer such Reasons and Proofs for the Support of these Principles, as will naturally occur.

III. To direct to the Performance of the Work with Instruments less intricate, more plain, cheap and commodious, than those used and described by Mr. *Tull.*

15. Eliot, "Preface," *Essays,* ed. Carman and Tugwell, 4. See Donald R. Johnson, "The Proper Study of Husbandry: Dryden's Translation of the *Georgics,*" *Restoration: Studies in English Literary Culture, 1660–1700,* VI (1982), 94–104; and, especially, Anthony Low, "New Science and the Georgic Revolution in Seventeenth-Century English Literature," *English Literary Renaissance,* XIII (1983), 231–259. For a discussion of the relationships between the familiar and experimental essay, see James Paradis, "Montaigne, Boyle, and the Essay of Experience," in George Levine, ed., *One Culture: Essays in Science and Literature* (Madison, Wis., 1987), 59–91. On the literary practices of Robert Boyle and the Royal Society, see also Steven Shapin and Simon Schaffer, *Leviathan and the Air Pump: Hobbes, Boyle, and the Experimental Life* (Princeton, N.J., 1985).

Every Sabbath for nearly half a century Eliot had preached to his congregation by explaining a biblical text, supporting the doctrine drawn from it with reasoned arguments, and applying the message to the everyday lives of his parishioners. Like a sermon, the tripartite essay had its text, doctrine, and application or "improvement." [16]

The sermonic form of the fifth essay might have been Eliot's wry response to a complaint Benjamin Franklin had made about a draft of the fourth. Eliot had called a section that addressed practical applications the "improvement" by analogy to a sermon's last section. "I object to the Word *Improvement*," Franklin wrote, "which in the Sense you use it is peculiar to New England and will not be understood elsewhere." Eliot wrote his next essay sounding more like a New England clergyman than ever, building a sermon and an essay upon a single frame, just as he had combined the two drills on his drill plow. [17]

The sermon and the essay, however, disseminated knowledge in different, even contradictory ways, and in Eliot's agricultural work it was the essay that essentially prevailed. The sermon extracted truth from an authoritative text and applied it to life; the essay recorded the exploration of life, in which truth is but glimpsed, assent is provisional, and credence is based on probability. Eliot compared Tull's "Principles or Doctrine" to "important Truths" early on but later in the essay admitted that he discussed doctrine only to help persuade farmers to experiment with new tillage practices. Eliot set Tull aside as an authoritative and innovative "Instructor" when explaining that "Tullian" tillage of the wheat field was, after all, very similar to how Americans had tilled Indian corn all their lives. "The Culture of Indian Corn" thus replaced the English book of husbandry as that which "holds forth much useful Instruction." Sentences that began "Mr. *Tull* saith" ended with, "I am satisfied by Experience," or, "Of this we can have no Certainty but by Tryal." Text and doctrine were subordinated to "Experience," a word Eliot repeated thirteen times in a ten-page section of his first essay. [18]

Eliot's invocations of "Experience" reflected a specific philosophical attitude; they were not assertions of his authority to speak upon farming issues. Claiming decades of practical experience and condemning all other writers as "book farmers" more familiar with the library than the field was standard

16. Eliot, *Continuation of Essay* (1754), 8, 9.

17. Benjamin Franklin to Eliot, Feb. 11, 1752, in Labaree, ed., *Papers of Benjamin Franklin*, IV, 265–266. Eliot's letter to Franklin is not extant.

18. Eliot, *Continuation of Essay* (1754), 6, 7, 28–29, 35–36; see also 18: "But so long as Experience shews that all this is true, it will be to no Advantage to the Farmer to say any more about it; Nor should I have entered so far into the Philosophy of Tillage as I have done, were it necessary for a practical Farmer to understand it so far as to make a Judgment."

practice among eighteenth-century agricultural writers. By contrast, Eliot made clear that, although thirty years of medical rounds had allowed him to make "many Observations" of farming in Connecticut and Long Island, he had been "in a great measure prevented hereby, from making Trials and Experiments of those things which occurred to my Mind." He was careful to note that "what hath been inserted in this Essay only upon hear-say, is not offered as certainly to be depended upon; but only as probable and worthy to be tryed." Although what "Persons of Worth and Ingenuity" told him might prove useful, "Experience is Authority, to whom we are to submit, [and] I am not forward to believe without Trial." He urged his readers to "value Things or disregard them just so far as they are found (by *Experience* that faithful Instructor) to be useful or unprofitable," and he promoted the tenets of experimental philosophy: "A Discovery of the Nature and Property of Things, and applying them to useful Purposes, is *true Philosophy*: A great deal of what has passed in the World for Learning, is *Philosophy falsly so called*. . . . *Experimental Philosophy* being founded in Nature and Truth is obtain'd no way, but by Time and Diligence: The *Knowledge of Things Useful* are gained by little and little." [19]

At times, Eliot wrote as if he were logging sequential observations in a diary. He allowed passages of his text to resemble the unrevised notes a farmer might add to the pages of his almanac, and he had an epistemological motive for doing so. In his first essay, which discussed draining swampland, he paused to explain what he was doing to readers who "may think this long Hystory of two pieces of Meadow, this tedious Detail of so many minute Particulars to be needless, trifling and impertinent." Rather than simply providing a set of instructions for others to follow, Eliot wanted to convey something of the workings of his own mind in solving particular problems and especially to capture the uncertainty haunting every new decision and trial. He hoped his recorded experience would serve as a guide: "If others save where I lost, and mend wherein I was mistaken, it answers my design in Writing." But beyond the solution of specific problems, Eliot wanted his "Hystory of Facts (as imperfect as it is)" to give readers who wanted to become experimental husbandmen "Light, Courage, and Instruction." [20]

In his sixth essay, Eliot used the word "essay" as a synonym for "trial" or "ex-

19. The quotations are from Eliot, *Essay upon Field-Husbandry* (1748), ii, 23, 24–25, appendix. See also Eliot, *Sixth Essay* (1759), 9; and Eliot, *Essay on Iron*, 12. On agricultural writers and "experience," see G. E. Fussell, "The Farming Writers of Eighteenth-Century England," *Agri. Hist.*, XXI (1947), 3. Tull made a similar remark in 1736; see Joan Thirsk, "Plough and Pen: Agricultural Writers in the Seventeenth Century," in T. H. Aston et al., eds., *Social Relations and Ideas: Essays in Honour of R. H. Hilton* (Cambridge, 1983), 318.

20. Eliot, *Essay upon Field-Husbandry* (1748), 10, 12, 13.

periment": "Experience in little esays will enable a person to judge of greater works of the same kind." The literary form and the experimental action it reports, both called "essays," function in similar ways. The farmer who experiments on two trees can extrapolate with some degree of probability about a whole orchard; the reader of the essay about the experiments can with some degree of probability expect similar results from his own trials. The writer who describes an experiment may, in the very act of composition, engage in yet another experimental act: "What I have further to write on this Subject, not only for the Sake of Order and greater Precision, but even from Necessity too, will be in the Manner of a Journal. For now entering on the Borders of *Terra incognita*,—[I] can advance not one Step forward, but as Experience my only Pole Star shall direct, am obliged to write as poor Men live, from Hand to Mouth, and as Light springs up before me as I advance." [21]

In other passages, Eliot the storyteller stepped forward, for he believed that public discourse ought to imitate the friendly exchanges of private conversation. When waiting with skeptical neighbors for the results of his attempt to make iron out of black sea sand, he told a story about "a certain whimsical Enthusiast" who informed his wife that with enough faith they could turn a stone into bread. When they failed, the enthusiast blamed his wife's unbelief, but she asked, "Why is it not half Bread?" Eliot defended the inclusion of "such trivial Stories" against the objection that they were "below the Dignity of Writing." The charge must mean "that when a Person is to write a Letter or a Book, he must ascend into the Clouds, think himself going about something quite different from the common Actions of Life: That he must divest him himself of that Sociability, that easy Freedom, that Familiarity which is so much the Support and Pleasure of Conversation; must now put on a distant and forbidding Air, assume a solemn Mein, a formal stiffness, as if clad in Buckrum; and being thus equipt is in Appearance like a Hog in Armour." [22]

Eliot's story about the "whimsical Enthusiast" made several points about the

21. Eliot, *Sixth Essay* (1759), 8; Eliot, *Essay on Iron*, 12.

22. Eliot, *Essay on Iron*, 16 (dialogue italicized in the original), 17. For another example, see *Continuation of Essay* (1749), 23–24. Benjamin Franklin to Eliot, Aug 31, 1755, in Labaree, ed., *Papers of Benjamin Franklin*, VI, 176, commented upon Eliot's friendly conversation: "I remember with Pleasure the chearful Hours I enjoy'd last Winter in your Company, and would with all my heart give any ten of the thick old Folios that stand on the Shelves before me; for a *little Book* of the Stories you then told with so much Propriety and Humour." In the funeral sermon preached at Eliot's death, his friend Thomas Ruggles remembered him as a "charming and engaging" man who communicated his ideas in a peculiarly "animated" and "entertaining" way. See Ruggles, *The Death of Great, Good, and Useful Men Lamented* ... (New Haven, Conn., 1763), 16–17.

epistemological and social contexts of practical knowledge. The radical subjectivism of the religious fanatic, who believed that he could break God's natural laws through the power of "primitive Faith," was repudiated by the common sense, kick-the-stone empiricism of his wife. Yet Eliot was also poking fun at his own experiment with black sea sand. The analogy was clear to the workman who doubted that sand could become iron and had to be promised a bottle of rum before even trying it in the forge. Too much skepticism discouraged experiments and attempts at innovation. One should neither listen to the enthusiast's promise of miracles nor silence the innovator with contempt. One should, Eliot believed, cultivate sociability, easy freedom, and familiarity through personal exchanges, private correspondence, and public discourse. Sometimes, too, a bottle of rum could help.

WRITERS AND READERS

Agricultural writing as it developed in Britain was marked by a bifurcated rhetoric: with varying degrees of emphasis, farm books tried to appeal to both the unsophisticated husbandman and to the gentleman farmer. Early-eighteenth-century writers inherited the Commonwealthman's desire to draw practicing farmers into conversations about agricultural reform and the Restoration royalist's paternalism. Agricultural texts became cheaper, and reformers wrote with confidence that they were dispensing valuable information to at least some farmers. But reaching and influencing the common husbandman remained a problem. Writers viewed farm laborers and small-scale yeomen as ignorant clodhoppers who continually opposed innovation. Improving landholders trying to promote the latest practices recommended by the textbooks could still be stymied by tenants who suspected a scheme to raise rents and by laborers who balked at deviations from the tried and true.[23]

23. Thirsk makes the point about the "improving" language of the Commonwealth and the Restoration by comparing Hartlib's circle and the work of Walter Blith to the Royal Society and the agricultural writing of John Worlidge. See "Agricultural Innovations," in Thirsk, ed., *Agrarian History of England and Wales*, V, pt. 1, 547–557; and "Plough and Pen," in Aston et al., eds., *Social Relations and Ideas*, 306–308. Blanche Henrey discusses the late-seventeenth-century movement away from expensive folios to smaller, cheaper volumes in *British Botanical and Horticultural Literature*, I, 214. Thirsk notes the eighteenth-century appearance of the four-page pamphlet in "Agricultural Innovations," in Thirsk, ed., *Agrarian History of England and Wales*, V, pt. 1, 574. See Charles W. J. Withers, "William Cullen's Agricultural Lectures and Writings and the Development of Agricultural Science in Eighteenth-Century Scotland," *Agri. Hist. Rev.*, XXXVII, pt. 2 (1989), 144–156. In the 1750s, Sir Archibald

English agricultural texts gestured toward a wider readership, but their primary audience remained gentlemen with country estates and well-to-do gentry with capital to invest in improvements and plots set aside for experiments. Tull wrote in a "low" "Stile," but not to the "low Life"; he aimed at the "Persons of Rank" who had shown an interest in his "Engines." He complained in passing about insolent and treacherous plowmen, deceitful servants, and lazy laborers. He built his drill plow to save labor, not just seeds, and seemed to wish that he could "contrive *Automata* to do the business appertaining to Tillage without hands."[24]

Addressing an audience that included both common farmers and gentlemen "of Worth, Capacity and Learning," Eliot displayed none of Tull's class antagonism. Eliot's farmhands wondered at some of his projects, and local farmers formed a skeptical chorus, but all were pleased when something he tried actually worked. He cited the advice of men like Colonel Saltonstall, Esq., the Reverend Mr. Todd, and Captain Fisk, but also many anonymous "experienced farmers," "an honest judicious Neighbour," and even "a Woman of Experience." He kept his pamphlets small and inexpensive for the common farmer, but he was delighted by encouragement from scientifically inclined gentlemen like "*B. Franklin* Esq; of *Philadelphia*."[25]

Grant launched a pamphlet campaign against tenant apathy in Scotland. But in 1772, agricultural reformer Arthur Young was still complaining that not one in five thousand farmers bothered to read at all. See Fussell, *More Old English Farming Books*, 34; and Thirsk, "Agricultural Innovations," in Thirsk, ed., *Agrarian History of England and Wales*, V, pt. 1, 588.

24. Tull, *Horse-Hoing Husbandry*, i, vi–vii, 134–135. Tull did remark that his method should appeal to the common husbandman, since it would employ more of them to hoe, but that is disingenuous. Tull developed his drill plow because he was disgusted with his workers, who refused to abandon the broadcast method and bend over to plant wheat in rows. Thirsk, in "Agricultural Innovations," in Thirsk, ed., *Agrarian History of England and Wales*, V, pt. 1, may overstate the case when she writes that Tull's "obsessive suspicion and hatred of servants bordered on paranoia" and about "the vexation, verging on neurosis, that he felt toward his expensive and unreliable laborers" (552, 585). According to Hidden, "Jethro Tull I, II, III," *Agri. Hist. Rev.*, XXXVIII, pt. 1 (1989), 32, local villagers supposedly smashed Tull's drill plow and threw it down a well. If so, they might have been motivated more by hatred of Tull than of his machine. On English agricultural improvers more generally, see J. D. Chambers and G. E. Mingay, *The Agricultural Revolution, 1750–1880* (New York, 1966), 17–18. There were a few hundred great landlords in England and many lesser landlords. Usually only the smaller country gentlemen were practicing farmers. The vast majority of landowners farmed fewer than twenty acres, and half the farmers in England and Wales were tenants.

25. Eliot, *Continuation of Essay* (1749), 1; Eliot, *Essay upon Field-Husbandry* (1748), 15, 21; Eliot, *Continuation of Essay* (1751), 16; Eliot, *Sixth Essay* (1759), 11. Eliot's "public" could include women. See Eliot, *The Blessings Bestow'd on Them That Fear God . . .* (New London,

By defending his prose style with references to "sociability" and "familiarity" in the "Hog in Armour" passage, Eliot signaled his larger social and rhetorical purposes. His Scottish contemporaries were developing an analysis of society built upon man's natural sociability. Eliot's model of an easy, conversational style, however, is the prose of Sir William Temple (1628–1699), a writer "who relates the common Incidents of Life, in such an easy agreeable Manner, as to engage the Attention, captivate the Mind, and excite the Admiration of every Reader." Temple, a diplomat, essayist, and patron of Jonathan Swift, wrote "Upon the Gardens of Epicurus; or, Of Gardening, in the Year 1685," an essay combining a discussion of Epicurean ethics with details about cultivating fruit trees and grapevines. He also entered what Swift would call the battle of the books with "An Essay upon the Ancient and Modern Learning" (1690), which attacked Baconian experimental philosophy and which Eliot must have found less congenial. One literary critic has described Temple's style as "poised between formality and informality," giving the "impression of plainness and simplicity." Temple, like Eliot, was fond of proverbs and personal comments. He avoided affectation and overrefinement with "Augustan lucidity and elegance." In Temple's essays, as another scholar has written, one hears the voice of a "humane, cultivated, cosmopolitan man of taste" in conversation with other gentlemen. This much-admired post-Restoration prose style was a precursor to Joseph Addison's *Spectator*. Addison's periodical essays had shorter sentences, a simplified vocabulary, and a literary style reminiscent of coffeehouse conversation, and they reached far broader audiences than writing like Temple's. Eliot's style, too, can be seen as a simplification of Temple's; his essays were purposely written in a plain style that would be useful and intelligible to New England farmers. Eliot wanted to do more than help gentlemen chat about their gardens; he was trying to create a dialogue that crossed social classes and had a practical effect upon public affairs.[26]

Conn., 1739), a funeral sermon for Mrs. Elizabeth Smithson, who, as a midwife and because of her virtue, is described as a "Publick Character" (25–26). On the public roles of women in what was generally (but not exclusively) defined as a male sphere, see Patricia Crawford, "Public Duty, Conscience, and Women in Early Modern England," in John Morrill, Paul Slack, and Daniel Woolf, eds., *Public Duty and Private Conscience in Seventeenth-Century England: Essays Presented to G. E. Aylmer* (Oxford, 1993), 57–76.

26. Eliot, *Essay on Iron*, 17; Richard Faber, *The Brave Courtier: Sir William Temple* (London, 1983), 144–147; Samuel Holt Monk, "Introduction," in Holt, ed., *Five Miscellaneous Essays by Sir William Temple* (Ann Arbor, Mich., 1963), xxxiii. The difference between Temple and Eliot's work, too, illustrates the difference between an aristocratic/aesthetic and a public/rhetorical *sensus communis*. See David S. Shields, *Civil Tongues and Polite Letters in British America* (Chapel Hill, N.C., 1997), chap. 3. See also Lawrence E. Klein, *Shaftesbury and*

The battles over "Virgilian" husbandry that Tull's text provoked showed that practical agricultural writing in Great Britain was still entwined with literary debate, despite advertisements of a "low" style. Old versus new husbandry became yet another round of ancients versus moderns. Virgil's *Georgics* was still consulted as a practical handbook, and Tull, a self-proclaimed *"Anti-Virgilian,"* spent a chapter denouncing the habit of relying on classical quotations and ancient advice.[27]

Eliot admired the way that *"old Romans"* like Virgil "regarded the Study of *Husbandry,* and the Improvement of their own *Language"* as two extremely important—and interconnected—branches of learning. Husbandry was the foundation of society, and the vernacular language was the medium of culture, and it was not beneath the dignity of any writer to try to improve both.

> Whereas with us there is so little care to Cultivate our own *Language,* . . . And *Husbandry* is left to the Invention and Conduct of *Common Labourers.* The product of Husbandry is Necessary to Life, is the Basis of Trade, and Sinnews of War: And our own *Language* is the ordinary Channel of Conveyance for Divinity, Law, and Politicks; it is that by which Commerce, Conversation, and all the important Affairs of Life are managed: Therefore both deserve our Attention and Regard.

In this passage, Eliot emphasizes the importance of cultured men's turning their attention to agriculture and devalues the efforts of common farmers. Just as the *"Mother Tongue"* could not be "improved" without the literary efforts of "Great and Learned Men" in the commonwealth of learning, farming would never advance if left to common practices and traditional habits.[28]

Rather than old Romans and the new philosophers, though, the ancients and moderns that mattered most to Eliot's audience were the New England forefathers and their mid-eighteenth-century descendants. His first essay frankly discusses the early settlers' lack of knowledge and experience. They came "from an old Cultivated Country, to thick Woods, [and] rough unim-

---

the Culture of Politeness: Moral Discourse and Cultural Politics in Early Eighteenth-Century England (Cambridge, 1994); and John Dwyer, "Introduction—A 'Peculiar Blessing': Social Converse in Scotland from Hutcheson to Burns," in Dwyer and Richard B. Sher, eds., *Sociability and Society in Eighteenth-Century Scotland, Eighteenth-Century Life,* XV (1991), 1–22.

27. Tull, *Horse-Hoing Husbandry,* chap. 9, "Remarks on the Bad Husbandry, That Is So Finely Express'd in Virgil's First Georgic." See also Fussell, *The Classical Tradition in West European Farming,* 143–148. Eliot, in *Continuation of Essay* (1749), 10, noted simply that Virgil's *Georgics* "is a better piece of Poetry than a Book of Husbandry; in which he hath taken more care to imbelish his Poem than to instruct a Farmer."

28. Eliot, *Continuation of Essay* (1751), 28, 29.

proved Lands, . . . Unskill'd in every Part of Service to be done." They chose the worst land to farm, tried the most expensive methods of cultivation, and hacked down the trees, "impoverishing the Land." The second essay counters this picture by suggesting that some of the knowledge New England's pioneers brought with them had been lost. They knew how to roll their barley, protect their orchard trees from mice, and preserve their cut timber with methods forgotten in less than a century. On balance, Eliot tried not to dim the virtuous efforts of New England's golden age even while he argued against the slavish perpetuation of traditional farming practices.[29]

Despite his appeal to "Great and Learned Men," Eliot generally sought to attract readers of almanacs, not translators of Virgil and Cato. Almanacs offered a smattering of pastoral poetry, satirical verse, proverbs, aphorisms, and other didactic material, but little practical farming advice. They became farmers' handbooks primarily for their astronomical and astrological charts, because husbandmen still planted and harvested according to the phases of the moon and positions of the planets. Almanac writers frequently ridiculed the idea that the stars ruled the fates of human beings, but "natural astrology," the belief that celestial bodies exerted some sort of physical influence over the growth of plants and the functions of animal bodies, was still discussed more seriously. Eliot might have been expected to scoff at the common farmer's reliance on his charts, but in fact he recommended that brush be cut at a particular time in the summer during *the old Moon that Day the Sign is in the Heart.* He wrote that "to shew such a Regard to the Signs, may incur the Imputation of Ignorance or Superstition; for the Learned know well enough, that the Division of the Zodiac . . . is not the Work of Nature, but of Art, contrived by Astronomers for Convenience." But the learned also knew "that the Moon's Attraction hath great Influence on all Fluids," including the sap in bushes, and a "Tryal" had shown this particular day better for killing off brush than other times. Therefore, Eliot concluded, "A Regard to the Sign, as it serveth to point out and direct to the proper Time, so it becomes worthy of Observation."[30]

Eliot shared the almanac writers' didacticism. He differed in giving his read-

29. Eliot, *Essay on Field-Husbandry* (1748), 1, 2; Eliot, *Continuation of Essay* (1749), 18–19.

30. Eliot, *Continuation of Essay* (1754), 39, 40, 41–42. On almanacs, see Chester E. Eisinger, "The Farmer in the Eighteenth Century Almanac," *Agri. Hist.,* XXVIII (1954), 107–112; Milton Drake, *Almanacs of the United States,* pt. 1 (New York, 1962), 18–59; Marion Barber Stowell, "The Influence of Nathaniel Ames on the Literary Taste of His Time," *Early American Literature,* XVIII (1983), 127–145. On the agricultural use of almanacs, see Frank Horsfall, Jr., "Horticulture in Eighteenth-Century America," *Agri. Hist.,* XLIII (1969), 163–164. On natural astrology, see also Herbert Leventhal, *In the Shadow of the Enlightenment: Occultism and Renaissance Science in Eighteenth-Century America* (New York, 1976), chap. 2.

ers not just something instructive to read but also lessons in how to read for instruction. He quoted old English proverbs to pass on "Truth and good Sense" to his readers, as long as the sayings were "founded on due Observation and Experience." He stitched together "scraps of History" to comment on ancient agricultural practices but paused to reflect upon the proper way to read about the past: "The Reader will see what use we are to make of *History,* and in what manner to improve it: For if we only read the Story without making Reflections or Improvement, *Religious, Natural or Political;* if we read only as a meer Amusement, without turning and improving the various Incidents to some useful Purposes, I cannot see why a Romance might not be as good or better than a true History."[31]

Eliot also directed readers to their Bibles and was surprised that no agricultural writer had taken notice of the "Rules of Husbandry" offered there. Eccles. 11:6 recommended that seed be sown in the morning and in the evening; Isa. 28:24–27 suggested a way to separate clover seed from its chaff. Although encouraging his readers to search the Scriptures for farming tips, Eliot also cautioned that husbandry was mentioned there only by way of comparison and illustration, not as the primary intention of a given passage. Furthermore, when the Bible seemed to support the case against drill husbandry, as in 2 Cor. 9:6 ("He that soweth sparingly, shall reap also sparingly"), Eliot noted that "in the application of this Rule we are to be under the conduct of Reason, Use, Prudence and Discretion."[32]

Eliot claimed that, when he first began his "small tracts," he had never expected that they "would ever extend farther than to a small Circle of Neighbours." But the essays found readers in New Jersey, Pennsylvania, Nova Scotia, and England. Published as pamphlets, as newspaper articles, and in the collected edition of 1761, the essays prompted some readers to write to the author, giving him material for future essays. Eliot's correspondents wrote optimistically about his work's importance. They believed his essays would influence agricultural practices in the colonies at two levels. Public-spirited gentlemen would be encouraged to experiment with improvements; their successes, in turn, would persuade others to try new techniques and experiments them-

31. Eliot, *Continuation of Essay* (1753), 27; Eliot, *Continuation of Essay* (1749), 8, 9.

32. Eliot, *Continuation of Essay* (1749), 10, 15–16. New Englanders were used to getting moral instruction from husbandry, not farming tips from Scripture. Eliot here inverts the tradition of Cotton Mather's *Agricola; or, The Religious Husbandman: The Main Intentions of Religion, Served in the Business and Language of Husbandry . . .* (Boston, 1727) and John Flavell's *Husbandry Spiritualized; or, The Heavenly Use of Earthly Things . . .* (London, 1669), which was first printed in America in 1709 (Boston), and reprinted in 1725.

selves. James Monk of Halifax was very eager to complete his set of Eliot's essays "that I may have an opportunity of receiving instruction and communicateing so useful a branch of knowledge to my neighbours in this country, where it is so much wanted; and so little understood." Peter Oliver reported that his "Enthusiasm for raising Wheat has spirited up my Neighbours to raise it," producing a bigger harvest than the previous ten years combined.[33]

Common farmers, however, might not be so easily "spirited up," according to Charles Read, a large landholder in New Jersey: "I perused your two Essays on Field Husbandry, and think the public may be much benefited by them; but, if the farmers in your neighborhood are as unwilling to leave the beaten road of their ancestors as they are near me, it will be difficult to persuade them to attempt any improvement . . . [even when] a gentlemen of a more public spirit has given them ocular demonstration of the success." Eliot's nephew in South Kingston had an even lower opinion of common farmers, though he believed that the drill plow would be a powerful "occular demonstration": "Indeed I am convinc'd that Agriculture will flourish in this Country if Gentlemen of Genius Leizure and Application will undertake it. The Soil is good, . . . but the Character of a Farmer in this Country is generally a Stupid one—their Minds are not to be inform'd but by occular demonstration. Reasoning on Farming to them is like Dancing a Jig in the Clouds."[34]

Not just an author addressing readers, Eliot undertook to provide a forum for farmers to communicate with each other. He offered to publish accounts of experiments, observations, discoveries, and even hints about small matters that "may be of publick Service." In the course of experience, he wrote, almost everyone discovers "Things valuable and useful, but for Want of some proper Method to communicate them, they die with the Discoverers, and are lost to Mankind." The public press, private correspondence, and personal contacts worked together to facilitate exchanges of information. Even without Frank-

33. Eliot, *Sixth Essay* (1759), 3; William Logan to Eliot, July 25, 1754, James Monk to Eliot, Sept. 17, 1757, Peter Oliver to Eliot, Nov. 30, 1759, Oliver to Eliot, November 1759, all in Eliot, *Essays*, ed. Carman and Tugwell, 228, 235, 241, 242; Richard Jackson to Eliot, ALS, June 12, 1760, Beinecke Library.

34. [Charles Read] to Eliot, n.d., 1749, in Eliot, *Essays*, ed. Carman and Tugwell, 223–224 (this edition of Eliot's essays follows older practice in misidentifying this unsigned letter as Franklin's, but it was subsequently shown to be Read's). See Woodward, *Ploughs and Politicks*, xi–xxiii; Robinson to Eliot, July 13, 1762, in Eliot, *Essays*, ed. Carman and Tugwell, 252. In *An Anxious Pursuit: Agricultural Innovation and Modernity in the Lower South, 1730–1815* (Chapel Hill, N.C., 1993), 131–140, Joyce E. Chaplin argues that agricultural innovation was promoted mostly by coastal planters trying to extend their power into the upcountry and that others were willing to experiment only in times of crisis.

lin's contacts, Eliot's essays brought him both informative correspondents and a wider circle of friends. Looking to examples in Ireland and Scotland, Eliot also urged that formal agricultural societies be organized in the colonies. Although nothing local took root, he and Oliver became corresponding members of the London Society for the Encouragement of Arts, Manufactures, and Commerce. With Thomas Clap, Eliot administered the society's attempt to promote silk production in Connecticut.[35]

Essays upon Field-Husbandry established a short-lived communications network for the exchange of agricultural information, seeds, and even farm implements between New England, Philadelphia, and London. Franklin was at the center of the web, though he confessed that he had little to add to the conversations about husbandry. He distributed or sold fifty copies of Eliot's first essay; he introduced Eliot to James Logan and John Bartram in Philadelphia and to Patrick Collinson and Richard Jackson in London, all of whom began corresponding with Eliot, often via Franklin. Eliot, in turn, introduced Jonathan Todd and Ezra Stiles to Franklin. Franklin sent Eliot rhubarb seeds, a specimen of "Alum Earth," and farm tools; Collinson sent him seeds from England. Nathan Bowen sent Eliot samples of wheat and marle from Massachusetts; Eliot sent wheat samples along with his drill plow to Philadelphia.[36]

The notebook of one of Eliot's correspondents shows how the essays supplemented advice from English farm books and might have influenced agricultural practice. Charles Read, a jurist and politician in New Jersey, was

35. Eliot, *Essay upon Field-Husbandry* (1748), 24. On the relationship of the press, letters, and personal contacts, see, for example, William Logan to Eliot, July 25, 1754, in Eliot, *Essays*, ed. Carman and Tugwell, 228: "As I take the N[ew] Y[or]k News Papers and have an Acquaintance with my kind Friend Benj Franklin, I have had the Opportunity of reading thy Several Essays on Husbandry." Eliot discusses the Irish Association in the "Preface," in Eliot, *Essays*, ed. Carman and Tugwell, 4, the Scottish societies and his desire for something like them in America in *Continuation of Essay* (1751), 28–29, and his involvement in the London Society in *Sixth Essay* (1759), 4–6. See also Peter Oliver to Eliot, Dec. 14, 1761, in Eliot, *Essays*, ed. Carman and Tugwell, 245; and Ezra Stiles to Eliot, Sept. 24, 1759, Stiles Papers. On the relationship between philosophical and improving societies in Scotland, see Kathleen Holcomb, "A Dance in the Mind: The Provincial Scottish Philosophical Societies," in Patricia B. Craddock and Carla H. Hay, eds., *Studies in Eighteenth-Century Culture*, XXI (East Lansing, Mich., 1991), 89–100. Eliot managed to cooperate with Thomas Clap on the matter of silk but resisted Clap's policies at Yale College (though not as vociferously as his son-in-law Benjamin Gale; see Chapter 3).

36. Eliot, *Continuation of Essay* (1749), 1. See Peter Collinson to Eliot, Jan. 27, 1753, Nathan Bowen to Eliot, Aug. 3, 1753, William Logan to Eliot, Sept. 23, 1758, all in Eliot, *Essays*, ed. Carman and Tugwell, 209, 210, 226–227. See also Eliot to Stiles, May 3, 1762, Stiles Papers; and the letters concerning Eliot in vols. III–VI of Labaree, ed., *Papers of Benjamin Franklin*.

William Logan's cousin and a member of Franklin's circle, but he introduced himself to Eliot in a 1749 letter merely as one who had "perused" the husbandry essays. Unlike Logan and other American readers, Read did not pause to praise Eliot's work as superior to English agricultural writing or at least as more suited to the climate and circumstances in the colonies. He launched right into the details of the experiments he had conducted on his three-hundred-acre Burlington farm. Read's farming notebook shows Eliot's essays were used by a practicing farmer—a farmer more interested in maximizing profits than in cultivating a philosophical attitude. Read's notebook is a heavily annotated copy of John Worlidge's *Systema Agriculturae* (1681), interleaved with notes and records dating from 1746 to 1777. Read drew from two dozen agricultural writers besides Worlidge, Eliot among them; he quoted Eliot on reclaiming swamps, cutting down elder bushes, and using red clover. The fifteen citations of Eliot's essays, compared to twenty-one references to Thomas Hale's *Compleat Body of Husbandry* (1756), suggest that Read relied less on Eliot's attempt to address colonial conditions than on the latest advice from England.[37]

Eliot had not written his essays only, or even primarily, for elite readers like Read. Like English agricultural writing, the essays probably circulated only among wealthier and more educated farmers. But his tone reduced the distance between the common plowman and the gentleman farmer, and his inclusive rhetoric encouraged his readers to consider poorer farmers as fellow husbandmen in a common enterprise rather than ignorant rustics needing instruction.

SCIENCE, RELIGION, AND NATURE

Charles Read's farming notebook does not reveal what Read, whom an associate described as a person who "knew no friend but the man that could serve him," made of Eliot's homespun moralism. Perhaps he took Eliot's advice and valued passages—the farming tips and the religious references alike—only so

---

37. John Worlidge, *Systema Agriculturae*, 3d ed. (London, 1681); Thomas Hale, *A Compleat Body of Husbandry* . . . (London, 1756); [Charles Read] to Eliot, [1749], in Eliot, *Essays*, ed. Carman and Tugwell, 223. Book 1 of Woodward's *Ploughs and Politicks* is a biography of Read; Read's notes on agriculture are printed as book 2. See William Logan to Eliot, July 25, 1754, in Eliot, *Essays*, ed. Carman and Tugwell, 228. Benjamin Franklin to Eliot, Sept. 12, 1751, in Labaree, ed., *Papers of Benjamin Franklin*, IV, 193, reported that Hugh Roberts described Eliot's essays as "preferable to any thing of late Years publish'd on that Subject in England." "The late Writers there, chiefly copy from one another, and afford very little new or useful."

far as they were found by experience to be "useful or unprofitable." Eliot certainly stressed the importance of *practical* knowledge over arcane scholarship, the kind of knowledge that would *"make a poor City rich, and a small City great."* His understanding of practicality and utility, however, did not just refer to material profit and progress but always included a moral and spiritual dimension. He began his first essay with the assertion that "the Cultivation of the Earth affords the most useful Philosophy, [it] opens to us a glorious scene and discovery of the Wisdom and Power of the Creator and Governor of the World." Husbandry could at once be made more scientific and "spiritualized." There was divine meaning in the natural world that human beings could discern; there was divine action on display that they could try to imitate. For Eliot, experimental philosophy and true religion reinforced each other.[38]

Yet in mid-eighteenth-century New England, the new science and the old faith interpreted the works of God, man, and nature in ways that were not always so easy to reconcile. On November 18, 1755, an earthquake shook Bostonians from their beds and rattled traditional conceptions of God's active role in the temporal affairs of New England. Eight days after the earth moved, John Winthrop, Harvard professor of mathematics and natural philosophy, delivered a lecture in the college chapel describing earthquakes as natural byproducts of the vegetative growth of minerals. Just as the plow breaks the ground for plants on the earth's surface, he explained, so earthquakes opened the subterranean "pores" of the earth necessary for mineral growth. "Fermenting materials" produced combustible vapors that eventually, and unavoidably, exploded. The process was all governed by general laws and was conducive to "the good of this globe in general"; even though a city might be occasionally leveled, God's wisdom and goodness were displayed.[39]

38. The remark about Read is from Aaron Leaming, Diary, Nov. 14, 1775, quoted in Woodward, *Ploughs and Politicks*, 53. The Eliot quotations are from "Preface," in Eliot, *Essays*, ed. Carman and Tugwell, 4; Eliot, *Essay on Field-Husbandry* (1748), ii, 25. Flavell's *Husbandry Spiritualized* and Mather's *Agricola* spiritualized husbandry by finding God's revealed will in nature and mixing metaphorical analogies with biblical typology. See Mason I. Lowance, Jr., *The Language of Canaan: Metaphor and Symbol in New England from the Puritans to the Transcendentalists* (Cambridge, Mass., 1980), 26; and Wallace E. Anderson, "Editor's Introduction," in Jonathan Edwards, *Typological Writings*, ed. Wallace E. Anderson and Mason I. Lowance, Jr., in Perry Miller et al., eds., *The Works of Jonathan Edwards*, XI (New Haven, Conn., 1993), 23.

39. John Winthrop, *A Lecture on Earthquakes . . .* (Boston, 1755). The discussion about the fermentation of metals is on 30. Winthrop also argued by drawing on an analogy between the explosions in "the entrails of the earth" (29) and an animal body evacuating its bowels, a function "of absolute necessity to maintain life and health," yet fatal in extreme cases (28). The discussion of God's goodness is on 27–29. Leventhal, *In the Shadow of the*

The Reverend Thomas Prince of Boston played Calvinist Jeremiah to Winthrop's Pangloss. He suggested that the Boston fashion for lightning rods had drawn an electrical charge from the clouds to the earth, causing a subterranean thunderclap, and he described the shrieks of terror in Boston with the care that Winthrop took to calculate the earthquake's epicenter. Rather than marvel at God's ingenious method of underground tillage, he urged the inhabitants of New England to repent their sins in the aftermath of what was obviously God's dreadful judgment upon them.[40]

Eliot wrote on the subject in a letter to Ezra Stiles on March 24, 1756: "I think Mr Winthrop has laid Mr Prince flat on his back, and seems to take some pleasure in his mortification. The Professor has in my opinion given the best summary of the Laws of Electricity that I have ever seen; and accounted for earthquakes upon Principles founded on Experience." Eliot simply believed that Winthrop had demolished Prince's hypothesis about the connection between

---

Enlightenment, 223–231, discusses the various theories, which held throughout the eighteenth century, on the growth of metals and minerals: "All theories, again excepting that of direct creation by God, held that minerals, in some sense, developed and grew. Moreover, the gestation period of minerals generally appeared to be calculated not in geological eons but in periods comparable to those of animal and plant life. This in itself tended to bridge the gap between the animate and inanimate worlds" (225).

40. Thomas Prince, *An Improvement of the Doctrine of Earthquakes, Being the Works of God, and Tokens of His Just Displeasure . . .* (Boston, 1755). This is a reprint of Prince's second 1727 earthquake sermon, with an attached letter, which appeared seven days after the Nov. 18, 1755, earthquake. On Dec. 5, Prince reprinted the first of his 1727 sermons as *Earthquakes the Works of God, and Tokens of His Just Displeasure . . .* (Boston, 1755), with a new appendix and postscript discussing electricity as a probable cause. Winthrop takes aim at Prince in an appendix to his *Lecture on Earthquakes.* Prince responded with a letter published in the *Boston Gazette,* Jan. 26, 1756. Winthrop answered with a pamphlet, *A Letter to the Publishers of the Boston Gazette . . .* (Boston, 1756). These works are ably discussed in Eleanor M. Tilton, "Lightning-Rods and the Earthquake of 1755," *New England Quarterly,* XIII (1940), 85–97. Charles Edwin Clark, in "Science, Reason, and an Angry God: The Literature of an Earthquake," *NEQ,* XXXVIII (1965), 340–362, correctly describes this material when he writes that the twenty-seven relevant publications do not reflect a three-way theological split between liberals, Old Calvinists, and New Lights, although his phrase "unanimity in interpretation" (355) glosses over significant differences in tone and emphasis. Maxine Van de Wetering, in "Moralizing in Puritan Natural Science: Mysteriousness in Earthquake Sermons," *Journal of the History of Ideas,* XLIII (1982), 417–438, claimed that eighteenth-century clerics followed a paradigm illustrated by Thomas Doolittle's *Earthquakes Explained and Practically Improved . . .* (London, 1693). Doolittle divided earthquakes into two categories: those caused by God's direct intervention, which should produce fear in people, and those that arose through second causes, which ought to prompt human admiration. But this model clearly does not describe the 1755 sermons, which described earthquakes from second causes that nonetheless should provoke fearful awakenings.

electricity, lightning rods, and earthquakes. Eliot did not comment on the religious use of earthquakes, which was indeed the larger question. The earthquake prompted a discussion of the proper moral improvement of divinely ordered natural phenomena. It was not a contest between science and religion, if that means the opposition of natural and supernatural explanations. Both Winthrop and Prince tried to explain the phenomenon scientifically, and both gave it a moral and religious significance.[41]

Winthrop's criticism of Prince went beyond the dispute over earthquakes; it challenged what Winthrop called the "complex character of *Philosopher* and *Divine*." Although it is difficult to separate Winthrop's contempt for Prince personally from his general opinion about clergymen who tried to speak authoritatively about scientific questions, the professor's main point was that the true relationship between the natural and moral worlds is properly expounded by the scientific philosopher, not the minister playing with the latest scientific fad. Winthrop refused to let divines characterize natural philosophy as merely the consideration of natural or material causes. "The consideration of a DEITY is not peculiar to *Divinity*, but belongs also to *natural Philosophy*." Winthrop compared Prince's "panic" over lightning rods to the "unreasonable terrors" of "the more *timorous Sex*." When lecturing about comets four years later, he further developed the contrast between the "alarm" and "natural superstition" of "Those who see with unphilosophic eyes" and the "rectitude" and "firmness" of the "reasonable being" who turns his thoughts to "that consummate WISDOM, which presides over this vast machine of nature."[42]

Clergymen continued to consider science the handmaiden of theology and

41. Eliot to Ezra Stiles, Mar. 24, 1756, in Franklin Bowditch Dexter, ed., *Extracts from the Itineraries and Other Miscellanies of Ezra Stiles, D.D., LL.D., 1755–1794, with a Selection from His Correspondence* (New Haven, Conn., 1916), 480. Clifford K. Shipton, in *Biographical Sketches*, V, 200, claimed that Jared Eliot "applauded when Professor John Winthrop 'laid Mr Prince flat on his back' for using earthquakes for purposes of religious terrorism." But this misrepresents comments Eliot made and distorts the nature of the argument about God's activity in the world.

42. Winthrop, *A Letter*, 2, 4, 6, 7; John Winthrop, *Two Lectures on Comets . . .* (Boston, 1759), 40–44. See also Winthrop to Ezra Stiles, Apr. 17, 1756, Stiles Papers. Thirty years later, the argument continued. In the *Connecticut Courant* (Hartford), June 15, 1789, the Reverend Joseph Huntington of Coventry argued that an unusual optical phenomenon (multiple haloes around the sun) was a "loud, speaking occurrence of divine providence." Turning to list the sins that might have provoked the sign, he asked, "What do we behold among God's covenant people?" An article entitled "Some Strictures on the Piece Published by Dr. Huntington" (*Conn. Courant*, July 20, 1789), however, challenged this interpretation and argued that such natural phenomena merely testify to the existence of God and cannot bear the moral arguments that Huntington thrust upon them.

did not seem to be worried (as Winthrop suggested) that the handmaiden might divert too much attention from the earthquake's "awaken[ing] apprehensions." "In the Earthquake, we have had a practical Sermon, preached to us in very awful Accents," the Reverend Thomas Foxcroft wrote, and all other clergymen who published on the event agreed. Although some earthquakes mentioned in the Scriptures seemed to be miraculous, there was no reason why God could not work through second causes with the materials at hand. An earlier generation of learned clergymen, clinging like Prince to the "complex character of *Philosopher* and *Divine,*" spent more time discussing the second causes, but, in 1755, clerics were more content to leave the scientific aspects to "Disputers" like Winthrop. How God shook the earth was much less important than the message he was trying to send. The "doctrine" to be found in God's "practical sermon" was, not Winthrop's general law about the fermentation of metals, but the Bible's general rule that God sends earthquakes as tokens of divine wrath; and, although Winthrop chided Prince's pathos, other clergymen, too, considered the proper "application" to be fear and trembling, followed by solemn repentance. Jonathan Mayhew's earthquake sermons promised to address, not the passions and superstitions, but the heart and conscience through the door of the understanding, yet he was much more skeptical than Winthrop about the ability of human understanding to penetrate God's mysteries. Charles Chauncy's *Earthquakes a Token of the Righteous Anger of God* argued that earthquakes were, not part of God's wonderful machine-world, but part of a natural world maimed by the sin of man and that they ought to inspire fear.[43]

Whatever Eliot's experimental philosophy, like Winthrop's scientific explanations of natural phenomena, might have contributed to the demystification of the natural world, Eliot himself still saw God's hand very active in the affairs

43. Winthrop's mention of "awaken[ing] apprehensions" is in *A Letter,* 6; Thomas Foxcroft, *The Earthquake, a Divine Visitation . . .* (Boston, 1756), 46. Van de Wetering, in "Moralizing in Puritan Natural Science," *Jour. of the Hist. of Ideas,* XLIII (1982), 428, claimed that earthquake sermonizers in 1727 "gave over a disproportionate amount of space to natural causes," but that was not the case in 1755. Foxcroft was content to leave such questions to the "Disputers" (30). Jonathan Mayhew, in *The Expected Dissolution of All Things, a Motive to Universal Holiness . . .* (Boston, 1755), 57–58, wrote that a discussion of the natural cause or causes of earthquakes was "quite foreign from the business of preaching." See also Mayhew, *A Discourse on Rev. XV, 3d, 4th. Occasioned by the Earthquakes in November 1755 . . .* (Boston, 1755); Charles Chauncy, *Earthquakes a Token of the Righteous Anger of God* (Boston, 1755); John Burt, *Earthquakes the Effects of God's Wrath . . .* (Newport, R.I., 1755); Mather Byles, *Divine Power and Anger Displayed in Earthquakes . . .* (Boston, 1755); James Cogswell, *The Danger of Disregarding the Works of God . . .* (New Haven, Conn., [1755]); and John Rogers, *. . . On the Terribleness, and the Moral Cause of Earthquakes* (Boston, 1756).

of men. The 1744 victory of New England and British forces over the French at Cape Breton, Eliot had rejoiced, was a wonderful display of "God's Marvellous Kindness." Eliot enumerated a long "train of Providences" that had carried the day and thanked God for providing good weather, keeping the troops healthy, and confusing the enemy. Like both Charles Chauncy and Thomas Prince, Eliot described God's producing the marvel of the Cape Breton victory providentially, not miraculously—that is, by working through second causes.[44]

Eliot sought to awaken an awareness of the divine providences and moral instructions offered daily in the common occurrences of life, not just in extraordinary events like earthquakes and military triumphs. "The supreme Ruler of the Universe takes Care of the whole Race of Mankind," he wrote in closing his fifth husbandry essay. "His Goodness, in a special Manner, meets us with Instruction, and lays it in our Way, that we may find it in our ordinary Vocation, for our Profit and Improvement, whether it be Merchandise or Farming." Farmers and merchants learned the same moral lesson: the former were told to "sow to yourselves Righteousness" and the latter to seek the kingdom of heaven like a pearl of great price. Only on this allegorical level, however, could Eliot bring himself to regard the merchant's and the husbandman's vocations of equal value. The fifth essay had begun with a discussion of nominal versus real value, where pearls, gold, and diamonds were dismissed as overvalued baubles, and oyster shells (used in medicines), iron, and grindstones were hailed for their practical utility and real "intrinsick Worth." Similarly, husbandry was described as the foundation of all commerce, communication, social advantages, and earthly pleasures and as the basis for the merchant's activities and the generation of artificial wealth.[45]

Like Winthrop, Eliot believed that a humble inquiry into the natural world promoted religious sentiments. Peat showed that God had preserved wood from before Noah's time for use in the present and also offered evidence that the Mosaic account of the Flood was true; limestone found twenty miles inland "is an Evidence that the World is made and governed by a Kind, Wise and Intelligent Being"; the different forms and states of iron and mercury demonstrated that the doctrine of the Resurrection was not inconsistent with scientific principles. Winthrop stressed that science (natural philosophy) increased

44. Jared Eliot, *God's Marvellous Kindness* . . . (New London, Conn., 1745), a sermon preached in Killingworth on the July 25, 1745, thanksgiving for the victory at Louisbourg (June 17, 1745); Charles Chauncy, *Marvellous Things Done by the Right Hand and Holy Arm of God in Getting Him the Victory* . . . (Boston, 1745); and Thomas Prince, *Extraordinary Events the Doings of God, and Marvellous in Pious Eyes* . . . (Boston, 1745).

45. Eliot, *Continuation of Essay* (1754), 1, 44, quoting Hos. 10:11–12 and Matt. 13:45–46.

one's appreciation of divine greatness, majesty, power, and goodness. Comets, he declared, when seen by the philosophical eye, can "raise in our minds most sublime conceptions of God, and particularly display his exquisite skill." Eliot praised planted groves as "proper places for retirement, study, and medita-tion" for "those, who love contemplation," describing the moral use of pas-toral scenes the way that Professor Winthrop characterized the psychological effect of investigations in natural philosophy: "These Views serve to waft away the Soul upon the Wings of exulting elevated Thoughts and warm Desires, to-wards the Great Creator and Beneficent Ruler of the Universe. . . . *This* affords a Pleasure . . . which the Stranger to serious Thought and Reflection inter-meddles not with-all." Both Winthrop and Eliot described an intellectually re-fined contemplation that wafted consciousness into the realm of the sublime.[46]

More commonly, however, Eliot urged his readers to imitate God's creative action, not just to admire the Almighty's handiwork. In most areas of life, the proper moral response to God's wonders was neither passive contemplation nor paralyzing fear, but practical moral action. He celebrated the gentleman's pastoral retreat as the product of the husbandman's hard labor. The best ex-ample was offered by Eliot's favorite "Branch of Husbandry," the swamp recla-mation he had described in his first essay. "Take a View of a Swamp in its orig-inal Estate," he began. It was "full of Bogs" and overgrown with "poisonous Woods and Vines"; its "miry Bottom" harbored snakes, toads, "and other creeping Vermin"; its brambles and thickets were "a Cage of every unclean and hateful Bird."

> Now take another Survey of the same Place, after the Labour of Clearing, Ditching, Dreining, Burning, and other needful Culture has passed upon it.
>
> Behold it now cloathed with sweet verdant Grass, adorned with the lofty widespreading well-set *Indian*-Corn, . . . fine Ranges of Cabbage; the deli-cious Melon . . . a wonderful Change *this!* and all brought about in a short Time; a Resemblance of Creation, as much as we, impotent Beings, can at-tain to, the happy Product of Skill and Industry.

Eliot warned that there were limitations to what people could or should do to a landscape: "We many Times, as it were, commit a Rape upon our Land, by forcing it to that Improvement for which it is not fitted by Nature." Yet he had no affection whatsoever for some natural ("unimproved") environments: "Frog-Ponds spoil the Beauty of a Field; and are undesirable, like *Ulcers* or

46. Eliot, *Continuation of Essay* (1749), 23–27 (peat), 29 (limestone); Eliot, *Essay on Iron,* 12n (iron and mercury); Winthrop, *Two Essays on Comets,* 38; Eliot, *Sixth Essay* (1759), 30; Eliot, *Continuation of Essay* (1753), 33.

Sores in a Man's Face." The husbandman is called to work for aesthetic reasons if not monetary rewards: "It is not only worth while to Drein and Subdue such Places on the account of the *Profit* that may be made hereby, but also for the sake of the *Deformity* that is hereby Removed." Eliot directed, while his farm laborers actually performed, the "needful Culture." Like God, he worked through second causes.[47]

NEW ENGLAND VIRTUE AND THE NEW HUSBANDRY

Eighteenth-century New England had both subsistence- and market-oriented farmers. In Connecticut, towns along the coast and in the Connecticut River valley produced for markets in commercial centers such as New London and Hartford, whereas, according to one study, the towns planted in the rocky soil of present-day Windham, Tolland, and Litchfield Counties "remained largely self-sufficient." Although historians disagree about the timing of the transition to commercial farming, most acknowledge that, as market opportunities expanded, farmers gradually adopted intensive agricultural techniques to produce larger surpluses. Richard L. Bushman has argued that the commercialization of agriculture was more than the result of "a raw desire for profit"; it was driven as much by cultural aspirations for a higher standard of living, for "urbanity, refinement, and middle-class values." Eliot certainly wanted to open rural America to the best that English culture had to offer, but he was even more concerned to preserve New England's traditional pattern of nucleated villages and middling family farms because of the social and moral benefits he believed they bestowed. He tried to show his local audience how New England could retain its commitment to the virtues of the yeoman freehold even as population soared, land prices rose, and war altered the region's political and economic relationship to the mother country. Many of his Connecticut neighbors shared his faith that New England virtue could withstand new economic pressures and opportunities, but few were as willing to bow to imperial restrictions on expansion.[48]

47. Eliot, *Continuation of Essay* (1753), 32; Eliot, *Continuation of Essay* (1751), 12, 22.

48. Carolyn Merchant, in *Ecological Revolutions: Nature, Gender, and Science in New England* (Chapel Hill, N.C., 1989), 150, 308–310, assessed the long debate over the relative importance of subsistence- and market-oriented farming and argued that the two economic extremes coexisted and varied by region. Jackson Turner Main, *Society and Economy in Colonial Connecticut* (Princeton, N.J., 1985), 379, discussed the self-sufficiency of Windham, Tolland, and Litchfield. Richard L. Bushman, "Opening the American Countryside," in James A. Henretta, Michael Kammen, and Stanley N. Katz, eds., *The Transformation of Early*

Between 1730 and 1760, Connecticut's population almost doubled, and the price of farmland rose while acreage per family declined sharply. Eliot offered Tullian tillage and fertilization to improve exhausted soil, crop rotation and plantings of red clover and grasses to keep land productive, and swamp draining to bring more land under cultivation. Others pinned their hopes to the Susquehanna Company and the cheap land in Pennsylvania's Wyoming Valley that they hoped the sea-to-sea clause in Connecticut's 1662 charter would allow them to settle. Eliot bought a share in the company, but Richard Jackson warned him from England that the home government would never allow Connecticut's expansion. Although many were "inclined to Remove to new Places," Eliot was determined to make Connecticut economically productive even with its increasing population density and smaller parcels of land.[49]

Connecticut, however, was preoccupied with wars that took "off men from their husbandry business" and burdened the colony with debt. Eliot began writing on husbandry during King George's War in 1747, and his plan of publishing annual essays was interrupted after 1754 by the Seven Years' War. He rationalized these disruptions by lodging them in lessons from Roman history. Like "the old *Romans,*" men moved "from the plow to the war, and from the war to the plow again." Eliot's correspondents worried about the effect that war and the libertine manners of British officers would have upon American virtue. His nephew rejoiced in 1762 to finally hear that "the Military Men . . . draw their Minds off of Blood and Slaughter and turn to the more Pleasing and Profitable Task of Cultivating the Lands for the Support of Man." Throughout the difficulties, Eliot had remained optimistic. In 1749, after acknowledging a scarcity of corn and hay, he reminded his readers: "The Country may be considered as Improving and Advancing very much: There is now a great deal of Silver and Gold in the Country; we have better Houses, publick and Private,

American History: Society, Authority, and Ideology (New York, 1991), 239–256, argued for commercialization stemming from a desire for refinement.

49. On Connecticut population, see Bruce C. Daniels, *The Connecticut Town: Growth and Development, 1635–1790* (Middletown, Conn., 1979), 47; and Main, *Society and Economy in Colonial Connecticut*, 13–14. On the land-to-man ratio, see Bruce C. Daniels, "Economic Development in Colonial and Revolutionary Connecticut: An Overview," *WMQ*, 3d Ser., XXXVII (1980), 432, 446. On price, see Main, *Society and Economy*, 33. Eliot, according to Benjamin Franklin in a letter to Richard Jackson of Dec. 6, 1753, believed that Killingworth's population was doubling every fifteen years, without much immigration (Labaree, ed., *Papers of Benjamin Franklin*, V, 148). Eliot bought one share in the Susquehanna Company for nine dollars, according to the "List of Persons Added to the Susquehanna Company, Nov. 20, 1754," in Julian P. Boyd, ed., *The Susquehanna Company Papers*, 4 vols. (Wilkes-Barre, Pa., 1930–1933), I, 1750–1755. See Jackson to Eliot, Aug. 13, 1755, Beinecke Library. Eliot's reference to removing to new places is in *Continuation of Essay* (1749), 5.

richer Furniture, better Food and Cloathing; better Bridges and High-ways, fatter Cattel and finer Horses, and Lands bear an higher Price: These things are matters of Fact, and Facts are stubborn Things, which will not bow nor break." A decade later, he took delight in planting a new grove of trees and imagining the pleasure the trees would provide when they matured, though he knew that he himself would not live long enough to see them flourish. In 1762, a year before his death, he marveled at the age of progress he lived in and continued to promote his experimental philosophy: "Every Week's Experience affords a new Accession of Knowledge, and opens a new Scene of Wonders, and furnishes out a new Set of Ideas." [50]

If war endangered American morals, victory offered the chance of redemption. As Quebec fell into English hands on September 17, 1759, Eliot wondered whether William Pitt's administration would combat the corruptions of "luxury" with the "economic virtues" of temperance and frugality. Ezra Stiles told him he had high hopes that "the Alterations in Husbandry and facilitating the Acquisition of property both in Britain and America may retrieve both from Vice; especially if national Measures be taken for promoting universal Industry." Eliot, too, was looking west and thinking about new land as well as new husbandry.[51]

Pondering in his last husbandry essay how the new land ought to be settled and farmed, Eliot opposed suggestions to carve "the extensive, uninhabited, parts of *North-America*" into plantations of several thousand acres each so that the land would be "eminently beneficial, to our mother Country." He described the advantages of the small yeoman freehold. It took hard work to clear, drain, and cultivate the land, and nothing would inspire men to persevere "like the pleasure, and the advantage, of having a right to call it their *own*." Echoing his friend Franklin's analysis in "Observations concerning the Increase of Mankind" (1751), Eliot argued that, when men can support a family by their own labor, they marry young and populate the land and thus "increase the trade of *Great-Britain*, and add strength to the community." Closely settled areas become towns, towns build schools and colleges, trade flourishes, and men and women enjoy the benefits of civilization and "social worship." "Stragling, scattered, distant settlements" were not conducive to "virtue, and order." Consonant with these views, Eliot objected to slavery, though for eco-

50. Eliot, *Sixth Essay* (1759), 4, 29–33; Ezra Stiles to Eliot, Sept. 24, 1759, Stiles Papers; H. W. Robinson to Eliot, July 13, 1762, in Eliot, *Essays*, ed. Carman and Tugwell, 252; Eliot, *Continuation of Essay* (1749), 20; Eliot, *Essay on Iron*, 24.

51. Eliot to Ezra Stiles, Sept. 17, 1759, Stiles to Eliot, Sept. 24, 1759 ("economic virtues"), both in Stiles Papers.

nomic and practical reasons rather than moral ones. Glancing south while he pondered the new lands in the West, he acknowledged that slave labor could be used to plant and harvest export crops but argued that, "as slaves spent but little, there will not be a proportionable demand for *English* Goods." Furthermore, slaves "are not constitutional members of the common wealth" and "cannot be rely'd on, in a time of common danger."[52]

Eliot's main concern was to revitalize the "economic virtue" of the older New England settlements that he offered as a model. Like colonial "improvers" in other regions, he wanted the benefits of commercial modernization while preserving the social and moral benefits of an agricultural society. Developing domestic manufactures, he argued, would help the farmer, for, "if great Numbers were employed in and about Manufactures in Iron," they would depend upon the farmer for their food and create "the most sure and certain" home market. The scheme to plant mulberry trees and produce silk would not take men away from husbandry because much of the labor could "be performed by women, children, cripples, and aged persons." Children would be rescued from the dangers of idleness, the old and the lame from feeling like "a dead weight" upon the community. The poor could work at home in an occupation that required "no stock to set up with, except virtue and diligence."[53]

Eliot's proposals balanced self-interest with the needs of the community. He was neither a Boston liberal urging that self-interested entrepreneurs be unleashed in a free market nor an Edwardsean Calvinist demanding nothing less than disinterested economic benevolence. These two views might characterize clerical polemics over economic issues—just as historians' models of a nostalgic classical republicanism and modern liberal capitalism can describe opposing theories of political economy—but Eliot tried to mediate between the ideological extremes. In his 1738 election sermon, he tried to show "how our Interest and Duty are interwoven and joined together." In his husbandry

52. On tenant farmers, see Eliot, *Sixth Essay* (1759), 15, 16, 17. Indeed, it was hard to secure tenant farmers for a 600-acre parcel Eliot had purchased for Richard Jackson. William Samuel Johnson described the continuing problem in a letter to Jackson in 1772 (Boyd, ed., *Susquehanna Company Papers*, IV, 329–330). Cheap land in the north was draining farm labor out of the colony. Main, in *Society and Economy in Colonial Connecticut*, 33, notes that at the end of the colonial period the same sum that bought 50 acres in Connecticut bought 640 in Ohio. On slavery, see Eliot, *Sixth Essay* (1759), 17. Eliot also explained why "the introduction of great numbers of slaves is not good policy" in a letter to Stiles, May 25, 1761, Stiles Papers.

53. Eliot, *Essay on Iron*, 33; Eliot, *Sixth Essay* (1759), 13, 14. For a discussion of agricultural improvement and the ambivalence about progress in the colonial Lower South, see Chaplin, *An Anxious Pursuit*, 23–65.

essays, he argued that a "prospect of reasonable gain to themselves and their posterity" was an acceptable motive to economic activity, especially when joined with the chance to do "publick service to the colony" as well as "what may be useful and acceptable to our mother country." He criticized the self-love that led many to overvalue their abilities and live beyond their means. He denounced the selfishness that made others refuse to support public projects "unless you can promise mountains of gold." Eliot's efforts to promote silk and iron manufacture in Connecticut appealed to both private profit and public service. The London Society's encouragement of both schemes showed how a transatlantic spirit of cooperation could support the development of local husbandry and commerce. Cash rewards and institutional recognition could promote, to use Eliot's words, "a new Sort of Improvement" of the interest first cultivated by private correspondence and publication.[54]

As he balanced self-interest and the public good, Eliot also accommodated New England's interests to the requirements of the home government—an accommodation that soon rendered his vision obsolete. His political understanding was more clearly expressed in his 1738 election sermon than in his later essays. The Hobbesian state of nature he described in 1738 was not unlike the noxious frog pond in his agricultural essays years later: a natural but miserable state of affairs requiring diligent human effort to improve it. Those improvements led first to patriarchal government and then, finally, to a civil government of law and restraints upon power, which was best exemplified by

54. The quoted phrases from Eliot are in *Give Cesar His Due; or, The Obligation that Subjects Are under to Their Civil Rulers . . .* (New London, 1738), 19, 43; Eliot, *Sixth Essay* (1759), 12; Eliot, *Essay upon Field-Husbandry* (1748), appendix. Mark Valeri, in "Self-Love and Self-Denial: New England and the Social Crises of the Mid-Eighteenth Century" (paper presented at the American Historical Association's Annual Meeting, New York, December 1990), divided clerical economic opinion between the liberal and Edwardsean positions. On liberalism and republicanism, see, especially, Daniel T. Rodgers, "Republicanism: The Career of a Concept," *Journal of American History*, LXXIX (1992–1993), 11–38; James T. Kloppenberg, "The Virtues of Liberalism: Christianity, Republicanism, and Ethics in Early American Political Discourse," *JAH*, LXXIV (1987–1988), 9–33; Robert E. Shalhope, *The Roots of Democracy: American Thought and Culture, 1760–1800* (Boston, 1990), and "Republicanism and Early American Historiography," *WMQ*, 3d Ser., XXXIX (1982), 334–356. Eliot's involvement with silk and iron is briefly discussed in Rodney True's biographical introduction to Eliot, *Essays*, ed. Carman and Tugwell, li–lvi; and in Herbert Thoms's biographical sketch, *Jared Eliot, Minister, Doctor, Scientist, and His Connecticut* (n.p., 1967). Eliot was awarded a gold medal for his *Essay on Iron* by the Society for the Encouragement of Arts, Manufactures, and Commerce of London, receiving notification of the award nine days before his death. That was ironic, True noted, for a regulation forbidding ironworks and steelmaking in the colonies had been passed in 1750 (lvi). E. H. Jenkins, in "Jared Eliot: A Pastor-Physician, 1685–1763," typescript, Beinecke Library, confuses this society with the Royal Society.

the British Constitution. Patriarchal government had arisen from the natural rights parents had over their children and their dependents. Patriarchy was found to be too despotic (even King David could not be trusted with arbitrary power) and in modern times had "by degrees dwindled away," though it had not disappeared. Eliot still called subjects to obey their civil fathers according to the fifth commandment. And patriarchal government still existed in families. He explained the relationship between the patriarchal family and civil society with an agricultural metaphor: "Yet *Family Government,* as it is limited by the *Civil Government,* is of mighty Advantage to mankind. This is the Nursery from whence Plants are removed into the Common Wealth: if they are Unpruned, Uncultivated, Crooked, Stunted, Knotty, Crabbed, As the Tree is, so will be the Fruit." Similarly, the colonies were "*British* Plantations," with governments that were "little Models of that Excellent and great form at Home." Sketching an analogy linking contemporary and New Testament politics in his 1738 sermon, he seemed far more sympathetic to the Herodians (the Court Party and colonial placemen) than to the Scribes and Pharisees (the Country Party), zealots who pretended great zeal for the law and for the rights of the people but who twisted civil and religious controversies together and caused popular turmoil. As the crises of the 1760s approached, pamphlets and editorials began to urge New Englanders to buy fewer imported goods and to dress in homespun. Eliot argued that "this would make us less useful to *England,* from whom we derive; and from whom we have receiv'd such favours and assistance, when we were surrounded by our encroaching enemies." The best solution for all concerned, he contended, was for New England to export more, not import less. His entire program of intensive agriculture, too, can be seen as an act of deference to the imperial authority that in 1763 would nullify Connecticut's Susquehanna land claims and forbid settlements west of the Appalachians.[55]

For Eliot's neighbors, struggling to make old land new made sense only if new land could not be had. Acquiring new property, not developing a new husbandry, remained the most popular means to economic prosperity, and the mother country was blocking the way. The men elected to replace the governor and assistants who had taken the Stamp Act oath in 1765 were Susquehanna men, not experimental farmers, and this new leadership would guide Connecticut through the coming years of resistance and revolution.

Post–Stamp Act Connecticut proved to be stony ground for Jared Eliot's program of agricultural renewal. The British finally did receive some Connecticut iron (though not from black sea sand) in the form of cannonballs

---

55. Eliot, *Give Cesar His Due,* 2–10, 27–28, 31, 34, 36–37; Eliot, *Sixth Essay* (1759), 12.

fired by the Continental army. Silk production, which New Englanders found to be a difficult, labor-intensive business, never thrived. The cooperation between the scholar and the artisan that had marked the construction of the drill plow ended in a 1771 lawsuit between Eliot's son-in-law Benjamin Gale and the wheelwright Benoni Hylliard over the rights to the device. Drill plows did not come into general use until improved designs and standardized parts were introduced in the nineteenth century. Rather than develop a staple crop, as Eliot also urged, many Connecticut farmers turned to livestock, changed occupations, or left the colony. Those who stayed and farmed continued the wasteful practices of their grandfathers.[56]

Eliot's essays did not immediately inspire other American writers to spread the word about agricultural improvement. The few farmers who read agricultural texts still read British books. The next important work on colonial agriculture was the two-volume *American Husbandry* (1775), which claimed to be by "An American" but was probably written by Arthur Young, an Englishman who had never crossed the Atlantic. Connecticut's leading agricultural improver after the Revolution, Jeremiah Wadsworth, who helped found the Philadelphia Society for Improving Agriculture and the Connecticut Agricultural Society in 1785, had been inspired by a library of English agricultural books purchased during a tour of England in 1784. A letter in the *Connecticut Courant* in 1789 argued again that population pressures demanded new methods of agriculture and challenged learned men to conduct experiments, publish their results, and show laborers how to improve their farms. Samuel Deane's *New-England Farmer* (1790) drew upon Eliot's work, modified English advice to suit American conditions, and addressed "persons of a liberal or polite education" as well as "the common people." Still, it was "ocular demonstration" rather than literature that influenced the average farmer. Only when Wadsworth in 1795 successfully introduced a new strain of wheat that resisted the devastating

56. Joseph Ewan described the difficulties involved in silk manufacture in "Silk Culture in the Colonies: With Particular Reference to the Ebenezer Colony and the First Local Flora of Georgia," *Agri. Hist.*, XLIII (1969), 129–142. See also Edmund S. Morgan, *The Gentle Puritan: A Life of Ezra Stiles, 1727–1795* (New Haven, Conn., 1962), 147–151, 164–165; Chaplin, *An Anxious Pursuit*, 158–165. On the dispute over the drill plow, see George C. Groce, Jr., "Benjamin Gale," *NEQ*, X (1937), 708; J. Hammond Trumbull and Charles J. Hoadly, eds., *The Public Records of the Colony of Connecticut*, 15 vols. (Hartford, Conn., 1850–1890), XIII, 566. On drill plows more generally, see Marshall, "Jethro Tull," *Econ. Hist. Rev.*, II (1929– 1930), 55–57; Timothy Dwight, *A Statistical Account of the City of New-Haven* (New Haven, Conn., 1811), 23: "*Drills* are not used, except to drop onion seed." On New England agricultural practices in the later eighteenth century, see Daniels, "Economic Development," *WMQ*, 3d Ser., XXXVII (1980), 445–450.

Hessian fly did Connecticut farmers begin to show the enthusiasm for improvement that Jared Eliot tried to promote a half-century before. Even then improvers had to endure the jeers of scoffers like David Daggett, a prominent lawyer and politician:

This species of [modern] enterprise, and this spirit of [new] learning, has entered deeply into the business of agriculture. Discoveries have been made which have rendered sowing and reaping unnecessary. The plow, harrow, spade, hoe, sickle and scythe, have undergone a thorough change, on mathematical principles, and the speculative husbandman has yearly expected to see the fields covered with grass, and the hills and vallies with corn and wheat, without the clownish exercise of labour. With Varlow on Husbandry, in his hands, and a complete collection of philosophical farming utensils, he has forgotten that by the "sweat of his brow he was to eat his bread," and is hourly expecting to "reap where he hath not sown, and gather where he hath not strawed." [57]

Eliot's *Essays*, however, distinctly impressed at least one influential New Englander. John Adams's first published essays, as the rustic "Humphrey Plough-

57. David Daggett, *Sun-Beams May Be Extracted from Cucumbers, but the Process Is Tedious; An Oration, Pronounced on the Fourth of July, 1799* . . . (New Haven, Conn., 1799), 8–9. On *American Husbandry* . . . , 2 vols. (London, 1775), see Carl R. Woodward, "A Discussion of Arthur Young and American Agriculture," *Agri. Hist.*, XLIII (1969), 65. See also Rodney C. Loehr, "Arthur Young and American Agriculture," ibid., XLIII (1969), 43–56. On Wadsworth, see Chester McArthur Destler, "The Gentleman Farmer and the New Agriculture: Jeremiah Wadsworth," ibid., XLVI (1972), 135–153. In the 1790s, Wadsworth ordered all twenty-four volumes of Young's *Annals of Agriculture*. Although gentleman farmers questioned the suitability of England's intensive practices for America, agricultural improvers generally relied on English advice at least until the War of 1812. "A Connecticut Citizen," *Conn. Courant*, Sept. 7, 1789: "It is the duty of *men* of *leisure*, of *knowledge*, of *influence*, and *independent property* to point out to the laboring part of the community the best means of improving their farms." The quotations from Samuel Deane are from *The New-England Farmer; or, Georgical Dictionary* . . . (Worcester, Mass., 1790), 1, 5. Deane refers to Eliot's essays in seventeen different entries. Robert B. Thomas, who published his first *Farmer's Almanack* in 1792, was another "cultural mediator who bridged the gap between cosmopolitan and localist cultures," according to Jaffee, "The Village Enlightenment in New England," *WMQ*, 3d Ser., XLVII (1990), 331. On the new wheat, see Chester McArthur Destler, "'Forward Wheat' for New England: The Correspondence of John Taylor of Caroline with Jeremiah Wadsworth, in 1795," *Agri. Hist.*, XLII (1968), 201–210. Agricultural items and farming tips begin to appear more frequently in Connecticut newspapers in the 1790s. "The Farmer," in the Stonington *Journal of the Times*, July 2, 1799, cited Eliot's essays and paraphrased his advice about cutting bushes.

jogger" and the learned "U" in 1763, had paraphrased Eliot's preface and recommended his 1761 volume. Forty-eight years later, the Massachusetts Society for Promoting Agriculture under Adams's leadership reprinted Eliot's first five essays. After a dozen years of pleading for contributions from New England writers and apologizing for presenting so many extracts from foreign publications, the society had the satisfaction of publishing a domestic production. The society since its founding in 1792 had echoed Eliot's original aims. It tried to steer between "a wild spirit of innovation" and a "blind adherence to the beaten track," as Eliot had done. It argued that theory counted for nothing unless supported by experience, called for "a spirit of more liberal inquiry and communication," and tried to draw practical knowledge from naturalists and chemists as well as common farmers. Soon after the 1811 volume, the society's leadership acknowledged that its efforts had failed. In that same year, local farmers' groups were on the rise—societies that disseminated knowledge about new plows and practices through demonstrations at county fairs rather than in literary journals. Like Eliot, "Ploughjogger" Adams must have seen how difficult it was to create a community of farmers and philosophers, and a discourse that addressed both.[58]

Eliot's work is significant because it sheds light on a lost moment on the eve of the American Revolution. His rhetoric adumbrates the shifting relationship between learned writers and the audiences they addressed during the Revolution and the early Republic, when the authoritative ministerial voice was challenged by plain speakers exploring new genres. His experimental philosophy of farming anticipates attitudes about efficient land use and farm management that would become widespread in the nineteenth century as New England farmers competed more aggressively in a capitalist market. But Eliot's cultiva-

58. Helen Saltzberg Saltman, "John Adams's Earliest Essays: The Humphrey Ploughjogger Letters," *WMQ*, 3d Ser., XXXVII (1980), 125–135; Robert J. Taylor, ed., *The Papers of John Adams*, I (Cambridge, Mass., 1977), 63–69. Adams's essays appeared in March, June, and September 1763 in the *Boston Evening-Post* and in July 1763 in the *Boston Gazette*. See *Papers for 1811, Communicated to the Massachusetts Society for Promoting Agriculture* (Boston, 1811). The 1811 preface misidentified Eliot's work as a "Treatise" written "in 1747 . . . from a Journal of thirty years experience" and also described the essays as "diffuse" and somewhat dated. On the relation of theory and experience, see the prefaces to the society's *Papers* for 1793, 1797, 1799, 1804, and 1809. See Tamara Plakins Thornton, *Cultivating Gentlemen: The Meaning of Country Life among the Boston Elite, 1785–1860* (New Haven, Conn., 1989), chaps. 2, 3, for a discussion of the Massachusetts Society for Promoting Agriculture. The agricultural societies "on the Berkshire plan," promoted by Elkanah Watson and first founded in Pittsfield, Mass., in 1811, are discussed in Percy W. Bidwell, "The Agricultural Revolution in New England," *American Historical Review*, XXVI (1921), 686; and in Loehr, "Arthur Young," *Agri. Hist.*, XLIII (1969), 54–55.

tion of Connecticut, taken in a broader sense that includes its social, moral, and political dimensions, failed because the Revolutionary crisis altered the cultural landscape. He had hoped that experimental husbandry could foster communal solidarity among local elites who might differ over religious or political questions, social cohesion among men of different status who shared the common experience of tilling the soil, and a spirit of cooperation between Britain and the colonies for the good of the national economy. His promotion of intensive agriculture was part of an accommodationist stance toward imperial colonial policies that restricted access to cheap western land. After his death in 1763, committees of correspondence were formed to oppose British economic policy, not to promote it; Connecticut's citizens were "spirited up" to bring about political independence, not an agricultural revolution.[59]

59. On the more aggressively capitalistic nineteenth-century New England farmer, see Merchant, *Ecological Revolutions*, pt. 2.

CHAPTER 5

Christian Knowledge and

Revolutionary New England

The Education of Ezra Stiles

Ezra Stiles noted in his diary that he had spent most of June 2, 1770, sitting for portraitist Samuel King and transcribing his *Discourse on Saving Knowledge* for the press. The portrait, like the sermon, would become an effort to depict Christian knowledge, for Stiles designed special "Emblems" that King would add when he finished the work a year later. In the painting, a bookshelf displayed Stiles's favorite titles in science, divinity, and, especially, history. A diagram etched on a background pillar denoted the solar system, and his private hieroglyph for the spiritual universe floated on the back wall. Taken together, these emblems represented three areas of knowledge: history, the material world, and the spiritual world. All united in the seated figure in the foreground, Ezra Stiles, scholar of voracious curiosity, amateur scientist, and pastor of Rhode Island's Second Congregational Church. "These Emblems are more descriptive of my Mind," Stiles wrote, "than the Effigies of my face."[1]

Like his portrait, Stiles's *Discourse on Saving Knowledge* was in part an effort of self-representation. It attempted to assure his Connecticut friends that his theological sentiments had not radically changed since his days as a student and tutor at Yale, despite rumors to the contrary. But the sermon was much more than that, because Stiles himself was something of an emblem of Christian union in the ecclesiastical and theological arena of New England Congregationalism. Ezra Stiles, son of bitter Old Light Isaac and once reputed to be an

---

1. Ezra Stiles, *The Literary Diary of Ezra Stiles, D.D., L.L.D. President of Yale College*, 3 vols., ed. Franklin Bowditch Dexter (New York, 1901), I, 131–133 (quotations); Stiles, *A Discourse on Saving Knowledge . . .* (Newport, R.I., 1770).

Arminian heretic, had preached the *Discourse* at the Newport installation of the Reverend Samuel Hopkins, disciple of Jonathan Edwards and a leading New Divinity Calvinist theologian. Stiles was determined to show New England that harmony could exist between Congregational pastors and churches of different theological and ecclesiastical sentiments—that the "Wound" opened after the Awakening had "well nigh heald." His ability to elicit support from different religious and political factions would be as important as his reputation for scholarship when he was called to the Yale presidency in 1777. At Yale until his death in 1795, Stiles tried to redefine the place of the learned clergyman in New England by drawing from his own experience and further separating the knowledge of the scholar's study from the truths preached in the evangelical pulpit.[2]

Sifting through the voluminous manuscript material he left behind, modern scholars have used Stiles to represent "the life of the mind" in eighteenth-century America. Edmund S. Morgan's superb biography portrayed Stiles as "an intellectual" and focused upon "his adventuring in ideas." Morgan described young Ezra's thirteen years as a Yale student and tutor and concluded that "the Yale Library had produced . . . a child of the Enlightenment." Two decades at Newport and hundreds of pages of notes on the ecclesiastical history of New England molded the "Gentle Puritan" of Morgan's title: Stiles's antiquarian scholarship led him toward the theology of his Puritan forbears, but with an enlightened aversion to their "overweening dogmatism"; he combined demands for freedom of thought with a pious faith in the Scriptures. But if Morgan's portrait of Stiles highlighted the shelf of books behind Stiles's development, Herbert Leventhal's suggestive study looked to the other side of Stiles—to the curious emblem of the universe, to the Stiles drawn to Neoplatonism, angelology, and the mystic theology of Dionysius the Areopagite. For Leventhal, Stiles's manuscripts show the persistence of older currents of thought and occult beliefs running beneath the Enlightenment. Rather than an enlightened Puritan, Leventhal's Stiles appears as a Renaissance man clinging to anachronistic ideas before they turned to dust in the dry air of the modern world.[3]

The Ezra Stiles Papers, however, offer another Ezra—the Stiles in the King

2. Stiles, *Discourse on Saving Knowledge*; Stiles to Noah Welles, Aug. 26, 1769, in *Literary Diary*, ed. Dexter, I, 20n–21n. Stiles's Connecticut correspondents included Chauncy Whittelsey, John Devotion, William Hart, James Dana, and John Hubbard, all considered Old Lights.

3. Edmund S. Morgan, *The Gentle Puritan: A Life of Ezra Stiles, 1727–1795* (New Haven, Conn., 1962), vii, 77, 177; Herbert Leventhal, *In the Shadow of the Enlightenment: Occultism and Renaissance Science in Eighteenth-Century America* (New York, 1976).

Figure 9. *Portrait of Ezra Stiles.* By Samuel King, 1771. Courtesy, Yale University Art Gallery, New Haven, Conn.

portrait sitting in front of the emblems "in a teaching attitude . . . holding a preaching bible." The Yale tutor who studied Newton and tracked comets also filled empty pulpits during school vacations. The ecclesiastical historian in Newport also preached two sermons a week for more than twenty years. As Yale president, Stiles lectured in church history and Westminster divinity, counseled students with spiritual concerns, and still spent about half his Sundays preaching. Approximately 350 extant manuscript sermons, along with the records of his preaching and lecturing on religious topics, show the relationship between the study and the pulpit. Alongside his diaries, notebooks, and letters, Stiles's sermons reveal the tension between private and public selves that shaped his development and also the changing relationships among religion, learning, and politics that reshaped Revolutionary New England.[4]

Stiles's conversion from Christian philosophe to evangelical Puritan was not as gradual as his biographers, following Stiles's own recollections, have portrayed. Nor was it initially the product of his biblical studies or his research into New England's past. The demands of his congregation, more than the knowledge gleaned from his library, prompted him to adopt a more evangelical preaching style in 1765. The historic events of the Stamp Act crisis in that same year, more than the history he wrote in his study, rewrote *him* as a Puritan. When he accepted the Yale presidency in 1778 to promote *"Learning* in conjunction with *Religion,"* and when he resisted what he thought was a deist political campaign to marginalize clergymen in the 1780s and 1790s, he drew upon an understanding of the minister's role in New England culture that was shaped in the mid-1760s.[5]

Ezra Stiles presents a case study of the webs of ideas and cultural styles known as "Puritanism" and the "Enlightenment." The Enlightenment can be typified by the belief that the cultivation of critical intelligence is the key to human progress. But as many historians have argued, the Enlightenment must be understood as an experience as well as a set of propositions about man, nature, and history. Indeed, many enlightened philosophes saw their private experience of intellectual development and the course of human progress as mirror images.[6] Puritanism, too, needs to be seen as both a set of ideas and a type of

4. Unless otherwise indicated, all manuscripts cited are from the Ezra Stiles Papers, Beinecke Rare Book and Manuscript Library, Yale University, New Haven, Conn. Short citations are patterned after the format of Harold E. Selesky, ed., *A Guide to the Microfilm Edition of the Ezra Stiles Papers at Yale University* (New Haven, Conn., 1978).

5. Stiles, *Literary Diary,* ed. Dexter, II, 264.

6. My definition of the Enlightenment follows Henry F. May, *The Enlightenment in America* (New York, 1976), xiv; Ernst Cassirer, in *The Philosophy of the Enlightenment,* trans. Fritz C. A. Koelln and James P. Pettegrove (1932; reprint, Princeton, N.J., 1951), though he focused upon the ideas of the Enlightenment, also argued that it must be understood as an experience (164); see Peter Gay, *The Enlightenment: An Interpretation,* II, *The Science of Freedom* (New York, 1969), 502. On Enlightenment practices, see also Margaret C. Jacob, *The Radical Enlightenment: Pantheists, Freemasons, and Republicans* (London, 1981); Jacob, *Living the Enlightenment: Freemasonry and Politics in Eighteenth-Century Europe* (New York, 1991); Charles Camic, *Experience and Enlightenment: Socialization for Cultural Change in Eighteenth-Century Scotland* (Chicago, 1983); Jerome Christensen, *Practicing Enlightenment: Hume and the Formation of a Literary Career* (Madison, Wis., 1987); Dena Goodman, *The Republic of Letters: A Cultural History of the French Enlightenment* (Ithaca, N.Y., 1994); Rich-

experience. For Stiles, the word denoted a list of Calvinist doctrines about sin and salvation, a powerful preaching style, a political force against civil and religious tyranny, and a personal experience of self-transcendence through God's free grace. That his education in Revolutionary New England led him from the eighteenth century's Enlightenment to a self-conscious embrace of his Puritan heritage highlights the paradox of a culture that was simultaneously building a new future and resuscitating the myths of the past.[7]

THE STUDY AND THE PULPIT

Stiles's sermons before 1765 attempted to mediate between what polemicists of his day set up as dichotomies: Arminianism versus Calvinism, intellect versus the affections, and deism versus scriptural faith. He at first dismissed the Arminian-Calvinist controversy as name-calling without much substance, and he then tried to minimize the real theological differences between the two points of view for the sake of Christian union. The relationship between head and heart in religious experience, always a matter of personal temperament as well as pulpit style, had become politicized in the aftermath of the Awakening, when the learned opposers of the revivals were charged with being all light without heat, and Whitefield's fiery supporters were accused of being all heat without light. Stiles's early sermons were not displays of cool reasoning that neglected to address the passions, although they did blur the distinction between religious affections and what he called philosophic rhapsody. But it was Stiles's personal and professional commitment to a rational defense of Chris-

ard B. Sher and Jeffrey R. Smitten, eds., *Scotland and America in the Age of the Enlightenment* (Princeton, N.J., 1990); John Dwyer and Richard B. Sher, eds., *Sociability and Society in Eighteenth-Century Scotland, Eighteenth-Century Life*, XV (1991); John Bender, "A New History of the Enlightenment?" *Eighteenth-Century Life*, XVI (1992), 1–20; Daniel Brewer, *The Discourse of Enlightenment in Eighteenth-Century France: Diderot and the Art of Philosophizing* (Cambridge, 1993); Anne Goldgar, *Impolite Learning: Conduct and Community in the Republic of Letters, 1680–1750* (New Haven, Conn., 1995).

7. The problem of defining Puritanism is discussed in David D. Hall, "Understanding the Puritans," in John M. Mulder and John F. Wilson, eds., *Religion in American History: Interpretive Essays* (1970; reprint, Englewood Cliffs, N.J., 1978), 1–16; John Morgan, *Godly Learning: Puritan Attitudes towards Reason, Learning, and Education, 1560–1640* (Cambridge, 1986), chap. 1; Peter Lake, "Defining Puritanism—Again?" and Stephen Foster, "Not What But How—Thomas Minor and the the Ligatures of Puritanism," in Francis J. Bremer, ed., *Puritanism: Transatlantic Perspectives on a Seventeenth-Century Anglo-American Faith* (Boston, 1993), 3–29, 30–54.

tianity against deism that placed him in a transatlantic debate among the learned and polite and extracted him, or so he thought, from the narrower theological battles raging in New England.[8]

Between 1746 and 1754, Stiles, as he later described it, "passed thro' the cloudy darksom valley of scepticism, and stood on the precipice . . . of deism." Upon what rational basis do we declare the Bible to be the revealed Word of God? What if the Scriptures, and thus Christianity itself, were human inventions, fables like other religions? A minister's son in post-Puritan New England had stopped to wonder. Ezra was licensed to preach in 1749, but his confidence in the faith of his fathers received a serious blow when "an ingenious deist" in late 1749 or early 1750 "excited doubts about revelation." Continuing to preach occasionally but plagued by doubts, he set aside his plans to settle as a minister in 1752 and decided to become a lawyer. By the end of 1754, however, having continued his Bible study and historical research, he began to find answers to his questions. His doubts had vanished, he later claimed, several months before the spring of 1755, when Newport's Second Congregational Church asked him to be their pastor. He told his New Haven friends years later that, as soon as he had emerged from the darkness of skepticism, he had returned to the faith he had been raised in, a faith based upon the doctrines of human depravity, Redemption by Christ, and regeneration through the influences of the Holy Spirit. His theological development, he argued, including his refined un-

8. As Stiles understood it, deism was the belief in a benevolent but detached Creator, the attempt to understand that Creator only through reason and nature, and the rejection of the Scriptures as divinely inspired; it was a step beyond the skeptic's doubts about the Bible and a step closer to the atheist's mechanistic universe. On deism in America, see Herbert M. Morais, *Deism in Eighteenth Century America* (New York, 1960), 85–119; May, *Enlightenment in America,* esp. 122–126, 136–149, 230–233, 326–334; Kerry S. Walters, "Introduction," in Walters, ed., *The American Deists: Voices of Reason and Dissent in the Early Republic* (Lawrence, Kans., 1992), 1–50. Stiles defined Arminianism as a set of doctrines about human will and God's prescience and decrees, whereas some of his contemporaries applied the term to almost any deviation from rock-ribbed Calvinism that seemed to elevate the status of man. See Conrad Wright, *The Beginnings of Unitarianism in America* (Boston, 1955), chap. 1; Gerald J. Goodwin, "The Myth of 'Arminian-Calvinism' in Eighteenth-Century New England," *New England Quarterly,* XLI (1968), 213–237; Trenton Wayne Batson, "Arminianism in New England: A Reading of the Published Sermons of Benjamin Colman, 1673–1747" (Ph.D. diss., George Washington University, 1974); David A. Weir, *The Origins of the Federal Theology in Sixteenth-Century Reformation Thought* (Oxford, 1990), 20; and Ava Chamberlain, "The Theology of Cruelty: A New Look at the Rise of Arminianism in Eighteenth-Century New England," *Harvard Theological Review,* LXXXV (1992), 335–356. On evangelical and rational preaching styles, see Harry S. Stout, *The New England Soul: Preaching and Religious Culture in Colonial New England* (New York, 1986), 218–222.

derstanding of the Atonement and the Trinity, could be described, not as "change," but as "progress" in the same system, "enlargements" upon the same principles, a deepening of faith and an "Education in the Truth." [9]

But Stiles's autobiographical story of illumination and education misses the creative tension between public and private selves that arose as he simultaneously worked out his own system of beliefs in his private notebooks and sought to establish a public reputation through preaching and scholarly correspondence. His early years of doubt as a Yale tutor highlighted the incongruities that could exist between personal belief and public doctrine. In the early 1750s, he preached what he thought were the gospel doctrines, but he was not sure that the gospel was true. He always "made a Distinction between what I *believed to be Verity,* and what I *believed to be Christianity.*" Even on what was thought to be his deathbed during an illness in 1751, he gave orthodox answers to a minister's questions about his understanding of Christianity, but he told neither the minister at his bedside "nor any mortal, that I had not a satisfactory belief that Christianity was divine." There was always, he thought, a veil between the truth a man perceived in his study and what he was willing to proclaim in public, and as late as 1764 he was still hoping that one of his descendants could be privately funded to study the Bible, insulated from the public pressures for orthodoxy. Against the Whitefields and the Tennents who ranted against an unconverted ministry, Stiles believed with the Puritans and Augustine that a man's private sentiments did not necessarily hamper his efficacy as a preacher. But the stench of hypocrisy was still too strong, and in the early 1750s he "Tho't much concerning the inconsistency of preaching . . . while in doubt of Revelation." [10]

As Stiles kept his doubts hidden from even his closest friends, he also learned that what a man preached on Sundays was not necessarily reflected by the label the public pinned upon him, whether Old Light or New Light, Calvinist or Arminian. Like his father and a circle of his father's friends, Stiles had

9. The "darksom valley" remark is in Ezra Stiles, *The United States Elevated to Glory and Honor . . .* (New Haven, Conn., 1783), 85. Such a personal aside was very unusual in an election sermon. The passage is absent from the manuscript version and was probably not delivered orally. The reference to the "ingenious deist" is in Ezra Stiles, autobiographical reflection, Apr. 5, 1765, 5. This paragraph is also based upon Stiles's "Birthday Reflections" for 1767 and 1768, "Series of Occurrences in My Life," Dec. 28, 1767, and "Review of the Authors I Read and Admired during the Rise, Height, and Decline of My Scepticism from about 1749 to 1755," Dec. 12, 1768. There is some variation in the dates Stiles gives to mark his period of skepticism. The quotations in the last sentence are from Stiles to Chauncy Whittelsey, Mar. 6, 1770.

10. Stiles, "Series of Occurrences," Dec. 28, 1767, 1, 3.

earned a reputation as an Arminian heretic by 1751, and for twenty years thereafter people who quizzed him on his doctrinal positions were surprised to find him so orthodox. It was true that he and his father's friends had all been reading "Arminian books" since about 1745 and that their sentiments on some questions had broadened, but none had ever renounced specific Calvinist doctrines. Ezra refused to parrot the pet phrases of the confessions and catechisms but still considered himself doctrinally orthodox. Furthermore, his tutors at Yale had been called Arminians too, whereas President Thomas Clap was known as a staunch Calvinist, and yet all were friends and seemed, to Stiles, to have the same religious beliefs. Stiles concluded that the charge of Arminianism was little more than "New Light hocus-pocus" hurled at anyone who opposed raving revivalism. Before 1755, Stiles believed, he had been a skeptic in the study, a Calvinist in the pulpit, and an Arminian by reputation.[11]

In fact, Stiles's early sermons reveal both Calvinist doctrines and an Arminian tone. Two sermons written in the summer of 1752, for example, and preached several more times through the decade, discussed man's helplessness, Christ's all-sufficient Atonement, and the regenerating power of the Holy Spirit. Textual evidence therefore supports Stiles's contention that he preached his father's Calvinism. But his sermons also reveal his private sentiments: "That Man was of a sublime Order of rational Beings capable of glorious exercises and Imployments . . . [and] not in so sinful and deplorable an Estate as Divines represented." He argued that Christianity had been designed to put the body back under the control of the mind and the dictates of reason, and he implied that man rather than God did most of the work. One sermon, preached to seventeen different congregations between 1749 and 1763, explained that frequent meditation upon moral topics could "beget such a Relish and Tast for Moral Excellence as to encourage us in the Pursuit of Religion." Another sermon stressed "that by due Culture, we should be formed into the divine Image in Knowledge as well as *Holiness*." Although he denied that salvation could be attained by good works, he emphasized that rewards in the next world depended upon behavior in this one. Therefore, if "an elevated confidence in freedom of choice, a sharply upward revised estimate of human nature, and a form of commonsense moralism" marked a preacher as an Arminian in eighteenth-century New England, it is not surprising that Stiles's early preaching raised charges of heterodoxy.[12]

11. Stiles, "Another Review," Nov. 21, 1769; Ezra Stiles, "Memoirs and Anecdotes of the Life of the Reverend Isaac Stiles," June 15, 1760.

12. Ezra Stiles's early sermons with a Calvinist tone are MS sermon on Titus 3:5, preached at Kensington, July 12, 1752 (also preached July 19, Aug. 2, 1752, October 1754, Feb. 6, 1757,

Privately, Stiles denied that the controversies between Calvinists and Arminians had done much to influence his religious development, and he refused to take sides: "I have for years passed [as] a reputed Arminian," he wrote to John Holt in 1759, "which however I equally disclaim with that of calvinism." Publicly, in his *Discourse on the Christian Union* the following year, he argued that the whole dispute arose from ultimately unimportant differences in "manner and phraseology." He saw no real difference between the two parties—certainly nothing that should have kept Presbyterians and Congregationalists from banding together against the threat of episcopacy. He called for a union of New England Protestants based upon liberty of conscience and similar notions of polity, but he did not begin stressing the importance of Calvinist doctrine to that union until the mid-1760s.[13]

Stiles's pre-1765 sermons also belie the overdrawn dichotomy of head-centered and heart-centered homiletics that arose during the Awakening. He argued that Christianity was a form of moral cultivation that reasserted the

---

Aug. 14, 1763); and MS sermon on 1 John 3:7, 10, preached at Kensington, July 12, 1752 (also preached July 26, 1752, December 1752, Jan. 6, 1753, July 1756, Apr. 13, 1760), Ezra Stiles Papers, Massachusetts Historical Society, Boston. Stiles asserts that as a young minister he had preached his father's Calvinism in "Another Review," Nov. 21, 1769. His recollection about his earlier, more optimistic view of man is in Stiles, "Review of the Authors I Read and Admired," Dec. 12, 1768. On the control of reason, see MS sermon on John 6:27 (undated, but in an early hand); on the moral taste for excellence, see MS sermon on Ps. 119:23, written June 12, 1749, and preached seventeen times in various pulpits between Aug. 20, 1749, and May 1, 1763, Mass. Hist. Soc.; on heavenly rewards for good behavior, see MS sermon on Prov. 2:10–11, "The Right Conduct of Life," July 23, 1751, Mass. Hist. Soc. The "loose" definition of Arminianism was offered by Clyde A. Holbrook, "Editor's Introduction," in Jonathan Edwards, *The Great Christian Doctrine of Original Sin Defended . . .*, ed. Holbrook, in Perry Miller et al., eds., *The Works of Jonathan Edwards*, III (New Haven, Conn., 1970), 4n. Morgan, in *Gentle Puritan*, 111–112, 168–169, used Stiles's first Newport sermon as a kind of benchmark. A sermon that "had fallen little short of deism" made it clear that, at the very least, "the man was an Arminian." After a few years in Newport, Morgan argued, "the Arminian tendency which had often characterized his writing was giving way to an insistence upon human corruption and the atonement of Christ." This is accurate as a broad generalization, but it obscures the relationship between private belief, pulpit doctrine, and public reputation of which Stiles was keenly aware.

13. Stiles to John Holt, Aug. 10, 1759; Ezra Stiles, *A Discourse on the Christian Union . . .* (Boston, 1761). In ["Birthday Reflections"], Apr. 5, 1765, Stiles wrote: "I was little concerned about Calvinism or Arminianism or any other *Ism*." Early notebooks, however, show his comparing Calvin and Arminius on God's prescience and decrees, and he also helped collect subscriptions for Moses Dickinson's *Inquiry into the Consequences Both of Calvinistic and Arminian Principles, Compared Together . . .* (Boston, 1750). See Dickinson's letter to Stiles, Dec. 26, 1749, and Stiles's response of Jan. 1, 1750.

rule of intellect over passion and molded moral beings to what was right and true "in the Nature of Things." He used the words "mind" and "intellect" as synecdoches for the whole person, not to ignore or extinguish the passions, but to put them in their place and emphasize the intellect as the main doorway to the soul. That doorway was blocked by "bias" and "prejudice," which in Stiles's early preaching seemed to loom as the biggest obstacles left by original sin. Stiles urged all who heard him to contemplate religious questions and search after truth with an "unbiased Openess of Mind for Liberal Inquiry." Such a frame of mind opened the way for both natural and gracious "impressions and infusions" that would influence the heart, affections, and moral conduct. In describing the experience of these impressions and infusions upon the heart, Stiles was not content to fill his auditors' heads with coolly reasoned arguments.[14]

Stiles oscillated between two different vocabularies of heart language: the Pietist tradition of Reformed Protestantism, which spoke of the necessity of infused grace, and British "sentimentalist" philosophy, which spoke of cultivating an inherent moral sense. From the beginning of his career, Stiles had preached what New England simply called the doctrines of grace. An open mind was not enough; fallen man needed the aid of the Holy Spirit even to apprehend the truth. The Spirit "dispels the mists which becloud and darken the understanding." In regeneration, it infuses the soul with a new inward principle of wisdom and holiness; it sets the regenerated Christian on the path of true virtue and keeps him there. Yet, for Stiles, all that was a gradual process that unfolded over a lifetime. Spiritual insight was indistinguishable from "the

14. Stiles, MS sermon on Prov. 2:10–11, "The Right Conduct of Life," July 23, 1751, Mass. Hist. Soc. See also MS sermons on John 6:27 (no #, n.d., but written in an early hand); Rev. 5:13 (#32), Feb. 1, 1756; Prov. 10:1 (#41), Apr. 4, 1756; Prov. 14:12 (#149), July 17, 1757; "Discourse on the Study of the Scriptures," Jan. 29, 1758, 80; Phil. 3:13–14 (#213), June 11, 1758; Ps. 1:14 (#259), Nov. 23, 1758; Ps. 106:44–45 (#293), Apr. 5, 1759; Rev. 3:20 (#159), Aug. 5, 1759; 1 Cor. 2:15 (#348), Nov. 18, 1759; Rom. 12:2 (#434), Feb. 19, 1764; and *Discourse on Christian Union*, Apr. 23, 1760, 17–18, 25. His first biographer noted only that Stiles's "early discourses were philosophical and moral" and that he gradually "'became a serious, zealous, and powerful preacher'" (Abiel Holmes, *The Life of Ezra Stiles, D.D., LL.D.* [Boston, 1798], 237). Holmes quotes a phrase from a letter to him by the Reverend Benjamin Trumbull. But the "philosophical and moral" Stiles had been just as serious, and, in his own way, just as passionate. Stiles articulated what Norman Fiering has described as the "intellectualist" position in seventeenth- and eighteenth-century moral philosophy. See Fiering, *Moral Philosophy at Seventeenth-Century Harvard: A Discipline in Transition* (Chapel Hill, N.C., 1981), 113, 125, 195. On the relationship between ethics and aesthetics, see Robert E. Norton, *The Beautiful Soul: Aesthetic Morality in the Eighteenth Century* (Ithaca, N.Y., 1995).

native Elucidations of Reason." Theoretically distinct, the divine communications of grace were experientially identical to the sublime "rapture" that could fill the soul when contemplating nature and the "Ideas of Moral Dignity, beauteous Order, and perfect Goodness" found there. In one sermon, Stiles would mark out the privileged experience of the saint, and in the next he would describe the same experience as available to everyone. The sentimentalist philosopher cultivating his moral sense and the Christian growing in grace and preparing for glory in the next world seemed to be on the same path. Stiles mentioned human depravity but focused on the accessible rapture of the sublime; he decried sin but avoided a rhetorical posture that evoked and dwelt upon humiliation before God.[15]

The passion of Stiles's own religious and intellectual experiences made its way into his public performances. The man who looked to the heavens and was thrilled by Newtonian vastness and order wanted to share his enlarged understanding with others; the man who sensed God's presence in the joy he felt when gleaning knowledge from books wanted to enlighten those who had little time for reading. As a young man pondering his vocation, Stiles wished that every community could afford to pay "a Gentleman of Genius and Learning" to tutor groups of other young men. Local mechanics and farmers could meet with a scholar on winter evenings for "agreeable philosophic Discourses, Lectures, Conversation, and Amusement." Stiles argued that philosophy and astronomy could bring even those with only "a vulgar Education" to see the or-

15. Stiles, *Discourse on Christian Union,* 13, 18; Stiles, "Discourse on the Study of the Scriptures," 1758, 80; Stiles, "Oration," June 4, 1754, 5. See also Stiles's MS sermons from the Mass. Hist. Soc. on Matt. 22:37–38 (#25), Mar. 27, 1756; Matt. 22:37–38 (#27), June 5, 1756; John 14:21 (#28), June 12, 1756; Eph. 3:17 (#333), Sept. 9, 1759; and Beinecke MS sermon on James 3:7 (#266), Dec. 31, 1758. The term "sentimentalist" is from Norman Fiering, *Jonathan Edwards's Moral Thought and Its British Context* (Chapel Hill, N.C., 1981), 10, who defined the word as "the emphasis in early eighteenth-century British literary and philosophical culture on the constructive role of the affections and passions (in French, *sentiment,* feeling) in the moral life." See also Peter J. Diamond, "Witherspoon, William Smith, and the Scottish Philosophy in Revolutionary America," in Sher and Smitten, eds., *Scotland and America in the Age of Enlightenment,* 115–132; John Dwyer, "Introduction: 'A Peculiar Blessing': Social Converse in Scotland from Hutcheson to Burns," Susan M. Purviance, "Intersubjectivity and Sociable Relations in the Philosophy of Frances Hutcheson," Dwyer, "Enlightened Spectators and Classical Moralists: Sympathetic Relations in Eighteenth-Century Scotland," all in Dwyer and Sher, eds., *Sociability and Society, Eighteenth-Century Life,* XV (1991), 1–22, 23–38, 96–118; G. J. Barker-Benfield, *The Culture of Sensibility: Sex and Society in Eighteenth-Century Britain* (Chicago, 1992); Lawrence E. Klein, *Shaftesbury and the Culture of Politeness: Moral Discourse and Cultural Politics in Early Eighteenth-Century England* (Cambridge, 1994); Norton, *The Beautiful Soul,* 9–54.

der, beauty, and wisdom of creation. Students would see that their own purpose as thinking beings was "studying and imitating infinite perfection." They would be inspired to venerate the Deity, be prepared to embrace the gospel, and be equipped to commence the growth toward perfection that begins in an imperfect world. In a 1754 oration, he explained that these "sublime apprehensions" differed from "the rapturous Sallies of an Enthusiastic Mind" that sprang from "the warmth of Fancy and Imagination" because they had an objective correlative: like the "pleasing Sensations" that arose when a harmonious melody filled the ear, this "rapt pleasure" filled a mind attuned to the harmony of nature.[16]

Before 1765, Stiles's religious thought was shaped less by post-Puritan theological and homiletic debates than by the pagan Enlightenment's challenge to the grounds of Christianity itself. The ability to suspend judgment and submit all traditional truth claims to the bar of reason, so essential to Stiles's program of "Liberal Inquiry," had initially inclined him toward deism. Even after he had accepted the gospel as God's Word, he continued to find the deist's arguments powerful and seductive. His battle with skepticism actually lasted longer than he cared to admit in his later recollections, which tended to bring the skeptical phase of his intellectual and religious development to a close with the end of 1754. One brief autobiographical reflection notes that he had "sustained the last capital shock from the Artillery of Deism" in 1756, when he read David Hume, Henry St. John, Viscount Bolingbroke, and other writers on the subject of miracles.[17]

But Stiles's continuing doubts are better preserved in a remarkable letter he

16. Ezra Stiles, "Notes on Education," July 3, 1750, Mass. Hist. Soc.; "Oration," June 4, 1754. Since New England was not ready for lyceums, Stiles made use of the pulpit. He never paraded his erudition, but he did try to communicate the "sublime apprehensions" that could be derived from philosophic or scientific inquiry. See, especially, the MS thanksgiving sermons for Nov. 25, 1756 (#111), Nov. 17, 1757 (#177), and Sept. 25, 1760 (#366).

17. Stiles, "Series of Occurrences," Dec. 28, 1767, 3. Peter Gay, *The Enlightenment: An Interpretation,* I, *The Rise of Modern Paganism* (New York, 1966), argued that at the heart of the Enlightenment was a dialectical movement involving the rejection of Christianity and the embrace of classical paganism. Margaret Jacob, who focused upon the popular enlightenment (rather than the elite Enlightenment of the philosophes) in *The Radical Enlightenment* and *Living the Enlightenment,* found radical departures from Christianity and a secular orientation. Other studies downplay the antagonism to Christianity or the centrality of the Enlightenment's radical strain. See John Redwood, *Reason, Ridicule, and Religion: The Age of Enlightenment in England, 1660–1750* (Cambridge, Mass., 1976); Robert E. Sullivan, *John Toland and the Deist Controversy: A Study in Adaptations* (Cambridge, Mass., 1982); Richard B. Sher, *Church and University in the Scottish Enlightenment: The Moderate Literati of Edinburgh* (Princeton, N.J., 1985); May, *Enlightenment in America.*

wrote on August 16, 1756, to Jared Ingersoll, who had been his law tutor. What was the purpose of human life? "The more we think and examine, the more perplext and at a loss. The present scene is so confused, that I scarce know what Path to travel." Where was God? "I can't see him," Stiles wrote, unless it was when he saw that *"ineffable Something blaze* in the Face of Man, that looks like *Divinity,"* or in "that *Divinity,* which I daily discern in the Face of Nature." The Scriptures, whose divine inspiration he had worked so hard to prove, seemed only to republish the religion of nature. "The Substance of Christianity (if there is any Thing in it) is as Old as Creation," wrote a man who had been preaching the gospel in Newport for more than a year—crossing out, but still leaving clearly legible, the parenthetical phrase. If restoring man to moral virtue was Christianity's "ultimate Design," why was religion so intermixed with "Fiction" and "Fooleries," with superstitions for "fanciful Priests, who use them to amuse and gull Mankind out of a subsistence"?[18]

Stiles was either more guarded or more of a Christian when he wrote to Jared Eliot the following year. Claiming only that he wanted to muster arguments to silence the deists and "put the Truth of Christianity beyond dispute," Stiles seemed frustrated that the New Testament was contradictory about the nature of Christ's divinity and that the apostles altered the original meanings of most of the Old Testament prophecies they applied to Jesus. Eliot thought Stiles was taking the deists' objections too seriously, and Stiles himself later admitted that in 1757 he still had doubts about the "real Deity," or divinity, of Jesus Christ.[19]

Stiles's preoccupation with the question of the Bible's divine inspiration is shown by what was intended to be his first major publication, an expansion of his "Discourse on the Study of the Scriptures" delivered in 1758. The manuscript ballooned to more than 140 pages as Stiles poured in nearly a decade's worth of study. Stiles set out to support the proposition that "believers of Revelation" ought to derive their religious principles from the Bible alone. Instead, as his friend William Vinal's unflinching critique of the manuscript pointed out, most of Stiles's pages laboriously demonstrated that the Scriptures were divine, something that "believers" would have taken for granted. Moreover, Stiles's method was to authenticate the sacred text like any other historical document and to draw matters of fact from it as from other authentic histories, a process that would eventually "lead us up to the agency and inspiration of

18. Stiles to Jared Ingersoll, Aug. 16, 1756.

19. Stiles to Jared Eliot, Apr. 5, 1757, with Stiles's note dated 1783 (where he admitted that his doubts were still lingering in 1757). See also Eliot to Stiles, Apr. 12, 1757; and Eliot to Stiles, Sept. 17, 1759.

God." The faithful, however, as Vinal argued, could not fail to perceive the Bible's divinity on every page. Stiles left the 1758 lecture unpublished, but his enthusiasm for a rational defense was undaunted.[20]

The deist controversy not only engaged him on a personal level but defined, for Stiles, the role of the mid-eighteenth-century Christian scholar. "Besides the ordinary Labors of the Christian ministry," he wrote to a friend in Edinburgh in November 1758, clergymen were called to "persist in the rational Defence of the Gospel" against the rising tide of infidelity in Western Europe. To Thomas Clap nearly a year later he wrote that deism was being quickly propagated in America, too, and that "the only way left to conquer and demolish it, is to come forth to dispute the matter on even footing." A 1759 letter to Eliot placed the clergy's rational defense of Christianity in a broader intellectual context. The poets of the day, Stiles argued, had few great works to boast about, and the philosophers and mathematicians were still busy digesting Newton and popularizing the previous century's science. But the "Disquisitions on Revelation seem to be the most learned and truly great." In England, "the greater Geniuses among the Ministers are ranging the Evidences of Revelation to the public View." The "small folks indeed keep warming up the old Pye," arguing about Calvinism and orthodoxy like Clap or making "a pother" like Whitefield. But the colonies will follow the mother country, and, "instead of the Controversies of Orthodoxy and Heresy, we shall soon be called to the defence of the Gospel itself." Against deism, the New Divinity theologians like Joseph Bellamy, with all their "cant orthodox phrases" and "unintelligible Metaphysics," would not stand a chance. The New England of the near future, it seemed, would require a different style of clerical genius.[21]

The battle for revelation against the "Contagion" of deism was not just an argument among the learned, Stiles believed; it would shape the pulpit divinity of the coming generation. The "rational Defence" would be articulated both in learned treatises and in ordinary sermons. One of Stiles's earliest sermons, dated February 24, 1749, and preached five times before being delivered in Newport in 1755, was devoted to the topic. It offered a list of rules for discovering "certain *Signs and matters of Fact*" that "*positively and directly proved*" the Scriptures were from God at a time when Stiles was far from certain or positive himself. After his unpublished 1758 "Discourse," his next major effort was a sermon series on 2 Pet. 1:16 begun on November 25, 1764, which he intended

20. William Vinal to Stiles, Sept. 2, 1758; Stiles, "Discourse on the Study of the Scriptures," 1758, 98.

21. Stiles to Patrick Cummings, Nov. 8, 1758; Stiles to Thomas Clap, Aug. 6, 1759 (copy 2); Stiles to Jared Eliot, Sept. 24, 1759 (copy).

to preach on successive Sundays through the second week of December. These sermons would prove the existence of God by the evidence of the visible universe and argue that the system of moral government offered in the Scriptures, even considered only as a hypothesis, was far more rational and sublime than anything in other religions and philosophies. Stiles would then proceed to show that the objections the deists made against revelation would hold equally against their natural religion and conclude by demonstrating that the prophesies and miracles proved the Scriptures were divine. He addressed the complaint Vinal had made to his 1758 "Discourse" by very briefly mentioning the special "evidence" of divinity that the Bible manifested to those who had already "felt the power of the divine Truth." [22]

This ambitious sermon series, however, came to a halt before the last two sermons could be written or delivered. "The Last sermon disgusted my people as containing too much history and astronomy unintelligible to the Audience," Stiles noted in the sermon booklet. "I desisted from the prosecution of this subject and left the two last heads unfinished." He immediately began a new sermon series, this time on the subject of repentance. Delivered in six installments through the second week of January 1765, these sermons would mark a turning point in Stiles's preaching. "It seems I am not to conceive of you my Friends as otherwise than believing the Bible with unquestionable Certainty to be a divine Revelation," he told his congregation. But if they were not closet skeptics as he had been, why were they not more visibly affected by the scriptural message? The Bible told them that without Christ they would be "cast into a Lake burning with Fire and Brimstone." If they already saw that this doctrine was part of God's Truth, why were they not begging for forgiveness in fear and trembling? The answer, as Stiles like many preachers before him discovered, was that, "tho' popularly believed," the doctrine of the soul's eternal damnation in hell "is not realized." The preacher needed, not to convince them that it was true, but to help bring the truth "so home to the mind" that they would perceive its terrible reality. [23]

22. Stiles, MS sermon on Luke 28:36, Feb. 24, 1749, Mass. Hist. Soc.; MS sermons on 2 Pet. 1:16 (#442–445), Nov. 25–Dec. 29, 1764. The scriptural text reads as follows: "For we have not followed cunningly devised fables, when we made known unto you the power and coming of our lord Jesus Christ, but were eyewitnesses of his majesty." Stiles had devoted four sermons to a single text only once before, on John 16:33 in 1758. See Stiles's Notebook List of Sermons Preached, May 10, 1755–1756, October 1775.

23. Stiles, MS sermons on 2 Pet. 1:16 (#442–445), Nov. 25–Dec. 9, 1764, [30]; MS sermons on Acts 10:20–21 (#446–451, #453), Dec. 16, 1764–Jan. 12, 1765, Mass. Hist. Soc. (remarks to his congregation are on 41–43 of the booklet, 4–6 of the sermon). On the truth's needing to be "realized," cf. Wilson H. Kimnach, "Jonathan Edwards's Pursuit of Reality,"

Hellfire preaching was not Stiles's forte, but he did his best to turn his congregation's attention inward to the vileness of their sin and forward in time to the torment that could await them. It was a "terrible thing to fall into the hands of the living God." To then sink into hell would bring agonies beyond description: "There is a very terrible Account given of them in Scripture. . . . Let us believe they are far more awful and terrible than can be described by the language of Mortals." The last sermon in the series was devoted to exhortation and advice, building emotional intensity through a series of rhetorical questions and "expostulations." He admitted in a footnote, and presumably to his congregation, that this section had been extracted from the published sermons of Simon Brown. Although he borrowed passion for his pulpit, the preacher, if not the congregation, had learned some lessons by the time the series had been completed.[24]

Those lessons would be reformulated into a new philosophy of preaching by the fall of 1766. In arguing with the deists, he wrote to an English Dissenter, perhaps the Presbyterians were "conceeding too much," and the emphasis on "Rationality with a certain aim after Elegance and Politeness in Composition, may have taken up too great a portion of their labors." It was better to dwell on the doctrines of human depravity, redeeming grace, and regeneration in the Holy Spirit. The best pulpit strategy, "considering the Inattention of Mankind [was] to rouse[,] call upon[,] and alarm them with Anticipation of the tremendous Torments of Damnation." Stiles urged that those who had adopted "a less pathetic and what is called a more rational and polite manner of preaching" should "resume those *evangelical Doctrines* for which their learned and pious Ancestors were eminent, and especially that close manner of address [and] the *powerful Preaching*." He expressed similar sentiments to Joseph Jennings on January 20, 1767: labored explications of Christianity as a moral system have "Engrossed the Modern Preaching." Determining God's will should be enough, Stiles argued, "whether I can enter into the Rationale of it or not." He now believed that arguments for revelation would not influence the deists anyway and that the whole effort was less important because, as he wrote again to Thomas Wright, "the Period of Deism is almost at an End."[25]

---

in Nathan O. Hatch and Harry S. Stout, eds., *Jonathan Edwards and the American Experience* (New York, 1988), 102–117.

24. Stiles, MS sermon on Acts 10:21 (#449), 62, 72 of the booklet.

25. Stiles to [Thomas Wright], Nov. 18, 1766, 1–3 (see also Stiles to [Wright], Nov. 22, 1766, presumably a later draft); Stiles to Joseph Jennings, Jan. 20, 1767, [1]; Stiles to Wright, Dec. 22, 1767 (copy 2), [5]. Stiles published the same opinion about preaching God's will whether he could explain the rationale of it or not in *A Sermon, Delivered at the Ordination of the Reverend Henry Channing* . . . (New London, Conn., 1787), 14. By the date of this ser-

Between 1765 and 1767, his own methods of sermon composition and delivery also began to change. After a decade of fully writing out the sermons he delivered in the pulpit, Stiles started reducing his written texts to outlines. Although he still wrote out lectures and sermons delivered on special occasions, the texts for his regular Sunday sermons became more and more condensed, the major points filling no more than a page by 1772 and requiring as few as fifty words two years later. In 1768, Stiles carefully recorded details about how Solomon Stoddard, who was remembered in New England as a dynamic preacher (and not just for his ecclesiastical innovations) and who had discouraged reading from the pulpit in 1724, had composed the sermons he delivered without referring to notes. Preaching without notes had been the hallmark of the revivalists during the Awakening, and perhaps Whitefield's visit to Newport in August 1770 made Stiles try preaching "without Notes or premeditation" three months later.[26]

Some historians have argued that the Awakening's evangelical rhetoric ushered in a new mode of egalitarian communications that set the rhetorical style of the American Revolution's public discourse. But Stiles's new preaching style did not likely diminish his clerical authority; nor was it more popular because it reduced the distance between the minister and his congregation. And, although Stiles was not, through oral performance, reconstituting his authority

---

mon, and its placement in Morgan's *Gentle Puritan* (445–446), this opinion can be mistakenly thought of as something Stiles arrived at much later in life. Stiles's preaching during 1765 and into 1766 had been unusual, not because he rained down fire and brimstone upon his congregation, but because most of the sermons written in that period were chapter-by-chapter expositions of the gospel of John and the book of Acts. Rather than focus on doctrine or proposition drawn from a biblical verse or two, in other words, his expositions focused on paraphrasing, explicating, and better understanding a whole chapter.

26. Stiles noted this change at the beginning of his Notebook Listing of Sermons Preached, May 10–Oct. 6, 1775. For early examples, see his MS Sermon on Ps. 119:71 (#504), Nov. 30, 1766, and on Luke 12:32 (#506), Nov. 16, 1766. See also Stiles's MS sermon booklets begun July 23, 1769 (#729–#740), Mass. Hist. Soc., and Sept. 6, 1772 (#987–#1002). His MS sermon on John 1:29 (#1200), October 1774, Beinecke Library, is little more than a thumbnail sketch. On Stoddard, see Stiles, "Itineraries," Sept. 5, 1768, II, 446; and Solomon Stoddard, *The Defects of Preachers Reproved in a Sermon Preached at Northampton, May 19th, 1723* (1724), 2d ed. (Boston, 1747). On George Whitefield's visit, see Stiles, *Literary Diary*, ed. Dexter, I, 77. Whitefield preached from Stiles's pulpit on Aug. 5, 1770 (I, 61). Perhaps Stiles had also been inspired by the Reverend Samuel Maxwell, an eighty-one-year-old former Baptist minister who preached for Stiles on May 18, 1769. Maxwell "always wrote his Sermons at full length and read them in delivery" until his eyes weakened in his eightieth year. He then had to learn how to preach without notes, although "verbatim memoriter" and not "extemporaneously" (I, 12). By 1773, congregations were *requesting* that Stiles preach without notes (I, 378).

as a man of religious feeling rather than as a scholar, the new style does evoke from Stiles's portrait the image of the preacher holding the Bible rather than the shelf of scholarly books behind him. Stiles was not attempting to imitate the passionate theatricality of Whitefield, but he was trying to become a more affective—and thus effective—preacher of the Word. He self-consciously connected his new rhetoric of persuasion to Puritan (not New Light) evangelicalism. His sermon outlines are not fragments that by their very form represent the breakdown of cultural narrative in the chaos of the Revolutionary era. They show how Stiles adopted a new public identity and fashioned a place for himself in a historical narrative that had more to do with Puritanism than with the English Enlightenment.[27]

Stiles's shift from rationalist to evangelical preaching had both theological and psychological dimensions, for it was more than just a question of technique. After 1765, Stiles never failed to connect "powerful" and "pathetic" preaching with "the good old Puritan Doctrines." In the pulpit, he began to focus more intently on doctrines he had previously accepted as propositions of Christian philosophy but now seemed to speak more directly both to his experience as a preacher and as a private Christian: the total depravity of mankind, Redemption through Christ, and regeneration by irresistible grace. He more carefully distinguished the saint's experience from the sinner's, and speculative knowledge from the new understanding wrought by grace; he delineated and reconciled the operations of truth and of the Holy Spirit in the preparation for conversion, conversion itself, and in the sanctified soul.[28]

Stiles never had a conversion experience like Paul's on the road to Damas-

27. On evangelical preaching and the cultural style of the Revolution, see Alan Heimert, *Religion and the American Mind: From the Great Awakening to the Revolution* (Cambridge, Mass., 1966), 159–236; Harry S. Stout, "Religion, Communications, and the Ideological Origins of the American Revolution," *William and Mary Quarterly*, 3d Ser., XXXIV (1977), 519–541; Stout, *The New England Soul: Preaching and Religious Culture in Colonial New England* (New York, 1986), 218–222; Donald Weber, *Rhetoric and History in Revolutionary New England* (New York, 1988). Weber claimed that "fragmentary" sermons were "the grammatical reification of the spiritual and social upheaval" of both the Awakening and the Revolution (27). On elites' using speech to reconstitute cultural authority, see Jay Fliegelman, *Declaring Independence: Jefferson, Natural Language, and the Culture of Performance* (Stanford, Calif., 1993). As I will discuss in subsequent chapters, by the 1760s evangelical preachers were not the only ones concerned about oratorical delivery and appeals to sentiment.

28. See, for example, Stiles's MS sermons on Ps. 86:4–5 (#499), Aug. 10, 1766; Col. 3:2 (#505), Nov. 9, 1766; Luke 12:32 (#506), Nov. 16, 1766; Ps. 119:125 (#527), Feb. 8, 1767; John 1:13, "Regeneration" (no #), Aug 16, 1767, Mass. Hist. Soc.; 1 John 3:1 (#566), Sept. 6, 1767; 1 Tim. 1:16–17 (#1018), Feb. 21, 1773; 1 John 4:1 (#996), Feb. 28, 1773; Ps. 145:9–12 (#1229), Dec. 15, 1774; Matt. 13:23 (no #), Nov. 11, 1781.

cus, nor did he ever achieve a solid assurance that he was among the elect. But after 1765, the personal religious experiences that he recorded had less to do with the Shaftesburian sublime than with a desire to be cleansed of sin by the blood of Christ and to "annihilate" himself in an "intire Submission to the infinitely holy Will of God." The transformation in Stiles's spiritual life was not merely a response to his new experiences in the pulpit; both the private Christian and the public preacher, rather, were on parallel courses and, along with his research in New England's ecclesiastical history, carried him back toward Puritanism. By 1770, the year he sat for his portrait, published his *Discourse,* and recorded his "considerable success in the ministry," Stiles's private and public selves were more closely integrated than ever before.[29]

THE SELF AND HISTORY

The spiritual needs of Stiles's congregation helped reshape his public persona in the mid-1760s. But the personal and political events of 1765 also transformed the scholar in the study and his vision of history. The theme of the empowered self had been woven through his philosophical, historical, and personal writings before the Stamp Act crisis. As he wrote abstractly about how knowledge empowered the mind, he tested his own intellectual powers and constructed an identity as an enlightened thinker. His published demographic projections, which ensured the continuing dominance of New England Congregationalism, fueled his private fantasies about himself as a New World Abraham fathering an extensive family dynasty. As late as January 1765, his resistance to overtures by the Anglicans a decade earlier still stood out for him as a shining moment of "self-determination." But, because his Anglican neighbors wrote to London accusing him of treason during the heated months of the Stamp Act, the resolution of the crisis for Stiles marked nothing less than an "astonishing" inter-

29. Stiles, "Birthday Reflections," Dec. 10, 1769 (contrast to language in Stiles, "Oration," June 4, 1754), Dec. 10, 1770; I am using "Shaftesburian sublime" here as shorthand for that author's manner of describing the perception of beauty that elevates the cultured soul to an apprehension of the divine. Shaftesbury's view of the sublime is actually quite complex; he criticized the sublime style but seemed to distinguish between true and false sublimity as he distinguished between true and false enthusiasm. See Samuel H. Monk, *The Sublime: A Study of Critical Theories in Eighteenth-Century England* (1935; reprint, Ann Arbor, Mich., 1969), 59, 208–209; Stanley Grean, *Shaftesbury's Philosophy of Religion and Ethics: A Study in Enthusiasm* (n.p., 1967), 24–32; Klein, *Shaftesbury and the Culture of Politeness,* 203–206; Norton, *The Beautiful Soul,* 26–50. On Stiles's early appreciation of Shaftesbury, see Morgan, *Gentle Puritan,* 66–67.

position of "a merciful God . . . [who] bro't about the Deliverance of me and my Country." In Stiles's post-1765 writing, the empowered self's stamping its image onto history was replaced by a receptive soul's seeking divine communications of truth; the British colonial philosophe became a New England Puritan in righteous dissent.[30]

Stiles's conception of the empowered self developed through his early efforts to unite natural and moral philosophy in a personal credo. He drafted a six-part essay titled "The Universe" in the early 1750s that built a cosmology from a phenomenology of perception. By beginning with the individual's experience as a bodied soul, Stiles could approach the universe as "one *intire* WHOLE" and try to avoid theories that divorced spirit and matter or methods that kept natural and moral philosophy at arm's length. Astronomy had taught him that the earth was just a tiny point in a visible cosmos probably teeming with other populated planets. Yet God's creation was grander still, for the invisible part of the universe "may be superior to the material in Extent as it is in sublimity or Excellency." The ontological category that man inhabited, which Stiles called the "moral world," linked the invisible realm of unbodied spirits ("the intellectual world") with the sensible world of matter and nature.[31]

"The Universe" began with an analysis of the individual's "sensible world,"

30. Stiles, "Birthday Reflections," Dec. 10, 1767, 16. Robert A. Ferguson notes that "the Enlightenment in America is sometimes conveyed in a single phrase, the political right of self-determination realized." See Ferguson, "The American Enlightenment, 1750–1820," in Sacvan Bercovitch, ed., *The Cambridge History of American Literature* (Cambridge, 1994), I, 347–537 (quotation on 368).

31. Quotations are from Stiles to [James Abraham Hillhouse], Feb. 20, 1750; Stiles, [Notes on the Population of the Universe], May 8, 1765. See also ["Birthday Reflections"], Apr. 5, 1765, 16: "Astronomy had convinced me this World was a very minutesimal part [of the universe]." The "moral world" consisted of all bodied and unbodied beings who were conscious and thus capable of responding to God's moral laws. The moral beings who found themselves on earth had been born into a material world in order to be prepared for a future incorporeal life. He drafted early sketches entitled "The Universe" dated Aug. 7, 1750, and Dec. 28, 1750. He wrote "The Universe: or Moral View of the Intellectual World and the Analogy of Nature" in six parts in March 1752. The publication of three parts in 1785 (*New-Haven Gazette,* Mar. 10, 17, 24, 1785), suggests that Stiles continued to think highly of the work that Morgan, in *Gentle Puritan,* 74, aptly called a "cosmic hatrack on which to hang his ideas." See also Stiles's letter to James Abraham Hillhouse, Feb. 22, 1750, which is an early discussion of the project. Morgan notes the Berkeleyan influence on the essay, but a more direct influence on the 1752 draft might have been George Turnbull's *Principles of Moral Philosophy* . . . (London, 1740), which Stiles read in 1752. Turnbull, too, tried to stitch together Isaac Newton, John Locke, George Berkeley, Anthony Ashley Cooper, 3d earl of Shaftesbury, Frances Hutcheson, and Alexander Pope's *Essay on Man* . . . (London, 1733–1734) (see, especially, chap. 1, on "the law of power" and "spheres of activity").

the "sphere of activity" open to a person through his five senses. Although the "Theater of our Being" is "emblazoned with the Character . . . of the *Universal Mind*," our sensible worlds are always individual, and we can deduce a connection between what we perceive and the sensible worlds of the similar beings around us only by analogy. Experience shows us that our volitions are somehow connected to change in the world we perceive, while "Reason and the General Glory of the Universe evince that every created Intelligence is made and designed for *Progress*." Therefore, Stiles concluded, the individual has the power, derived from God, to expand his sphere of activity and "enlarge into Intellectual Greatness." Power, knowledge, and progress reinforced each other in a system that rewrote Stiles's love of learning and intellectual growth as the telos of conscious being in God's universe. An individual has an internal "mental power" called understanding, will, or memory, depending upon the objects that power is directed toward; he also has an external or "constitutional" power to act within the sensible world. Both powers, borrowed from God yet possessed by finite minds, work together and increase with knowledge.[32]

Stiles used his notion of the individual's mental power to navigate through the rocky shoals of the debate over free will and determinism. A few years after his essay "The Universe," he tried to construct an argument for what he experienced as "self-determination." He rejected both the idea of an indifferent self's determining a course of action through a bloodless moral calculus and the idea of the self as a rudderless ship impelled by the winds of motive. Virtue and liberty, he wrote, were rooted in the mind's power of suspension: the ability to resist acting one way or another until a problem has been thought through. To say with the free will philosophers that the understanding determines the will, however, improperly separates the mental faculties of understanding and will, because ordering ideas in consciousness involves the will as much as moving physical objects in the sensible world. Yet to define liberty as merely the freedom to embrace the greatest apparent good, as so-called determinists like Jonathan Edwards or Henry Home, Lord Kames, did, slights the "greater Liberty" of being able to delay compliance with an external motive until all the facts are in.[33]

32. Ezra Stiles, "The Universe" (1752), "No. 1: Phenomena and Laws," 1–7, "No. 3: Power," 9–18.

33. Ezra Stiles, Miscellaneous Papers, undated fragment beginning, "His Ldshp thinks Liberty consists in Spontaneity." Internal evidence suggests that this undated fragment among Stiles's miscellaneous writings was probably written sometime shortly after he read [Henry Home, Lord Kames], *Essays on the Principles of Morality and Natural Religion* (Edinburgh, 1751), between 1756 and 1758. Stiles's "power of suspension" was both spontaneous, which is what the determinists stressed about the will, and able to be cultivated and

Stiles's stress on the mind's power of suspension both reflected and helped him understand his own experience. He described his skeptical phase as an extended period of mental suspension. Deists' arguments made him doubt but never converted him to deism: they "did not overset my mind, but only suspended it, till I could find positive and determining Evidence" for the Scriptures as divine revelation. While sketching out his philosophical ideas, he gave as an example of self-determination a "hypothetical" attempt by Anglicans to induce him to take orders in the Church of England. The motives they offered were a huge salary and the chance to be a bishop. Even if he had no immediate motives to counter their offer, he could, as he put it, hold up one side of the scale to balance the weight of motives on the other side until he found his counterweights. "I can defer or suspend my Compliance 'till I have studied and thoroughly tho't the Thing." Then, after seeing that episcopacy was unscriptural and bad policy, "I can continue my suspension into fix[ed] Resistance of a Motive whose Influence however I cant at once cease to feel." Tutor Stiles, in fact, had been approached twice by the Church of England with lucrative offers. Family and friends said nothing to sway him. "Self-determined at first I was left to self-determination at last."[34]

The self's constitutional power to act within the sensible world grew with experience. But experience for Stiles included something far loftier than a brutish adaptation to the environment. When he wrote that "without experimental Knowledge of the Connexions of Nature this [constitutional] Power could not be exercised to good Purpose," the word "experimental" meant "experiential" and signified the more rationalized accumulation of facts and discovery of laws demonstrable by scientific experiments. The power to reason and the ability to act within the world combined to increase power *over* the world: "The greater our Insight into Nature and its Laws, the greater will be our

---

strengthened, which was how their opponents talked about the understanding. But he did not seem to care whether philosophers spoke of the self's freedom to resist motives or the will's embrace of self-determination itself as a motive. See Allen C. Guelzo, *Edwards on the Will: A Century of American Theological Debate* (Middletown, Conn., 1989). For the relationship of Edwards's argument to Kames's, see "Remarks on the *Essays on the Principles of Morality and Natural Religion . . . ,*" in Edwards, *A Careful and Strict Enquiry into the Modern Prevailing Notions of that Freedom of the Will . . . ,* ed. Paul Ramsey, in Miller et al., eds., *Works of Jonathan Edwards,* I (New Haven, Conn., 1957), 453–465.

34. Stiles, ["Birthday Reflections"], Apr. 5, 1765, 12, 14 (hyphens added). The offers had come from the Stratford, Conn., parish in 1752 and from the Anglican church in Newport, Rhode Island, in 1755. "I was alone," he recalled, and because none of his friends shared his doubts, "Nor could I unbosom myself to any for Relief." "I set myself to a thoro' Discussion of the deistical Controversy, alone and without any help." See Stiles, "Birthday Reflections," Dec. 10, 1767, 7; Stiles, "Series of Occurrences in My Life," Dec. 28, 1767, 1.

Power over its Laws, in altering, suspending or counteracting them." From the time he had been an undergraduate concentrating on science rather than theology, Stiles had labeled the most refined form of this disciplined intellectual activity "Newtonian."[35]

For the young man pursuing knowledge by studying comets with Thomas Clap and chatting about electricity with Benjamin Franklin, Christian apologetics did not measure up to Newtonian rigor. Because he "had been taught by the Newtonian demonstrations to discard the authority of great Names and ingenious Hypotheses in philosophy," he refused to give any special weight to the Westminster Confession of Faith. When he read Samuel Clarke's *Demonstration of the Being and Attributes of God,* Stiles "did not perceive his reasonings so strong and conclusive, as I had been accustomed to perceive those for the solar system, mathematics and experimental philosophy." George Turnbull's *Principles of Moral Philosophy,* too, was "far from being decisive," although Stiles admired Turnbull's attempt to treat *"moral,* as Newton had treated *natural philosophy."* But if Newtonian science had raised Stiles's criteria for moral certainty too high for religious questions, it also offered an initial escape from skepticism:

> At first and in the Depth of Scepticism, I found myself ready to demand too much. I wanted to have displayed before me [that] every Word, or at least every sentiment in the Scriptures was [inspired], and was able to have my faith of the whole overset if I found one insuperable Difficulty. Newton tho't whether the power by which a stone falls to the Ground might not retain the Moon in her Orbit; and then went on and investigated the Law of Gravity demonstrably obtaining in the solar system and probably thro' out the stellar universe. In like manner some one principle may be a [fact] upon which the whole system of Revelation may be firmly supported.

35. On Newton as a model and cultural hero, see Gay, "The Enlightenment's Newton," and "Newtons of the Mind," in *The Enlightenment,* II, *Science of Freedom,* 128–140, 174–187; Henry Guerlac, "Newton's Changing Reputation in the Eighteenth Century," in Raymond O. Rockwood, ed., *Carl Becker's Heavenly City Revisited* (n.p., 1968), 3–26; Rom Harré, "Knowledge," and Simon Schaffer, "Natural Philosophy," in G. S. Rousseau and Roy Porter, eds., *The Ferment of Knowledge: Studies in the Historiography of Eighteenth-Century Science* (Cambridge, 1980), 11–54, 55–91. To most of Newton's admirers from the eighteenth century to the present, Newton was a model of austere mathematical rationality, though he might actually have been closer in spirit to Stiles's later hero, the mystical theologian Dionysius the Areopagite, than the *Principia* suggests. See Betty Jo Teeter Dobbs, *The Foundations of Newton's Alchemy; or, "The Hunting of the Greene Lyon"* (Cambridge, 1975); and Dobbs, *The Janus Faces of Genius: The Role of Alchemy in Newton's Thought* (Cambridge, 1991); on Dionysius, see 157–159.

Once Stiles had established that the Resurrection of Jesus was a historical fact as verifiable as the assassination of Julius Caesar, he was able to begin his journey back to faith.[36]

Stiles's essay "The Universe" tried to reduce the phenomena of experience to general laws, but Stiles was even less of a Newton for moral philosophy than George Turnbull. Stiles was no metaphysician, and he knew it; he was much more interested in gathering facts about the world around him than in philosophical hairsplitting and abstract speculation. He had gone far enough, however, to reconcile a metaphysics and a physics that painted man as passive, with a moral view that empowered the self. He was able to argue, at least to his own satisfaction, that a person could not blink an eyelid or think about lunch without the direct exercise of God's power and that natural laws operated upon a man mechanically, imprinting his mind with sensible ideas—but also that human liberty and virtue were rooted in self-determination.

Self-determination was also the key to religious liberty. Like Elisha Williams, Stiles grounded liberty in the individual's conscience, not in the norms of a covenanted community, and he opposed his old friend Thomas Clap and the New Divinity's Joseph Bellamy on the subject of orthodoxy tests. In a drafted response to Bellamy's "Paulinus" essay in the *Connecticut Gazette*, Stiles argued that communities had no right to formally establish an "orthodox" interpretation of the Scriptures, "Because they have no common Mind to judge for them." A community was an aggregate of individual minds that could in no way combine to form "one simple Principle of Intelligence," and only a single mind was capable of thinking for itself and making religious choices.[37]

But Stiles's moral view of politics and history, his understanding of God's moral government of the world in the gospel dispensation, was initially so individualistic that he was unprepared for the rhetorical demands of the wartime

36. Samuel Clarke, *Demonstration of the Being and Attributes of God . . .* (London, 1705); Stiles, ["Birthday Reflections"], Apr. 5, 1765, 5; Stiles, "Review of the Authors I Read and Admired," Dec. 12, 1768, 24, 27, 37. Stiles here demonstrates a great shift in biblical hermeneutics, focusing on the text's "ostensive reference" to historical facts rather than upon the meaningful story itself. See Hans W. Frei, *The Eclipse of Biblical Narrative: A Study in Eighteenth and Nineteenth Century Hermeneutics* (New Haven, Conn., 1974), esp. chap. 4. Stiles's effort to place his trust in the Scriptures on a continuum stretching from "opinion" to "moral certainty" draws from English thought of the late seventeenth century. See Barbara J. Shapiro, *Probability and Certainty in Seventeenth-Century England: A Study of the Relationships between Natural Science, Religion, History, Law, and Literature* (Princeton, N.J., 1983); and Gerard Reedy, *The Bible and Reason: Anglicans and Scripture in Late Seventeenth-Century England* (Philadelphia, 1985).

37. Ezra Stiles, "To the Gentleman Who Inserted the Piece Subscribed Paulinus in the Connecticut Gazette No. 149," [ca. February 1758].

pulpit. Instead of a single corporate entity that had reality in God's eyes, and a historical mission that he blessed, Stiles envisioned society as a collectivity of individuals whose aggregate virtue might, or might not, add up to victory. In 1752, he believed that Israel had been unique among the nations of the world. Because the Jews alone lacked the idea of immortality and future retribution, God ruled them through an *"equal Distribution"* of justice under the Mosaic plan, rewarding them in this world for their virtue and vice. But, as the doctrine of *eternal* rewards and punishments became known, the old plan faded, and in this world vice was allowed to triumph while virtue was oppressed. Thus, droughts, diseases, wars, and earthquakes were no longer necessarily signs of God's displeasure. When he first came to Newport, Stiles was willing to concede that, although the Jewish "moral economy" had ceased, public blessings still depended upon "the public Temper of a People," but only to a degree. All nations were still obliged to give public thanks and ask forgiveness, but primarily because such rituals made individuals reflect upon their sins and blessings.[38]

His fast sermon on General Edward Braddock's defeat in August 1755 was remarkably detached. Evils, like wars between nations, he argued, often have little to do with a people's misconduct. But it was natural that nations, like little children, should go before their Father and ask him to arbitrate their disputes. As other New England ministers beat the war drum for a crusade against the minions of Antichrist, Stiles reminded his congregation that the enemy were also "Children of the same common Father, apprehending themselves an equal claim to his protection." Perhaps if the English colonials "roused up all the *Briton*" within themselves, God would reward their bravery and give them dominion over an American empire.[39]

Fifteen months later, in 1756, it had become clear to him that "all manner of societies, communities, and public Bodies as such are capable of Rewards and Punishments in this World." By 1758, he was celebrating the defeat of the Roman Catholic "Enemies of God" at Louisbourg, and, in 1759, although he still

38. Stiles writes of the "equal distribution" of justice in "A View of the Moral Government of the World," Jan. 29, 1752; Stiles, "Fast Sermon on the Occasion of the Defeat of General Braddock at the Ohio, July 9, 1755," on Joel 2:2:15–17, Aug. 28, 1755, Mass. Hist. Soc. See also Stiles, MS sermon on Ps. 1:1–4 (#6), Aug. 10, 1755; and MS sermon on Ps. 100:3–5 (#19), Dec. 4, 1755. Professor John Winthrop's letter to Stiles on earthquakes, Apr. 17, 1756, indicates that both men agreed about the moral interpretation of such natural phenomena (see my discussion of Winthrop and earthquakes in Chapter 4).

39. Stiles, MS "Fast Sermon" (Braddock's defeat) on Joel 2:15–17, Aug. 28, 1755, Mass. Hist. Soc.

believed that the Jews were the only ones ever to be in a national covenant of works, he held up Israel as an example of how God's smiles and frowns varied according to the public virtue of any nation. After the victory at Quebec in September 1759, Stiles began stressing the similarities between Britain and Israel, not just as exemplars of God's universal moral government but as peculiarly chosen nations with divine historical missions. He never argued that Britain or New England was an elect nation in the sense that Israel was, or that either was a type of Israel. But he discovered the rhetorical uses of the "striking Analogy and Similitude" between "Israel's possessing the Land of promise; and british protestants possessing this american Canaan."[40]

He articulated the conception of manifest destiny, not by celebrating a covenantal promise to New England's pious founders or by trying to read the American experience through the dark glass of scriptural prophecy, but by extrapolating present "facts" into future dominion. Certainly New England's founding, within the larger British story of the struggle for religious and civil liberty, took on an increasing significance for Stiles. But it was evidence from the "sensible world" that led him to believe that "a few Generations more shall sweep [the Indians] off the face of the Earth" and open the American continent as an asylum for British liberty all the way to the Pacific.[41]

He believed that the study of population, or what we would call demogra-

---

40. On societies rewarded and punished in this world, see Stiles, MS sermon on Ps. 67:3 (#111), Nov. 25, 1756, 2. On the Roman Catholic enemies of God, see MS sermons on Judg. 5:31 (#233, 234), Aug. 20, 1758; Ps. 106:44–45 (#293), Apr. 5, 1759, "At a Fast; When Part of the Regiment under Colonel Babcock was Present"; Heb. 7:22 (#353), Nov. 25, 1759. See also MS sermons on Lam. 3:39–41 (#363), Apr. 3, 1760; and Ps. 96:8 (#408), Nov. 18, 1762. The reference to the American Canaan is in MS sermon on 2 Chron. 20:6–7 (#366), Sept. 25, 1760, after "Montreal Capitulated Sept. 8, 1760," 3. See also MS sermon on 1 Chron. 29:26–28 (#371), Jan. 20, 1771 (on the death of George II and the accession of George III), 3. Stiles never compared the "New" and "Old" Israels without making careful distinctions, and the parallel remained primarily a heuristic exercise rather than an assertion about British America's role in sacred history. He believed that God had condescended to the Jews, a nation without letters and at an immature stage of intellectual development, and allowed them to think that his will varied according to their behavior. In eighteenth-century New England, it could still be useful to think in this way, especially for children: "Let our children be often taught to read [Deut. 26:6–9] with parallel application to the history of our ancestors. Let the great errand into America never be forgotten" (Stiles, A Discourse on Christian Union, 116–117).

41. Stiles, MS sermon on Ps. 48:9 (#345), Oct. 15, 1759, 13–22. See also MS sermons on 2 Chron. 20:6–7 (#366), Sept. 25, 1760, 17; and on Ps. 27:6 (#424), Aug. 25, 1763, where he raises the possibility that God might permit the Indians to survive as a chastisement to the British.

phy, was a systematic branch of philosophy founded on hard facts and having much to offer philosophers and politicians. The human race was divided into various stocks, with their national differences bred into the bone by climate and culture. Nations grew numerous, reached "patrical maturity," and then declined according to regular laws. The current state of any nation in this rise-and-fall cycle could be determined by an analysis of birth and death records. His forays into pre-Malthusian demographics assured him that the Indians would continue to conveniently vanish from the American landscape, and that dissenters would continue to hold the reins of power in New England, over-whelming the Church of England and all other sects by sheer numbers. There-fore, the facts supported an optimistic vision of the future and buttressed his call for "Christian union" among New England Dissenters in his 1760 sermon — a call that earned him the enmity of the Anglicans. The natural laws of procre-ation in such a favorable environment would produce the exponential growth of New England stock, and the spirit of "Christian union" among the clergy would keep those future generations in the pews, thereby ensuring cultural as well as genetic continuity. The material "sphere of activity" of New England's churches would expand through natural procreation, and its intellectual or spiritual greatness would enlarge through progress in Christian knowledge.[42]

This vision of New England's progress had enormous personal resonance for Stiles, and it could almost be said that New England was merely Ezra Stiles writ large. For in the privacy of his study, Stiles created an elaborate fantasy in which he achieved a kind of secular immortality by founding a large family bound together by blood and by the laws, institutions, and rituals Father Ezra had framed. In this fantasy of the empowered self, Stiles was both Abraham and Moses, patriarch and lawgiver, shaping the future in his own image through his loins and by the power of his mind.

The series of writings Stiles called his "Family Constitutions" began in 1762, two years after his father's death, with a plan to buy a parcel of Susquehanna land in order to establish a trust fund for his posterity. "The wisest Precepts en-joyned upon offspring by the father of a family will lose their Influence in the Dissipations of Posterity," he wrote. But a small Canaan might keep the dias-poric forces at bay and maintain his family as "a distinct Body combined in firm Alliance and Union for the Reception of those ancestral institutions." Every four years, or "Stilesian Olympiad," after his death, his descendants

42. Stiles, *A Discourse on Christian Union*, 120–127; Stiles, MS "Itineraries," [ca. 1760–1761], I, 295–302. For a general survey of colonial attitudes about demography, see James H. Cassedy, *Demography in Early America: Beginnings of the Statistical Mind, 1600–1800* (Cambridge, Mass., 1969).

would attend a meeting during the autumnal equinox to cultivate their collective virtue and manage the family funds. Before the gathered branches or "tribes" of the family, who would be seated according to genealogy and rank, the family historian and census collector would display a parchment copy of Ezra's "Institutes" written in the founder's own hand. With time and the accumulation of wealth, the family could patronize the arts like the Medici and found a library and a learned society, endowing their own chair for scriptural research. That would make the family members not only beacons of virtue but "repositors of Truth and a Blessing to the World."[43]

Such an experiment in family virtue had never been attempted in the history of the world; it would distinguish the family "to eternal ages in distant regions of the moral world with a name above all the families of this Earth, not accepting even the family and natural offspring of Abraham." It might earn the Stileses "very distinguished blessings in the millennial state." Stiles even offered to return to earth with Christ to serve as head of the family during the millennium. The position would open a very large sphere of activity indeed because of the intoxicating mathematics of population increase. If each of his five children had five children, and their children had five, and so on, down through the generations, several million Stileses would inhabit the earth before the 350th anniversary of his 1757 wedding.[44]

In 1860, however, long before the family grew so large or Stiles expected to return with Christ, the celebration of the Stilesian Olympiad would have to become more formal. Father Ezra's "Institutes" would be printed, and a thirty-foot marble obelisk would be erected in the center of a walled plot of land somewhere in Connecticut. Stiles's design for the monument, along with his designs for other family icons like medals and stone tombs, is itself emblematic of the whole project. Anticipating the stone column in his 1770 portrait, the monument represents the material world inscribed by consciousness. Like the parchment copy of his "Institutes" displayed as a sacred object, the stone would stand in for the bodily presence of Father Ezra until his millennial return; like the text of the "Institutes," which enjoined the family to plant mulberry trees and keep accurate census records, the obelisk would be "deeply en-

43. Ezra Stiles, "Family Constitutions—Thoughts on Raising a Family," Mar. 10, 1762, with subsequent entries dated Mar. 14, May 10, Aug. 25, Dec. 20, 1762, Jan. 17, 1763, Jan. 23, 1765, and one undated entry (quotations from "Family Constitutions," n.d.). The meeting would be presided over by the eldest male or female, and leaders of every tribe would be appointed. All males and females in the direct bloodline over the age of fourteen could vote on business matters, including any white "bastards" but excluding the offspring resulting from any copulation with Indians or blacks.

44. Stiles, "Family Constitutions," Mar. 10, 1762, 35.

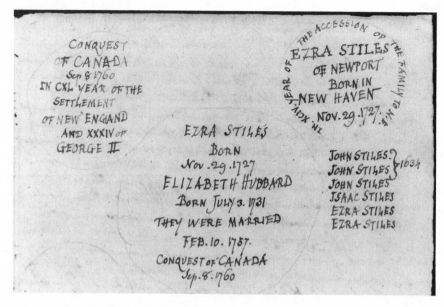

Figure 10. Ezra Stiles's Sketch of Medallion; or, Monument Inscriptions Commemorating the Stiles Family and the British Conquest of Canada. On a draft of a letter to an unknown correspondent, Jan. 15, 1765. Courtesy, Beinecke Rare Book and Manuscript Library, Yale University, New Haven, Conn.

graved" with maps of New England and the Susquehanna lands, with population figures and the names of the Stiles family leaders since the founder's birth in 1727.[45]

The obelisk shows how the empowered self and New England's rising glory commingled in Stiles's imagination. A notebook draft of inscriptions, too, marked both the rise of the Stiles family and the conquest of Canada as the beginning of a new era in New England's history. A mood of cultural optimism for New England's expansion after the fall of Quebec merged with a mood of personal independence after his father's death in 1760 and became, for Stiles, an index of personal and historical progress.

The devastating news of the Stamp Act reached Newport during the last week of March 1765. In the pulpit, as he later told his congregation, he refused to address the issue directly, being "Influenced by Timidity partly, partly by Judgement," and he devoted much of his preaching during the fourteen months un-

45. Ibid., 9. Stiles noted that the etymological roots of his name signified both "pen" and "pillar." See Stiles, *Literary Diary*, ed. Dexter, III, 75.

til the act's repeal to benign, chapter-by-chapter expositions of the books of John and Acts. In his study, Stiles recorded every scrap of news that he could collect about the colonial resistance to the act, and he privately raged that Parliament's passage of it "sealed the loss of American liberty" and began an era "of American slavery." "Henceforth the *European* and *American* Interests," he concluded, "are separated[,] never more to be joyned."[46]

On a trip to Connecticut in October, he was told that a letter had been sent to the Lords of the Treasury in London, naming him as one of the instigators of the Newport Stamp Act riots of August 29. Frantically, he drafted a letter to his friend Benjamin Franklin in London, denying the "malicious Rumor"; he denied it again to the Lords of Trade and declared that he would "continue to make it as a part of my pastoral Labors in my little sphere to inculcate and perpetuate . . . Allegiance and Obedience to the King." But he felt powerless, just as he felt America would be powerless if pushed into a "civil war." The Newport Anglicans, who had become his enemies since his *Christian Union* predictions in 1760, were ready, Stiles believed, to supply false witnesses for any accusation. They had been behind the letter to the Lords of Treasury and the "capital charge" against him, "designing as they said to take my Life for Treason." If the act had not been repealed, Stiles recalled, "I should have been sent for and carried home in Chains to Sustain a Trial for my Life." The repeal was an astonishing act of God's mercy—a personal and national deliverance. "Our fathers saw great Things in their day," he wrote in 1766, "but their sons have seen greater manifestations of the power and protection of Heaven."[47]

In private and in public, Stiles began to identify himself with Puritanism. The flurry of letters beginning in November 1765 that praised "the good old Puritans" made a political statement as much as they commented on theology or preaching style. Before 1765, he had spoken of the emigration to America as an escape from Stuart tyranny and of British liberty's reaching its fullest expression in the more tolerant New England of the eighteenth century. Now he spoke of Puritanism as a *continuing* resistance to the forces of British tyranny operating in the present. "This is the 200th year of Puritanism," he proclaimed

46. Stiles, MS sermon on Jer. 30:19–22 (#496), June 26, 1766, 57; Notebook Listing of Texts Preached, May 10, 1755–Oct. 6, 1775 (of more than 1,100 sermons, Stiles composed only 54 "expositions," which he listed separately: those written on John and Acts between Apr. 28, 1765, and May 8, 1766); "Stamp Act Notebook," July 17, 1765.

47. Stiles to [Benjamin Franklin], draft, Oct. 23, 1765 (copy 2, dated Nov. 6, 1765); Stiles to "The Right Honourable the Lords of the Treasury," Nov. 6, 1765 (if sent, the letter to Franklin has been lost—it is not printed in Leonard W. Labaree, ed., *The Papers of Benjamin Franklin*, 33 vols. to date [New Haven, Conn., 1959–]); "Birthday Reflections," Dec. 10, 1767, 16; Stiles to Chauncy Whittelsey, June 1766.

from the pulpit, and Jesus Christ was "the Head of the Sons of Liberty." Before the crisis, Stiles had held up Jonathan Mayhew as an intellectual model, a doctrinally heterodox clergyman who championed free inquiry and attacked the Church of England; the bookshelf in his 1770 portrait, however, held New England's "primaeval Divines": President Charles Chauncy of Harvard, John Cotton, John Davenport, and Richard Mather.[48]

The enemy was clearly defined: "*Stamp Act, Episcopal Hierarchy, and military Government* were all Branches of the same Policy." Sometimes he simply denounced his opponents as the "anti-American party." Liberty of conscience and the laws of procreation would not be enough to protect against the Anglicans, who schemed to get American bishops and secretly desired to "subordinate" and "police" dissenting sects. He worked behind the scenes for an intercolonial congress of Congregationalists and Presbyterians, who could unite not only upon similar doctrines and forms but on a shared contempt for episcopacy. He hoped that the spirit of unity that had inspired Americans in 1765 would spread to the churches, but he also tried to cultivate an "inseparable Affection," a bond that transcended politics, "between Dissenters in England and that Branch of Puritanism which has been exiled into America." To New England friends, Stiles announced that the time was ripe "to dispute the whole Reformation over again," which would probably be necessary two or three times each century—not to convert Anglicans, but "to confirm our Brethren and establish the rising Generation in Puritanism."[49]

---

48. See the following letters from Stiles: to [Thomas Wright], Nov. 18, 22, 1766, Dec. 22, 1767; to Noah Welles, Nov. 22, 1766; to Joseph Jennings, Jan. 20, 1767; to [Benjamin Gale?], May 2, 1767; to John Barnard, Oct. 3, 1767; to John Hubbard, Jr., Dec. 15, 1767; to [Abigail W. S. Dwight], Nov. 30, 1770. In three letters to Massachusetts governor Thomas Hutchinson, who was writing his history of New England, Stiles justified the New England uprising against Governor Edmund Andros during the Glorious Revolution. See Stiles to Hutchinson, Mar. 29, Oct. 5, 1765, Nov. 26, 1767. For the quotations from Stiles's sermons, see MS sermon on Jer. 30:19–22 (#496), June 26, 1766, 40; MS thanksgiving sermon on Ps. 145:3–13 (#507), Nov. 27, 1766, 9. On Stiles's early opinion of Mayhew, see "Family Constitutions," Mar. 10, 1762, 28: "*Mayhew* is the most open and honest and undisguised of the American Divines; he is learned and you are in no doubt whether you have his honest and full Opinion, tho Error, and yet he will be found very nearly right." Stiles describes the contents of the portrait bookshelf in Stiles, *Literary Diary*, ed. Dexter, I, 131–133.

49. The quotation connecting the Stamp Act, episcopacy, and military government is in Stiles to Charles Chauncy, Oct. 24, 1766. Stiles talks about the "American" and "anti-American" parties in letters to William Hart, Feb. 27, 1767, and to [Benjamin Gale?], May 2, 1767, although he acknowledges that *Southern* Anglicans were on the side of liberty. On Congregationalist-Presbyterian unity, see Stiles to [Chauncy Whittelsey], July 27, 1767; Stiles to Francis Allison, Aug. 27, 1767 (copy 2). Stiles had sketched out a much cooler argument

The language and tone of his self-reflections changed too. Before the mid-1760s, he had considered diary writing a hypocritical exercise that recorded how the writer would like to be seen by others rather than the true state of his soul. But on his birthday in 1767, he sat down to write a page or two and found that his thoughts "flowed hastily thro' the pen" for nearly four hours. In the twelve-page manuscript he reread the next morning, he found truth mixed with "some Partiality, Hypocrisy and self-delusion, pride and Vanity." The exercise had been worthwhile, he decided, because it made him "see and feel how frail I am." "How absolutely contemptible is Man glorying in some Little Eminency among his fellow worms, while in Comparison with the Immensity of the Universe, and in the view of superior spirits, and above all in the contemplation of God, he must appear nothing, less than nothing and vanity!" His "Family Constitutions" were precepts to be handed down to posterity by Father Ezra, the Great Patriarch. The birthday reflections were attempts at candid intellectual and spiritual self-examination. No doubt the annual reflections were partially written for the eyes of posterity too. But those readers would discover short essays by a flawed human being trying to learn and grow, not monuments and constitutions by a founding father trying to teach—and control—the future.[50]

In 1771, he reviewed his "Family Constitutions" notebook, which he had not supplemented since early in 1765. "I was carried away with this family Projection," he wrote in disgust. "I am so sick of this pleasing vanity." He planned to destroy the manuscript and merely recommend to his posterity the Congregational way and "the love of Jesus." In his notebooks, plans for the "Stilesian" learned society were replaced by drafts for American philosophical and scientific associations; sketches of family medals and obelisks were supplanted by descriptions of public monuments to liberty.[51]

"Self-determination" and the power of "suspension" dropped from Stiles's philosophical vocabulary, and by 1770 his friends complained that he sounded like a New Divinity determinist. As early as 1759, Stiles had defended Jonathan

---

against episcopacy in his "Reflections, I. On the Present State of the Protestant Religion," Dec. 12, 1759, pt. 2. For a discussion of Stiles's role in developing the unsuccessful "Plan of Union," see Morgan, *Gentle Puritan*, chap. 16; and Carl Bridenbaugh, *Mitre and Sceptre: Transatlantic Faiths, Ideas, Personalities, and Politics, 1689–1775* (New York, 1962). The comment about the bond to English Dissenters is in Stiles to Joseph Jennings, Aug. 8, 1767. Quotations to New England friends are from Stiles to Hart, Feb. 27, 1767; Stiles to Noah Welles, Nov. 22, 1766.

50. Stiles, "Birthday Reflections," Dec. 10, 1767, 4–5.

51. See the notes dated June 11, 1771, and Aug. 29, 1772, appended to the Dec. 20, 1762, draft of the "Family Constitutions," 1, 60.

Edwards and Lord Kames against the charge that their schemes made man the pawn of fate. Both "place[d] the Universe under the Controll of Deity," and both offered ideas about liberty and necessity that could be accepted by a "Christian and Revelationist." Late in 1764, Stiles discussed these "metaphysical points" with his father-in-law, Connecticut physician John Hubbard. Moral liberty, Stiles now argued, consisted in the ability to choose and act accordingly. Hubbard held the Arminian position that virtue rested in the liberty of indifference and the power to choose between two courses of action, or else the whole notion of choice was a sham. Stiles countered that God could reveal irresistible motives that overwhelmed a man and, like moral gravity, drew him toward the center of truth. If God opens before me a ravishing vision of moral excellency and it excites within me and draws out of me a prevailing tendency to choose what is virtuous, and if, "in Consequence of this[,] I am swallowed up in virtue and absorbed in Moral Perfection . . . what matter is it to me . . . whether a contrary choice and pursuit were equally within my Power."[52]

In 1764, Stiles could still dismiss his differences with Hubbard over "the metaphysical modus of operation of the mind" as having little practical importance, but by 1768 such discussions were at the center of New England theological debate. The New Divinity men were championing Edwards's treatise on the will as the keystone of Calvinist orthodoxy, Chauncy Whittelsey complained, and denouncing Arminian missteps as *damnable* errors. When Stiles welcomed Samuel Hopkins to Newport with his *Discourse on Christian Knowledge* in 1770, and spoke of holiness as a miraculously given idea that God "pours down" into the elect soul, Stiles's Connecticut friends groaned. William Hart complained that Stiles made "holiness" an idea that could not possibly be "believed or gained by reasonings from God's works or words," an idea that transcended human discourse and could be implanted only by immediate inspiration. James Dana was sorry to see that Stiles's sermon was so Edwardsean in the way it described regeneration as God's physical operation upon a passive human mind. For John Hubbard, that passivity destroyed everything that could be meant by "intelligence" and "moral agency."[53]

Stiles was stunned. He did not understand why his sermon "had proved very unacceptable and even offensive" to his best friends. He insisted that anyone who compared his 1760 *Christian Union* to his 1770 *Saving Knowledge* would find the same opinions in both. (John Devotion responded to the chal-

52. Stiles to "Mr. Bennet, Edinburgh," Sept. 14, 1759; Stiles to Jared Eliot, Sept. 24, 1759; Stiles to John Hubbard, Nov. 14, 1764.

53. Chauncy Whittelsey to Stiles, June 30, 1768; [William Hart] to Stiles, Sept. 17, 1770; James Dana to Stiles, 1770; John Hubbard to Stiles, Apr. 25, 1771.

lenge, compared the two sermons, and disagreed.) Stiles had always held that a human mind needed supernatural assistance to apprehend divine things. But the earlier Stiles had acknowledged God's grace and then focused upon the actions of the empowered self. Stiles emerged from the trials of the 1760s "wishing with the greatest Ardor that my Will, my soul, my All may be intirely swallowed up in the divine Will."[54]

Writing to a friend in February 1772, Stiles seemed frustrated that publication, instead of effectively communicating his sentiments, had threatened to draw him into "the Battle of Words and terms," the kind of "befogged" metaphysical controversy that he believed was impossible to clarify for the public. If he had more confidence in his ability to communicate face to face with his own congregation—preaching, teaching, counseling—that confidence would not last. Stiles's sense of his powers as preacher and pastor received a shock when in October 1772 he returned from a visit to Connecticut to find his Newport congregation "in flames." In his absence, a universalist named John Murray had preached from Stiles's pulpit and seemed to have undone what Stiles had labored to cultivate for seventeen years: belief in sound doctrines and warm affection for the pastor. How could it be? He reviewed his old sermons, to see if anything he had said could have made his flock "Tinder for some of Mr Murray's Sparks," but found nothing. Losing the love and support of about a dozen families seemed to hurt more than knowing his congregation had been so easily swayed by false doctrines. From the beginning of his ministry in 1755, he had believed that a prudent, hard-working minister could secure the affections of his flock. "I have no more any Dependence on my own prudence," he wrote in 1773, "or on the stability of the Affections of Man, but rely alone on God."[55]

In December 1777, after war had scattered Stiles's congregation and forced him from Newport, he preached on America's future and privately pondered his own. The Revolution called forth all the powers of mind and body, he argued, yet Americans could rely on something far greater than the strengths of human nature. "God has been pleased to pour down among the Body of this people a very singular and diffuse Knowledge of their political Rights and Liberty"; he also filled them with "vigor," "a Spirit of Enterprise," and a "pro-

54. Stiles to [John Devotion], Mar. 12, 1771 (more likely an unfinished draft of a letter to John Hubbard, although subsequent letters indicate that Stiles communicated the same sentiments to Devotion); John Devotion to Stiles, July 8, 1771; Stiles to Chauncy Whittelsey, Mar. 6, 1770, 10.

55. Stiles to Abigail W. S. Dwight, Feb. 7, 1772; Stiles to Chauncy Whittelsey, Mar. 6, 1770; "Birthday Reflections," Dec. 10, 1773.

phetic enthusiasm" for their own future as a great nation. God's plan for America seemed clear, but what was his will for Ezra Stiles? If left to choose for himself, Stiles would have retreated into his study, where, freed from the narrow chauvinism of scholarly, religious, and political affiliation, from the "Affairs, Enterprizes, and Revolutions" of the world, his soul could unite "with the whole Body of the Mystical Church." But as God guided America to Independence, he also seemed to be calling Ezra Stiles to the Yale presidency.[56]

MYSTICISM AND POLITICS

Stiles's experiences had taught him that the learned man in Revolutionary New England must be able to retire with his books and his visions of God's intellectual world. But the scholar must also be able to reach out to others, "in a teaching and preaching attitude," to shape what Stiles began to call the "public mind." A dialectical tension between scholarship and preaching shaped Stiles's sense of himself. From 1777 until his death in 1795, however, constructing the identity of the learned man was more than just a personal project. He agreed with James Madison that the colleges of the young Republic would lay the foundation for the future glory of America, and, by the 1780s, Yale was the largest college in the land. One of his major goals was to redirect the energies of New England's clerical intellectuals. But as Yale's president, Stiles would also be thrown into the midst of struggles to realign church and state, to redefine the power of clergymen and "civilians" over higher education, and to recast the relationship between religious and political life in the young Republic.[57]

Stiles brought to Yale the belief that hermeneutics rather than systematic theology would be the best buttress for orthodoxy and a reputation as a linguist that had developed only after he had received an honorary doctorate from Edinburgh in 1765. Embarrassed that a doctor of divinity should know so little Hebrew, he embarked on a study of Semitic languages and, with some initial help from Newport rabbis, mastered Hebrew, Syriac, Chaldee, and Arabic. He believed he found new evidence for the Athanasian understanding of

56. Stiles, MS sermon on Gen. 49:22–26, Dec. 18, 1777; "Birthday Reflections," Dec. 10, 1777; Stiles, *Literary Diary,* ed. Dexter, II, 115; and his acceptance letter to the Yale Corporation, Mar. 20, 1778, II, 267–269.

57. Stiles to James Madison, July 12, 1780; Madison to Stiles, Aug. 1, 1780, in Stiles, *Literary Diary,* ed. Dexter, II, 445–449. Morgan, in *Gentle Puritan,* 359, notes that by 1784 Yale was "the most popular and flourishing college in the United States. . . . Yale had some 270 students, the largest enrollment there had ever been at one time in an American college, over a hundred more than the current number at Harvard."

the Trinity in the Old Testament and for the Anselmian view of Christ's Atonement in the ancient prophecies of a suffering Messiah. His daily study of the Scriptures in Hebrew and Syriac confirmed his faith in the King James translation, and his Talmudic research led him to think that additional allegorical meanings might be concealed in the Hebrew vowel points.[58]

An eighty-seven-page letter to the renowned Orientalist Sir William Jones in 1794 shows how Stiles's linguistic studies had reframed his search for truth. As a young Newtonian, Stiles had focused on gathering facts from the material world, believing that the lost tribes of Israel, for example, might be discovered through the examination of physical characteristics like skin color and even bodily odor. To Jones he wrote that the tribes might be traced by a talented Hebraist who could perceive the remnants of nationality in "the Structure[,] Syntax and Formation of Language." The search had more to do with the possibility of recovering an ancient copy of the Pentateuch than in discovering the carnal seed of Israel. For the young Stiles, culture had literally been embodied; for the Yale president, culture was embodied as literature—as the preservation, not of bloodlines, but of languages and texts.[59]

Stiles believed that, in the infancy of the world, heaven had taught mankind "all Literature, and all the Arts and Improvements of secular as well as religious life," perhaps in an original encyclopedia of "Adamical books," subsequently lost. The scholar's quest was to recover the scattered fragments of that primeval knowledge hidden in the archives of the world's great civilizations and among its scattered peoples.[60]

Stiles understood the fragmentation of knowledge and language in the world in Neoplatonic terms, as part of a universal plurality emanating from a single unity. This idea was represented in Stiles's portrait by the emblem of the

58. Ezra Stiles, "Memoir concerning My Learning Hebrew," May 12, 1768; [Notes on the Name of God], n.d.; Stiles to Rabbi Raphael Haim Isaac Carigal, July 19, 1773 (in Hebrew with English translation); Stiles to John Lewis, Feb. 15, 1775; "Birthday Reflections," Dec. 10, 1774. Stiles discusses the rabbinical titles on the bookshelf of his 1771 portrait in his *Literary Diary*, ed. Dexter, I, 131–133; see also I, 7, 74–75, 555–556. Stiles's Hebraic studies are discussed in Arthur A. Chiel, "Ezra Stiles: The Education of an 'Hebrician,'" *American Jewish Historical Quarterly*, LX (1971), 235–241.

59. Stiles to Sir William Jones, Jan. 18, 1794. Cf. "Itineraries" notebooks, July 22, 1761, where he speculates that the different skin colorations among the English, Indians, and Jews might be due to the different densities of "perspirable Effluvia." He also discussed skin color and his theory that different races had different smells in letters to John Winthrop, July 19, 1759, Jan. 7, 1760. In his "Family Constitutions," Mar. 10, 1762, 24–25, Stiles recorded his belief that the tribes ought to be distinguishable by characteristic marks, just as he could "infallibly distinguish by smell an Indian, a negro, and a Jew."

60. Stiles to Jones, Jan. 18, 1794, 30–56, 123–149 of the booklet.

intellectual universe, which showed the tetragrammaton ("Yahweh") in the center of a circle of light, surrounded by a multiplicity of tiny white spots on a field of blue. But the emblem also shows the Neoplatonic countermovement, the return of consciousness to that central truth. Hairlines ascend from each spot, "denoting the Tendencies of Minds to Deity." The human minds clustered on earth, however, were turned away from God and toward "self and created good"; a small crucifix stood for their means of redemption, and a small black spot for the fate of "the finally wicked." Stiles had first drafted the emblem in 1766. After he purchased two folio volumes by the mystical theologian Dionysius the Areopagite in 1771, subsequent drafts of the emblem would become more complex as Stiles developed his understanding of how consciousness returned to God through knowledge.[61]

Stiles had long been attracted to Platonic and Neoplatonic thought, but when he publicly recommended that his brethren in the ministry become well-read in Plato and Plotinus, the suggestion was not well received. John Devotion found it surprising that "Christians should be sent to Plato and the infidel Jews to be confirmed in the doctrines of the Trinity" and charged that Stiles had "affected to become a believer" of Henry More, the seventeenth-century Cambridge Platonist. Stiles pleaded his case to other friends by trying to side-step the dispute. No theological system demanded universal assent the way a system of astronomy did, and so, beyond the list of fundamental Christian doctrines, one should expect that different tastes would respond to different phraseology and modes of inquiry. Dionysius and Aquinas, Frances Hutcheson and Jonathan Edwards, each had their own peculiar idiom, and Stiles refused "to fight the Battle of Words and Terms" that other men used to clothe the truth.[62]

Privately, however, Stiles thought that Dionysius's synthesis of Neoplatonism and Christian theology was much more than a personally congenial idiom. Contemporary scholarly opinion considered the works of Dionysius to be a

61. Stiles, *Literary Diary*, ed. Dexter, I, 131–133, 225, III, 470.

62. As a young skeptic, Stiles had esteemed only "pure Christianity," considered as an "imagined system," superior to Platonism (["Birthday Reflections"], Apr. 5, 1765, 5). In a letter to Jared Eliot on Apr. 5, 1757, Stiles argued that Plato, Philo, and the early Christians alike were drawing from antediluvian knowledge of the Trinity preserved in the Old Testament. In *Saving Knowledge*, 18n, Stiles recommended "the *platonic writers*, and the *rabbinical literature*" by first arguing that "Our fathers, the first Ministers of New-England" were "well read in Plato and Plotinus, among the ancients" (see also 16–18). Quotations from John Devotion are in Devotion to Stiles, Jan. 21, 1771, Feb. 15, 1772. On differing theological tastes, see Stiles to Chauncy Whittelsey, Mar. 6, 1770, 12; the quoted phrase is from Stiles to Abigail W. S. Dwight, Feb. 7, 1772.

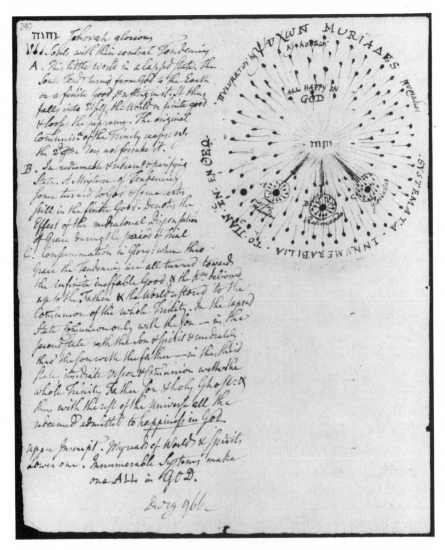

Figure 11. Ezra Stiles's Sketch and Explanation of His Symbol of the Spiritual Universe, Dec. 19, 1766. Courtesy, Beinecke Rare Book and Manuscript Library, Yale University, New Haven, Conn.

fifth-century forgery, but Stiles was convinced that they were penned by the disciple of Paul mentioned in Acts 17:34. Dionysius, he believed, was an Athenian philosopher, a Platonist who retained his philosophical idiom as he discussed the truths of Christianity. Dionysius wrote almost like Paul himself, who could rise above "calm coolness in Reasoning and Discourse," above "philosophic Dulness" to "listen to Messengers from the Throne of God, all alive with Energy, and animated and even inflamed with a sense not only of the

Truth, but of the Importance and Glory of it." Like the apostle John, with whom, Stiles believed, Dionysius was also in close contact, the Areopagite could penetrate the mystery of Christ as the incarnation of the divine Logos. Again and again Stiles returned to *The Divine Names, The Mystical Theology,* and *The Celestial Hierarchy,* calling his "beloved Dionysius" a "lofty and sublime Writer" in 1790 as in 1773.[63]

Dionysian negative theology best captures Stiles's intellectual outlook and private spiritual practice in the last twenty-five years of his life. The Areopagite, "from the Mouth of St. Paul," supplied an angelic typology and triadic hierarchy for Stiles's emblem of the intellectual universe, so after 1772 the angels who swam through Stiles's cosmos transmitted spiritual light to lower beings in a more orderly fashion. More important, Dionysian mysticism fused the scholar's active pursuit of truth with the saint's passive reception of divine knowledge through grace. As one scholar has explained, Dionysian mystical theology was not the ecstatic mysticism of the Middle Ages, which described "a private, emotional, and supra-rational experience." It was a cognitive process, a spiritual elevation coincident with the act of interpretation itself. The "negative theologian" gradually strips the deity of the perceptible characteristics offered in the Scriptures and in the idioms and metaphors of human discourse. The interpreter's epistemological movement from a plurality of false analogies to a single pure idea of God, therefore, mirrors the Neoplatonic return of being from the plurality of creation to the oneness of the Creator.[64]

Stiles acknowledged that his admiration for Dionysius seemed like a scholar's eccentricity, completely out of step with the academic tastes of the

63. Ezra Stiles, [Dissertation on and Translation of Two Letters of Dionysius the Areopagite], [Nov. 30, 1793], a manuscript apparently intended for posthumous publication; Stiles, *Literary Diary,* ed. Dexter, I, 242–243, 368–369, III, 399–400. The repeated notations of "reading Dionysius" in the *Literary Diary* almost confirm Morgan's exaggeration in *Gentle Puritan,* 447, that Stiles in his later years "read Dionysius almost as regularly as he read the Scriptures." Stiles was studying *The Divine Names* six weeks before his death in 1795 (Stiles, *Literary Diary,* ed. Dexter, III, 561).

64. Stiles, *Literary Diary,* ed. Dexter, III, 470. On Stiles and angels, see Leventhal, *In the Shadow of the Enlightenment,* 251–257. Stiles was also drawing from Hebrew cabalistic works like the *Zohar.* The quoted description of Dionysian theology is from Paul Rorem, *Biblical and Liturgical Symbols within the Pseudo-Dionysian Synthesis* (Toronto, 1984), 137; Rosemary Ann Lees, *The Negative Language of the Dionysian School of Mystical Theology: An Approach to "The Cloud of Unknowing,"* 2 vols. (Salzburg, Austria, 1983). See also Andrew Louth, *Denys the Areopagite* (Wilton, Conn., 1989); and the introductions by Jaroslav Pelikan, Jean Leclerq, Karl Froehlich, in Pelikan et al., eds., *Pseudo-Dionysius: The Complete Works* (New York, 1987).

times. But he also predicted that, in another generation, the writings of Jonathan Edwards, then in vogue among the best and brightest theology students, would pass into near oblivion, "and when Posterity occasionally comes across them in the Rubbish of Libraries, the rare Characters who may read and be pleased with them, will be looked upon as singular and whimsical, as in these days an Admirer of Suarez, Aquinas, or Dionysius Areopagita." For the most part, Stiles seemed content to be a singular and whimsical admirer. But in the 1790s, he drafted his "Dissertation on and Translation of Two Letters of Dionysius the Areopagite," a far-fetched attempt to make the mystic's long-discredited writings palatable to the late eighteenth century. The letters, which discussed the miraculous eclipse during Christ's Crucifixion, would show Dionysius, not as a mystic, but as "an unprejudiced scientific and even astronomic observer" and "an historian of *facts*." If intrigued by what Dionysius had to say about astronomy, Stiles reasoned, modern readers might then be more inclined to read the Areopagite's discussions of the Trinity.[65]

Yet Stiles continued to insist that a scholar's personal tastes should never be translated into an ecclesiastical or political platform. That, he believed, had been the mistake of the New Divinity men, who practically canonized Edwards's texts and used his major treatises to club other Calvinists into submission. Samuel Hopkins, Stiles complained, condemned all the ministers of Protestant Christendom as erroneous and corrupt except forty or fifty Edwardseans. Joseph Bellamy stubbornly sought a union among New Divinity men, shunning other New England Calvinists. Jonathan Edwards, Jr., obstructed the rising spirit of cooperation among New Haven–area churches headed by Old Calvinists, Arminians, and other New Divinity pastors. Other Edwardseans regularly refused to communicate with "Unchristian" Congregationalists.[66]

Stiles objected to more than the New Divinity's myopic and uncharitable allegiance to Edwards. "They all want to be Luthers," he wrote in 1787, as he watched the third generation of Edwardseans struggle for preeminence among themselves. The New Divinity had dropped some of the "Shocking Positions

65. Stiles, *Literary Diary*, ed. Dexter, III, 275; Ezra Stiles, "Dissertation on and Translation of Two Letters by Dionysius," 7, 13, 30. A separate, 158-page manuscript written between July 30, 1790, and Jan. 3, 1792, containing translations of Dionysius, Ignatius, Justin Martyr, Tertullian, and Origen, was dedicated: "To The most Learned, most Enlightened, most holy and most profound and yet most humble Theologians."

66. Stiles, *Literary Diary*, ed. Dexter, I, 363, II, 7–8, III, 4–5, 208, 247, 273–275, 286, 343–344. Stiles estimated that, of the 215 ministers in Connecticut, 168 were consociating Congregationalists, and, of these, 58 or 60 were New Divinity men (III, 463).

and Assertions" of the New Light radicals of 1741, but they still held to tenets that, "altho' provable by Reasonings to Strict Demonstration," should "never be made by Man." Stiles found particularly dangerous New Divinity formulas that made God the author of sin and those that discouraged unregenerate sinners from seeking grace in their churches and prayers. Stiles did not, however, condemn all New Divinity pastors as dry metaphysicians who alienated their congregations. He did believe that Samuel Hopkins's theology and the rigidity of Jonathan Edwards, Jr., had turned the people in the pews against them. But other New Divinity pastors had considerable success in the pulpit, success that Stiles attributed to their good old Puritan piety—the straightforward preaching of hellfire and salvation through Christ that had softened in some of the moderate Calvinists and had evaporated from the polite discourses of the Boston-based Arminians.[67]

Revolutionary New England, Stiles believed, needed preachers in the old Puritan mold to revitalize its churches. Neither New Divinity theologians, itinerant revivalists, nor genteel Bostonians would be strong enough pillars for an independent Christian republic. In 1777, Stiles himself had been considered the best candidate to reunite the "broken" congregation in Portsmouth, New Hampshire. A parade of candidates had come and gone, and each "pleased some and disgusted others." The "more polite part were ambitious of having a learned sensible man, the middling and lower people were for an Evangelical preacher whether learned or not—they had not found these united in one

67. Ibid., II, 114–115 (New Divinity doctrines), 504 (their preaching), III, 273–275 (on the third generation's wanting to be Luthers); Ezra Stiles, "Shocking Positions and Assertions, Which However True Ought Never Be Made by Man: Altho' Provable by Reasonings to Strict Demonstration," n.d. (pre-1776). On the New Divinity, see Joseph Haroutunian, *Piety versus Moralism: The Passing of the New England Theology* (New York, 1932); Joseph A. Conforti, *Samuel Hopkins and the New Divinity Movement: Calvinism, the Congregational Ministry, and Reform in New England between the Great Awakenings* (Grand Rapids, Mich., 1981); William Breitenbach, "Unregenerate Doings: Selflessness and Selfishness in New Divinity Theology," *American Quarterly*, XXXIV (1982), 479–502; Breitenbach, "The Consistent Calvinism of the New Divinity Movement," *WMQ*, 3d Ser., XLI (1984), 241–264; Breitenbach, "Piety *and* Moralism: Edwards and the New Divinity," in Hatch and Stout, eds., *Jonathan Edwards and the American Experience*, 177–204; Bruce Kuklick, *Churchmen and Philosophers: From Jonathan Edwards to John Dewey* (New Haven, Conn., 1985); Mark R. Valeri, "Joseph Bellamy: Conversion, Social Ethics, and Politics in the Thought of an Eighteenth-Century Calvinist" (Ph.D. diss., Princeton University, 1985); Valeri, *Law and Providence in Joseph Bellamy's New England: The Origins of the New Divinity in Revolutionary America* (New York, 1994). On New Divinity pastors as dry metaphysicians, see Morgan, *Gentle Puritan*, 410; Richard D. Birdsall, "Ezra Stiles versus the New Divinity Men," *AQ*, XVII (1965), 250.

man." Stiles, who had a reputation as a scholar and had developed something of an evangelical pulpit manner, became the only minister the congregation would agree to. But Yale called too, and Stiles was told that he was the only candidate that Connecticut's Arminians, Old Calvinists, and New Divinity men could unite behind.[68]

Yale under Stiles was no den of deism and French infidelity awaiting rescue by Stiles's successor, Timothy Dwight. Indeed, although they were men of different temperaments and interests, the son of Old Light crusader Isaac Stiles and the grandson of Jonathan Edwards actually held very similar theological and pedagogical opinions. Dwight, like Stiles, would stress practical divinity over theologizing and emphasize the moral and social importance of religion in New England. Stiles had hopes that Yale would expand into a university, but he did not secularize higher education in Connecticut any more than Dwight did. Sounding like his predecessor Thomas Clap, Stiles was quite sincere when he told the Yale Corporation that he considered the presidency "an Employment near akin to the Sacerdotal office, as the primary and great Design of Yale College was the Education of Ministers for the Churches."[69]

Stiles loved all the pomp and ceremony of the academy, the annual ritual of Latin orations, public disputations, and commencement processions that helped set Yale graduates apart from the New Haven boys who broke a few college windows every commencement eve. He hoped that new professional organizations and learned societies would foster the continued association of ministers, lawyers, physicians, and other learned men who would cultivate the best of the world's art and science in America. Yet, in a republican society, which depended upon the diffusion of knowledge to the whole body politic, exclusive societies of learned elites aroused suspicion, and the learned man had to be more careful not to flaunt his classical education or expect deference for it. As lawyers and physicians worked out their professional identities by balancing between service as useful republican citizens and status as liberally educated intellectuals, Stiles found his own balance in the learned *and* evangelical minister. His portrait, with its esoteric emblems and books with foreign titles, displayed a world inaccessible to most New Englanders. But it also portrayed a local clergyman, right hand over his heart and left holding the

68. Stiles, *Literary Diary*, ed. Dexter, II, 183, 227, 260.

69. Stiles to the Corporation of Yale College of New Haven, Apr. 18, 1778, in Stiles, *Literary Diary*, ed. Dexter, II, 267–269. Edmund S. Morgan demolished the historiographical myth of a deistic Yale under Stiles reformed by Dwight in "Ezra Stiles and Timothy Dwight," Mass. Hist. Soc., *Proceedings*, LXXII (1957–1960), 101–117 (from a paper read March 1958).

Bible, leaning slightly forward to the viewer with a warm smile and an attentive gaze.[70]

For President Stiles of Yale, pursuing the Puritan balance of piety and intellect meant, to some extent, the compartmentalization of pulpit divinity and liberal scholarship. Ministers, like lawyers and physicians, needed to ground their vocation in a liberal education. Although philological and historical research should continue to inform their work, however, the minister's vocation was primarily as pastor to his flock and preacher of the simple gospel message. Do not let favorite studies take time away from pastoral duties, he warned in a published 1787 ordination sermon. Treatises for the learned world on any subject ought to be considered a private pursuit.[71]

In gauging the relationship between education and vocation, Stiles was little different from the Puritans themselves or from his predecessors at Yale. But he was so concerned about the political and ecclesiastical dangers of polemical theology that he went to the other extreme from the New Divinity, reducing theology to a question of personal taste and draining it of intellectual interest. Great discoveries and advancements were being made daily in political philosophy and natural science, Stiles argued in his well-known 1783 election sermon, but theologians had not found anything new in the Scriptures since the apostolic age. Other sciences and arts were progressing, but divinity was at a standstill, and would probably remain so until the Second Coming. Fashions came and went—Augustine, Aquinas, Luther, Calvin—and theological insight appeared new to each generation because the same sentiments were "cloathed in different diction." Thus, the eighteenth century despised the Middle Ages and thought it had advanced in Christian knowledge, "while it is only possessing the knowledge familiar to our predecessors." Posterity will surely treat the present's favorite theological authors, he argued, in the same way.[72]

70. On lawyers, see Robert A. Ferguson, *Law and Letters in American Culture* (Cambridge, Mass., 1984), who looks at Connecticut's John Trumbull. On Connecticut physicians, see Peter Dobkin Hall, *The Organization of American Culture, 1700–1900: Private Institutions, Elites, and the Origins of American Nationality* (New York, 1984), chap. 7. I will discuss the professionalization of both groups in Chapter 8.

71. Stiles, MS sermon on 2 Tim. 3:17 (#1397), a farewell sermon to candidates for the baccalaureate, Sept. 9, 1781; MS sermon on Matt. 25:20–21 (no #), funeral sermon for Chauncy Whittelsey, July 26, 1787; Stiles, *Sermon . . . at the Ordination of . . . Channing*, 16.

72. Stiles, *United States Elevated to Glory and Honor*, 95–97. On the Puritan and later New England relationship between education and clerical vocation, see John Morgan, *Godly Learning: Puritan Attitudes towards Reason, Learning, and Education, 1560–1640* (Cambridge, 1986); David D. Hall, *The Faithful Shepherd: A History of the New England Ministry in the Seventeenth Century* (Chapel Hill, N.C., 1972); J. William T. Youngs, Jr., *God's Messengers: Religious Leadership in Colonial New England, 1700–1750* (Baltimore, 1976); Richard

Systematic theology in the study might have been an intellectual dead end, but, if carried into the pulpit, it could also warp a minister's public calling and destroy his effectiveness. "It is not the greatest theological knowledge" that makes ministers useful, Stiles preached in 1784, but an "indefatigable Zeal or Engagedness in the Lord's Work." Three years later, he urged ministers to lay aside their "human reasonings" and to teach "didactically and directly from the BIBLE with a *thus saith the Lord*." He wished that congregations could be indoctrinated with the great truths of Christianity "instead of being addressed with long and laborious discussions of subjects whose *intricacies* baffle the efforts of the strongest and most learned reasoners."[73]

Politics and religion, like scholarship and evangelical preaching, had to be balanced by the prudent minister. Stiles wanted to insulate scholarship within a private sphere separate from politics, which would at once prevent the demands of the state from crushing intellectual inquiry and hinder the firebrands among the learned from launching socially divisive ideologies. At the same time, he argued against any coerced limitation of free expression or association, echoing the calls he had made decades earlier for unfettered intellectual and religious liberty and seemingly endorsing the Madisonian view that competing factions in a large republic would cancel each other out. By limiting preaching to salvation, civil obedience, and ecumenical moralism, he wanted to place the Congregational clergyman on the moral high ground above the ferment of religious sects, political arguments, and philosophical opinions.

Although Stiles's 1794 argument that "the common people will generally judge right" and that "general liberty is safe and secure in their hands" might indicate faith in the common man as an abstract principle, it expressed something quite different when translated into actual political practice in Connecticut. Stiles wrote:

> The common people will generally judge right, when duly informed. . . . It is not from deficiency of abilities to judge, but from want of information, if they at any time as a body go wrong. Upon information from an abundance of enlightened characters always intermixt among them, they will ultimately always judge right, and in the end be the faithful guardians and support and security of government.

S. Warch, *School of the Prophets: Yale College, 1701–1740* (New Haven, Conn., 1973); Donald M. Scott, *From Office to Profession: The New England Ministry, 1750–1850* (Philadelphia, 1978), chap. 1.

73. Stiles, MS sermon on Phil. 1:21 (no #), from the funeral of the Reverend Allyn Mather (Yale A.B. 1771, A.M. 1774), Dec. 12, 1784; Stiles, *Sermon . . . at the Ordination of . . . Channing*, 12, 14.

Stiles's private writings show more clearly than his public pronouncements who those "enlightened characters" ought to be, how they ought to be educated, and the nature of the "information" they ought to disseminate to the body politic. Stiles's "gentle Puritanism" did not make clergymen less political after all—just more discrete.[74]

In the 1780s and 1790s, Stiles believed that the threat of deism loomed large again. As the war ended and the states reconsidered questions about religious establishment and religious oaths for public office, deistic articles began appearing more frequently in American newspapers and magazines. Ethan Allen's notorious *Reason the Only Oracle of Man,* published in 1784, only seemed to confirm what many had whispered through the 1770s: some of the leaders of the patriot cause were not Christians. Although Stiles argued that the actual number of deists was quite small, he thought that they had risen to positions of power in European and American politics, and even threatened Connecticut and Yale College itself. Analyzing Connecticut voting returns in 1794, Stiles found only thirty "religious Characters" among the eighty-five men earning more than one hundred votes. Forty of the eighty-five were lawyers, and of those at least a third were deists and another third were doubtful. Some of those deist lawyers, he believed, had been behind the campaign two years earlier to wrest control of Yale from the Congregational clergy. The political duty of Connecticut's Yale-trained clergymen was clear: Connecticut's citizens "may be waked up to elect a *religious* as well as otherwise well informed Magistracy; especially if the Ministers of the Gen[eral] and particular Associations should exert themselves properly in the Nominations and annual Elections." The pulpit, particularly in the smaller towns and villages where Stiles himself preferred to preach, was still a powerful political weapon. Especially after the campaign against Yale, ministers had "a particular and special Reason now to preach up for and recommend the Election of religious and undeistical Councillors," and politicians with the wrong religious principles "may be hunted down in a future Election."[75]

Behind Stiles's enthusiasm for liberty was a desire to preserve Connecticut's institutional status quo and even to recommend it as a model for other states and societies. His *United States Elevated to Glory and Honor* (1783) was, after

74. Ezra Stiles, *A History of the Three Judges of King Charles I . . .* (Hartford, Conn., 1794), 274–275. Morgan's *Gentle Puritan* concluded on an exultant note with Stiles as a champion of democracy and American progress.

75. Stiles, *Literary Diary,* ed. Dexter, III, 451–466 (quotations on 457, 466), 545–546; Ethan Allen, *Reason the Only Oracle of Man; or, A Compenduous System of Natural Religion . . .* (Bennington, Vt., 1784).

all, an argument for religious establishment, despite its tacit acknowledgment that religion had been shoved to the periphery of civic life in Revolutionary America. Seemingly returning to his pre-1755 ideas about God's moral government, Stiles acknowledged that a nation's prosperity was not necessarily connected to its moral state. A "well governed and prosperous empire" was a "superstructure" whose "foundation" was laid in population increase, the just distribution of property, and "a good system of *polity* and *jurisprudence*." But the American experiment "must receive its finishing from religion." America ought to aim even higher than at the secular happiness it seemed destined to achieve in the natural course of things. Americans should augment their political experiment and reach for "additional glory," dedicating themselves to becoming a holy people. To achieve this, magistrates and ministers, like Moses and Aaron, ought to walk together.[76]

In Connecticut, that meant maintaining tax-supported churches and the legal preference given to Congregationalism, with toleration extended to other Christian sects. Stiles failed to condemn Connecticut's church-state system, and, moreover, he considered establishment and toleration, as opposed to the complete religious freedom he had called for in his younger days, as an enormously important safeguard in a Christian republic committed to civil liberty. The numerical supremacy of Presbyterians and Congregationalists was not enough to ensure that new immigrants would be smoothly assimilated into New England's culture without changing its complexion. The Standing Order needed to continue its control over Connecticut's civil and religious institutions—and especially over the institution that supplied both with leaders, Yale College.[77]

For Stiles, therefore, democracy's free market of ideas and opinions should still be contained by Standing Order institutions, and public opinion should be shaped by and expressed through the "enlightened characters" Yale produced. Stiles proudly reported that during the Revolution there had been about two thousand college graduates mixed among the New England population, communicating knowledge to more ordinary folk, and he hoped that in the future there would be enough "erudite men" to illuminate the public councils of every community. Stiles's confidence that a free press and a profusion of voluntary associations would, despite the mischief they could cause, "frame the public mind to wisdom" was built upon an even firmer confidence in the

---

76. Stiles, *United States Elevated to Glory and Honor*, 34, 68–69, 75, 87.

77. Morgan, *Gentle Puritan*, 451. Morgan briefly conceded that Stiles "moved a step backward in his views of the relationship between church and state" when he "failed to condemn the favored position that the Connecticut law gave to his own denomination."

learned Christian's ability to enlighten his neighbors and influence them by "fraternal persuasions," if not by paternal instruction.[78]

Private and public selves, personal experience, scholarship, and preaching—Stiles hoped these elements could be balanced in life as the esoteric symbols, the shelf of books, and the friendly human figure were in his portrait. As a young preacher, Stiles had described the connections of public and private life by examining the three kinds of character a person had to cultivate: private, "familistic," and public. In 1751, he spent most of his sermon discussing private character, but under that category he argued that the first purpose of gaining knowledge was to be serviceable to the public (the second was pleasure). He also inserted into his section on private character extracts from Bolingbroke on patriotism, yet he spoke of the patriot as the guardian of public liberty. In this sermon, as in his "Family Constitutions" of the early 1760s, Stiles seemed more concerned about shielding the individual's or the private group's free inquiry from coercive authority and the pressures of religious and political bigotry and faction than he was about scholars' using their knowledge to shape the public mind. And, despite the extracts from Bolingbroke, Stiles's early writings certainly lack the political engagement of his later work. His "Family Constitutions," in fact, urged the family to "Ever avoid Politics or taking part as a family in any Revolution in the state." If individual family members felt compelled to participate, he thought it would be best if the family as a whole were divided in its political sentiments, so it could not act or take an official public position. Yet the enlightened young scholar at midcentury projected his own experience onto public discussion and debate. He privately struggled with skepticism and therefore felt that the defining intellectual issue of his age would be a rational defense of Christianity against deistic doubt. He reasoned his way back to God and Christ via modern astronomy and world history and assumed his congregation could follow the same path. He participated, through his correspondence, in a scholarly republic of letters devoted to the free exchange of information, ideas, opinions, and criticism and argued that this model should be applied to the broader public as well.[79]

The Revolutionary Puritan who emerged after 1765 still saw connections between his private experience and public culture. A deeper awareness of sin and grace, of personal vanity and vulnerability, coincided with his advocacy of the old Puritan doctrines, preaching style, and political engagement. He believed

78. Stiles, *United States Elevated to Glory and Honor,* 34; Stiles, *History of the Three Judges,* 273–283.

79. Stiles, MS sermon on Prov. 2:10–11, "The Right Conduct of Life," July 23, 1751; "Family Constitutions," Mar. 14, 1762 (quotation on 16).

that a scholarly elite needed to do useful work and help promote practical knowledge and social progress, like the agricultural improvement his friend Jared Eliot had championed (Stiles, too, was heavily involved in promoting silk production), while keeping more speculative matters to itself. Yet, Stiles came to understand that the enlightened republic of letters could not broaden to become the public sphere of the American Republic without institutional safeguards protecting religious orthodoxy and church tradition. State support of the church and clerical control of higher education would help ensure that learned and Christian men would continue to guide the public toward wisdom. These learned and godly men, mixed with the population, would also allow America to absorb foreign people and new ideas without threatening its own identity. In this way, Stiles believed as he pictured America's future, scholarly inquiry and public discourse, elitism and democracy, intellectual cosmopolitanism and American nationalism could all be balanced.[80]

After Stiles's death in 1795, few clergymen would share his enthusiasms for Christian knowledge as exemplified in Dionysius or in the revolutionary spirit as it was being played out in France. Although by 1800, most of the leading evangelical Christians would trace their lineage to the New Divinity spawned by Edwards rather than the moderate Calvinism promoted by Stiles, the sober revivalism and social control of Connecticut's "Second Great Awakening" derived from both. As anticlericalism and partisan politics intensified in the closing years of the century, the Congregational clergy had to be even more cau-

---

80. Goldgar, in *Impolite Learning,* argued that the republic of letters before the mid-eighteenth century was a private "community" based upon scholarly correspondence and journals that tried to shield its members from the demands of political allegiance, religious affiliation, and personal interest. It tried to create the conditions whereby ideas could be exchanged freely without the bigotry and persecution that broader public inspection would bring. As other historians argue, this and other structures of civility and sociability, developed in private life, provide space for political discussion and help create the public sphere of discussion and debate that would oppose the authoritarian state. See Jacob, *Radical Enlightenment;* Joan Landes, *Women in the Public Sphere in the Age of the French Revolution* (Ithaca, N.Y., 1988); Jacob, *Living the Enlightenment;* Dwyer and Sher, eds., *Sociability and Society, Eighteenth-Century Life,* XV (1991); Anthony La Vopa, "Conceiving a Public: Ideas and Society in Eighteenth-Century Europe," *Journal of Modern History,* LXIV (1992), 79–116; Dena Goodman, "Public Sphere and Private Life: Toward a Synthesis of Current Historiographical Approaches to the Old Regime," *History and Theory,* XXXI (1992), 1–20; Brewer, *Discourse of Enlightenment;* Klein, *Shaftesbury and the Culture of Politeness;* Goodman, *Republic of Letters;* Margaret C. Jacob, "The Mental Landscape of the Public Sphere: A European Perspective," *Eighteenth-Century Studies,* XXVIII (1994), 95–113; the essays on the public sphere in *Eighteenth-Century Studies,* XXIX (1995), 1–4, 5–24, 25–44, 69–96, 97–109.

tious than Stiles had been in expressing political sentiments without appearing to be party spokesmen. While sharing his faith in the power of the pulpit, learned and pious men also explored other ways to "frame the public mind to wisdom"—through newspaper essays and through the belles lettres that Stiles had never held in very high esteem. Ezra Stiles had not redefined Christian knowledge for Revolutionary New England. But he as much as anyone understood that the relationships between politics, religion, and higher learning had been thrown into question.[81]

81. On moderate Calvinism and the "Second Great Awakening" in Connecticut, see Sidney Earl Mead, *Nathaniel William Taylor, 1786–1858: A Connecticut Liberal* (Chicago, 1942); Stephen E. Berk, *Calvinism versus Democracy: Timothy Dwight and the Origins of American Evangelical Orthodoxy* (Hamden, Conn., 1974); Mark A. Noll, "Moses Mather (Old Calvinist) and the Evolution of Edwardseanism," *Church History*, XLIX (1980), 273–285.

PART 3

Revolution and Steady Habits

Connecticut entered the Revolutionary War without changing its political leadership or altering the structures of government established by its 1662 royal charter. Its established ministers strongly supported the patriot movement, rallying the troops and the local congregations with descriptions of the battle for Independence as a moral crusade against tyranny. As coastal towns like Fairfield, New Haven, New London, and Groton suffered enemy attacks, the booming wartime economic activity shifted to the interior of what came to be called "the provisions state." Hartford expanded as a trade and transportation hub during the war; Norwich grew as a provisions depot, a shipbuilding center, and a locus of manufacturing interests. The state's speakers and writers, representing a wartime coalition of moderate and radical whigs, elite officials and populist Sons of Liberty, celebrated victory both as the opening of a new era in world history and as a validation of New England's traditional ways of life. Yet, despite the continuing stability of the state's social and political Standing Order, some of Connecticut's steady habits began to change. The population of towns and villages shifted and changed as the number of transient laborers increased, and out-migration again surged as speculators promoted a renewed interest in western lands. The diverging economic interests of merchants, commercial planters, artisans, and small farmers created political antagonism during the economic slump of the mid-1780s. By the end of the century, the preachers, poets, orators, and newspaper essayists who had promoted the cause of liberty in the 1770s, debated policy in the 1780s, and fueled the heated partisanship of the 1790s were engaged in a bitter contest over the meaning of New England tradition and the legacy of the American Revolution.[1]

Between 1770 and 1800, the greatly increased activity of the printing press and the crucial importance of the dissemination of print to Revolutionary politics ensured that learned men would no longer try to offer moral instruction to the public solely from pulpits and printed sermons. The number of imprints

1. Richard J. Purcell, *Connecticut in Transition, 1775–1818* (1918; reprint, Middletown, Conn., 1963); Norman Levaun Stamps, "Political Parties in Connecticut, 1789–1819" (Ph.D. diss., Yale University, 1950); Gaspare John Saladino, "The Economic Revolution in Eighteenth Century Connecticut" (Ph.D. diss., University of Wisconsin, 1964); Harvey Milton Wachtell, "The Conflict between Localism and Nationalism in Connecticut, 1783–1788" (Ph.D. diss., University of Missouri, 1971); Richard Buel, Jr., *Dear Liberty: Connecticut's Mobilization for the Revolutionary War* (Middletown, Conn., 1980); Stephen Reed Grossbart, "The Revolutionary Transition: Politics, Religion, and Economy in Eastern Connecticut, 1765–1800" (Ph.D. diss., University of Michigan, 1989).

increased more than threefold; the number of active printers rose from three (in Hartford, New Haven, and New London) to two dozen in fourteen different towns. The colony had produced five newspapers by the eve of the Revolution; the state would see thirty-five different papers published by the end of the century. During the era of the American Revolution and the founding of the new American Republic, Connecticut's citizens witnessed a dramatic increase in the volume, variety, and accessibility of print along with a proliferation of occasions for formal public speech. But they also came to understand the political significance of public discourse in new ways. This new sovereign people emphasized the importance of circulating knowledge and information throughout the entire society. Symbolically, the "public" came to be seen, not as a body ruled by a sovereign head, but as a mind that ruled itself. Citizens began to conceive of public discourse not just as the speech and writing of learned elites *to* the people but the expression of the opinions and desires *of* the people through representative voices chosen from among them. These developments have been described by scholars as part of the structural transformation of the public sphere in an age of democratic revolutions. What was the significance of these changes for public speakers and writers in Connecticut?[2]

The career of poet and satirist John Trumbull, and his relationship to local newspapers like Hartford's *Connecticut Courant,* offers a window into the rise of the local press and the development of a new Connecticut literary culture. Both Trumbull and the local press tried to refine the public taste, which meant opening a middle way between the bickering fueled by clerical controversies and the shallow cosmopolitanism affected by the sons of the wealthy. As the *Courant* evolved from community bulletin board to republican political forum, Trumbull's *M'Fingal* (1776, 1782) satirized the town meeting and celebrated republican themes; as the *Courant* came to be identified as a partisan weapon of the local merchant class, the second edition of *M'Fingal* (published by the *Courant*'s owners in 1782) became the center of a debate over copyright laws and literary property. Together, poetry and newspapers show the rapid transformation of public writing during a revolutionary age.

The sermons, poetry, and prose of Timothy Dwight, grandson of Jonathan

---

2. The towns are Bridgeport, Cheshire, Danbury, East Windsor, Farmington, Hartford, Litchfield, Middletown, Newfield, New Haven, New London, Norwich, Stonington, Suffield, and Windham (revised list of Early American Imprints, American Antiquarian Society, Worcester, Mass.). On newspapers, see Clarence S. Brigham, *History and Bibliography of American Newspapers, 1690–1820,* I (Worcester, Mass., 1947); Sidney Kobre, *The Development of the Colonial Newspaper* (1944; reprint, Gloucester, Mass., 1960), 177; Donald H. Stewart, *The Opposition Press of the Federalist Period* (Albany, N.Y., 1969), 869–871. Stewart lists eight active papers in 1790 and eighteen in 1800 (652).

Edwards and president of Yale after 1795, address the central concerns of this study: the place of the learned man in the new Republic, the relationship between religion, politics, literature, and intellectual life, and the continuity or change in the rhetoric of moral order and corporate identity. Like Thomas Clap, Dwight was a conservative advocate of deferential society with an exalted conception of the learned ministry and of Yale as Connecticut's fountain of knowledge and religion. He, too, believed that New England's character had been shaped by the civil, scholastic, and ecclesiastical institutions established by the founders. But he argued that assessing that character involved looking to the superior intelligence of the common people, not just weighing the achievements of the ingenious few. For Dwight, New England's learned men were products of the larger culture and needed to be understood as such. Like their fellow citizens, they were men of business and action, devoted to practical invention rather than speculative musing, men who read books but were usually too busy to lock themselves in garrets to write them.[3]

The different perspectives of Thomas Clap in 1740 and Timothy Dwight in 1795 reflect the different cultural contexts in which they labored to uphold religious orthodoxy and New England tradition. Dwight's conception of public institutions was not Clap's static, three-tiered fortress of church, state, and college. For Dwight, New England's institutions were progressive. New literary, medical, and missionary societies, law schools, academies, and moral associations all offered new ways to promote wisdom and virtue. He praised local libraries and more warily noted the proliferation of newspapers that cultivated new habits of reading and learning. The contrasting views of Clap and Dwight also resemble the contrast between the intellectual history of Perry Miller's era and later cultural histories of printing, writing, literature, and knowledge—the shift from discourse as a repository of ideas that define the "mind" of an epoch to discourse as a cultural product sustained by social and material practices. If asked to describe intellectual life in Connecticut, Clap would have pointed to sermons, synods, statutes, and the "user's manual" to his catalog of Yale's library. Dwight would have spoken about pastors and pious conversation, the general diffusion of knowledge, the state of the literary market, the lack of scientific and literary institutions to support authors and researchers, and the influence of local lending libraries. Dwight's New England mind was less a system of ideas than a set of social and intellectual habits.

Ultimately, we cannot understand the late-eighteenth-century transformation of public discourse by focusing exclusively upon either the ideas inform-

3. Timothy Dwight, *Travels in New England and New York* (1821–1822), 4 vols., ed. Barbara Miller Solomon (Cambridge, Mass., 1969), IV, 225–226, 271.

ing an evolving New England mind or the realignment of social and political structures that created a cultural "space" for those ideas to be articulated. Discourse both emerged from and helped to create post-Revolutionary structures. Discussions and publications about popular sovereignty, political character, and party politics drew from and sustained both a new American politics and a renewed anxiety about the relationship between public and private life. This new politics was manifested in popular conventions, a partisan press, new rhetorical occasions for political speech (like July Fourth celebrations), and a new speaking aristocracy that included anonymous pamphleteers and lawyer-orators as well as clergymen. The men playing leading roles in this post-Revolutionary political culture argued about the nature and control of public language and over the often conflicting demands of republican publicity and the rights of privacy. In the 1790s, as the division between Federalists and Republicans became more acrimonious and partisans on both sides worked harder to mobilize popular support, words were weapons, and formal public speech and writing, more than ever before, became wedded to the exercise of political and cultural power.

CHAPTER 6

Print, Poetry, and Politics

John Trumbull and the Transformation of

the Public Sphere

When John Trumbull and Timothy Dwight, two aspiring young men of letters at Yale, sent off their "Meddler" essays to the *Boston Chronicle* in 1769, they aimed at "instructing the unlearned, diverting and improving the learned, rectifying the taste and manners of the times, and cultivating the fine arts in this land." The series ended abruptly after the ninth essay. Their stiff imitations of Joseph Addison's *Spectator* and bookish commentaries on manners, morals, and belles lettres seemed out of place in a weekly paper preoccupied by British taxes and colonial resistance. When Trumbull wrote his "Correspondent" column in the early 1770s, he tried to pay less attention to literary models and more to the world around him. It was a world where the social role of the published writer, the rhetoric of public persuasion, and the powers of the printed word were being transformed.[1]

Trumbull's literary career coincided with the rapid expansion of Connecticut printing and publishing and, in that context, reveals the interrelated developments of literary and political culture through the last three decades of the eighteenth century. He had been a popular Yale tutor in the 1770s and had campaigned for curricular reforms to shift academic emphasis away from Latin, Greek, and mathematics and toward English literature, composition, and pub-

---

1. [John Trumbull and Timothy Dwight], "The Meddler," *Boston Chronicle*, Sept. 4, 1769 – Jan. 15, 1770; "The Correspondent," *Connecticut Journal, and the New-Haven Post-Boy*, Feb. 23 – July 6, 1770, Feb. 12 – Sept. 3, 1773. These essays have been reprinted in John Trumbull, *The Meddler (1769 – 70) and The Correspondent (1770 – 73)*, ed. Bruce Granger (Delmar, N.Y., 1985); unless otherwise indicated, however, quotations are from the original newspapers.

lic speaking. He wrote verse early in the Revolutionary War to support the patriot cause and revised his poetry as the war ended to secure a national reputation as an American poet. In the early 1780s, Trumbull moved to Hartford and built a law practice. He continued writing and tried to see how the post-Revolutionary reading public, with its astonishing appetite for newspapers and novels, pamphlets and plays, would patronize its indigenous authors. By 1785, Trumbull's fame was already established with *M'Fingal*—yet his literary career was virtually over.[2]

In Trumbull's works and career, however, as in the growth of Connecticut's newspapers, we can see how conceptions of what public writing was (and ought to be) changed with new social, political, and economic relationships between writers and readers. Those changes can be described by observing how Trumbull adopted or commented upon four models of discourse: the social community of polite letters, the political community of speakers, the civic forum of the press, and the literary marketplace of print. In the social community of polite letters, conversation, correspondence, and the circulation of belles lettres in manuscript were all related practices among ladies and gentlemen cultivating genteel sociability and refining their taste for the arts. In the political community of (male) speakers, exemplified by the New England town meeting, writing could be substituted for speech but did not essentially change the nature of communication, which remained grounded in the face-to-face exchanges of small, hierarchical communities. The speaker's or writer's powers of persuasion drew upon the personal authority he had earned within society or the institutional authority conferred by his office in church or state. The civic forum of the local press, however, was characterized by the distinctive discourse of the republican public sphere: the usually anonymous writing that contributed to a public forum distinct from the mechanisms of the state and from the concerns of private life. Writing in the civic forum was, at least ideally, a disinterested and virtuous participation in the commonweal. In the literary marketplace of print, writing became an expression of individual interests within a highly competitive marketplace of ideas and opinions; it also became a form of regulated intellectual property that provided financial gain to authors.[3]

2. Leon Howard, *The Connecticut Wits* (Chicago, 1943), remains the single best study of Yale literary and intellectual life during the 1760s and 1770s and of the subsequent development of the major writers who studied there, known as the "Connecticut Wits" (Trumbull [1750–1831], Dwight [1752–1817], David Humphreys [1752–1818], and Joel Barlow [1754–1812]).

3. Michael Warner, *The Letters of the Republic: Publication and the Public Sphere in Eighteenth-Century America* (Cambridge, Mass., 1990), applied Jürgen Habermas's model

Trumbull is best known as the author of *M'Fingal* (1775, 1782), an enormously popular Revolutionary poem that turned a debate between a whig and a tory during a New England town meeting into a comic epic. But, during his brief career as a public writer, Trumbull also argued for the virtues of polite letters and tried to shape the local press into something more than a New England town meeting in print. He contended that the cultivation of literary taste was connected to the struggle for liberty. He also insisted that, if the press was to be a civic forum for disinterested debate, it could not just transfer to a new medium a community of speakers mired in personal and local concerns. Creating the civic forum of the press involved redefining what public discourse was and how it functioned in politics and culture. That redefinition, however, had to contend with forces beyond the lofty rhetoric of the republican ideal. The commercialization of public writing and the atmosphere of bitter partisan debate in the post-Revolutionary marketplace of print threatened to turn every text into a commodity and every declared opinion into party propaganda. From Trumbull's earliest verse and prose in the late 1760s and early 1770s, which satirized false politeness and sought to improve literary taste, to his 1783 letter to the *Connecticut Courant,* which complained of pirated editions of his poetry and called for copyright laws, Trumbull moved uneasily among these different conceptions of public writing.[4]

In literary histories describing the Revolutionary era as a "false literary dawn" before the American Renaissance, Trumbull is a familiar, if minor, figure: a wit wielding a pen for political independence from Britain while revealing his cultural dependence upon Britain in every imitative line. Studies less concerned with the place of Revolutionary writers in the canon have tried to restore texts like Trumbull's *M'Fingal* to their late-eighteenth-century context. One approach tries to recover both the "lost poetic language" and the "lost world of silent assumptions" that made these texts meaningful and gave them cultural power. Another study argues that publications in the seventeenth-century colonies, in the Revolutionary republic of letters, and in the nineteenth century's literary marketplace were perceived in radically different ways and that eighteenth-century texts need to be understood as discourse within a republican public sphere. But both the sharp discontinuities drawn from Jürgen

---

(*The Structural Transformation of the Public Sphere: An Inquiry into a Category of Bourgeois Society,* trans. Thomas Burger [Cambridge, Mass., 1962]) to eighteenth-century America and distinguished between the traditional, republican, and liberal constructions of the "public sphere."

4. [John Trumbull], "For the Connecticut Courant," *Connecticut Courant, and Weekly Intelligencer* (New Haven), Jan. 7, 1783.

Habermas's notion of the "public sphere" and the more static portraits of a "lost world" obscure the transformation of public discourse as it was experienced by the Revolutionary writers themselves. Trumbull's work is significant in precisely this context: it shows the traditional, republican, and liberal public spheres, not as three epochs, but as overlapping rhetorical possibilities in a dynamic age.[5]

THE SOCIAL WORLD OF POLITE LETTERS

As a young man, John Trumbull had seemed destined for literary greatness. The sickly son of a wealthy Westbury minister, he was a child prodigy who had read through the Bible, memorized Isaac Watts's "Lyrics," and begun writing verse by his fourth year. He passed Yale's entrance exam at age seven, read Milton and *The Spectator* at eight, and, by the time he actually began his studies at Yale at the ripe age of thirteen, he was steeped in Homer, Horace, and Cicero. Not surprisingly, he thought most of his classmates were dullards. A new crop of students and tutors who shared his interest in poetry and polite letters, however, was able to invigorate the college after the resignation of President Thomas Clap in 1766, Trumbull's junior year. The attractions of the college library and of a literary society that would include aspiring wits and writers like Dwight, David Humphreys, Lemuel Hopkins, and eventually Joel Barlow would keep Trumbull at Yale for five years beyond his bachelor's degree, as a Berkeley scholar and tutor. This group, Trumbull would recall in later years, effected "a material change . . . in the taste and pursuits of the students." Their campaign to excite an interest in polite letters at Yale was outlined in Trum-

5. Robert E. Spiller et al., eds., *Literary History of the United States,* 3d ed., rev., 2 vols. (New York, 1963), I, 129, used the phrase "false literary dawn." For similar views, see also Richard Ruland and Malcolm Bradbury, *From Puritanism to Postmodernism: A History of American Literature* (New York, 1991), 50–52, 61. Emory Elliott, in *Revolutionary Writers: Literature and Authority in the New Republic, 1725–1810* (New York, 1982), was still apologetic about aesthetic failures and concerned to make an argument for the Revolutionary writers' formative influence in American literature (3–18). John McWilliams's "Poetry in the Early Republic," in Elliott, gen. ed., *Columbia Literary History of the United States* (New York, 1988), sketched the historical context but noted that, from the perspective of the late twentieth century, "nearly all American verse of the Revolutionary era seems a desert where no art can bloom" (166). William C. Dowling, *Poetry and Ideology in Revolutionary Connecticut* (Athens, Ga., 1990), xv, xvi, explores "the lost world" and "lost poetic language" of eighteenth-century texts.

bull's *Essay on the Use and Advantages of the Fine Arts,* the master's oration he delivered at the college commencement in 1770.[6]

Trumbull's call for academic reform in the *Essay* reversed the customary relationship between the fine arts and what were considered "the more solid branches of Learning." Ancient languages, mathematics, and metaphysics had long been the pillars of an undergraduate education, but the fine arts, "especially those of Polite Literature," were "perhaps too much undervalued by the public, and neglected by the youth in our seminaries of science." New Englanders tended to dismiss belles lettres as trifling amusements and concentrate on what they considered to be more serious scholarly pursuits. That, Trumbull argued, was a mistake. The traditional subjects were important, of course, and deserved the devoted attention of rare geniuses like Francis Bacon, Isaac Newton, and John Locke. But, in the hands of many scholars, it was the so-called solid branches, not polite letters, that became "amusements" rather than useful contributions to society. When traditional scholarly subjects "are carried beyond a certain point; when they are of no advantage to the common purposes of life; when they are employed upon questions which human Reason can never with certainty determine, they degenerate into meer speculations of amusement, and become no farther valuable, than as they serve to enlarge the mind, clear the understanding, and entertain us in the hours of leisure from the important avocations of business." The fine arts, by contrast, did not flatter finite beings into thinking that by exercising their reason they could travel beyond a circumscribed world of practical moral action and empirical experience. Metaphysical speculation, especially, Trumbull believed, falsely inflated the human intellect in a misguided pursuit of truth; the fine arts, on the other hand, elevated and ennobled human nature by refining the natural pursuit of pleasure.[7]

As he described the fusion of aesthetic and moral experience that the fine arts offered, Trumbull echoed the language of Scottish Enlightenment thinkers

6. [John Trumbull], "Memoir of the Life and Writings of John Trumbull, LL.D.," in *The Poetical Works of John Trumbull, LL.D. . . . ,* 2 vols. (Hartford, Conn., 1820), I, 12 (this memoir, though anonymous and written in the third person, was clearly penned by Trumbull himself); [Trumbull], *An Essay on the Use and Advantages of the Fine Arts . . .* (New Haven, Conn., 1770). For studies of Trumbull's life and works, see Alexander Cowie, *John Trumbull: Connecticut Wit* (Chapel Hill, N.C., 1936); Howard, *Connecticut Wits;* and Victor E. Gimmestad, *John Trumbull* (New York, 1974). For a discussion of the relationship between Trumbull's legal vocation and literary avocation, see Robert A. Ferguson, *Law and Letters in American Culture* (Cambridge, Mass., 1984).

7. [Trumbull], *Essay,* [3].

like Henry Home, Lord Kames, whose *Elements of Criticism* (1762) strongly influenced the young Yale literati in this period. The key word in Trumbull's Kamesian lexicon was "taste." People had a natural and unceasing thirst for happiness, he told the commencement assembly, a thirst that served as the "universal spring" of their actions. Unfortunately, human beings in their fallen state could become too easily attached to the low—and often vicious—enjoyments of the senses as they tried to quench that thirst. However, "the Divine Being, to raise us above these low desires, hath implanted in our minds a taste for more pure and intellectual pleasures." "These pleasures have their source in the fine Arts, and are more especially found in the elegant entertainments of polite Literature. They ennoble the soul, purify the passions, and give the thoughts a better turn. They add dignity to our sentiments, delicacy and refinement to our manners." Turning away from the speculative scholarship that could ultimately deify human reason, Trumbull focused attention upon the taste for civilized "delights, which humanize the soul."[8]

Like the New Light evangelicals who had shaken Thomas Clap's Yale nearly three decades before, Trumbull's literary circle used the language of sentiment to counter the stale, overly rationalized academic culture that still lingered four years after Clap's resignation. To certify that refined aesthetic perception was indeed connected to moral behavior, Trumbull, not unlike the evangelical preachers who tied inner religious feeling to moral action, asked the members of his audience to reflect upon their own experiences: "I appeal to all persons of judgment, whether they can rise from reading a fine Poem, viewing any masterly work of Genius, or hearing an harmonious concert of Music, without feeling an openness of heart, and an elevation of mind, without being more sensible of the dignity of human nature, and despising whatever tends to debase and degrade it?" Unlike the evangelical's "new sense," which was infused by the Holy Spirit and limited to the elect, Trumbull's "taste" for intellectual pleasure was a universal human propensity cultivated by education. Yet, just as the New Lights had at times been torn between nurturing piety within a close-knit com-

8. [Trumbull], *Essay,* 4–5; Henry Home, Lord Kames, *Elements of Criticism,* 3 vols. (Edinburgh, 1762). On taste, sociability, and sensibility in the eighteenth century, see John Dwyer and Richard B. Sher, eds., *Sociability and Society in Eighteenth-Century Scotland, Eighteenth-Century Life,* XV (1991); G. J. Barker-Benfield, *The Culture of Sensibility: Sex and Society in Eighteenth-Century Britain* (Chicago, 1992); Lawrence E. Klein, *Shaftesbury and the Culture of Politeness: Moral Discourse and Cultural Politics in Early Eighteenth-Century England* (Cambridge, 1994); Leslie Ellen Brown, "The Idea of Life as a Work of Art in Scottish Enlightenment Discourse," in Carla H. Hay and Syndy M. Conger, eds., *Studies in Eighteenth-Century Culture,* XXIV (Baltimore, 1995), 51–67; David S. Shields, *Civil Tongues and Polite Letters in British America* (Chapel Hill, N.C., 1997).

munity of saints and preaching to convert a wider world of sinners, Trumbull's reform project betrayed a tension between elitist exclusion and broader social reform. His phrasing revealed a fondness for the aristocratic tone of Anthony Ashley Copper, the third earl of Shaftesbury's descriptions of sentimental culture: "elegant," "polite," "dignity," "delicacy," "refinement"—the language of gentility that aspiring men and women of "quality" in eighteenth-century America, following the British gentry, had adopted. Trumbull also argued, however, that America's future literary and artistic greatness would grow because learning was, not confined to an elite few, but diffused through all ranks, with most Americans occupying "the middle station of life," avoiding the ignorance of peasants and the unthinking dissipation of the wealthy.[9]

The taste Trumbull described, therefore, was both aesthetic and moral, universal and elitist, psychological and sociological. Even within a single person—even within himself—it referred to two dimensions of the mind that were at times in tension. Tasting intellectual pleasures was an emotional experience. It involved, in the words of the *Essay, feeling* the openness of the heart and the elevation of the mind, *sensing* the dignity of human nature, and *despising* anything that debased or degraded humanity. To have (good) taste, though, was also to possess a power of critical discernment, the ability to discriminate between the elegant and the inelegant style, differentiate the polite and the impolite performance, distinguish the "masterly work of Genius" from the conventional or the extravagant production. These two aspects of taste—the sentiments of aesthetic experience and the critical judgment about beauty and excellence—are related to two impulses Trumbull felt in his own life: his poetic sensibility and his exacting critical judgment.

Trumbull remembered that, in his youth, his flights of creative imagination were always paired with a relentless, critical self-scrutiny. "That one must be born a Poet is an old adage, but that any one, tho' formed with the keenest sensibility, and the most extravagantly romantic feelings, should have an innate attention to the minutiae of Criticism, is perhaps uncommon. I was born the dupe of imagination. My satirical turn was not native. It was produced by the keen spirit of critical observation, operating on disappointed expectation and avenging itself on real or fancied wrongs." This insightful comment about the origins of his satirical skills may also help explain his thin-skinned sensitivity to criticism—why he lashed out at "malicious" misreadings of his work and real or imagined "slanders," why he seemed, even in an age obsessed with honor, so fearful of the damage that public words could do to his reputation. By setting his work before the public, he risked exposing the products of his poetic

9. [Trumbull], *Essay*, 4–5, 12.

"sensibility" and "most extravagantly romantic feelings" to the meticulous scrutiny of critics like himself. Even worse, he risked exposing himself to vengeful readers whose expectations of greatness had been disappointed and to enemies who wanted to thrust their daggers through the curtain of language to wound the author behind it.[10]

Some of Trumbull's early poems illustrate the poet's fear of critical scrutiny and sense of public vulnerability. "On the Vanity of Youthful Expectations," written in December 1771, speaks of wild ambition's swelling a young man's heart as, simultaneously, slander raises the envenomed dart. Four years later, he compared the ambitious poet's risking public criticism to Ulysses' traveling through the valley of death. In "Lines Addressed to Messrs. Dwight and Barlow, on the Projected Publication of Their Poems in London" (December 1775), he described the bard's long and dreary "pilgrimage of fame," where "each judging dunce reviews, / And every critic wars with every Muse." Faults and weaknesses, he warned, were fair game in this struggle between poets and critics, but, especially in Britain, the poet had to expect that the critical attack would be anything but fair:

> The cloud of Critics on your Muse descends!
> From every side, with deadly force, shall steer
> The fierce Review, the censuring Gazetteer,
> Light Magazines, that pointless jests supply,
> And quick Gazettes, that coin the current lie.
> Each coffee-house shall catch the loud alarms,
> The Temple swarm, and Grub-street wake to arms.
>
> . . . .
>
> The pamper'd critic feeds on slaughter'd names,
> And each new bard a welcome feast proclaims.
>   Such men to charm, could Homer's muse avail,
> Who read to cavil, and who write to rail;
> When ardent genius pours the bold sublime,
> Carp at the style, or nibble at the rhyme;
> Misstate your thoughts, misconstrue your design;
> And cite, as samples, every feebler line?

A key difference between the heroic poet and the vultures writing in the gazettes and magazines was that the critics could hide in the protective shadows of anonymity. The poet, "Pleased with the vision of a deathless name," seeks "a

10. John Trumbull Papers, Moses Coit Tyler Collection, Cornell University Library, MSS, 6, in Cowie, *John Trumbull*, 18.

flowery road to fame"; the dangers and fears waiting on that road to fame, however, are "of unknown name." The anonymous critics could destroy a writer's reputation—feed on his "slaughter'd" name—without risking their own.[11]

Ideally, the poet and the discerning critic (not the Grub Street hack) would converse within the same community of refined sentiment and elevated understanding. For both, the cultivation of taste was an essentially social process. Sentiments, as Shaftesbury and the Scottish school after Frances Hutcheson argued, are not just felt but expressed and measured against the standards of the community. Sensibility could be elevated and purified by the right kinds of sociability. The polite conversation of ladies and gentlemen, therefore, became a paradigm that shaped both the ideal of the refined moral community and the literary practices—the composition and circulation of manuscript poems, letters, and essays—that helped sustain that community.

Many of Trumbull's early poems were firmly rooted in his immediate social context, the intimate world of familiar conversation and polite sociability. Rather than merely exposing the parochialism of a bookish young poet, the poems reveal the very purposes of literary practice in polite society. Exchanging artful letters, passing around manuscript poems, and conversing with other men and women who were enthusiastic about belles lettres were all different aspects of the same process: creating and sustaining a community of shared sentiment based upon the virtuous pleasures of the fine arts. Some of Trumbull's poems marked local occasions. His elaborate burlesque "Epithalamion Stephani et Hannae" (August 1769) was written for the wedding of Yale tutor Stephen Mix Mitchell and Hannah Grant. Filled with humorous literary allusions, the poem also included some schoolboy snickering about the wedding bed, which (along with a reference to Miss Grant's attractive dowry) reportedly angered the groom. One of Trumbull's first poems in print, *An Elegy on the Death of Mr. Buckingham St. John, Tutor of Yale College,* was written to mourn a close friend and former roommate who had drowned on May 5, 1771.[12]

Other poems, which circulated in manuscript among Trumbull's Yale and New Haven friends and acquaintances, grew out of familiar conversation and epistolary exchange. If the "Epithalamion" started a quarrel, "Advice to Ladies of a Certain Age" (July 1771) was intended to end one. Trumbull composed it, he later wrote, after he "had interposed in vindication of some young ladies, who were injured, as he believed, by malicious slanders. He became in conse-

11. [Trumbull], *Poetical Works,* II, 105–108, 165.
12. [John Trumbull], *An Elegy, on the Death of Mr. Buckingham St. John, Tutor of Yale College . . .* [New Haven, Conn., 1771]. Trumbull's "Epithalamion" would be published twenty years later as "The Wedding, an Epithalamium" in *Columbian Magazine,* June 1789.

quence implicated in the quarrel. The poem was written (to use a mercantile phrase) to close the concern." Trumbull quarreled poetically again in "Epistle Addres[s]ed to Mr. I. J." (1771), which attacked an opponent for slandering him. "The Owl and the Sparrow" (1772) was part of "a poetical correspondence with a friend" who had sent him "a very humorous letter in ridicule of Love." When away from school, he also carried on a poetical correspondence with fellow Yale poet David Humphreys. He wrote "To a Young Lady" (September 1774) for a local girl who asked Trumbull to "draw her Character" in verse.[13]

Trumbull's social world included young women as well as his fellow Yale men. As an ardent student of polite literature and gentility, Trumbull knew that the society of women and the polite conversation they afforded was essential to polish the young gentleman and refine the writer's art. Although collegiate subjects like mathematics and astronomy were still considered the province of male scholars, and public disputes over parliamentary power or the Half-Way Covenant remained the domain of male politicians and divines, the literary public increasingly included, and was increasingly influenced by, women. Like the Scottish literati, the English "polite Whigs," and the French philosophes in their Parisian salons, the aspiring young men of the Anglicized Connecticut gentry understood that "the fair" were a powerful civilizing force.[14]

Trumbull and his Yale friends conversed with and courted young women who themselves corresponded about manners, morals, literature, and the refined pleasures of Connecticut's "better sort." Trumbull, Dwight, and other Yale men were involved with a circle of young women who called themselves the "Union Club." The club members, sisters and cousins living in Stamford, Connecticut, and in Oyster Bay and Queen's Village, Long Island, were united by kinship and intimate friendships; they regularly conversed and exchanged carefully crafted letters. They traded poems, discussed current literature, shared sentiments, monitored each other's moral and spiritual development, and pondered a future of marriage and childbirth. The Union Club has been described as a sisterhood of confident, assertive, upper-middle-class women who were cultivating friendship as a genteel art and striving to forge relationships—both romantic and familial—based upon mutual respect and esteem. Trumbull's assessment of the Union Club supports this view. In a somewhat flirtatious letter to Sally Lloyd, apparently the most charming and popular member of the group, he credits the club with containing the most sensible young ladies in the country, ladies who had risen far above the "common level"

13. [Trumbull], *Poetical Works*, II, 123, 149, 171; Cowie, *John Trumbull*, 65n–66n.
14. For France, see Dena Goodman, *The Republic of Letters: A Cultural History of the French Enlightenment* (Ithaca, N.Y., 1994).

of their sex. To other local young women, however, he was less generous. He later recalled seeing some of the letters these young ladies exchanged, and he found them filled with extravagantly romantic notions about courtship and matrimony of the type found in popular sentimental novels; the young women wrote as if interested in only the highest perfection of male virtue but would act like coquettes in front of an audience of coxcombs, fops, and fools.[15]

Although Trumbull's satirical poems depicting coquettes and fops can strike readers as merely imitations of English stock characters, those character types helped shape the young poet's perceptions of his social experience. The unpublished "Epitaph to Be Inscribed on the Marriage Bed of Miss S . . . W . . ." (1773–1776) describes a coquette who married at the age of twenty-four because she feared becoming an old maid. This was precisely the fate of the fictional Harriet Simper, the coquette in the third part of Trumbull's *Progress of Dulness,* published in September 1773. Trumbull recommended this printed poem to Sally Lloyd and her club, calling it a just description of most of the females in the colony. The work began with a preface insisting that the author, unlike other satirists and wits on the subject of coquetry, had no intention of ridiculing the fair sex. His target was, not the nature of women, but the education that perverted their taste and manners. "The sprightliness of Female genius, and the excellence of that Sex in their proper walks of science are by no means inferior to the accomplishments of Men. And although the course of their education ought to be different, and writing is not so peculiarly the business of the sex, yet I cannot but hope hereafter to see the accomplishment of my prediction in their favor." The "prediction" referred to lines (which he proceeded to quote) from his "Prospect of the Future Glory of America," the poem that concluded his 1770 commencement oration:

> Her Daughters too the happy land shall grace
> With pow'rs of genius, as with charms of face.
> Blest with the softness of the female mind,
> With fancy blooming and with taste refin'd,
> Some *Rowe* shall rise and wrest with daring pen,

15. On the Union Club, see Karen Sue Kauffman, "'In the Society of Our Friends': Two Generations of the Hillhouse Family, 1770–1840" (Ph.D. diss., University of Connecticut, 1996), chap. 1. On Trumbull's relationship to local women, see Gimmestad, *John Trumbull,* 70–72. Trumbull's letter to Sally Lloyd, Sept. 10, 1773, is included in the Hillhouse Family Papers, Manuscripts and Archives, Yale University Library, New Haven, Conn. Trumbull's reflections upon the young ladies he knew while in college, dated 1776, is in a draft of an essay, "I've Seen an End of What We Call Perfection Here Below," in Woodbridge Papers, Burton Historical Collection, Detroit Public Library, Detroit, Mich.

The pride of genius from assuming men:
While each bright line a polish'd beauty wears;
For ev'ry muse and ev'ry grace is theirs.

But, while Trumbull's oration and preface were condescendingly optimistic about the progress of female genius, the tale of Harriet Simper mocked the false taste and artificial gentility he saw all around him that retarded that progress.[16]

The Progress of Dulness, Part Third, subtitled *Sometimes Called the Progress of Coquetry; or, The Adventures of Miss Harriet Simper of the Colony of Connecticut*, complains that "The Fair are nurst in Folly's school." Six-year-old Harriet's taste is initially warped by the "council of Ladies" discussing her education at the beginning of the poem. The speaker, Harriet's aunt, criticizes the girl's choice of reading. Why pour over a primer? "'Tis quite enough for girls to know, / If she can read a billet-doux." Besides, too much reading produces wrinkles, marring a girl's most important asset: a pretty face. As she grows, Harriet fills her mind with little besides dress and dancing and wastes her time embroidering handkerchiefs. After a trip to the city, she copies the formal manners she sees there, demonstrating, according to the narrator, that "The half-genteel are least polite." Her education is finished by the sentimental novels she reads, romances "With whims that in no place exist, / But author's heads and woman's breast."[17]

In several ways, Harriet is a perverse reader. At the tea table, she reads tea leaves, thinking that "fate displays its book" about future beaux in the patterns left in her cup. In periodicals and letters, instead of reading about political economy and paying attention to important news from the wider world like a virtuous young man, she studies "The trade and politics of fashion" and learns to discern the precise moment a hat or a shoe falls out of style. She establishes committees of correspondence, but not, like the politically engaged men of her time, to protect liberty:

> A Patriot too, she greatly labours,
> To spread her arts among her neighbours,
> Holds correspondencies to learn

16. John Trumbull, "Epitaph to Be Inscribed on the Marriage Bed of Miss S . . . W . . . ," in "I've Seen an End to What We Call Perfection Here Below," [3]–[4], Woodbridge Papers; [Trumbull], "Author's Preface," *The Progress of Dulness, Part Third, and Last: Sometimes Called the Progress of Coquetry; or, The Adventures of Miss Harriet Simper of the Colony of Connecticut* . . . (New Haven, Conn., 1773), vii–viii; for the "Prospect of the Future Glory of America," see [Trumbull], *Essay*, 15. "Rowe" refers to Elizabeth Singer Rowe (1674–1737), English poet and author of several devotional works.

17. [Trumbull], *Progress of Dulness, Part Third,* ll. 35–36, 130, 206, 381–382.

> What facts the female world concern,
> To gain authentic state-reports
> Of varied modes in distant courts.

The novels she reads are dangerous not only for their fanciful subject matter but because of the way she reads them: she sympathetically identifies with swooning heroines like Samuel Richardson's Pamela and sits before the text as she stands before the mirror, admiring herself. At social occasions, she misreads the slightest gesture or expression, and, like the malicious critics Trumbull warned Dwight and Barlow about, fixes upon these trifles to destroy reputations. She

> Points out what smiles to sin advance,
> Finds assignations in a glance;
> And shews how rival toasts (you'll think)
> Break all commandments with a wink.[18]

Trumbull had sketched Harriet's male counterpart, Dick Hairbrain, in the second part of *The Progress of Dulness*. Dick, the son of a wealthy farmer who had purchased his way into local respectability, comes to college but receives his real education from the fops and coxcombs of the town. In such company, and with a fat enough allowance to pay the tailor, barber, and dancing master, "ev'ry money'd Clown and Dunce / Commences Gentleman at once." Trumbull criticizes the artificiality of this "Clockwork-Gentleman" who is made by his clothing and his affected manners. By describing how Dick achieves social success through his "studied elegance of phrase," the poet also jabs at the polite society of men and women too easily fooled by appearances. Whereas Harriet's misreadings display the perversion of politeness, Dick's speech betrays a false gentility.

> To grace his speech, let *France* bestow
> A set of compliments for show;
> Land of Politeness! that affords
> The treasure of newfangled words,
> And endless quantities disburses
> Of bows and compliments and curses:
> The soft address, with airs so sweet,
> That cringes at the Ladies feet;
> The pert, vivacious, play-house style,
> That wakes the gay assembly's smile.

18. Ibid., ll. 228, 241–246, 337–340, 355.

From "loads of Novels," Dick can sprinkle his speech with "simpring tales of am'rous pain"; from John Wilmot, the earl of Rochester's poetry and Laurence Sterne's *Tristram Shandy,* he has a ready supply of double entendres; from magazine reviews he can speak like a critic about the faults of books he has not read; from a smattering of David Hume, Voltaire, and clerical debate, he can play the daring freethinker. After a trip to Britain, he is at the top of his form, and Harriet has met her match.[19]

Unlike the ideal polite society, the social world where the likes of Harriet and Dick meet is not portrayed as a sociable sphere where men and women are mutually enlightened and civilized—where friendship and a taste for the finer things are cultivated. The artificial gentleman has been shaped outside the society of women, mostly molded by the arts of the other local fops who had smoothed and polished the rough surface of the rich country clown. Harriet, in turn, was primarily educated by other empty-headed women like her aunt, mother, and the friends who write to her about fashion. When the fop and the coquette meet, they do not communicate their sentiments; they perform for each other. Dick is a "Player" who knows "the play-house style"; Harriet, "rising on the stage, / Learns all the arts, that please the age." Harriet had enjoyed misleading suitors and then breaking their hearts by professing only friendship, claiming that they had misread her intentions. But she had so often imagined herself a love-struck character that she ultimately becomes one. When Dick, his heart unmoved beneath all the artful flattery, moves on to other pretty faces, and Harriet's mirror begins to show a face revealing the "tracks of age," she marries the dull preacher Tom Brainless to avoid, like Trumbull's acquaintance S. W., becoming an old maid.[20]

By exposing false gentility with satire, Trumbull's poems reinforced the values of polite society: sociability, shared sentiments, and the cultivation of taste in both men and women for the higher intellectual and aesthetic pleasures. The immediate social context—the organic community—of polite letters, however, and especially the central role of women within it, was mostly absent from Trumbull's 1770 *Essay on the Use and Advantages of the Fine Arts.* In that work, broad political and historical conditions, not the refined conversations of tea tables and parlors or the literary correspondence of friends and clubs, provided the fertile soil for the fine arts. Trumbull does not describe women as contributors to literary culture and an active civilizing force; he only hopes

19. [John Trumbull], *The Progress of Dulness, Part Second; or, An Essay on the Life and Character of Dick Hairbrain of Finical Memory . . .* (New Haven, Conn., [1773]), ll. 169–170, 217–226, 235–236.

20. Ibid., ll. 225, 229; [Trumbull], *Progress of Dulness, Part Third,* ll. 225–226, 642.

that someday, in the distant American future, the progress of civilization will enable women to take up the "daring pen." Like the enlightened Scots in the 1760s, Trumbull took pains to distance polite letters from "luxurious effeminacy" and fuse it to "manly fortitude." In America, an unreconciled tension existed between politeness and virtue as social values. Politeness marked status; virtue, moral commitment to the public good. The elevated sensibilities, cultural progress, and refined manners of the polite were rarely praised without strong qualifiers, for sturdy American whigs did not want to be seen aping the manners of the British aristocracy. The recent struggle for liberty in America, Trumbull argued, had "rectified the manners of the times" and had prompted America "to distinguish itself in literature." Whereas cosmopolitan effeminacy had "introduced a false taste in writing" to Britain, "America hath a fair prospect in a few centuries," he predicted, "of ruling both in arts and arms." His brief history lesson, beginning with Greece and Rome and linking the cultivation of the arts to martial vigor, tried to balance politeness with the classical values of civic virtue. Most of Trumbull's printed prose and verse in the 1770s, in fact, would help shape a male civic forum, not a heterosocial society of polite letters.[21]

BUILDING A CIVIC FORUM IN THE CONNECTICUT PRESS

As Trumbull and Dwight began to devote their extracurricular energies to studying Lord Kames's *Elements of Criticism* and John Ward's *System of Oratory*, the colony's presses were putting more weekly newspapers into local circulation. In 1765, Benjamin Franklin's nephew Benjamin Mecom revived the *Connecticut Gazette* in the teeth of the Stamp Act, hoping the zealous whiggery of the times would support the return of what had been the colony's first newspaper a decade earlier. The first full year for the *Connecticut Courant* in Hartford was also 1765, and by 1766 the three-year-old *New-London Gazette* had

---

21. [Trumbull], *Essay*, 11, 12. On the tension between virtue and politeness, see Warner, *Letters of the Republic*, 132–138. See also J.G.A. Pocock's description of "polite Whigs" in chaps. 6, 7, and 11 of *Virtue, Commerce, and History: Essays on Political Thought and History, Chiefly in the Eighteenth Century* (Cambridge, 1985); Peter J. Diamond, "Rhetoric and Philosophy in the Social Thought of Thomas Reid," and John Dwyer, "Enlightened Spectators and Classical Moralists: Sympathetic Relations in Eighteenth-Century Scotland," both in Dwyer and Sher, eds., *Sociability and Society in Eighteenth-Century Scotland, Eighteenth-Century Life*, XV (1991), 57–80, 96–118; Kathleen Wilson, "Citizenship, Empire, and Modernity in the English Provinces, c. 1720–1790," *Eighteenth-Century Studies*, XXIX (1995), 69–96.

expanded its format. In the fall of 1767, New Haven got its second paper, the *Connecticut Journal, and the New-Haven Post-Boy,* and, in 1773, Norwich got its first, the *Norwich Packet.* During this same period, Connecticut entrepreneurs began making their own paper (1766), casting type (1769), and building presses (1775).[22]

Connecticut newspapers were products of commercial expansion and the turbulent political climate. Newspapers grew and multiplied as farmers and merchants became willing and able to pay for more information, entertainment, and advertisements. The imperial crisis turned the journals, chronicles, and gazettes into forums of political debate and cultivators of civic consciousness. Local papers—begun as collections of battlefield dispatches, extracts from the presses of neighboring provinces, miscellanies from the London papers, and commercial notices—grew into public arenas of political commentary and economic argument. The context for Trumbull's published literary efforts in the 1770s was created by the expansion and politicization of the local press in the late 1760s.

What one writer called "the Grand Debate" over the postwar economic troubles of the 1760s (little hard currency and large debts) sometimes pitted one sector of society against another—merchants against farmers, for example, or town against country. But, for the most part, newsprint moralists castigated the colony as a whole for its lack of industry and frugality or offered schemes to promote those virtues. When the Stamp Act threatened to make a bad situation worse, letters from sympathetic London merchants or extracts from the Boston, New York, or Philadelphia papers made the case against it in the pages of the *Courant.* More Connecticut pens set to work after August 12, 1765, when the names of the colonial Stamp distributors were published, giving the unpopular measure a local face—that of lawyer Jared Ingersoll. Nevertheless, the texts of town resolutions and reports of anti–Stamp Act protests, rather than locally written harangues, provided most of the Connecticut print about the Stamp crisis until the act's repeal in the spring of 1766.[23]

---

22. John Ward, *A System of Oratory . . . ,* 2 vols. (London, 1759). See Jarvis Means Morse, *Connecticut Newspapers in the Eighteenth Century* (New Haven, Conn., 1935); Sidney Kobre, *The Development of the Colonial Newspaper* (1944; reprint, Gloucester, Mass., 1960), 176–177; J. Eugene Smith, *One Hundred Years of Hartford's Courant: From Colonial Times through the Civil War* (New Haven, Conn., 1949), pts. 1, 2; Stephen Botein, "Printers and the American Revolution," in Bernard Bailyn and John B. Hench, eds., *The Press and the American Revolution* (Worcester, Mass., 1980), 11–57. Also helpful have been Lyon N. Richardson, *A History of Early American Magazines, 1741–1789* (New York, 1931); and Arthur M. Schlesinger, *Prelude to Independence: The Newspaper War on Britain, 1764–1776* (1957; reprint, Boston, 1980).

23. "A. C.," *Connecticut Courant* (Hartford), Apr. 29, 1765, discusses "the Grand Debate."

Yet, early in 1767, the press was suddenly filled with local writers trying to shape the legacy the Stamp Act would have upon Connecticut politics. Governor Thomas Fitch and four councillors had been turned out of office for taking the Stamp oath. Pseudonymous disputants, beginning with "Plaind Facts," "a Mekannick" who professed to tell "real Truths," battled over the wisdom of that political purge and of the hardening east-west division within the colony. A year later, letters to the *Courant* bemoaned that only "fierce combatants for an election" bothered to write to the press and urged that writers pick up their pens once again to oppose Parliament or to write more nonpartisan essays to promote industry and frugality. "O.E.K." offered a verse fable and suggested that similar contributions could be inoffensive diversions yet still serve the public good. Early in 1768, the "Complainant," a regular ostensibly nonpolitical essayist, was encouraged to continue his weekly efforts in the Hartford paper because several gentlemen assured the printer that "nothing can be more beneficial to the public, or add a greater reputation to a paper like his, than periodical essays, humurous, satyrical and instructive." [24]

Trumbull's Correspondent essays first appeared in 1770 during another cycle of virulent political debate over the Townshend Acts and then reappeared in the so-called Quiet Period before the Tea Act in 1773. His promotion of the "non-political" essay, however, does not signal a retreat to a detached, belletristic world. Trumbull wanted to make the weekly press into a vehicle for local "moral, critical, and poetical" writing, but not by divorcing this content from the context of political influence or the realities of material production. His Correspondent invited readers of the *Connecticut Journal* in 1773 to send material for the column, if "in these times of liberty, while the praise of home manufactures is not yet quite forgotten, there be any Gentlemen who are desirous of encouraging new attempts of literary production." For Trumbull, "literary production" was intimately connected to economic development ("home manufactures") and political opposition ("these times of liberty"). [25]

24. Letters by "Plaind Facts," "A. Z.," "Senex Quondam Senatorius," "Icabod," "Justice," "Constant Customer," "Freeman," "Philo-pacis et Veritas," "Mr. Plain Truth," "Cadddo," "Thomas Moderation," "H. L.," "Pacificus," "A Son of Liberty," "General Plan," "Ballander," "Titus Moderate," and "Your Constant Customer," in *Conn. Courant*, Feb. 16 – May 18, 1767; letters from "A Tradesman" and "Liber Nov-Anglus," ibid., Jan. 4, 11, 1768; letter from "O.E.K.," ibid., Feb. 8, 1768. The "Complainant" series began on Jan. 18, and the notice about its continuation appeared on Feb. 15, 1768.

25. See Kenneth Silverman, "Culture in British America during the 'Quiet period,' 1770 – 1773," in *A Cultural History of the American Revolution: Painting, Music, Literature, and the Theater in the Colonies and the United States from the Treaty of Paris to the Inauguration of*

Trumbull's Correspondent column, which called for local contributions even as it addressed "the World" as its audience, also recapitulated the newspapers' evolution from community bulletin board to center stage in the republican public sphere. When the *Courant*'s printer, Ebenezer Watson, or his partner at New Haven's *Journal,* Thomas Green, urged their readers to bring in old linen rags to the print shop in order to make new paper, they were stepping from behind their printed pages as any other local merchant or craftsman might step away from his work to greet a customer. When Watson apologized for errors, or for the low quality of his paper or type, or when he pleaded with his subscribers to pay their debts promptly because peculiar expenses had become an added burden, he embedded his work in personal and local concerns. Trumbull's Correspondent essays, too, were conscious of their local audience. Writing the column was an act of local boosterism, for he complained that New Haven, despite being the colony's "seat of literature" because of Yale, produced fewer essays in its public papers than any other town with a printing press on the continent. And Trumbull himself could not help becoming personally singed by the fires of local controversy fanned by the Correspondent.[26]

Trumbull's call for contributions, like the newspapers' call for linen rags, made the domestic production of paper and the domestic production of literature for the newspapers something of a community project. But it was a community that took both private interests and the loftier motives of civic virtue into account. Notices that promised "Ready Money" for linen rags also reminded readers that "the public Utility of this Undertaking" transcended the local: "If you really love your country, then, my brethren," beseeched "A Housholder" in a half-column appeal, "if you really love those advantages which made that country dear to you," you will save all your rags. Trumbull appealed to private motives in his "gentle Reader" by arguing that the reader-turned-writer would personally profit by quenching "the heart burnings of an author" or the desire for revenge upon the satirist. Nobler motives, of course, existed in "a truly patriotic concern" for "the welfare of the public."[27]

George Washington, 1763–1789 (1976; reprint, New York, 1987), 153–161; "Correspondent," IX, *Conn. Journal,* Feb. 12, 1773.

26. "Cash Given for Rags at the Printing-Office," *Conn. Courant,* July 14, 1766, became a regular notice in both the *Conn. Courant* and Thomas Green's *Conn. Journal.* The partnership between Green and Ebenezer Watson was dissolved on Dec. 18, 1770. Eugene Smith mentions Watson's "personal tone" in *One Hundred Years of Hartford's Courant,* 10. Quotation from "Correspondent," IX, *Conn. Journal,* Feb. 12, 1773.

27. When Watson announced the expansion of the *Conn. Courant* on Nov. 13, 1770, he reminded his readers that, although they would have to pay an extra shilling per year, "they

Despite references to the personal and the local, which could model public writing after the social exchanges of polite society or mimic the town meeting's "community of speakers," Trumbull and the Connecticut press were primarily engaged in creating a republican civic forum. Historians have described the "republican paradigm," in which key tenets of republican ideology like civic participation and disinterested virtue along with new uses of print reconstructed the idea of authorship, the act of addressing an audience, and the practice of participating in public debate. Print was no longer seen as merely substituting for the writer's presence, the way that Cotton Mather thought that his printed sermons simply preached a second time to a reader or functioned like an additional pastoral visit, or the way that the artful letters of polite society continued conversations. As the continual use of pseudonyms like "Cato" or "Mr. Freeman" in republican discourse emphasized, language was detached from the person who wrote it; social status, personal characteristics, and private concerns were intentionally bracketed out. Although often written in the *form* of private correspondences or personal dialogues, an essay's intended audience was actually an abstracted and universalized "public" made up of innumerable and unknowable readers. In the public forum of print, as opposed to the parlors of polite society or a New England town meeting, fictional personae like "Boltrope" and the Correspondent could air dissenting opinions without risking personal reputations or social harmony.[28]

For Trumbull, even the physical appearance of the newspaper essay signaled its republican appeal. In contrast to books, the newspaper essay lacked the showy display of pompous prefaces, long-winded dedications, descriptive title pages, tables of contents, and portraits of the author—all of which tended to "raise expectation, excite curiosity, and often contribute greatly to the sale."

> This paper being forced to make its appearance in the world, without any of these advantages, without the name of the writer to defend it, or of any great man to patronize it, throws itself upon the mercy of the public, and desires only a fair and unprejudiced perusal.

themselves will be reaping the benefit." When he revived the "Correspondent" in the *Conn. Journal* on Feb. 12, 1773, Trumbull invited all his readers who could write to "join hands, to assist me in this work." Other quotations are from *Conn. Courant*, Jan. 11, 1768; "Correspondent," IX, *Conn. Journal*, Feb. 12, 1773.

28. See Warner, *Letters of the Republic*, chap. 1, esp. 19–26, and 46: "The [traditional or Puritan] ideal of a social order free from conflictual debate" was transformed "into an ideal of debate free of social conflict."

The newspaper essay, like the independent republican, did not depend upon the arts of display, authoritative names, or wealthy friends, but rose or fell in the public sphere by its own merits.[29]

The Correspondent series, despite its local references, displayed the abstracting and universalizing characteristics of republican print. That was clear in the way Trumbull introduced the epistolary format. It was an age of letter writing, he began: "Party and politicks take upon them the form of letters to Lords and members of Parliament; religion and morality, of letters to a friend." He would assume the character of a "universal Correspondent," receiving letters from the public and crafting his own essays in the form of letters inscribed "to the World." The Correspondent was a rhetorical persona, detached from Trumbull the person, and therefore without his name, social status, and private interests; he addressed an abstract public, and encouraged discussion and debate about anything that was not grossly personal. The earlier "Meddler" series had begun, like the *Spectator* upon which it was modeled, with descriptions of the fictional circle of friends whose conversation and correspondence would supposedly supply material for the column: the country gentleman Thomas Freeman, the serious John Manly, Esq., the sprightly Jack Dapperwit, and the elegant clergyman. The Correspondent dispensed with this fictionalized reflection of polite sociability. The Correspondent was an anonymous author writing to the public, not a polite writer pretending to send epistles to intimate friends.[30]

Of course, Trumbull was not inventing a new form of cultural politics; his newspaper column resembled those that had circulated through the coffeehouses of early-eighteenth-century London, and the style he had copied had been raised to an art by writers like Joseph Addison and Jonathan Swift. Furthermore, the Addisonian essay had not been truly new in New England since young Benjamin Franklin's "Silence Dogood" essays in the 1720s. Even in Connecticut's much more recently developed weekly press, Trumbull had been preceded by the *Courant*'s "Complainant" essays. What set Trumbull apart (besides the wit that the "Complainant" lacked) was his self-conscious effort at once to establish this model of public discourse and to pursue a specific program to reform Connecticut's intellectual foundations. Trumbull was trying to radically alter both the form and the content of public debate.[31]

29. "The Meddler," I, *Boston Chronicle*, Sept. 4–7, 1769.

30. "Correspondent," I, *Conn. Journal*, Feb. 23, 1770.

31. William Hazlett wrote that the eighteenth-century periodical essay was to manners what experiments were to natural philosophy (quoted in Terry Eagleton, *The Function of Criticism: From The Spectator to Post-Structuralism* [London, 1984], 20). John Trumbull was

The young critic aimed his arrows at the group of learned men who continued to dominate intellectual life and public debate: the clergy. Trumbull was
neither a skeptic, a libertine, nor even an enemy of Calvinism. But he thought
that clerical incompetence and contentiousness were twin sores on the body
public—the two most serious threats to the vitality of intellect and religion
in the colony. He saw Connecticut pulpits being filled by dunces who dozed
through four years of college and by barely literate blunderers who were licensed to preach by their brethren as long as they could recite the Calvinist
creed. The few clerics with some brains scrambled them with metaphysical
speculation and plunged the colony into violent controversies—disputes that
"savouring so highly of vanity and ostentation, and breathing a spirit so opposite to christian benevolence, hath done more hurt to the cause of religion, than
all the malice, the ridicule, and the folly of its enemies." Trumbull addressed
other important social issues as well. The Correspondent launched a Swiftian
attack on slavery, which was printed a page away from a not-uncommon advertisement for the sale of "a likely, healthy, active Negro Boy." He ridiculed
quacks and confidence men who peddled health tonics and elixirs, and he
included a serious call for state medical licensing. He complained about how
quickly the public spirit had cooled, as seen in the weakening support for the
nonimportation agreements, although Parliament's threats to American liberty
remained. But Trumbull was preoccupied by the clerical domination of higher
learning and public discourse.[32]

---

no more the stylistic innovator than Jared Eliot was the inventor of the experimental
method, but both helped popularize new ways of writing and thinking in Connecticut. According to Bruce Granger, "Introduction," in Trumbull, *The Meddler (1769–70) and The
Correspondent (1770–73)*, ed. Granger, 3, "In the half-century separating the first American
essay serial, Benjamin Franklin's *Doogood* papers (1722), from the efforts of John Trumbull
(1750–1831) in this genre, no fewer than twelve important serials appeared in the [colonial]
press."

32. Trumbull's published writings indicate that he thought the official manual of ortho-
dox divinity at Yale, William Ames's *Medulla Theologica (The Morrow of Sacred Divinity,
Drawn Out of the Holy Scriptures, and the Interpreters Thereof, and Brought into Method . . .*
[London, 1642]) was a solid explication of the gospel. His unpublished "Speculative Essays"
reveal his assent to the Calvinist doctrines of foreordination and foreknowledge (see Cowie,
John Trumbull, 81). Quotations from [John Trumbull], "Author's Preface," *The Progress of
Dulness, Part First; or, The Rare Adventures of Tom Brainless . . .* (New Haven, Conn., 1772),
vi; "Correspondent," VIII, XIV, XVI, XX, *Conn. Journal*, July 6, 1770, Mar. 9, Apr. 2, 30, 1773.
Trumbull inserted jabs at clerical controversialists in unexpected places. A verse fable on
falling in love, written to a friend in 1772, speaks of a time when all animals had speech, and
"Each Ass [was] a gifted met'physician" who could "Write *Halfway-covenant Dialogues*"
("The Owl and the Sparrow: A Fable," in [Trumbull], *Poetical Works*, II, 150). In his un-

The Correspondent fired his opening shot in his second essay, when he announced that besides his own writings he would publish from some manuscripts by writers who had recently become famous in the literary world. These included "The Art of Quarrelling," "Creeds and Catechisms Made and Mended, by D. D. and Company" (probably a reference to the Reverend Joseph Bellamy), and the following:

> The Art of Second Sight; shewing an easy and infallible method of discovering, by intuition, any person's character, principles, practices, state of body or soul, future happiness or misery etc. . . . first invented by a reasoned Stage-player, and since brought to perfection by the united labours of a certain set of Philosophers.

The "Stage-player" probably referred to revivalist George Whitefield, known for his theatricality and for acting in plays in his youth; the "Philosophers" were the New Divinity theologians, followers of Jonathan Edwards whose works continued to stir up controversy.[33]

Subsequent essays contained extracts from a manuscript entitled "A New System of Logic," whose author championed the new vogue for labyrinthine metaphysical argument and derided common sense. The new method, this author explained, was "to split every word into so many distinctions, and to give it so many different meanings, marking it on all sides like a die." The favored form was the dialogue, the author of the "New System" advised: "In that way you must take some pains in forming an under character for an objector. Let him be as awkward and ignorant as you can make him. . . . Let your Parishioner doubt, and your Minister dogmatize." It was also important to advertise a pompous title:

A Vindication of True Religion
Being an Answer to the Remarks of
The Rev'd Dunscotus,

Wherein is shewn, that the remarker hath wholly mistaken the nature of the subject, and that he hath been guilty of the most palpable blunders and absurdities; Concluding with a Catalogue of his Contradictions, and an

---

finished novel, the main character, a hermit trying to reduce theology to mathematical formulae, criticizes the apostle Paul for his writing abilities. If Paul had been able to study with Connecticut's New Divinity theologian Joseph Bellamy, the hermit declared, "Instead of plain common talk, he might perhaps have been a good writer of Sermons and Essays, or had a tolerable hand at a Halfway-covenant Dialogue." See John Trumbull, "The Mathematical Metaphysician," John Trumbull Papers, Burton Historical Collection, [8].

33. "Correspondent," II, *Conn. Journal,* Mar. 2, 1770.

appendix proving the coincidence of his opinions with those of *Hobbs,* *Spinoza,* and the Atheists and Deists of all ages.

Right beneath this burlesque, in the same column of the *Journal's* April 27, 1770, issue, appeared an actual advertisement for Joseph Bellamy's *Fourth Dialogue between the Minister and His Parishioner.* Trumbull's spoof, however, also strikingly resembled a notice by an opponent of the Edwardseans that had appeared a week earlier: James Dana's *Examination of the Late President Edwards' Enquiry on Freedom of the Will . . . with an Appendix, Containing a Specimen of Coincidence between the Principles of Mr. Edwards' Book, and Those of Antient and Modern Fatalists.* Trumbull was not taking sides in this tedious battle of Old and New Divinities; he was holding up the clerical controversy itself to ridicule.[34]

The Correspondent also introduced a character called "Dogmaticus," whose favorite exercise was religious disputation and who condemned all who differed from him on points of doctrine as enemies to Christianity. But Trumbull's sharpest attack came during the Correspondent's hiatus, with the anonymous publication of the first part of *The Progress of Dulness.* The 450 lines of octosyllabic satire, printed just in time for Yale's commencement in 1772, would provoke more public response than its author could handle.[35]

The first installment of *The Progress of Dulness* detailed the adventures of "Tom Brainless," a dull and lazy country lad who slept and stumbled through four years of college, yet got his degree. Aiming at the ministry, Tom then "settles down with earnest zeal / Sermons to study, and to steal." He either mimics the grave preaching style "Safe-handed down from *Cromwell's* days" or flies "Aloft in metaphysic sky" to explain the system of the universe. After six months, he appears for licensing before the clerical association.

> What though his learning be so slight,
> He scarcely knows to spell or write;
> What though his skull be cudgel-proof!
> He's orthodox, and that's enough.

Tom gets his wig, pulpit, salary, and the deference due his office. Each Sunday he yokes dullness to dogmatism, "And while above he spends his breath, / The yawning audience nod beneath."[36]

Connecticut's reverend gentlemen were not amused. The virulence of their reaction seems to have stunned Trumbull, who was prompted to define and de-

---

34. Ibid., VI, Apr. 27, 1770.
35. Ibid., III, Mar. 9, 1770.
36. [Trumbull], *Progress of Dulness, Part First,* ll. 307–308, 318, 322, 351–354, 443–444.

fend the public role of the satirist and critic and to explain how his work should be read and understood. When the Correspondent returned, he reiterated: "To expose vice by general animadversions, and not to brand characters by personal satire, was the principal design of these essays." He repeated the "old allegory" of the arts and sciences' conquering the New World. Sense and Genius landed first, then Fancy and Invention, and, finally, in a later stage of civilization's triumph over barbarism, Humor and Satire. These last two were just beginning to make their appearance in America but could be very useful in battling the new enthusiasms of the ignorant. New England no longer hanged witches or Quakers and no longer glanced anxiously at astrological charts. Even the period of religious enthusiasm, when men set themselves up as prophets who could peer into souls, seemed to be a thing of the past. But new demons of enthusiasm were rising in the land: Uncharitableness and Controversy, Arrogance and Libertinism, Foppery, Riot, and Lewdness. "Now these spirits are not to be driven away by nailing horse-shoes at our doors . . . or saying over the Lord's prayer either forwards or backwards." They had to be *shamed* out of the society, "and those who would turn a deaf ear to the calls of reason are often checked by the arrows of satire."[37]

The satirist's role was not an easy one. Because of the very nature of public writing, he was bound to be misunderstood: "It may be, Gentle Reader, you have never seen yourself in print, or known the heart burnings of an author on his first appearance upon the stage. . . . to hear the strange guesses, and misbegotten conjectures of the world." Trumbull tried to use the problem of misinterpretation to his advantage to preempt complaints and criticism. "'Pray what does the author mean?' is the first question most readers will ask, and the last they are able to answer," he wrote. The Correspondent had argued that it was the reader, not the writer, who would take the barbs aimed at "fictitious characters" and apply them to real people. The writer only asked that the reader first apply the remarks to himself to see if they fit. In the "Author's Preface" to the first part of *The Progress of Dulness,* Trumbull tried to clarify the writer's contribution to this process by setting out the "general errors" that the poem would condemn in the story of Tom Brainless.[38]

Reacting to the resentment that greeted the poem, Trumbull dedicated the second part's preface "To the Envious and Malicious Reader." He lashed out at those clergymen who had groaned at the bitter medicine of his first satire. Since "the old trite way" of arguing by "calling men Heretics, Deists and Ar-

37. "Correspondent," XXXVIII, *Conn. Journal,* June 25, 1773, XXIX, July 2, 1773.
38. Ibid., IX, Feb. 12, 1773; [Trumbull], "Author's Preface," *Progress of Dulness, Part First,* vi.

minians" had been "lately so much hackneyed and worn out by some Reverend Gentlemen," he offered his malicious readers a lesson in literary criticism so that they might focus their attention upon the writing instead of the presumed character of the anonymous writer. But he fully expected them to misrepresent the motives behind the composition again, since the poems themselves would offer no evidence to support their charges that he was ridiculing truth, religion, and morality or trying to tear down Yale College and the Ten Commandments. Within the poem's third part, he compared the clergy's malicious attempts to read infidelity between his lines of verse to the coquette Harriet Simper's perverse misreading:

> So Priests drive poets to the lurch
> By fulminations of the church,
> Mark in our titlepage our crimes.
> Find heresies in double rhymes,
> Charge tropes with damnable opinion,
> And prove a metaphor *Arminian,*
> Peep for our doctrines, as at windows,
> And pick out creeds of innuendoes.[39]

Trumbull complained that his opponents did not understand the ground rules for public debate: impersonal authorship, general criticism of character types rather than particular attacks upon individuals, and the restriction of the argument to the public sphere itself. Debates conducted in print's civic forum should not spill over into the social world of polite conversation. Trumbull contended that his "impartial observations" had been answered by "the personal violence of unprovoked slander"; his "good wishes to the morals of mankind" had met with "private censures and insinuations" by cowards unwilling to enter the public lists. Writers on both sides of the controversy, however, strained at the leash of propriety. The writer who signed himself "The Lover of Virtue and Good Manners" complained in the *Journal* that the author of *The Progress of Dulness* made personal attacks, but he then demanded that the poet name names once and for all. The poet himself singled out two of his enemies and dared them to "throw off the mask" of anonymity and step forward by name from behind the "screen" of the crowd. The Correspondent called another opponent ("L. H.") a liar for denying that he was a clergyman. L. H. was called a

---

39. [John Trumbull], "Author's Preface: To the Envious and Malicious Reader," *Progress of Dulness, Part Second*, vi–x. In the "Author's Preface" to *Progress of Dulness, Part Third*, Trumbull again wrote that he expected his designs "will by many be ignorantly or wilfully misunderstood" (vii). The quotation is from *Progress of Dulness, Part Third*, ll. 341–348.

hypocrite, too, for applauding the Correspondent's essays "in private conversation, where you thought I should hear of it," while "in public," behind the mask of two initials, railing at them "with such expressive malevolence." By referring to private conversations, singling out individuals, and asking for names, Trumbull was violating the very standards he had explicitly tried to set.[40]

The question of the satirist's true motives kept recurring, and Trumbull's responses tried to locate the writer's social role in the gray area between literary entertainer and social reformer. When friendly letters wondered why he bothered debating knaves and fools, whom he could only antagonize rather than educate, he admitted the limited effects of public writing and celebrated the play of wit for its own sake. When opponents accused him of writing only to gratify his vanity, he trumpeted his high moral purpose. Trumbull's basic contention, however, was that every author writes both to honor himself and to benefit mankind.[41]

The tension between the writer's private interests and the public good was played out with mercantile metaphors as the Correspondent series drew to a close. Planning his move to Boston to study law with John Adams, Trumbull placed this notice in the Correspondent's column for July 30, 1773: "As the Co-partnership between the Correspondent and the Public will soon be dissolved, all persons, that have any accounts to settle with said 'Partnership, are desired to send them in as soon as possible." One writer regretted the Correspondent's departure, praising his plain dealing and "Choice of Commodities" and offering to barter for some "Remnants" with some verse of his own. Another letter compared the Correspondent to a small boat loaded with goods that had run aground at New Haven and planned to depart for Boston as soon as possible, "as the market is very low in this town, and little or nothing can be got for those rough materials for fabricating essays, songs, sonnets, odes, etc." "Boltrope" charged that the Correspondent's personal estate contained only "Vanity and Importance": "If upon settling your Account with the public, you find them indebted to you for one new Idea, one generous Sentiment, or one useful Remark, you may draw upon Mess. Fame and Reputation, Bankers in Boston, for the full Amount . . . but no patch'd Plagiarism will be admitted as a just Charge in the Account." Like a character in the earlier "Meddler" series, the Corre-

40. "Correspondent," XXVIII, *Conn. Journal*, June 25, 1793, XXX, July 9, 1773, XXXIV, Aug. 6, 1773, XXXVI, Aug. 20, 1773; "Author's Preface," *Progress of Dulness, Part Second*, ix; "To My Good Catechist," Trumbull's letter in the *Conn. Journal*, Feb. 5, 1773, in response to a letter "To the Author of the Progress of Dulness, Parts First and Second," ibid., Jan. 29, 1773; "L. H." to the *Conn. Journal*, Aug. 13, 1773.

41. "Correspondent," XXVII, *Conn. Journal*, June 25, 1773, XXX, July 9, 1773; "To My Good Catechist," *Conn. Journal*, Feb. 5, 1773.

spondent was accused of being a mere "peddler of wit," foisting London trifles upon the public for private gain.[42]

SATIRIZING THE COMMUNITY OF SPEAKERS

Trumbull's move to Boston in November 1773 placed him, as he later wrote, "in the centre of American politics." Studying with Adams and rooming with Thomas Cushing, the speaker of the house, Trumbull spent his leisure hours "writing essays on political subjects, in the public gazettes" (and being very careful to conceal his identity) instead of polishing his translation of Virgil, as he had planned. Massachusetts printers like Isaiah Thomas had realized that a moderate position would be untenable for publishing a newspaper. When the whig press unfurled its banners proclaiming "Open to ALL PARTIES, but not under the INFLUENCE OF ANY," the familiar slogan was by this point, as one historian has written, "an empty gesture." To men who had come to consider the press an institution of "the people," safeguarding their liberties against executive usurpation, the press was indeed open to "all parties" *except* those seeking to undermine the popular (that is, whig) cause. "The violence of party was extreme," Trumbull remembered. His poetic contribution to the partisan battle was the stiffly serious "Elegy on the Times," written in opposition to the Boston Port Bill and printed in Thomas's *Massachusetts Spy*.[43]

42. "Correspondent," XXXV, *Conn. Journal*, Aug. 6, 1773, and "n. b." beneath L. H.'s letter in the same issue; "Boltrope" to the "Correspondent," *Conn. Journal*, Aug. 20, 1773. See also letters from "Philatros," "Tim Grocer," "Moderatius," "Fusee," and "Twig," ibid., August through Sept. 3. The "Schemer" was a character in the "Meddler" series, a self-described "retailer" or "pedlar of wit," who would praise any gentleman's character or any aspect of (false) politeness for the right price. See "The Meddler," III, VII, *Boston Chronicle*, Oct. 23–26, Dec. 18–21, 1769.

43. [Trumbull], "Memoir," *Poetical Works*, I, 15, 16, 17. These political essays, which Trumbull carefully disguised "to prevent any discovery of the real author," have not been identified. Before moving to Boston, Trumbull mentioned his "somewhat inelegant" translations of Virgil in a letter to Samuel Quincy, who was looking for submissions for a "Poetical Miscellany" (Trumbull to Quincy, July 22, 1773, Beinecke Rare Book and Manuscript Library, Yale University, New Haven, Conn). "An Elegy on the Times" was first published in *Massachusetts Spy*, Sept. 22, 29, 1774. On the "open" whig press, see Botein, "Printers in the American Revolution," in Bailyn and Hench, eds., *The Press and the American Revolution*, 42. See also in this volume Richard Buel, Jr., "Freedom of the Press in Revolutionary America: The Evolution of Libertarianism, 1760–1820," 71, 80–81, and Robert M. Weir, "The Role of the Newspaper Press in the Southern Colonies on the Eve of the Revolution: An Interpretation," 115. The *Conn. Courant* used the "Open to ALL PARTIES" slogan as a byline from June 7, 1774, to Apr. 24, 1775 (Smith, *One Hundred Years of the Hartford Courant*, 9, 271n).

Trumbull returned to New Haven in late 1774 and wrote his most famous work, *M'Fingal,* in the spring and summer of 1775. His friends John Adams and Silas Deane, attending Congress in Philadelphia, had Trumbull's comic epic published there the following winter. This first version of *M'Fingal* was a fourteen-hundred-line burlesque, set in a New England town meeting and featuring a debate between a whig spokesman named Honorious and a pompous and ridiculous tory, Squire M'Fingal. The debate ends in riotous shouting and confusion, but not before the tory cause and the British troops who defended it were thoroughly ridiculed, mostly by the bumbling M'Fingal himself. The cantos added for the 1782 edition bring M'Fingal to the liberty pole for a tar-and-feathering and detail his prophetic vision of whig victory. Readers have long noted that, in these later cantos, M'Fingal plays much less the fool and in fact offers a devastating critique of a political world where "Each leather-apron'd clown" thinks he is a politician.[44]

Certainly *M'Fingal,* even in the 1775 version, ridiculed both the hypocrisy of the tory moneychangers and the leveling zeal curdling the patriotism of the lower orders. But it was also a satire on speech itself—on speech as a medium of politics, prophecy, and poetry. The detachment of the satirist and the decorum of his heroic couplets contrast sharply with the passion and chaos of the town meeting he describes. *M'Fingal* the poem seeks to triumph in the republic of print by describing how M'Fingal the character flounders in the personal politics of speech.

Skilled in making speeches and claiming the Scottish highlander's gift of "Second-sight," or the prophetic ability to see the future, M'Fingal was the town oracle and the leader of the tory faction. His lungs were stronger than his powers of reasoning,

> Yet at town-meetings ev'ry chief
> Pinn'd faith on great M'Fingal's sleeve,
> And as he motion'd, all by rote
> Rais'd sympathetic hands to vote.

Gazettes no sooner printed the news, "But strait he fell to prophesying." The poem opens with M'Fingal's leaving Boston for his native town, feeling that his presence was needed there after a string of British embarrassments beginning with Lexington and Concord. Sermons by Anglican clergymen had made few

44. [John Trumbull], *M'Fingal: A Modern Epic Poem: Canto First; or, The Town-Meeting* (Philadelphia, 1775 [1776]); [John Trumbull], *M'Fingal: A Modern Epic Poem in Four Cantos* (Hartford, 1782), canto 3, l. 117. Canto 1 from the 1776 version was split in half to form cantos 1 and 2 in 1782 (all references hereafter are from the 1782 edition).

Figure 12. A Gentleman Riding into Town as the Deferential Townsfolk Bow before Him.
Drawn by E. Tisdale. M'Fingal, predicting a quick British victory, refers to Abijah White,
who, Trumbull's note explains, "was a representative of Marshfield [Mass.], and was
employed to carry to Boston their famous town-resolves, censuring the Whigs and
reprobating the destruction of the Tea." "He armed himself in as ridiculous military array,
as a second Hudibras, pretending he was afraid he should be robbed of them" (66). The
text reads, "In awful pomp descending down / Bore terror on the factious town" (canto 2).
    The illustration also suggests the opening scene of the poem, where "Great 'Squire
M'Fingal" left Boston "And graced with ensigns of renown, / Steer'd homeward to his
native town" (4). From *The Poetical Works of John Trumbull, LL.D.*, 2 vols. (Hartford,
Conn., 1820), I, facing p. 66. Courtesy, Beinecke Rare Book and Manuscript Library,
Yale University, New Haven, Conn.

converts among the whigs; the "earthly reas'ners," the tory "scriblers" who "Fill'd ev'ry leaf of ev'ry paper" and rose to "The summit of news-paper wit," had also been ignored. M'Fingal's "debate" with Honorious, however, was less a dialogue than a verbal brawl, interrupted by shouting and disorder, finally dissolving into a chaos of voices, "like the variegated gabble / That craz'd the carpenters of Babel." [45]

Honorius and M'Fingal, as Trumbull explained to Adams and Deane, were fictitious characters: they did not allude to any particular individuals but allowed the poet more room for "Invention" and made their points with more "spirit" than would "an unvaried harangue in the Author's own person." The chaotic scene, however, was not a spectacular event, imagined or dramatized, but politics as usual in a New England town meeting: "The Picture of the Townmeeting is drawn from the life, and with as proper lights, shades and Colouring as I could give it, and is I fancy no bad likeness." [46]

> The town, our Hero's scene of action,
> Had long been torn by feuds of faction,
> And as each party's strength prevails,
> It turn'd up diff'rent, heads or tails;
> With constant rattl'ing in a trice
> Show'd various sides as oft as dice:
>
> .   .   .   .
>
> So did this town with stedfast zeal
> Weave cob-webs for the public weal,
> Which when compleated, or before,
> A second vote in pieces tore.
> They met, made speeches full long winded,
> Resolv'd, protested, and rescinded.

Gathered in the meetinghouse, the freemen were likened to a den of thieves in the house of God; as a political body, they resembled the barbarians of Gaul rather than the Roman Senate. An ineffectual moderator stood in the pulpit, and

> Beneath stood voters of all colours,
> Whigs, tories, orators and bawlers,
> With ev'ry tongue in either faction,
> Prepared, like minute-men, for action.

45. [Trumbull], *M'Fingal*, canto 1, ll. 79–80, 107–110, 508, 511, 538–539, canto 2, ll. 795–796.
46. Trumbull to Silas Deane, May 27, 1775, Trumbull to John Adams, Nov. 14, 1775, reprinted in Gimmestad, *John Trumbull*, 81–82, 88.

Figure 13. *Town Meeting*. Shows M'Fingal, with sword raised, as the town meeting turns to chaos after the whig Honorious's speech enrages the tories. From John Trumbull, *M'Fingal: A Modern Epic Poem in Four Cantos* (New York, 1795), first illustrated edition. Courtesy, American Antiquarian Society, Worcester, Mass.

As portrayed by Trumbull's pen, this New England tradition of local oration and personal persuasion was demagoguery, not participatory politics; it was a Babel of bombast and nonsensical noise that had little to do with reason, order, and virtue.[47]

M'Fingal's oracular visions connect him with another of Trumbull's favorite targets: religious enthusiasts, whose prophetic speech claimed supernatural perception and manipulated a gullible public schooled in superstition. Like the second-sighted "Stage-player" (Whitefield) who peered into men's souls, M'Fingal professed to see the future. Like the backwoods preachers who made the country folk tremble at every comet or eclipse, M'Fingal pointed to a meteor and the aurora borealis as signs of impending doom. He also repeated reports of mysterious "or'tors in the air" who rumbled biblical verses from the clouds. All these portents, M'Fingal contended, confirmed his prophetic warning of a swift and merciless tory victory.[48]

M'Fingal the prophetic speaker recalled "the days of antient fame / [when] Prophets and poets were the same." His bardic presence and Delphic certitude contrast sharply with the personal detachment and ironic distance of the poet who tells the epic tale in octosyllabic rhyme. M'Fingal the poet-prophet proclaims a special ability to speak the truth about the future; the neoclassical poet-critic winks at his own artifice, his own poetic fictions and inventions, as he pretends to record the past in writing. To Honorius's earnest but inflated oratory, which gets drowned out by the clamor of the town meeting, Trumbull offers Horace's dictum: "Ridicule often settles a matter of importance more forcefully and effectively than grave severity."[49]

M'Fingal had changed both stylistically and ideologically when it reemerged from the press in 1782. Trumbull had settled in Hartford as a lawyer in 1780 and, within two years, had doubled the length of the poem by writing two

47. [Trumbull], M'Fingal, canto 1, ll. 111–116, 121–126, 153–156.

48. Ibid., canto 2, ll. 555–598.

49. Ibid., canto 1, ll. 71–72. In canto 1, l. 78, M'Fingal is called "The very tripod of his town," and Trumbull's note reminds the reader, "The tripod was a sacred three-legged stool, from which the antient priests uttered their oracles." An earlier, unpublished poem mocked the oracular model of poetic inspiration by describing ancient poets sitting on the sacred tripod over a hole that vented subterranean gasses: "Th' inflation rising from behind, / It came out verse, which went in wind" (printed in Cowie, John Trumbull, 39–40). On the poet's artifice, see [Trumbull], M'Fingal, canto 1, ll. 373–403, a long aside where the poet argues for the accuracy of his transcription, claiming that the muses had recorded every word, and then asks his "critic-brothers" to blame any poetic flaws in the speeches on the speakers. For Horace's dictum, see Satires 1.10.14–15, quoted in Latin on the title page of the 1782 edition of M'Fingal and translated in Edwin T. Bowden, ed., The Satiric Poems of John Trumbull (Austin, Tex., 1962), 217.

Figure 14. M'Fingal at the Liberty Pole. Drawn by E. Tisdale. He is defying the whig crowd preparing to tar and feather him (note the goose being plucked in the lower left). The tory constable, hoisted aloft, has just recanted. Three men sit as a "Committee" on a "Bench of Justice" and decide M'Fingal's punishment. Trumbull's 1820 annotation notes that "an imitation of legal forms was universally practised by the mobs in New-England, in the trial and condemnation of Tories. This marks a curious trait of national character."
From *The Poetical Works of John Trumbull, LL.D.,* 2 vols. (Hartford, Conn., 1820), I, 112n, facing p. 112. Courtesy, Beinecke Rare Book and Manuscript Library, Yale University, New Haven, Conn.

more cantos ("The Liberty Pole" and "The Vision"). Although more broadly humorous, canto 3 is also more thoroughly steeped in literary allusions. The scene at the liberty pole where M'Fingal condemns the "dirtbred patriots" waging war against the rights of property, where he is bested by the "stoutest wrestler on the green" wielding a shovel against his sword, and where, finally, M'Fingal is tarred, feathered, and stuck to the liberty pole like a barnacle to the side of the boat, bristles with references to Homer, Ovid, Virgil, and Milton. Canto 4, "The Vision," is even more deeply mythological and Miltonic. Yet, more noticeable is the shift in the later two cantos' ideological thrust. When M'Fingal denounces paper currency, weak government, and vulgar democracy, his speech is no longer inflected by the unintended ironies and self-defeating absurdities so prevalent in the first half of the poem. From 1775 to 1782, *M'Fingal* evolved from Revolutionary verse propaganda to conservative American literature.[50]

COMPETING IN THE LITERARY MARKETPLACE

The poem that for the next twenty years would be reprinted, excerpted, and even drummed into the heads of schoolchildren by Noah Webster's *Grammatical Institute* was first published in its complete form in early September 1782 by Hudson and Goodwin, Hartford printers of the *Connecticut Courant*. Trumbull assumed the financial risk for 2,024 copies, and Hudson and Goodwin ran weekly advertisements in their newspaper. But the relationship between the poet and the printers goes beyond *M'Fingal* to reveal the changing politics of publishing in the post-Revolutionary era.[51]

The *Courant* under Ebenezer Watson had been a fiercely pro-whig paper whose circulation increased rapidly during the British occupation of New York, quickly surpassing most other papers in North America. When Watson died in 1777, his widow formed a partnership with George Goodwin and a new marriage with Barzillai Hudson, and the *Courant* continued with the same political sympathies but a less personal tone. By the end of the war, and by the time their monopoly on Hartford printing was challenged, Hudson and Goodwin owned interests in two paper mills, had expanded the line of merchandise they offered for sale in the store beneath the print shop, and had published *M'Fingal*

<hr />

50. [Trumbull], *M'Fingal,* canto 3, ll. 130, 358. For discussions of the literary allusions in *M'Fingal,* see Cowie, *John Trumbull,* chap. 7; and Gimmestad, *John Trumbull,* chap. 4.

51. Noah Webster, *A Grammatical Institute of the English Language . . . ,* 3 vols. (Hartford, Conn., 1783); Gimmestad, *John Trumbull,* 102; Cowie, *John Trumbull,* 167.

and Webster's spelling book. When Trumbull denounced two of Hudson and Goodwin's new rivals for selling pirated editions of *M'Fingal*, he was serving his printers' interests as well as his own.[52]

Trumbull's long, unsigned letter appeared on the front page of the *Courant* on January 7, 1783, arguing for copyright laws as a matter of national importance and natural justice. The civilized world valued "works of Literature and Genius," he began, because such works regulated manners and provided "rational entertainment." Foreign nations would form their opinion of the American character not just by looking at "military genius" and "ardour of liberty" but by assessing the literary productions of the United States. No state was more ready to lead the effort to encourage that production than Connecticut, where knowledge and a taste for polite letters had been broadly diffused. The problem, Trumbull wrote, was money. Whereas a dozen years earlier he had argued that the elite's failure to patronize literature highlighted the virtues of republican print, now it was almost the occasion for regret: "As we have in this country no gentlemen of fortune sufficient to maintain [authors] in the sole pursuit of literary studies, it is certainly necessary for the encouragement of Genius, to secure to every author the profits that may arise from the sale of his writings." Yet the need for copyright protection arose from more than circumstantial necessity. It was based upon "a principle of natural justice." "Surely there is no kind of property, in the nature of things, so much our own, as the writings which we originate meerly from our own [creative] imaginations."[53]

What had been a mercantile metaphor for the Correspondent now became a fundamental truth: literature was a commodity produced by individual labor, and it deserved just compensation in the marketplace. "A work of Genius is a work of time," Trumbull wrote, "the effect of long labor, study, and application." When an author "risques both his money and reputation in the publication of works, which cost him much labor in the production, [he] should be entitled to the profits arising from their sale." In the current state of publishing, no printer would offer an author "so much as the common day wages of a laborer" because profits would immediately be drained away by rival editions. The author had to take the financial risk himself, only to find that he was at the mercy of rogue printers out to enrich themselves by injuring and defrauding him.[54]

Concern for profits, reputation, and class prerogative mingled in Trumbull's

52. Smith, *One Hundred Years of Hartford's Courant,* 12, 14–16, 36.

53. *Conn. Courant,* Jan. 7, 1783. The text has "creature," rather than "creative," probably a misprint.

54. Ibid.

attack on the "mean and ungenerous Printer." Such a man lacked the refined taste and liberal education even to appreciate or understand the work he stole, "reprinting it in so mangled and inelegant a manner, that the author must be ashamed of the edition." Hardly rallying to the defrauded author's support, members of the reading public were all too quick to buy a cheaper edition, even those readers who had originally subscribed for one of the author's books.[55]

Gone was the hope that anonymous contributions to the public sphere would remain anonymous. No rhetorical masks could shield the identity of the author, and therefore the reception of the work inevitably affected his personal standing within society: "He is known and stands forth the butt at which all the arrows of criticism and censure are aimed." If his performance fails to please, "he stands on record, as a dull writer[,] the object of ridicule for a mistake of his abilities." The republican ideal of a forum for debate without social conflict had evaporated. Even if the author's work succeeds,

> the world immediately divide[s] into parties. . . . Those whose sentiments, or practices he has opposed, are at once his enemies, and employ their whole endeavours to blast his reputation. . . . If he attempt humour and ridicule, he is at once dreaded and hated as a satirist, and every witty passage in his writings shall be wrested and distorted to sound a charge of irreligion and profligacy.

The writer's attempt to use the reader's inevitable misreadings to his advantage, and the satirist's artful dodge behind literary conventions, would no longer avail.[56]

Trumbull's complaint acknowledged the partisan atmosphere that the *Courant* itself tried to deny. Although the *Courant* kept up its nonpartisan "open to all" rhetoric until Thomas Jefferson's election, it quickly became a mouthpiece for the state's socially conservative mercantile establishment after the Revolution. Bavil Webster, one of the rival printers who pirated *M'Fingal,* began publishing a dissenting paper called *Freeman's Chronicle* on September 1, 1783. The *Chronicle* endorsed a popular convention in Middletown convened to denounce the elite Society of the Cincinnati and bonus pay for military officers. The *Courant* condemned the convention, prompting some delegates to call for a boycott of the paper. As Trumbull recalled in his memoir:

> In Connecticut, mobs were raised to prevent the officers from receiving their certificates for the five years' pay. A self-constituted Convention as-

55. Ibid.
56. Ibid.

sembled to second the views of the populace, and for that purpose, to effect a revolution in the State, and fill every office with the leaders of disorganization. . . . A considerable proportion of the people of Connecticut were prepared to join in a general opposition to government, and involve the country in the horrors of civil war. The friends of order, justice and regular authority, endeavoured to counteract this spirit by every effort in their power—by remonstrance, argument, ridicule and satire.

The decade's greatest debate, of course, was over the new federal Constitution. The *Courant* neglected to publish Antifederalist letters or essays, all the while maintaining its "impartiality" in the face of criticism by another rival paper, the *American Mercury*. With this nonpartisan partisanship, the *Courant* strained the notion of an open republican press as a vehicle for disinterested debate in ways that its exclusion of tory opinion had not, for now the dissenters could point to the Revolution and their own patriotic pedigree.[57]

Along with his printer, the *Courant*'s Barzillai Hudson (another self-styled friend of order, justice, and authority), Trumbull entered local politics in 1784, when Hartford was incorporated as a city and both men were elected to the Common Council. M'Fingal was called up for duty in the partisan battles too. The *New-Haven Gazette* in 1786 and the *Massachusetts Centinel* in 1788 reprinted passages from his speech to the rabble at the liberty pole to ridicule Daniel Shays and other dirt-stained democrats. In 1786, Trumbull and his circle of Hartford Wits published a series of some fame known as "American Antiquities" (which included "The Anarchiad"), a literary vehicle for partisan attacks upon local politicians and national symptoms of "anarchy." He also wrote some dull and dignified essays for the *Courant* in 1793 under the title "The American," which expressed starchy disapproval of Jefferson, Thomas Paine, and the French Revolution. Connecticut's Jeffersonian opposition finally turned satire against the satirist with a character known as "M'Fingal, a Poet,—late Student with J. Adams" in a popular play called *Federalism Triumphant in the Steady Habits of Connecticut Alone* (1802). By this time, however, Trumbull "declined any interference in the politics of the state" because he had been appointed as a judge of the superior court, and he believed "that the character of a partizan and political writer was inconsistent with the station of a judge."[58]

57. [Trumbull], "Memoir," *Poetical Works*, I, 19–20. Smith, *One Hundred Years of Hartford's Courant*, 59–65; Morse, *Connecticut Newspapers*, 19.

58. Cowie, *John Trumbull*, 192–194. The first of twelve installments of what was entitled "American Antiquities" appeared in *New-Haven Gazette, and the Connecticut Magazine*,

The same parties who waged ideological warfare over the meaning of the new Republic continued to fight economic battles over print. Connecticut did pass a copyright act in 1783, but charges of pirating and monopolization continued to fly back and forth between the state's printers. The law would prove to be more helpful to writers like Webster and geographer Jedidiah Morse than it would be to Trumbull, who gained fame from *M'Fingal* but because of illness and his public duties produced no more major works. When he published his *Poetical Works* in 1820, he was still complaining about the way that *M'Fingal,* soon after its publication in 1782, had become "the prey of every bookseller and printer, who chose to appropriate it to his own benefit." "Among more than thirty different impressions, one only, at any subsequent time, was published with the permission, or even the knowledge of the writer; and the poem remained the property of newsmongers, hawkers, pedlars and petty chapmen."[59]

When Trumbull had first published his call for a copyright law in 1783, the commercialization of the literary marketplace of print was just beginning. Trumbull acknowledged the lack of an American system of aristocratic literary patronage and seemed to want to become a "market professional" able to negotiate contracts and royalties with a publisher. If authors had to continue to take the financial risk of publication upon themselves, he argued, they should at least be guaranteed the right to profit from their work as independent producers. Trumbull was not, however, espousing an artisanal ideology, equating the professional writer to carpenters and cobblers. The tension was between writing as a disinterested contribution to the public from an anonymous pen and writing as an author's property, produced by his labor and genius, linked to his personal reputation, and up for sale in a competitive marketplace. Trumbull's complaint anticipated the liberal public sphere, which prized the consumption of literary works as luxury items and encouraged a private and imaginary (rather than public and actual) participation in the civic order. In the

---

Oct. 26, 1786, purporting to be excerpts from an ancient epic entitled "The Anarchiad." The pieces were written by Trumbull, David Humphreys, Joel Barlow, and Lemuel Hopkins, and also ran in the *Conn. Courant* and other papers. They were first published in book form as *The Anarchiad: A New England Poem,* ed. Luther G. Riggs (New Haven, Conn., 1861). See Howard, *Connecticut Wits,* chap. 7; and J. K. Van Dover, "The Design of Anarchy: *The Anarchiad,* 1786–1787," *Early American Literature,* XXIV (1989), 237–247. See also [John Trumbull], "The American," *Conn. Courant,* Jan. 7–Apr. 17, 1793. [Leonard Chester], *Federalism Triumphant in the Steady Habits of Connecticut Alone . . .* ([New York], 1802), is discussed in Cowie, *John Trumbull,* 208n. Trumbull commented upon the "character of a partizan" in his "Memoir," *Poetical Works,* I, 22.

59. [Trumbull], "Memoir," *Poetical Works,* I, 18–19.

terms of the civic forum the Correspondent tried to build, Trumbull's 1783 letter certainly articulated a "post-republican" conception of public discourse.[60]

RHETORICAL POSSIBILITIES

John Trumbull was no more the innovative creator of new modes of discourse than Hudson and Goodwin were the inventors of commercial publishing. He was a skillful writer who adopted rhetorical strategies and new modes of print to cultivate a new, politicized reading public. The different conceptions of public writing that his work employs did not cause the printing business to change any more than changes in printing produced these new conceptions. Medium and message mutually influenced each other: a newspaper like the *Courant,* initially a local vehicle for commercial and miscellaneous information, expanded when it became a medium of political discussion and cultural criticism; a poem like *M'Fingal* was perceived differently as a freely circulating political pamphlet than as a literary commodity. It is in this relation to the growth of Connecticut's press and the development of its literary culture that Trumbull's work reveals some of the complexity of the transformation of public discourse in the Revolutionary era.

In Trumbull's works and career, we can at least glimpse the three constructions of the public sphere described by writers following Jürgen Habermas. By satirizing prophetic oratory and the New England town meeting's political community of speakers in *M'Fingal,* Trumbull glanced back to traditional conceptions of face-to-face communication. By working to establish a civic forum in the local press with the Correspondent column, he promoted the ideals of republican print. By complaining about copyright and the author's control over his literary property, he anticipated the liberal literary marketplace. However, that Trumbull did all of this in a dozen years suggests that these traditional, republican, and liberal constructions of public writing—along with a conception of literary practice drawn from the sociable community of polite

60. Raymond Williams distinguished between different forms of authorial production in *The Sociology of Culture* (New York, 1982), 44–51; Lawrence Buell applied them to late-eighteenth- and early-nineteenth-century America in *New England Literary Culture: From Revolution through Renaissance* (Cambridge, Mass., 1986), 57. Cathy N. Davidson, in *Revolution and the Word: The Rise of the Novel in America* (New York, 1986), 34, sees the problem of the writer's self-definition in the late eighteenth century as a vacillation between artisanal republicanism and the older notion of the gentleman author. On the liberal public sphere and its literary aesthetic, see Warner, *Letters of the Republic,* 114, 142, 172–176.

letters—should be considered less as successive stages or distinct epochs than as overlapping and even concurrent possibilities. But we need to be as cautious of the notion of "concurrent possibilities" as of "discontinuous epochs." After the rise of Grub Street and English coffeehouse culture in the late seventeenth century, English-speaking authors and readers everywhere did not necessarily have all these options available to them. Hypothetical rhetorical options can become actual rhetorical strategies only if the local cultural and socioeconomic circumstances of print production and public speech are right. A Connecticut writer could not have used the rhetoric of a republican civic forum in the local press before 1755, for example, because no Connecticut newspapers were yet being printed.

The genteel community of polite letters, the political community of speakers, the periodical press's civic forum, and the literary marketplace were not unrelated discursive spaces. They constructed overlapping audiences that the Revolutionary-era writer learned to address in different ways. After moving to Hartford in June 1781, Trumbull helped to establish a literary society not unlike the social circle he had enjoyed in college. He called it a "friendly club" that "assembled once a week for the discussion of questions on proposed subjects, legal, philosophical and political," and he described himself as "one of its most active members." It was the members of this club who urged Trumbull to revise and complete *M'Fingal* and then circulated a subscription for the poem, which in 1820 Trumbull would proudly describe as having survived "the ordeal of criticism" both in England and America to be enjoyed by a broader reading public for more than forty years. The installments of "American Antiquities" were written collaboratively in 1786 by club members Trumbull, David Humphreys, Joel Barlow, and Lemuel Hopkins, initially for newspapers in Hartford and New Haven. These anonymous publications were addressed to the political turmoil of the moment and had, Trumbull noted, "considerable influence on the public taste and opinions; and by the boldness of their satire . . . [had] checked and intimidated the leaders of disorganization and infidel philosophy." The political discussions of the Friendly Club, no doubt, also aided Trumbull when he served in the state legislature in 1792 and "took an active and influencial part in their debates and deliberations," especially those concerning the alteration of the Yale College charter. Club conversation, therefore, helped define the contours of legislative debate, newspaper satire, and American poetry.[61]

The different notions of authorship, literature, and audience suggested by polite society, republican politics, and literary publication, however, did not

61. [Trumbull], "Memoir," *Poetical Works,* I, [7], 18, 21.

coexist without tension. In his 1770 *Essay*, Trumbull had to work hard to disassociate polite letters from idleness, luxury, and effeminacy and to identify them with martial vigor and public virtue so that belles lettres would appear useful and advantageous to the community at large. The different motives of the republican propagandist and the literary author were also demonstrated by the two versions of *M'Fingal*: the first, in 1775, he wrote to "crush the efforts of the Tory party and to prepare the public mind for the declaration of independence"; the second, in 1782, the poet described as his intellectual property, the expression of his genius. The relationship between the writer and the writing also differed as a text moved from the literary circle to the newspaper column to the bound volume. Circulated among local friends and acquaintances, an unsigned manuscript would nevertheless carry the imprint of its author. Published in the newspaper under a pseudonym for a larger regional audience, the text's paternity was supposed to be irrelevant, but anonymity was difficult to maintain, and critics would often find out who wrote a particular piece and then attack the writer's character rather than his arguments. Politically biased literary critics who did not know the author personally could also use information about him to savage a literary work. That was illustrated, according to Trumbull, when British journals showered him with "obloquy and contempt" only after they discovered that *M'Fingal* had not been written by an Oxford scholar or a British officer but by a native of New England. Yet, Trumbull ultimately decided that the broader literary public sometimes needed more rather than less biographical information about an author. Even after the name of *M'Fingal*'s author had become generally known in the United States, Trumbull wrote,

> many false anecdotes, and several erroneous accounts of his life, have been printed by those, who had no other information, than rumour and hearsay. Hundreds of essays have been charged upon his pen, containing principles which he never held, abuse on persons whom he respected, and low attempts at humour, which would have disgraced the scurrility of Peter Pindar. In a word, to him have been ascribed, as he once complained, 'Jests he ne'er utter'd, deeds he ne'er atchiev'd, / Rhymes he ne'er wrote, and lives (thank heaven) he never lived.'[62]

After the turn of the century, Trumbull stayed out of print, confining his wit to the Friendly Club and to the parlors of Hartford's elite. In 1819, his political career ended as a Republican purge of Federalists forced him from the bench. The following year he published his two-volume *Poetical Works*, which con-

62. Ibid., I, [7], 8, 17.

tained some verse that had circulated in manuscript during his Yale days. He also included his brief memoir, which tethered the poems to the name and proper character of the poet and helped secure a literary reputation. Yet, when restored to their original eighteenth-century context, Trumbull's works show how the overlap of discursive models is accentuated—and the transformation of public discourse especially compressed—in Connecticut, with its powerful traditional culture of preaching and the Anglicized gentry's taste for belles lettres merging with the rapid development of printing and literary production during the Revolutionary era. Connecticut's local press blossomed in the 1760s, an ambitious literati emerged in the 1770s, and competing entrepreneurial publishers were waging economic and political battles by the 1780s and 1790s. Perhaps focusing on Trumbull's work and the growth of the Connecticut press through the Revolutionary era exaggerates how suddenly and thoroughly the politics of writing and publishing were transformed. But one writer's essays and poems, and the presses that published them, do show how cultural patterns drawn from the New England town, genteel society, an ideal republic of letters, and the partisan marketplace of a commercializing America overlapped, competed, and constructed different roles for writers and readers in a Revolutionary age.

CHAPTER 7

Reawakening the Public Mind

Timothy Dwight and the Rhetoric of New England

Two years after John Trumbull delivered his *Essay on the Use and Advantages of the Fine Arts* at Yale's commencement in 1770, his friend and sometime collaborator Timothy Dwight stood in the same spot and told his audience that he was going to do something novel. He would discuss the excellence of the Bible—not its "purity and holiness," but its excellence as "fine writing" that "finds the shortest passage to the human soul" by appealing to the imagination through imagery and metaphor. He held up the "sacred Penmen" as exemplary writers and the apostle Paul, with his "unstudied language of affection," as the unequaled Christian orator. In the years ahead, as Trumbull wrote his essays and satires, Dwight studied the biblical power of eloquence and especially noted the ability of a speaker or writer "to suit his addresses to time, place, and audience." Whereas Trumbull tried to set the ground rules for public discourse, Dwight crafted a figurative language drawn from Augustan literature, republican politics, and New England biblicism that tried to establish the meaning of the Revolutionary experience.[1]

Dwight has proved a convenient transitional figure for historians writing about eighteenth- and early-nineteenth-century America. A grandson of Jonathan Edwards, he lived through the Revolution and glorified America; a conservative New England clergyman looking back to the Puritans, he wrote about evangelizing the new American frontier. Historians have called him a key figure in the consecration of America as a redeemer nation. Yet, for all the hope-

1. [John Trumbull], *An Essay on the Use and Advantages of the Fine Arts* ... (New Haven, Conn., 1770); [Timothy Dwight], *A Dissertation on the History, Eloquence, and Poetry of the Bible; Delivered at the Public Commencement, at New-Haven* (New Haven, Conn., 1772), 3, 4, 5, 10, 11.

ful expansiveness associated with Dwight, he has also become a representative Federalist crank, a man whose "mind was closed as tight as his study windows in January," in Vernon Parrington's memorable phrase. Kenneth Silverman saw Dwight's writing alternating between "total hopes and total despairs" and explained it as the expression of a Manichaean temperament. Dwight "lived only on birthday or doomsday," Silverman argued. "For each occasion he owned a separate voice: for doomsday, the language of the Puritan Jeremiads: for birthdays, the couplets and balanced sentences of neo-Classic verse and prose."[2]

Understanding how Dwight's rhetoric tried to shape the moral order involves more than hearing the "two voices" of a divided temperament. Discussions of Dwight have often drawn freely from his poems and sermons, as if differences in genre or rhetorical context had little bearing on the thought being expressed. Other works have kept the theologian too separate from the poet. A fine study of Dwight's politics and theology declared Dwight's poetry writing "incidental" to his career. An exposition of "literary Augustanism" has countered that, for Revolutionary poets like Dwight, poetry was a crucial attempt to construct an ordered world in the midst of ideological crisis—yet these insights are not applied to Dwight's prose. Focusing on Dwight's rhetorical strategies as he moved through a new world of public discourse can better illuminate the interconnections between poetry, politics, and theology in his work.[3]

Dwight saw the rising popularity of literature and journalism as an oppor-

2. Ernest Lee Tuveson, *Redeemer Nation: The Idea of America's Millennial Role* (Chicago, 1968), 103; Sacvan Bercovitch, *The American Jeremiad* (Madison, Wis., 1978), 129; Vernon Louis Parrington, *Main Currents in American Thought: An Interpretation of American Literature from the Beginnings to 1920*, I, *The Colonial Mind, 1620–1800* (New York, 1927), 361; Kenneth Silverman, *Timothy Dwight* (New York, 1969), ix, x, 152. Silverman's perceptive but brief study did not examine these two rhetorical voices in isolation and is the best discussion on Dwight's writing and thought since Leon Howard, *The Connecticut Wits* (Chicago, 1943). For Dwight as a Yale minister and educator, see Roland H. Bainton, *Yale and the Ministry: A History of Education for the Christian Ministry at Yale from the Founding in 1701* (New York, 1957), chap. 6; Ralph Henry Gabriel, *Religion and Learning at Yale: The Church of Christ in the College and University, 1757–1957* (New Haven, Conn., 1958), chaps. 3–4. The standard biography is still Charles E. Cuningham, *Timothy Dwight, 1752–1817: A Biography* (New York, 1942).

3. Stephen E. Berk, *Calvinism versus Democracy: Timothy Dwight and the Origins of American Evangelical Orthodoxy* (Hamden, Conn., 1974), 24; William C. Dowling, *Poetry and Ideology in Revolutionary Connecticut* (Athens, Ga., 1990). See also Robert D. Arner, "The Connecticut Wits," in Everett Emerson, ed., *American Literature, 1764–1789: The Revolutionary Years* (Madison, Wis., 1977); A. Owen Aldridge, *Early American Literature: A Comparatist Approach* (Princeton, N.J., 1982), chap. 6; Emory Elliot, *Revolutionary Writers: Literature and Authority in the New Republic, 1725–1810* (New York, 1982), chap. 2.

tunity for learned men to instruct the public in new ways. Newspaper essays and patriotic poems could function as moral and political catechisms in a society where, because the people were sovereign, public happiness depended on the broad diffusion of knowledge and the inculcation of virtue. In the 1770s and 1780s, his own publications reworked literary language and biblical images to shape a myth of America's rising glory. But in the last dozen years of the century, Dwight turned from the promise of America to the traditions and institutions of New England, fashioning the New England way into an ideological weapon. As the century drew to a close, Dwight, who became Yale's president in 1795, began to fear that French Revolutionary atheists were pumping propaganda into America to corrupt the minds of its youth. The battle against the contagion of French infidelity, he argued, had to be fought on several fronts: preaching in local revivals, writing in periodicals, and distributing Bibles, religious tracts, and hymns. While French "Jacobinism" and sectional rivalry were threatening the national power of New England Federalists, in Connecticut the Standing Order of magistrates and Congregational ministers that his Puritan forebears had built was being attacked by religious dissenters and ambitious politicians who called for a new state constitution. Learned and pious men like Dwight who spoke and wrote to instruct the "public mind," hoping to restore a more coherent moral order, competed with other voices and had to find ways to reach different audiences.[4]

Dwight began his annual summer travels through New England and New York in 1796 and experienced some of that complexity. But what he saw and heard only further convinced him of the superiority of New England's social and cultural institutions—its clusters of middling family farms, state-supported local churches and schoolhouses, and tradition of learned leadership in church and state. For Dwight, the New England way was both the "true

4. I am following Richard Slotkin's distinction between "myth" and "ideology" in *The Fatal Environment: The Myth of the Frontier in the Age of Industrialization, 1800–1890* (Middletown, Conn., 1985), 19, 22. A myth "implies a theory of cause and effect, a theory of history; but these implications are only rarely articulated as objects of criticism, since their operation is masked." A myth does not set out the logical connections of an argument; "it projects models of good or heroic behavior" and supports them with "the powerful force of tradition and habits of feeling and thought." Ideological language often appears when the premises of a mythic structure are no longer taken for granted. "Ideology proper" relies heavily on persuasive appeal and provides a firmer base for programs of action. As appeals are made more explicit, the logical connections of past, present, and future are more systematically expressed. See also Slotkin, "Myth and the Production of History," in Sacvan Bercovitch and Myra Jehlen, eds., *Ideology and Classic American Literature* (Cambridge, 1986), 70–90.

means of establishing public happiness" in this world and the best means for preparing communities of men and women to receive the Spirit and look forward to the next world. If America was rising to millennial glory, only New England manifested the means through which that glory could be obtained. So Dwight preached the faith to his Yale boys, for they would need to reawaken New England before New England could awaken America and America could redeem the world.

THE MYTH OF AMERICA

The Dwights, like the Trumbulls, had their stories to tell about their child prodigy. Young Timothy, it seems, was studying Latin grammar during breaks in his regular lessons at age six, was reading through his father's library at ten, and was more than ready for Yale when he entered at thirteen. Yet his early years at college exemplified prodigious industry rather than budding genius. His daily fourteen hours of study would begin long before dawn, after four hours of sleep, with a hundred lines of Homer. He practiced penmanship during his lunch break, allowed himself only twelve mouthfuls of vegetables for dinners, and then studied by candlelight into the night. Coupled with a touch of smallpox, this regimen nearly killed him and permanently damaged his eyes. After 1775, he had to dictate his works to amanuenses. For Timothy the orator, writing was, quite literally, merely the representation of speech.[5]

Dwight's *Dissertation on the History, Eloquence, and Poetry of the Bible* (1772) was his first chance to distinguish himself before the learned and powerful of Connecticut. In the argument he presented, the criteria of excellence for each of his three categories (history, oratory, and poetry) were based upon the effect produced upon or within the individual reader. He recommended, moreover, that historical and poetic writing ought to be combined to fuse moral instruction to the reader's experience of the sublime. The biblical chronicle of God's dealings with Israel, for example, was important in its own right as a series of historical facts and as a sequence of moral lessons. But to "catch the attention

5. On Dwight's youth, see Cuningham, *Dwight*, 14–44. In later life, Dwight would define "genius" as "the power of making mental efforts." See Dwight, *Travels in New England and New York* (1821–1822), ed. Barbara Miller Solomon, 4 vols. (Cambridge, Mass., 1969), IV, 219. Ezra Stiles commented sarcastically to himself about how Dwight composed his election sermon by dictating while he sat "wrapt up in Sentiment with his Eyes shut absorbed in fictitious Contemplation and Study." See Stiles, *The Literary Diary of Ezra Stiles, D.D., L.L.D. President of Yale College,* 3 vols., ed. Franklin Bowditch Dexter (New York, 1901), III, 393n.

of the Reader," the scriptural writers knew to appeal to "the earthly part of the human soul" in order to "extend its regard" to the ethereal plane. Therefore, they added poetic passages and dramatic scenes to the narrative, making the "General History" less "dry and unentertaining" by focusing on the particular. Once drawn into the work, the "Contemplator may find most excellent patterns" of human nature and divine power. If poetry made history lively, history gave "weight and dignity to Poetry." So did prophecy, which in the Bible was the true chronicle of the future, just as the Bible's history was the true record of the past.[6]

Dwight's first important poem, *America; or, A Poem on the Settlement of the British Colonies; Addressed to the Friends of Freedom, and Their Country,* first written in 1771 and published in 1780, followed the precepts that the *Dissertation* had set out. It demonstrated how history and prophecy united in visionary poetics to become the vehicle for an overarching rhetorical intent: to communicate sublime and ennobling ideals to the reader. *America* looks backward to "the Settlement of the British Colonies"; it also invites "the Friends of Freedom" to share a vision of America's happy future. The myth of America constructed by this "rising glory" poem urges Americans to find their heroic identity in the struggle occurring *between* the idealized past and the prophesied future that the poem itself represents.[7]

The poem begins with the speaker's turning away from the stock images of the pastoral to contemplate the idea called "America":

> From sylvan shades, cool bowers and fragrant gales,
> Green hills and murm'ring Streams and flowery vales,
> My soul ascends of nobler themes to sing;
> AMERICA shall wake the sounding string.

In the next thirty-two lines, the speaker describes a land that was dark and barbarous until the arrival of Christopher Columbus. Settlers under Walter Raleigh and William Penn and colonists in New England and Georgia survive "the horrors of the desert" and transform the "dreary Wilderness" into peace-

---

6. [Dwight], *Dissertation,* 5–6, 7, 16. Dwight's rhetorical theory was greatly influenced by Henry Home, Lord Kames, whose *Elements of Criticism* (Edinburgh, 1762) appeared in New Haven in 1762. See Howard, *Connecticut Wits,* chaps. 1, 3. Dwight's later opinions on rhetoric are preserved in one of his student's notebooks. See Vincent Freimarck, "Rhetoric at Yale in 1807," American Philosophical Society, *Proceedings,* CX (Philadelphia, 1966), 235–255.

7. [Timothy Dwight], *America; or, A Poem on the Settlement of the British Colonies; Addressed to the Friends of Freedom, and Their Country; by a Gentleman Educated at Yale-College* (New Haven, Conn., [1780]).

ful communities through their "Labour fearless." After reviewing the suffering and heroism of the Seven Years' War, and a peace secured by the arm of the Almighty, the speaker builds through a description of prosperous towns, commercial expansion, and the spread of liberty, religion, and justice to his concluding apostrophe:

> O Land supremely blest! to thee tis given
> To taste the choicest joys of bounteous heaven;
> Thy rising Glory shall expand its rays,
> And lands and times unknown rehearse thine endless praise.[8]

At this point, the speaker has gone too far. He has gone beyond chronicling the past, and his "guiding fancy" has begun to speculate on the bright, bustling future that ought to follow a secure peace. Here his reverie ceases, and he finds himself back "in a lonely vale, with glooms o'erspread," where "Deep silence" reigns. The colonies' struggles with Britain following the defeat of France are represented by only the movement from the potentially prosperous community to the lonely vale, from light to darkness, from "endless praise" to "Deep silence." The historical telos that the poet's vision of the past had begun and his fancy had completed actually remains unfinished, and America's future glory remains uncertain.[9]

At the last moment, a radiant figure carrying a scepter marked "Freedom" makes a timely arrival and completes the poem and the myth of America with nearly one hundred lines of prophecy. Freedom explains that her heroes shall triumph after a terrible battle. Peace, Religion, History, and the Arts will follow as America grows in power and glory. New Columbuses shall sail to every region on the globe and fill their vessels with the treasures of the earth. "Hail Land of light and joy!" Freedom exclaims, matching the first speaker's earlier apostrophe,

> thy power shall grow
> Far as the seas, which round thy regions flow;
> Through earth's wide realms thy glory shall extend,
> And savage nations at thy scepter bend.[10]

Like the first speaker, Freedom draws upon the neoclassical motifs of *translatio imperii* and *translatio studii,* the movement of empire and culture to the West. But in the poem's last fourteen lines, she invokes biblical eschatology and

8. Ibid., 3, 4, 5, 9.
9. Ibid., 9.
10. Ibid., 10, 11.

points to the millennium of earthly happiness connected to Christ's Second Coming. After American culture and commerce have blissfully engulfed the earth, "Then, then an heavenly kingdom shall descend," and the Savior's glory shall reign triumphant until the last trumpet of the Judgment Day. The poem had begun with the soul's poetic ascension to a noble theme, and it ends as "God's happy children mount to worlds above, / Drink streams of purest joy and taste immortal love." [11]

The poem does *not* explicitly link the Revolutionary War to the apocalyptic struggle that Freedom foretells, nor does it link the "Friends of Freedom" addressed in the poem's title to Freedom's "Heroes" who battle in the poem. In other words, the poem does not claim that the Revolution would usher in the millennial age. Though published in 1780, Dwight had first drafted it in 1771. Yet, the 1780 version had not been revised to assign meaning to the Stamp Act crisis, to Revolutionary events, or to the America that Independence would create within "the stream of ever rolling time." The poem's first speaker surveys the past from pre-Columbian darkness to 1763; the radiant figure unfolds an unspecified future. The poet and his audience occupy the lonely vale, the interpretive silence of the time between past and future, history and prophecy. The meaning of "America" would be created by those readers who could ascend with the poet to praise a noble past and could, as Freedom's friends, share her vision of the future. [12]

Dwight's 1776 *Valedictory Address* to Yale seniors followed the same pattern. The "deduction of reason" and the declaration of the Scriptures both strongly indicated that America would be the site of God's millennial kingdom, he declared, and he focused on the non-scriptural arguments for America's rise as a glorious Christian empire. But then he paused to explain why, "in this description of America, I have mentioned several things as present, whose existence is future."

11. Ibid., 12. On millennialism, see James West Davidson, *The Logic of Millennial Thought: Eighteenth-Century New England* (New Haven, Conn., 1977); Nathan O. Hatch, *The Sacred Cause of Liberty: Republican Thought and the Millennium in Revolutionary New England* (New Haven, Conn., 1977); John F. Berens, *Providence and Patriotism in Early America* (Charlottesville, Va., 1978); Stephen A. Marini, *Radical Sects of Revolutionary New England* (Cambridge, Mass., 1982); Ruth H. Bloch, *Visionary Republic: Millennial Themes in American Thought, 1756–1800* (Cambridge, 1985).

12. Dwight, *America*, 10. Eric Wertheimer, in "Commencement Ceremonies: History and Identity in 'The Rising Glory of America,' 1771 and 1786," *Early American Literature,* XXIX (1994), 35–58, notes that, in the 1771 version of the rising glory poem by Philip Freneau and Hugh Henry Brackenridge (in contrast to the 1786 version), "the uncertainties of what would result as America rose are overwhelming" (53).

The reason is, that with respect to the end, which I propose in this description, the distinction is immaterial. For our actions ought all to be inspired, and directed by a comprehensive regard to this scene of glory. . . . It is here described to you, that you may not be ignorant or regardless of that great whole, of which each of you is a part.

The history lesson and the glimpse into the glorious future are means to a rhetorical end: to motivate present action.[13]

For Dwight the poetic mythmaker, the specifics of millennial prophecy were secondary to rendering a sublime experience to fire the imagination and motivate behavior. He used biblical history in similar ways in his most ambitious work, the Miltonic, eleven-book *Conquest of Canaan*. His preface announced that he had taken the liberty to rearrange and relocate various events in the Old Testament history of Joshua and the Israelites. Historical accuracy was clearly subordinated to his primary rhetorical intention: to "furnish the fairest opportunities of exhibiting the agreeable, the novel, the moral, the pathetic, and the sublime." His epic would represent timeless ideals like godly heroism and virtue; his characters would display "such manners, as are removed from the peculiarities of any age, or country, and might belong to the amiable and virtuous, of every age." Though epic poetry in the sublime style had fallen from fashion in England, Dwight hoped that his countrymen's recent experience would prepare them to appreciate it.[14]

Dwight explained in a footnote that in 1776 he had "annexed" to a draft of the poem "comparisons" to Revolutionary War heroes "to indulge the Author's own emotions of regard to the persons named in them." But readers in 1785 pointed to many more parallels and read the five thousand heroic couplets about biblical Israel as an allegory for recent American experience. The allegorical reading irritated Dwight. He had announced in his preface that he had chosen "a subject, in which his country had no national interest." Dwight did not want the new American nation to look at Israel and see itself behind the flimsy mask of art. An eleven-book allegorical link between Israel and America, he wrote to Noah Webster, would be a tedious exercise; furthermore, he insisted, it was absurd to allegorize the conquest of one country with the de-

13. [Timothy Dwight], *A Valedictory Address to the Young Gentlemen Who Commenced Bachelors of Arts at Yale-College, July 25, 1776* (New Haven, Conn., [1776]), 14, 15.

14. Timothy Dwight, *The Conquest of Canaan; A Poem, in Eleven Books* (Hartford, Conn., 1785), preface. On Dwight's intentions and Philip Freneau's criticism of this poem, see John P. McWilliams, Jr., *The American Epic: Transforming a Genre, 1770–1860* (New York, 1989), 43–53.

fense of another. The *Conquest* was not supposed to link America and Israel as sacred "types" within God's chronology of redemptive history, nor was the poet merely dressing American heroes in ancient costumes as a dramatic device. The poem was intended to be an imaginative meditation upon a biblical story that encouraged American readers to contemplate the sublime ideals of a Christian republic.[15]

Not surprisingly, in 1785 Dwight's rhetorical intentions were misread. During the Revolution, the links between Israel, America, and the millennial kingdom were continually made but rarely scrutinized. In the 1770s, Dwight's Revolutionary rhetoric and millennial message sounded nearly the same whether he was delivering a graduation speech, composing songs for the military camps, preaching to soldiers, or writing poetry. He blurred much of the distinction between the poet's license to use prophetic imagery and a preacher's contemporary application of scriptural prophecy. To an age anxious to understand Revolutionary change within the narrative of redemptive history, however, that distinction was an important one.[16]

As the war ended, some clergymen tried to cool the millennial zeal that wartime rhetoric had inflamed and deflate some of the overblown comparisons between the "New Israel" and the Old. In his 1785 election sermon, Samuel Wales reminded his audience that the ancient Israelites "were under a dispen-

15. Dwight, *Conquest*, 3, note for l. 76; Dwight to Webster on allegory is quoted in Silverman, *Timothy Dwight*, 31. Mason I. Lowance, Jr., *The Language of Canaan: Metaphor and Symbol in New England from the Puritans to the Transcendentalists* (Cambridge, Mass., 1980), 4–5, distinguished between the "type" and the "trope" as modes of representation. "The trope was a Platonic representation of one thing by another." The trope primarily represents abstractions, and "the essential relation between [it] and that which it represents involves no historical continuity." In contrast, the type "exists in the historical context of time, and its relation to the substance it represents is that of foreshadowing, or adumbration." Lowance also acknowledged the many "shades of grey between these two extremes" of type and trope and was sensitive to how each generation struggled to rewrite the rules distinguishing one from the other. See also Erich Auerbach, "Figura," *Scenes from the Drama of European Literature: Six Essays* (New York, 1959), 11–78; Ursula Brumm, *American Thought and Religious Typology* (New Brunswick, N.J., 1970); Sacvan Bercovitch, ed., *Typology and Early American Literature* (n.p., 1972); Joseph A. Galdon, *Typology and Seventeenth-Century Literature* (The Hague, 1975); Earl Miner, ed., *Literary Uses of Typology from the Late Middle Ages to the Present* (Princeton, N.J., 1977); and the introductions by Wallace E. Anderson and Mason I. Lowance, Jr., in Jonathan Edwards, *Typological Writings,* ed. Anderson and Lowance, in Perry Miller et al., eds., *The Works of Jonathan Edwards,* XI (New Haven, Conn., 1993).

16. Donald Weber discusses the anxiety of interpretation in *Rhetoric and History in Revolutionary New England* (New York, 1988).

sation of grace different from ours. . . . National blessings are not promised, and national judgments are not threatened under the gospel in like manner." Then Wales turned to the millennial language of America's rising glory:

> It has lately become very fashionable to prophesy about the future of this country; its astonishing progress in science, in wealth, in population and grandeur. . . . Such representations may perhaps be beautiful in poetry and declamation, but cannot with equal propriety be admitted, in an unqualified sense, into serious and didactic prose.

Even Ezra Stiles, in the soaring optimism of *The United States Elevated to Glory and Honor* (1783), had been careful to qualify his "prophetic zeal," clearly marking his rhetorical shift from "serious and didactic prose" to poetic exclamation by quoting from Joel Barlow's epic *Vision of Columbus*. Stiles and, more explicitly, Wales recognized the need for clearer rhetorical boundaries within the prophetic and metaphorical "language of Canaan." [17]

The introduction to Dwight's next major work, *Greenfield Hill: A Poem in Seven Parts* (1794), specified his rhetorical intention and defended literary mythmaking. "Poetry may not, perhaps, produce greater effects in promoting the prosperity of mankind, than philosophy," he wrote. But where truth required few proofs and arguments, "and only needs to be set in a strong and affecting light,"

> Poetry appears to be as advantageous an instrument of making useful impressions, as can be easily conceived. It will be read by many persons, who would scarcely look at a logical discussion; by most readers it will be more deeply felt, and more lastingly remembered.

Dwight's contrast between poetry and philosophy (or "logical discussion") derives from the distinction between rhetorical appeals to the head and the heart, a distinction that had been formed by a tradition combining classical rhetoric,

---

17. Samuel Wales, *The Dangers of Our National Prosperity; and the Way to Avoid Them . . .* (Hartford, Conn., 1785), 25, 27. Ezra Stiles, MS sermon on Deut. 26:19, May 8, 1783, 28, Ezra Stiles Papers, Beinecke Rare Book and Manuscript Library, Yale University, New Haven, Conn.: "We have *reason* to expect that our new Republic bids fair to rise high in Honor among the Kingdoms of the Earth. (I had almost said in the spirit of Prophecy, *the Zeal of the Lord of Hosts will accomplish this.*)" This passage was immediately followed by a quotation from Barlow's *Vision of Columbus . . .* (Hartford, Conn., 1787), bk. 4. The election sermon was later printed as *The United States Elevated to Glory and Honor . . .* (New Haven, Conn., 1783). The quoted phrase in the paragraph's last sentence refers to Lowance, *Language of Canaan.*

faculty psychology, and moral philosophy. But in his self-conscious defense of poetry's moral and didactic purpose, we can see the tensions that were preparing Dwight for ideological battle—a battle that would need to be waged in what Samuel Wales had called "serious and didactic prose."[18]

Greenfield Hill, written while Dwight was a pastor and schoolteacher in the Fairfield County parish of that name, took the vague abstraction of American progress and glory and stamped its past, present, and future with New England's cultural identity. The Revolutionary War entered heroic experience in the poem's third part, which described the burning of Fairfield. The allegorical figure who appeared with a vision of the future at the end of the poem was, not "Freedom," but "The Genius of the [Long Island] Sound." At least half of the poem, however, including the 744-line section entitled "The Flourishing Village," examined the present. In *America,* the present is a virtually empty moment between the retrospect of the past and the vision of the future, filled only by the reader's elevation to the sublime; in the *Valedictory Address,* it is an unspecified open field for the inspired acts of the listener. In *Greenfield Hill,* the present—New England, circa 1790—is the focus of attention. Dwight's New England village is certainly idealized, but it nevertheless represents what he considered the social and cultural heart of New England life: church, school, and family farm. When the last section returned to the vision motif, most of the qualities of America that the "Genius" praised had already been identified as New England characteristics.[19]

In the endnotes he added to the poem in 1794, Dwight further dissipated poetic ambiguity with the hard "facts" of New England superiority. He glossed, for example, a reference in the poem to "plain and honest manners" with a sketch of New England hegemony:

> The manners of Virginia and South Carolina cannot be easily continued, without the continuance of the negro slavery; an event, which can scarcely be expected. The manners of New England appear to be rapidly spreading through the American republic. . . . When the enterprize, industry, economy, morals, and happiness, of New England, especially of Connecticut, are attentively considered, the patriotic mind will perhaps find much more reason to rejoice in this prospect, than to regret it.

A notation on a line mentioning the "general weal" made it clear that "the peculiar prosperity of New England in general, and particularly of Massachusetts

18. Timothy Dwight, *Greenfield Hill: A Poem in Seven Parts* (New York, 1794), 7.
19. Ibid., pt. 2, pt. 7, l. 26.

and Connecticut, undoubtedly arises from the equal division of property, the universal establishment of schools, and their peculiar manner of supporting the gospel." Lines that began "Fair Verna! loveliest village of the west; / Of every joy, and every charm, possess'd" were glossed by a note referring to Connecticut's inheritance laws.[20]

The endnotes were more than an afterthought tacked onto the poem as it headed for the press in 1794. Dwight's movement from the lofty rhetoric of the poem to the sociological prose of the notes indicates a shift in rhetorical strategy that would characterize Dwight's work after he was named president of Yale the following year. In 1795, he would even sneer that the theories of liberty being publicized by "visionary" philosophers "ought to be placed on the same level with the professed fictions of poets, and to be written in verse, and not in sober prose."[21]

RELIGIOUS TOLERATION AND THE THREAT OF INFIDELITY

Dwight's rhetorical shift was prompted in part by his response to two post-Revolutionary developments: attacks on Connecticut's religious establishment and the contagion of infidelity that he perceived to be spreading in the late 1780s and 1790s. For Dwight, calls for complete religious freedom and the separation of church and state were not unconnected to the radical Enlightenment's assault upon Christianity itself. The tolerant liberal acceptance of diverse sects and opinions that many advocated after the Revolution could be the top of a slippery slope toward religious indifference and, finally, practical atheism. He came to see that Connecticut's besieged Standing Order churches and orthodox Calvinists were fighting local battles in Christianity's epic struggle against the thrashings of Antichrist. In 1788, he anonymously published *The Triumph of Infidelity*, a satirical inversion of the "rising glory" poem that put liberal Boston minister Charles Chauncy in Satan's regiments next to Joseph Priestly, Voltaire, and David Hume. A decade later, his panic had escalated to a point far beyond where poetic satire would be an appropriate response. Con-

20. Ibid., pt. 1, ll. 296, 297, pt. 2, ll. 1–2, "Notes," 171–172.
21. Silverman, *Timothy Dwight,* 60–63, discusses Dwight's footnotes in *Greenfield Hill;* [Timothy Dwight], *The True Means of Establishing Public Happiness . . .* (New Haven, Conn., [1795]), 20–24 (quotations on 23, 24). Slotkin would call this a shift from the "fictive-mythological" genre to the "discursive-ideological" genre; see "Myth and the Production of History," in Bercovitch and Jehlen, eds., *Ideology and Classic American Literature,* 85. See also Slotkin, *Fatal Environment,* 22.

spirators seemed to be everywhere, and the fundamental premises of Christianity and civilization were threatened by a massive attack.[22]

Dwight's campaign to revivify New England's steady habits and combat dangerous heterodoxies relied heavily on the use of the increasingly influential local press, but the newspaper as civic forum, it turned out, did not necessarily aid his efforts. As one anticlerical writer noted rather smugly, ministers were not used to this new model of public discourse: "Their custom of preaching from sabbath to sabbath unanswered and having all the talk to themselves" led some of them to "imagine they only have the knowledge of the arts and sciences and it is uncivil to contradict them, [and] that they alone are intitled to the liberty of censuring without being censured." In the newspapers, people talked back. Editors did their best to keep religious controversy out of their pages, printing plenty of banal moralism but avoiding pieces with a sectarian slant. But even apparently safe attacks upon deistic straw men provoked responses from actual deists who, under the cover of newspaper pseudonyms, boldly challenged orthodoxy.[23]

If a minister expected reverent silence when he preached from the pulpit,

---

22. Timothy Dwight, *A Discourse on Some Events of the Last Century* . . . (New Haven, Conn., 1801), 16. See also Azel Backus, *Absalom's Conspiracy* . . . (Hartford, Conn., 1798), 46; [Dwight], *The Triumph of Infidelity: A Poem* (n.p., 1788). Thomas Paine's *Age of Reason: Being an Investigation of True and Fabulous Theology* was published in Paris in 1794. Elihu Palmer helped found the Deistical Society of the State of New York in 1796–1797.

23. *Connecticut Courant* (Hartford), July 28, 1778. Dwight did contribute didactic essays to the *New-Haven Gazette, and the Connecticut Magazine* in 1786: "The Friend," nos. 1–14, Mar. 23, 30, Apr. 6, 20, 27, May 4, 25, June 8, 15, 22, July 6, Sept. 21, Oct. 12, 19. The editors of the *New-Haven Gazette* explained their antisectarian editorial policy: Christians were only 20 percent of the world's population; Protestants were only a part of Christianity; Calvinists were only a part of all Protestants; and Congregationalists were only one branch of Calvinism (Aug. 4, 1785). The *Conn. Courant*'s editors refused to print a letter from "A Friend to Reason," which challenged a pamphlet discussing Mosaic history, claiming that it was their rule to keep religious controversies out of the newspaper (June 10, 1799). A satirical jab at the creed of "The Infidel, Alias Deist, Alias Freethinker" in the *American Mercury* (Hartford, Conn.), Sept. 26, 1785, was answered a week later (Oct. 3, 1785) by a creed written for "The Puritan, Alias Calvinist, Alias Orthodox Thinker," who delighted in the doctrine consigning all who believed anything except "the way I was brought up in" to eternal torment in hell. Verse satirizing Ethan Allen's deistic *Reason the Only Oracle of Man; or, A Compenduous System of Natural Religion* . . . (Bennington, Vt., 1784) in 1786 was followed by verse portraying it in a more favorable light a month later (*American Mercury*, July 24, Aug. 21, 1786). When sneers at Thomas Paine's *Age of Reason* in the *Conn. Courant*'s "Companion" column were answered by an actual deist, the columnist and the paper's editors backed off and urged religious controversialists to go at each other in pamphlets rather than in the weekly newspaper (Jan. 19–Feb. 9, 1795).

his sermon, if reprinted in the newspaper, became fair game in the give-and-take of public debate. Dwight's own 1798 July Fourth sermon, printed in the *Middlesex Gazette*, was followed by a complaint by "Democratus" about the "tautological, bombastic, ranting, canting, self-righteous sufficiency, which has foamed from a thousand puritanical pulpits since Cromwell's time"—remarks that parishioners would not have dared to shout back at Dwight from the pews. Yet, perhaps the way that newspapers encouraged people to answer the speaking aristocracy of clergymen was best illustrated in 1799, when, after a proclamation for a national fast day was read from the pulpit, a Middlebury man stood up in his pew and read an address from the New London *Bee* denouncing the practice of civic fasts as an improper mix of religion and politics.[24]

The medium, therefore, reinforced what was in Dwight's eyes a dangerous message. By encouraging open debate, the press legitimized the existence of diverse opinions; yet by ruling religious controversy out of bounds, it implied that religion was merely a matter of personal taste, that it amounted to a collection of disparate, privately held preferences that were unsuitable for rational public debate. The press, in other words, seemed to be moving toward the notorious standard of genteel politeness Dwight and other conservatives attributed to Lord Chesterfield's *Letters Written . . . to His Son*, which held that religious topics were not suitable for social conversation and that denouncing impiety was bad form. For clergymen like Dwight, removing religion from the center of sociable conversation and public discussion resembled the deistic effort to remove God from the center of daily life.[25]

The Standing Order clergy's concerns about the direction of post-Revolutionary society deepened as they endured three successive debates that challenged the relationship between church and state in Connecticut: first, the movement for disestablishment and religious freedom coming from Virginia in 1786 and enshrined in the federal Constitution; second, the uproar by reli-

24. *Middlesex Gazette* (Middletown, Conn.), Sept. 14, 28, 1798, Apr. 19, 1799. Similarly, according to a report in the *Bee* (New London), May 13, 1801, after a New London County minister in a sermon at a freemen's meeting went beyond praise for good government and named the Federalist candidates voters should elect and the Republicans they should not trust, a merchant then rose "to unsay all the fine things [the minister] had advanced."

25. "Libertines and Deists," *Norwich Packet; and the Country Journal,* July 26, 1787. Dwight, too, denounced Philip Dormer Stanhope, earl of Chesterfield's *Letters Written . . . to His Son,* 2 vols. (London, 1774) in *A Sermon Preached at Northampton . . .* (Hartford, Conn., [1781]). As William G. McLoughlin wrote in *New England Dissent, 1630–1833: The Baptists and the Separation of Church and State,* 2 vols. (Cambridge, Mass., 1971), II, 915, the decade after the Revolution in Connecticut was marked by a "mood of 'catholicity,' 'candor,' and 'toleration.'" The local press gave these sentiments a public forum.

gious dissenters to Connecticut's revised certificate law in 1791; and, third, the controversy over an appropriation of state funds for the support of the ministry, which began in 1793 and was finally settled in 1795.

While Connecticut's revised laws in 1784 silently dropped the Saybrook Platform's confession of faith and ecclesiastical organization (but maintained tax support for the churches), debate in Virginia redefined the American argument about religious establishment. After 1776, most states had moved to establish Christianity rather than a single sect. The Massachusetts Constitution of 1780, for example, established the public worship of Christianity, despite a campaign led by the Baptists against it. But in Virginia, an alliance of rationalists (who considered religious opinions a private matter and wanted to preserve the state from religious disputes) and evangelicals (who considered religion a spiritual matter and wanted to preserve Christ's church from interference by the state) passed Virginia's Act for Establishing Religious Freedom, characterizing state aid to religion as an infringement of natural rights.[26]

Connecticut papers printed the act, after already publishing a series of essays by English Presbyterian Richard Price calling for the United States to lead the way toward the full protection of religious freedom. The sudden prominence of what one critic called the "modish" demand for universal toleration (or complete disestablishment) prompted essays in the Connecticut press defending the state support of Christianity as prudent policy and the fulfillment of religious duty. When William Williams, a delegate to the state ratifying convention, complained that the proposed federal Constitution ignored God and banned a religious test for public officials, a political writer assured him: "The business of civil government is to protect the citizen in his rights, to defend the community from hostile powers, and . . . to promote the general welfare. Civil Government has no business to meddle with the private opinions of the people." But others argued that legislating complete religious freedom and failing to acknowledge the divinely ordained system of moral order would be like "hanging God's bible to the Devil's girdle" and creating a "Hell above ground."[27]

26. On church and state, see Jon Butler, *Awash in a Sea of Faith: Christianizing the American People* (Cambridge, Mass., 1990), 258–268; Thomas E. Buckley, *Church and State in Revolutionary Virginia, 1776–1787* (Charlottesville, Va., 1977); Edwin S. Gaustad, "Religious Tests, Constitutions, and 'Christian Nation,'" in Ronald Hoffman and Peter J. Albert, eds., *Religion in a Revolutionary Age* (Charlottesville, Va., 1994), 218–235.

27. Virginia's 1786 act was published in the *American Mercury*, Feb. 27, 1786. See also "Dr. Price's Observations, Continued: Of Liberty of Conscience and Civil Establishment of Religion," *Conn. Courant*, Feb. 22, 1785. A fable by Voltaire promoting religious toleration was

Calls for disestablishment and religious liberty were not "modish" new proposals to Connecticut's dissenting religious groups, who had for years petitioned the General Assembly and decried the ecclesiastical tax and other religious legislation as an infringement upon the rights of conscience. The campaign for disestablishment had *not* been immediately launched by the "Great Awakening": petitions by Separates and Baptists before the 1750s, despite some dramatic language, asked for toleration under an established church, not the complete separation of church and state and total religious freedom. Even compulsory religious taxation was not an issue for dissenters before mid-century. Worn down by continued persecution and borrowing slogans from political radicals between 1765 and 1775, however, Separates and Baptists began calling for disestablishment and full religious liberty—unmolested liberty for all Christians at least—by the Revolution. Their most successful attack upon Connecticut's ecclesiastical establishment resulted from their reaction to new legislation concerning dissenting certificates in 1791.[28]

---

printed in the *American Mercury,* Nov. 14, 1785, and in the *Norwich Packet; or, The Country Journal,* Dec. 28, 1785. The *Conn. Courant* published a five-part response to Price, entitled "The Establishment of the Worship of the Deity, Essential to National Happiness" (Aug. 28, Sept. 4, 11, 18, Oct. 2, 16, 1786). The six installments of "An Essay on Toleration" carefully worked through the major arguments for and against establishment, concluding that the state should support the public worship of Christianity (nos. 1–6, *American Mercury,* Feb. 16, 23, Mar. 9, 16, Apr. 6, 13, 1789). The description of toleration as "modish" is in "Senex," *Conn. Courant,* May 9, 1789. The response to Williams is in *American Mercury,* Dec. 17, 1787. See also "Impartialis," *Norwich Packet; and the Country Journal,* Apr. 17, 1789. William Williams was thought to be an Antifederalist, though he ended up voting for the Constitution despite his scruples about Article VI, clause 3. See his exchange with the author of the "Landholder" essays, *Conn. Courant,* Feb. 4, Mar. 3, 1788. The "Devil's girdle" quotation is from *American Mercury,* Jan. 31, 1791. See also Ibid., Apr. 14, 1788; and "Horatious" and "Calvenist" in the *Norwich Packet; and the Country Journal,* Apr. 17, 24, 1789.

28. McLoughlin, *New England Dissent,* I, 247–587. See also C. C. Goen, *Revivalism and Separatism in New England, 1740–1800: Strict Congregationalists and Separate Baptists in the Great Awakening* (1962; reprint, Middletown, Conn., 1987). Solomon Paine, *A Short View of the Difference between the Church of Christ and the Established Churches in the Colony of Connecticut . . .* (Newport, R.I., 1752), seems to militate against the whole idea of establishment, but the 1748 petition to the General Assembly, reprinted in this tract, seems to request only toleration (see McLoughlin, *New England Dissent,* I, 390–391). Separate (Strict Congregational) Ebenezer Frothingham, in *A Key to Unlock the Door, That Leads in, to Take a Fair View of the Religious Constitution Established by Law, in the Colony of Connecticut . . .* ([New Haven, Conn.], 1767), did call for disestablishment and religious freedom for Protestants. McLoughlin argued that "the Baptists did not produce a clearly developed theory of complete separation of church and state until 1773" (*New England Dissent,* I, 613). John Leland's *The Rights of Conscience Inalienable . . .* (New London, Conn., 1791), called for complete liberty of conscience for Roman Catholics, Jews, Muslims, and atheists as well, but this

The certificate law passed in the spring of 1791 tightened the requirements for legal religious dissent in an effort to slow an apparent post-Revolutionary exodus of the disaffected from the Standing Order churches. The previous revision of ecclesiastical laws in 1784 had done away with the fines levied against dissenters for not attending the parish church on the Sabbath and dropped the statute requiring state licenses for dissenting societies; it extended tax-exempt status to *all* persons of *any* Christian denomination and allowed dissenters to get their certificates signed by their deacons or clerks as well as their ministers. Members of the Standing Order complained that this lax system, ushered through the Assembly in the giddy mood of modern liberality after the war, had simply allowed the growing numbers of loose and irreligious men and women to dodge religious taxes. The General Assembly in 1791 accordingly changed the certificate process, requiring those who wished to leave the Standing Order church to submit certificates to two *civil* officers in the town (often hostile Congregationalist justices of the peace) and to prove that they were dissenting in good conscience and were attending another religious congregation. "Pandor" in the *Courant* and Baptist John Leland in a powerful pamphlet entitled *The Rights of Conscience Inalienable* denounced not just the revised law but the whole idea of the state's establishing one form of worship and merely tolerating others: establishment was anti-Christian and a tyrannous infringement of rights worse than anything the British had done in 1775, they argued. The *Norwich Packet* printed an extract from Thomas Paine's *Rights of Man* on religious liberty and a remonstrance condemning the new act as inconsistent with the idea of liberty, the federal Constitution, the practice in most other states, and the teachings of Christ. It was rumored that outraged dissenters throughout the state held meetings and corresponded about getting the law repealed. As the legislature met for its fall session in Hartford, Massachusetts Baptist Isaac Backus addressed a mass protest meeting at the courthouse. After much wrangling in the Assembly, the revised bill that emerged was the most liberal certificate law imaginable and a sharp blow to establishment Congregationalists: dissenters would now simply notify the authorities of their dissent by filling out the certificate themselves and filing it with the clerks of their own religious societies.[29]

---

opinion, as McLoughlin writes, was atypical among New England Baptists (*New England Dissent*, II, 928–935).

29. On tax dodgers, see, for example, "Baptistos," "An Address to the Baptists, Separates, Quakers, Rogerenes, and All Other Denominations of Christians, Freed by Law from Supporting, What Has Been Called, the Established Religion," *Conn. Courant*, Apr. 20, 1789, which uses satire to suggest that people were buying and selling dissenters' certificates merely to dodge ecclesiastical taxes. Answered in the *Conn. Courant* by "Coercio," May 11, 1789,

The state still collected ecclesiastical taxes, and Congregationalism was still the de facto established denomination. Supporters of religious establishment responded to the uproar over the certificate law with what would become the Standing Order's central argument for establishment through the 1790s:

> The legislature has the same right to lay a tax, or enforce those laid by a corporation for the purpose of supporting the preaching of the gospel, as for supporting schools. It is the *civil* effect of such preaching that gives the *civil* magistrate jurisdiction. The law has nothing to do with *conscience* nor *principles;* but the preaching of the gospel is found to contribute to the *good order of society,* and therefore it is proper it should be countenanced by law. Every man is left to *think and worship as he pleases;* but if he will not worship at all, he shall contribute to support the worship of others, because such worship produces *good effects in society,* of which every man enjoys his share.

State support for the public worship of Christianity (not for Congregationalism per se), justified by its social utility, with liberal allowances for dissent, became the rallying cry of Congregational conservatives like Timothy Dwight. But this modified relationship between government and religion also met stiff resistance and was quickly attacked during the debates over the Western Lands Appropriation bill in 1793. Dwight and his fellow establishmentarians found their most potent opponents this time were, not pietistic Baptists and a few scattered Methodists, but the liberal rationalists—the men that Dwight, like Ezra Stiles, considered closet deists and libertine lawyers, the men who were increasingly dominating discussion in the General Assembly and the local press.[30]

"Tertious," June 1, 1789, and "Catholicus," June 22, 1789. See "Pandor," ibid., May 23, 1791, answered by a letter on May 30, 1791; Leland, *Rights of Conscience Inalienable; Norwich Packet,* Sept. 8, 1791. See also "Naphtali," *Conn. Courant,* Sept. 12, 1791. On the revised bill, see "Hushai," ibid., Aug. 29, 1791, "Plain Dealer," Sept. 12, 1791; McLoughlin, *New England Dissent,* II, 935–938.

30. Hartford correspondent to the *Norwich Packet,* Sept. 8, 1791. "Moral History of Connecticut, Contrastical Sketches, No. V," *Conn. Courant,* Apr. 1, 1793, noted the importance of public worship and complained about its neglect, as did the seventh article in this series (May 20, 1793). The effort to justify state-supported public worship, the social utility of Christianity, and the toleration of Christian dissent marks the election sermons of the 1790s. Martha Louise Counts, in "The Political Views of the Eighteenth Century New England Clergy as Expressed in Their Election Sermons" (Ph.D. diss., Columbia University, 1956), also noted that, whereas the Revolutionary sermons had stressed the actions of human beings in the course of historical events, the post-Revolutionary sermons returned to the earlier emphasis upon God's role in determining human fate (198). As discussed in Chapter 1, this does not necessarily imply a return to a "public covenant" with God.

The Appropriation Act began as an effort to fund the ministry with money from the sale of Connecticut's western lands. To make the proposal more palatable, and to reinforce the connection between preaching and general education, the bill would have established a fund to support public worship *and* the state's public schools. The first version of the bill narrowly passed in October 1793; the final version, which passed in June 1795 after a year and a half of public debate, directed all the money to local schools. Although no money ever reached the clergy, the debates the measure stirred up in the Assembly, in town meetings, in the newspapers, and most likely in taverns and coffeehouses as well affected religious and political life in the state perhaps more than the funds ever could.[31]

Essays discussing the Appropriation Act filled the state's two leading papers, and, for the first time in Connecticut's history, citizens were also able to read extended excerpts from speeches and floor debates delivered in the General Assembly. Despite lengthy discussion about the economic wisdom of the land sale and the proper use or investment of the funds, the fundamental issue at stake, as "A Farmer" wrote in the *Courant*, was the relationship between civil government and religion. But whereas proponents of the Appropriation Act developed broad philosophical arguments justifying close ties between Christianity and republican government, opponents focused their criticism upon the Congregational ministry and its role in Connecticut politics and public life. The bluntly anticlerical tone of the comments that circulated freely in the press stunned and embittered the clergymen, many of whom, two decades earlier, had proudly considered themselves the vanguard of the patriot movement.[32]

Some speakers and writers blamed the ministers themselves for the post-Revolutionary religious malaise that the preachers complained about and doubted that supporting clerical salaries was the answer to the problem. "The curse upon us is that we have so many men in the pulpit who are so incompetent to the duties of their profession," Litchfield deputy John Allen told the lower house. "Civis" in the *American Mercury* suggested that instead of more pay clergymen needed more training in precisely the kind of rhetorical instruction that Dwight had championed as a Yale tutor: "If the Clergy would pay more attention to the study of their profession; particularly to that simple ele-

31. The final version of the bill, printed in the *Conn. Courant* and the *American Mercury*, June 8, 1795, stipulated that funds apportioned to a local society could be used to support the ministry if two-thirds of the society so voted, if the state legislature also approved, and if all denominations benefited equally. No society ever went through all the trouble to have some of its share of the money go to its local preachers (McLoughlin, *New England Dissent*, II, 969).

32. "A Farmer," *Conn. Courant*, May 4, 1795.

gance in composition, and natural, engaging delivery, which is calculated to gain attention, we should find fewer disputes between ministers and people, less complaint of societies broken to pieces by different sectaries, and of the unwillingness of people to support the preaching of the gospel." Several critics, like representative Charles Phelps of Stonington, bluntly charged that the Standing Order ministry's very vocal and nearly unanimous support for the act betrayed a hunger for wealth and power rather than a pious regard for the common good. Shall this public money, "Catiline" asked incredulously, "go to these lazy black-coated fellows, who never did a days work in their lives?" "Cato" charged that the act was part of a plot hatched by an unholy alliance of Congregational clergymen, especially those connected to Yale College, and key legislators, especially those in the Council. Their scheme revealed "aristocracy in the bud."[33]

Opponents differed in their assessment of the clergy's current political power, but not about what that power *should* be. Canterbury deputy Elisha Paine, who was a religious dissenter, contended: "The influence of the clergy has been gradually declining for half a century; and had its fatal stab when the famous act was passed known by the name of the conscience bill. Fifty years ago no office either civil or military could be obtained, unless the candidate bowed to the shrine of superstition, and yielded tamely to the yoke of ecclesiastical tyranny, the established religion of this state." But Paine's Canterbury colleague Moses Cleaveland believed that, although things were not so bad "in this enlightened age" as in previous years, when the clergy could ruin a man's political career because he opposed the Yale College charter, the ministers still "have sometimes resolved among themselves, whose election they would favour and whom they would oppose" and thus continued to be courted by power-seeking politicians. Both Cleaveland and Paine conceded that ministers were "useful men in their place" and "confined in their proper sphere." Appropriation opponents, though, defined that "proper sphere" very narrowly.

33. Legislative debates, *Conn. Courant,* May 19, 26, 1794, "Catiline," Aug. 11, 1794; "Civis," *American Mercury,* Feb. 24, 1794 ("Cimon" in the *American Mercury,* Apr. 14, 1794, answered that meager salaries made dull preachers), "Cato," Apr. 6, 1795. The resolution against the act from the town of Cheshire also objected to making "a certain and permanent *civil* provision, for a certain and permanent *sacerdotal* order" (*Conn. Courant,* Jan. 26, 1795). Some earlier discussion had also blamed the perceived post-Revolutionary religious malaise upon the clergy. "Juvenis," in the *American Mercury,* May 26, 1788, blamed hellfire preaching and sectarian bickering; "A Reply to the Address of the Ministers of the State of Connecticut" blamed the Standing Order's Calvinism (Sept. 1, 1788); "The People" blamed the New Divinity's distortion of Calvinism (Dec. 22, 1788).

As John Watson of Canaan argued, ministers were to prepare men for a future state, "but to form the manners and improve the morals of men, was a proper and important object of legislative care." Civil rulers schooled in the science of law and republican politics, not clergymen trained in theology, were in charge of making people good members of society.[34]

Dwight entered the fray with "Extracts from a Thanksgiving Sermon Preached at Greenfield, with Some Additional Observations," an extended, blatantly political argument in favor of the Appropriation Act that was printed by the *Courant* in three installments in the spring of 1795, half a year before he became Yale's president. The newspaper "sermon," with its explicit policy recommendations (to invest the funds in deferred stock of the United States, for example), support for the incumbents in the upper house in the forthcoming election, and commentary on the political maneuvering of lawyers in the Assembly, probably did more to establish Dwight's reputation as a political preacher than his separately printed sermons. Wading into the middle of the newspaper debate, Dwight defended the broader public role of the parish pastor: "To him every parishioner, as of right, applies for instruction, advice, and consolation, and from him derives not only knowledge in morals and religion, but information on every subject of use, or curiosity, to which his own inclinations lead, and to which the ministers understanding is adequate." In answer to those who contended that the minister's proper sphere of activity concerned only preparation for the afterlife, he reminded his fellow New Englanders "that in this, the freest state in the world, the whole state of society was in great measure contrived by clergymen."[35]

The way that Dwight and other clerical establishmentarians characterized their opponents, however, was at least as significant to the development of Standing Order ideology as their defense of the clergy. He charged that those who supported the act's repeal were "men who wish public worship not to be supported, and who are indifferent, and perhaps opposed, to the establish-

34. Legislative debates, *Conn. Courant,* May 19, June 2, 1794. Extended extracts from the debate in the legislature can also be found there, May 26, 1794. For examples of town resolutions, see the *American Mercury,* Dec. 22, 1794 (Killingworth); and *Conn. Courant,* Jan. 5, 1795 (Granby and Wethersfield). Some of the other notable discussions are: *American Mercury,* Mar. 17, 31, May 19, Oct. 13, 1794; *Conn. Courant,* Feb. 10, Apr. 14, May 3, 12, June 30, Sept. 15, 1794, Feb. 9, 23, Mar. 9, 16, 30, Apr. 6, 1795. In *Conn. Courant,* Apr. 17, 1795, the editors say they have more articles to print about the controversy, but readers told them they had made up their minds and asked them to stop.

35. Timothy Dwight, "Extracts from a Thanksgiving Sermon Preached at Greenfield, with Some Additional Observations," *Conn. Courant,* Mar. 16, 23, 30 (quotations), 1795.

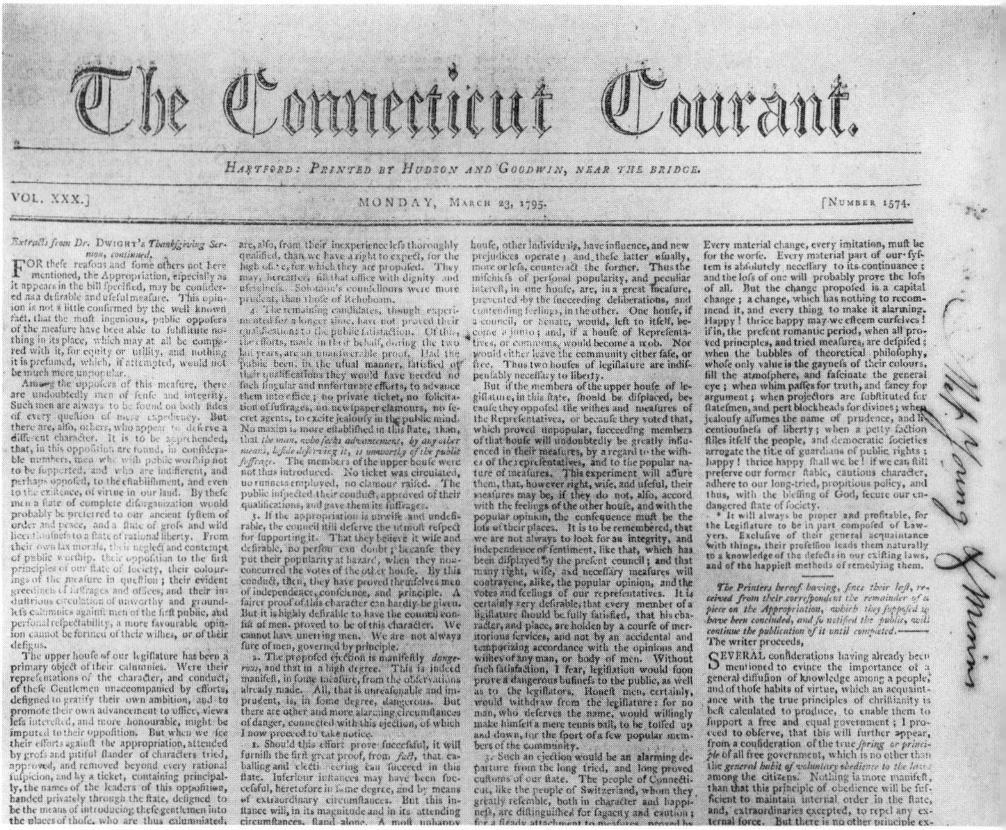

The Connecticut Courant.

Hartford: Printed by Hudson and Goodwin, near the Bridge.

VOL. XXX.] MONDAY, March 23, 1795. [Number 1574.

Extracts from Dr. Dwight's *Thanksgiving Sermon, continued.*

FOR these reasons and some others not here mentioned, the Appropriation, especially as it appears in the bill specified, may be considered as a desirable and useful measure. This opinion is not a little confirmed by the well known fact, that the most ingenious, public opposers of the measure have been able to substitute nothing in its place, which may at all be compared with it, for equity or utility, and nothing it is presumed, which, if attempted, would not be much more unpopular.

Among the opposers of this measure, there are undoubtedly men of sense and integrity. Such men are always to be found on both sides of every question of mere expediency. But there are, also, others, who appear to deserve a different character. It is to be apprehended, that, in this opposition are found, in considerable numbers, men who wish public worship not to be supported, and who are indifferent, and perhaps opposed, to the establishment, and even to the existence, of virtue in our land. By these men a state of complete disorganization would probably be preferred to our ancient system of order and peace, and a state of gross and wild licentiousness to a state of rational liberty. From their own lax morals, their neglect and contempt of public worship, their opposition to the first principles of our state of society, their colourings of the measure in question; their evident greediness of suffrages and offices, and their industrious circulation of unworthy and groundless calumnies against men of the first public, and personal respectability, a more favourable opinion cannot be formed of their wishes, or of their designs.

The upper house of our legislature has been a primary object of their calumnies. Were their representations of the character, and conduct, of these Gentlemen unaccompanied by efforts, designed to gratify their own ambition, and to promote their own advancement to office, views less interested, and more honourable, might be imputed to their opposition. But when we see their efforts against the appropriation, attended by gross and pitiful slander of characters tried, approved, and removed beyond every rational suspicion, and by a ticket, containing principally, the names of the leaders of this opposition, handed privately through the state, designed to be the means of introducing these gentlemen into the places of those, who are thus calumniated, are, also, from their inexperience less thoroughly qualified, than we have a right to expect, for the high office, for which they are proposed. They may, hereafter, fill that office with dignity and usefulness. Solomon's counsellours were more prudent, than those of Rehoboam.

4. The remaining candidates, though experimented for a longer time, have not proved their qualifications to the public satisfaction. Of this, the efforts, made in their behalf, during the two last years, are an unanswerable proof. Had the public been, in the usual manner, satisfied of their qualifications they would have needed no such singular and unfortunate efforts, to advance them into office; no private ticket, no solicitation of suffrages, no newspaper clamours, no secret agents, to excite jealousy in the public mind. No maxim is more established in this state, than, that *the man, who seeks advancement, by any other means, beside deserving it, is unworthy of the public suffrage.* The members of the upper house were not thus introduced. No ticket was circulated, no runners employed, no clamour raised. The public inspected their conduct, approved of their qualifications, and gave them its suffrages.

5. If the appropriation is unwise and undesirable, the council still deserve the utmost respect for supporting it. That they believe it wise and desirable, no person can doubt; because they put their popularity at hazard, when they non-concurred the votes of the other house. By this conduct, then, they have proved themselves men of independence, conscience, and principle. A fairer proof of this character can hardly be given. But it is highly desirable to have the council consist of men, proved to be of this character. We cannot have unerring men. We are not always sure of men, governed by principle.

2. The proposed ejection is manifestly *dangerous*, and that in a high degree. This is indeed manifest, in some measure, from the observations already made. All, that is unreasonable and imprudent, is, in some degree, dangerous. But there are other and more alarming circumstances of danger, connected with this ejection, of which I now proceed to take notice.

1. Should this effort prove successful, it will furnish the first great proof, from *fact*, that caballing and electioneering can succeed in this state. Inferiour instances may have been successful, heretofore in some degree, and by means of extraordinary circumstances. But this instance will, in its magnitude and in its attending circumstances, stand alone. A most unhappy

house, other individuals, have influence, and new prejudices operate; and these latter usually, more or less, counteract the former. Thus the mischiefs of personal popularity, and peculiar interest, in one house, are, in a great measure, prevented by the succeeding deliberations, and contending feelings, in the other. One house, if a council, or senate, would, left to itself, become a junto; and, if a house of Representatives, or commons, would become a mob. Nor would either leave the community either safe, or free. Thus two houses of legislature are indispensably necessary to liberty.

But if the members of the upper house of legislature, in this state, should be displaced, because they opposed the wishes and measures of the Representatives, or because they voted that, which proved unpopular, succeeding members of that house will undoubtedly be greatly influenced in their measures, by a regard to the wishes of the representatives, and to the popular nature of measures. This experiment will assure them, that, however right, wise, and useful, their measures may be, if they do not, also, accord with the feelings of the other house, and with the popular opinion, the consequence must be the loss of their places. It is to be remembered, that we are not always to look for an integrity, and independence of sentiment, like that, which has been displayed by the present council; and that many right, wise, and necessary measures will contravene, alike, the popular opinion, and the votes and feelings of our representatives. It is certainly very desirable, that every member of a ligislature should be fully satisfied, that his character, and place, are holden by a course of meritorious services, and not by an accidental and temporizing accordance with the opinions and wishes of any man, or body of men. Without such satisfaction, I fear, legislation would soon prove a dangerous business to the public, as well as to the legislators. Honest men, certainly, would withdraw from the legislature: for no man, who deserves the name, would willingly make himself a mere tennis ball, to be tossed up and down, for the sport of a few popular members of the community.

3. Such an ejection would be an alarming departure from the long tried, and long proved customs of our state. The people of Connecticut, like the people of Switzerland, whom they greatly resemble, both in character and happiness, are distinguished for sagacity and caution; for a steady attachment to measures, proved by

Every material change, every imitation, must be for the worse. Every material part of our system is absolutely necessary to its continuance; and the loss of one will probably prove the loss of all. But the change proposed is a capital change; a change, which has nothing to recommend it, and every thing to make it alarming. Happy! thrice happy may we esteem ourselves! if in, the present romantic period, when all proved principles, and tried measures, are despised; when the bubbles of theoretical philosophy, whose only value is the gayness of their colours, fill the atmosphere, and fascinate the general eye; when whim passes for truth, and fancy for argument; when projectors are substituted for statesmen, and pert blockheads for divines; when jealousy assumes the name of prudence, and licentiousness of liberty; when a petty faction stiles itself the people, and democratic societies arrogate the title of guardians of public rights; happy! thrice happy shall we be! if we can still preserve our former stable, cautious character, adhere to our long-tried, propitious policy, and thus, with the blessing of God, secure our endangered state of society.

* It will always be proper and profitable, for the Legislature to be in part composed of Lawyers. Exclusive of their general acquaintance with things, their profession leads them naturally to a knowledge of the defects in our existing laws, and of the happiest methods of remedying them.

The Printers hereof having, since their last, received from their correspondent the remainder of a piece on the Appropriation, which they supposed to have been concluded, and so notified the public, will continue the publication of it until completed.——The writer proceeds,

SEVERAL considerations having already been mentioned to evince the importance of a general diffusion of knowledge among a people, and of those habits of virtue, which an acquaintance with the true principles of christianity is best calculated to produce, to enable them to support a free and equal government; I proceed to observe, that this will further appear, from a consideration of the true *spring or principle* of all free government, which is no other than the *general habit of voluntary obedience to the laws* among the citizens. Nothing is more manifest, than that this principle of obedience will be sufficient to maintain internal order in the state, and, extraordinaries excepted, to repel any external force. But there is no other principle ex-

Figure 15. *Connecticut Courant* (Hartford), Mar. 23, 1795, front page. Shows the continuation of "Extracts from Dr. [Timothy] Dwight's Thanksgiving Sermon." Courtesy, American Antiquarian Society, Worcester, Mass.

ment, and even to the existence, of virtue in our land." He had remarkably nice things to say about religious dissenters, which was probably a calculated effort to drive a wedge between the pietistic and rationalistic opponents of the Standing Order and to form a political coalition of Christians against those he considered "infidels." The Standing Order's real opponents were, not the overly enthusiastic sectarians who had complained about the certificate law, but the morally lax "enemies of Christianity" who were out to destroy public worship.[36]

Dwight and most other Standing Order clergymen who commented on public affairs believed that skepticism, deism, and infidelity lay at the heart of

36. Ibid. (quotations from Mar. 23, 30, 1795).

the religious declension they perceived after the war. Historians have usually told a different story, highlighting the evangelical dissenters' long struggle for religious liberty. The parish system in this reading seems to suffer an inevitable decline in an increasingly pluralistic and individualistic society; established churches lose adherents to competing Christian groups that emphasized religious voluntarism and revivalism. The Baptists and Methodists simply preached a populist Christianity, it is said, that was more suited to a democratic age. But the spectacular growth of Baptism and Methodism in the nineteenth century should not cause one to overestimate the power of religious dissent in eighteenth-century Connecticut. Dissenting groups were certainly growing faster than the Standing Order, but established Congregationalists outnumbered all dissenters combined through the end of the century. In 1792, according to one estimate, there were 10 Separate churches, 55 Baptist societies (in 1795), and a single Methodist church. Episcopalians, who in this period were closer socially and politically to the Standing Order, had 30 churches; the Standing Order had 168 churches. By 1800, according to another survey, 17 percent of the churches were Baptist, 9 percent were Methodist, and 52 percent were established Congregational. But even these numbers might exaggerate dissenter strength, because they do not account for the size of the churches being counted: 2 of the new Methodist churches in Stratfield and Redding, for example, had only three members each. A historian counting clergymen rather than churches found that almost 85 percent of the ministers in 1790 and nearly 75 percent in 1800 belonged to the Standing Order.[37]

37. On evangelical dissent and democracy, see M. Louise Greene, *The Development of Religious Liberty in Connecticut* (Boston, 1905); Goen, *Revivalism and Separatism in New England;* McLoughlin, *New England Dissent;* Marini, *Radical Sects of Revolutionary New England.* This interpretation has been put forward most prominently by Nathan O. Hatch, *The Democratization of American Christianity* (New Haven, Conn., 1989). On the number of churches in the 1790s, see McLoughlin, *New England Dissent,* II, 919. McLoughlin noted that, even in 1818, the fact that dissenters had more churches than the Standing Order (215 to 204) does not mean they had more voters. Figures must be read with McLoughlin's caveat: "Statistics vary widely for all denominations" (II, 919n). On the churches in 1800, see Stephen Reed Grossbart, "The Revolutionary Transition: Politics, Religion, and Economy in Eastern Connecticut, 1765–1800" (Ph.D. diss., University of Michigan, 1989), 3. The problems involved in estimating church adherence by counting churches and ministers in late-eighteenth-century Connecticut are discussed in Edmund B. Thomas, Jr., "Politics in the Land of Steady Habits: Connecticut's First Political Party System, 1789–1820" (Ph.D. diss., Clark University, 1972), 213–220. Jonathan Douglas Sassi, "To Envision a Godly Society: The Public Christianity of the Southern New England Clergy, 1783–1833 (Congregationalism)" (Ph.D. diss., University of California, Los Angeles, 1996), stressed the continuing power of

Dwight was more concerned with infidelity than with radical pietism because the former seemed to be making inroads among the elite. Libertine legislators and Yale students duped by Denis Diderot were more dangerous than backwoods farmers who weeped with semiliterate itinerant Methodists; a new breed of learned men was infiltrating Connecticut's natural aristocracy, and their hands were reaching for the levers of power. Standing Order clergymen like Dwight in the mid-1790s also might have underestimated the strength of evangelical dissenters, and focused so much upon anticlerical deists, because of incomplete tallies published in newspapers and Timothy Green's yearly *Register for the State of Connecticut,* which underrepresented religious groups outside the Standing Order. Anticlerical liberals were more vocal and politically engaged; they, not Baptists and Methodists, were the most vigorous spokesmen against the Western Lands Appropriation Act. Although larger numbers of individual evangelical dissenters became more politically active in the 1790s, the dissenting churches and associations in their formal statements and petitions "went out of their way to avoid becoming embroiled" in political disputes. Although the Reverend James Cogswell of Scotland, Connecticut, confided to his diary fears about the Baptists' being as disruptive as the Separates had been after the revivals of the early 1740s, the prevailing winds of skepticism and the growing political clout of men who cared little for religion concerned him at least as much. Deism and religious skepticism did not, as it turned out, overwhelm Christianity in the early nineteenth century, but the Standing Order could not have known that in the 1790s.[38]

National and international events between 1793 and 1798 allowed Dwight and the Standing Order to connect their local troubles to the seemingly apoca-

---

the corporatism at the heart of Standing Order ideology and showed that, aside from the issue of compulsory taxation, the established Congregationalists and the dissenters had much in common.

38. McLoughlin, *New England Dissent,* II, 988. McLoughlin, II, 983, writes: "It is difficult to explain why the dissenters in general, particularly the Baptists, did not make a more vigorous attempt to organize their denominational voices and votes to defeat the bill. The minutes of various Baptist associations make no mention of the debate. No one established special committees to prepare petitions. There is a tradition that at the May 1794 session of the legislature the Baptists and other dissenters staged a great rally on the steps of the Hartford State House and that John Leland addressed the throng with a stirring speech. But there is no record of this event in contemporary newspapers or any other source." Grossbart, "The Revolutionary Transition," 307, however, argues that, in the 1790s, "Baptists and other dissenters were admitted freemen at disproportionately high rates." See James Cogswell, Diary, Mar. 3, 1788, Sept. 8, 1789, Connecticut Historical Society, Hartford, Conn., Mar. 3, 1788, Sept. 8, 1789 (the latter entry is also quoted in McLoughlin, *New England Dissent,* II, 925).

lyptic developments affecting Christianity throughout the world. Clergymen turned against the French Revolution in the mid-1790s, especially after the Reign of Terror. Their worst fears about the rise of infidel politics seemed to be coming true as the crusade for liberty devolved into anti-Christian anarchy in Europe. "With astonishment the world has beheld a novel and bold experiment made by the French politicians, to establish their new government on the foundation of a merely civil and atheistical morality," a correspondent to the *Courant* remarked in December 1795. Francophobia intensified as relations between America and France soured, reaching its peak in the response to the XYZ affair and the Adams administration's military buildup in the spring of 1798.[39]

On July 4, 1798, Dwight preached a sermon from Rev. 16:15 entitled *The Duty of Americans, at the Present Crisis*. He recounted for his New Haven audience the prophecy that described "teachers of unclean doctrines" spreading through the world in "an open, professed enterprise against God Almighty." He then tried to fit a brief sketch of church history to the periods of the "seven vials" mentioned in the Scripture and concluded that the design of Voltaire, Diderot, and others to destroy Christianity might very well be what the prophet foresaw in the pouring out of the sixth vial. The Yale president believed that, in France, revolutionary atheists had taken up the methods and instruments for cultivating virtue and diffusing knowledge through a community and had turned them against God. The teachings of Voltaire and Diderot turned the human will away from piety, temperance, and the common good and toward atheism, anarchy, and the guillotine. Their "philosophic" sects were a distortion of the voluntary societies that were being formed in America. Their artful sophistry mimicked and mocked the rational discourse of enlightened Christianity. The unrestrained debates they encouraged among the youth played out the very pedagogical techniques Dwight used, but without the guidance of the paternal

39. *Conn. Courant*, Dec. 7, 1795. See Gary B. Nash, "The American Clergy and the French Revolution," *William and Mary Quarterly*, 3d Ser., XXII (1965), 392–412; Ann Butler Lever, "Vox Populi, Vox Dei: New England and the French Revolution, 1787–1801" (Ph.D. diss., University of North Carolina at Chapel Hill, 1972). For political developments in the 1790s more generally, see Simon Peter Newman, "American Popular Political Culture in the Age of the French Revolution" (Ph.D. diss., Princeton University, 1991); James Roger Sharp, *American Politics in the Early Republic: The New Nation in Crisis* (New Haven, Conn., 1993); Stanley Elkins and Eric McKitrick, *The Age of Federalism* (New York, 1993); David Waldstreicher, *In the Midst of Perpetual Fetes: The Making of American Nationalism, 1776–1820* (Chapel Hill, N.C., 1997); Waldstreicher, "Rites of Rebellion, Rites of Assent: Celebrations, Print Culture, and the Origins of American Nationalism," *Journal of American History*, LXXXII (1995–1996), 37–61.

Christian instructor. In France, these anti-Christian vipers had "insinuated themselves into every place of power and trust, and into every literary, political, and Friendly society." They had taken over the educational institutions, literary journals, booksellers, printers, and licensers of the press, spreading the contagion that flowed from their pens.[40]

The diseases of atheism and subversion, Dwight argued, were entering America in two ways. One was through a conspiratorial society of freethinkers called the Bavarian Illuminati, which Scottish anti-Jacobin John Robinson had decried in a polemic that Dwight took for proof. With the famous New England geographer Jedidiah Morse and Harvard's Hollis Professor of Divinity David Tappan as well as other New England leaders, Dwight spread the alarm about the Illuminati, which was rumored to have already grafted itself onto some American Masonic orders.[41]

The second method of subversion was through the printing press, which flooded the world with the writings of the radical Enlightenment. Infidel philosophes had clouded the bright vision of the new republic of letters that

40. Timothy Dwight, *The Duty of Americans, at the Present Crisis, Illustrated in a Discourse, Preached on the Fourth of July, 1798* (New Haven, Conn., 1798), 7, 9, 11, 13. Dwight calls deists, lovers of sophistry, and the followers of Voltaire "philosophists" to distinguish them from true philosophers (11). The governor's speech to the General Assembly in 1798 echoed Dwight's warning: "Among numberless other artifices which at this time are brought into operation, two great engines which are made use of by our enemies against us, are French infidelity and French Philosophy; the one operating to the destruction of all religious sentiments; the other unhinging every social and human tie by which societies are cemented; both together, tending to introduce universal disorder and confusion" (*American Mercury*, Oct. 18, 1798).

41. See Richard Buel, Jr., *Securing the Revolution: Ideology in American Politics, 1789–1815* (Ithaca, N.Y., 1972), 171–172; see also Amos Hofman, "Opinion, Illusion, and the Illusion of Opinion: Barruel's Theory of Conspiracy," *Eighteenth-Century Studies*, XXVII (1993), 27–60. Ironically, according to Steven Bullock's *Revolutionary Brotherhood: Freemasonry and the Transformation of the American Social Order, 1730–1840* (Chapel Hill, N.C., 1996), the order was becoming more rather than less explicitly Christian in this period. For examples of anti-Illuminati sermons other than those by Dwight and Morse, see A[mos] Stoddard, *An Oration Delivered before the Citizens of Portland, and the Supreme Judicial Court of the Commonwealth of Massachusetts, on the Fourth Day of July, 1799 Being the Anniversary of American Independence* (Portland, Maine, 1799), 11; Zechariah Lewis, *An Oration on the Apparent, and the Real Political Situation of the United States, Pronounced before the Society of Cincinnati . . .* (New Haven, Conn., 1799), 17. The newspaper debate over the Illuminati can be followed in the *Conn. Courant*, Aug. 6, Sept. 3, 1798, May 27, June 17–Oct. 7, Nov. 4, 1799. In the *American Mercury*, see Aug. 9, 16, 1798, June 6, Aug. 21, 29, Nov. 14, 1799. For the Republican response, see the New London *Bee*, Feb. 27, June 19, Sept. 11, Oct. 9, 16, 30, Nov. 20, 27, Dec. 4, 11, 1799, Jan. 15, 22, 1800, Mar. 4, 1801.

Dwight, like his fellow Yale tutor John Trumbull, had enthusiastically supported in the early 1770s. The success of infidelity had dampened the hope that the broad dissemination of print and the diffusion of knowledge would emancipate the minds of millions from the shackles of ignorance and that the active participation of citizen-writers within a vigorous public sphere would help sustain the virtue of a republic. The French infidels would force man back into his savage state to wallow with the swine, not, at first, by persuading readers that their doctrines were true, but by stripping words of their meaning. Dwight described "infidel philosophy" as "a system of abstract declarations, which violated common sense, delivered in an abstract style, equally violating all just taste and sober criticism"; its language, "like the signs of unknown quantities of Algebra, is without meaning." The French were leading men to an idolatry even worse than that of the heathen:

> The idolatry of the present day, still more stupid and unmeaning, is the worship of abstract terms. To the astonishment of every sober man, France has exhibited the spectacle of twenty-five millions of the human race prostrating themselves with religious reverence before the word REASON. . . . A multitude of the Americans have paid their devotions to the word liberty. This word has a real and important meaning, but in the minds and mouths of most men appears to have no meaning at all.[42]

Dwight was not pitting piety against the Age of Reason; he saw the project of the radical philosophes as a promulgation of a *false* rationalism, a seductive appeal to would-be intellectuals that played upon their desires for enlightenment. Azel Backus developed this theme in his 1798 election sermon. Demagogues, like those who had worn the cloak of fervent piety a half-century earlier, now manipulated the impressionable by adopting the fashionable pose of the skeptic. Zealots and crusaders once knelt before crucifixes; now it was the fashion "to worship, and adore human reason, falsely so called; and, the rage for relics, is now spending itself . . . in search for Mammoth bones, making experiments on air, or casting the age of the world from the lava of burning mountains." The superstitious enthusiast, with his holier-than-thou displays of godliness, and the intellectual skeptic, with his learned conceits, were not polar opposites. They were different examples of the same delusion: "He who

42. Dwight, *Travels,* ed. Solomon, IV, 265, 268. See also Timothy Dwight, "The Nature and Danger of Infidel Philosophy; Preached to the Candidates for the Baccalaureate in 1797," in *Sermons,* 2 vols. (New Haven, Conn., 1828), I, 310–342. On the importance of language to civilization, see Dwight's "Observations on Language," in Connecticut Academy of Arts and Sciences, *Memoirs,* I (New Haven, Conn., 1816), 365.

once believed in legends, and he who now doubts of self-evident [religious] propositions, are the same characters."[43]

Dwight, who had once argued in favor of poetry's appeal to the passions and the imagination, now saw these faculties being duped:

> Whatever [the unwary reader] reads is uttered with the gravity and confidence of superior wisdom, and an imposing air of mystery, and with continual hints of something, immensely important, in due time to be revealed. Thus he wanders on, a dupe to artfully excited expectation, and loses himself "in a wilderness where there is no way" . . . so thoroughly estranged from truth and virtue as never to return.

As a writer, Dwight had tried his hand at a variety of literary forms, from the Addisonian essay to the epic poem, and had contemplated the comparative strengths and weaknesses of the different forms of public address. But infidelity had infected them all:

> Their writings have assumed every form, and treated every subject of thought. From the lofty philosophical discourse it has descended through all the intervening gradations to the newspaper paragraph; from the sermon to the catechism; from regular history to the anecdote; from the epic poem to the song; and from the formal satire to the jest of the buffoon.

In *Greenfield Hill* and *The Triumph of Infidelity,* Dwight used footnotes and endnotes to complement or counterpoint the poetic voices in the text. But the infidels had turned this device into a technique of subversion. A casual remark or reference in an otherwise legitimate work could unravel an entire argument. Dwight saw this as the diabolical method behind the *Encyclopédie,* in which "decently written" articles about theology were "entirely and insidiously overthrown" by "references artfully made to other articles." In a footnote, in a remark, "in a hint, in a book of travels; or a stroke, in a letter of civility . . . the reader was intended to be taken by surprise, and to yield his judgement before he was aware, that he was called to judge."[44]

---

43. Backus, *Absalom's Conspiracy,* 30–32 (quotations on 32). Cf. Andrew Lee, *The Declensions of Christianity* . . . (Norwich, Conn., 1794), 17: "The places most infested, by this delusive spirit, fifty years ago, now afford the strongest marks of irreligion."

44. See Dwight, *Discourse on Some Events of the Last Century,* 26, for all quotations except the reference to Denis Diderot and Jean d'Alembert, eds., *Encyclopédie, ou dictionnaire raisonné des sciences, des arts et des metiers* (1751–1765), which is from Dwight, *Duty of Americans,* 10. Dwight is borrowing freely from English archdeacon William Paley, whose description of infidel discourse was excerpted in the *Conn. Courant,* Sept. 9, 1799: "Infidelity is served up in every shape, that is likely to allure, surprize, or beguile the imagination; in a

Dwight's work in the 1790s attests to a continued reverence for the power of the printed word but also to an increasing uneasiness about the anonymity of the civic forum that the press had constructed. Rather than celebrating a public sphere in print that abstracted debate from the personalities and social relationships of those involved, his was a "politics of sincerity and authenticity" that regrounded discourse in the character and sensibility of the author. A text could (should?) convey "that glow of feeling . . . which prove[s], at once, the peculiar sincerity of the writer." Print, like oratory, could derive much persuasive power from the character of the speaker. Virtuous men created virtuous discourse.[45]

Dwight countered the infidel's artful seduction of the reader with appeals to the intellect and to "common sense." He preached to his Yale seniors in 1797 on "The Nature and Danger of Infidel Philosophy" and spent half of his first sermon merely describing a discordant and contradictory infidel tradition stretching from the Stoics through Hume. But Dwight was not just waging an academic battle of the books. Alongside the new emphasis of his rhetorical appeal was the new focus of his message: New England tradition instead of the American millennial future that had inspired the mythic strains of his rousing wartime addresses and his poetry. Since Dwight worried that the godly would lose control over public debate and politics, his preaching aimed at both religious exhortation and political catechism. His political message was adumbrated by two sentences from the endnotes to *Greenfield Hill:* "A thorough and impartial development of the state of society, in Connecticut, and a complete

---

fable, a tale, a novel; a poem; in interspersed and broken hints; remote and oblique surmises; in books of travels, of philosophy, of natural history; in a word, in any form, rather than the right one, that of a profession and regular disquisition." Daniel Brewer discusses subversive cross-referencing in *The Discourse of Enlightenment in Eighteenth-Century France: Diderot and the Art of Philosophizing* (Cambridge, 1993), 48–49.

45. The phrase "politics of sincerity and authenticity" is from Jay Fliegelman, *Declaring Independence: Jefferson, Natural Language, and the Culture of Performance* (Stanford, Calif., 1993), 128–129; Timothy Dwight, *Virtuous Rulers a National Blessing* (Hartford, Conn., 1791), 26–27. Dwight is referring here to Psalm 72 but, in this comment, is primarily concerned with its poetic impact rather than its divine inspiration. The difference between John Trumbull's civic forum in the 1770s and Dwight's New England public mind in the 1790s bears some resemblance to the contrast Anthony J. La Vopa draws between Immanuel Kant's public sphere in "What Is Enlightenment?" (1784), which was ideally rational, universalistic, and freed from the constrictions of social context, and Herder's "Publikum," which was nationalistic and grounded in the particular social and cultural experiences of a community. See La Vopa, "Herder's *Publikum:* Language, Print, and Sociability in Eighteenth-Century Germany," *Eighteenth-Century Studies,* XXIX (1995), 5–24. For Kant's essay, see Isaac Kramnick, ed., *The Portable Enlightenment Reader* (New York, 1995), 1–7.

investigation of the sources of its happiness, would probably throw more light on the true methods of promoting the interests of mankind, than all the volumes of philosophy, which have been written. The causes, which have already produced happiness, will ever produce it." [46]

THE NATURE OF TRUE NEW ENGLAND VIRTUE:
THE POLITICAL PROBLEM

When Timothy Dwight stood before an assembly of veteran officers of the Revolutionary War on July 7, 1795, addressing the anxieties of the audience and the age, he focused on the implications of the American, not the French, Revolution. An unstable national Republic and an unsettled social order had prompted Dwight to enter the continuing discussion about the merits of the new federal and state constitutions. The desperate times clearly demanded a solution to "that political problem, which has so long perplexed the rulers of mankind": how to make a "free government" endure. Dwight turned to "the most respectable political writers" to argue that the root of public happiness was the virtue of individual citizens, and he turned to Isa. 33:6 to counsel that "wisdom and knowledge" shall be "the stability of the times." His *True Means of Establishing Public Happiness* was a bid to shove aside all the constitutional tinkerers and visionary policy planners and reestablish citizen virtue as the central issue for public discussion. Dwight's particular brand of virtue, moreover, was rooted in his evangelical faith and his vision of Connecticut as an ideal Christian republic.[47]

46. Howard, *Connecticut Wits*, 234–235, 361, described how Dwight's use of "common sense" sometimes referred to an "intuitive perception," as in the Scottish philosophy of Thomas Reed and Dugald Stewart, although usually it meant "cautious reasoning." See Dwight, Sermon 19, "The Nature and Danger of Infidel Philosophy," in *Sermons*, I, 314–375; Dwight, *Greenfield Hill*, 172. Millennialism continued to offer him a language with which to construct an American cultural identity and a common purpose for the new nation. But, as Ruth Bloch has noted in *Visionary Republic*, 81, "thoughts about future perfection did not easily lend themselves to immediate practical application."

47. [Dwight], *True Means of Establishing Public Happiness*, 5, 13, 27. The three central studies in what came to be known as "republicanism" are Bernard Bailyn, *The Ideological Origins of the American Revolution* (Cambridge, Mass., 1967); Gordon S. Wood, *The Creation of the American Republic, 1776–1787* (Chapel Hill, N.C., 1969); J.G.A. Pocock, *The Machiavellian Moment: Florentine Political Thought and the Atlantic Republican Tradition* (Princeton, N.J., 1975). Reviews of the literature these works influenced can be found in Robert E. Shalhope, "Toward a Republican Synthesis: The Emergence of an Understanding of Republicanism in American Historiography," *WMQ*, 3d Ser., XXIX (1972), 49–80; Shalhope,

Dwight's first two published sermons, preached in 1777 and 1781, focused more upon the lack of virtue in the British than upon the moral or political character of Americans. The earlier sermon, on Joel 2:20–21, found an "exact" Old Testament "parallel" for the haughty British tyrant with an insatiable demand for tribute money. The 1781 sermon, occasioned by the surrender of General Charles Cornwallis, explained the peculiar evil that had just been conquered: it was "wickedness methodified . . . deceit reduced to a system, and wrought into maxims, or established rules of practice." Although selfishness characterized the human heart, modern philosophers (perhaps Dwight had Bernard Mandeville in mind) had spread the idea that it was a justifiable spring of action, and Sir Robert Walpole, believing that every man had his price, had made selfishness a principle of government—the very principle that led the British to usurp American rights. Selfishness was the root of corruption, the corruption decried by the radical Whigs and the "country" opposition to the Walpole regime: the political domination of self-interested men who pursued wealth and power at public expense. Yet, by also criticizing Lord Chesterfield's "scheme" of education in his *Letters Written . . . to His Son,* Dwight suggested that British society and not just government, private morals and not just the public virtue of government officials had been corrupted.[48]

When Dwight called for a republic of Christian virtue in the 1790s, he was doing more than merely making an argument that had been heard from New England pulpits for a generation. It is true that New England Congregational clergymen had for years identified republican virtue with Christian piety and benevolence, and the ideal republic with the model Christian commonwealth.

"Republicanism and Early American Historiography," *WMQ,* 3d Ser., XXXIX (1982), 334–356; Daniel T. Rodgers, "Republicanism: the Career of a Concept," *JAH,* LXXIX (1992–1993), 11–38. For revisions that move away from the notion of a self-contained republican "paradigm," see Robert E. Shalhope, *The Roots of Democracy: American Thought and Culture, 1760–1800* (Boston, 1990); Gordon S. Wood, *The Radicalism of the American Revolution* (New York, 1991); Milton M. Klein, Richard D. Brown, and John B. Hench, eds., *The Republican Synthesis Revisited: Essays in Honor of George Athan Billias* (Worcester, Mass., 1992). Arguments against the predominance of classical republicanism in Revolutionary America can be found in Joyce Appleby, *Capitalism and a New Social Order: The Republican Vision of the 1790s* (New York, 1984); Appleby, *Liberalism and Republicanism in the Historical Imagination* (Cambridge, Mass., 1992); Isaac Kramnick, *Republicanism and Bourgeois Radicalism: Political Ideology in Late Eighteenth-Century England and America* (Ithaca, N.Y., 1990); Paul A. Rahe, *Republics Ancient and Modern: Classical Republicanism and the American Revolution* (Chapel Hill, N.C., 1992); Michael P. Zuckert, *Natural Rights and the New Republicanism* (Princeton, N.J., 1994).

48. [Timothy Dwight], *A Sermon, Preached at Stamford . . . December 18th, 1777* (Hartford, Conn., 1778), 10; [Dwight], *A Sermon, Preached at Northampton,* 1.

It is also true that late-century clerical Federalists argued against the anarchic forces of democracy in the mid-1790s with the same vehemence and from the same general principles that they had used to preach against Britain's tyrannical usurpation of liberty in the mid-1770s. Although the ministers' Revolutionary rhetoric could sometimes blur the distinctions between the Christian, classical republican, and modern moral virtue, however, in the 1790s the clergy emphasized how woefully inadequate "pagan" virtue was for sustaining a stable political life and, in some cases, argued that it was even a deceptive euphemism for pride and selfishness. They contrasted modern benevolence, resting on a natural moral sense rather than grace or the gospel, to the vastly superior public virtue cultivated by Christianity. Clergymen also had to answer the nonclerical political commentators who were deemphasizing virtue altogether as the keystone of republican politics. Dwight's effort to move debate away from constitution making and back toward a Christian public virtue was also an attempt to reclaim control over the public agenda, to recast political arguments as social and moral problems and give ministers rather than magistrates the stronger voice.[49]

Dwight tried to stifle calls for a new state constitution, which would threaten to change Connecticut's existing political structure—including its provision for the compulsory support of religion and official preference for Congre-

49. Hatch, *Sacred Cause of Liberty,* 117, 135, notes that New England clergymen—"Arminian and New Divinity, urban and rural, Harvard- and Yale-trained"—had long associated republican virtue with Christian piety and benevolence. On clerical Federalism, see also Buel, *Securing the Revolution,* 167–172, 231–233. Stephen A. Marini, looking at the religious connections of Federalism and Antifederalism in the earlier ratification debates, argues that the former tended toward a political theory emphasizing strong government and conflict resolution and the latter toward virtue and consensus management ("Religion, Politics, and Ratification," in Ronald Hoffman and Peter J. Albert, eds., *Religion in a Revolutionary Age* [Charlottesville, Va., 1994], 184–217). Dwight and Connecticut's Standing Order, however, cut across these categories. Earlier sermons comment on the inadequacies of Greco-Roman (or at least not explicitly Christian) citizen virtue, although this theme is not as prominent as in the 1790s; see election sermons for 1768, 1772, 1778, 1779 (see Appendix for citations). Some seemed to have a less jaundiced view of citizen virtue; see election sermons for 1764, 1766, 1775, 1776, 1780, 1783, 1787; and Enoch Huntington, *Political Wisdom; or, Honesty the Best Policy . . .* (Middletown, Conn., 1786). The election sermons for 1791–1798 agree with the sentiment expressed by John Smalley, *On the Evils of a Weak Government . . .* (Hartford, Conn., 1800), in Ellis Sandoz, ed., *Political Sermons of the American Founding Era, 1730–1805* (Indianapolis, Ind., 1990), 1438: "Too many choose to take their instructions from heathen philosophy, rather than from the oracles of God." Articles in the *Conn. Courant,* May 27, June 17, 1793, for example, also noted that voters were choosing men with political ability over men with virtue and wondered how Christians could elect infidels to represent them.

gationalism. Whereas all other states except Rhode Island had called constitutional conventions following Independence, Connecticut merely proceeded under its 1662 royal charter and substituted loyalty to the state for loyalty to the king. In 1786, the General Assembly debated whether the charter was in fact a constitution. In 1792, a writer in the *Middlesex Gazette* complained that a decade had passed "without any amelioration of the system of government." Another in the *Litchfield Monitor* charged that the charter was an antirepublican document. In 1795, Judge Zephaniah Swift denounced these "visionary theorists" who denied that the charter could be considered a legal constitution because it had not been ratified by the people. When Dwight described Connecticut as a model republic for the rest of America, he was also warning a local audience not to tamper any further with the status quo.[50]

Dwight's 1795 argument presupposed a symbiotic relationship between society and government, noting that political systems help mold the character of a people and that character in turn maintains political health. But the time had come for a change of emphasis from constitution making to character building. Granting that "a free government has been always, and justly, supposed to be a primary source of national happiness," he pointed out that in a dozen years of political freedom there had been several unhappy instances where "we seem to have approached the verge of dissolution." In the 1780s, Ezra Stiles and Samuel Wales had described political institutions as the "foundation" and religion a part of the "superstructure" of a republic. Dwight inverted that formula.[51]

50. Proceedings of the General Assembly, in the *Conn. Courant,* Nov. 13, 1786. The two newspaper articles and a passage from Zephaniah A. Swift, *A System of the Laws of the State of Connecticut,* 2 vols. (Windham, Conn., 1795), are quoted in Richard J. Purcell, *Connecticut in Transition: 1775–1818* (1918; reprint, Middletown, Conn., 1963), 115–116, and discussed in Grossbart, "The Revolutionary Transition," 279. Comments from the Boston *Gazette, and the Country Journal* calling absurd the idea that the charter was a constitution were reprinted by the *Norwich Packet,* Oct. 6, 1791. "Hambden's" thirteen-part series on the need for a new state constitution ran in the *Middlesex Gazette; or, Foederal Adviser* from June 16 to Sept. 8, 1792. The author of *The Security of the Rights of Citizens in the State of Connecticut Considered* (Hartford, Conn., 1792), thought the dispute was over words more than substance (61). See also "An Answer to the Querist No. 1," *Conn. Courant,* Mar. 30, 1795.

51. [Dwight], *True Means of Establishing Public Happiness,* 5, 6. Cf. Stiles, *United States Elevated to Glory and Honor,* 34; Wales, *Dangers of Our National Prosperity,* 27. Similarly, an essay entitled "The Utility of Social Worship, Historically Illustrated" ("Moral Sentiments, No. IX"), in *American Mercury,* Nov. 1, 1790, described the formation of the mythical republic of "Eucoria," where Christianity was superadded to previously established republican institutions and the moral teachings of "natural" religion. Dwight would neither have elevated civic over social life (Aristotle's *zoon politikon*) nor the opposite (as in Thomas Paine's *Com-*

Dwight clearly recognized the distinction between *establishing* a free government and *perpetuating* it, seeing the former task as "sufficiently easy" and the latter as "very difficult." Here he confronted what has been considered the central problem of the republican tradition: How can an essentially static model of the republic survive in a world of time and change? For the author of a one-hundred-page Connecticut pamphlet entitled *The Security of the Rights of Citizens in the State of Connecticut Considered* (1792), the answer was, not the continuous cultivation of citizen virtue, but political institutions that balanced interests and settled disputes by the rule of law. The political architecture this pamphlet proposed was similar to what was offered by John Adams in his *Defense of the Constitutions of the United States* (1787): the social struggle between a natural aristocracy and the poorer citizenry would be reflected in and controlled by a bicameral legislative body, which would govern with a strong executive. The author of *Security of the Rights* argued that Connecticut's government exemplified just such a system. Two classes—debtors and creditors—were represented in the two houses of the legislature. The wealthier, wiser, and more politically active men, who were usually creditors, took an interest in the elections to the upper house—the twelve-seat Council—and the Council, therefore, must be taken as representing "those who have been called the natural aristocracy of a country." Debtors were rightly more interested in the election of town deputies to the lower house. The interests of these two groups were balanced in the bicameral legislature: "The aristocracy, and the people, being the two great orders in society, compose the *public,* or the whole community; and the will of both is the public will." [52]

---

mon Sense . . . [Philadelphia, 1776], where government is only a necessary evil). Dwight would have agreed with the author of "Thoughts on the Alterations Which Have Taken Place in the Characters of Nations and of the Causes by Which They Were Produced," *American Mercury,* Dec. 5, 1796, Sept. 26, 1799, who argued that the form of government changes "the character and spirit of a people," and with the author of "On Party-Spirit," who wrote that "virtue begets republicanism—and republicanism begets equal rights and equal laws."

52. [Dwight], *True Means of Establishing Public Happiness,* 5; *Security of the Rights,* 41, 48n. One copy of this pamphlet contains a handwritten note attributing it to anticlerical Windham lawyer Zephaniah Swift, although hostile readers in this period tended to blame Swift even for works discussing rights and Connecticut government that he did not write. See *Conn. Courant,* May 30, June 6, 1791. J.G.A. Pocock defines the central problem of the republican tradition in *Machiavellian Moment,* viii. Jean Yarbrough, building on Pocock's *Machiavellian Moment* and Wood's *Creation of the American Republic* in "Republicanism Reconsidered: Some Thoughts on the Foundation and Preservation of the American Republic," *Review of Politics,* XLI (1979), 61–95, has argued that the founding fathers failed to understand in what way founding a new government and making it last were separate activities. The new order was brought forth by innovative action. But as "the activities of the

Was there a retreat from the politics of public virtue in the late 1780s and 1790s? Americans in 1787–1790 adopted the internal mechanisms of checks and balances in the Constitution, not Adams's explicit balance of social orders, to preserve the national Republic. Though few of the founders wanted to entirely discard the traditional emphasis on citizen virtue, they and the Constitution they devised were inclined, according to some interpretations, to sever virtue from political participation. They hoped that the people would be virtuous, but the virtue they described was not that of classical republicanism, which was constituted by activity in the civic arena. The Constitution, as Madison explained in "The Federalist" No. 10, depended for stability, not on virtue, but upon the counterbalanced energies of competing private interests. Some students of the period see 1787 as a turning point, when virtue becomes privatized, is spoken of more in terms of individual morality, and is implicitly removed from the sphere of public power relations. Others have argued that the classical republican notion of *civic* virtue does not really describe the ideology of 1776 well in the first place, so 1787 should not be seen as a dramatic departure from earlier sentiments and principles. Yet, if there was no paradigm shift from classical republicanism to a postclassical politics relying on institutional mechanisms, pamphlets like *Security of the Rights* suggested to clerical writers like Dwight that there had been a change of emphasis. Against those who put too much faith in political mechanisms, Dwight and others stressed the necessity of virtue and specified its necessarily Christian character.[53]

---

founding became the paradigm for all political activities," including the activities of ordinary citizens, "civic involvement" came to imply the violence and destruction required to tear down the old order and creative "innovation" to connote the radical challenge to fundamental principles involved in constitution making (87). The founders saw that tearing down and reconstituting were appropriate to the task of founding, but not of perpetuating the Republic. When they set these activities aside, they also set aside creative civic involvement as well. They, like Dwight, "made the question of preservation appear to be largely a question of stability" (87). The founders hoped to achieve stability through a political mechanism (the federal Constitution) that would preserve the system in response to historic change.

53. Pocock, in *Machiavellian Moment,* stressed the civic character of virtue; Wood, in *Creation of the American Republic,* marked 1787 as the end of classical republicanism. Yarbrough, "Republicanism Reconsidered," *Review of Politics,* XLI (1975), 61–95, argued that the Constitution institutionalized the distinction between civic and moral virtue as a result of its compromise between the liberal-democratic demand for liberty and the mechanisms of republican government. But we should be cautious about reading an ethos (economic individualism) and a social formation (the more rigid separation of public and private) of a later, industrializing America as inevitable consequences of Constitutional structures. Rahe's *Republics Ancient and Modern* argued: "Gordon S. Wood's contention that the con-

Security of the Rights purposefully displaced the politics of virtue. Free governments, the author contended, did not rest on the "mere personal integrity" of the leadership, and "corruption, over which the good have often wept with fruitless lamentation," resulted from a bad form of civil government, not from moral declension. Systems of manners and principles were a sandy foundation for political stability because they could not be enforced, and, at any rate, they would be undermined by the natural forces of social change. What remained constant was that society was made up of competing, self-interested individuals. Equal justice, administered by the legal and political system, not the benevolence cultivated by moralists, held society together by preserving the balance between interests. Vibrations to the scales of justice, the author wrote, citing Adam Smith's *Wealth of Nations*, caused civil commotions. Referring the reader to Publius's "Federalist," he contended that "the public interest is the aggregate of private interest," even when those particular and partial interests remain irreconcilably hostile, as long as they are contained and balanced in a properly constituted legislature.[54]

---

stitutional proposal of 1787 embodied a repudiation of the principles of 1776 is not borne out by the evidence" (966 n. 78). Kramnick, in *Republicanism and Bourgeois Radicalism*, 200–259, argued that scholars following Wood have misread calls for private Christian virtue in central texts like James Burgh's *Political Disquisitions . . .* (Philadelphia, 1775) as republican civic virtue. Zuckert in *Natural Rights and the New Republicanism*, 297–319, argued that John Trenchard and Thomas Gordon's *Collection of Cato's Letters, in the British Journal . . .* (London, 1723) had also been misinterpreted in light of the republican paradigm. Although containing some exhortations to public virtue, Zuckert argued, *Cato's Letters* are founded upon Lockean rights and interests.

54. *Security of the Rights*, 10, 11, 22, 77. To this analysis the author added a frank—perhaps even cynical—reading of "the language of power." In different kinds of governments, "there is a difference in the *forms* as well as the substance of public communications" (28n). Monarchs justify their actions with rhetoric that refers to their own "splendid elevation." Legislation in a republic benefits a great proportion of the population; the interests of this proportion are called the "general interest," and arguments about power are conducted using the language of "liberty" (49–50). "Honorious," in "An Address to the Thinking, Judicious, Inhabitants of Connecticut," *Conn. Courant*, Sept. 16, 1783, also pushed the politics of virtue aside. Montesquieu taught that popular governments must have public virtue for their basis, "and[,] since there never was and never will be such a thing, as a permanent general principle of *public virtue*, there never was and never will be such a thing as a permanent democracy." "Self-interest is the ruling principle of all mankind—when this becomes generally connected—that is, when the private interests of individuals, all unite to pursue the same object, it assumes the name of *patriotism* or *public spirit*." John Treadwell of Farmington countered a week later (Sept. 23, 1783) that virtue was the essential force keeping a government and its people united. Nathan Strong, in *A Sermon, Delivered in Presence of His Excellency Samuel Huntington . . .* (Hartford, Conn., 1790), agreed that the business of gov-

The dependence upon constitutional systems for stability in America or Connecticut formed the pretext for Dwight's 1795 speech. In his 1791 election sermon, he had argued that the success of the first years under the federal Constitution owed less to the nature of the Constitution itself or to the specific functions of the government it established than to the virtuous character of George Washington, who had done so much to mold a virtuous citizenry by example. In 1795, Dwight faced the problem of a free government's long-term durability.

> Hence most of the political knowledge and labour of freemen has been employed, and exhausted, in endeavouring to give stability to their respective political systems. Hence have arisen the numerous checks, balances, and divisions of power and influence, found in our own political constitutions, and in those of several other nations. In other nations, these have been generally insufficient to accomplish the end. Whether they will issue more happily in our own is uncertain.

Dwight found any system that merely checked and balanced power between governmental bodies, like the state and federal constitutions, or tried to divide and control it among antagonistic socioeconomic classes, like Adams's *Defense,* was insufficient:

> The formation and establishment of knowledge and virtue in the citizens of a Community is the first business of Legislation, and will more easily and more effectually establish order, and secure liberty, than all the checks, balances, and penalties, which have been devised by man.

Dwight believed that, since virtue was the only foundation of a free constitution, the republic must mold the character of its citizens. Knowledge must be generally diffused, vice extinguished, virtue inspired. Dwight denied the perfectibility of man (an idea bandied about by "infidel philosophers") but dedicated his life to the belief that the grace of God could work through human efforts to inculcate a Christian disposition to do good.[55]

The solution to the problem of the unstable republic, Dwight argued, was clear once one stepped back and put governmental institutions into a larger context. The real problem was not how to stabilize a republican government; it was how to establish and stabilize public happiness, which was the ultimate

---

ernment is to check and balance a diversity of interests, but "for this it needs the assistance of some pervading social bond, and this bond can be no other than religion" (11).

55. Dwight, *Virtuous Rulers a National Blessing,* 21, 30; [Dwight], *True Means of Establishing Public Happiness,* [5]–6, 33.

goal of government in the first place. Government as such, though not in any particular form, was instituted by God to preserve the happiness of his creatures so that he could better take delight in his creation. Since men in chains had no opportunity to become happy by living a virtuous life, the creation of a free government provided that opportunity. The real work, though, since "happiness is produced through Knowledge and Virtue," is the "diffusion of these through a Community." Government must devote itself to actively inculcating virtue and disseminating knowledge, but these tasks are also (and more importantly) carried on by church, school, and family. The relationship between virtue and political participation becomes a false dilemma, since public action includes much more than active participation in legislative decision making. The public sphere includes, but is considerably larger than, the domain of politics and civil government.[56]

Individual families were metonymically related to the republic, since governmental authority was parental authority on a larger scale, but the difference in scale did not make the family as an institution any less important. "Few persons can be concerned in settling systems of faith, moulding forms of government, regulating nations, or establishing empires," Dwight declared in his 1798 Fourth of July oration, "but almost all can train up a family for God," and in doing so offer him the "most lovely" sign of virtue and public service. Parents nurturing, educating, and governing their children were not just performing private tasks with public consequences, but tasks that were simultaneously public and private. The family and the state had interrelated tasks in sustaining the life of the social organism. They were not just analogously related to one another, and compared as distinct entities, but were both images of an all-embracing divine paternalism.[57]

56. Dwight, "Sermon XCIX: The Law of God; The Second Great Commandment; Utility the Foundation of Virtue," in *Theology; Explained and Defended, in a Series of Sermons...,* 5 vols. (Middletown, Conn., 1818), III, 439–455; [Dwight], *True Means of Establishing Public Happiness,* 27. A letter in the *Conn. Courant,* Nov. 6, 1797, similarly described social habits and institutions outside government as performing the crucial work of cultivating virtue: "The family, the school, the college, the church, the town, and the state, successively bid [the citizen] a welcome reception, and enroll him a member of their several institutions. To these we may add the restraint of public opinion, which compels even profligates to be outwardly virtuous. Habits and institutions like these, though generally under-rated, as subordinate means of securing virtue and order, have ever possessed the highest efficacy.... When they have taught him the course of conduct, which he ought to pursue, little is left for the magistrate. The business of government is already performed. From the moral culture of the heart, is derived the chief sorce of moral obligation, and of course, the chief support of human laws."

57. Dwight, *Duty of Americans,* 17. Jay Fliegelman discussed the familial metaphors of

Dwight put a public Christian virtue (not the private virtue of Christian domesticity) in the place of a civic virtue that overemphasized political participation. Individuals did not have to be virtuous by arguing at a town meeting, joining a crowd protest, or picking up their guns for liberty; they could signify their public virtue through their daily social behavior. They could participate in the public sphere, not primarily by electing representatives to act virtuously for them in the political arena, but by consciously investing their nonpolitical actions with public significance. Individuals, even of the lowest station, Dwight argued, could participate in public life just by attending Sunday worship, which was a sign and rallying point of social solidarity: "Every man, therefore, who loves his country, or his religion, ought to feel, that he serves, or injures, both, as he celebrates, or neglects, the Sabbath."[58]

The central institution of communal identity for Dwight and the Standing Order clergy was, not surprisingly, the church, for "the house of God is also the house of social prayer." Religion provided the ritual to bring public and private together. Attending the Sabbath was "the bond of union to christians; the badge by which they know each other." Piety, righteousness, and temperance were private matters, but Christian virtue was the bridge from the private to the public sphere:

If each man conducts himself aright, the community cannot be conducted wrong. If the private life be unblamable, the public state must be commendable and happy. . . . Individuals are often apt to consider their own private conduct as of small importance to the public welfare. This opinion is wholly erroneous and highly mischievous.[59]

In the closed, culturally homogeneous community of Dwight's ideal New England town, virtue could be signified in silent exchanges that gave people "confidence" in one another. A tidy farmhouse and neat, simple clothing reinforced the mutual confidence among fellow citizens who shared Christian virtue. Each would be assured that his neighbor would endeavor to subordinate private passions for the common good and pursue the good through the application of enlightened common sense. The citizen would be satisfied and secure with the ability to "approve" wise policies; the legislator, on his "lofty summit," where he "stands as a Watchman for the welfare of millions,"

Revolutionary politics in *Prodigals and Pilgrims: The American Revolution against Patriarchal Authority, 1750–1800* (Cambridge, 1982). Dwight's story of the three-generation decline of a family serves as a political parable in *Greenfield Hill*, pt. 4, ll. 596–784.

58. Dwight, *Duty of Americans*, 19.

59. Ibid., 16–23 (quotations on 16, 19).

would be confident that he could govern by rational persuasion rather than force.[60]

Although Connecticut would never distinguish itself by the extent of its territory, its wealth, or its population, Dwight proclaimed in 1795 that "it may rise to preeminence in knowledge, virtue, and happiness." A large republic with a diverse population would lack a homogeneous citizenry that could speak with one voice, and it would require too complex a government to manage. A republic devoted to commerce as the means of its prosperity would soon be calculating virtue and vice in gold coin, perverting individual morals with excesses of luxury, and corrupting the corporate character by inciting greed. Carthage and Holland had fallen under the burden of their commerce as easily as Greece and Rome had been ruined by conquest, he argued. Connecticut was rivaled only by the Swiss canton as a successful experiment in human government and society. Not created artificially through sudden constitutional fiat (as the United States had been), it had grown and developed gradually, applying the principles of the pious first planters and cautiously learning from the experience of 150 years. If it continued to cultivate virtue in its citizens, he believed, Connecticut would become the Athens of "a world enlightened, refined, and christian."[61]

THE NATURE OF TRUE NEW ENGLAND VIRTUE:
THE RELIGIOUS SOLUTION

Dwight's calls for public virtue meshed in distinctive ways with the moral government theology and practical divinity that he preached to his Yale students

60. Ibid. The epigraph to Dwight's *Virtuous Rulers a National Blessing,* from "Gov. Patterson's Answer to the Address of the Presbytery of New Brunswick," expresses a similar sentiment: "Our holy religion makes good men; from thence the transition is easy and natural to regular citizens, and obedient subjects. *Where private virtue cannot be found, it is in vain to look for public; and laws are of little efficacy without good examples.*" Silverman, *Timothy Dwight,* 65–66, remarks on Dwight's symbolic use of clothing in *Greenfield Hill.* The quotations in the paragraph's last sentence are from [Dwight], *True Means of Establishing Public Happiness,* 25, 27.

61. [Dwight], *True Means of Establishing Public Happiness,* 39. For an argument similar to Dwight's, see "A Querist, No. III," *Conn. Courant,* Mar. 23, 1795 (reprinted from the New London *Conn. Gazette):* "Human invention has been on the rack for many centuries to perpetuate republicanism; many trials have been made in different parts of the civilized world; all the ancient, and most of the modern ones have failed. Our country is an exception. . . . Experience teaches, that men verge towards the savage state in proportion as they scatter

beginning in 1795. His stress on the social utility—indeed, the political neces-sity—of public worship and Christian virtue is also representative of the Stand-ing Order's main themes after 1784. Historians often portray Dwight and his clerical cohort as either desperately clinging to old models of the relationship between religion and the public realm, like Puritan covenant preaching or the "civil millennialism" developed during the Seven Years' War, or as tentatively stepping forward into the new era of revivalism and religious voluntarism known as the "Second Great Awakening." But, after the abrogation of the Say-brook Platform in 1784, the still-powerful Standing Order did not preach about a national covenant with God or rely on revivalism; Congregational clergy-men did not advocate either a retreat into a pure church or the sacralization of America as an elect nation. What they did preach—and what is especially evi-dent, though often misunderstood, in Dwight's work—is a more complex dia-lectic of memory and hope, combining an ideological defense of New England institutions with ever more anxious projections of America's possible rise to glory in a millennial future.[62]

Dwight both invoked and moved away from New England's theologian of

---

their setlements in a wilderness.... And would not that have been the case here, had not the institutions in question, instamped on our people a far more dignified character." Pennsyl-vania and New York, the "Querist" thought, were starting to learn lessons about political stability from New England.

62. Historians have argued, in the words of J. Earl Thompson, Jr., that "a radical change transpired in the Protestant mind—a change involving the substitution of the presupposi-tions of the Revival for the covenant assumptions of the politico-religious sermons" ("A Perilous Experiment: New England Clergymen and American Destiny, 1796–1826" [Ph.D. diss., Princeton University, 1966], 207). Perry Miller's "From Covenant to Revival," in Miller's *Nature's Nation* (Cambridge, Mass., 1967), 90–120, placed this transition in the late eighteenth century; Thompson argues for the period between 1816 and 1826. These and other interpretations, whether focusing on a covenant-to-revival or *ecclesia*-to-*polis* shift, miss the Connecticut Standing Order's distinctive formulations in the period between the abrogation of the Saybrook Platform in 1784 and complete disestablishment in 1818. An ex-ception is James Fulton Maclear, in "'The True American Union' of Church and State: The Reconstruction of the Theocratic Tradition," *Church History*, XXVIII (1959), 41–62. Later studies also suggest that previous historians have exaggerated the idea of America as re-deemer nation (or what would come to be called American manifest destiny) in the religious thought of the eighteenth and nineteenth centuries. See Gerald R. McDermott, *One Holy and Happy Society: The Public Theology of Jonathan Edwards* (University Park, Pa., 1992); David W. Kling, *A Field of Divine Wonders: The New Divinity and Village Revivals in North-western Connecticut, 1792–1822* (University Park, Pa., 1993); Mark Y. Hanley, *Beyond a Chris-tian Commonwealth: The Protestant Quarrel with the American Republic, 1830–1860* (Chapel Hill, N.C., 1994).

"true virtue," his grandfather Jonathan Edwards. Dwight studied theology with his uncle, Jonathan Edwards, Jr., and by the late 1780s Ezra Stiles still considered him one of the "would-be Luthers" of the New Divinity movement. But no single Edwardsean social and political theory guided the thought and practice of New Divinity men in the later eighteenth century. Samuel Hopkins's evangelical social criticism proclaimed an uncompromising, self-denying benevolence that condemned all the moral strivings of the unregenerate as worthless. Joseph Bellamy, however, called the unregenerate as well as those born again to their moral duty under God's law and preached a politically engaged communalism that meshed with Revolutionary republican ideology. Benjamin Trumbull's preaching on social virtue, according to one interpretation, shifted from republican communalism to a liberal vision stressing individual self-interest and supporting the values of a free market economy. Challenged by political and social upheavals that Edwards himself had not faced, New Divinity men in the last quarter of the eighteenth century found different ways to apply the tenets of Edwardsean Calvinism, even as they joined together in the patriot cause and, later, in the Federalist party.[63]

63. Stiles, *Literary Diary,* ed. Dexter, III, 273–275, Aug. 10, 1787. On Dwight's endorsement of Edwards, see Dwight, *Travels,* ed. Solomon, IV, 228–229. On Dwight's theology, see Frank Hugh Foster, *A Genetic History of the New England Theology* (Chicago, 1907); Wayne Conrad Tyner, "The Theology of Timothy Dwight in Historical Perspective" (Ph.D. diss., University of North Carolina at Chapel Hill, 1971); Berk, *Calvinism versus Democracy;* John R. Fitzmier, "The Godly Federalism of Timothy Dwight, 1753–1817: Society, Doctrine, and Religion in the Life of New England's 'Moral Legislator'" (Ph.D. diss., Princeton University, 1986); Annabelle S. Wenzke, *Timothy Dwight (1752–1817)* (Lewiston, N.Y., 1989). See also Sidney Earl Mead, *Nathaniel William Taylor, 1786–1858: A Connecticut Liberal* (Chicago, 1942); Sidney E. Ahlstrom, *A Religious History of the American People* (New Haven, 1972), chap. 26; Conrad Cherry, "Nature and the Republic: The New Haven Theology," *New England Quarterly,* LI (1978), 509–526; Bruce Kuklick, *Churchmen and Philosophers: From Jonathan Edwards to John Dewey* (New Haven, Conn., 1985), chaps. 4, 7; and Allen C. Guelzo, *Edwards on the Will: A Century of American Theological Debate* (Middletown, Conn., 1989). Gerald R. McDermott, in *One Holy and Happy Society: The Public Theology of Jonathan Edwards* (University Park, Pa., 1992), 172–176, speculates about the influence of Edwards's "social and political theory." On Hopkins, Bellamy, and Trumbull, see Joseph A. Conforti, *Samuel Hopkins and the New Divinity Movement: Calvinism, the Congregational Ministry, and Reform in New England between the Great Awakenings* (Grand Rapids, Mich., 1981); Mark Valeri, *Law and Providence in Joseph Bellamy's New England: The Origins of the New Divinity in Revolutionary America* (New York, 1994); James Dale German, "The Preacher and the New Light Revolution in Connecticut: The Pulpit Theology of Benjamin Trumbull, 1760–1800" (Ph.D. diss., University of California at Riverside, 1989); German, "The Social Utility of Wicked Self-Love: Calvinism, Capitalism, and Public Policy in Revolutionary New England," *JAH,* LXXXII (1995–1996), 965–998.

In his 1795 sermon, *True Means of Public Happiness*, Dwight seemed to translate Edwards's difficult prose into more accessible language. Edwards had compacted his dissertation on true virtue into two sentences:

> True virtue most essentially consists in benevolence to Being in general. Or perhaps to speak more accurately, it is that consent, propensity and union of heart to Being in general, that is immediately exercised in a general good will.

Dwight defined virtue as "the Love of doing good"; it is "the mental energy, directed steadily to that which is right." Since it is a single "disposition" or "Attribute of mind," we can only talk about different *kinds* of virtue by looking at what object this mental energy is focused upon. Directed toward God, we call it piety, toward mankind, goodwill or benevolence, and toward ourselves, self-government or temperance. True virtue for Edwards had to be grounded in the "propensity and union of heart to Being in general"; Dwight called this necessary disposition "Piety," and simply said that, "without Piety, the other branches of virtue are never found."[64]

But as Dwight preached his ostensibly Edwardsean theology to a post-Revolutionary generation, he "Arminianized" it, or gave more importance to human agency, even as he battled the Boston Arminians in his grandfather's name. Dwight's God was a Moral Magistrate, a Benevolent Father in the Republic of Grace. This God did not overwhelm the hearts of his children with a "new spiritual sense" but rationally persuaded them that his Law was just and offered "motives" for them to "relish" him and his moral government. The Holy Spirit did not act upon the human soul in a flood of irresistible grace but cooperated with the soul in the act of regeneration. Christ died for the sins of mankind, but men still had the human freedom and moral ability to accept or reject the offered pardon. In this context, Dwight's descriptions of the virtuous disposition, of how one becomes virtuous, and of how to speak of virtue in relation to the unconverted dull the sharp edge of Edwards's theological propositions and make Christian virtue a more practical foundation for social and political life.[65]

---

64. Jonathan Edwards, "The Nature of True Virtue," in *Ethical Writings*, ed. Paul Ramsey, in Miller et al., eds., *Works of Jonathan Edwards*, VIII (New Haven, Conn., 1989), 540; [Dwight], *True Means of Establishing Public Happiness*, 14, 21.

65. On the "new spiritual sense," see Jonathan Edwards, *Religious Affections*, ed. John E. Smith, in Miller et al., eds., *Works of Jonathan Edwards*, II (New Haven, Conn., 1959), 205–206; on the heart's ability to "relish" spiritual objects, see Dwight, "Sermon LXXIV: Regeneration—Its Nature," in *Theology*. Howard, in *Connecticut Wits*, 363, argued that Dwight's often ambiguous and contradictory language, his "characteristic looseness of thinking," enabled him to make the "broad outline" of Edwards's system attractive to the early nine-

Dwight's definition of virtue as "the love of doing good" does not itself place more emphasis on either the heart's disposition ("the love") or the person's act ("doing good"). But his discussions quickly turn to the *effects* of virtue: temperance restrains the evil desires of the self, goodwill makes good laws and social relations. Certainly in the 1795 sermon to former Revolutionary War officers, this emphasis is partially due to the audience and the occasion, both of which required practical suggestions rather than metaphysical distinctions. The theology Dwight taught at Yale, however, continued to modify his grandfather's scheme. A later sermon by Dwight, included in his posthumously published *Theology*, gave virtue a further utilitarian twist: "VIRTUE IS FOUNDED IN UTILITY," he declared; it draws all its value from the happiness it produces in the human world, thus giving glory to God.[66]

For Edwards, only the saved could be truly virtuous. The disposition of the heart toward being in general was the direct result of the Holy Spirit's penetrating a soul, regenerating (though not perfecting) human nature in a second birth that turned the heart toward God. Dwight maintained the same absolute distinction between the virtuous saint and the sinner, but he modified its severity by describing conversion as being readily available to almost everyone in the Christian community. Dwight did not rest his hopes for social stability upon heathen virtue and reserve Christian virtue for the chosen few. Like other election day preachers in the late 1780s and 1790s, he argued that the republican virtue of the Greeks and Romans, which lacked true piety, had no foundation "beside the changing power of fashionable opinion, the slippery dependence of personal honour, and the accidental coincidence of selfishness with duty." The modern philosopher's natural benevolence came up short too: man's natural moral obligations to other "worms of the dust" were flimsy motivations to good behavior. Instead, Dwight argued that the "immediate duty of *all* men" is faith and repentance. All men are called so they can be filled with "the spirit of obedience" and restored "*to the character of good subjects.*" Only the atheist was a hopeless case. All others needed only to be convinced of their sin and the righteousness of God's moral law. Possessed of this conviction, only "a

---

teenth century through his ability "to hold on to old-fashioned orthodoxy with one hand while he kept the other on the pulse of a new age." Guelzo, in *Edwards on the Will,* 221–229, suggests that Dwight was more self-consciously distancing himself from the New Divinity and moving closer to Old Calvinists by the time of his ascension to the Yale presidency. Dwight either shrugged in "metaphysical ignorance" at the problems regarding regeneration and volition that continued to perplex New Divinity thinkers or explicitly moved his theology in a different direction (226).

66. Dwight, "Sermon XCIX," in *Theology,* III, 439–455 (quotation on 440).

very small number" would return to their sinful ways. Regeneration, and true Christian virtue, regularly followed the prayers of convinced sinners.[67]

Man can as easily be a saint as a savage, Dwight indicated, depending upon the human efforts to build a Christian civilization and culture in which a spiritual awakening can take place. Dwight came to see that a virtuous environment provided the fertile ground for the seeds of saving grace. What some theologians had defined as man's ability to prepare the soul for grace, Dwight placed in a social and cultural context. The Spirit remained the agent or efficient cause of regeneration, but Dwight emphatically stressed that it acted on the soul through natural means like preaching, religious education, or the general influence of other religious people.[68]

In Dwight's ideal Christian community, like the one described in *Greenfield Hill* where virtue was actively cultivated, conversion did not have to follow the "violent torrent" of the soul that Edwards witnessed. Conversion could be a "consummation of the Christian character" following a progress more like "a river silently, and uniformly, moving onward, and never delaying its course a moment in its way toward the ocean." All would be taught how to turn toward saving grace as their only hope, and many would in fact be converted. Virtuous behavior would characterize the lives of the saints, who would continue to grow in grace. Truly virtuous acts would be valued by the effects they produced in society. Virtue would be cultivated by carefully tending a thoroughly Christian society and by following the wisdom of the Divine Father as revealed in the Scriptures. The peace, justice, and happiness of God's moral government could be reflected on earth in the new United States if the whole country, like New England, established the proper institutions and social habits.[69]

67. On the distinction between saint and sinner, see, for example, Dwight, "Sermon LXXVI: Regeneration; Its Attendants; Generally Considered," *Theology,* III, 96–110: "Nothing can be virtuous, which does not proceed from a heart, good in the Evangelical sense" (102). For the "worms of the dust" reference, see [Dwight], *True Means of Establishing Public Happiness,* 19, 21. On the spirit of obedience, see Dwight, "Sermon CXXXIV: Faith and Repentance; Necessary to Restore Us to Obedience," *Theology,* IV, 470–484 (quotation on 471). On the small number of unredeemed, see Dwight, "Sermon LXX: Regeneration; Its Antecedents," *Theology,* III, 78–95 (quotation on 88).

68. Berk, *Calvinism versus Democracy,* 87. Dwight embraced an individualist "preparation" as well, though human efforts are always aided by the Holy Spirit. See Sermons LXX to LXXXI on regeneration in *Theology,* I. On the means of grace, see Dwight, "Sermon CXXXV: The Means of Grace; Ordinary Means of Grace; Proofs That There Are Such Means," *Theology,* IV, 485–499.

69. Dwight, "Sermon LXXV," *Theology,* III, 78–95 (quotations on 87). The Connecticut General Assembly's special address, written to accompany the annual thanksgiving procla-

Although often held up as an apostle of the American redeemer nation, for Dwight the *church* was the primary corporate entity under God's moral government. North America was the probable location for the dawn of the millennial kingdom; the United States had only the potential to share in that glory if they supported the work of the church. Dwight was no federal theologian extending the Puritan national covenant to the American Republic. In describing God's moral government, Dwight did not speak of nations making covenants with God; they made formal professions acknowledging God's ultimate sovereignty. The same scriptural passages that federal theologians quoted when they pointed to ancient Israel's national covenant, Dwight argued applied to the "Jewish Church," not to the nation of Israel. The whole Old Testament, Dwight argued, defined such covenants as oaths or professions by members of a church.

> As, therefore, there is no hint of any other oath, ever taken to God by this people, as a nation; as there is no conceivable occasion, upon which a whole nation can be supposed, throughout its successive generations, to enter into any other oath to God; it is plain, that the precepts, requiring them to swear to God, required them solely thus to take upon them this covenant.

Under the Christian dispensation, God's sole covenant existed with his true (Protestant) Church, into which all Christians were baptized and in which they were recognized as full members when they professed their faith as adults.[70]

---

mation and to be read from all the pulpits in the state, accurately reflected the sentiments of Dwight and the Standing Order clergy: "This Assembly taking into consideration the ancient laws and institutions of this State, and especially those which relate to the observation of the Sabbath, and to the morals and manners of the people, are deeply sensible that they are wisely calculated to form the habits of virtue, to promote social order, and of consequence, to support our free and happy constitution of government; that they have, by producing a prompt and voluntary obedience to the laws, in every period, greatly contributed to the peace and prosperity of the State, and that they still continue, though their energy is sensibly diminished, to contribute in a degree to the same end" (*Conn. Courant*, Nov. 12, 1798).

70. Dwight, "Sermon CXLIX: The Extraordinary Means of Grace; The Character of Members of the Church," *Theology*, IV, 147–166 (quotation on 156). Beginning with Gen. 2:26, Dwight observed terms like God's "children" or God's "people" and noted that "this phraseology is ever afterwards used to denote the Church" (V, 151). Reading especially Deut. 26 and Jer. 31 and supporting his point with reference to 2 Chron. 23:16 and many other passages, Dwight concluded: "*The Oath*, here sworn by all the people of *Israel*, was no other than *a Religious Covenant* between God, and *them* as members of his Church" (V, 155). See my discussion of the national or public covenant in Chapter 1; on Dwight specifically, see also Wenzke on Dwight's ecclesiology in *Timothy Dwight*, 207–220.

In a fast sermon delivered late in his life, Dwight reaffirmed that the title of "people of God" belonged not just to New Englanders or Americans but to the Protestant Christians of the world. But he added that "the nations in which they are found, and which publicly profess the same religion, are also included, as a body, in this phraseology." No Christian state or people was an elect nation with exclusive privileges; all Protestant nations had been given the opportunity to support the evangelical work of their churches. But at a time when so many Protestants in the international Church were disobeying the voice of God, which nation, which people, which region of the globe would truly be the keeper of the gospel flame by strengthening its churches?[71]

After 1776, Dwight would never again describe America as a place "inhabited by a people, who have the same religion, the same manners, the same interests, the same language, and the same essential forms and principles of civil government. . . . a people, in all respects one." When the nineteenth century began, Dwight exhorted "the great Body of People in New England" with language he could never use for the country as a whole:

> Your ancestors . . . laid here such foundations of human happiness, under his guidance, as were probably never laid elsewhere. In their establishment of rational freedom, just government, and perfect order, in their schools and their colleges, their churches and their worship, their exemplary life and fervent prayers, they left a glorious inheritance to *you*.

The New Englander could follow the advice given in Deut. 32:7: "Remember the days of old . . . ask thy father, and he will shew thee, thy elders, and they will tell thee." American glory was a possible future, a theme suited to the speculative interpretations of millennial prophecy and the soaring strains of vision poetry. New England success was a present reality, derived from habits and institutions established in the colonial past. Americans outside New England, without its history and its "glorious" institutional inheritance, had to turn to New England itself for paternal wisdom.[72]

A dozen years into the nineteenth century, when Dwight again assessed the state of true religion in the world, most of his optimism was rooted in New England and some regions of New York, where piety was reviving and missionary and Bible societies were expanding. To the rest of America, however, Dwight again spoke, not of completed accomplishments, but of distant potential. He

71. Timothy Dwight, *A Discourse, in Two Parts, Delivered August 20, 1812, on the National Fast, in the Chapel of Yale College* (New York, 1812), 38.

72. [Dwight], *Valedictory Address*, 10; Dwight, *Discourse on Some Events of the Last Century*, 42, 43.

described the sinful character of a nation where more than three million people lived without religion and warned that God might inflict additional judgments. He wavered over the question of whether the New England states, along with their hinterland in New York, would be better off if they were separated from the rest of the country:

> Should they be separated from their sister states, there cannot be a doubt that their citizens will hereafter find in their local situation, soil, and climate; in their religious and political systems; in their arts, literature, and science; in their manners and morals; in their health, energy, and activity, ample, perhaps peculiar sources of national greatness and prosperity.[73]

The rhetoric of New England that Dwight preached to America might be called a rhetoric of redemptive provincialism. Through the Revolution, Dwight and other clerical writers tended to portray all America as New England writ large. They embraced a hazy millennial vision of the future and wrote soaring verse about the nation's rising glory. But just as they increasingly distinguished the politician's civic virtue from the gospel's virtue, they also differentiated between the moral status of New England and America. Just as many of Dwight's Puritan forefathers had distinguished between full church members, Half-Way Covenanters, and the unchurched inhabitants who *ought* to be filling the back pews, Dwight drew his concentric circles around church members, New Englanders, and those Americans in other states still refusing the preacher's call. His rhetoric of redemptive provincialism, of course, would have rung hollow even to him if the province itself had remained spiritually dead.

POPE DWIGHT AND THE NEW ENGLAND MIND

Dwight's rhetoric of New England exceptionalism, when addressed to a local audience, tried to reawaken in what had come to be called the "public mind" a

---

73. Timothy Dwight, *A Discourse, in Two Parts, Delivered July 23, 1812, on the Public Fast, in the Chapel of Yale College* (New Haven, Conn., 1812); Dwight, *Discourse . . . August 20, 1812, on the National Fast;* Dwight, *Travels,* ed. Solomon, IV, 373 (quotation), dated 1811. In 1813, he said that the "evils of disunion would be so great, that nothing like an advantage which appears to be promised by it, is worthy of a moment's regard" (Timothy Dwight, *President Dwight's Decisions of Questions Discussed by the Senior Class in Yale College, in 1813 and 1814,* ed. Theodore Dwight, Jr. [New York, 1833], 103). In Dwight's anonymously published *Remarks on the Review of Inchiquin's Letters . . .* (Boston, 1815), he identified himself only as "a Federalist and a New Englander" (14).

proud sense of regional identity and cultural heritage. References to a public mind became commonplace by the 1790s, sometimes referring to the shifts in public opinion or attention and other times to a more stable sense of a people's collective intellectual and moral character. This conception of the public replaced the earlier references to the traditional "body politic," which, as Joseph Huntington described in 1781, subordinated the common people (the legs) to the magistrates and ministers (head and vital organs). The symbolic shift from a fixed hierarchy of body parts to a single corporate mentality left the role of the clergymen and statesmen unclear. Did they speak *to* and act *upon* the public mind—instructing, persuading, leading? Or did they speak and act *for* the public as its servants, representing its will? As Standing Order clergymen defended their role as civil officers who conducted state-sanctioned public worship, opponents criticized the inappropriate power that preachers had over the political attitudes and opinions of the people. Dwight was singled out and condemned as a political "pope." But as clerical commentary upon electoral politics became increasingly controversial toward the end of the century, Dwight's other activities demonstrated new ways for ministers to influence the public mind.[74]

For Dwight and other conservative commentators, the public mind, like an individual's mind, could occasionally become clouded, confused, or diverted

74. Joseph Huntington, *A Discourse Adapted to the Present Day, on the Health and Happiness, or Misery and Ruin, of the Body Politic, in Similitude to That of the Natural Body* . . . (Hartford, Conn., 1781). For Huntington, the legislature was the "seat of thought" in the political body (13). In the ecclesiastical body, ministers were in both the head and the vital organs (prevailing principles); in the civil community they were in only the latter. Elias Perkins, in his "Oration Delivered at Commencement," Sept. 13, 1786, spoke of extraordinary events (the Revolution) shaping individual minds and creating "national manners and national principles" (Elias Perkins Papers, Manuscripts and Archives, Yale University Library, New Haven, Conn.). Sometimes writers urged the members of the political body to speak with one mind ("Paul," *Conn. Courant*, Apr. 20, 1789). For examples of uses of "the public mind," see "Proceedings of the [Middletown] Convention, Address to the People at Large," *Conn. Courant*, Mar. 30, 1784, Feb. 3, 1794, "New Appropriation," Mar. 30, 1795, announcement of a new newspaper, the Suffield *Impartial Herald*, Apr. 24, 1797, "An Address to the Citizens of Connecticut, by Gideon Granger, jun., No. 1" (reprinted from the Suffield *Impartial Herald*), Apr. 23, 1798, Letter from Dan Harrison (reprinted from the Litchfield *Farmer's Monitor*), Mar. 31, 1800, "An Old Assembly-Man," Aug. 25, 1800; "D.I.O." (reprinted from the New Haven *Conn. Journal*), *American Mercury*, Sept. 12, 1791; "Don Quixote No. 1" (reprinted from the *American Mercury*), *Bee*, Mar. 28, 1798, Address from the editor, June 6, 1798, "Non-Exterminator," July 24, 1799; "Political Miscellany," *Courier* (Norwich, Conn.), June 8, 1800; *Journal of the Times* (Stonington, Conn.), Apr. 9, Aug. 13, 1799; *Connecticut Evangelical Magazine* (Hartford), I (July 1800–June 1801), 5, 21.

from its proper business despite the best education and the finest advantages that New England's institutions could offer. Their solution to the problem was summed up by articles in the *Mercury and New-England Palladium,* a newspaper Dwight helped to establish in 1800, and the *Connecticut Evangelical Magazine,* which also began publication in that year. "Let the public mind be firmly fixed upon the sage and virtuous maxims of the fathers of *New-England,*" one writer counseled. "We know that the great body of the *New England* people are of one mind," wrote another, and "that they still reverence and cherish, and support the institutions of their venerable forefathers." A third (who might have been Dwight himself) argued: "The happiness of *Connecticut* has been attributed to three causes:—Their peculiar manner of supporting religion; the general establishment of schools; and the equal distribution of property." The *Connecticut Evangelical Magazine* demonstrated how the first of those causes of public happiness—the state's support of Christian worship—was once again bearing fruit, as God's grace, after a long drought, seemed to rain down upon the Congregational churches. Bristol pastor Jonathan Miller, describing a local religious "awakening" that began in 1799, wrote that not only were church members "animated to greater exertions for proficiency in holiness" but more generally that "the public mind becomes impressed with the importance of real religion."[75]

A Connecticut revival beginning in Milford in 1796 gave Dwight fresh hope that he could, as one of his literary biographers put it, "Connecticutize the world." Preaching the four-year cycle of sermons that would become his *Theology,* Dwight finally enjoyed a campus revival in 1802. Of his 230 students, 63 joined the college church. Benjamin Silliman, then an undergraduate, wrote home to his mother that Yale College had become "a little temple: prayer and praise seem to be the delight of the greater part of the students, while those who are unfeeling are awed into respectful silence." The college revival, like revivals in the surrounding Connecticut churches, was calm and decorous, un-

75. "Address to the Public," *Mercury and New-England Palladium* (Boston, Mass.), Jan. 2, 1801, "Remarks on the Causes of the Happy State of Society in New-England," Jan. 6, 1801, "The New England Politician, No. 1," Nov. 10, 1801; Jonathan Miller, revival narrative, *Conn. Evang. Mag.,* I (July 1800–June 1801), 21–22. Dwight is known to have contributed anonymous essays to the *Mercury and N.-E. Palladium,* not all of which have been identified. The Jan. 6, 1801, *Mercury and N.-E. Palladium* citation above includes Dwight's favorite themes, as expressed in *True Means of Establishing Public Happiness,* his *Travels,* and other works. On Dwight's connection to the *Mercury and N.-E. Palladium,* see "Communication," *Bee,* Jan. 28, 1801; "Eschiness," *American Mercury,* Apr. 23, 1801; Robert Edson Lee, "Timothy Dwight and the Boston *Palladium,*" *NEQ,* XXXV (1962), 229–239.

like the divisive Awakening that Dwight's grandfather had tried to control more than sixty years earlier.[76]

But, as Connecticut parishes began reporting religious stirrings in the late eighteenth century, Dwight's efforts to spread the Word and stamp out infidelity were denounced in attacks far more scathing than anything Thomas Clap had seen as the reigning Yale autocrat during the first Awakening. In a series of anonymous pamphlets and newspaper articles, John C. Ogden, an Episcopalian minister and Republican political writer, lashed out at Dwight, Yale, and Connecticut's Standing Order. *An Appeal to the Candid, upon the Present State of Religion and Politics in Connecticut,* probably printed in 1798, charged that "President Dwight is making great strides, after universal controul in Connecticut, New-England, and the United States, over religious opinions and politics." Dwight was "a divine, a poet, eloquent, talkative, and undaunted." He used "discipline, missions, the College, and [the] predicted millennium"; he employed "the scorpions of polemic divinity, party politics, poetry, satirical writings, the Triumph of Infidelity, and the prejudices circulated by young men and young divines taught by him." It was all "Pope" Dwight's attempt "to direct all the public affairs, civil, ecclesiastical, literary, military, and political."[77]

The Republican press amplified Ogden's charges. One writer attacked Dwight's 1798 July Fourth address as "one of the most uncharitable antichrist-

---

76. "Connecticutize the world" is Silverman's phrase, in *Timothy Dwight,* 113; Benjamin Silliman to Mary Silliman, June 11, 1802, Silliman Family Papers, Manuscripts and Archives, Yale University Library, cited in Chandos Michael Brown, *Benjamin Silliman: A Life in the Young Republic* (Princeton, N.J., 1989), 92. Dwight himself dated the beginning of the revivals historians would come to call the "Second Great Awakening" with the Milford stir in 1796. See *Discourse . . . July 23, 1812, on the Public Fast,* 40.

77. [John Cosens Ogden], *An Appeal to the Candid, upon the Present State of Religion and Politics in Connecticut* [New Haven, Conn.? 1798?], 9, 11–12, 14, 15. See also [Ogden], *Friendly Remarks to the People of Connecticut, upon Their College and Schools* ([Litchfield, Conn.?], 1799); [Ogden], *A View of the Calvinistic Clubs in the United States* [Litchfield, Conn.? 1799?]. Ogden's earlier charges that New England's college presidents were improperly using their influence in political affairs were printed and discussed in the *Conn. Courant,* July 18, Aug. 1, 8, Sept. 17, 1796. Federalist writers responded to the pamphlets by calling him a "half crazy, half ideot priest" and "the Rev. Liar" (Feb. 11, 1799, May 27, 1799). Ogden was jailed for debt in what Republicans considered to be a politically motivated prosecution. One writer charged that Dwight had used his influence to keep Ogden in jail. Rumors also circulated that a group of young Federalists hatched a plan to drag him from the jail to tar and feather him. See the *Bee,* Apr. 24, May 22, June 9, 1799. For Ogden's role in Connecticut's Republican opposition, see Alan Vance Briceland, "Ephraim Kirby, Connecticut Jeffersonian, 1757–1804: The Origins of the Jeffersonian Republican Party in Connecticut" (Ph.D. diss., Duke University, 1965), 221–233.

ian sermons ever printed," a "perversion of the prophesies, of revelation, of the institution of preaching, and all the solemn rights and obligations of Christianity." Another contended that "in the *ecclesiastical carcass* of Connecticut, the President of Yale is the *grand pablum, and fountain head* of political and religious orthodoxy, from which thro' associations, and consociations to smaller vehicles and minuter channels, flow the *dignified results of wisdom,* and the cautious *intrigues* of party." These attacks on Dwight were part of a campaign by opposition writers who by the end of the century were intensifying their efforts to break the church-state alliance and appeal to religious dissenters by flogging the Federalist clergy. Republican writers feared that the Standing Order was whipping up "Zeal for federalism and awakening" to raid the school fund established by the sale of western lands. They wondered why clergymen escaped taxes and military service and why the best and most lucrative positions in the government seemed to go to sons of ministers. They charged that the clergy monopolized the press, manipulated the Council, and sent missionaries to the west to speculate in land. Their most sustained criticism, however, aimed at political preaching, which, they argued, prostituted the ministry to party purposes and polluted the house of God. Connecticut's Congregational clergy, the Philadelphia *Aurora; and General Advertiser* declared, never failed to attack Republicans "with the most violent abuse from the pulpit, the press, and in conversation, and the people who have been taught to reverence and respect the *Ministers,* above any other created being, generally conclude that what *they* say must be true." The political opposition and many of the state's dissenters saw in every Congregational program a hidden effort to maintain tax funding and restore the Standing Order authority that the liberalized certificate law was eroding. Since Dwight's politics and religion blended together in a single structure of moral order that depended upon virtue within a community and deference to authority, the fears of the opposition were to a certain degree justified.[78]

78. "Philalethes" (reprinted from *Aurora; and General Advertiser* [Philadelphia]), *Bee,* Feb. 13, 1799, May 8, 1799, "Illuminati Sermons," June 19, 1799; "Eschiness," *American Mercury,* Apr. 30, 1801. Other criticism of the Standing Order clergy can be found in the following: Republican protests about the Federalist fast day, *Bee,* Apr. 4, May 16, 23, 1798, the charge that the *Conn. Courant* was under the direction of "Pres, Dwight and Co." (reprinted from a Philadelphia paper), Jan. 30, 1799, "On Political Sermons," May 8, 1799, "Strictures on Missions," May 20, 1799, an open letter to Dwight from "An Old Friend," May 22, 1799, "Communications," May 22, 1799, "On Infidelity," June 5, 1799, on the bigotry of Dwight and Jedidiah Morse, Dec. 4, 1799, "New-England Portraits" (reprinted from *Aurora; and General Advertiser*), May 20, 1801, July 29, Sept. 9, 16, 1801, "To the Clergy of New England" (reprinted from *Sun* [Pittsfield, Mass.]), Sept. 16, 1801, "Thanksgiving," Dec. 9, 1801; "To the

Dwight tried to defend the civic role of ministers. *Mercury and New-England Palladium* essays addressed "To the Farmers and Mechanics in New-England" argued that "the people of *New-England* have always hitherto adopted the same opinion on general political subjects, which have been generally adopted by the clergy," not because of clerical power or priestcraft, "but because the opinions were just and right." The men who attacked the clergy for political meddling and promoting aristocracy therefore must be "infidels" who "frequent public places, taverns, and corners of the streets." He described the clergyman's proper political role again in his *Travels,* and tried to distinguish between "influence," which derived from office, conduct, and persuasive abilities, and "power," which Dwight defined as rule by force. The clergy had influence among the people, he concluded, but no actual power. But the influence of preaching and teaching should not be underestimated. Ministers and schoolmasters "to a great extent" molded "the manners and habits of the people," and in turn "the manners support the ministers and schoolmasters." Dwight did not repeat Jedidiah Morse's mistake by describing the clergy as an aristocracy at a time when that term had become a dirty word in political discourse. Dwight probably agreed with the much-criticized sentiment that Morse had expressed in his *Geography:* "The [Connecticut] clergy who are numerous, able, harmonious and very respectable, as a body, have hitherto preserved a kind of aristocratical balance in the very democratical government of the state: This has happily operated as a check upon the overbearing spirit of democracy." Instead, Dwight described clergymen as Federalists were beginning to describe their candidates: not as an elite order of men expecting deference, but as citizens who shared the same values and interests as their neighbors. New Englanders, he wrote, were all "men of business," devoted to the active life, and the minister was the quintessential businessman, laboring incessantly for his flock with little time for extra studies.[79]

Historians have been intrigued by the claim in Ogden's *Appeal* and else-

---

Clergy of Connecticut," *American Mercury,* June 4, 1801; Letter from "Amicus ejus Patriae," *Journal* (Stonington), Oct. 9, 1801. Much of the criticism of "Pope" Dwight related to his defense of state tax support for Congregational churches. See *Travels,* ed. Solomon, IV, 279–291. The Federalists' monopoly on political power was broken in 1818, a year after Dwight's death, in part because Episcopalians had finally joined Methodists and Baptists in a Democratic-Republican opposition. The new constitution that was drafted in 1818 did away with Congregationalism's preferential treatment. See Purcell, *Connecticut in Transition,* chap. 9.

79. [Timothy Dwight], "To the Farmers and Mechanics of New-England," *Mercury and N.-E. Palladium,* May 26, June 5, 1801; Dwight, *Travels,* ed. Solomon, IV, 225–226, 297–298; Jedidiah Morse, *The American Universal Geography* (1793), 4th ed., 2 vols. (Boston, 1802), I, 432, cited in Norman Levaun Stamps, "Political Parties in Connecticut, 1789–1819" (Ph.D.

where that Dwight exercised "controul over rulers and elections," especially because it seemed to be corroborated by Lyman Beecher, one of Dwight's protégés. Beecher's *Autobiography* recalled Connecticut religion and politics from Dwight's era:

> The ministers had always managed things themselves, for in those days the ministers were all politicians. . . . On election day they had a festival. All the clergy used to go, walk in procession, smoke pipes, and drink. And, fact is, when they got together, they would talk over who should be governor, and who lieutenant governor, and who in the Upper House, and their counsels would prevail.

Some have doubted the reliability of Beecher's recollections, which were written decades after the events he described, and it has been argued that Beecher's political interest was unique rather than representative. Although the average country parson would not be found smoking pipes with the governor, the inbreeding of Connecticut's elite makes it hard to imagine the state's secular and religious leadership did not share a number of concerns and counsel one another. One study has described an apolitical ministry, arguing that an important clerical theme in the early Republic was that politics was corrupt and that ministers had no business in the political arena. The question of clerical political involvement, however, depends upon one's definition of politics. Dwight condemned political clergymen, too, even as he (anonymously) charged that Jefferson was "a Spaniel" "drivelling" with "infatuation" for France and preached that a national policy linking the United States to that pestilent corpse of a country would stain America with sin. It was the opposition, he indicated, who played politics, created factions, and hurled charges at authority—accusations and slanders that demanded a response from the community's sober leaders.[80]

Criticized for preaching politics, the Federalist clergy argued that part of

diss., Yale University, 1950), 136 (for criticism of Morse's statement, see *American Mercury*, Feb. 12, 19, 1801; and *Bee*, Feb. 11, 1801).

80. Ogden, *Appeal to the Candid*, 19; Lyman Beecher, *The Autobiography of Lyman Beecher*, 2 vols., ed. Barbara M. Cross (Cambridge, Mass., 1961), I, 190; [Dwight], *Remarks on the Review of Inchiquin's Letters*, 16; Dwight, *Duty of Americans*, 18. See Keller, *Second Great Awakening in Connecticut*; and Lois W. Banner, "Religious Benevolence as Social Control: A Critique of an Interpretation," *JAH*, LX (1973–1974), 23–41. Banner described an apolitical ministry. In contrast to Dwight, North Branford pastor Matthew Noyes tended toward general moral lessons rather than explicit political references. See MS fast sermons on Prov. 14:34, Apr. 17, 1793; Luke 14:4–5, Oct. 20, 1793 (preached again Mar. 22, 1799); 2 Chron. 28:10, Apr. 3, 1795; Jer. 25:31, Apr. 14, 1797; Rom. 13:7–9, Apr. 6, 1798; Gen. 22:14,

their ministerial duty involved speaking to all matters of broad public concern. Along with this traditional restatement of their obligation to "blow the trumpet in Zion," however, they added an important new defense. Ministers, Boston's Samuel Stillman argued, "are *citizens,* members of *civil* society; have civil rights as well as other men." "They have interest[s], families, liberties, as dear to them as to any other citizens. Shall they see all these in danger, and be silent?" Nathanael Emmons asserted that it was "unreasonable" to object to preachers' speaking out in support of the Adams administration's controversial policies, "because ministers have the common right of citizens, to form their own opinions, and to speak their own sentiments, upon such public measures, as relate not merely to the local politics of a town or parish, but to the great body of the nation." In the 1740s, ministers warned the common people not to cloak themselves with the authority of public discourse. By 1800, they had to defend their speech and writing by wrapping themselves in the rights of the common man.[81]

For Dwight, preaching, teaching, and revivals were not enough, for the battle against ignorance and irreligion had many fronts, and infidelity had many faces. He launched parallel attacks by writing for the press, establishing voluntary reform societies, and working to influence political opinion and public policy.

After the "infidel" Jefferson gained the presidency in the Federalist defeat of 1800, Dwight helped Jedidiah Morse found the Federalist *Mercury and New-England Palladium* and contributed anonymous poems and essays. In 1805, the *Panoplist,* a religious magazine also directed by Morse and strongly influenced by Dwight, became a party organ for New England Trinitarian evangelicals. In 1808, the *Connecticut Evangelical Magazine* aligned itself more closely with Dwight's moral activism to begin building a more explicit evangelical social agenda. Dwight lent his support to Bible societies, which began printing and distributing Bibles by the thousands, and presided over the Connecticut Reli-

---

Apr. 25, 1799; Jer. 14:12, Apr. 11, 1800; 1 Kings 20:32, April 1803, all in Matthew Noyes Papers, Manuscripts and Archives, Yale University Library.

81. Samuel Stillman, *A Sermon, Preached at Boston, April 25, 1799; the Day Recommended by the President of the United States for a National Fast* (Boston, 1799), 19; Nathanael Emmons, *A Discourse, Delivered on the Natinoal* [sic] *Fast, April 25, 1799* (Wrentham, Mass., 1799), 18. Dwight also appealed to the clergyman's right as a common citizen to speak out about politics in "To the Farmers and Mechanics in New-England," *Mercury and N.-E. Palladium,* May 26, 1801. For another defense of political preaching, see "A Humble Citizen," *Conn. Courant,* Mar. 17, 1800.

gious Tract Society, which distributed short, simple interdenominational messages to those who had strayed from the faith. As one writer proclaimed, Voltaire's "engine"—the ceaseless printing press—"has proved the downfall and destruction of his own infidelity." [82]

Reform societies began to take root in the fertile ground between private families and governmental structures, where Dwight had always said that Christian virtue should blossom. In 1803, Dwight's student Lyman Beecher published *The Practicability of Suppressing Vice, by Means of Societies Instituted for That Purpose* and began a crusade that would grow, by fits and starts, to a movement seeking to curb profanity, intemperance, and Sabbath breaking, to improve prisons, schools, and the treatment of the handicapped and the insane, and to end slavery. Dwight lent his skills in persuasion and bombast to the early temperance movement, thundering that drunkards would not inherit the kingdom of God. [83]

In these years too, the work of the western missions movement, which Congregationalists had launched in the late 1780s, accelerated, and Dwight turned his attention beyond the Connecticut state line to the frontier settlements in western New York. He had a low opinion of the "pioneers," seeing them as men of loose morals, little religion, and democratic politics. As one historian put it, "If the white clapboard house roused Dwight's hopes, the log cabin sank them. . . . In the log cabin he foresaw impermanence, anarchy, sloth." The pioneers' only use was to clear the way for settlements of family farms, churches, and schools—for, in other words, the transplantation of New England towns. [84]

Dwight agreed that ministers should be sent west, because preaching was the primary "means" for calling men and women to faith and obedience, but the itinerant minister, even with his crate of Bibles and pocketful of religious

82. Berk, *Calvinism versus Democracy*, 168–172; Keller, *Second Great Awakening in Connecticut*, 117–118 (quotation from *Religious Intelligencer* [New Haven, Conn.], II, no. 22 [Oct. 25, 1817], 350).

83. Keller, *Second Great Awakening in Connecticut*, 147.

84. Silverman, *Timothy Dwight*, 131 (quotation). The General Association of Congregational Churches tried to promote a subscription for missionaries to the new settlements in the western wilderness in 1774 but realized the following year it was not practical. They revived the idea in 1788, began funding itinerants in 1793, and formally constituted a mission society in 1798. See *An Address to the Inhabitants of the New Settlements in the Northern and Western Parts of the United States* (New Haven, Conn., [1793]); and *The Records of the General Association of the Colony of Connecticut; Begun June 20th, 1738; Ending June 19, 1799* (Hartford, Conn., 1888), 76, 85, 125, 177. On a tour of the region with Dwight in 1799, Jeremiah Day found a prejudice against state support for public worship (Diary, 1797–1801, entry for Sept. 28, 1799, Day Family Papers, Manuscripts and Archives, Yale University Library).

tracts, would not succeed alone. Christian virtue was tied to wisdom and knowledge, Dwight argued, and therefore schools were required. Areas ought to be settled in village communities, not in scattered plantations, because the "solitary mind" would be "sluggish, contracted, austere, or in some other unhappy manner defective." Christians needed to be "invigorated by their frequent intercourse with each other." Therefore, he urged in his "Address to the Emigrants from Connecticut," it was not enough to settle new lands, or even to sow the seeds of the gospel in new soil. New England's institutions of religion and education must be planted as well. "Long established institutions and habits have a mighty influence over the whole population," he reminded his audience. "Every man acts under the public eye, and feels a responsibility, which restrains sinful inclinations, and serves to regulate his daily deportment." Remaking the wilderness into the image of New England, he argued in his *Travels*, was the last best hope for America, and perhaps for the world:

> The manners of the people of New England, unless I mistake, are already more gentle, more softened, in the middle and inferior classes than in those of the same classes in most other countries. . . . The institutions which have given these characteristics to the people of New England will give them to any other people, and these institutions are spreading both their reputation and their efficacy through the United States; their progress is silent indeed, and is made amid many prejudices and difficulties, but, as I believe, is real.[85]

Although Dwight had hoped to transplant Greenfield Hill to the frontier, New England itself was changing. Even in his rosy rhetoric of New England virtue, the emphasis on the yeoman farmer and landed property began to be replaced: "The New-England people are fitted by Providence for commerce," he told his Yale students. The family farm, as a primary hub of industry and virtue, would be joined by the factory: "Manufacturers should be compelled to guard the morals of their work people," he argued. "Manufactories besides would furnish employment to many children who now run about the streets, as well as to many men and women who do nothing." By linking "softened" manners, progress in the arts and sciences, and commerce, Dwight was fashioning an enlightened gentility that would be very palatable to nineteenth-century New England's middle class.[86]

As the missions movement and westward emigration wore away the idea of

---

85. Dwight, "Sermon CXLV: The Ordinary Means of Grace; Intercourse with Religious Men," *Theology*, V, 81–99 (quotations on 93); [Timothy Dwight], *An Address to the Emigrants from Connecticut* . . . (Hartford, Conn., 1817), 5; Dwight, *Travels*, ed. Solomon, IV, 371.

86. Dwight, *Decisions*, ed. Dwight, 101, 285, 287.

Connecticut as a self-contained republic and replaced it with the rapidly developing New England–New York region that he surveyed in his travels, Dwight was forced to become more specific about the ethnic makeup of his society. He had hope for the Indians and the blacks. He thought the Indians might be raised from savagery by adopting the white man's love of Christ and property. If love for Christ did not take hold in primitive minds, the pursuit of property might better appeal to a race so fond of competing for personal glory. The indolent, ignorant, and vicious lives that he imagined blacks led were the result of slavery, he believed, and to him the white man's duty to educate and uplift was obvious. He was cheered by reports of both blacks and Indians who, in the right environment, had literally "turned white." Dwight approved of the scattered Dutch, French Protestants, and Scotsmen he encountered, since they seemed to measure up to the New England standard. He had more doubts, however, about Germans and the southern Irish. But as it would be hard enough to assimilate the foreigners already in the region, he believed that further immigration should not be encouraged. Some foreigners with proof of their good character might be naturalized, but the region certainly had no need of uneducated hordes with "profligate and corrupting" habits.[87]

In his 1801 "century sermon" and in later reflections, Timothy Dwight looked at the history of eighteenth-century New England. Unlike many modern historians, Dwight did not claim that the religious excitement of the early 1740s had been a trigger of momentous social, political, or intellectual transformation. Intermittent revivals, he argued, had ultimately strengthened the religious principles and moral character already in place. In the 1750s, however, external forces of immorality and irrationality had begun to work their mischief. "Degeneration," which he defined as moral declension and intellectual befuddlement, began during the Seven Years' War and intensified through the Revolutionary period. Moral principles were unhinged and habits of rational thought broken by economic instability, corrupt British policy, war, an infatuation with politics, and the spread of French infidel philosophy.[88]

Dwight credited the region's recovery to New England institutions, religious revivals, and the public discourse of learned and pious men. The New England "mind," Dwight argued, molded by New England institutions "operating everywhere and every moment," had "an elastic tendency toward the recovery

87. On Dwight's regarding blacks and Indians, see Dwight, *Decisions*, ed. Dwight, 127–128; Barbara Miller Solomon, "Introduction," in Dwight, *Travels*, ed. Solomon, I, xxxvi–xxxviii (quotation on xxxvii). They supposedly "turned white" both epidermally and culturally. On European ethnic groups, see ibid., xxxvi. On foreign immigration, see Dwight, *Decisions*, ed. Dwight, 19.

88. Dwight, *Discourse on Some Events of the Last Century*, 10–12, 17–25.

of its original position." Revivals beginning in 1796 and gradually spreading throughout New England had reformed manners, refocused public attention upon religious matters, and swelled church membership. To answer the infidel philosophes, "a great multitude of judicious discourses were preached throughout the country, and not a small number published." Although Dwight acknowledged that most of the books doing the philosophical heavy work against infidelity had been written by "men of talents and worth in Great Britain" rather than by New Englanders, he quickly turned a New England deficiency into a virtue. New England lacked the institutions "for the support of ingenious and speculative men, in the pursuits of learning and science." But that meant learned New Englanders, like their neighbors, cultivated practical intelligence and never drifted too far from the common concerns of daily life.[89]

Many nineteenth-century Americans, educated and uneducated, immigrant and native born, would find a way to avoid Dwight's rhetorical persuasions and resist the cultural imperialism of New England's institutions. Blacks did not turn white, Southerners failed to develop a Yankee twang, and even New England itself neglected to sacrifice profit for elevated piety as Pope Dwight had prescribed. Young Timothy had labored hard to acquire the "power of eloquence" and had learned to "suit his addresses to time, place, and audience." But, since the day of Dwight's first major oration in 1770, a fair portion of his audience had come to believe that his literary talents had been "swallowed up in ecclesiastical politics." The times had changed, and America—even New England—had become a different place.[90]

89. Dwight, *Travels*, ed. Solomon, IV, 273; Dwight, *Discourse on Some Events of the Last Century*, 15–16.

90. After an article lamenting the state of American literature, a newspaper commentary in the *Bee*, Mar. 27, 1799, examined the fate of the bright young poets of the 1770s—David Humphreys, Joel Barlow, Philip Freneau, John Trumbull, and Timothy Dwight. Where were they now? The first two were abroad, the third struggling to make a living. Trumbull had "degenerated into a village lawyer," and Dwight had been "swallowed up in ecclesiastical politics." On the limited success of Dwight's brand of religious culture on the northern New England and western New York frontiers, see Randolph A. Roth, *The Democratic Dilemma: Religion, Reform, and the Social Order in the Connecticut River Valley of Vermont, 1791–1850* (Cambridge, 1987), chaps. 1–2; Richard W. Pointer, *Protestant Pluralism and the New York Experience: A Study of Eighteenth-Century Religious Diversity* (Bloomington, Ind., 1988); and James R. Rohrer, *Keepers of the Covenant: Frontier Missions and the Decline of Congregationalism, 1774–1818* (New York, 1995).

CHAPTER 8

Political Characters and Public Words

An untitled play, written by college sophomores and performed for their class-mates at a Yale College quarter day exhibition on June 9, 1784, captured some of the anxiety of the new political world the Revolution had created. The first scene begins with a discussion between two gentlemen, Mr. Irvin from Con-necticut and Mr. McPherson from a neighboring state, who are worried about the debates over a proposed impost, veterans' pay, and the Society of the Cin-cinnati, the fraternal order of Revolutionary War officers that was denounced as an attempt to create an American aristocracy. Irvin fears that the inflamed political passions are leading toward demagoguery and social unrest. He la-ments that citizens no longer defer to the wise decisions of the legislature: "We have a maxim with us that the voice of the people is the voice of God, and [an] act of the Delegates not coinciding with the voice of the people is deemed null and void." McPherson receives a letter, signed like a newspaper essay with the pseudonym "Philanthropos," that warns him against speaking publicly in fa-vor of the "aristocratic" position in the current debates. "I must confess," Irvin, the Connecticut man, remarks, "this is something very singular, that a person must be cautioned against speaking his sentiments upon any political point in a free state.—but, sir, we have a new set of folk lately come upon the stage."[1]

1. Yale College, Class of 1786, Class Play, 1784, Yale Miscellaneous Manuscripts, 6, 15, Manuscripts and Archives, Yale University Library, New Haven, Conn. The play was never published, although it might have circulated in manuscript among the students, as was not uncommon for such productions. Although forbidden by Yale College statutes, students had been giving plays at least since midcentury. The rage for drama at Yale soared in the 1780s, though President Ezra Stiles tried to temper it, forbidding the Linonia Society to per-form in 1782. See Yale University Linonia Society Records, YRG 40-A-96, Secretary's Records, Minutes, Dec. 21, 1782, Manuscripts and Archives, Yale University Library; Brooks Mather Kelly, *Yale: A History* (New Haven, Conn., 1974), 107–108; Edmund S. Morgan, *The Gentle Puritan: A Life of Ezra Stiles, 1727–1795* (New Haven, Conn., 1962), 366. By the mid-1790s,

The gentlemen do not know what to make of Philanthropos's letter or, more generally, of the "new set of folk" unsettling political life. Some answers, however, are provided by a strange character called Mr. Writer, who is introduced as "a Clerk of the Mind," a man with the ability to read minds and the task of committing other people's thoughts to a record book. Using Benedict Arnold as his example, Mr. Writer explains that, beneath the apparent confusion and variety of any person's conversation, writing, or thought, lies a fixed motive—a singular, real character, like a uniform canvas beneath many hues of paint. The trick is to discern the character behind the surface of language. Mr. Writer is able to see through the "bare signification" of Philanthropos's benevolent pseudonym and expose the "real character" behind the letter. It is a threat that comes from a Middletown conventioneer, he declares, a member of a new, self-created political body that for months had been shamelessly trying to influence voters. Although "Tis the part of a Gentleman to act his own opinion," Irvin explains, conventioneers "have delivered their consciences in keeping to this body" and simply accede to the faction's collective will. With Mr. Writer's help, Philanthropos is rescued from the temporary "phrenzy" and "mad enthusiasms" of partisan politics, and the play's characters are left with the hope that other Americans, too, will "hear the voice of reason" and turn from the path of anarchy and confusion.[2]

The play reflects anxieties about the control of public and political language. Without having recourse to mind reading, the young college students themselves would soon have to master the perplexing dramaturgy of post-Revolutionary political life. They would assert that individuals had the right—even the duty—to speak their minds about public matters, but they would agree with the play's Mr. McPherson when he counseled that it was "not always prudent for a man to express his thoughts." They were eager to master the speech and writing that helped define the public characters of gentlemen, and the

the college societies seemed to be sharing the administration's concern: in 1795, the Brothers in Unity voted twenty-four to thirteen that theatrical exhibitions were not beneficial (Yale University Brothers in Unity Records, YRG 40-A-5, Secretary's Records, Book II, Minutes of Meetings, 1783–1803, Nov. 5, 1795, Manuscripts and Archives, Yale University Library). Connecticut writers outside the college remained ambivalent about the theater. One writer in the *Conn. Courant*, Mar. 9, 1795, thought plays as dangerous as novels, especially for women and impressionable youth, connecting them to party spirit and immorality and suggesting that they be regulated by a board of censors that would carefully screen for any offensive material. Half a year later, notices in the same paper certified the theater as respectable and even described it as "a NATIONAL SCHOOL" of morals (*Connecticut Courant* [Hartford], July 27, Aug. 31, 1795).

2. Yale Class Play, 16–21.

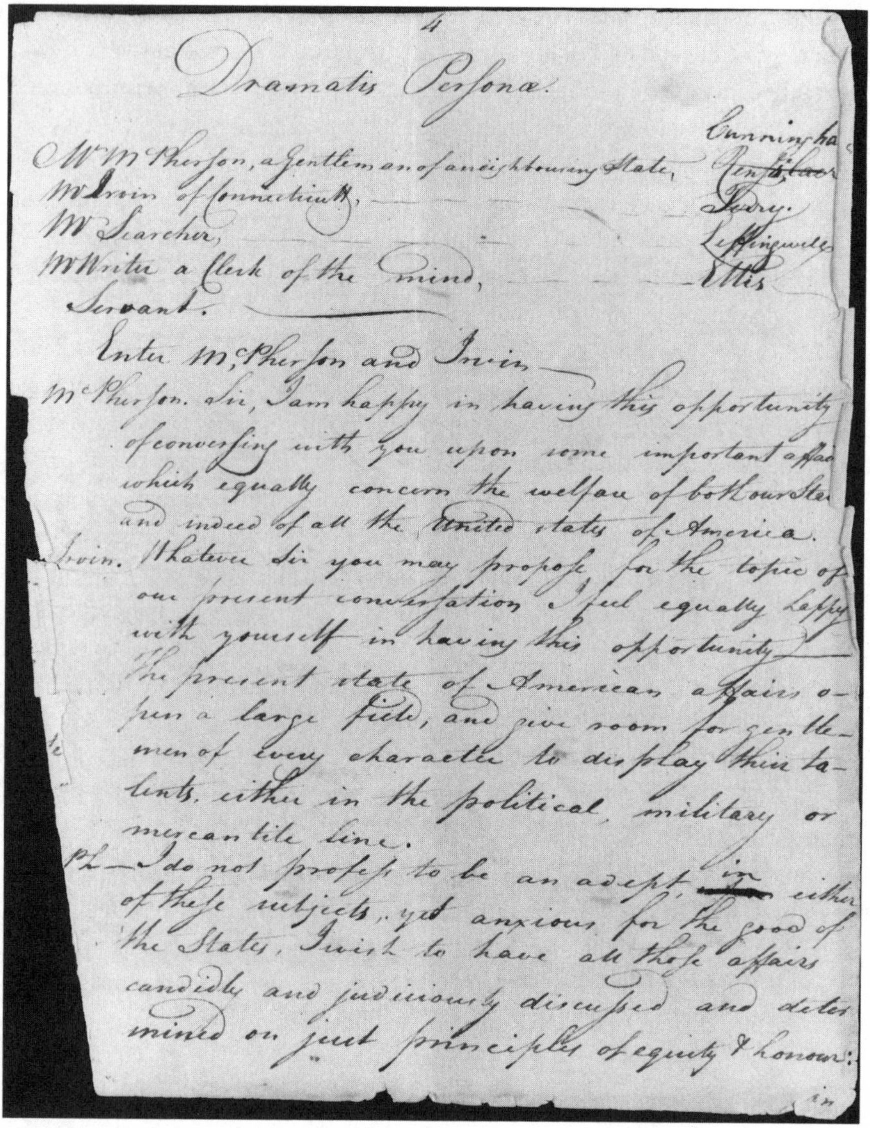

Dramatis Personæ

Mr McPherson, a Gentleman of a neighbouring State,
Mr Irvin of Connecticut, —
Mr Searcher, —
Mr Writer a Clerk of the mind, —
Servant.

Cunningham
~~Van~~
Terry.
Leffingwell
Ellis

Enter McPherson and Irvin

McPherson. Sir, I am happy in having this opportunity of conversing with you upon some important affairs which equally concern the welfare of both our States and indeed of all the United States of America.

Irvin. Whatever Sir you may propose for the topic of our present conversation I feel equally happy with yourself in having this opportunity. The present state of American affairs open a large field, and give room for gentlemen of every character to display their talents, either in the political, military or mercantile line.

McP. I do not profess to be an adept in either of these subjects, yet anxious for the good of the States, I wish to have all those affairs candidly and judiciously discussed and determined on just principles of equity & honour.

Figure 16. Dialogue at Quarter Day, June 19, 1784. Yale College Class of 1786. Of the performers listed in the upper right of the play's first page, Jonathan Ellis became a minister and then a teacher in Maine, serving in the General Assembly and giving patriotic (Republican) orations after the turn of the century; William Leffingwell became a wealthy merchant and stockbroker in New Hampshire and New York City; Nathaniel Terry became a Hartford lawyer, a bank president, and a United States congressman; Jacob Van Rennsselaer (crossed out on the MS) became a New York lawyer, state representative, and New York secretary of state. There is no Cunningham listed in Franklin Bowditch Dexter's *Biographical Sketches of the Graduates of Yale College with the Annals of the College History,* 6 vols. (New York, 1885–1912), IV, for 1786. Courtesy, Manuscripts and Archives, Yale University Library, New Haven, Conn.

college disputations, compositions, orations, and expositions would prepare many of them to walk onto the public stage at a time when public address had gained a political significance unlike anything their fathers had known. They were concerned about the influence gentlemen would continue to have over the political words that expressed the will of a sovereign people, and, although they would continue to mouth the *vox populi est vox Dei* slogan, many of them would rail against meetings, conventions, or associations that presumed to discern or express the public mind. They held up the ideal of government by virtuous and disinterested statesmen, even as it clashed with the experience of bitter factional politics; their speeches and writings continually shaped and reshaped conceptions of political character, even as they criticized the projection of false character through the manipulation of language. They would fantasize that public writing could record the voice of reason, becalming and enlightening the Republic, but they used the press to arouse political passion and partisan frenzy. For the young Yale students in 1784, the dramatic dialogue on politics was an exercise in writing and public speaking. In the world they entered upon graduation, public discourse was an exercise of political power.

ANXIETIES ABOUT PUBLICITY

The 1784 college play connected public deliberations on political questions to the private thoughts the mind reader discerned and presented both within a sociable world of friends in conversation. The letter Mr. McPherson receives and discusses with his friend Irvin is a private communication signed like a letter published in a newspaper; it warns that McPherson's personal reputation will be threatened if he publicly expresses his political opinions. Another character in the play, Mr. Searcher, also represents the passage from the public into the private. He is a traveler bringing political news from across the state into the "apartment" where Irvin and McPherson had sat in friendly conversation, news of absurd schemes that would extend public policy into the realm of private life in new ways. There is talk, he says, of taxes on both courtship and celibacy along with fines for any who would "harbour, conceal, abet, or any way assist that turbulent phrensy called Love." When he meets Mr. Writer, who works as a clerk in an office "faithfully record[ing] all affairs of the mind," Searcher wants to use Writer's mind-reading technique to gain an advantage when courting—or attempting to seduce—three young ladies. The play's vaguely defined "apartment," the intimate setting for the characters' conversations, becomes, on stage, the place where the audience can glimpse the exaggerated interpenetration of the public and the private: secret sentiments becoming public and public matters intruding upon the affairs of the heart.[3]

The Yale students of 1784 had grown up during the Revolutionary War, when questions about the proper domains of the public and the private had taken on a special urgency. What was *public* speech or writing? More words and symbolic actions came to be considered part of the public domain as the heat generated by social conflict and political divisiveness rose. Things said and written that might once have been ignored became a public concern in times of crisis. During the war, the only tolerated public opinions were those that assented to the Revolutionary course pursued by the patriot government. First the Sons of Liberty, acting upon the imperatives of vigilante justice, and later local committees of inspection, acting on a mandate by the Continental Congress, monitored their neighbors and published the names and offenses of any whose speech or behavior revealed sentiments opposed to the cause. The Sons of Liberty in Farmington pressured the Reverend John Smally to apologize for calling the Bostonians rebels and complaining about a Sunday militia muster in 1774. Requesting tea in a tavern got Seth Bird of Litchfield and Martha and Solomon Cowles of Farmington in trouble in the spring of 1775. Silvanus Griswold, overheard grumbling about a Continental fast day in the middle of harvesttime and seen laboring on that fast (he only threw up a fence rail, he claimed, to prevent his cows from straying into a flax field), found himself obliged to apologize publicly and declare his patriotism in the newspapers. People who dared speak ill of a committee of inspection, like Captain William Gaylord Hubbell of New Fairfield who said committeemen were prejudiced and partisan and Daniel Gray of Stamford who called them "damn'd rascals," were quickly posted as slanderous tories. In 1776, the editor of the *Connecticut Courant* printed the names of offenders in a box on the front page; names would be removed only after the shamed citizens duly confessed and apologized before their local committees and paid the editor a one-dollar indulgence. Like the Puritans a century before, who used public shaming to curb sinful behavior, the whigs were very effective at using publicity as a disciplinary tool.[4]

Sometimes politically incorrect speech would be punished more spontaneously. Whig newspapers in Connecticut reprinted a story from New York about a young man who cast aspersions upon the Continental Congress before a group of women. In what the article gleefully applauded as a feminine version of tar and feathering, the women stripped the man to the waist and cov-

---

3. Ibid., 9.

4. *Conn. Courant,* Oct. 17, 1774, Jan. 2, Apr. 3, 24, Aug. 28, Sept. 18, 1775, Apr. 15, May 27, June 17, 1776, Nov. 11, 1777.

ered him with molasses and the downy tops of flag plants from a nearby meadow. On the evening of February 14, 1775, two men from Ridgefield made the mistake of stopping at a Wethersfield tavern. Conversing with some of the locals, they "boldly justified the vote of the *late Town of Ridgefield,* in disapproving of the Doings of the Continental Congress." Such a remark, uttered in a "public House," was considered "by a Number of Gentlemen present" to be "a direct Breach of Association of said Congress." At nine o'clock that evening, the two Ridgefielders were run out of town, "amid the hisses, Groans, etc. of a respectable Concourse of People,—the Populace following them out of Town, beating a dead march." [5]

Informal, or even private, conversations, especially when conducted in public spaces like taverns and coffeehouses, were considered matters of public concern when the opinions expressed in any way seemed to denigrate the patriot cause or the Revolutionary authorities. On July 15, 1776, the same day the *Courant* published the Declaration of Independence, it carried a notice about the case of Amasa Jones of Hartford, called before a committee because a bystander had overheard him utter a single questionable sentence while in conversation with another person. Although the bystander did not know the context of the remark, it sounded suspicious enough to merit the attention of the committee and the press. The authorities were very sensitive to the potentially damaging effects of unregulated public discourse in a time of war. In 1782, a stranger in an Enfield tavern, claiming he was from Middletown, told people that one of Governor Jonathan Trumbull's vessels was trading with the enemy. Instead of running the man out of town, the townspeople, more bitter and cynical than the Wethersfield citizens of 1775 after years of seeing wartime profiteers and price-gougers, quickly passed along the man's rumor, which eventually launched a special investigation by the General Assembly. Although both Amasa Jones and Governor Trumbull were cleared, both had seen how a few remarks in conversation could quickly become dangerous public speech. [6]

The history of whig repression during the Revolution would be replayed in the 1790s, not by the popular demagogues that the student playwrights had warned about in 1784, but by Federalist gentlemen, who, like the play's Irvin and McPherson, spoke for law and order. A newspaper correspondent in 1795 announced that he intended to collect and publish "Anecdotes of Democrats" and "Anecdotes of Democratic Clergymen" in the Federalist papers, exposing

5. Ibid., Feb. 20, Oct. 2, 1775.

6. Ibid., July 15, 1776, Mar. 26, 1782. Rumors about Trumbull might have been circulating as early as 1780, but the investigating committee blamed the tavern conversation of the Enfield stranger.

their "leading traits" and "private characters" and proving that Democrats, like the tories of old, were worse than murderers because they tried to destroy the whole community. Three months later, the same writer wrote again to solicit information and assure readers that this project in character assassination was no joke. In the bitter partisan atmosphere at the turn of the century, casual remarks (and even inappropriate silence) would again be held up for public censure. Upon receiving news at the post office of a British victory against the French, Noah Webster, along with an unnamed merchant and a clergyman, cried "Huzza for John Bull[!]" A bystander who did not spontaneously join in the cheer was immediately labeled a vile Democrat.[7]

Just as the distinction between private and public conversations was blurred in the taverns, coffeehouses, and post offices, the distinction between a private and a public letter depended more upon the content of the letter and the general animus of the political climate than upon the intentions of the letter writer. Certainly, there was a long-standing assumption in the eighteenth century that gentlemanly correspondence containing news or information of public interest ought to be circulated beyond a single addressee. Some letters, especially those from Europe, were written with the expectation that they would be read aloud to others, handed around, or eventually published (usually without the writer's name) in the local press. Historians have noted that "even sealed letters were opened and resealed in transit, sometimes with a postscript added by the person who was transmitting the letter on to the next hand." Yet, political expediency or suspicions of partisan intrigue seemed to give license to abandon any notion of private correspondence whatsoever. Printers usually justified the unauthorized publication of a private letter if they deemed its content to be about "public matters" and therefore interesting to everyone. Dr. Benjamin Gale of Killingworth charged that his letter to Colonel Gurdon Saltonstall had been "piratically seized" by the local committee of inspection in 1775. In the *Connecticut Journal,* William Williams condemned the interception and subsequent publication of a political letter he wrote in 1786, calling the act a violation of the norms of civilized society. The Reverend Stanley Griswold was appalled to see a 1798 letter to his congressman appear in the local press, and the Connecticut poet Joel Barlow saw his reputation among former Federalist friends destroyed by the unauthorized publication of his letters from France. The New London *Bee* described in approving detail how a scheming letter between two prominent Federalists, left by accident in Lee's Tavern, was passed around by Republicans, copied, and published; the *Bee*'s editor, however, was

7. Ibid., Nov. 23, 1795, Feb. 15, 1796; *American Mercury* (Hartford, Conn.), May 28, 1801.

outraged to learn that letters to him were being opened and copied by the local Federalist postmaster.[8]

The characters in the Yale play of 1784 registered this concern about private sentiments' being publicized. Mr. Irvin asserts that no person in a free state should be afraid of "speaking his sentiments upon any political point," though his friend McPherson, with an eye on the anti-aristocratic "Inquisition" being established by popular rabble-rousers, warns that it is not always prudent to speak. When Mr. Searcher learns of Mr. Writer's special talents, he initially seems less worried about the mind reader's privately discerning his thoughts while they speak together than about his thoughts' being written down in an official record book: "Curious! . . . the thoughts of men committed to writing! If this is the case, a person cannot be too careful of thinking." As much as the play fantasizes about peering into people's minds, it also records real anxieties about publicity: not minds, but letters being opened and read; not the contents of consciousness, but the sentiments expressed in private conversation being published to the wider world. The play suggests the tension between the republican suspicion of secrecy and the gentleman's insistence upon privacy and a social life that was at least partially shielded from inspection by the broader public. The Yale students and the leading men they emulated needed ways to show the world that things hidden could still cultivate virtue, that secrecy was not necessarily conspiratorial, that privacy need not be suspected as a screen for selfish designs. The fraternal societies that were so popular at Yale were designed in part to help resolve this tension: secret rituals and private meetings allowed boys living away from home and family to cultivate warm sentiments among "brothers" within exclusive groups; public performances allowed the members to display themselves as virtuous young gentlemen before a wider audience.[9]

---

8. Richard D. Brown, *Knowledge Is Power: The Diffusion of Information in Early America, 1700–1865* (New York, 1989), 177, 339 (which cites an example in Joy Day Buel and Richard Buel, Jr., *The Way of Duty: A Woman and Her Family in Revolutionary America* [New York, 1984], 45); *Conn. Courant*, Sept. 18, 1775, William Williams, "To the Good Citizens of Connecticut," Oct. 30, 1786 (reprinted from *Connecticut Journal* [New Haven]), June 4, Aug. 27, 1798 (on the justification for printing Joseph Priestly's private correspondence); *American Mercury*, May 1, 1800; *Bee* (New London, Conn.), Apr. 25, 1798, June 19, 1799.

9. Yale Class Play, 12–13, 15. Another unpublished Yale College quarter day play, performed in the chapel on Mar. 13, 1793, humorously addressed the ethics of opening private letters. One of the characters, Captain Anthony, argues that "no man has the right to demand of another what he conveys by letter, no more than he has to demand what his thoughts are" (Quarter Day Play, Mar. 13, 1793, Bates Family Papers, Manuscripts and Archives, Yale University Library). On the relationship between privacy and publicity, see Jay

When the Revolutionary War had ended and the soldiers had put down their arms, young men like the Yale students in 1784 sensed that professional achievement and public reputation would now more than ever before depend upon mastery of the arts of oral persuasion. In the scramble for membership in the post-Revolutionary speaking aristocracy, speakers, institutions, and rhetorical occasions multiplied. Yet, the enthusiasm for rhetoric was related to more than personal ambition. Speeches, proclamations, and addresses were rooted in institutions—colleges, churches, the legislature, town governments, the courts, the militia, voluntary societies—and were given on ritualized occasions that conveyed social meanings far beyond the speaker's or writer's particular message to his audience. The Phi Beta Kappa lecturer and the Fourth of July speaker distinguished themselves by their affiliations to institutional authority as much as through any appeal to popularity.[10]

In the winter of 1783–1784, Noah Webster placed advertisements in the Connecticut papers for "A Rhetorical School," with classes to be held two or three evenings per week to instruct "young Gentlemen and Ladies in the most elegant modern pronunciation" and "a just and graceful elocution." But Connecticut's most important school of the rhetorical arts would remain Yale College, where Webster himself received his bachelor's degree in 1778. In their classes, public exhibitions, and fraternal societies, college students honed their skills in public address.[11]

The collegiate enthusiasm for rhetorical study and practice arose from several sources. The theatrical preaching of George Whitefield, who continued to tour the colonies until his death in 1770, impressed even his opponents with his display of the power of voice and gesture over an audience. The British elocutionary movement, exemplified in Thomas Sheridan's *Course of Lectures on Elocution* (1762), which tried to reduce oratorical delivery to a science of vocal modulation and gesture, also had an effect upon the colonies as theatrical per-

---

Fliegelman, *Declaring Independence: Jefferson, Natural Language, and the Culture of Performance* (Stanford, Calif., 1993), 117–129.

10. Enos Cook and Abel Flint, for example, debated before the Linonia Society in 1784 whether a military or a literary character was more meritorious; Hendrick Dow decided in favor of the latter ("A Dispute Spoken at Anniversary April 2d, 1784," Yale University Linonia Society Records, YRG 40-A-96).

11. *Conn. Courant*, Dec. 30, 1783.

formances themselves began to be produced and, gradually, accepted. Plays like the one written by the members of the sophomore class at Yale in 1784 were wildly popular at the college in the 1770s and 1780s. It would be a mistake, however, to overemphasize theatricality and place the elocutionists at the heart of the eighteenth-century rhetorical revolution. The admiration for the Roman republic sustained a lingering interest in the classical rhetoric of Cicero and Quintilian, which had supplemented the Puritans' truncated Ramist rhetoric by midcentury. Elementary Ciceronian rhetoric was available in John Ward's *System of Oratory* (1759), a text that had an important and lasting influence upon the Connecticut Wit David Humphreys at Yale in the late 1760s and that remained popular until about 1780. Juniors at Yale, moreover, recited from Cicero on oratory under Ezra Stiles (1778–1795).[12]

More important, as modern historians of rhetoric have written, in the curriculum at Yale and other American colleges in the late eighteenth century

12. Thomas Sheridan, *Course of Lectures on Elocution . . .* (London, 1762); John Ward, *A System of Oratory . . . ,* 2 vols. (London, 1759). On George Whitefield and the theater, see Harry S. Stout, *The Divine Dramatist: George Whitefield and the Rise of Modern Evangelicalism* (Grand Rapids, Mich., 1991). On the elocutionary movement and theater, see Frederick W. Haberman, "English Sources of American Elocution," in Karl R. Wallace, ed., *History of Speech Education in America: Background Studies* (New York, 1954), 105–126. On the rise of the theater in the Revolutionary era, see Kenneth Silverman, *A Cultural History of the American Revolution: Painting, Music, Literature, and the Theater in the Colonies and the United States from the Treaty of Paris to the Inauguration of George Washington, 1763–1789* (1976; reprint, New York, 1987); and Joseph J. Ellis, *After the Revolution: Profiles of Early American Culture* (New York, 1979). Fliegelman's *Declaring Independence* tends to overemphasize the elocutionists. For a corrective, see Wilbur Samuel Howell, *Logic and Rhetoric in England, 1500–1700* (1956; reprint, New York, 1961); Howell, *Eighteenth-Century British Logic and Rhetoric* (Princeton, N.J., 1971); and George A. Kennedy, *Classical Rhetoric and Its Christian and Secular Tradition from Ancient to Modern Times* (Chapel Hill, N.C., 1980). On Ramist and classical rhetoric at Yale, see Richard Warch, *School of the Prophets: Yale College, 1701– 1740* (New Haven, Conn., 1973); and Morgan, *Gentle Puritan,* 51. On Humphreys and Ward, see Leon Howard, *The Connecticut Wits* (Chicago, 1943), 31–32, 120–122, 130–131. On other classical rhetorical texts used at Yale, see Warren Guthrie, "Rhetorical Theory in Colonial America," in Wallace, ed., *History of Speech Education in America,* 48–59. On the classical rhetorical influence generally, see Walter J. Ong, "Forword," Winifred Bryan Horner, "The Eighteenth Century," and Donald C. Stewart, "The Nineteenth Century," in Horner, ed., *The Present State of Scholarship in Historical and Contemporary Rhetoric* (Columbia, Mo., 1983), 1–9, 101–133, 134–136. That the classical influence lingered beyond the end of the eighteenth century is shown by the publication of John Quincy Adams's *Lectures on Rhetoric and Oratory . . . ,* 2 vols. (1810; reprint, New York, 1962), which argued that Aristotle, Cicero, and Quintilian were immediately relevant to the early Republic (see, esp., lectures 1, 2, 15). On Stiles and Cicero, see Morgan, *Gentle Puritan,* 388.

"rhetoric fulfilled its classical *function* as the art of communication, one which synthesized material from a wide variety of fields." Appreciative of the status and synthetic function of classical rhetoric, the young writers and orators at Yale in the 1770s like John Trumbull and Timothy Dwight nevertheless used the classical apparatus of topics and proofs as a foil in their promotion of the new philosophical rhetoric of Henry Home, Lord Kames's *Elements of Criticism* (1762). Kames's text built its analysis of the verbal arts upon the new psychology of sentiment and taste developed by Anthony Ashley Cooper, third earl of Shaftesbury, and Francis Hutcheson. Students of *Elements* and of the enormously popular study that supplanted it in the 1780s, Hugh Blair's *Lectures on Rhetoric and Belles Lettres* (1783), edged away from the emphasis on rhetoric as the productive art of oral discourse and toward rhetoric as stylistic literary criticism.[13]

Far more than any particular rhetorical theory, new rhetorical *practices* promoted the interest in public discourse at Yale and other American colleges in the last quarter of the eighteenth century. The two most important developments were the rise of student societies and the curricular movement away from Latin disputation and toward English forensic argument. The Critonian Club at Yale lasted from 1750 to 1772; the more important and longer-lasting Linonia Society began in 1753 and was joined by its rival Brothers in Unity in 1768. The Phi Beta Kappa honor society, which began at the College of William and Mary in 1776, opened a Yale chapter in 1780. In these fraternal societies, which became especially popular after the Revolution, young men, away from the direct supervision of college authorities, could come together under their own rules, perform their own ceremonies, and discuss their own books. The

13. Robert J. Connors, Lisa S. Ede, and Andrea A. Lunsford, "The Revival of Rhetoric in America," in Connors, Ede, and Lunsford, eds., *Essays on Classical Rhetoric and Modern Discourse* (Carbondale, Ill., 1984), 2, 3 (emphasis added). See also Ian Thomson, "Rhetoric and the Passions, 1760–1800," in Brian Vickers, ed., *Rhetoric Revalued: Papers from the International Society for the History of Rhetoric* (Binghamton, N.Y., 1982), 143–148; Vincent M. Bevilacqua, "Lord Kames's Theory of Rhetoric," in Donald G. Douglas, *Philosophers on Rhetoric: Traditional and Emerging Views* (Skokie, Ill., 1973), 115–139; Kennedy, *Classical Rhetoric*, 235–240. In 1783, John Cotton Smith spoke with President Ezra Stiles about Henry Home, Lord Kames's *Elements of Criticism . . .* , 3 vols. (Edinburgh, 1762), a book that Smith "idolized" but Stiles hated (John Cotton Smith, Diary, Nov. 7, 1782–March 1783, Feb. 20, 1783, John Cotton Smith Papers, Manuscripts and Archives, Yale University Library [typescript]). Yale adopted Hugh Blair's *Lectures on Rhetoric and Belles Lettres,* 2 vols. (London, 1783) as a rhetoric textbook in 1785 (Morgan, *Gentle Puritan,* 388). For Timothy Dwight's views on Kames, Blair, and rhetoric generally, see Vincent Freimarck, "Rhetoric at Yale in 1807," American Philosophical Society, *Proceedings,* CX (Philadelphia, 1966), 235–255.

clubs combined individual competition and communal conviviality, secrecy and public display, ritual repetition and an active engagement with contemporary debate. A secretary of the Brothers in Unity wrote that, in the society, members sharpened their abilities to reason and speak about religious, political, and literary questions: "We transact in miniature the most important business in life."[14]

These "little republics" opened an avenue for the ambitious student eager for both self-improvement and the chance to stand out among his peers by displaying his learning, eloquence, and wit. The chief end of the Linonia Society, a pragmatic Aaron Dutton claimed in the 1790s, "is that we may bring into action and fix in our minds what we have learned in our studies." Yet, the activities were intended to cultivate sentimental attachments as much as develop speaking and writing skills. "Here we have had an opportunity of gather[ing] the flowers of Literature and fruits of friendship," Richard Storrs told his fellow Linonians in 1782. Regular meetings and ritual occasions were intended to forge and strengthen the bonds of affection among members and to create a sense of belonging to a special group. The recording secretary for the Phi Beta Kappa was overcome, or pretended to be overcome, with the sentiments stirred by a 1787 induction ceremony: "Language would fail, should we attempt to describe the nameless emotions of the Fraternity. Friendship glowing in each breast caught an additional ray and appeared in her most lovely robes." An-

14. Timothy Mather Cooley, Yale University Brothers in Unity Records, YRG 40-A-5, Secretary's Records, Valedictory Oration, June 28, 1792. Chauncy A. Goodrich's "Report of the Professor of Rhetoric and Oratory," Sept. 7, 1818, however, which commented on the study of rhetoric and belles lettres at Yale in the previous twenty years, complained that the curriculum still devoted only a fifth of the time to those subjects compared to the amount of attention given ancient languages and mathematics. He estimated that students participated in twenty forensic disputes and turned in fifteen compositions over their college career (Goodrich Family Papers, Manuscripts and Archives, Yale University Library). The Linonia Library catalog in 1784 included Ward's *System of Oratory,* Kames's *Elements of Criticism,* Edmund Burke's *Philosophical Enquiry into the Origin of Our Ideas of the Sublime and Beautiful* (London, 1757), Philip Dormer Stanhope, earl of Chesterfield's *Letters Written . . . to His Son,* 2 vols. (London, 1774), William Enfield's *The Speaker; or, Miscellaneous Pieces, Selected from the Best English Writers . . . ,* 2 vols. (London, 1774), *The Spectator,* essays by Oliver Goldsmith, and Whitefield's sermons ("A Catalogue of Books in the [Linonia] Library, March the 19th, 1784," Yale University Linonia Society Records, YRG 40-A-96, Secretary's Records). In 1790, the catalog contained eighty-seven titles in history, twenty-nine in divinity, twenty-eight in poetry, and eleven novels. An undated eighteenth-century catalog listed twenty-five titles in history (eighty volumes), eighteen in divinity (thirty volumes), seventeen in poetry, twelve novels, seven law books, and fifty-six miscellaneous titles (Yale University Linonia Society Records, YRG 40-A-96, Librarian's Records).

other hand wrote in the margin of the record book "Oh Sublime! Sublime! Sublime!"[15]

The tension between being a secret or exclusive society on one hand and embodying the values of and trying to benefit a broader public on the other marked the college societies just as it marked the fraternal organizations outside the college like the Society of the Cincinnati or the rapidly growing Freemasons. Speakers explained that secret rituals and transactions allowed members to be freer with their sentiments. Secrecy offered the kind of protective cocoon for free intellectual inquiry that Ezra Stiles had dreamed of a generation before; it provided an opportunity for the open expression of feeling while shielding members from undesirable publicity. Secrecy also created a special bond among members and piqued the interest of outsiders. But a fraternal society's relationship with the broader public was just as important. Phi Beta Kappans were concerned that their organization benefit the college as a whole, and Linonians worried about exhibitions that might make the college authorities, the civil magistrates, and the people in general uneasy.[16]

15. David Potter, "The Literary Society," in Wallace, ed., *History of Speech Education in America*, 256. Aaron Dutton, "A Dissertation on the Means of Rendering the Exercises of the Linonian Society Pleasing and Useful," n.d. [c. 1785–1802, probably 1790s], Yale University Linonia Society Records, YRG 40-A-96; Richard Storrs, Oration, April 1782, ibid.; Yale University Phi Beta Kappa Records, YRG 40-A-11, Records of the Phi Beta Kappa in 1787, Manuscripts and Archives, Yale University Library. The Brothers in Unity similarly proclaimed that they joined together for "the improvement of science and friendship"; the Linonia Society secretary wrote that the organization was "for the promotion of Friendship and social Intercourse and for the Advancement of Literature"; and the Phi Beta Kappa declared that they met "to cultivate and cherish Friendship and Literature; to enquire after the Brothers wellfare that they might know how to fulfill their mental engagements" (Yale University Brothers in Unity Records, YRG 40-A-5, Secretary's Records, Book II, Minutes of Meetings, 1783–1803; Yale University Linonia Society Records, YRG 40-A-96, Secretary's Records, Constitutions, 1792–1825, c. 1792; Yale University Phi Beta Kappa Records, YRG 40-A-11, Records of the Phi Beta Kappa in 1787, June 23).

16. Yale University Phi Beta Kappa Records, YRG 40-A-11, Constitution 1787, Initiation Oath: "Here you may disengage yourselves from scholastic cares and communicate without reserve whatever observations you have made upon a variety of objects. . . . Here too you may indulge in Speculation, that freedom of inquiry." On secrecy, see also Timothy Mather Cooley, Yale University Brothers in Unity Records, YRG 40-A-5, Secretary's Records, Valedictory Oration, June 28, 1792; and Yale University Linonia Society Records, YRG 40-A-96, Secretary's Minutes, Mar. 22, 1782. On the effect of secrecy upon nonmembers, see Yale University Phi Beta Kappa Records, YRG 40-A-11, Phi Beta Kappa Records in 1787, July 10: "The repeated attacks by the envious and malicious upon the secrets of the Phi beta Kappa will eventually give dignity and add importance to the Society"; and July 16 on the benefits to Yale College as a whole.

The Yale societies were also symbolically related to public life outside the college. The fraternal associations were elite idealizations of the new American Republic, little republics sustained by written constitutions and the cultivation of mutual sentiment. The way that Linonians and their rival Brothers in Unity competed for members and traduced each other's character can be seen as a juvenile analogue to the partisan division in America during the 1790s. More significant, though, the societies trained future leaders in the habits of elite voluntary association at a time when no combination of men could be considered politically innocent. Federalists, beginning with George Washington, denounced the "self-created" Democratic-Republican societies as subversive, and Republicans countercharged that elite associations and clubs like the anti-slavery Society for the Promotion of Freedom and even the Connecticut Academy for the Arts and Sciences were fronts for political intrigue. Toward the end of the century, when President Dwight and other Federalist clergymen were casting a suspicious eye upon the secretive Masons and preaching about French infidel conspiracies, Connecticut's Phi Beta Kappa met and even considered dissolving on the chance that one day the society might fall into the wrong hands. These fears became something more than Federalist paranoia about the Illuminati when New Haven politician Abraham Bishop used his 1800 Phi Beta Kappa address to launch the most open and forceful attack upon Connecticut federalism and the Standing Order clergy that the state had yet seen.[17]

The college societies' public exhibitions and ceremonies were intended to

17. The 1772 Linonian anniversary oration charged that "Luxury and Prophaneness" were "the darling objects" of the Brothers in Unity, and, by 1776, the Linonians were calling the Brothers "Plutonians" (Yale University Linonia Society Records, YRG 40-A-11, "An Oration by Alden Delivered at the Anniversary 1772," Anniversary Oration, ca. 1776, Secretary's Records, Minutes, Apr. 9, 1776). On July 6, 1796, a committee of Brothers met with Linonians to clean up their recruiting practices (Yale University Brothers in Unity Records, YRG 40-A-5, Secretary's Records, Book II, Minutes of Meetings, 1783–1803). But the societies would still go to great lengths to get new members. On his way to New Haven to attend college in 1799, Thomas Davies Burrall was met by a few Linonian brothers who, he wrote, "had travelled miles on foot from the City solely to guard me from the artful wiles of certain unprincipled young 'scamps' who styled themselves the '*Brothers in Unity*'—forsooth! who lay in wait to mislead the unwary aspirants for fame. I was kindly assured that every young gentleman who hoped for honors in College or distinction in life must *of course*, be a *Linonian*" (Burrall to the Secretary of the Linonian Society, Mar. 8, 1861, with Burrall's manuscript copy of Cyrus Pearce's "The Yaliad," Yale Miscellaneous Manuscripts, Manuscripts and Archives, Yale University Library). On the condemnation of self-created societies, see *American Mercury*, Nov. 27, 1800. On disbanding the Phi Beta Kappa, see *Conn. Courant*, July 29, 1799. See Abraham Bishop, *Connecticut Republicanism: An Oration on the Extent and Power of Political Delusion* . . . ([New Haven, Conn.?], 1800). The oration was also published in Newark, N.J.,

allay any suspicions that these groups were self-interested factions or morally dangerous associations. Whereas their private performances and rituals kindled fraternal sentiments and a gentleman's warm affection for the arts and sciences, their public exercises, with their genteel decorum and patriotic themes, supported the broad values of the Republic by advancing and diffusing knowledge and cultivating civic virtue. Sometimes, however, the private sentiments and the public display were in conflict. In 1782, President Stiles noted in his diary that, in both the Linonian Society and the Brothers in Unity, "many have had an ardent Desire to act Tragedies and other dramatical Exhibitions at their Anniversaries." "They have carried all Things secret in the Anniversaries hitherto. Yet lately [they have been] inviting Gentlemen and Ladies in To their Entertainments and dramatic Exhibitions have become of Notoriety no longer to be concealed." Theater was still notorious for treating questionable subjects and for arousing suspect emotions in the audience. A compromise was eventually reached: women would be excluded. In 1790, the Brothers in Unity performed two plays, written by students, at Abraham Bishop's New Haven theater: a comedy about a crafty lawyer and a tragedy about the capture of Germans at the battle of Trenton. According to the Brothers' recording secretary: "The Tutors, all the Literati of the City, and many respectable Citizens of the place, together with the members of the college composed a very respectable audience. No Ladies were admitted, it being prohibited by the President and Tutors." The young men were allowed to play their characters in front of a larger fraternity of respected citizens and gentlemen scholars, but not in the polite society of women.[18]

At the center of all the fraternal activities both private and public were the arts of discourse: parliamentary procedure and poetry readings, extempore arguments and formal orations, written compositions and dramatic dialogues. Members met and practiced in their rooms once or twice a week, and when the groups became too large they held meetings in New Haven's courthouse or the nearby Sandemanian meetinghouse. They drew their topics from the liberal arts, the advances in science, or current political news. In the early 1770s, for example, Linonians calculated the length of the earth's shadow, discussed the revolutions of the moon, and argued about the cause of thunder and lightning.

Philadelphia, and Albany, N.Y., and excerpts appeared in the *New-Jersey Journal* and the Hartford *American Mercury*, Oct. 23, 1800.

18. Ezra Stiles, *The Literary Diary of Ezra Stiles, D.D., L.L.D. President of Yale College*, 3 vols., ed. Franklin Bowditch Dexter (New York, 1901), Apr. 6, 1782, III, 14–15; Yale University Brothers in Unity Records, YRG 40-A-5, Secretary's Records, Book II, Minutes of Meetings, 1783–1803, July 28, 1790.

In 1788, they considered the following questions: whether education promoted religion, whether it was wise to entrust the army to the president rather than Congress, whether there ought to be a tax on hogs, and "whether it is not as much our duty to exterminate the savages of America as it was for the Children of Israel to exterminate the Canaanites." The Brothers in Unity elected officers responsible for history, geography, mathematics, composition, and oratory and chose a critic to respond to each performance. Linonians and the Brothers would also produce quarter day or anniversary exhibitions that became quite elaborate by the 1780s. The Linonian anniversary celebration in 1782 consisted of a procession from the college chapel to the statehouse, two orations, a tragedy (*Tamerlane*), a meal, another oration, a comedy (*A Bold Stroke for a Wife*), and a concluding oration. At the December quarterly exhibition in 1788, the Brothers in Unity presented three orations and two dramatic dialogues; the first dialogue was on the adoption of the Constitution, and a second was on Shays's Rebellion. Phi Beta Kappa orations, sometimes given on the day after commencement, were also special events. These speeches often addressed familiar themes in familiar ways, but the series included, besides Abraham Bishop's partisan manifesto, T. William Johnson's perceptive critique of classical republicanism in 1793 and Ebenezer Grant Marsh's 1797 dissertation on language.[19]

The interest in the arts of public discourse that was promoted by the fraternal societies also helped change the college curriculum. Daily recitations, twice-weekly declamations, and, for juniors and seniors, twice-weekly disputations had characterized student work at Yale since its founding. For recita-

19. Linonians and Brothers in Unity met in their rooms or in the Sandemanian meetinghouse, but Phi Beta Kappans met fortnightly off campus with postgraduate members living in the New Haven area. See Yale University Linonia Society Records, YRG 40-A-96, Secretary's Records, Minutes, Dec. 16, 23, 1772, Feb. 10, 1773; Yale University Linonia Society Records, YRG 40-A-96, Secretary's Records, Minutes, Dec. 15, 1768–July 8, 1790, entries for Apr. 18, 1782, Mar. 2, Apr. 3, Aug. 14, 1788; Yale University Brothers in Unity Records, YRG 40-A-5, Secretary's Records, Book II, Minutes of Meetings, 1783–1803, entry for 1787, Dec. 22, 1788. Simeon Baldwin's Phi Beta Kappa oration on the day after commencement in 1787 dealt with the diffusion of knowledge and the sublime ideas conveyed by nature. J. Walter Edwards in 1791 argued that national peace elevated the general taste in architecture, poetry, and painting, and he cheered the revolutionary spirit taking hold in France and Poland. The following year, Timothy Pitkin described the advancement of knowledge and the international progress toward universal brotherhood. T. William Johnson delivered his oration on Sept. 12, 1793. For all of the above, see Yale University Phi Beta Kappa Records, YRG 40-A-11, Phi Beta Kappa Orations. See also Ebenezer Grant Marsh, *An Oration Delivered before the Phi Beta Kappa Society, at Their Anniversary Meeting in New-Haven, on the Fifth of December, A.D. 1797* (Hartford, Conn., 1798).

tions, students stood with the textbook open in their hands as the tutor or professor quizzed them on the day's assignment. A half-dozen students each week also submitted written declamations in English, Latin, Greek, or Hebrew and then delivered them from memory to the class. The centerpiece of the upper-level curriculum was disputation. Half the class prepared affirmative arguments and the other half negative ones for an assigned topic; a chosen few presented their arguments in front of the class, and then the tutor or professor rendered a decision. Before midcentury, disputations were always conducted in Latin as formal exercises in syllogistic reasoning. President Clap supplemented these by introducing English forensic debate but still confined the debated topics to timeworn "brain-teasers" in ethics, divinity, and natural philosophy. In 1779, just a few years after the students had formally requested more curricular attention to English rhetorical training and literary study, President Stiles began introducing English forensic debates on the public issues of the day. By 1782, Latin syllogistic disputes had been reduced to once a month, and, by 1789, the same year seniors began studying civil policy, Latin disputes had ceased completely, much to President Stiles's regret.[20]

This change in the language, form, and topics of academic debate at Yale, which mirrored developments at colleges throughout the country, joined the students' collegiate work to contemporary political discussion. In the syllogistic disputations, as a historian has noted, the "pattern was extremely stereotyped and allowed no essential adaptation for the persuasion of the audience." English forensic debate, however, was far better adapted to the demands of "the pulpit, the courtroom, the legislative hall, the town meeting, and the stump," all of which "claimed as much flexibility, knowledge of current issues, and skillful speaking as the best students could learn." That was especially true when the forensic disputations focused upon topics of immediate public concern. During the 1794–1795 school year, Nathan Perkins recorded disputes on traditional ethical and philosophical questions—on the nature of virtue, the just war doctrine, and whether animals could think, for example—that were similar to the disputations another Yale student, Joseph Camp, had recorded thirty years earlier. But, unlike Camp, Perkins spent about half of his time arguing about the pressing questions of the day: the ecclesiastical tax, the proper relationship between a representative and his constituents, and the extent of federal power over the states. The topic that Perkins in the mid-1790s approached only begrudgingly, complaining that it was potentially limitless

20. Kelly, *Yale*, 78–83; Morgan, *Gentle Puritan*, 390–399. Morgan aptly characterizes the traditional topics as "brain-teasers" (395).

and often incomprehensible, was the one that appeared much more frequently in Camp's list of student exercises for 1764–1765: theology.[21]

Topics with more contemporary relevance and forms of address with more popular appeal also began to dominate collegiate commencements in the 1780s. Before the 1770s, student exercises exhibited to the public on quarter days and at commencement primarily consisted of Latin syllogistic disputations. They were called *quaestiones* for the undergraduates and *theses* for the master's degree candidates and were organized into categories labeled *Technologicae* (which related the arts and sciences to one another in a comprehensive view of knowledge), *Logicae, Grammaticae, Rhetoricae, Mathematicae, Physicae,* and (after 1757) *Theologicae.* Syllogistic disputation gradually receded in prominence through the 1780s, and in the 1790s commencement day presented a much more varied display of learning and eloquence:

Yale Commencement 1796

Morning:	Afternoon:
1. Procession	1. Sacred Music
2. Sacred Music	2. Poetical Oration
3. Salutatory Oration (Latin)	3. Humorous Oration
4. Forensic Disputation	4. Degrees Conferred
5. Oration	5. Sacred Music
6. Dialogue	6. Prayer
7. Oration	
8. Sacred Music[22]	

The college was, in effect, representing knowledge and the character of the learned man to the public in new ways. In the older emphasis upon ancient languages and scholastic argument, the *quaestiones* and *theses* paid homage to tradition; the participants showed how dexterously they could handle the forms of logical argumentation and the intricacies of an ancient tongue. The knowledge on display was an inheritance, and the college's public exercises demonstrated that it had been successfully handed down to the rising generation. The newer modes of academic performance, though still formal and stylized, were far more attuned to the practical application of academic learning

21. George V. Bohman, "Rhetorical Practice in Colonial America," in Wallace, ed., *History of Speech Education in America,* 71, 73; Nathan Perkins, College Notebook, 1794–1795, Jones Library, Amherst, Mass.; and Joseph Camp, College Notebook, 1764–1765, Yale Miscellaneous Manuscripts, Manuscripts and Archives, Yale University Library.

22. Louis Leonard Tucker, *Puritan Protagonist: President Thomas Clap of Yale College* (Chapel Hill, N.C., 1962), 158–159; *Conn. Courant,* Sept. 26, 1796.

to the public problems of contemporary life. The young men who showcased their literary and linguistic abilities also demonstrated how they could reason and argue about topics that were immediately relevant to a broader public. In 1790, for example, students debated new laws for religious liberty and policies concerning the public debt; in 1799, they discussed the Alien and Sedition laws and the emancipation of slaves.[23]

A published description of the 1784 commencement is notable for the writer's emphasis on the appeal the performances had for the audience (as well as his transparent boosterism): "The Assembly was brilliant and very numerous. The House was so crowded that several hundreds were prevented from obtaining Seats. There was a degree of Silence and Attention which could scarcely have been expected from so large a collection of people." The audience did have to sit through a brief Latin syllogistic disputation. But it also heard a forensic disputation on whether the Society of the Cincinnati was dangerous to American liberty. Then four students began a dialogue, "interspersed with a variety of sentiment and humour, and exhibiting a specimen of that natural prejudice and partiality which arises from different principles of Government, and systems of Education." The morning's exercises closed with an oration on the "Arts of Peace"; the afternoon session opened with another oration "on the Origin and Progress of Commerce, and its influence on Government and Manners." According to the newspaper account, "The literary exhibitions received general approbation and applause." The writer concluded that these learned discourses, "together with the decent and polite behaviour and the number of the students and the Candidates for the Academic honours, must convince every unprejudiced mind that the College established in this city is in a flourishing condition, and that it is the best and brightest ornament of the State." Like fine young gentlemen in polite society, the performers displayed sentiment appropriately, discussed timely topics, and even engaged in a bit of genteel humor. The behavior of the audience—the silent attention and approving applause—was remarkably polite as well, considering that the size of the crowd indicates that the occasion drew spectators from beneath the ranks of the elite. The exercises not only displayed but could teach polite manners.[24]

Like election sermons or Phi Beta Kappa orations, commencement speeches could sometimes produce revealing commentary about changing values. The master's disputation on sumptuary laws in 1786, for example, explored some of the contradictory tendencies within New England's political sensibility. In arguing about whether the modern state should have laws regulating and re-

23. *American Mercury,* Sept. 20, 1790; *Conn. Courant,* Sept. 16, 1799.
24. *American Mercury,* Sept. 13, 1784.

stricting the kinds of clothing, food, and other luxury items citizens bought and used, Jedidiah Morse, a geographer and divinity student, made the case for Christian Sparta and a return to the Puritan moral supervision of everyday life. He argued from the "rational principles of republicanism" and the maxims of Montesquieu's *Spirit of the Laws* that a republic was sustained by citizen virtue and that luxury was virtue's bane. The scramble for fine wines, silks, and carriages made people weak, selfish, and jealous of one another; a nation of unrestricted consumption would soon suffer the return of monarchy, the advent of social revolution, or both. David Daggett, a lawyer who would soon have political ambitions, argued that sumptuary laws were unwise, impractical, and a violation of the individual's natural rights of property. More akin to Adam Smith's *Wealth of Nations* than to Montesquieu, Daggett's argument contended that "dress, diet, and equipage, must regulate themselves." Luxury was a natural part of the progress of empire and, at the right stage of social maturity, could coexist with and even help promote the advancement of liberty and literature. It also had economic benefits: "The luxury of the rich furnishes the tables of the indigent of every description. It tends to circulate money among those who otherwise would procure it by no possible means." Although it is unclear whether or not the assignment of the affirmative and negative arguments to Morse and Daggett was arbitrary, both men argued positions that did not deviate too far from their personal sentiments. Their arguments would find a second audience when published in the *New-Haven Gazette,* and both men would go on to achieve regional if not national reputations as Federalist orators and writers by the end of the century.[25]

The college curriculum, the fraternal societies, and the multiplying opportunities to enhance one's reputation after college through public speech and

25. *New-Haven Gazette, and the Connecticut Magazine,* Oct. 5, 12, 1786. A letter from Morse to his friend John Cotton Smith on July 27, 1786, indicates that Smith was initially chosen to speak at commencement with Morse and includes some discussion about which one should argue the affirmative rather than the negative (John Cotton Smith Papers). *New-Haven Gazette* printed extracts from Adam Smith's *Inquiry into the Nature and Causes of the Wealth of Nations,* 2 vols. (London, 1776) on Nov. 2, 1786, three weeks after it printed Daggett's commencement address. Commencements, like the other rhetorical occasions, could sometimes fill the air with little more than inflated platitudes and the self-congratulatory pedantry for which Yale was already well known. The young scholars' customary flattery of their elders demonstrates the perpetuation of polite rituals in a deferential society. "Letter, from an American Officer, to His Brother, Who Had Just Finished His Education; Feb. 16, 1781," in *American Mercury,* Feb. 10, 1794, refers to the "pedantry (for which by the way N. H. College has ever been famous)." A satirical poem about the Yale commencement describes the Yale Corporation members' "Licking their lips to taste the sweet oration" filled with "brazen Flattery" for their efforts (*Conn. Courant,* Sept. 26, 1791).

print all made public discourse an important part of many students' lives. By the 1790s, some were even entering Yale with experience in public speaking and performance. Schoolmasters began holding scholastic exhibitions for the lower grades and training their students—both boys and girls—in public speaking, practices some newspaper critics found ridiculous. College diaries show how large a role rhetorical practice could play in student life at Yale. In the month of January 1796, John Hooker went to a Phi Beta Kappa meeting and a Linonia Society meeting; he attended or participated in class disputes on interest rates, ancient languages, capital punishment, and the college commons; he heard (at least) two sermons, a "speaking recitation" and a "Composition recitation"; and he listened to President Dwight lecture on voice, gesture, dialogue, courtroom oratory, defining terms in an argument, and novels. In a college diary entry for 1782, John Cotton Smith, a future congressman and Connecticut governor, fantasized about becoming a great orator. He was transported, he wrote, after reading a study of Demosthenes and Cicero:

> With what a thirst for eloquence am I fired when I read what miraculous effects it produced in these great personages [and] on the minds of their audience. How would they lead triumphant wherever their inclinations prompted [their audience, which was] . . . blinded and ravished with their transcendent excellence of speech! Could I hope to arrive at that summit of oratory to which their genius attained, not an expedient Demosthenes made use of should be untried, nor would I be deficient in the unbounded application of Cicero.

Smith here focuses, not on decorum, rational persuasion, and controlled appeals to the sentiments of listeners, but on powerful—and empowering—emotions. He has gotten more than just oratorical techniques from his reading; a passionate desire has been aroused within him, a "thirst for eloquence." He imagines audiences "blinded and ravished" rather than enlightened and persuaded and speakers who do not just prove a point but feel the "miraculous effects" of their speech within their own breasts as well. He admires oratorical genius because of the powerful passions speech could arouse and the power over audiences that accomplished speakers could wield.[26]

After graduation, young Yale men, especially law students, paid close attention to the power of public speech. Abraham Bishop wrote David Daggett

<hr />

26. *Norwich Packet; or, The Chronicle of Freedom* (Conn.), July 29, 1784; "The Companion," no. 21, *Conn. Courant*, Apr. 27, 1795; John Hooker, Diary, 1796–1797, entries for January 1796, Hooker Family Papers, Manuscripts and Archives, Yale University Library; John Cotton Smith, Diary, Nov. 7, 1782, John Cotton Smith Papers.

from London in 1787 and provided detailed descriptions of the speakers he heard in Parliament, in the courts, and in the six-hundred-person debating society that met in "Coach Maker's Hall." Two years earlier, John Cotton Smith had written Daggett a very long description of a trial in order "to exhibit a fine specimen of the eloquence" of the lawyers. Smith again concentrated, not on the lawyer's command of rational argumentation, but on his power to move the emotions of his audience. One counselor, Smith wrote, warned the jury about his opponent's oratorical skills: "Prepare yourselves for the shock—I caution you against the fascinating influence of his rhetoric—I have seen the effects of it—I have seen a Jury shake on their benches with the agitations of grief—and I have seen the judges cheeks wet with tears." And, indeed, when the great courtroom orator spoke, Smith was impressed: "He spoke almost five hours to my inexpresable entertainment. I did not see a single wandering eye in the whole assembly. . . . His language was moving and pathetic—and his manner affecting and altogether irresistible—I would not, neither could I refuse him the tribute of a tear." Congressman Zephaniah Swift wrote letters to Daggett from Philadelphia that described "the rage of speech making" in the United States House of Representatives. Overall, Swift rated congressional oratory as inferior to what he had heard in Connecticut's General Assembly. James Madison had "a hollow feeble voice, an awkward uninteresting manner—a correct stile without energy or expressiveness." Fisher Ames, however, had delivered "the most sublime and eloquent harangue which I ever heard—and Ames is the most accomplished Orator in the United States."[27]

Young professional men recognized the ways that speakers had power over audiences through persuasive appeals to sentiment, but they also understood that the context in which a speech was delivered helped endow the speaker and his words with authority. Still new to a world of public communications that before the Revolution had been defined by preaching, secular oratory remained closely affiliated with respected institutions, and those institutions cultivated that respect with increasingly elaborate public rituals. Yale College commencement in September, like election day in May, would remain one of the state's most important rhetorical occasions through the end of the century. Like election sermons, commencement addresses were surrounded by a ritual that included processions, hymns, and prayers and by social festivities that, by the 1780s, included a ball and, by the 1790s, a fireworks display. The ceremonial rituals helped create a solemn mood that reinforced the authority of the gath-

27. Abraham Bishop to David Daggett, Mar. 10, 1787, John Cotton Smith to Daggett, Dec. 1, 1785 (copy), Zephaniah Swift to Daggett, Jan. 28, Mar. 5, Dec. 13, 1794, all in David Daggett Papers, Manuscripts and Archives, Yale University Library.

ered dignitaries; the decorous celebrations that followed the commencement exercises associated the college with the sociability of high society and displayed that connection to the rest of the town. Common townspeople, however, did not necessarily stare at all the pomp and finery with slack-jawed awe. New Haven boys traditionally threw rocks through the illuminated college windows. Perhaps the fireworks display was added to distract the vulgar from their annual rites of vandalism.

Other rhetorical occasions began to cluster around commencement and election days, as other organizations borrowed from their prestige and took advantage of the biannual gatherings of the elite from around the state. It was no accident that the Connecticut Society for the Promotion of Freedom, established in 1790, decided to meet twice a year, on the day after commencement and the day after the anniversary election. This group organized men who, for political and moral reasons, had become increasingly opposed to slavery during the Revolutionary struggle for liberty and the constitutional compromise with the South over national power. The society drew together clergymen and politicians, in effect helping to shore up Connecticut's Standing Order elite. By sponsoring and publishing antislavery addresses, the society provided an important forum for lawyer-politicians like Zephaniah Swift and ministers like Jonathan Edwards, Jr. It was whispered that Swift was irreligious—a deist, perhaps an infidel—but his attack upon the inhumanity of human bondage helped establish his moral credentials. Edwards, whose preaching and theology were criticized as abstruse and dogmatic, tried to persuade his audience, not with New Divinity doctrine, but on the basis of the American principles of liberty. By having its list of elected officers (almost all of whom were "reverends" or "esquires") published alongside the state's election results, and by having its addresses delivered along with the commencement exercises, election sermons, and Phi Beta Kappa orations, the society established its social, political, and intellectual legitimacy.[28]

28. Zephaniah Swift, *An Oration on Domestic Slavery* (Hartford, Conn., 1791). A writer in the *Conn. Courant*, May 30, 1791, accused Swift of trying to flatter and "tickle" the clergy for political reasons. "A Late Orator" (Swift) responded in the same paper the following week (June 6). See also Jonathan Edwards, Jr., *The Injustice and Impolicy of the Slave-Trade, and of the Slavery of Africans*... (Providence, R.I., 1792). Edwards preached from Matt. 7:12 ("do unto others"), but quickly turned to the principle that, he contended, had become generally acknowledged since the beginning of the Revolution: *"that all men are born equally free"* (5). "We all dread political slavery," he wrote, but it would be infinitely better than what the African endures; Great Britain's attempt to enslave America was "a very small crime indeed, in comparison with the crime of those who enslave the Africans" (23–24). To the argument that their pious forefathers had held slaves (including, an objector might have said,

The General Association of Ministers in Connecticut had instituted a *concio ad clerum*—a special sermon addressed to the state's Standing Order clergy— in the early 1750s that was held on the day following the college commencement. In 1785, the association complained about poor attendance. But, instead of discontinuing the annual sermon, they added another: a yearly address on an essential point of Christian doctrine, which was initially proposed for election day afternoon but then switched to the day preceding college commencement. The new annual sermon was, of course, part of the clergy's continuing effort to school the public in Christian orthodoxy. But it had two other purposes as well: to strengthen the clergy's voice at public occasions and to provide another incentive for pastors and parishioners from around the state to join together in a mutual affirmation of shared principles and sentiments. This addition to the commencement week calendar meant that a visitor to New Haven in September 1793, for example, could have heard the following in a single three-day span: Timothy Dwight's sermon on the authenticity of the Bible, a Latin salutatory oration, an oration on the moral revolution in the United States, an oration on the progress and utility of literature, a poem in praise of poets, a forensic disputation on the federal union of states, a *concio ad clerum* sermon, an antislavery address, and T. William Johnson's Phi Beta Kappa critique of classical republicanism.[29]

Other organizations, like the college fraternal societies, tried to combine public display and service with secrecy or exclusive membership. Freemasonry, which grew rapidly after the Revolution, was increasingly seen and heard by Connecticut's citizens. Masonic celebrations and speeches displayed the order's growing public self-confidence and its attempt to closely identify with the ruling elite. A celebration in Hartford on December 31, 1787, began with a procession from the Masonic lodge to the courthouse, where the brothers and perhaps nonmembers as well assembled to hear a discourse on Masonry. The return procession to the lodge for the feast included the state secretary and treasurer, the clergy of the town, the mayor, several aldermen, and many other "Gentlemen of Character," who together spent the rest of the day "in that har-

---

Edwards's own slaveholding father, the revered Jonathan, Sr.), Edwards pointed to the Old Testament patriarchs, who not only held slaves but took more than one wife. The world had received more light and had seen the sinfulness of polygamy. Now in the age of liberty men were beginning to understand that even the best Christians of the previous generation had been ignorant on this matter. "You therefore to whom the present blaze of light as to this subject has reached, cannot sin at so cheap a rate as our fathers" (27).

29. Congregational Churches in Connecticut, General Association, *The Records of the General Association of the Colony of Connecticut; Begun June 20th, 1738; Ending June 19, 1799* (Hartford, Conn., 1888), 30, 131, 138, entries for 1753, 1789, 1791; *Conn. Courant*, Sept. 23, 1793.

mony and decent hilarity peculiar to Masonry." A Norwich lodge festival in the 1790s consisted of a procession, a sermon, an oration, music, and an elegant dinner on the town green. The first Masonic stone laying and installation of officers in the state included an oration, a sermon, hymn singing, and a feast at the New London courthouse, all of which, according to the newspaper report, "excited the curiosity of the multitude." [30]

As Freemasonry became more prominent in the public eye just as political tensions were rising in the 1790s, curiosity could sour into suspicion. *The Free-Mason's Pocket Companion,* published by New London brother Samuel Green in 1794, tried to address the uneasiness that Masonic secrecy aroused in the public, explaining that the order strictly avoided political and religious disputes and was dedicated to promoting charity and benevolence throughout the world. Yet, in that same year—and still a few years before the Illuminati scare—"an attempt was made to convert the [Connecticut] Lodges into political meetings or democratic clubs, to influence the elections," according to the Masonic brother who wrote "A Hint to Free Masons." The Reverend Azel Backus warned in a sermon to Masons in Litchfield: *"Clubs cannot rule among a free people.* Should you convert your Society into a *political Cabal,* the jealousy of a free and enlightened people will search it out, and evil will return on your own heads." By the end of the century, Masons were confidently telling ministers to mind their own business. They warned the clergy that in "making insidious attempts at the overthrow of masonry, by attempting to insinuate into the minds of the public that masonry is a dangerous society, who wishes to overthrow all order, government, and religion in the world," ministers were antagonizing a formidable opponent: "An institution which hath outstripped all others that have started up at different periods of the world." Masonic orations continued to stress the order's support of true Christianity and good government, but they also defended the dignity and heritage of Masonry itself.[31]

The similar suspicions raised about the Cincinnati, though they seemed to

30. *American Mercury,* Dec. 31, 1787, July 6, 1795; *Bee,* July 3, 1799. Masonic funeral processions were another form of public display; participants were identified by white aprons, wands, sashes, gloves, and various other insignia ("A Brother," *Norwich Packet,* Oct. 10, 1799). One Mason estimated that there were more than fifteen hundred of his brethren in forty-four Connecticut lodges by the end of the century (*Norwich Packet,* Oct. 10, 1799). On Freemasonry, see Steven C. Bullock, *Revolutionary Brotherhood: Freemasonry and the Transformation of the American Social Order, 1730–1840* (Chapel Hill, N.C., 1996).

31. *The Free-Mason's Pocket Companion; or, Elements of Free-Masonry Delineated* (New London, Conn., 1794); *Norwich Packet,* Oct. 10, Nov. 14, 1799; "Extracts from a Sermon Preached by the Rev. Azel Backus, Sept. 27, 1794, to the Free-Masons at Litchfield," *American Mercury,* Mar. 9, 1795.

have temporarily abated in the late 1780s and early 1790s, returned at the end of the century and eventually killed the society. Again distrustful of what the Republican press was calling the "Julius Caesar" Society, the General Assembly refused to allow the Cincinnatians to incorporate and protect their funds. Until its dissolution in 1804, however, the society went about its primary business: providing charity to indigent members or their families (handled at a yearly business meeting held on the day before the Yale College commencement in New Haven) and celebrating the Fourth of July. Independence Day festivities conducted by the Cincinnati in Hartford began with a procession from the council chamber in the statehouse to one of the local meetinghouses, where a large audience assembled for prayers, songs, a sermon, a reading of the Declaration of Independence, and the keynote oration. The ceremony, and the feast and patriotic toasts that followed in a nearby tavern, was annually reported by the press and helped establish the form of other July Fourth ceremonies in the state. Yale-trained orators with established or rising reputations delivered the orations, which were usually published; they evolved from paeans to the progress of liberty and enlightenment (Joel Barlow's in 1787) to harsh partisan diatribes against Jeffersonian republicanism (Theodore Dwight's in 1798).[32]

The July Fourth oration emerged as a new political-rhetorical form that rivaled the election sermon as a presumptive expression of consensual values and political orthodoxy. Orators who had often studied together in college corresponded about the rhetorical challenge of giving their local July Fourth address. Calvin Goddard and David Daggett exchanged copies of their orations by mail, Goddard acknowledging "that *Oration makers* feel a unusual interest in each other's productions." Henry Channing approved of Daggett's use of "burlesque" rather than sober political analysis in 1787: "Indeed our political situation is become too serious to be contemplated on a day devoted to festivity." A decade later, John Cotton Smith disliked feeling obliged to rehearse the noble military exploits of the Revolutionary heroes: "I have however waded thro' up to the armpits in blood—and of course when I come on the stage, reeking with gore, how many salt tears will be shed." Thomas Dawes, Jr., confessed to throwing a few "flowers" into his discourse, "which are not displeas-

32. Connecticut State Society of the Cincinnati, *Records of the Connecticut State Society of the Cincinnati, 1783–1807* (Hartford, Conn., 1916), [3]; Connecticut State Society of the Cincinnati, *Papers of the Connecticut State Society of the Cincinnati, 1783–1807* (Hartford, Conn., 1916); *Bee*, July 1, 1801; Joel Barlow, *An Oration, Delivered . . . at the Meeting of the Connecticut Society of the Cincinnati, July 4, 1787* (Hartford, Conn., 1787); Theodore Dwight, *An Oration Spoken at Hartford . . . on the Anniversary of American Independence, July 4, 1798* (Hartford, Conn., 1798). The title page does not identify Dwight's oration as an address to the Cincinnati, but see Conn. St. Soc. of the Cin., *Records.*

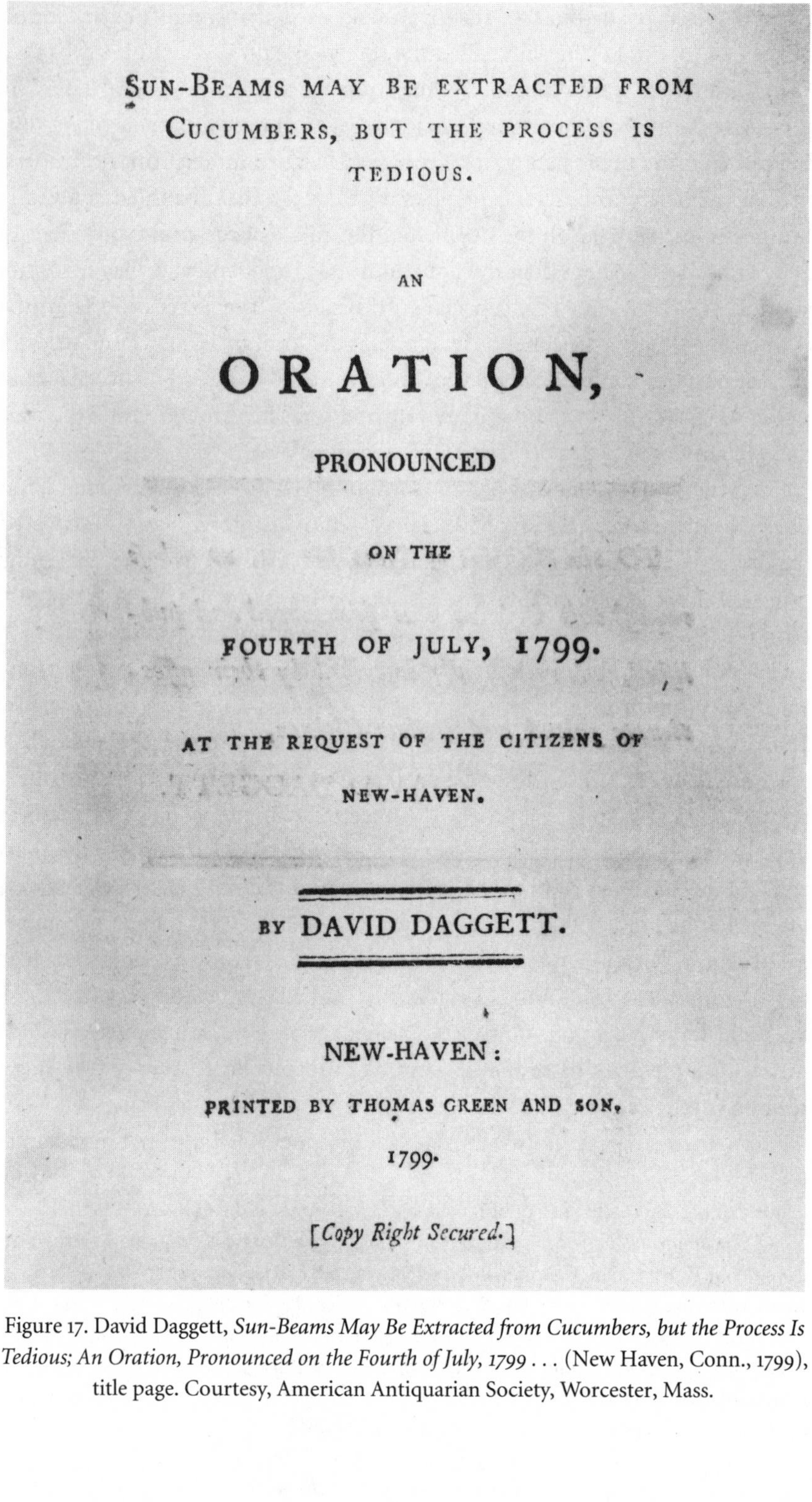

SUN-BEAMS MAY BE EXTRACTED FROM
CUCUMBERS, BUT THE PROCESS IS
TEDIOUS.

AN

ORATION,

PRONOUNCED

ON THE

FOURTH OF JULY, 1799.

AT THE REQUEST OF THE CITIZENS OF
NEW-HAVEN.

BY DAVID DAGGETT.

NEW-HAVEN:

PRINTED BY THOMAS GREEN AND SON,

1799.

[Copy Right Secured.]

Figure 17. David Daggett, *Sun-Beams May Be Extracted from Cucumbers, but the Process Is Tedious; An Oration, Pronounced on the Fourth of July, 1799* . . . (New Haven, Conn., 1799), title page. Courtesy, American Antiquarian Society, Worcester, Mass.

ing in a *popular* assembly, tho' they are not always sufficient for the chaste eyes of a *schollar*." Each writer addressed the difficulties of balancing the demands of the occasion, the subject matter, and the audience. They wanted to assess the progress of American liberty and discuss serious political questions, yet they were being called to speak in the middle of a celebration. They felt the pressure to meet the popular audience's expectations for extravagant sentiment, yet worried about embarrassing themselves in front of the learned.[33]

A generation earlier, the only regular public addresses in Connecticut were sermons and the governor's fast and thanksgiving day proclamations, which were usually read from the pulpit by the local minister. The preaching and government proclamations continued, of course. But they did so along with newer forms of occasional discourse that also projected the power of the state or were similarly embedded in ritual displays of status and authority. Just as sermons were joined by secular orations and addresses, printed proclamations were supplemented by the governor's addresses, legislative speeches, and congressional debates that the press circulated throughout the state. Although militia sermons by the local pastor had long been preached and published, newspapers by the 1790s also began printing the speeches of military officers to their troops. Courtroom oratory, too, found a larger audience when the press began printing or commenting upon speeches delivered there. Chief Justice Eliphalet Dyer's address to the convicted rapist Joseph Mountain in 1790, which went on and on about the three types of government described by Montesquieu, the ancient origin of juries, and the settling of New England, no doubt had this larger audience in mind. The newspaper account of a Litchfield trial in 1799, in which eighty-three-year-old Gideon Washburn was convicted on four counts of bestiality, focused on "the zeal and eloquence of the advocates, [which] wrought upon a very crouded house with irresistible effect," as did "the remarks of Chief Justice Root, and the ceremony of passing Sentence." Eloquent discourse, it seems, had the power to elevate even the spectacle of a crime that degraded human nature below "the most beastly monsters." Even such a trial could become a rhetorical occasion to instruct the public and move the emotions of an audience, and the courtroom could become a rhetorical school.[34]

33. Thomas Dawes, Jr., to David Daggett, July 21, 1787, Henry Channing to Daggett, Aug. 7, 1787, John Cotton Smith to Daggett, June 22, 1798, Calvin Goddard to Daggett, Aug. 16, 1799, all in David Daggett Papers. See also the letters from William May, Oct. 15, 1787, and Jirah Isham, Aug. 7, 1799, in the same collection.

34. Lieutenant Colonel Zephaniah Swift's "Recommendatory Orders for the 5th Regiment of Militia," *American Mercury*, Apr. 29, 1793 (reprinted from the *Phenix; or, Wind-*

The 1784 play written by Yale sophomores records the authors' support for elite or "aristocratic" notions of virtuous citizenship. Although Irvin and McPherson speak initially of the generic person's right to political speech in a free society, they quickly shift to assumptions about how a *gentleman* ought to speak his mind and act in the public forum and contrast this to the language and behavior of the "new set of folk lately come upon the stage." The gentleman forms his opinions and political sentiments by consulting his conscience; he expresses those opinions rather than parroting some party line; he acts conscientiously, and he casts his votes for men he knows and trusts, not for the names circulated by printed propaganda. The "new" men of Connecticut's post-Revolutionary politics, however, "have delivered their consciences in keeping to this body [the Middletown Convention]; so that without any concern, whatever it prescribes, they readily acquiesce in and discharge themselves of the trouble of reason and common sense; and the difficulty of being obliged to act their own opinion." If, as Irvin remarks, it is "the part of a Gentleman to act his own opinion," then the conventioneer who wrote to them was playing some other part upon the public stage.[35]

McPherson wonders why the conventioneer "concealed his real name if he meant to act as a friend." Irvin answers: "There are some persons who like to have a pompous name, the base signification of which implies benevolence towards their fellow creatures. . . . A Destroyer of his country will not stile himself a tyrant, and a Villain often assumes the name of a Gentleman." Perhaps Irvin believes that the pen name "Philanthropos" is only appropriate for

---

ham Herald [Conn.]); Brigadier General Cleaveland's Address to the Brigade of the Militia, *American Mercury*, Nov. 1, 1798 (reprinted from the *Connecticut Gazette* [New London]); Lt. Col. Ephraim Kirby's Regimental Orders to the Seventeenth Regiment of Connecticut Militia, *Bee*, Oct. 7, 1801; *Conn. Courant*, Aug. 23, 1790, Sept. 9, 1799; *Journal of the Times* (Stonington, Conn.), Sept. 17, 1799. The *Conn. Courant* also published judicial remarks like the "Extract from an Address Delivered in Court by Judge Rush at Reading . . ." (Apr. 25, 1796), which attacked Thomas Paine's *Age of Reason: Being an Investigation of True and Fabulous Theology* (Paris, 1794) and declared that "a Judge may at *any time,* without stepping aside from the path of duty, illustrate [Christianity's] precepts and enforce its evidences." On Apr. 1, 1799, the paper devoted all five columns of page 1 and half of page 2 to "A Charge to the Grand Juries of the County Courts of the Fifth Circuit of the State of Pennsylvania, at December Sessions, 1798, by Alex. Addison . . . ," which concerned the Alien law.

35. Yale Class Play, 17–18.

gentlemen because only they can be truly philanthropic, or because only they wrote political letters in the press bearing such signatures, where, presumably, assuming such a name was less "pompous." In any case, Irvin and McPherson conflate proper gentlemanly behavior and the standards of good citizenship, and in their eyes the new folk attending conventions and claiming that they speak the voice of the people measured up to neither.[36]

Not only were these new political troublemakers not acting like gentlemen, according to McPherson and Irvin they were not even acting like free, rational, moral agents. By blindly following the dictates of their political faction, they forfeit their consciences, their reason, and their common sense; they forgo forming private judgments and acting independently and instead follow the baying herd. The characters in the play diagnose the problem with language similar to that of the Old Lights who condemned the excesses of the Awakening four decades earlier. It is a "mad enthusiasm," a passionate "phrenzy" that makes the afflicted unable "to hear the voice of reason." Mr. Writer samples the thoughts of the enthusiast Philanthropos and finds them heterogeneous and absurd. Possessed by their own passions, political enthusiasts unman themselves. The mental chaos of Philanthropos resembled a lady's mind that Mr. Writer also mentions, a mind that wore "a thousand different aspects in a day—and many more in the night." When political enthusiasm became epidemic, mental chaos created social chaos. Irvin is ready to find Philanthropos and apply a few swift kicks to his backside to "extract the vapours from his head." The gentlemen, however, are cheered when Philanthropos writes to apologize and announce that the "phrenzy which then possess'd my mind, has left me." McPherson was pleased "that men, after having been led away with mad enthusiasms, are, in their cooler moments, willing to listen to the voice of reason; and retract from folly and errour; and it would be well for America, and well for many individuals at the present day, if reason has a seat in their breasts."[37]

Theoretically open to all members of the body public, in practice formal public discourse in Connecticut after the Revolution remained thoroughly dominated by a speaking aristocracy of propertied white men like Mr. Irvin and Mr. McPherson. According to republican principles, any citizen could make a speech to a public assembly or publish opinions and commentary in the press. Like Irvin when he commented upon the rights of a person in a free state to speak out, newspaper writers from the 1770s through the 1790s insisted that speaking or writing upon matters of public concern was a citizen's natural

36. Ibid., 16.
37. Ibid., 13, 19–21.

or constitutional right, and often his patriotic duty. Some, like McPherson when he warned that speech ought to be tempered by prudence, qualified their support for free expression by saying that speaking out was appropriate only when the community was in danger, when public measures might injure the state, when a decent respect toward government was maintained, or only before (rather than after) a proposed bill became law. Others, however, became convinced that the average citizen needed to relearn how to keep his mouth shut and his quill pen dry. A writer in the *Norwich Packet* told his fellow citizens in 1797: "It cannot be supposed that the voice of one individual will command thousands in this country. . . . Your talking, your opinions and your arguments, are of no avail, therefore you will do well to desist from such unprofitable attempts."[38]

If everyone, or at least every citizen, had the right to speak or write to the public, these activities continued to be considered most appropriate for gentlemen—and not only the gentlemen themselves thought so. The elite domination of public speech and writing, however, did not go unchallenged. In 1777, a writer representing laborers, mechanics, and small tradesmen complained that, although these common men made up the majority "upon the open ground," majorities in public meetings and assemblies always seemed to be commanded by men with very different interests. A newspaper essay fifteen years later entitled "Vox Populi, Vox Dei" still concluded with frustration that "the common people are always hushed into a thoughtless lethargy."[39]

The most forceful effort to give poorer workingmen a public voice in eighteenth-century Connecticut was led by Walter Brewster, a twenty-eight-year-old Canterbury shoemaker who wrote a remarkable series of essays that ran in Connecticut papers between 1791 and 1794. Brewster charged that the state's gentleman's club of public discourse and aristocratic politics remained locked in place because of the numbing force of custom, the ingrained preju-

38. *Conn. Courant,* May 27, 1776, May 19, 27, 1777, Sept. 19, 1780; *Norwich Packet,* Oct. 10, 1797, May 4, 1779, Jan. 17, 1788, Apr. 2, 1790; *American Mercury,* Oct. 24, 1784, Sept. 8, 1794. Nancy Fraser examined the difference between the ideal of Jürgen Habermas's bourgeois public sphere and actual practice in "Rethinking the Public Sphere: A Contribution to the Critique of Actually Existing Democracy," in Bruce Robbins, ed., *The Phantom Public Sphere* (Minneapolis, Minn. 1993), 1–32. The central irony: "A discourse of publicity touting accessibility, rationality, and the suspension of status hierarchies is itself deployed as a strategy of distinction" for a reformulated elite of white males (6). See also Anthony J. La Vopa, "Conceiving a Public: Ideas and Society in Eighteenth-Century Europe," *Journal of Modern History,* LXIV (1992), 79–116; Kathleen Wilson, "Citizenship, Empire, and Modernity in the English Provinces, c. 1720–1790," *Eighteenth-Century Studies,* XXIX (1995), 69–96.

39. *Norwich Packet,* May 26, 1777, "Vox Populi, Vox Dei," by "A Traveller," May 10, 1792 (Supplement).

dices of the many, and the schemes of the elite few. Learned men who monopolized political discussion and power had passed laws to keep mechanics poor; men who worked with their hands therefore lacked the suffrages to send representatives who could speak for their interests in the legislature. Even if a mechanic did gain a seat in the Assembly, "it is ten to one if he dare speak, for he is illiterate." Brewster attacked the popular prejudices that automatically associated mechanics with "the ignorant, vulgar and partial," prejudices that dissuaded men of his class from writing and speaking about politics. Even old women, he despaired, who had not seen any of his essays thought it was ridiculous for a mechanic to try to "write on the great and mysterious subjects of taxation and government." He challenged the craftsman and laborer to think and reason for himself rather than look to "an EARL DUKE OR ESQUIRE" to tell him that two and two make four; he challenged the mechanic to speak out for his rights and not to be frightened "by the pert sneer of the vain coxcomb, or by any person of a more grave deportment, who with a magisterial shrug and sententious puff, will tell him he can do nothing, and make him believe it." [40]

By the mid-1790s, Brewster was discouraged because artisans and other laboring men did not rally around his calls for economic and political justice and because other essayists refused to engage him in serious intellectual debate. His fellow mechanics, Brewster concluded, were still too inhibited by *the fear of man.* The patrician's response to Brewster's well-wrought arguments about

40. [Walter Brewster], "A Mechanic, Not Yet a Free-Man," *Norwich Packet,* Sept. 8, 1791 ("Illiterate" here probably means "not being a man of letters" rather than "unable to read"), [Brewster], "The Mechanick on Taxation, No. I," Apr. 4, 1792, [Brewster], Apr. 16, 1792 (call for a mechanics meeting), "The Mechanick on Taxation, No. VI," Sept. 13, 1792, [Brewster], "The Mechanick on Taxation, No. VIII," Apr. 4, 1793.

Walter Brewster wrote sixteen essays published in the *Norwich Packet* between Sept. 8, 1791, and May 15, 1794 (he signed his name to "The Mechanick on Taxation, No. V"). "The Mechanick on Taxation" Nos. I through [IV] ran in the *Conn. Courant,* Apr. 23–May 14, 1792; a slightly altered series of three essays by Brewster also ran in the *American Mercury,* Apr. 9–23, 1792. James P. Walsh, in "'Mechanics and Citizens': The Connecticut Artisan Protest of 1792," *William and Mary Quarterly,* 3d Ser., XLII (1985), 68, prints a list of Brewster's publications in the *Norwich Packet* but leaves out the final essay, "The——on Taxation, No. XII and Last" (pts. 1, 2), May 1, 15, 1794, so titled because Brewster had, by this time, he claimed, given up being a mechanic because it was so unprofitable. Walsh reports that the Danbury *Farmer's Journal* and the *Phenix; or, Windham Herald* also printed some of Brewster's essays. Stephen Reed Grossbart, in "The Revolutionary Transition: Politics, Religion, and Economy in Eastern Connecticut, 1765–1800" (Ph.D. diss., University of Michigan, 1989), 283–285, argued that the complaints Brewster raised had been discussed since the late 1770s. Nevertheless, the length of the series, its publication throughout the state, and its powerful Paineite critique of aristocratic domination were unprecedented.

the poll tax, the assessment on craftsmen, and new tax breaks for large manufacturers was expressed in a letter to the *Courant,* which dismissed "The Mechanick" as "absolutely *insane*" and suggested that he be confined to his workshop for a year and kept away from pen, paper, and political conversations. Once again, political discourse from voices and pens outside the elite was dismissed as a kind of madness.[41]

By the century's end, however, other common men were beginning to speak out and answer for themselves in print. When a newsprint moralist huffed that door-to-door salesmen were money-grubbing reprobates and a threat to the community, a traveling tin peddler wrote back to the newspaper, arguing that tin peddling was certainly as respectable as land speculation and *"the pedling of sermons."* Other writers began proclaiming the rights of craftsmen and laborers and harshly denouncing the oppressive learned elite in the public prints. Whereas Brewster had appealed to common reason and an inclusive notion of the public good, a later address to farmers and mechanics described society as permanently divided into two warring classes: those who labored and the "artful class of citizens"—merchants, speculators, lawyers, clergymen—who lived like parasites off the fruits of everyone else's labor. By 1802, letters in the New London *Bee* were describing society as a mortal contest between rich and poor and asking the poor and disenfranchised to look around to see how the elite avoided public service and manipulated political power:

> Militiamen of Connecticut! look through the ranks of your companies. How many freemen are there? How many of the well-born? Where are the ministers? A dining with the officers. Where are the members of the council and assembly? They made the law and prudently excused themselves. . . . Where are the justices of peace? Lolling with laziness on the step-stones of the sanctuary. Where are the lawyers? Looking contemptuously at you from the windows of their offices. . . . Where is the child of fortune, the member of college? Walking in his gown on the smooth shaven green with some soft nymph; early excused from all public burdens, he never feels their weight, and is one day destined to be a legislator . . . without any sympathy for the poor.

On election day, the scene was quite different, as the speaking aristocracy of clergymen, politicians, and college literati closed ranks:

41. [Brewster], "The——on Taxation, No. XII and Last (cont.)," *Norwich Packet,* May 15, 1794; *Conn. Courant,* May 14, 1792. A letter signed "A Shoemaker" in the *American Mercury,* Apr. 23, 1792, also encouraged Brewster to quit wasting his time trying to write about politics and return to his trade.

Where are your ministers now? Writing votes. . . . Where is the young man of fortune, the member of college? With powdered head, out-turned toes and self-sufficient strut, he goes from rank to rank with packages of votes, nicely copied from the Pope's [Yale President Timothy Dwight's] last bulls.

Although elite men were fractious, divided, and continually arguing among themselves, this writer indicates that, to the men who worked with their hands, professional men ought to be perceived as a united order continually working to secure their own power and prestige.[42]

Like the role of the common working man, the place of women in public discourse and political life became a topic of discussion after the Revolution as women themselves helped transform the content and form of the public sphere. Male educators, writers, and printers began to reevaluate women as thinkers and readers. Yale College students under President Dwight pondered the intellectual capacity of women. Benjamin Silliman described himself in his 1795 college diary as a "strenuous advocate" for the idea that women were not intellectually inferior to men; he, like John Trumbull nearly a quarter-century earlier, attributed the vacuous conversation that he heard from New Haven girls as the fault of inadequate education. Ten days after Silliman penned his diary entry, a fraternal society debated the question, and twenty-four of thirty-seven members came to Silliman's conclusion. John Hooker reported a class discussion on the same topic in his diary a year later and attributed a similar opinion to President Dwight. Newspaper writers also discussed the education of women. A 1787 article in the *Norwich Packet* complained that female education was "limited to trivial, unworthy objects," reinforced "an unparalleled degree of stupidity," and made women "a blank in useful conversation, and in society [they] are little better than parrots." A "young Lady" writing in the *Courant* as "G. V." argued in 1795 that, in this new age of liberty and learning, women should be freed from the despotism of ignorance.[43]

42. "A Real Patriot" complained about peddling in the *Conn. Courant*, Sept. 23, 1799 ("A Tin-Pedlar" responded Oct. 7, 1799, and see also the response by "Berlin," Sept. 30, 1799); "To the Farmers and Other Industrious Citizens of America, Particularly Those of Connecticut," *Bee*, Apr. 4, 1798 (reprinted from *Middlesex Gazette* [Middletown, Conn.]), with the following heading: "Farmers! Mechanics! attend! Read the following piece with deliberation, and let its contents sink deep into your minds"; *Bee*, Mar. 31, 1802.

43. Benjamin Silliman, Diary, 1795–1796, Silliman Family Papers, Manuscripts and Archives, Yale University Library: on female intellectual equality, see Nov. 9, 1795; on young women and frivolous conversation, see Jan. 7, Apr. 8, 1796. See also Brothers in Unity Records, YRG 40-A-5, Secretary's Records, Book II, Minutes of Meetings, 1783–1803, Nov. 19, 1795 (but, on June 24, 1790, the Brothers had affirmed, after debate, that "females ought to be excluded from a share in the Civil Government"); John Hooker, Diary of Senior Year at

As readers, women were increasingly being courted by writers and printers. Literary historians have described the rising cultural importance of sentimental fiction and the growing popularity of novels for and about women in the new nation. The weekly newspapers, too, acknowledged and tried to cultivate a female readership as the war's end reduced the amount of military and political news. Writers in the press acknowledged the key role women played in civilizing behavior and polishing manners. Both Hartford papers banned advertisements and discussions deemed improper for the mixed company that the editors wanted to serve. The author of the *Courant*'s "Companion" column imagined that his moral fables and general advice would be read and discussed at the tea table and in the parlor by groups of men and women together. Sentimental tales about women enduring the trials of courtship and marriage or suffering the evils of seduction or even prostitution appeared in the papers whenever there was a lull in political news. In 1798, Lazarus Beach of Newfield advertised a fortnightly journal "calculated entirely for the Ladies" called the *Humming Bird; or, Herald of Taste*. In the same year, Charles Holt, editor of the New London *Bee*, tried to launch a similar literary magazine "particularly recommended as a COMPANION FOR THE LADIES," promising that it would avoid all the political discussion and controversy that was again filling the regular newspapers in the late 1790s. Women, who dominated the world of polite conversation, were reshaping the world of print.[44]

Yale, 1796–1797, June 25, 1796, Hooker Family Papers; "Of Female Education," *Norwich Packet,* Oct. 18, 1787; "On Female Education," *Conn. Courant,* Nov. 23, 1795. Compare these to a series of essays before the Revolution advising that girls needed to learn household economy from their mothers, delicate taste and correct speech from polite literature, and arithmetic no further than fractions because "deeply to study the mathematics is unsuitable for ladies" ("On Female Education," Letter IV, Letter V, *Conn. Courant,* Jan. 5–12, Jan. 19–26, 1773). In 1782, Massachusetts essayist Judith Sargent Stevens (later Murray) anonymously published *Some Deductions from the System Promulgated in the Page of Divine Revelation* in Norwich. In 1790, thirty-nine members of the Chelsea Congregational Church in Norwich formed a "sisterly" society to read, pray, and sing hymns together. This group was reformulated in 1800 as the Ladies Literary Society. See Barbara E. Lacey, "Women in the Era of the American Revolution: The Case of Norwich, Connecticut," *New England Quarterly,* LIII (1980), 527–543.

44. On female readers, see, especially, Cathy N. Davidson, *Revolution and the Word: The Rise of the Novel in America* (New York, 1986). See "The Companion," no. 1, *Conn. Courant,* Nov. 3, 1794, no. 4, Nov. 24, 1794, no. 18, Mar. 2, 1795, no. 25, Jan. 1, 1798 (after an eighteen-month hiatus): "The fair sex will claim a large share of my attention." Beach ran his advertisement in the *Bee,* Mar. 28, 1798. The first issue of *Humming Bird; or, Herald of Taste* (Newfield, Conn.), Apr. 14, 1798, carried an address "To the Patrons of the Humming Bird," apparently written by a female editor (Mrs. Beach?): "I know it will be argued that it is a woman's business to attend to her family concerns, and that she has no business to be in-

Women were welcomed as readers and began to appear more frequently as writers, but the question of their political participation was another matter. In the 1780s, as in the Revolution, women's political power as *consumers* was acknowledged. But even those writers who challenged the idea that "the Fair Sex ought not to take any part or concern in public affairs" spoke of women's *indirect* influence upon men and manners rather than their direct participation in public discourse and political decision making: "As to party and faction, those minds which ought ever to diffuse gentleness and cheerfulness around them, and those voices which ought ever to be tuned with the accents of mildness and sweetness, have no part in such a troubled and intemperate region." The editors of the *New-Haven Gazette* went out of their way to welcome the prose and poetry submitted by a female correspondent in February 1786. But, three weeks later, they published a scathing satire of women in politics. The essay began by arguing that the Republic was a male aristocracy that needed to open the doors of political power to women if society was ever to be truly democratic. Voting rights for women in the proposed new order would be based, not on property requirements, but upon childbearing (three illegitimate children counting as one legitimate birth); a new, separate statehouse would need to be built for a female legislature and staffed with a sheriff who could administer pills for hysteria and padlocks for mouths that talked too much. More than misogynist ridicule, this essay was trying to stem the tide of post-Revolutionary democracy by showing the idea taken to an absurd extreme. It also demonstrated the different (though overlapping) composition of the literary and political publics and the awkward position of publications that tried to address both.[45]

---

quisitive about what is going forward in the world. I acknowledge that domestic affairs is her business; and this business, with industry she may conduct properly, and have much time to read." The editor promised that she herself would "not neglect my spinning wheel, even to compile the Humming Bird, for I think you had better be without entertainment, than my children without clothes." She promised that "the news which will be published in this paper will only be of a Domestic kind, and such as concerns ladies only. Political and commercial details will be excluded." She wanted to solicit articles from ladies but hoped that literary gentlemen would contribute too. The *Humming Bird* seems to have survived for only a few issues. Holt first advertised and described "The Honeycomb" in the *Bee*, Nov. 14, 1798, and issued a "last chance" for subscriptions on June 19, 1799; he announced the first issue on Sept. 11, 1799, and explained that the second would be delayed because of his sedition trial (Dec. 4, 1799).

45. "An Observer," *Conn. Courant*, Nov. 20, 27, 1786; *New-Haven Gazette*, Feb. 15, 1786, "Lycurgus," Apr. 6, 1786. An unnamed Norwich woman even delivered a July Fourth address to a female audience, which was printed in the Norwich, Conn., *Courier*, July 10, 1799. She described the social benefits of elevating women to be the "intellectual companions" of

Denigrating comments about women did not always go unanswered. A few sarcastic insinuations about female inferiority in the New London *Bee* in 1797 were quickly countered by a writer under the name "Maria." Maria's opponent, "Juvenis," had told a parable in the form of a dream about a town under siege where the women, allowed by the enemy to leave town with only the possessions they could carry on their backs, carried their husbands out the front gate. "I have been determined, ever since I saw the vision of Juvenis," Maria wrote, "to convince the public that women, if they can't speak and write, can at least *dream* as well as any man." In Maria's vision, men are allowed to leave a town under siege carrying their dearest possessions, and many walk out carrying prostitutes, bottles of grog, maps and charts, sacks of speeches and essays, tailors, barbers, and horses. Besides answering a young male "witling" with a bit of his own medicine, Maria had a serious argument to set before her male readers: "You are hereditary masters, not by virtue of sexual excellence, but in consequence of an ancient established system of tyranny and usurpation," she wrote. Men's advantages arose, not from natural superiority, but from an education and broader experience that women were denied—women who, according to God and nature, were entitled to equality. A writer signing herself "Maria" next appeared, however, not in Charles Holt's *Bee,* but in Samuel Trumbull's Stonington *Journal of the Times.* The Stonington Maria began a series of "Lectures" directed principally to young ladies (because, she wrote, addressing her own sex would be "more proper") but withdrew after being

men but was careful to define the woman's sphere: "Let us appreciate justly the rank of our sex, not indeed by an affectation of political science. . . . In the narrow but liberal walks of domestic life our sphere lies . . . as mothers, wives, sisters, and daughters." The theme of intellectual companionship was seconded by a *Conn. Courier* letter of Apr. 9, 1800. In the United States, the writer argued, "Science lies open to all; and 'tis *there* that Woman is found as in her original formation, a meet help to her husband." On Mar. 13, 1775, "Philanthropist" in the *Conn. Courant* emphasized female industry, frugality, and economy in running the household. An "Oeconomical Association" formed by more than one hundred Hartford women declared in 1786 that "while the Gentlemen are anxiously devising other and more extensive plans of policy for the salvation of this and the United States, the Ladies may unite their influence in effecting the same desirable purposes by a strict attention to domestic oeconomy and frugality" (*Conn. Courant,* Nov. 6, 1786). A letter to the *New-Haven Gazette* in 1785 cut through the gendered language of economic virtue that hailed the manly exertions for liberty and independence in the 1770s but blamed the problems of the mid-1780s on the "idleness and extravagance" of women who had an unquenchable appetite for frivolous imported luxuries. Women made the tea boycott work, the writer argued, showing "what the women will do when they know the true interest of their country," and men with their expensive habits were just as much to blame for current problems (reprinted in *American Mercury,* Sept. 19, 1785).

"critically examined and severely censured." Not until the publication of the *Connecticut Evangelical Magazine* in July 1800 did local women become regular contributors to, and primary subjects of attention within, the Connecticut periodical press—and here, of course, the focus was upon piety, not upon explicitly political questions.[46]

Irvin and McPherson, like most of the speakers and writers who dominated public discourse in late-eighteenth-century Connecticut, had a conception of the person who speaks his mind in a free society that was heavily marked by class and gender. In some ways, the play's notion of the gentleman citizen was also quite individualistic: though conforming to polite standards of behavior, the gentleman must act upon his own conscience, reason, common sense, and personal experience. The gentleman determined how he should act for the public good; he was not swayed by the shifting winds of public opinion or bullied by groups who claimed to speak the voice of the people. Like the assumptions about class and gender, this gentlemanly vision of magisterial political leadership would collide with the popular politics of the Revolutionary era.

THE VOICE OF THE PEOPLE

Thus, *what* speech and writing were considered public varied with context and political climate, and the customary constraints upon *who* spoke or wrote publicly were weakening by the century's end. The question of who could speak *for* the public was answered in different ways as Connecticut citizens emerged from the Revolution. Preserving the institutions established by their colonial charter and the traditions of the New England town meeting, citizens nevertheless had to try to work out the meaning of, and the political practices entailed by, popular sovereignty. In the struggle for Independence, town meetings often claimed to express the local voice of the people. When the towns began passing resolves upon controversial postwar issues, however, critics in the press

---

46. "Maria," *Bee*, July 6, Aug. 23, 1797, responding to "Juvenis," *Bee*, June 21, 1797; "Maria's Lectures," nos. 1, 2, 3, *Journal of the Times*, Jan. 16, 23, 30, 1799. Charles Holt, the *Bee*'s Jeffersonian editor, might have been sympathetic to Maria's point of view. Some of the toasts Holt's fellow Democratic-Republicans made at political celebrations called for equal rights for women; see the toasts given at Berlin, Connecticut's July Fourth dinner in 1800, reported in the *American Mercury*, July 10, 1800, and at a Mar. 4, 1801, celebration in Tolland, in *American Mercury*, Mar. 12, 1801. In one issue, Holt himself asked that his office copy of Mary Wollstonecraft's *A Vindication of the Rights of Woman: With Strictures on Political and Moral Subjects* (Boston, 1792), be returned (*Bee*, Sept. 13, 1797).

challenged their legitimacy. The Middletown Conventions in 1783 and 1784, which struggled to be recognized as expressing the voice of the people to the government, were condemned by many not just as an attempt to organize an oppositional political party but as an effort to create a competing legislature.

In the early years of resistance and Revolution, the proceedings of town meetings, which for the most part had previously been confined to local affairs, began to contain resolves about the imperial crisis that were published in the newspapers to signify each locality's formal assent to the patriot cause. Usually the work of local elites—the patriot counterparts to the fictional town-meeting orator M'Fingal—the resolves were publicized as expressions of the entire community. Even Connecticut's western colony along the Susquehanna proclaimed its solidarity with the mother state by mailing a declaration of principles to the *Courant,* summed up on an eight-foot banner that flew from a ninety-foot liberty pole: "UNITY AND INDUSTRY BRINGS, PEACE AND PLENTY. LIBERTY AND CONNECTICUT LAWS! NO TAXATION!" Some town resolutions, like one from Windham, read more like long persuasive essays written by a single hand and approved in assembly rather than a list of decisions that were discussed and voted upon individually. Other towns found persuasive language elsewhere and made it their own: on May 27, 1776, the town of Canterbury declared its independence five weeks before the Continental Congress did by unanimously adopting the principles contained in Thomas Paine's *Common Sense.* Loyalists recognized the rhetorical power these resolves had. The Reverend Samuel Peters of Hebron wrote a loyalist list of resolves, but the town spurned them. In Stratford, the local printer refused to print Isaac Foster's approved draft of patriot resolves, calling them treasonous and heretical, which gave the town's loyalist faction time to organize and get the resolves tabled.[47]

When the war drew to a close, the published resolves of Connecticut town meetings again expressed popular resentment of policies that seemed to exalt the few by oppressing the many. A debt-ridden Congress facing a crippled economy promised five years of bonus half-pay to military officers, including Connecticut officers who had, it was argued, already accepted a generous settlement with the state. Many ordinary citizens who had suffered and sacrificed through the war and now felt as though they were drowning in public and pri-

47. On Peters's loyalist town resolves, see *Conn. Courant,* Sept. 12, 1774, Isaac Foster letter, Oct. 31, 1774, Susquehannah letter, Jan. 30, 1775, Canterbury resolution, May 27, 1776; Windham resolution, *Norwich Packet; and the Connecticut, Massacusetts, New-Hampshire, and Rhode-Island Weekly Advertiser,* June 30, 1774. Towns also sent delegates to special multicounty meetings, like the nonconsumption meeting in Hartford on Sept. 15, 1774, where towns in Hartford, New London, Windham, and part of Litchfield Counties were represented (*Conn. Courant,* Sept. 19, 1774).

vate debt considered the seven-million-dollar giveaway to the military elite outrageous. The specter of a government that taxed the people into poverty and opened the public coffers to a privileged class was all too familiar. When Connecticut's General Assembly was officially silent on the matter, townsmen returned to the language and the practices of Revolutionary politics. A long address from the town of Torrington, published on July 29, 1783, asked, "Is it not high time, for that patriotic fire, which has so often blazed forth, to the confusion of our adversaries, now to flash with redoubled violence?" It was time, according to Torrington, for the people to act again against tyrannical rule, just as they had done in the 1770s; it was time to remind legislators that "in a popular government, all power is delegated by the people; so that unanimity among the people, is all that is necessary to make any alteration, by them judged necessary, for the common good." Two weeks later, the town of Farmington also condemned this latest threat to American liberty, and the principles of popular sovereignty the town's address cited justified the town resolutions as the voice of the people: "There is an original, underived and incommunicable authority and supremacy, in the collective body of the people, to whom all delegated power must submit, and from whom there is no appeal." These protests against government actions could not be condemned or ignored as merely the complaints of a disgruntled minority, Farmington declared: "When the sense of the people collectively is opposed to measures adopted by the ruling power, it cannot be denominated faction, but the judgment of the community, by which, that power ought to be controlled." Addresses from Killingworth, Southington, and Simsbury soon followed. Through the publication of these resolutions, townsmen claimed that they were expressing the "sense of the people collectively" and "the judgment of the community."[48]

If town resolves were ignored, then the disgruntled townsmen would form committees of correspondence and assemble in a special convention, just as they had done during the struggle for Independence. The call for a general convention went out in late August, and, on September 3, 1783, less than two weeks before the fall election, representatives from twenty-eight of Connecticut's seventy-four towns met in Middletown. Because the delegates determined that, without more complete representation, "the full sense of the state cannot, at this time, be collected," they adjourned until the end of the month and encouraged all towns to meet and instruct their state representatives on the matter. Reconvened on September 30, the Middletown Convention, now with delegates from a majority of the towns, reasserted the right of a free people

48. Torrington resolution, *Conn. Courant*, July 29, 1783, Farmington resolution, Aug. 12, 1783, Sept. 2, 9, 30, Oct. 14, 1783.

to confer together in this manner "in times of general complaint against public measures" and felt able to call themselves the representatives of "the People at Large." [49]

With the war over, the economy nearly at a standstill, and the state bankrupt, this perpetuation of Revolutionary popular politics—the town resolutions, special conventions, and committees of correspondence—came to be seen by men in power as a prescription for anarchy. Already glimpsing the implications of popular political conventions a year earlier, Governor Trumbull warned in 1782 of the "danger of running into extream equality—when each citizen would fain be upon a level with those he has chosen to govern him— then the people, incapable of bearing the very power they have delegated, want to manage every thing for themselves—to debate for the senate—to execute for the magistrates—and to decide for the judges." The governor's published speech to the General Assembly in November 1783 complained about the excessive jealousy people were showing toward their elected officials. The British had been beaten, but "in our present temper of mind, are we not rather to fear ourselves?" The best guide to public happiness, Trumbull argued, was in "the steady good sense of the virtuous public, wisely exercised in a judicious choice of their representatives, and a punctual observance of their collected counsels." In other words, the people should vote, and then keep quiet and do as they are told. According to Noah Webster, writing as "Honorius" in the state papers, Connecticut's citizens needed to relearn "that a few wise men may direct public measures for the good of the State—that people in general are not *historians, politicians* or *legislators*." Sounding like an old election sermon, Honorius's essays reminded readers that the citizen's sacred obligation was to obey rulers as long as they were acting within the bounds of the constitution. Other writers mocked the convention's claim to represent and speak for the people. One published letter sarcastically proposed still another convention, which would petition the Middletown Convention to petition the Assembly to petition Congress: "The *voice* of the people will be fully known; for three distinct setts of representatives, *fully instructed,* will surely be able to eccho forth the sentiments of their constituents." [50]

---

49. *Conn. Courant,* Sept. 16, Nov. 4, 1783.

50. Jonathan Trumbull, Speech to the General Assembly, October 1782, Jonathan Trumbull Papers, Connecticut State Archives, Hartford, 20:336a–c, quoted in Richard Buel, Jr., *Dear Liberty: Connecticut's Mobilization for the Revolutionary War* (Middletown, Conn., 1980), 288 (Trumbull's concern in 1782 was the town associations and convention formed to prevent illegal trade with the enemy); *Conn. Courant,* Sept. 30, Oct. 21, 28, Trumbull, "An Address," Nov. 25, 1783.

REVOLUTION AND STEADY HABITS

By the spring of 1784, the Middletown Convention was being ridiculed as populist demagoguery, as it was in the Yale students' play of that year. Although the convention's messages made an impact upon the previous fall's elections, prevented the state from supporting officers' pay, and probably encouraged Governor Trumbull to retire, anticonvention rhetoric effectively undermined the body's legitimacy. By the December meeting, the convention's delegation had shrunk to ten towns, and its resolves had turned to attacking the increasingly popular federal impost as further congressional tyranny and the increasingly irrelevant Society of the Cincinnati as an engine of aristocracy. Writers in the press noted that the convention no longer presumed to speak *for* the people; it even stopped addressing its resolves *to* "the People at Large" and wrote only for the attention of "the good people of Connecticut." One writer responded that "as the *good people* of Connecticut never meet in *Conventions,* you cannot expect an answer"; another wag wrote a satire of the convention's resolves, addressed: "To the bad People of the State of Connecticut." The town meetings and committees of correspondence of 1783 and 1784 were also denounced. "Town meeting resolves have no more effect in removing the evil, than puffs of wind," one published letter declared. The model town meeting had been held in Coventry, opponents said, where citizens quickly decided that Congress's commutation pay was none of their business, adjourned the meeting, "and went home like men of sense." Another writer charged that the Farmington town resolution, which had served as something of a conventioneer's manifesto, had come, not from the sober citizens of Farmington speaking in a duly appointed town forum, but from a frenzied mob that had been pulled indoors and temporarily leashed by smooth-sounding words. A writer signing himself "Brother and Friend" taunted the corresponding committee of Killingworth and charged that what was trumpeted as the people's voice—God's voice—in that town was actually more cantankerous squawking from a single old man, Dr. Benjamin Gale, who read papers aloud to his presumably illiterate neighbors and then penned addresses in their name: "You remember he has often told you, that the voice of the people is the voice of God. This is what we call a sublime moral precept, and should always be uttered with rolling up the eyes and laying the hand on the breast." Behind the discourse of committees, meetings, and conventions, opponents saw only designing men and demagogues, mobs and conspiring factions.[51]

51. *Conn. Courant,* Aug. 19, 26, Sept. 2, Oct. 14, 1783. A writer also mocked those who claimed to speak for the people: "As I am an advocate for the People, I am the Voice of God" (Sept. 30, 1783). On the Middletown Convention, see Grossbart, "The Revolutionary Transition," 197–240.

Supporters of the convention movement and the popular politics of 1783–1784 stood by their "Revolution principles." Some felt the very idea of popular sovereignty was being threatened. "But a few years past *the voice of the people was the voice of God,*" the "Respondent" remarked in the pages of the *Courant,* "but now Sir, a town-meeting regularly convened" expresses opinions that are immediately derided as falsehoods, and a convention of concerned citizens is abused as a junto. A writer to the *American Mercury* in 1784 wondered why those who had so recently proclaimed that the voice of the people was everything were now so worried that government might be changed by "the POPULAR BREATH" and were clamoring for a more powerful government. Critics, however, decried this "new era in politics" and warned that, by presuming to instruct representatives to the General Assembly, town meetings, committees, and conventions were trampling on the rights of freemen and dabbling in irregular political practices that could only lead to chaos and confusion.[52]

The convention movement was more than the result of unprincipled politicians' seeking a popular hobbyhorse to ride to power in a time of social and economic instability, as opponents charged; it was Connecticut's struggle with the contradictions embedded in the notion of popular sovereignty, its struggle to write the rules for the normal science of politics in post-Revolutionary America. Men in power and those who supported them wanted to make it clear that the sovereign people ruled itself through its elected representatives; the voice of Connecticut's people could legitimately be spoken and heard only in the General Assembly. Now that Britain's external threat to Connecticut's rights and liberties had been removed, the state could return to popular elections by deferential freemen and rule by a benign magistracy. The conventioneers agreed that ideally, as John Treadwell of Farmington wrote, "the body of the rulers are a perfect mirrour, in which the features and lineaments of the people are most accurately discovered." When government turns to pursue other motives, however, the people need to act. As the resolves of Torrington and Farmington made clear, nothing but a direct attack by the government upon the vital principles of the constitution could justify open and violent opposition. Between silence and violence, though, there was the option of public discourse—the discourse of the public *to* the government, the voice of the people expressed in extralegislative assemblies.[53]

52. *Conn. Courant,* Sept. 30, Oct. 7, 1783; *American Mercury,* Nov. 22, 1784.

53. *Conn. Courant,* Sept. 23, 1783. As historian Richard Buel in *Dear Liberty* has concluded, "A certain mystery shrouds the question of exactly who did promote the convention movement." From the fifteen names appearing in public documents, Buel points to men who had been radicals during the Stamp Act crisis but had faded from view during the Revolution

REVOLUTION AND STEADY HABITS

The collapse of the Middletown Convention had less to do with political principles than with the particular slate of issues being championed and the deepening economic crisis that consumed everyone's attention. The question about officers' pay was settled, and the attack on the Cincinnati lost some of its sting as people came to understand that the original provision making exclusive membership inheritable was dropped. The argument made by Noah Webster and others that a federal impost would end up lowering the overall tax burden upon Connecticut citizens became more persuasive. The demise of the convention movement did not, however, doom all citizen conventions or town meetings that addressed regional or national issues. The mechanics' meetings promoted in 1792 by Canterbury shoemaker Walter Brewster were not condemned out of hand as subversive organizations, because the mechanics, unlike the Middletown delegates, were recognized as a particular order of society associating to petition the legislature; they were not an ad hoc collection of the disgruntled challenging the government's legitimacy by claiming to represent the sovereign people or usurping the government's authority by threatening to veto its legislation. The town meetings that passed resolves about Connecticut's western lands in 1795 were not criticized for overstepping their jurisdiction, because the appropriation of money derived from the sale of those lands would be administered by the towns themselves. The uproar over the Middletown Convention, therefore, did not eliminate special meetings and conventions, but it did inspire a more cautious self-regulation of the political functions of those associations. Debate and confusion about the place of extralegislative assemblies and the legitimate expression of the voice of the people would continue nationally through the 1790s. In Connecticut after the Middletown Convention, and especially after Shays's Rebellion in western Massachusetts, citizens seemed far more wary about claiming to speak or act for "the people."[54]

---

and others who had been tainted by toryism or emerged from the war with less than sterling reputations. Buel ends up calling them "men in ruthless pursuit of political rehabilitation," echoing the anticonvention rhetoric (311–312). Yet, clearly that alone does not explain why passions were so roused in towns across the state on both sides of the question. On the contradictions entailed by the idea of popular sovereignty, see Gordon S. Wood, *The Creation of the American Republic, 1776–1787* (Chapel Hill, N.C., 1969), chap. 9; and Edmund S. Morgan, *Inventing the People: The Rise of Popular Sovereignty in England and America* (New York, 1988).

54. On Webster's argument, see Buel, *Dear Liberty*, 317. Buel attributed the settlement of the commutation issue to the persuasive powers of Congress. But a writer in the *Conn. Courant* on Nov. 20, 1786, suggested that people began to realize that, with depreciation, Congressional commutation would turn out cheaper than the original deal the state had

The most important issue submitted to "the people" in Connecticut in the last dozen years of the century was the new federal Constitution. The state ratified easily and with comparatively little rancor. Federalists engaged mostly out-of-state Antifederalists in the press. Dr. Benjamin Gale spoke against the Constitution at a town meeting but did not publish his remarks. James Wadsworth whipped up some Antifederalist sentiment in New Haven County but was the only leading speaker against ratification at the state convention. Men like Oliver Ellsworth, William Samuel Johnson, and Roger Sherman, Connecticut's delegates to Philadelphia, along with a host of the state's leading characters, easily carried the six-day debate toward a lopsided vote for ratification, 128 to 40. Even men with antifederal sentiments like William Williams, a signer of the Declaration of Independence who was jeered as "William Wimble" in Federalist satirical verse, voted for the Constitution against the wishes of his townsmen. For a state still in deep financial trouble, the promised economic benefits of the new Constitution were too much to resist.[55]

As political minds wondered about who would speak for the people of Connecticut in the new national politics of the 1790s, "The Apologizer" in the *American Mercury* suggested that the old political nomenclature would no longer serve. The binary oppositions of whig and tory in the 1770s and Federalist and Antifederalist in the 1780s needed to be replaced in the 1790s by a "scale of minds," rising from parish and county intellects to state and, finally, "Federal intellects." The new political era placed a premium upon federal in-

---

worked out with the soldiers of the Connecticut Line. On the national debate about extralegislative assemblies, see James Roger Sharp, *American Politics in the Early Republic: The New Nation in Crisis* (New Haven, Conn., 1993), 124–125.

55. On the argument in the press, for example, Connecticut supporters of ratification argued against the objections of Elbridge Gerry of Massachusetts and George Mason of Virginia and against the "Centinel" pamphlet by George Bryan of Pennsylvania, which was being circulated from New York "in the same covered, secret, and insidious manner as British proclamations, pardons, and manifestos were in the days of yore," a Federalist complained, painting antifederalism with the brush of toryism (*American Mercury*, Nov. 26, 1787; *Norwich Packet; or, The Country Journal*, Dec. 6, 1787). On Benjamin Gale, see "Dr. Gale's Objections to the New Plan of Government Proposed by the Convention Holden at Philadelphia, at a Town Meeting Holden at Killingworth the 12 Day of Nov. for the Choice of Delegates," Beinecke Rare Book and Manuscript Library, Yale University, New Haven, Conn.; Christopher Collier, "Connecticut and the Constitution, 1787–1788," *Connecticut Bar Journal*, LXI (1987), 206. On Connecticut ratification more generally, see ibid., 182–209; Collier, *Roger Sherman's Connecticut: Yankee Politics and the American Revolution* (Middletown, Conn., 1971), 131; and Buel, *Dear Liberty*, 331–332. For a detailed analysis of the "extremely fluid" political factions in Connecticut in the 1780s, see Grossbart, "The Revolutionary Transition," chaps. 6, 7.

tellects. Members of the state's upper house could not be men "who would scarce distinguish a College from one of our distilleries," wrote an "Apologist" in 1792, and a "Freeman" added that congressmen, even more than members of the state Council, "should be possessed of a more enlarged *acquaintance with books*, with *men*, and with the *general policy of the United States*." Writers also stressed that a political leader needed to be a good speaker, or he would "not have half the influence his other qualifications may deserve." It is not surprising, then, that young, ambitious men would spend so much energy polishing their public address and that Yale College, once a school of the prophets and recently a school of poets, became a school of orators and politicians.[56]

CHARACTER AND THE MANIPULATION OF LANGUAGE

Character—especially the character of society's leaders—was an important theme for orators and writers in the early Republic. Character referred in part to an individual's moral traits and distinguishing intellectual features and also to the public presentation of those traits and features. Although in the eighteenth century character might have been more closely allied to reputation than to personality, the possible disjunction between a man's public character and his real character disturbed those who yearned for virtuous leadership and feared conspiracy and corruption. Personal integrity and public persona could be identical as, apparently, they were in George Washington, America's living Cincinnatus, the Roman patriot who left his farm to serve his country. Connecticut's Benedict Arnold, who played the role of the courageous hero before revealing himself as Washington's Judas, demonstrated the opposite extreme. Some said that the techniques for constructing a false public character—the appearance only of virtue and honor—were to be found in the order of eloquent men who had quickly risen to dominate post-Revolutionary politics: the lawyers. Without having a mind reader on hand, as the Yale students imagined in their 1784 play, people feared the potentially wide gap between the artful projection of character and the truth.[57]

56. *American Mercury*, Feb. 22, 1790, "Apologist," Mar. 26, 1792; "A Freeman," *Conn. Courant*, Apr. 2, 1792. See also *American Mercury*, Sept. 6, 1790.

57. Exemplary character was often discussed as an abstracted cluster of desirable qualities that would-be leaders should approximate as closely as possible. Character types—the good ruler, the military hero, the republican leader—all defined models for the behavior and attitude of public men. The ideal character of the good Christian ruler had long been described in sermons on election days, at freemen's meetings, and at funerals for departed magistrates. On George Washington and Cincinnatus, see "A Short Account of Lucius

In the Yale play, self-interested men who disguised their true motives be-hind "benevolent signification" were even more dangerous than "mad enthu-siasts." Mr. Writer's description of the structure of the mind helped explain why. He makes the distinction between "aspects of mind," which change— sometimes rapidly—according to circumstances and the objects of attention, and the mind itself, which "never is changed." This explanation resembles the distinction made by clerical writers during the Awakening between the tran-sient state of awakened affections and the inclination or principle of the heart, which could be changed only by supernatural regeneration. Enthusiasm, either religious or political, is usually temporary. The enthusiast's objects of atten-tion are confused and misinterpreted; his overheated passions and imagina-tion prevent him from thinking rationally. Like Philanthropos at the end of the play, the enthusiast can cool down and be restored to reason. The self-interested "villain," however, is neither confused nor frenzied. He manipulates the passions of the impressionable in a single-minded pursuit of his selfish goals. Behind all of Benedict Arnold's different words, thoughts, and actions, Mr. Writer explains, his mind was the same: he was a villain—black as night— and his one object was money. Irvin and McPherson worry that the political unrest of the 1780s is being used by similar men as "a cloak under which . . . [they] may screen themselves while their ultimate aim is self-aggrandizement and popularity." Such "designing men" are always busy: "Self-interest often outweighs publick justice with private characters."[58]

Quintus Cincinnatus, with his Character—from the Beauties of History," *Norwich Packet; or, The Chronicle of Freedom*, Mar. 11, 1784; "An Essay towards the Character of the Presi-dent of the United States," *Conn. Courant*, June 20, 1791; "Character of Washington, Drawn by the Pen of a Master," *American Mercury*, Sept. 20, 1798. On character and reputation, see Stanley Elkins and Eric McKitrick, *The Age of Federalism* (New York, 1993), 37; Steven Watts, *The Republic Reborn: War and the Making of Liberal America, 1790–1820* (Baltimore, Md., 1987), 270. On Arnold, see *Conn. Courant*, Oct. 31, Dec. 12, 1780, Oct. 23, 1781, Dec. 2, 1783; *Norwich Packet; or, The Chronicle of Freedom*, Dec. 10, 1783. The preface to *The Fall of Lu-cifer: An Elegiac Poem on the Infamous Defection of the Late General Arnold* (Hartford, Conn., 1781), apologizes for perhaps inflating Arnold's heroic character before his fall but explains that the author did so to sharpen the contrast. The poet explains that he did not know Arnold personally and, at any rate, is more concerned with general character traits, particu-larly manifestations of *"public spirit* in *obscure life."* Chesterfield's *Letters Written . . . to His Son* was also characterized as a textbook for the construction of false character. See [Royall Tyler], *The Contrast* (Philadelphia, 1790). Timothy Dwight vigorously condemned Chester-field in *A Sermon Preached at Northampton . . .* (Hartford, Conn., [1781]). "Chesterfieldians" are criticized in passing in "Sobriety," *American Mercury*, May 12, 1794; and in "The Com-panion," no. 27, *Conn. Courant*, Jan. 15, 1798.

58. Yale Class Play, 5, 13, 19, 21.

In the 1780s and 1790s, Connecticut's political writers were concerned with the characters of the men who were seeking or holding political power. A writer signing himself "Algernoon Sidney" in the *American Mercury* argued in the spring of 1793 that Connecticut needed a "public discussion of the qualifications and merits of candidates for office" so that every voter could choose wisely and well. Sidney and writers who offered similar arguments were especially concerned about the governor's chair, the twelve seats in the upper house, and the state's Congressional delegation. Voters were personally acquainted with the town representatives that they sent to the lower house, but the men filling other offices, elected at large by the whole state, were often just names on a ballot. How could a freeman cast an intelligent and responsible vote without knowing more about these men and what they stood for? Yet, Connecticut's political tradition dictated that such a public discussion about the state's leading men was "political heresy." Men were expected to rise gradually from local prominence and through the seniority system in the lower house before they stepped into a higher office made vacant by death or retirement. Years of service—not speech making and public writing—had traditionally been considered the proof of character. How could a younger man with new ideas establish a public reputation and find a shortcut through this system? If men set their political ideas before the public in the newspapers, they were expected to do so under pseudonyms: signing one's real name while in office was said to be an insult to readers because it appeared as an attempt to persuade from the authority of office rather than the strength of argument. A correspondent to the *Courant* in 1787, for example, complained about state treasurer Erastus Wolcott's signed essays about revenue laws: "His setting his name to a piece of that kind is an insult upon the people.—The language is clearly this:—There—You Plebean Rascals—Contradict a Tribune, if you dare!" Signed essays produced while out of office were considered political self-promotion. It was a "POLITICAL MAXIM" that any man who showed himself eager for office was unworthy of it, because he probably had selfish views rather than the public good in mind. The office seeker and his "abetting orators" were "lost to all sense of *decency* and *honor*" and were to be held in contempt.[59]

59. *American Mercury,* Apr. 1, 1793 (this argument was extended the following year by "Cassius," Aug. 11, 18, Sept. 1, 8, 1794, and in "The Querist, No. 1," *Conn. Gazette,* May 9, 1798); "Cassius Unveiled," *American Mercury,* Apr. 6, 1795. Erastus Wolcott's critic appeared in the *Conn. Courant,* Oct. 8, 15, 1787; *American Mercury,* Apr. 8, 1793, Apr. 6, 1795; *Norwich Packet,* Apr. 6, 1786. A letter to the *Conn. Courant,* May 21, 1798, sneered at Republicans Abraham Baldwin and Gideon Granger for writing signed essays defending their political positions and principles: "The last Connecticut Courant exhibits a singular spectacle to the

Any attempt to organize political discussions about potential candidates, even by men who were not themselves interested in higher office, was branded as the intrigue of a faction improperly trying to influence the vote. A dialogue in the papers in 1786 tried—without much success—to distinguish between campaigning for candidates and enlightening the public about the characters of prominent men. But through the mid-1790s, there was no legitimate way for voters to learn and talk about public men without appearing to campaign for a candidate or manipulate the electorate. The relationship between personal character traits and public service could occasionally be scrutinized when something went wrong: when longtime Litchfield legislator Jedediah Strong was convicted of wife beating and endured an acrimonious—and much publicized—divorce trial, for example, questions were raised about character and the qualifications for public office. But political biographies would only begin to appear toward the end of the century, as the partisan newspapers struggled to puff politicians who lacked Washington's national reputation and acclaim.[60]

Connecticut's political discussion was not organized around the banners of dominant political figures until national politics mobilized support for Thomas Jefferson and John Adams late in the century. Certainly, power brokers worked behind the scenes in state politics, but in print the clash of inter-

world—two persons of *great political significance* in the United States, pleading their own causes before the public bar, upon a voluntary arraignment, with as much engagedness, as if they stood charged with crimes of the deepest dye."

60. *Conn. Courant,* Apr. 6, 1786: "Particular and personal influence [upon voters] was unlawful and reprehensible," but "general characteristic influence was lawful and commendable." On Strong, see *American Mercury,* Aug. 30, Sept. 6, Oct. 11, Nov. 15, 1790. The case eventually made it to the General Assembly, taking up seven or eight days of the session, according to the Nov. 15 article. See also *Conn. Journal,* Sept. 8, 1790. The Republican press ran essays on Albert Gallatin, Aaron Burr, and, especially, Thomas Jefferson; the Federalist press smeared Jefferson, defended John Adams, and tried to launch Charles Cotesworth Pinckney. Individual Connecticut politicians received less attention until a series of short, scathing character sketches of Connecticut Federalists appeared in the Republican press in 1801. On Gallatin, see *Bee,* Mar. 12, 19, 26, 1800; on Burr, see *Bee,* Dec. 24, 1800; on Jefferson, see, for example, *Bee,* Feb. 7, 1798, Sept. 24, Oct. 4, 1800; on Pinckney, see *Conn. Courant,* Oct. 27, 1800. "New England Portraits" of the governor, lieutenant governor, and four members of the upper house were published in the Philadelphia *Aurora* and reprinted in the *Bee,* May 20, 27, June 3, 1801. The short biographies of French generals in the Republican press of the late 1790s did not yet describe the officers as unique Romantic personalities. Yet, the press did devote an increasing amount of attention to a compelling figure named Napoleon, whom John Fellows (Yale, 1783) believed to be a native of Middletown, Conn., who had sailed on a French merchant ship at the age of twelve (*American Mercury,* Feb. 13, 1797).

ests and the contests over policy were portrayed as struggles between generic figures: the social stock characters like the Farmer and the Merchant, who were particularly lively debaters in the late 1770s, and the polemical caricatures of Jacobin and Aristocrat, each of whom considered the other the political Antichrist of the 1790s. In the first group, the Farmer and the Merchant (and the Mechanic as well) were distinguished by social and vocational differences, and, although they might have argued vehemently about legislation, each acknowledged the other's right to exist as a legitimate part of society. The Aristocrat and the Jacobin, however, were separated by opposing ideological commitments, and each believed that the other posed a dangerous threat to the very existence of the Republic. Another figure arose in the 1780s that had characteristics of both groups: the Lawyer. The Lawyer, of course, represented an occupation with its own set of interests in society. But as lawyers multiplied quickly after the Revolution and rapidly filled political offices, the stereotypical Lawyer often became a whipping boy in polemics attacking all that was wrong with contemporary society and politics.

Young men seemed to flood into all the learned professions after the war—"Priests, Lawyers and Doctors, are thick enough to ride two upon a horse," the shoemaker Walter Brewster complained in 1791—but the lawyers were the ones who were most noticed. Whereas about 20 percent of Yale graduates pursued a legal career in 1770, by 1800 the profession claimed more than half the graduating class. These men built upon the work of their predecessors in the 1760s and 1770s and further professionalized their vocation by forming new associations, organizing a body of knowledge to be mastered, and standardizing requirements for training and admission to the bar. Thirty-two Hartford County attorneys founded a bar association in 1783, and Tapping Reeve's famous Litchfield Law School opened in 1784. Publications like Ephraim Kirby's *Reports of Cases,* Jesse Root's *Reports,* and Zephaniah Swift's *System of the Laws* established the intellectual caliber of Connecticut legal practice, and expectations of two years of postbaccalaureate legal study before admission to the bar were in place by 1795. But, if the number of lawyers and the social status of the profession were rising, so was the public's resentment of these learned men who mostly seemed to profit from the financial misfortune of others. Some writers blamed the swarm of lawyers upon the state's inefficient judicial system, but others pointed at Connecticut's citizenry, forever in debt and notoriously litigious over even the smallest sums of money. Hostility to the legal profession, however, was high throughout the new nation and would remain so into the next century. Campaigners for legal reform called for a simplified legal language that the common American could understand; they argued that the crafty manipulators of abstruse legal jargon were carrying their bag of verbal tricks from the courtrooms to the legislative halls, where they would warp legislation to serve their selfish interests just as they had perverted justice to fill their purses.[61]

As more and more lawyers filled elective office, the character of the Lawyer came to be shorthand for the politics of self-interest, faction, and artful intrigue. According to a letter in the *Courant*, all but a few of the fifty new advancing candidates in state politics in the late 1790s were members of the bar. The writer explained that "the business of their profession more than any other, favors a political combination" and then pretended to excuse, while pointing out, the lawyers' self-interested motives: "We must expect them to be more than men, not to improve their advantage of this combination in procuring their own election to stations of honor and emolument." A "Green-Woods Ploughman" writing in 1795 worried that "we are going to have a government made up entirely of one sort of men, and that sort I am afraid the worst there is in the country, I mean LAWYERS." He found thirty-six attorneys on the list of men who had received votes for the upper house, a half dozen of them—only

---

61. *Norwich Packet*, Sept. 8, 1791. Tapping Reeve trained 118 students before the end of the century; one of them, Seth P. Staples (1798), opened Connecticut's second law school in New Haven in 1800 (Marian C. McKenna, *Tapping Reeve and the Litchfield Law School* [New York, 1986], 168–170, 187–197). See Ephraim Kirby, *Reports of Cases Adjudged in the Superior Court of the State of Connecticut from the Year 1785, to May 1788; with some Determinations in the Supreme Court of Errors* (Litchfield, Conn., 1789); Jesse Root, *Reports on Cases Adjudged in the Superior Court and Supreme Court of Errors from July A.D. 1789 to June A.D. 1793 . . .*, 2 vols. (Hartford, Conn., 1798); Zephaniah Swift, *A System of the Laws of the State of Connecticut . . .*, 2 vols. (Windham, Conn., 1795). On legal education in Connecticut, see Anton-Hermann Chroust, *The Rise of the Legal Profession in America*, II, *The Revolution and the Post-Revolutionary Era* (Norman, Okla., 1965), 36, 146n. Gerard W. Gawalt, in *The Promise of Power: The Emergence of the Legal Profession in Massachusetts, 1760–1840* (Westport, Conn., 1979), reported that the Berkshire County (Mass.) Bar Association in 1792, "in order to staunch the influx of attorneys from Connecticut and to halt the outflow of law students to the Litchfield Law School, . . . refused to credit legal studies performed outside Massachusetts" (91). For general discussions of antilawyer sentiment after the Revolution, see Chroust, *Rise of the Legal Profession in America*, II, chap. 1; Richard E. Ellis, *The Jeffersonian Crisis: Courts and Politics in the Young Republic* (New York, 1971), chap. 8; and Maxwell Bloomfield, *American Lawyers in a Changing Society, 1776–1876* (Cambridge, Mass., 1976), chap. 2. On professionalization, see Samuel Haber, *The Quest for Authority and Honor in the American Professions, 1750–1900* (Chicago, 1991); Robert Dingwall and Philip Lewis, eds., *The Sociology of the Professions: Lawyers, Doctors, and Others* (New York, 1983). "Honorius" claimed that the county courts could be jammed with as many as eleven thousand lawsuits, 95 percent of them actions for debts of only five or six pounds (*Conn. Courant*, Sept. 30, 1783).

one of whom was past his mid-thirties—actually edging closer to seats on the Council. The Ploughman warned: "Their cunning and intrigue is become a bye-word, and their want of honesty an't much better. They are very good in their own places—when a man's got a crooked case they can help him out; but they are become very numerous, and they hang together so that they can do any thing in the state." Another writer a week later claimed that the young and ambitious men crowding the state bar were turning to politics because the number of lawsuits was dropping and therefore their incomes were declining. In the fall of 1797, "A Farmer" and "A Merchant" examined Connecticut's congressional delegation. In that year, as usual, the state's seven representatives and two senators were all lawyers. The reason, Merchant argued, was that "there is no set of men who are better acquainted with all our true national interests than the Lawyers," but the "Farmer," like Timothy Dwight two years earlier, believed that the interests lawyers advocated were too often their own and that other voices needed to be heard.[62]

The prominence of lawyers in politics and public discourse was related to, but not inevitably determined by, the growth of the legal profession generally. The increase in the number of doctors was even more spectacular. Between 1756 and 1790, for example, while the population of New Haven County grew by 55 percent, the number of physicians there rose 300 percent. To separate themselves from quacks, folk healers, and midwives—as lawyers had distinguished themselves from pettifoggers—physicians moved to professionalize the practice of medicine. They formed associations, published medical journals and treatises, and tried to control the certification and regulation of medical practitioners in the state.[63] Connecticut physicians, like Connecticut law-

62. *Conn. Courant*, Apr. 2, 1798; "Extracts from Dr. Dwight's Thanksgiving Sermon," *Conn. Courant*, Mar. 23, 30, Apr. 6, 1795, Nov. 20, 27, 1797. A writer in the *Norwich Packet* also reported that the number of lawsuits, after a high point in the late 1780s, was beginning to decline by 1791 (May 12, 1791). On the decline of the Connecticut lawyer's income after 1790, see Chroust, *Rise of the Legal Profession in America*, II, 87. A writer in 1800 challenged the general opinion that electing lawyers to almost all public offices was a problem: it spoke well of the profession that voters consistently sent their town lawyer to the Assembly as well as voted attorneys into higher office (*American Mercury*, Apr. 10, 1800).

63. Peter Dobkin Hall, *The Organization of American Culture, 1700–1900: Private Institutions, Elites, and the Origins of American Nationality* (New York, 1984), 129–130. About one in ten Yale graduates chose medicine between 1775 and 1800; see Franklin Bowditch Dexter, *Biographical Sketches of the Graduates of Yale College with the Annals of the College History*, 6 vols. (New York, 1885–1912). The physician's "illiterate" competitors are described in "The Companion," no. 28, *Conn. Courant*, Jan. 22, 1798.

In 1779, physicians from Massachusetts, New York, and Connecticut met and founded the Medical Society of Sharon, vowing to suppress "quackarism" and encourage medical

yers, succeeded in elevating their collective social status and boosting the integrity of their profession. As masters of a body of specialized learning and esoteric jargon that seemed as arcane and opaque to the uninitiated as the English common law, they used their claim of private knowledge to secure public reputations. They succeeded not so much by demonstrating their expertise before the public—that is, by healing people with their potions, purges, and bleedings—as by speaking a language of expertise and by allying themselves closely with the Standing Order clergy and Yale College. But, although an increasing number of doctors began sitting in the state legislature, doctors were never identified collectively as a powerful political force the way that attorneys were; unlike the Lawyer, the Physician never became a formidable character in public debate and a lightning rod for political dispute.[64]

By contrast, the Lawyer became the bogeyman of Connecticut politics in the early 1790s. The profession seemed to propel men into politics—not because legal expertise necessarily made men good legislators, it was argued, but because of the lawyers' talents for public speaking and writing. One writer contended that the lawyers' oratorical skill helped them win and hold public office,

---

knowledge and virtue (*Conn. Courant,* Sept. 14, 1779). New London County physicians gathered in 1774 to petition the Assembly for the right to license physicians; eleven years later, this same county society complained that it could not hold well-attended quarterly meetings because it was still not sanctioned by the state (*Norwich Packet; and the Connecticut, Massachusetts, New-Hampshire, and Rhode-Island Weekly Advertiser,* Mar. 10, 1774, Sept. 22, 1785). Physicians in Norwich (1763 and 1774), Litchfield (1766), and New Haven (1787) sent similar petitions (Hall, *Organization of American Culture,* 135). One representative to the Assembly, Colonel Burrall, spoke against the New Haven bill for incorporation in 1787, likening the medical society to the Cincinnati and the Freemasons, which might be "composed of cunning men, and we know not what mischief they may be upon." Abraham Granger voiced concerns about monopoly (*American Mercury,* June 4, 1787). The act for incorporation passed in May 1792, establishing an annual state convention and county societies empowered to examine candidates. The *Conn. Courant* published the full text of the act on July 2, 1792. On calls for a medical school, see *American Mercury,* June 15, 22, 1795; and Kelly, *Yale,* 131–133.

64. Hall, *Organization of American Culture,* 148, stresses the importance of Connecticut physicians' achieving social credibility through the alliance with the college and the clergy. Physicians might have had a specialized language, but they did not pretend to compete with lawyers as orators. James Potter, in *An Oration on the Rise and Progress of Physic in America . . .* (Hartford, Conn., 1781), delivered to a medical convention held at Sharon, Conn., in February 1780, referred to the "Roman eloquence" of the bar but apologized for his own performance: "Not having been accustomed to public speaking, the rules of my rhetoric having been deduced from the conversation of nurses, and the oritory of my life the groans of the sick" ([3], 11).

but it did not necessarily produce an effective government: "The art of speaking in public is better acquired in the practice of law in any other business. . . . [But] the long speeches which tire the patience and protract the business of Congress at the present day, have probably less influence than the pertinent and laconic arguments which formerly characterized a[n] [Oliver] Wolcott, a [Roger] Sherman and others whose fame is founded on a more permanent basis than stenographical reports." Again the public was warned that a reputation built upon artful language did not automatically signify the character of a good ruler. It should not be surprising, wrote a correspondent to the *American Mercury,* "that *Lawyers* should be the only characters elected, when we consider, that they have the means of making themselves more generally known than any other class of citizens." "Not that their general characters are known, so as to merit that confidence which is entrusted to a legislator. It is only their talent for public speaking, which is a trifling ingredient, in the composition of an able and virtuous ruler." A letter in the *Bee* counseled lawyers that a changed political climate would not hurt their fortunes. Legislative debates would still give them the opportunity to display their forensic eloquence; their "habits of public speaking" would still give them the advantage over men with more knowledge and better sense; and shifting their political sentiments should be no problem for professional men used to arguing both sides of a question.[65]

Even defenses of the profession acknowledged the disjunction between the rhetorical projection of character and the true man beneath the professional facade. In a short story published in 1793, an enthusiastic law student dreams that he overhears the tortured soliloquy of an eminent attorney. "How unhappy is the situation of the lawyer!" the dejected man moans. "However lively his sensibility, he must not *seem* to feel. And however gentle and amiable his own nature, he is obliged to embroil himself in the quarrels and express the passions of others." Advocates of legal reform, though, were not worried about tender-hearted men at the bar having to conceal their own "gentle and amiable" sentiments while they spoke the voice of reason to others who were

65. *Conn. Courant,* Apr. 2, 1798; *American Mercury,* Mar. 27, 1800 (the writer in this case was referring to elections to Congress); "Advice to Federalists, No. II," *Bee,* Jan. 28, 1801. Another writer had made a similar complaint about how the lawyers' habit of speech making bogged down the Connecticut General Assembly in 1790: "But you know we have a great many attornies in the House—they consider it a part of their trade to make *long speeches* on all occasions; indeed they generally make the *longest harrangues* where there is the *least* room for *argument.* Many of the *old* members do not chose to be out-done in this way: so they make long speeches too" (*American Mercury,* Nov. 15, 1790).

embroiled in passion. The critics charged that courtroom orators more often feigned emotion and played upon the passions of their audience and that these masters of legal jargon, while pretending to conduct a rational process, would exacerbate quarrels, prolong trials, and add to their fees.[66]

The first hint that the young and ambitious lawyers were forming "combinations" in order to thrust themselves into higher office came in the fall of 1790. A newspaper attack upon Congressman Roger Sherman was revealed to be the work of prominent New Haven lawyer Pierpont Edwards, thought to be eyeing Sherman's seat, aided by the pen of his fellow bar member, David Daggett. Edwards, the eleventh and youngest child of the elder Jonathan, turned forty that year but had already been a member of the state legislature since 1776, speaker of the house since 1787, a one-term congressman, and grand master of the Connecticut Freemasons. Letters under three different pseudonyms published in various papers around the state had charged that Sherman had publicly denounced a congressional pay hike and then secretly worked to secure it. Exposed as the author of two of the letters (the other was attributed to Daggett), Edwards then proceeded to engage Sherman directly, presenting his evidence before "the impartial public." Accused of smearing an opponent to promote his own political fortunes, Edwards was elected to Congress anyway, yet he surprised everyone—including, it was reported, his coadjutor Daggett—by refusing the seat and resigning as speaker of the Connecticut house as well. Daggett, fourteen years Edwards's junior, would not take a seat in the Assembly until 1791 but, like Edwards, was already "known to be as profuse in his mode of living as he is splended as to his abilities as a lawyer and speaker." A Yale Linonian and Phi Beta Kappan, he had debated Jedidiah Morse on sumptuary laws at the 1786 commencement and published a July Fourth oration of some renown in 1787. By the end of the 1790s, he would deliver two orations to the Cincinnati and, like Edwards, would achieve high Masonic office, serve as speaker of the Connecticut house, and refuse a seat in Congress. In 1790, after the Edwards-Sherman dispute, however, newspaper wits portrayed him as "Pimpy Catspaw," a man at once Edwards's tool and scheming to get Edwards into Congress in order to inherit the bulk of his colleague's New Haven law practice. Although much of the paper war that re-

66. "On the Profession of the Law," *American Mercury*, Apr. 1, 1793. Another writer warned the Federalist lawyer-politicians who were itching for war with France in 1798 that such a war would be "nothing like a contest of Lawyers, before a New-England court." In previous displays of French military might, "there was a more powerful rhetorick made use of, than 'may it please your Honors, and if your honors please'" (*American Mercury*, Apr. 5, 1798).

sulted consisted of juvenile taunting tossed back and forth between Hartford and New Haven, some writers perceived darker intrigues and more devious electioneering being plotted by lawyer-led cabals in New Haven County.[67]

The Edwards-and-Daggett incident demonstrates that the lines of opposition marked out by political debate were still not, in 1790, primarily ideological. Arguments pitted the ambitious lawyer against the traditional magistrate, public discourse and fame at the bar versus family connections and local reputation. In a few short years, Edwards, with out-of-state help from his nephew, Aaron Burr, would become the leader of Connecticut's Jeffersonian Republicans. Daggett, rumored to be a dangerous young insurgent in 1790, would become a pillar of the Standing Order. But at the beginning of the century's last decade, both were allies in what critics anxiously described as the new politics of post-Revolutionary Connecticut. The young lawyers, though symbols of this new, increasingly competitive, and sometimes devious political style, were not its masters, for their scheme to use the press to portray Sherman as a duplicitous insider blew up in their faces and turned public suspicion toward themselves.[68]

67. Quotation about Daggett is in "A Real Republican and Farmer," *American Mercury*, Sept. 20, 1790. For the controversy in the *American Mercury*, see "A Farmer," "The Observer, No. XX," Sept. 13, 1790, "A Real Republican and Farmer," letter from Roger Sherman, "Cato," letter from Pierpont Edwards, Sept. 20, 1790, letter from Pierpont Edwards, Sept. 27, 1790, "A Quaker," Oct. 4, 1790, letter from Pierpont Edwards, Oct. 11, 1790, "Reflections upon the Freedom of the Press," Oct. 18, 1790, letter, Dec. 6, 1790. In the *Courant*, see Sept. 13, 20, Oct. 11, 1790, "Vivat Respublica," Nov. 8, 1790, Nov. 10, 1790, [Daggett], "Neoportenis," Nov. 15, 1790, "The Improvements of Modern Times—A Rhapsody," Nov. 15, 1790, Dec. 13, 1790, Jan. 10, 17, 1791. In the *Conn. Journal*, see Sept. 22, 29, Oct. 13, Nov. 10, Dec. 8, 1790, Jan. 5, 1791. Henry Channing also wrote privately to Daggett that he had heard Daggett had become the "political Tool" of a certain gentleman. "Our political system is evidently no longer the free and uninfluenced voice of Freemen," Channing lamented, "but we are under the government of Rhode Island politics—party intrigues" (Channing to Daggett, Nov. 22, 1790, David Daggett Papers).

68. Sherman, however, did not himself represent the older model: he lacked extensive family connections and a college degree and was himself a lawyer. As a biographer of Pierpont Edwards notes, "While his brother Jonathan, on the east side of New Haven, wrote pamphlets and articles attacking slavery, Pierpont lived comfortably on the west side of town, attended by two slaves" (James McLachlan, *Princetonians, 1748–1768: A Biographical Dictionary* [Princeton, N.J., 1976], 640). Daggett became very active along with Jonathan Edwards, Jr., in the Society for the Promotion of Freedom. "Apologist" in the *American Mercury*, Mar. 26, 1792, sarcastically wrote that government "was very simple, while we were a Colony of Britain, and even during the war against her. . . . But a new era has commenced, the scale of policy is infinitely enlarged," and now they need to be led by men "able in politics and learned in the Law."

In 1792, the next manifestation of this new politics emerged in what news-paper satirists dubbed "The Nocturnal Society of Stelligeri," a caricature de-scribed as part political party and part secret fraternal society. Apparently, a group of restless young men, most of them lawyers holding seats in the lower house, had met one or more evenings during the sessions of the Assembly to discuss candidates for higher office. Among them, according to a private mem-orandum by Ezra Stiles, were Edwards, Daggett, and a half-dozen other Yale graduates. Writers in the press mocked the group by turning what appears to have been an informal gathering or two into a formal society, inventing ac-counts of the Stelligeri's proceedings (the meetings were held in a distillery cel-lar), resolves (to force the old guard out of office), and expenses (travel for covert campaigning, libelous printing, and liquor). The society was also said to offer prizes for the best essays or rumors that would "depress some characters and advance others." By the time the papers published a "Journal" describing the effects of public exposure upon the members (one vomits in a bucket, an-other drowns in a horse trough), the Stelligeri writings had evolved from po-litical satire to pure farce. For several more years, the term "Stelligeri" would be applied in discussions of self-interested lawyer-politicians and devious fac-tions. By 1795, however, the rumored formation of a secret political junto led by lawyers had become part of Connecticut's political mythology. Men like Ezra Stiles and Timothy Dwight glanced anxiously at the list of elected officials and thought that they saw scores of office seekers who believed, as the Stelligeri president had said in one of the satires, that success "depends entirely and solely upon our own address and intrigue."[69]

69. Morgan, *Gentle Puritan,* 414, apparently working from a memorandum summarized in Stiles, *Literary Diary,* ed. Dexter, III, 451n, identifies some of the Stelligeri: "Jonathan In-gersoll (Yale 1766), Pierpont Edwards (Princeton 1750), and David Daggett (Yale 1783) from New Haven, William Judd (Yale 1778) from Farmington, Ephraim Kirby and Uriah Tracy (Yale 1778) from Litchfield, Amasa Larned (Yale 1772) from New London, Elisha Hyde from Norwich, Zephaniah Swift (Yale 1778) from Windham, Moses Cleaveland (Yale 1777) from Canterbury, Jeremiah Halsey from Preston, and Philip Bradley from Ridgefield" as well as Middletown attorney Asher Miller. Stiles also mentions a Major Pumroy, whom Morgan fails to note; Morgan surmises Miller's involvement based on a letter from William Judd to David Daggett (415–416). See *American Mercury,* Mar. 26, Apr. 2, May 28, 1792; *Conn. Cour-ant,* Apr. 2, May 7, 14, 21 (quotation), 28, 1792. Some of these items were reprinted in the *Norwich Packet,* May 31, June 7, 1792; and the *Monitor* (Litchfield, Conn.), Apr. 4, June 6, 1792. For the continued use of "Stelligeri," see *Conn. Courant,* Apr. 1, 1793, Jan. 4, 1796, Jan. 8, 1798; *American Mercury,* Sept. 8, 1794; *Bee,* Nov. 14, 1798. The quotation from the Stelligeri president is in the *Conn. Courant,* May 21, 1792. Serious concern about the junto of lawyers is expressed in an essay published in the *Conn. Courant,* Apr. 6, 1795.

It is not surprising that there was tension between lawyers, as symbols of the new politics, and clergymen, as spokesmen for the old magistracy. This tension was reinforced from two other sources: the readjustments in the relationship between religion and politics and the professional rivalry that emerged as lawyers appeared alongside ministers as public speakers and moved ahead of them as the dominant intellectuals of the new Republic. A good example of how these broad political, social, and cultural strains could shape the interactions between individual lawyers and clergymen can be found in the early career of Zephaniah Swift. Less in his masterwork, *A System of the Laws in the State of Connecticut* (1795), than in an extended controversy with clergymen and in his reputation as a freethinking politician, Swift challenged the traditional notions about public character articulated by the ministry. Swift, a Windham lawyer who had first been sent to the Assembly in 1787 at the age of twenty-eight, became a congressman in 1793. Letters from Swift and fellow congressman Uriah Tracy to David Daggett joked about Swift's unorthodox religious sentiments: Tracy called him a "convert" for attending half a church meeting—on Christmas—since arriving in Philadelphia; Swift insisted that he was sampling all the denominations in town and that he "once devoutly attended and [had] been spiritually edified in a dutch [or *deutsche]* Church where I could not understand a word that was spoken." But he also described his soul's being most gratified after a trip to the theater. When ministers warned that men who were not true Christians, whatever other talents they had, could never be good rulers, they had candidates like Swift in mind.[70]

70. Uriah Tracy to David Daggett, 1794, Zephaniah Swift to Daggett, Dec. 31, 1793, Swift to Daggett, February 1794, all in David Daggett Papers. The Reverend James Cogswell of Scotland parish wrote in his diary on Sept. 8, 1789, that "Swift is a Man that totally disregards Religion—profligate, irreligious Persons, Baptists and Separates are all very fond of such men for Deputies chiefly because They are inimical to the Standing Ministries and Churches" (quoted in William G. McLoughlin, *New England Dissent, 1630–1833: The Baptists and the Separation of Church and State,* 2 vols. [Cambridge, Mass., 1971], II, 925). In the preface to Swift's two-volume treatise, *System of the Laws of the State of Connecticut,* Swift says that men on the state's higher courts would probably not benefit from his study, but he stated the opposite in a letter to David Daggett. He wrote the study, he told Daggett, in part because he was astonished at the ignorance of the judges on the superior court (Swift to Daggett, Sept. 16, 1796, David Daggett Papers). To Swift, a professional bar, a reformed judicial system, and the rule of law were the foundations of political and social happiness. As Everett C. Goodwin has argued in *The Magistracy Rediscovered: Connecticut, 1636–1818* (Ann Arbor, Mich., 1981), 98, Swift's conception of the law differed from the lingering Puritan vision of "the law as a tool for the chastisement of depravity, and the prevention of destruction" under God's rule. Swift understood the law *itself* "as a preserver of order and a ra-

Swift's dispute with Connecticut clergymen began with a controversy at the First Church in Pomfret in 1792. An ordination council was presented with charges against the Reverend Oliver Dodge, a local friend of Swift's and a candidate to be an assistant pastor with the aging Reverend Aaron Putnam. Dodge was accused of behavior unbecoming a minister: levity, profanity, dissipation, and disrespect to other ministers. One particular incident was singled out— a gathering where Dodge drank too much gin, sang songs and threw chairs about, and then made ungentlemanly advances toward a Miss Polly Peabody. The majority of the First Church Society accepted Dodge's apology and voted to renew their offer to him, but Putnam overruled the decision and refused to see Dodge ordained. Outraged members separated from the First Church and formed a new society with Dodge as their pastor. Anti-Dodge clerics took their case to the press. Swift, writing to the Windham *Herald* and in later pamphlets as the "Correspondent," counterattacked. The ordination council's declaration against Dodge was a false and malicious slander, and subsequent actions by Dodge's opponents were examples of clerical tyranny, he contended—but that was only the beginning. The resulting pamphlet war extended until 1796 and expanded to more than 375 printed pages. The arguments on both sides moved far beyond the charges and countercharges about what the ministers involved did or did not do to a much broader struggle to define the characters of the good clergyman, lawyer, and statesman. It was a battle between somber piety and polite sociability, ecclesiastical power and civil liberty, Calvinism and the Enlightenment.[71]

Swift claimed he was attacking clerical despotism, not the clergy as such. The old Saybrook Platform statutes, he reminded his opponents, "which were

---

tional basis for unbiased judgment." High praise for *A System* appeared in the *American Mercury*, June 20, 1796 (reprinted from the *Conn. Gazette*). On Swift, see also Donald F. Gerardi, "Zephaniah Swift and Connecticut's Standing Order: Skepticism, Conservatism, and Religious Liberty in the Early Republic," *NEQ*, LXVII (1994), 234–256.

71. [Zephaniah Swift], *The Correspondent . . . Together with an Appendix Containing Some General Observations Relative to the True Principles and Spirit of the Christian Religion* (Windham, Conn., 1793). The initial skirmish in the *Windham Herald* was also reprinted in the *American Mercury*, Jan. 21, Feb. 11, 1793. Details about a related dispute between Dodge and Woodstock pastor Eliphalet Lyman are related in a twenty-page appendix to Eliphalet Lyman, *Two Discourses Preached at Woodstock . . .* (Norwich, Conn., 1794). The controversy continued in Moses C. Welch, *A Reply to the Correspondent . . .* (Norwich, Conn., 1794); [Swift], *An Address to the Rev. Moses C. Welch . . .* (Windham, Conn., 1794); Welch, *The Addressor Addressed . . .* (Norwich, Conn., 1796); [Swift], *A Second Address, to the Reverend Moses C. Welch, Containing an Answer to His Letter to the Correspondent* (Windham, Conn., 1796). The general outline of the controversy is given in Dorothy Ann Lipson, *Freemasonry in Federalist Connecticut* (Princeton, N.J., 1977), 150–157.

enacted in the reign of puritanism, when clerical influence was at a higher pitch," had been repealed. In "this enlightened period" of civil liberty, he argued, Americans would no longer bow before ecclesiastics who trod upon the rights of conscience. "A most remarkable revolution has taken place in the human mind. Uniformity of sentiment, is no longer deemed necessary to the preservation of religion, nor an ecclesiastical establishment to the support of civil government." The popish tribunal that had denounced the pro-Dodge separatists as vile covenant breakers had confused civil contracts, which were enforced by legal sanctions, and religious covenants, which any individual could break at will, according to the dictates of his conscience. Attorney Swift then challenged his clerical opponents to point to any "page of Coke, Blackstone or Powell" that said otherwise. The Reverend Moses C. Welch of Mansfield, writing for the county ministerial association, agreed to try the controversy before the bar of the public and answered that Swift, however familiar with his law books, displayed a woefully inadequate grasp of the rules of ecclesiastical proceedings and completely bungled the topic of regulating church discipline: "It would be wise in him to retire from controversies of this nature, and attend wholly to the duties of his own profession, where it is agreed, on all hands, he makes more than an ordinary figure." [72]

Not surprisingly, Swift felt that the ministers were the ones who were stepping outside their proper sphere. They assumed that the laity would blindly respect a clergyman because of his office rather than his character as an individual. Swift wrote of "the rapid decline of the power of the clergy" and declared that "the deep and mysterious veil, which once hung round clerical usurpation, and concealed their iniquity from public view, has been rent asunder, and the priesthood are as assailable to the weapons of truth and justice, as any other class of men." People were beginning to see that preaching licenses did not signify "*superior minds*" or "a higher order of beings." Swift not only criticized the clergymen's hunger for power and intellectual pretension but their manners as well. "That austerity, reserve, distance and gravity of manners, which once had a powerful effect to *frighten children and deceive old women*, seem to be going out of fashion." The solemnity clergymen used to drape life in a mourning shroud was often a "subterfuge for slender abilities, superficial knowledge and forbidding manners." [73]

Swift also warned that the prevailing preaching styles and theological predilections of the Standing Order clergy were sweeping them toward irrelevance. To listen to their pulpit performances, it was no wonder that "men of

72. [Swift], *The Correspondent*, 32, 33, 43–45, 137; Welch, *A Reply*, 50.
73. [Swift], *Second Address*, 34 n. 6; [Swift], *The Correspondent*, 43, 45–46.

taste, and a relish for social happiness" were finding organized religion disgusting. Fanatic preachers ranted and raved like maniacs and were perhaps beyond help; others who followed along in the rut of "puritanical custom" needed to "pay more attention to the cultivation of eloquence and oratory":

> We find the pulpit is too generally the theatre of unanimated description, uninteresting exhortation, and lifeless declamation. Sermons are too often a cold unvaried round of common place topics, a dry repetition of threadbare sentiments, familiar to every old woman, presented in every possible shape, and expressed in every possible mode of dulness, to spin out the discourse to the ordinary [unbearable] length . . . and to inflict the usual anguish on the patience of the unhappy auditory.

The continual attempt to preach fear and terror, the "eternal din" of sin and depravity, human inability and self-denial, hell and damnation—this familiar pulpit oratory ultimately did nothing but cast a dismal, melancholy gloom over everyone. In this new age, Swift argued, ministers needed to become amiable, liberal, and eloquent men who urged their neighbors on a road to heaven "strewed with flowers and roses." Like the satirist John Trumbull two decades earlier, Swift was using the standards of politeness to castigate the clergy, but Swift's critique cut deeper. Not only the manner of address but the content of the Calvinist clergyman's message was inappropriate in an enlightened age for anyone other than old women and children. Men of taste would do more than just fall asleep in the pews, like the parishioners in Trumbull's *Progress of Dulness,* Swift implied; they would stop coming to church and ignore ministers as dullards and social misfits.[74]

Clergymen did not graciously accept this young lawyer-politician's criticism of them as thinkers, speakers, and public characters. The heresy intimated in *The Correspondent*'s appended "general observations" on Christianity was especially vulnerable to attack. Clergymen knew deism and infidelity when they saw it, and they said so. They also aimed their rhetorical artillery at Swift the writer, lawyer, and politician. The Reverend T. Byrne acknowledged Swift's talent for arrogant vitriol but wrote that it was—or should have been—beneath Swift's dignity as a member of the bar and holder of high office: "That he is possessed of distinguished abilities, at the mode of writing he has taken, no one disputes. But the question is, whether the public might have expected such a mode from a character rising to the first honors of the State?" More dismissive of Swift's air of argumentative prowess, Moses Welch took the measure of his

74. [Swift], *The Correspondent,* 131, 132, 134, 135.

opponent and announced that he was not impressed: Swift imagines that he wields "a sword of an enormous length," Welch wrote, "but, viewed with proper optics, it dwindles down to a pigmy size, and is not, from hilt to point, more than three or four inches." In contrast to the minister's apostolic duty to preach the gospel, popular or not, Swift was a scheming politician blinded by partisan views, "a mere political weather-cock" who sought the applause of "the unthinking, injudicious multitude." His attack on the clergy was a calculated plan by a self-exalted character "who has cajoled and riggled himself into public view, and who wishes to stand foremost in the list of fame." [75]

But Swift pointed the finger of political intrigue back at his pious accusers and had his reputation as a legislator, and the votes of the sovereign people, to speak for his character. He charged his opponents with preaching politics at freemen's meetings, trying to doom candidates with "the awful sound of deism from the oracular mouth of a minister." He argued that his own rise to political prominence had occurred without wealth, family connections, or intrigue and reminded them that all their insults were aimed at a man whom "the independent citizens of the most enlightened country on the globe, have elected . . . to an office of great importance and respectability." While he was away at Congress serving his country and debating Jay's Treaty—the most important question, he asserted, ever before the nation's legislature—a minister of the gospel was publishing "groundless calumny" throughout Connecticut and trying to ruin him. Such an attack, Swift seemed to suggest, was an attempt to debase more than the character of a single legislator. It was an assault upon the character of a free and enlightened people. [76]

Even as Swift wrote the dispute's last pamphlet in 1796, the distance between national debates over weighty issues like Jay's Treaty and the local, petty politics of character assassination was being breached. The national partisan divi-

75. Quotation from T. Byrne, in Welch, *A Reply*, 22; and see "Rev. T. B. to the *Windham Herald*, 2d of March, 1793," reprinted in [Swift], *The Correspondent*, 46–47; Welch, *The Addressor Addressed*, preface. For Welch on ministers and unpopularity, see *A Reply*, 60–62. Quoted phrases on Swift as political weathercock are from Welch, *The Addressor Addressed*, 6–7, 33n.

76. [Swift], *The Correspondent*, 64, 73, 91–92, 108 (quotation on deism), 114–116; [Swift], *A Second Address*, 4, 24. Nathaniel Niles, minister and congressman from Vermont, was also said to be attacking Swift's character (*Conn. Courant*, Dec. 1, 1794). A letter addressed "To Zephaniah Swift, Esquire," from "Falkland" appeared in the *Conn. Courant*, Aug. 5, 1793, calling him a fraud and a hypocrite; the charges were questioned by "Candour," Aug. 26, 1793. A notice in the *Conn. Journal*, Sept. 11, 1793, defended Swift against charges that he was a dangerous man, arguing that his abilities were first-rate, as he had demonstrated in the General Assembly.

sion between Federalists and Republicans came to dominate politics and discourse in the state. Quarrels in the press between the new Lawyer manipulating language and the old Magistrate and Clergyman expecting deference were replaced by an increasingly vicious brawl between the Federalist Aristocrat and the Republican Jacobin. Although Connecticut's elite were heavily Federalist, lawyers and clergymen were on both sides. Despite concerns of Federalist lawyers like Swift and Daggett about clerical despotism, and despite the established clergy's concern about a new politics dominated by the Stelligeri, they joined hands to preserve law and order against what they perceived to be the Francophile forces of licentious liberty and unrestrained democracy. Across the ideological divide, anticlerical lawyers like Pierpont Edwards and Abraham Bishop joined Republican preachers like Stanley Griswold. Speakers and writers on both sides urged their audiences to peel back the artful surface of their opponents' rhetoric to expose the real character of the minds at work—minds full of secret intrigue and villainy, pursuing power as their only object.

THE PRESS

Mr. Writer, the character imagined by the young Yale playwrights in 1784, represents fantasies about reading and writing. As a reader, he is able to make language utterly transparent. He can peer through the screen of words to gaze directly upon thought—and indeed, he can see beneath the chaotic surface of thought to the essence of mind beneath. He can discern an author's true intentions, a speaker's real character, a thinker's controlling motives. As a writer, though, he is able to make words reflect and record thought perfectly. He is able to preserve all the "evolutions, revolutions, and resolutions" in an individual mind like Benedict Arnold's, although he acknowledges that the text produced is "a very voluminous affair, [and] a very tedious book." When he reads, he is a purely objective eye that gazes through the shadows and illusions of language and material things. When he writes, he is merely a hand with a pen, a clerk who records, not an author, not a subjective intelligence who interprets and shapes and tells his own stories, but a mechanism accurately preserving the thoughts of others. Mr. Searcher asks him about the kind of ink he uses, but he answers that the ink does not matter—the material practices of writing are irrelevant. It is not the ink, pen, or hand but the mind being recorded "that gives the tincture and complection" to the writing.[77]

Mr. Writer's reading and writing comprehensively document people's men-

---

77. Yale Class Play, 11–13.

tal lives; his office of the mind is society's perfect archive. The nature of this office is unclear—is it connected to the state?—but, because we see him at the beginning of the play making extracts for a friend, we know Mr. Writer is not the only reader of his record books. Thus, the circle of communication is completed: thoughts are read and become writing; the writing is read, influencing further thought. The writing becomes a neutral medium of communication, linking minds separated by space, time, and circumstance; the office becomes an institution disseminating the truth about people, even truths they might not wish revealed.

This fantasy about reading and writing resembles some of the commentary about the role of the periodical press in the early Republic. Mr. Writer may be the antithesis of John Trumbull's "Universal Correspondent," who envisioned a civic forum in print that removed public debate from the personalities of its participants; if anything, the publication of Mr. Writer's records would mark the most extensive publicity of personality imaginable. To an eighteenth-century audience, Mr. Writer's record book might have recalled the book of sins opened on Judgment Day, and the office of the mind might have suggested the official surveillance of a despotic church or state (the play at one point mentions the Inquisition). Despite these negative connotations, and apart from his preternatural abilities, Mr. Writer is not unlike the ideal newspaper editor, a character that editors themselves, proclaiming their impartiality, liked to assume: a discerning reader who produces an accurate record and who uses the mechanism of the printing press to inform without injecting his own biased sentiments into the writing. Pondering the importance of print to a free society, commentators imagined that, in the hands of such men, the press could be a neutral medium of open communication, improving manners, diffusing knowledge, and rationalizing political behavior.

"Dr. Pull," a fictional character in a dramatic dialogue printed in the *Norwich Packet* during the summer of 1786, expressed this optimism about how the press could function and pointed out the importance of this neutral and open communication to a republic. The doctor is having a friendly conversation about public affairs with four other characters: Esquire Selfish, Deacon Honesty, Tom Taciturn's Wife, and Aunt Peg. The 'Squire would do away with all lawyers; the Deacon would abolish judges and physicians too. Dr. Pull, however, instead of prescribing that the public body be purged of particular noxious elements, offered a political physiology that stressed the importance of public discourse to the entire organic system. The body politic was like a natural body, he explained, with the General Assembly as the head. The head needs to receive knowledge from the various body parts—sensations carried by "nervous fluids" that, in the case of the American Republic or the states, were composed of newspapers. The Romans held public debates in large forums; in a modern republic, the press could serve the same purpose:

> I think by *instructing* our representatives, and by publishing all our thoughts on publick matters in a great news-paper made a purpose, and by making a law that the General Court should have this paper read clear through every day, before they went upon business: and by obliging them to publish before hand what they were going to do, that we might have an opportunity to express all our minds upon it in this news-paper—we might do almost as well as the Romans.

In the late 1780s and early 1790s, writers turned from fantasizing about the press to examining how the press actually functioned—or how it failed to function—as the nervous system of the new Republic. Far from the simple and transparent medium of communication between the state and the people that Dr. Pull described, the partisan press by the late 1790s helped shape what came to be, in effect, alternate political realities for Federalists and Democratic-Republicans. Instead of enlightening legislators, informing the citizenry, and providing the knowledge necessary for rational decision making, critics charged, the press fanned the flames of political passion.[78]

Not everyone stressed, as Dr. Pull had, the flow of political understanding *from* the extremities *to* the governmental head. Some still described political knowledge trickling from the top down. Verse satire in the *Courant* lampooned representatives who returned from the Assembly to lecture their constituents "like those who're fresh from College, / Spring to debate with fancied knowledge":

> Thus three weeks ends the legislature,
> When each turns home a commentator;
> Where he unfolds in learn'd debate;
> How he would ease the groaning State,
> For having mix'd among that croud,
> He's pack'd up knowledge by the load.
> As minds who've stor'd the *Encyclopedia*.

Other writers suggested that the political sentiments formed and expressed in legislatures created (rather than reflected) a similar spirit among the general population. A correspondent to the Republican *Bee* lamented: "There is a large

78. *Norwich Packet; or, The Country Journal,* June 22, 1786 (reprinted from the *Worcester Magazine*). Mrs. Taciturn liked the idea "because the women could write in this great newspaper, and so have a chance to speak their minds upon publick matters as well as the men."

proportion of people in every country who take their politics from their magistrate, just as they take their divinity from their parson, or their physic from their doctor; that is, without enquiry or affirmation." Writers who sent the newspapers brief reports on the Assembly also seemed to consider their summaries an opportunity to school the public in right political thinking. In the mid-1780s, news from the legislature was interlarded with commentary like the following: "The debates were managed with manliness and candor suited to the magnitude of the subject. . . . Never did people in general feel more satisfaction at any public measure than in consequence of this act." Some irritated readers began to complain about being spoon-fed political opinion along with the few facts concerning legislative deliberation. The newspaper editors explained that, although the proceedings of the lower house had finally been opened to public observers, there were still restrictions on the press. Captain Peter Bulkeley, a representative from Colchester, introduced a bill that would have formalized and even further tightened those restrictions by outlawing any publication of the Assembly's proceedings except an official account certified by the clerk of the house. But after this measure was rejected, detailed accounts of the lower house's debates began to appear. Former critics applauded the new openness and wrote that, thanks to the newspapers, members of the public could read the debates, see the vote tallies, check the positions taken and argued by individual representatives, and decide for themselves.[79]

The newspaper's role as the primary vehicle of political communication, however, was tainted by partiality and partisanship. One essayist complained that, although newspapers could create a forum of reasoned discussion and candid debate that "might afford a competent share of information respecting the affairs of the public to every individual," instead "a *mercenary groupe* of *Grubstreet Scriblers,* through the medium of a *prostituted press,*" filled the local sheets with grossly slanted irony, satire, and ridicule. Even without legislative censorship, another writer argued, freedom of the press suffered "from the ignorance, the caprice, or the partiality of officious Editors." A congressional debate in 1794 over the newspaper postal rate also addressed the problem of bias in local papers. Supporters of a rate reduction pointed to the crucial importance of diffusing knowledge in a republic but contended that the flow of

---

79. The verse is from "The News Lad's Address to the Readers of the Connecticut Courant," *Conn. Courant,* Jan. 2, 1792. On legislators' creating political sentiment, see *Journal of the Times,* Sept. 17, 1799. The quotation from the *Bee* is in the issue for June 12, 1799. The quoted report on the legislature is in the *Conn. Courant,* May 25, 1784. On printing house debates, see *American Mercury,* July 27, 1786, May 28, 1787; *Conn. Courant,* July 17, 1786 (reprinted from the *Conn. Journal*), Oct. 23, Dec. 18, 1786, May 28, 1787.

information from the capital and metropolis out to the country towns was hindered because most smaller towns had only one paper. These presses were "under the influence of the little lord of the village" and could freely print his opinion as fact without opposition. Perhaps no paper could be unbiased and impartial, but in cities readers had access to more than one publication and could hear arguments and opinions from different points of view. Reducing the postal rates would allow the competing metropolitan papers to penetrate— and enlighten—the countryside. But a rate reduction would also, opponents argued, destroy the business of every village editor. Country folk would still not be able to afford two papers or perhaps even one if they had to pay cash for it. Biased news from a single source was better than no news at all. And, besides passing on news from the bigger cities, the editor of the Norwich *Courier* argued a few years later, the small town newspaper had another function: close to the people and their interests, it serves the local public by expressing its interests to a wider audience. "The nearer a paper is printed, the more valuable; ... A Printing Office erected in any town, renders it more public, and consequently has a tendency to its future prosperity." According to the *Courier,* editors in small towns and villages were only "biased" and "partisan" in their concern for their local communities.[80]

Connecticut editors continued to struggle against charges of partiality and political bias. Elisha Babcock of the *American Mercury,* like his Hartford competitors Hudson and Goodwin of the *Courant,* vehemently denied the charge that he had slanted his coverage of local interests by purposely keeping Antifederalist arguments out of his paper in 1787. Through the 1790s, readers accused Babcock of being too afraid to reprint anything unless it came from a Federalist paper; then, in the spring of 1798, Federalists cursed him for switching sides and joining the Democratic-Republicans. But the editor insisted throughout that he kept his political opinions to himself and simply published respectable discussions about politics, letting readers judge for themselves: "I never supposed it belonged to me, as a printer, arogantly to assume to myself the *right of Judging* and dictating to the public, sentiments, either in politics, *religion,* or any thing else." Whether he admitted it or not, however, his selections (if not any direct editorial comment) did reveal the changing political character of his paper. For nearly a year and a half in 1796 and 1797, the front pages of the *American Mercury* were filled with George Washington's letters during the Revolutionary War, indicating a veneration for the principles of 1776

80. *American Mercury,* Apr. 1, 1793, May 14, 1796; Proceedings of the House of Representatives, Feb. 18, 1794, reported in *American Mercury,* Mar. 3, 1795 (opponents of the rate reduction won, forty-four to forty); *Courier* (Norwich, Conn.), Aug. 23, 1798.

and, because Washington had just completed his presidency, perhaps admiration for Washington's (as opposed to Adams's?) federalism. In January 1797, Babcock printed "Two Political Possibilities" that edged tentatively away from orthodox Federalist doctrine: that all zealous supporters of Independence (like the "monarchical" Adams?) were not necessarily friends of liberty and republicanism and that not all the staunch defenders of the Constitution supported the Adams administration. In that same month, Babcock printed opinion pieces from the Republican *Aurora* and the Federalist *Gazette of the United States* side by side. By 1798, cautious criticism of Adams began to be more prominent than support. Praise for Jefferson appeared in the early summer of 1800; by the end of that summer, Babcock's paper was campaigning for the Republican cause, and he feared that Federalists were trying to get him arrested for sedition under the infamous federal act passed two years earlier.[81]

When editor Samuel Trumbull of Stonington began the *Journal of the Times* in the fall of 1798, he attempted to produce what few printers even pretended to offer anymore: a truly impartial newspaper, devoid of party calumny and devoted to the public good. In his second issue, as he printed the Kentucky resolves against the Alien and Sedition Acts, he added an editorial note explaining that he refused to call the Kentuckians "deluded disorganizers" as did the Federalist press or "enlightened citizens" as did the Republican, but would call them only "men." He published July Fourth toasts from both sides of the ideological divide in parallel columns, labeled "Federal" and "Democratic," and printed articles like "The Parson's Cow—A Humorous Story" while other papers were filled with political diatribes. He complained that it was nearly impossible to get the facts about European events because the party zeal of his

81. *American Mercury*, Jan. 9, 1797, Elisha Babcock, "To the Public," May 31, 1798. On Babcock's fear of entrapment on the Sedition law, see *American Mercury*, Aug. 28, 1800. David Hackett Fischer, in *The Revolution of American Conservatism: The Federalist Party in the Era of Jeffersonian Democracy* (New York, 1965), surveyed the political positions of sixteen Connecticut newspapers on Oct. 1, 1800. He found three strongly Republican, eleven moderately Federalist, and two strongly Federalist (although the basis of his distinction between moderate and strong is not clear, and his table on 131 differs slightly from the breakdown on 416). Donald H. Stewart, in *The Opposition Press of the Federalist Period* (Albany, N.Y., 1969), 869–871, made a broader, but still selective, sample of Connecticut papers in the Federalist period and found, of the thirty-five printed, one was strongly Democratic, three Democratic, and four "independently" Democratic; ten were Federalist, seven independently Federalist, and five had a mild or fluctuating Federalist commitment. The remaining five were impartial, apolitical, or unknown. No tally of political affiliation at a particular moment like Fischer's, however, or even a broader-based assessment of a paper's position like Stewart's can convey how editorial positions shifted over time and for different reasons.

sources (the metropolitan papers) distorted everything concerning the French or the English. Like some of the few political letters his paper carried, Trumbull denounced the frenzied partisanship that characterized late-eighteenth-century American politics and tried to create a new category of Moderates between the polar opposition of Francophobe Aristocrats and Anglophobe Jacobins.[82]

Trumbull's appeal for moderation had little impact upon a region where, according to the "Rhode Island Farmer," almost every Connecticut and Rhode Island paper was violently partisan and busy "exaggerating everything which will serve to inflame the minds of readers and create opposition." But Trumbull's nonpartisanship and calls for moderation vanished when Jefferson's victory removed the Federalist threat of prosecution for sedition. After the *Journal* ceased publication in the fall of 1799, Trumbull returned in the summer of 1801 to print a periodical entitled *The Patriot; or, Scourge of Aristocracy* and immediately compared Federalist policy to British tyranny in 1776, lacerated John Adams, and spewed venom at clergymen like Timothy Dwight and other Federalist "Arnolds."[83]

Like Trumbull, Charles Holt began the New London *Bee* in 1797 with good intentions to provide an open forum. The political column of his first two issues carried "An American Republican's" criticism of John Adams and Oliver Wolcott as well as a Federalist response by a writer signing himself "Whip." But Holt quickly abandoned his impartial stance and began printing exclusively for the Republican opposition. He candidly explained why: "There are generally *two sides* to every subject.... And it is the duty of an impartial printer to communicate to the Public on *both sides* freely. But nine tenths of the newspapers in Connecticut are decidedly partial to *one side,* and keep the *other* out of sight. This is not fair." When the other papers started including some "democratical sentiment," he promised, he would again include some articles presenting the "aristocratical" point of view. The mighty *Courant* responded by doing its best to silence Holt and smother all political dissent in the state stirred up by the "leprosy" of Republican print. The *Bee* was supported by a half dozen "sans-culottes" in New London, one letter in Hudson and Goodwin's paper jeered, and hardly anyone living more than fifteen miles from that town had even

82. *Journal of the Times,* Oct. 10, 17, 1798, June 4, Aug. 13, 20, 1799. Tertius Dunning's *Middlesex Gazette* made some attempt to print both sides, but, when sixty Republicans canceled their subscriptions, he announced that he would henceforth "print a paper worthy of the most firm supporters of government" (Apr. 19, 1799).

83. *Journal of the Times,* Aug. 20, 1799; *The Patriot; or, Scourge of Aristocracy* (Stonington, Conn.), July 24, 31, Aug. 7, 14, 28, Oct. 9, 1801.

heard of it. In 1799, Hudson and Goodwin addressed Holt directly: "Holt, it will not do. All your plans will fail. The Jacobins are too poor, too few, and too dishonest to support you. . . . You have lately shifted from white paper to blue; you had better shift from blue to black, set your household in order, and like your great ancestor, *Judas Iscariot,* hang yourself." When yellow fever struck New London, forcing a bedridden Holt to suspend publication for nine weeks, the *Courant* cheered that the epidemic had done some good.[84]

A United States marshal came for Holt on a Saturday evening in September 1799 and arrested him for an allegedly seditious article printed in the *Bee* the previous May. The essay had raised the old whig moral objections to a standing army; the indictment charged Holt as "a wicked, malicious, seditious and ill-disposed person" purposely trying to stir up hatred against the government of the United States and to "excite an unlawful combination" against the laws designed to raise an army. The New London newspaperman spent three months in prison and paid $550 in expenses. According to Holt, the man who presented the offending issue of the *Bee* to the grand jury in Hartford and then sat on the trial jury and voted for conviction was none other than *Courant* editor George Goodwin.[85]

Even before Holt's arrest, Connecticut Republicans knew that a small and struggling paper like the *Bee* was not a sufficient forum for political dissent. Hartford's *Courant,* supported by moneyed arch-Federalists in power, boasted a subscription list of four thousand and a readership of several times that number in 1798. Other papers starting up in Connecticut quickly found, as one wit wrote, that if they wanted to keep subscribers on board they would have to sail

84. "Whip" and "An American Republican," in the *Bee,* June 14, 21, 1797. On July 19, 1797, the editor advertised his political section as "open to all parties"; Holt also introduced a column from the *Farmer's Weekly Museum* (Walpole, N.H.) called the "Lay Preacher," contending that, despite the author's "taint of European education, [and] tincture of aristocratical prejudices," the column was still profitable reading. Holt's explanation of his change of policy is in the *Bee,* Nov. 14, 1798. The "leprosy" reference is from an article first printed in another Federalist paper, the *Monitor,* and was reprinted in the *Conn. Courant,* Aug. 4, 1800. The reference to "sans-culottes" is in the *Conn. Courant,* Mar. 5, 1798, the reference to yellow fever is in Sept. 10, 1798, and *"Judas Iscariot"* is in July 29, 1799.

85. The allegedly seditious letter appeared in the *Bee,* May 8, 1799. The indictment, filed at the U.S. Circuit Court at Hartford, Sept. 17, 1799, was printed in the *Bee,* May 21, 1800 (Supplement). Holt's reference to Goodwin is in the *Bee,* Aug. 27, 1800, July 29, 1801. Ironically, one of Holt's attorneys was staunch Federalist David Daggett, and the prosecuting attorney was Republican Pierpont Edwards. For a discussion of the case, see James Morton Smith, "Political Suppression of Seditious Criticism: A Connecticut Case Study," *Historian,* XVIII (1955–1956), 41–56.

with the *Courant* rather than against it. The Reverend Stanley Griswold, a clergyman with Jeffersonian sentiments, sourly admitted that the *Courant* was
"the political thermometer of Connecticut." A frustrated Republican wrote to
the powerful Hartford paper in 1798 and tried to challenge the editors with
their old pretense to, at least, balanced reporting if not impartiality:

> You have long been considered . . . as entirely devoted to the court or aris-
> tocratic party—whose attempts to hoodwink the great body of the people,
> have been successful but too long. . . . A number of able and respectable men
> in this and other New-England states have of late, undertaken to offer their
> sentiments to the public on the great affairs of the nation. These are no
> hireling or party scribblers who act as second to some higher power . . . they
> are *determined* to be heard. They are sensible that your paper has an exten-
> sive circulation—you will therefore be requested to publish these senti-
> ments as they make their appearance.[86]

For Hudson and Goodwin, this was not a request to air a legitimate political
disagreement; it was a demand to broadcast the vile filth of Jacobinic treason,
anarchy, and atheism. They likened Republican discourse to the conspiratorial
mumbling of criminals, the ranting of madmen, and the howling of rabid
dogs. The Republicans in the state would have to be satisfied that Connecticut's
leading paper deigned to publish both sides of the Congressional debates.

As polemics drove partisans further apart, the newspaper a man read was
taken as a sign of his political affiliation—as a sign of his whole worldview, in
fact—and even the circulation of free papers was denounced as a political cam-
paigner's dirty trick. One newspaper correspondent declared that the whole
town of Suffield was dishonored because some of its citizens patronized opposition papers like the Philadelphia *Aurora* and the New London *Bee*. The excuse of liberally minded subscribers that they read several papers from various
points of view did not fool Dan Harrison, an angry writer in the Litchfield
Monitor. Furthermore, Harrison wrote, while subscription was a political
stigma, the distribution of gratis copies was even more reprehensible because
it could brand the innocent. Anxious because false publicity could so easily
ruin a man's reputation, Harrison was outraged that he had received an unso-
licited copy of a Republican paper from Richmond, Virginia. This tactic, he
wrote, had been borrowed from the leaders of the French Revolution and was

86. *American Mercury,* Jan. 3, 1799; *Conn. Courant,* Mar. 19, 1798, Griswold's third letter
to Congressman Joshua Coit, May 21, 1798. The *Conn. Courant*'s editors stated their position on Sept. 2, 1799: "Whenever persons are attacked in our paper, it is on *political,* not on
party grounds. . . . We are *partial* to government, order, and morals."

an attempt to make democrats in two ways: first, persuade weak minds by filling them with lies and misrepresentations about the government, or, second, start rumors at the post office about the political leanings of an innocent man who "finds himself suspected, and stigmatized as a *democrat*, till from mortification and resentment, he actually becomes one." Harrison's comments suggest the precarious relationship between private sentiment and public character. Not only could receiving a suspect newspaper publicize a misrepresentation of a person's political sentiments, but publicity could ultimately change those sentiments. The initially false public image could reconstitute the person's real inner character. Harrison might have been especially paranoid, but others, too, were concerned about what receiving papers in the mail signified to the public. The *Bee's* Charles Holt was accused of mailing out free copies and took the charge so seriously that he printed his sworn testimony, notarized by the mayor of New London, denying the accusation as a base slander.[87]

The very threat of disturbing Federalist control over Connecticut public discourse led to a brawl on the floor of the United States House of Representatives. Matthew Lyon was a fiery Republican from Vermont who as a youth had lived in Connecticut for a dozen years. On January 30, 1798, while in conversation on the floor of the House, Lyon bragged that he could effect a political revolution in the state if given six months and a printing press. Connecticut Congressman Roger Griswold overheard him and said that if Lyon tried to enter Connecticut he had better wear his wooden sword—an insulting reference to the Vermonter's dishonorable discharge during the Revolution. Lyon spat in Griswold's face. Federalists demanded Lyon's expulsion, one predicting that, if he was not driven from the House, it would be the last straw that the strained and divided political body could bear: the session would dissolve, the states would divide, and the country would be plunged into civil war. When the vote to expel Lyon fell short of the necessary two-thirds, Griswold, a Yale-trained lawyer, plotted his revenge. On February 16, on the floor of the House, right after prayers but before the session was called to order, he cracked Lyon several times over the head and shoulders with a large yellow hickory stick. After suffering a few more blows, Lyon grabbed some nearby fire tongs and lunged after Griswold. They ended up wrestling on the carpet, eventually dragged apart by fellow congressmen. A few minutes later, they were at it again over by the water table—this time Lyon had a cane and Griswold was without a weapon

87. *Conn. Courant*, Oct. 15, 1798, Aug. 19, 1799, Mar. 31, 1800 (reprinted from the Litchfield *Monitor* [Harrison's worries about being stigmatized probably explain why he had his own name, rather than a pseudonym, printed at the bottom of his letter]); *American Mercury*, Nov. 21, 1798; *Bee*, Apr. 4, 1798.

Figure 18. *Congressional Pugilists.* Philadelphia, 1798. Depicts the brawl on the floor of Philadelphia's Congress Hall between Congressmen Matthew Lyon, Republican from Vermont (holding the fire tongs), and Roger Griswold, Federalist from Connecticut (wielding a hickory cane). The fight began when Griswold heard Lyon say that he could cause a political revolution in Connecticut if he could operate a printing press there for six months. Courtesy, American Antiquarian Society, Worcester, Mass.

until a colleague threw him a walking stick from the crowd. As congressmen yelled "part them" and "don't part them," the speaker finally called the House to order.

The Republican and Federalist papers, each by this time addressing a readership trained to think that the opposition printed nothing but lies and distortions, viewed the scene from their opposing perspectives. A writer in the *Bee* taunted "the Honourable Roger Spittle, esq.," declaring: "If the frost had been severe enough to congeal the *saliva,* it might have been carried through the state, like relics in a catholic country, to engage the worship of cowards. . . . The people of Connecticut had rather have heard that you fell dead by a pistol shot." Griswold's refusal of Lyon's challenge to a duel after the second altercation, another correspondent wrote, revealed typical Federalist cowardice. Republicans denounced the move to expel Lyon, who had merely been defending his honor, as a Federalist conspiracy and suggested that the speaker of the house had helped plot the assault on the House floor. Writers in the Federalist press awarded wooden swords to members who voted against expulsion and threatened the *"Beast of Vermont"* himself with tarring and feathering if he ever set foot in Connecticut. A letter to the *Courant* warned that Lyon's remark about revolutionizing the state with newspapers might give credence to the rumor that Philadelphia Republicans were plotting to flood Connecticut with democratic propaganda. In the Litchfield *Monitor,* a writer used the incident to get out the Federalist vote: "It is presumed, that every man, who does not choose to be spit upon by a vile democrat Irishman—who wishes to preserve the government, to protect his life, family, and property from the horrors of anarchy, and the modern French tyranny," would do the right thing. The Griswold-Lyon affair could be considered a fitting emblem for the state of late-eighteenth-century Connecticut politics: discourse in many cases had become the verbal equivalent of spitting and caning.[88]

Unlike the Yale college play, the century did not end with the voice of reason neutralizing political enthusiasm and dissolving partisan division. In the play, Mr. Writer reveals the truth about character, and Philanthropos admits that his advocacy of new political men and measures in the name of "the people" was a mistake. Mr. McPherson and Mr. Irvin warn about "partisan politicians" and "private characters" who "assume the liberty of censuring with impunity our Continental and state bodies of legislation," and they exit the stage with the "hope that there is so much Virtue in the people of the United States of America, that they will despise the base insinuations of designing men." In late-eighteenth-century Connecticut, however, audiences heard voices who invoked reason but seemed more intent upon arousing political passions. There was no easy way to peer beneath the screen of language, and the relationship between real character and rhetorical disguise seemed more indiscernible than ever. To speakers and writers on both sides of the ideological divide, public writing was not a transparent, neutral medium of communication, a tool for enlightenment; it was a way to censure an opponent, a cane for clubbing an antagonist. The century ended with impassioned writers creating very different Federalist and Republican scripts for the new nation's political theater. Like the Yale boys in the competing fraternal societies, however, the gentlemen who wrote the language and played the leading roles were often very much alike.

88. *Bee,* Feb. 28, Mar. 7, 1798; *Conn. Courant,* Mar. 12, Apr. 2, 1798 (reprinted from the Litchfield *Monitor*).

Conclusion

The New Politics of Revolution and Steady Habits

Two New Haven orators in 1801 looked back upon the previous century and assessed both America's Revolutionary transformation and New England's steady habits. Timothy Dwight's *Discourse on Some Events of the Last Century,* delivered at the First Church in January, focused on change. He began by contrasting the obscure fringe of settlements on the edge of European civilization in 1700 with the rising American empire of 1800. Five of the united states were then but an uncivilized wilderness, he told his audience. Eighty thousand New Englanders had multiplied to nearly a million and a quarter, to say nothing of the tens of thousands who had emigrated to other states. Connecticut, then with 28 towns, now had 108. By any measure, the record showed tremendous growth and increased prosperity. But by "far the most interesting and prominent characteristic of the past Century," intoned the Yale president, was a change that could not be measured in figures from the census report or the customhouse. A more ominous change, a transformation in "religious character" and "habits of thinking," had affected not just Connecticut, New England, or America but the whole Christian world. Turning to the chaos and moral ruin of France, Dwight described the dangers of truly revolutionary change— a world turned upside down by the rise of infidel philosophy. New Englanders' only hope was in their inheritance: the laws, institutions, customs, and, most especially, the faith of their fathers.[1]

For Republican orator Abraham Bishop, speaking two months after Dwight at the Wallingford festival celebrating Thomas Jefferson's inauguration as president, these same New England steady habits had helped thwart the change promised by the American Revolution. Instead of joining the march toward equality and human rights, New England ended the eighteenth century just as

---

1. Timothy Dwight, *A Discourse on Some Events of the Last Century* . . . (New Haven, Conn., 1801), 18–19.

it had begun it: dominated by the same kinds of elite "political and clerical adventurers" who were engaged in "the same eternal struggle for power and wealth." An aristocracy continued to dupe the populace with tricks that were already old when similar "friends of order" condemned Christ as a revolutionary. For Bishop, New England's only hope was in abandoning its steady habits for the enlightened American politics of Jefferson and the spirit of democracy that was sweeping across Europe.[2]

Dwight and Bishop had evidence for both continuity and change right outside their study windows in New Haven. The city itself bore the marks of a lingering colonial past and yet clearly manifested signs of change that pointed to a future beyond the imagination of the town's Puritan founders. The New Haven that François Alexandre Frédéric, duc de La Rochefoucauld-Liancourt, described at the end of the eighteenth century sounded much like the one Sarah Kemble Knight had visited almost a hundred years earlier: the simple town green in the center of nine squares, the wharves and warehouses facing the shallow port, the surrounding small farms; a society without the extremes of dire poverty and opulent wealth; a generally sober and industrious people, like New Englanders elsewhere, though less refined and more "rigid and zealous in the discharge of their religious duties" than in Boston. Merchants and shopkeepers still bartered with their neighbors, farmers still read their almanacs, and mariners still read the seas. If the pace of life had quickened, the daily activities of many of New Haven's—and New England's—citizens remained much the same.[3]

But when Sarah Knight came to New Haven in 1704, the center of town had been marked by a single wooden meetinghouse with a painted roof, a single central space for the meetings of the town, the church, and, every October, the lower house of the colony's legislature. By 1800, the architecture on and around the New Haven town green proclaimed that church and state were close neighbors but distinct institutions and that religion, though still a dominating presence at the center of town life, was fragmented into competing denominations. Three structures stood next to each other on Temple Street in the center of the green. The brick First Church where Dwight spoke had replaced the old Puritan wooden meetinghouse in 1756. The dignified Georgian courthouse and statehouse had been constructed in 1763, as British American optimism

2. Abraham Bishop, *Oration Delivered in Wallingford . . .* (New Haven, Conn., 1801), 12, 29.

3. [François Alexandre Frédéric], duc de La Rochefoucauld-Liancourt, *Travels through the United States of North America . . .* , 2 vols., trans. H. Neuman, I (London, 1799), 509–537 (quotation on 536); [Sarah Kemble Knight], *The Journal of Madam Knight* (1704) (New York, 1935), 29–45.

soared after the fall of New France. The white Fair Haven Church had been built in 1770 by separating parishioners alienated by the New Divinity strictures on church membership preached by Jonathan Edwards, Jr. Two other churches faced the southeast and southwest corners of the green: the blue White Haven meetinghouse, whose congregation dated from a schism following the Awakening, and the Episcopalian Trinity Church, which, when built in 1753, strengthened the convictions of Connecticut's Standing Order Congregationalists that they had to worry less about post-Awakening Separatism and more about the growth of Anglicanism. Although at the end of the eighteenth century Congregationalists still outnumbered the members of all other denominations in the state combined, religious diversity was a fact of life. New Haven had received families of Catholics and Jews in the 1760s and 1770s and, by the 1790s, was witnessing the rapid growth of Baptists and Methodists.[4]

Commercial expansion and development also reshaped Connecticut's physical and cultural landscape, although the pace of change was much slower in more isolated rural communities than in larger towns like New Haven. By 1800, Connecticut was no longer a sleepy economic backwater; it had become integrated into the national and international economies. The city of New Haven, politically set apart from the largely rural township when it was incorporated in 1784, quickly came under the control of local merchants, who planted elms along the avenues and beautified the green by removing bushes, filling in wagon ruts, and fencing it off from messy herds of geese and swine. Stagecoaches arrived at and departed from a busy office on Church Street over roads and bridges in every direction that had been improved by the twenty-three Connecticut turnpike companies formed since 1795. The port had been booming since the expansion of the West Indies trade in the early 1790s, and by 1800 a fleet of twenty ships, each more than 250 tons and with crews of at least forty men, sailed from New Haven to the South Seas and China. By 1798, the city had 600 houses and 170 shops, up from 470 homes and 103 stores a decade earlier. Eli Whitney, whose Yankee ingenuity had produced the cotton gin that would change the economic future of the country, had a federal contract and a two-story gun factory two miles from the center of town, a business that employed twenty people and operated according to new ideas about mass production and interchangeable parts. The New Haven Cotton and Woolen Manufactory had a four-story building and employed fifty people.[5]

4. Rollin G. Osterweis, *Three Centuries of New Haven, 1638–1938* (New Haven, Conn., 1953).

5. Gaspare John Saladino, "The Economic Revolution in Late Eighteenth Century Connecticut" (Ph.D. diss., University of Wisconsin, 1964), 170, 257, 280, 312, 324, 354, 371; Oster-

New and old buildings, new and old institutions together greeted the dawn of the nineteenth century. The representatives who sat in the statehouse each October still operated under the 1662 charter, but the commissioner who sat in the customhouse a few blocks away occupied an important and lucrative position appointed by the president of the United States. The parishioners who attended the Congregational churches and heard the old Calvinist creed each Sabbath invested in the new bank, took out policies from the new insurance company, and perhaps even attended the new theater. Yale College, whose handsome brick buildings faced the green from College Street, enrolled as many students in a single year as the school had graduated in its first thirty years of existence, but, though it still supplied Congregational pulpits, more of its graduates headed for careers in law, medicine, and business.[6]

The thriving port, the improved roads, the political and economic ties to the federal government and international trade, all opened New Haven and Connecticut generally to a traffic not just in goods but in ideas. Like the towns and cities of the state, its books, speeches, sermons, pamphlets, and newspapers preserved many of the forms and attitudes of the Puritan past even as they opened onto a Yankee future. Booksellers offered election, fast, thanksgiving, funeral, and ordination sermons as well as discourses describing regeneration and revival, faith and the Judgment Day. Printers republished Calvinist catechisms and dissertations on the damnation of sinners. But the newspapers were filled with political essays. The libraries stocked their shelves with fiction, fables, travels, and histories. Printers published for Baptists and Freemasons as well as for Congregational clergymen; they sold satirical verse, political polemics, elocution manuals, and novels as well as almanacs, hymnals, and devotional tracts.[7]

Dwight looked at the world around him in 1801 and decried religious infidelity, but his chief sign of declension was the new radical politics of the post-Revolutionary age; Bishop inveighed against the entrenched power of the Connecticut aristocracy, but the boldness of his critique attested to the emergence

weis, *Three Centuries of New Haven*, 191. See also Charles H. Levermore, "The Town and City Government of New Haven," in Herbert B. Adams, ed., *Johns Hopkins University Studies in Historical and Political Science*, IV (Baltimore, 1886), 445–543; William L. Philie, *Change and Tradition: New Haven, Connecticut, 1780–1830* (New York, 1989).

6. Dwight, *Discourse on Some Events of the Last Century*, 14.

7. Early American Imprints, 1st Ser., Connecticut Imprints for 1799, 1801 (typescript courtesy of the American Antiquarian Society, Worcester, Mass.); Hudson and Goodwin, books for sale, in *Connecticut Courant* (Hartford), Dec. 9, 1799; *The Constitution and Bye-Laws of the Mechanic Library Society of New-Haven, with a Catalogue of Books and List of the Proprietors* (New Haven, Conn., 1793).

of a new political vision. Although each man paid close attention to economic changes and the progress of the arts and sciences through the eighteenth century, it was the partisan politics of the 1790s, more than anything else, that shaped their understanding of the century that had just drawn to a close.

THE NEW POLITICS

Although Connecticut's electoral practices and governmental institutions remained unchanged through the Revolution and the era of new constitutions, and, although compared to other states Connecticut was considered to be a bastion of political stability, many citizens felt that they were in the midst of a *new* politics and worried (or hoped) that they were teetering on the brink of even more profound change. People were defining themselves ideologically by professing their national and even international affiliations: federalism and England, republicanism and France. They struggled for political power locally by increasingly employing "electioneering" tactics to sway public opinion and influence the vote.[8]

The new politics of late-eighteenth-century Connecticut was about much more than voting and national policy; it threatened to redefine social life. Observers in the middle to late nineties seemed stunned and often worried about the popularity of political discussion and the interest in political news. "There is at all times among our people a curiosity to know the state of politics, and especially the temper of Congress," a writer in 1794 remarked. In 1797, according to one newspaper column, political writers and politicians were more in vogue than ever. People were conversing about politics in every public house and meeting place. On sunny mornings, they would be out by their shops, barns, and fences, even in the middle of the street, preoccupied with talk of aristocrats, Jacobins, and the fate of the Republic. By 1799, writers marveled at

8. Historians have argued about whether the politics of the 1790s gave birth to the first modern American political parties, or whether it is better characterized as the continuation of eighteenth-century patterns: deferential voters, noncompetitive elections, and legislative blocs' coalescing around cosmopolitan-commercial and localist-agricultural interests. See, for example, Richard Buel, Jr., *Securing the Revolution: Ideology in American Politics, 1789–1815* (Ithaca, N.Y., 1972); and Ronald P. Formisano, *The Transformation of Political Culture: Massachusetts Parties, 1790s–1840s* (New York, 1983). Certainly, when compared to the party machinery, popular participation, and enthusiasm for egalitarian democracy in the 1840s, late-eighteenth-century political culture seems closer to the elitist, patriarchal, court-versus-country mold from which it sprang. But the political actors themselves, of course, did not know that Alexis de Tocqueville's America was on the horizon.

"the present rage for Politics," where people were so frequently harangued in partisan orations, sermons, and newspapers, and where "every man seems to think himself born a Legislator and is generally so tenacious of his own darling sentiment that unless it is adopted, he is continually complaining." A traveler through the state in 1800 found someone preaching politics in almost every inn and tavern he entered. But perhaps the most revealing remark came from "Justinian" in the *American Mercury*, who argued that the new politics had even corroded the polite conversations of visiting parties. People now rarely spoke about religious or moral topics, he wrote, as they had thirty years before. If such topics did come up, young men, instead of listening quietly to their wise elders, turned the discussion into a forensic debate. Justinian believed that such manners had been shaped by the new demagogic methods of pursuing political power. Although these writers might have exaggerated the pervasiveness of political awareness in their society, they registered a growing interest and intensifying commitment that threatened to transfigure social relationships and infuse new sentiments into the common exchanges of daily life.[9]

The partisan nature of this political enthusiasm developed as New Englanders increasingly imagined themselves affiliated with national or even international political communities and felt compelled to exhibit these new political identities to their neighbors. The Connecticut press helped draw attention to national and foreign affairs. As the proceedings of the British Parliament and the French National Convention filled local papers, some men quickly and publicly recoiled from the radical turn taken by the French Revolution and old friends like Thomas Paine in 1793; others, like those in New London who celebrated French success in January 1794 with cannons, flags, and bells, continued to proclaim their support for French republicanism and the universal brotherhood of man. In 1796, after the press printed the angry legislative debates over John Jay's overly accommodating treaty with Great Britain, Connecticut writers began openly debating the possibility of dissolving the Union. The Adams administration's military buildup in 1798 was answered by supportive holy-war rhetoric and denounced in the tones of the old Country Party opposition to standing armies. Connecticut senator Uriah Tracy notoriously called for "a war of extinguishment" against the infidel French, and the newly formed Norwalk Republican Society proclaimed that it was prepared to fight to the death for the rights of man. Remonstrances for and against war with

9. *Conn. Courant*, Jan. 6, 1794, "Justinian," Oct. 13, 1800; "The Olio—No. IX," *Norwich Packet* (Conn.), June 8, 1797, Aug. 1, 1799, Oct. 21, 1800; *Journal of the Times* (Stonington, Conn.), Apr. 30, Sept. 3, 1799. See also *American Mercury* (Hartford, Conn.), Aug. 7, 1797 (reprinted from the *Farmer's Weekly Museum* [Walpole, N.H.]); *Norwich Packet*, Oct. 10, 1797.

France were circulated, and town meetings were held, pressuring people to signify their sentiments.[10]

As former allies joined opposing political camps in the 1790s, the common Revolutionary vocabulary—and the shared sensibility it had helped sustain—split apart. New Year's verse in the *American Mercury*'s first issue of 1799 put it this way:

> Strange changes! this [the Revolution] no sooner's done,
> Than *Whig terms* out of fashion run.
> Dame *Liberty* and *Rights of Man*
> Are slid down hill with *Thomas Paine.*
> *Democracy* and civil *Level*
> Are swiftly packing to the Devil.

Republicans still spoke of liberty and rights, but in a broader context of the international movement that had grown since the American calls for Independence a quarter-century before. They also invoked the Revolutionary ardor of 1776, with an added emphasis on equality. Federalists, because they thought "liberty" had become a code word for licentiousness and anarchy, stressed virtuous order and good government. They played down the idea that the Revolution had ushered in any kind of social or moral transformation and instead venerated the Constitution as the symbol of national identity. Like a writer in the Litchfield *Monitor* in 1800, Federalists warned that democrats were trying to "revolutionize" the state, and they urged Connecticut citizens to waken to the spirits of their fathers: "Kneeling before your altars, swear that you WILL maintain the *peace,* the *purity,* the *union,* the *stability,* the *order,* and the *reli-*

10. "The American," nos. 1, 2, *Conn. Courant,* Jan. 7, 14, 1793, criticizes the French and Thomas Paine; the New London "democratic sabbath" was reported and satirized in the *Conn. Courant,* Jan. 27, 1794. On Connecticut disunionism, see, for example, "Pelham," *Conn. Courant,* Nov. 21, Dec. 12, 1796 (reprinted Mar. 9, 26, Apr. 9, 1798), "Gustavus," Aug. 14, 21, Sept. 4, 11, 1797; see also John Hastings Chatfield, "'Already We Are a Fallen Country': The Politics and Ideology of Connecticut Federalism, 1797–1812" (Ph.D. diss., Columbia University, 1988), chap. 1. Tracy reportedly made his genocidal remarks while debating a bill annulling all treaties with France, June 23, 1798 (*Bee* [New London, Conn.], July 4, 1798). The *Bee* also noted that the *Conn. Courant* had reprinted the following sentiment by Peter Porcupine: "The *sword* and the *word* have often co-operated, and such a co-operation is at this time more necessary than ever. There ought to be, and there must be a real *Crusade,* a *Holy War* against the infidel reprobate French. To kill one of them in the field of battle will merit more in the eyes of God than praying and singing psalms for a hundred years" (July 25, 1798). The *Bee* printed the "Introduction to the Constitution of the Norwalk Republican Society" on Apr. 4, 1798, and discussed the remonstrances and town meetings on May 16, 1798.

gion of your ANCESTORS." Republicans labored toward a different sort of political awakening in Connecticut, toward a time when the scales would fall from citizens' eyes and they would "shake off the burthen, unjustly imposed upon them by the *'steady habits'* of PRIESTS, TORIES and FEDERALISTS."[11]

Federalists anxiously scrutinized public discourse for what they considered to be Jacobinic phraseology. Like the malicious critics that the poet John Trumbull had complained about, or like Timothy Dwight finding hints of infidel philosophy disguised in a footnote or a casual aside, Federalist critics scanned the surface of language for clues of a writer's or speaker's real motives. At a July Fourth celebration in New York, Yale professor Josiah Meigs was prompted to make some remarks about the bones of patriots who had suffered on British prison ships during the war. Noah Webster charged that this untimely reminder of British cruelty was actually a veiled political blast at the Anglophile Adams administration. Meigs responded in the *Courant* that he had had high hopes for the French Revolution, but that did not mean he had any less regard for the Constitution or the president. Besides, he wrote, "it has not, till very lately been unlawful for every citizen to express his opinion, what ever that opinion might be, of *public* measures, and the *public* conduct of *public* men." Webster answered that Meigs's seemingly impromptu speech had in fact been a premeditated Jacobin scheme and that by complaining about infringements upon his rights of free speech—an obvious swipe at the Sedition Act—he had shown the "cloven foot" once again.[12]

A July Fourth oration tainted with republicanism provided the opportunity for the *Courant* to publish an elaborate critique of democratic rhetoric and its thinly disguised political heresy. The *Courant*'s editors reported in 1799 that boys had been trained to deliver seditious July Fourth orations in Suffield. Gideon Granger, the Suffield Republican leader who had published a cautiously inoffensive Independence Day address two years earlier, wrote back defending the oration recently delivered by a youth named John Smith. Granger enclosed a copy of Smith's speech and challenged the paper to print it to let the public judge its honest patriotism. The editors did so, along with a lengthy rebuttal that occupied two issues. "Mr. S. evidently has taken for a model, the

11. "Ode on Ends; or, The Boy's Address Who Carries the American Mercury," *American Mercury*, Jan. 3, 1799; "To the People of Connecticut," *Conn. Courant*, Aug. 18, 1800 (reprinted from *Monitor* [Litchfield, Conn.]); "Brutus," *The Patriot; or, Scourge of Aristocracy* (Stonington, Conn.), Aug. 14, 1801. Other republican use of the phrase "steady habits," made popular in Governor Jonathan Trumbull's 1799 address to the Assembly, includes the editor's column in the *American Mercury*, Jan. 29, 1801; "On Steady Habits," *Bee*, Feb. 25, 1801, "Electioneering," Apr. 8, 1801; "An 'Ancient Habit' of Connecticut," *Patriot*, July 24, 1801.

12. Josiah Meigs letter, *Conn. Courant*, Oct. 15, 1798, response by "Odin," Oct. 22, 1798.

compositions of Revolutionary France," the critic charged. "There is a long display of such words and expressions as *philanthropy, energies, despotism, elements of society, rights of man, moral rectitude, relations of man, equal liberty, equality of nature,* etc. etc. These words in the mouth of a modern Republican, are intended only to impose upon the uninformed part of mankind." The critic found subversive intent lurking right below the surface of this supposedly patriotic oration. Smith's reference to government's rising from a state of nature where vices were "thinly sown" was actually a repudiation of the Calvinist doctrine of original depravity, making "a Savage" more virtuous "than the citizen of New-England." The audience or readers, the critic argued, should not be fooled by the young man's criticism of the British funding system and censorship laws, for "across the shoulders of poor Great Britain, our Government is flaggellated."[13]

A favorite Federalist technique for shooting down a democrat, once one had been flushed out in the open, was to expose his foolish attempts at argumentation and pick apart the ungrammatical ineptitude of his address. The Federalist "Whip" lashed a Republican opponent for not studying Demosthenes, Cicero, or English grammar; a Federalist paper spent forty lines sneering at the *Bee's* editor for misspelling "liquorice": "Mr. C. Holt, printer and democrat, gives us a fine specimen of the learning of his Publican tribe." The *Courant's* critic of John Smith's Suffield oration spent nearly half of his long essay playing the pedant and trying to prove that "the English language can scarcely furnish a work of no greater length than this Oration, with so many faults." Apparently, by ridiculing mistakes in pronoun reference and mixed metaphors like a sadistic schoolmaster, the critic hoped to show that men like Smith had no right to address the public, a privilege that should be reserved for the (Federalist) literary elite.[14]

Republicans like Abraham Bishop turned the Federalists' claim of linguistic and rhetorical expertise against them. Although Bishop had a Yale degree

13. Ibid., July 29, 1799 (the paper assured its readers that measures were being taken to have such speakers thrown into prison), Aug. 3, 1799; Gideon Granger, *An Oration, Spoken on Tuesday, the Fourth of July, 1797, at the East Meeting-House in Suffield: Being the Anniversary of American Independence* (Suffield, Conn., 1797). Smith's oration appeared in the *Conn. Courant,* Aug. 12, 19, 1799, the critic's "Remarks" on Aug. 19, 26. The editors defended their publication of the long and tedious critique on Sept. 2: "The critical remarks upon [the Oration], we think neither '*unnecessary,*' nor '*superfluous,*' as the Oration might *without them,* have been productive of some mischief; at least its character might not have been truly appreciated."

14. *Bee,* July 19, 1797; Federalist criticism of Holt's spelling is reprinted in *Bee,* Jan. 2, 1799; *Conn. Courant,* Aug. 19, 26, 1799.

and legal training himself, he charged that the learned men who dominated public discourse and who knew their grammar and their Cicero were chiefly responsible for propping up the system of political delusion that kept the lower nine-tenths of the population subservient to the upper tenth. Lawyers had somehow persuaded the people "that those who talk fluently must be knowing—and that through much debating cometh truth." Clergymen "always had address enough" to preserve their own interests, and knew how to cry, "THE CHURCH IS IN DANGER!" to rally the electorate to their cause. "These great men, who are to gain by every system injurious to freedom and equal government, are the *best informed* men in society. They are well versed in languages and history and political science, and are able to say *more,* and argue *better* on the wrong side of the question than the people are on either side of it." Such men perverted their powers of reason and eloquence to exalt themselves; their honeyd words painted pictures of happiness and prosperity while they picked the people's pockets. Learned eloquence, the liberally educated Bishop told his audience eloquently, was a sign of manipulation.[15]

When these "eloquent patriots" called the Constitution a fence around liberty, Bishop warned, their words should set off alarm bells. Language could not be fixed firmly enough to protect rights; a written document could not guard against abuses of power. "That constitution is perhaps as well wrought as language would admit; but language is very elastic. The men, whose interest it is to stretch it to the extent are, or have made themselves, the judges of it. They know well the force and power of every word—the east, west, north and south of every semicolon and can extract power from every dash or asterism." Since language was inherently elastic, good government and civil liberty could not be preserved by the professional masters of documents, letters, and law; these experts in legal obfuscation and rhetorical equivocation would always bend words to suit their interests. The people had to look behind the letter of the law

15. Abraham Bishop, *Connecticut Republicanism: An Oration on the Extent and Power of Political Delusion* . . . ([New Haven, Conn.?], 1800), 22, 27, 37, 39. "Philoveritas," a writer in the *Bee,* blamed the British bias and tendency to mix church and state found in New England congressmen upon their college education and legal training. They "are generally sons of a collegiate education, and have been in the usual manner hurried through the various fields of classic syllogisms, problems, propositions, and questions, at an age in which that maturity of judgment which is necessary to determine the most important of them accurately (being the result of much experience and observation) could not be expected." Their studies in ethics and law taught them how to construct warped systems from laying down first principles, and their studies from the English law libraries in every attorney's office inclined them toward the former mother country ("Adams's Defence of the American Constitutions," *Bee,* Jan. 29, 1800).

to the spirit—to *their* spirit, *their* sentiments. They had to see behind the life-less words that the elite arranged so artfully to realize that the life of a nation exists, not in a written document, but in the hearts and minds of the sovereign people. Despite what the public had been told, the Constitution was not a "sacred bulwark," Bishop argued: "You, the people, must be the bulwark of that Constitution, or it will never preserve your rights: your sentiments, your actions, your very souls must animate that constitution and give life and effects to its language. When the spirit of the people is lulled by the soft zephyrs of Delusion into security in the lap of the constitution—when it relies on inanimate paper for security of rights, that people is in the first stage of slavery." [16]

The Federalists' political delusion, the Republicans maintained, also relied on their viselike control over public speech and print. Connecticut Federalists were not only masters of legal language and persuasive rhetoric; they also controlled the social practices sustaining public discourse—the distribution of publications and the occasions for public address—so thoroughly as to nearly silence expressions of dissent. Charles Holt, editor of the *Bee,* claimed that Gideon Granger, perennial Republican congressional candidate, did not get votes in towns "where the avenues to political information are guarded with Cerberian vigilance, and republican newspapers held contraband by authority. . . . [and] especially in those towns where he has been vilified by name from the pulpit." The Federalist postmaster in Litchfield, according to Holt, banished *Bee* subscribers from the post office; in Middletown, opponents threatened to publish the names of subscribers, holding them up to all their neighbors as Jacobins. Holt also reported that Federalists tried to harass the post riders who carried his paper and prevented anyone connected with the state government from doing business with him, "some even avowing it to be their duty . . . to discourage the paper." Other Republicans pointed to the ways that Federalists had manipulated public occasions for their partisan purposes. Election day, when the Standing Order clergy (Federalist almost to a man) marched and dined with the magistrates at the public's expense and then flattered the civil rulers from the pulpit, was an annual scene of irritation. Republicans also found the Yale commencement so viciously partisan after 1798 that they finally boycotted the affair in 1803. But nothing irked Republicans more than the July Fourth celebrations that, Abraham Bishop argued, "have been perverted into days for chastising the enemies of [the] administration." [17]

16. Bishop, *Connecticut Republicanism,* 31, 33.
17. *Bee,* June 5, 19, 1799, Oct. 7, 1801, June 23, 1802; Bishop, *Connecticut Republicanism,* 43. On the boycott of commencement, see Franklin Bowditch Dexter, *Biographical Sketches of*

Independence Day rituals were intended to express—or enforce—public patriotism and political consensus. New Haven had celebrated the day in 1788 with "uncommon splendour" to mark the first July Fourth since the state's ratification of the Constitution. An elaborate parade displayed nearly every eighteenth-century trade and vocation: haymakers, butchers, coopers, and hatters marched with the tools of their trade; schoolmasters led their students, who read aloud from their books; cordwainers and blacksmiths went by in wagons, demonstrating their craft; physicians, Yale tutors, clergymen, and town officers brought up the rear. The day's theme was clearly portrayed by the model ship *Constitution,* pulled by boatbuilders through the streets, and by the silversmiths' urn, "beautifully engraved and spangled with ten stars emblematical of the ten States which had adopted the Constitution." Organizers had clearly tried to represent the components of a complex society working together in harmony. It was a harmony, a community, created by shared sentiments about the Constitution, and therefore political dissent could only be acknowledged as a perverse idiosyncrasy that was swept aside by the overwhelming will of the majority. According to the description in the press, "the most happy union of sentiment prevailed," and "an antifederalist would have been no more noticed on that day in the full blaze of federalism than the dim light of a taper in the midst of the bright luminaries of heaven." [18]

Public celebrations were usually far less elaborate, with simple processions that symbolically connected public spaces—courthouse, church, and coffeehouse or tavern—or, in some country towns, with even simpler promenades in the fields. Some towns ignored the Fourth altogether, like the small towns of Bozrah until 1799 and Berlin before 1800. Norwich did not mark the day before 1797, and a newspaper essayist had to argue that the celebration was not the useless custom that the locals thought it was: "You honor your country, you animate your children with a desire for History, and display to the nations of Europe, your political opinions, by reminding them that you yet remain an United people." A town could also "convince their fellow citizens of other towns" of its continuing devotion to the Republic. The Fourth became an important occasion in more and more towns and villages toward the end of the century, however, not just as an opportunity to demonstrate national unity,

the Graduates of Yale College with the Annals of the College History, 6 vols. (New York, 1885–1912), V, 623. On the politicization of such occasions, see Simon Peter Newman, "American Popular Political Culture in the Age of the French Revolution" (Ph.D. diss., Princeton University, 1991); David Waldstreicher, *In the Midst of Perpetual Fetes: The Making of American Nationalism, 1776–1820* (Chapel Hill, N.C., 1997).

18. *Conn. Courant,* July 14, 1788.

cultivate nationalistic affection, and honor the brave deeds of Revolutionary heroes but also as a ritual marginalization of political dissent.[19]

The Federalist orator's "great art" at these public occasions, according to Abraham Bishop, was to describe a character deformed by every possible vice, name him a Democrat (or Jacobin, or Republican), and then dub all holy men, past and present, as Federalists. Bishop did not exaggerate. Whereas Stonington planned an explicitly antipartisan commemoration in 1799, in the larger towns celebration became almost shrilly polemical. Litchfield townsmen heard Senator Tracy speak (a man dubbed "the exterminator" by the Republican press for his genocidal saber rattling) and then raised their glasses to support "non-resistance and passive obedience to the will of the majority." In Hartford, the orator flayed France, and the people toasted the Alien and Sedition Acts. In Norwich, the speaker celebrated "the genuine spirit of federalism" and warned of Jacobin intrigue and the Illuminati. Citizens in the town of Colebrook drank to *"Undeviating Federalism—May the democrats of Connecticut be transported to the Ancient Dominion."* But, since the Reverend Chauncey Lee's oration had just described Satan as the first Jacobin (and suggested that an American's failure to support the Adams administration was analogous to Adam and Eve's sin in the garden), the "Ancient Dominion" could have referred to either Virginia or hell. The Federalist press mentioned dissenting voices only rarely, and then only with ridicule. Federalist verse satirized vulgar, drunken Republican festivities that celebrated the guillotine and the "Southern Demos / Who represent our brother Negroes." A writer in the *Courant* was quick to deny reports that there had been a democratic celebration in Hebron, complete with French national cockades and seditious toasts, assuring the paper's Federalist readers that there was only a small, motley handful of democrats in town—a young merchant, a post rider, a blacksmith, a seventeen-year-old boy, and "two or three Negroes."[20]

Just as more and more July Fourth orations were printed as pamphlets and excerpted in the weekly newspapers in the late nineties, the lists of formal toasts given at these occasions were prominently featured in reports of the day's events. The *Courant* printed toasts from around the nation, claiming in 1799

19. "Olio, No. XI," *Norwich Packet,* June 29, 1797, "The Celebration of American Independence," July 11, 1799; *American Mercury,* July 10, 1800.

20. Bishop, *Connecticut Republicanism,* 44; *Journal of the Times,* July 9, 1799; *American Mercury,* Aug. 6, 1798 (reprinted from the *Farmer's Weekly Museum*), July 11, 1799; *Norwich Packet,* July 11, 1799; *Conn. Courant,* July 14, 1800; Chauncey Lee, *The Tree of Knowledge of Political Good and Evil: A Discourse Delivered at Colebrook, on the Twenty-Fourth Anniversary of American Independence, July 4th, 1800* (Hartford, Conn., 1800).

that they could be read like a political barometer: "Toasts, are the touchstone of politics in this country. We here learn the true sentiments of the people." Despite finding a few scattered Jacobin phrases, the editors concluded that the toasts showed strong support for the federal administration, abhorrence of France, reverence for religion, and approval of the new navy and the Alien and Sedition Acts. But Abraham Bishop argued that this toasting business was another of the Federalist's "delusive arts." The toasts were set in advance by a committee made up of each town's little Federalist aristocracy; no spontaneous sentiments could be offered during the feasts, and the man who did not raise his glass was hissed at as a Jacobin. Toasting was simply one more example of how Federalists controlled the social means of production of public speech and print. The *Bee* denied that the wine-soaked declarations by partisans "scorched with the fever of party rage" could legitimately represent public opinion. The New London paper, though, printed Republican toasts praising liberty, a free press, and religious toleration when it could get them. The editor also delighted in publishing examples of Federalist extremism, like the toast from Massachusetts that suggested making boots for the federal army from the skins of Frenchmen.[21]

When Federalists at the national level divided between the Hamiltonians and Adams's supporters, local Republicans thought they saw an opening and threw themselves into the effort to break the aristocratic lock upon Connecticut. Their covert tactics and open electioneering sent a chill through their Federalist opponents. An "Independent Elector" recognized that Republicans had become more daring in 1800: "Besides sending forth their rhetorical Missionaries to harangue the people in clubs and taverns, and exhibiting the best samples of their candidates for the Congress and Council in public show throughout the principle towns in the state, they have had the assurance to send out a printed list . . . as a *Voter's Guide.*" Such "impudent and dangerous" practices, the writer warned, would ultimately lead to the horror of rival candidates' openly soliciting votes. In June, the *Courant* reported, "a junto of second-rate lawyers and first rate Democrats" had met at Frick's Tavern in New London to plot strategy. Pierpont Edwards and his New York nephew Aaron Burr, the "prime movers in the Republican machine," reportedly visited the

21. *Conn. Courant,* July 22, 29, 1799; Bishop, *Connecticut Republicanism,* 50; *Bee,* July 31, 1799. The *American Mercury* started printing Republican toasts in 1800, and the editor wryly offered this explanation: "Most of the Editors of News Papers, in the United States, have served up to their customers a copious meal of *Toasts,* cooked for the 4th of July." But the best kind—mostly unknown in Connecticut—were made from Virginia wheat (*American Mercury,* July 17, 1800).

Democratic Societies of Stamford and Norwalk to rally their troops. An anxious Federalist traveler reported that he heard the same pandering Republican patter in tavern after tavern: "British influence—Standing Army—Direct Taxes—Funding System—Expensive Navy—Commerce can support itself—Congress have too high wages—Aristocracy—and Washington's Grave Stones." Republican candidate Gideon Granger was said to have spent the summer touring the state, ingratiating himself with the people and stirring up their animus against the government by complaining about high congressional salaries and burdensome taxes. An anonymous pamphlet by David Daggett charged that Abraham Bishop busily disseminated copies of his inflammatory oration on political delusion during the day and then distributed Republican nominations to area towns in the middle of the night.[22]

As election day neared, the New Haven opposition also dispatched candidates to different parts of the state and divided the city itself into districts for thorough canvassing right before the freemen's meeting. Republicans, the Federalist press concluded, had "ransacked every corner of the state and used every art that passion could dictate"; they called themselves "friends of the people" and had tried "to tamper with the lower class and the least informed of the freemen." In a frontal assault against Connecticut's customary political practices and its Federalist Standing Order, Republicans had imported the vulgar electioneering practices from Great Britain and the southern states, where "fair speeches and grog are furnished in abundance" on election day.[23]

Though obviously biased, this Federalist criticism clearly reveals Republican strategies in the face of the Federalists' continued domination of newspapers and public address. Silenced at formal occasions for public speech, Republicans spread their message through informal conversations in the sociable world of taverns and coffeehouses—like the Yale boys in their fraternal societies, who cultivated friendships and honed their speaking skills in private meetings even when prevented by the college authority from displaying their talents before a wider public audience. Outnumbered by Federalists in most towns, Republicans traveled like itinerant preachers and tried to build a translocal community of political dissent. Barred from publishing their opinions in the state's most-read newspapers, they covertly distributed campaign literature. Though usually elite and learned men themselves, democratic speakers fashioned a rhetoric that claimed to speak *for* the people, appealing to pop-

22. *Conn. Courant*, Sept. 1, 8, 1800; [David Daggett], *Three Letters to Abraham Bishop, Esquire, Containing Some Strictures on His Oration . . . with Some Remarks on His Conduct at the Late Election* (Hartford, Conn., 1800), 33–35.

23. *Conn. Courant*, Oct. 13, 1800, Feb. 2, 1801.

ular sentiments, flattering the capacities of the common man, arousing suspicions of aristocratic intrigue—"fair speeches," the Federalists worried, that could be as intoxicating as grog handed around on election day.

The Federalist Standing Order hoped that Connecticut's traditional electoral practices, which had always heavily favored incumbents, would negate the effects of Republican electioneering. Freemen assembled twice each year, in September and April, to vote for their representatives to the General Assembly. The twelve seats in the powerful upper house were elected in two stages (a system that was copied for the nomination and election of Connecticut's seven congressional seats as well). The statute stated that every freeman was to vote for twenty men for the Council during the fall nomination by writing out their names on a piece of paper, although towns altered this procedure by calling for a show of hands or dropping blank slips of paper into a hat. The twenty men with the most votes for the Council (and the fourteen for Congress) were then submitted to the towns in the spring for another vote. The names for the Council, however, were listed, not in order of the votes received, but in order of seniority. Freemen at the spring meeting received twelve slips of paper to elect assistants to the Council and seven slips for congressmen. As the names were read in order, the freemen turned in their votes. Lacking information about the policies and positions of candidates from other parts of the state, freemen tended to vote for the first names read. Therefore a man like Jonathan Ingersoll, a challenger who led the nomination for the upper house in the fall of 1790, was put at the bottom of the list in the spring and failed to attain a seat, whereas an incumbent like William Williams, who came in twentieth in the fall nomination but was listed at the top, was returned to office. If a voter wanted to cast a ballot for a nonincumbent, he would, in effect, be declaring his open rebellion against the Standing Order in front of his neighbors. It would be obvious if a voter held back one of his slips of paper as an incumbent's name was called. Only if the freeman sacrificed one of his votes by turning in a blank ballot could a man secretly express his disapproval of an incumbent.[24]

Other customs helped incumbents preserve their seats. Balloting for Council and Congress was not held until late in the day, after passions had been

24. *Conn. Courant*, Sept. 8, 1800. See Richard J. Purcell, *Connecticut in Transition: 1775–1818* (1918; reprint, Middletown, Conn., 1963), 127. Joy B. Gilsdorf and Robert R. Gilsdorf, in "Elites and Electorates: Some Plain Truths for Historians of Colonial America," in David D. Hall, John M. Murrin, and Thad W. Tate, eds., *Saints and Revolutionaries: Essays on Early American History* (New York, 1984), 207–244, argued persuasively that the "deference" operative in Connecticut elections was primarily a deference to political experience rather than to social or economic status.

spent on the election of deputies and after many of the less politically savvy had retired to the taverns. In one of the larger towns, it was reported, two-thirds of the freemen left the meeting before the votes for Congress came up. The freemen who did stay, according to Republicans, were carefully watched by the local Federalists running the meeting. The controlling powers made sure that an influential merchant sat in each pew with his creditors and any newly made freemen to direct their votes. Self-important men—sometimes the local Federalist sheriffs—patrolled the aisles, the opposition charged, with bunches of marked voting slips in their hands, which they submitted for unsuspecting freemen. Printed nomination lists, which freemen used by checking off names instead of having to write them out, had long been controversial, and each side charged the other with abuses. Federalists accused Republicans of printing several different counterfeit voting lists, trying to scatter votes and appeal to local interests; a Republican writer countered that prominent Federalists in Litchfield, including the law school's Tapping Reeve and three other lawyers, gathered at a printing office—on the Sabbath!—to fabricate voting tickets that left out the Republican candidates' names.[25]

In 1800, a writer in the *Norwich Packet* observed with foreboding: "So important an electioneering year was never known in this country, as the present. The Fate of America seems to hang by a thread." Republicans received votes that, in previous years, would have secured them seats in Congress and on the Council. But Federalists came to the polls in unprecedented numbers: the assistant who garnered the most votes had nearly two and a half times the leader's total in 1799. The leading Republicans placed eighth and ninth in the seven-seat congressional race, fourteenth and eighteenth in the contest for the upper house's twelve seats.[26]

The Federalist Standing Order had been shaken, but it was still standing. When the national electoral deadlock was finally broken in the spring of 1801, however, and Jefferson and Burr were proclaimed president and vice president,

25. *Conn. Courant*, May 12, Sept. 1, 1800; *Bee*, Apr. 18, 1798, May 1, 1799. The Council had introduced a bill preventing the circulation of nomination lists after an election upset in 1739–1740, but the bill failed in the lower house (Gilsdorf and Gilsdorf, "Elites and Electorates," in Hall, Murrin, and Tate, eds., *Saints and Revolutionaries*, 227). In response to the Republican campaigning of 1800, an electoral "reform" bill in 1801 further tightened Federalist control. Admission to freemanship would require written approval by the majority of the civil authorities and selectmen; freemen's meetings had to be presided over by an assistant, a justice, or a constable; to nominate, freemen had to stand up or raise their hands and be recognized; and voters dropped slips of paper, and tellers had to count their votes aloud (Purcell, *Connecticut in Transition*, 138–141).

26. *Norwich Packet*, May 20, 1800; Purcell, *Connecticut in Transition*, 150, 188.

Connecticut Democratic-Republicans had reason to celebrate. With strengthening ties to Jeffersonians in other states and federal support and patronage, they believed they would finally begin making inroads against the state's entrenched political elite. Hearing the news of Jefferson's victory upon his deathbed, Wallingford Republican Thaddeus Cook reportedly said, "I shall die in peace," and did. In Hartford on March 4, Republicans gathered on Charter Hill to fire sixteen rounds and cheer; in Killingworth, they fired rounds and toasted at intervals throughout the day, saluting the still-deluded New England states only after sundown. In Tolland, citizens enjoyed a public dinner at Smith's Tavern; in Norwich, men toasted at Lathrop's Inn. Suffield celebrated with music and feasting and another oration by John Smith. But the largest event was held in Wallingford, on March 11—the first of what would become an annual Republican festival.[27]

The Wallingford ceremony resembled election day and the Fourth of July; it combined the sentiments of Thanksgiving and a political rally. More than a thousand Republicans came from across the state, according to the *American Mercury;* the *Bee* claimed two thousand and added that many more would have attended but for the inclement weather. The day began with the sound of cannon and bells and the sight of a flag raised to the top of a one-hundred-foot liberty pole. After music and a prayer, Suffield lawyer and politician Gideon Granger read the Declaration of Independence. The Reverend Stanley Griswold offered a prayer and a sermon. A choir of fifty or sixty sang "The Gloomy Night before Us Falls." After a grand procession to Carrington's Inn and a feast complete with thoroughly Republican toasts, transparent paintings of Jefferson and Burr were illuminated in a vacant church building as the people sang patriotic songs like "Jefferson and Liberty." Pierpont Edwards then read the new president's inaugural address. Abraham Bishop, dubbed "the Connecticut Orator" after his famous address on political delusion the previous year, outdid himself with an oration "pronounced in a masterly and unequaled manner." The evening ended with a fireworks display.[28]

On the same day that Republicans celebrated in Wallingford, a group of New Haven Federalists rode out in the bad weather to a stagehouse where former president John Adams was staying on his way home to Quincy. Seventeen of them, including David Daggett and Noah Webster, had stayed late at a New Haven City meeting on fire safety after most of their fellow townsmen had gone home and had decided to compose an address to Adams on behalf of the city.

27. *American Mercury,* Mar. 12, 1801.

28. *Bee,* Mar. 4, 11, 25 (quotation), 1801; *American Mercury,* Mar. 5, 12, 26, 1801.

But Adams declined to receive them, and the address was not delivered. The *Bee* criticized this aborted performance with language that recalled a quarter-century of criticism about the "new politics" of Revolutionary and post-Revolutionary Connecticut. How dare this small group—this junto—try to manipulate a town meeting and presume to speak for the city of New Haven? Seventeen men in a city of 390 legal voters (about 165 of them Republican) and a population of 5,000 could not claim to speak for the sovereign people. The *Bee* also took the liberty of translating the address's lofty rhetoric into "plain republican English." These disgruntled Federalists came, not to show respect for the former president, but to demonstrate their hatred and contempt for the celebrating Republicans. The real meaning of the undelivered address, the critic argued, was to be found, not in the stage play of dignified gratitude and honor the Federalists had planned, but in the malevolent intent behind it.[29]

The opposition had not overturned the Standing Order, and would not for another fifteen years, but Federalists knew that politics and public discourse would never be quite the same. A sovereign people had demanded that government heed the public voice. Opposition leaders had their own rhetorical occasions. Political character appeared to be built less on local reputation and deference to long experience than upon speech making and a mastery of legal jargon. The press, rather than a forum for reasoned debate and the formation of consensus, had become a partisan weapon. National politics seemed to be the subject of every conversation, and electioneering seemed more blatant at each election. Still, a few might have questioned how different things really were—or, even, how different they would have been if the Republicans had taken control. Who had spoken at the Wallingford festival? Granger, Edwards, Griswold, Bishop—three prosperous lawyer-politicians and a minister, all with college degrees. Despite Bishop's forceful populist harangues, despite all the changes in political language and practice, some might have wondered why the people in power seemed so much the same.

In 1800, a twenty-five-year-old freeman decided that he wanted to attend his first election day in Hartford. Born at the beginning of the Revolution, he had come of age during a time of harsh partisanship. An avid reader of newspapers, he expected Federalists and Republicans to be vastly different political characters. At a tavern along the way, he noticed two sleek young gentlemen, finely attired—dressed like clergymen, he thought. Both were lawyers, and both were candidates for Congress, one a Federalist, the other a Republican. They each had silk purses "well replenished with cash" and seemed "as much alike

29. *Bee*, Mar. 25, May 20, 1801.

as twin brothers." He watched them ride off together toward Hartford, chatting happily.[30]

However, all the sermons, essays, dialogues, debates, and satirical verse that the young man had read in the press, which had led him to believe that the Federalists and Republicans were very different political animals with contrasting views of the world, cannot be dismissed as mere rhetoric masking the perpetuation of elite control. The partisan debates of the 1790s reflected many of the ways that public discourse in Connecticut had been transformed by the eighteenth century's evangelical preaching, legal reasoning, enlightened science, republican ideology, literary sensibility, and political press. Election sermons, once delivered as God's Word to his covenant people, were now considered by many to be polemical speeches deserving an answer in kind. The college-educated clergymen who preached them were not the only local speakers and writers respected for their scholarship, and, indeed, the intellectual caliber of the clergy had been openly questioned since the days of John Trumbull's *Progress of Dulness*. Some of the finely attired gentlemen attending the election day ceremonies were busily studying the sciences and the arts rather than theology. The scientist's experimental attitude, in fact, which had been promoted by Jared Eliot a half-century before, now inspired even unlettered Connecticut men to write tracts criticizing Isaac Newton. Some writers and speakers, like David Daggett, who penned a Swiftian satire of these philosophic farmers and other enthusiasts for Enlightenment science, wrote satirical essays and verse for newspapers that had become bitterly partisan. Many more who wrote for the press and spoke at public assemblies had mastered the style of the well-read lawyer, a style that Thomas Clap had exploited in the 1760s and that had come to dominate politics by 1800. The post-Revolutionary public speakers and writers had learned not only how to display their knowledge, wit, and professional expertise but had also learned how to appeal to the emotions; evangelical preachers, who had criticized scholarly sermons during the Awakening, were no longer the only ones who could arouse the passions of an audience.[31]

The sheer abundance and diversity of print and public speech had changed the very act of public address. Like so many preachers in the past, Timothy

30. "R.," *American Mercury,* May 29, 1800.

31. [John Trumbull], *The Progress of Dulness, Part First; or, The Rare Adventures of Tom Brainless . . .* (New Haven, Conn., 1772); Enos Blakeslee, *A System of Astronomy Wherein the Copernican System Is Refuted . . .* (Litchfield, Conn., 1794), which also determined that the Newtonian principle of gravitation was "groundless and absurd" (iv); David Daggett, *Sun-Beams May Be Extracted from Cucumbers, but the Process Is Tedious; an Oration, Pronounced on the Fourth of July, 1799 . . .* (New Haven, Conn., 1799).

Dwight addressed his audience of Yale students and members of the First Congregational Church in 1801 as if "the great Body of people in New England" were assembled before him. But other New Englanders, like Abraham Bishop, had come to resent ministers who still seemed to presume that they alone could define the meaning of New England, and these new voices derided the "multitudes gathered about the clergy, like children at a catechism, expecting oracular truths and infallible opinions even on secular subjects." Even "Pope" Dwight, though, seemed to realize that it was now too much of an "indulgence of imagination" to consider that his silent and reverent congregation could represent a vast harmonious, consensual New England public. He knew that the clergy could no longer easily claim to be New England's "speaking aristocracy" and that the "democracy" they addressed was fractious and anything but silent.[32]

Dwight believed that the public mind should be articulated by learned and godly men who had proven themselves to be the best and the brightest; Bishop dramatically renounced his affiliation to the elite and pledged to "join myself to the great community of unprivileged men" to serve as a voice of the people. Both men understood—and feared—that language, as Bishop had said, was elastic. They knew that the meanings given to the terms of public discussion were multiple and unstable and that the public they addressed had become increasingly diverse and complex. They realized that the ideas, values, and sentiments binding a community could not be easily regulated by a minister's or a magistrate's authoritative proclamations, which were answered, not by silent acquiescence, but by dialogue and debate. Nevertheless, despite the multiplicity of meaning and the fragmentation of cultural authority, the malleability of language still allowed those with the most access to public speech and print to shape public discussion and bend it to their own purposes. In 1800, those able to exploit the power of public discourse were still, for the most part, elite men like Dwight and Bishop. To do so, however, they had to appeal to the common sense and sentiments of people who were less likely than ever before to automatically acknowledge their authority to speak for God or good government. There was still a large audience for learned and pious men who, like Dwight, called New England to its steady habits. But there were other audiences, too, and other speakers and writers who had learned other lessons from the revolutions of the eighteenth century and now demanded to be heard.[33]

32. Dwight, *Discourse on Some Events of the Last Century*, 42; Bishop, *Oration Delivered in Wallingford*, 87.

33. Bishop, *Oration Delivered in Wallingford*, 107 (appendix).

Orations, circulated manuscripts, and publications in eighteenth-century Connecticut, as in many other places in eighteenth-century Europe and America, reveal the complicated and shifting realms of public and private experience. To speak of a single "sphere" or "public" is perhaps inaccurate, although eighteenth-century writers did just that. Historians have come to speak instead of many "publics" in complex relationships to each other, to the state, and to private life, which itself is constructed in various ways. Clearly, a simple opposition of public and private domains will not do. Private societies like Freemasonry had a public face (open to inspection by a broad audience or the whole community); public institutions, like the apparatus of government itself, had a private (secret, concealed) side. Still, the broader questions remain: How did new language, like the changing rhetoric of public and private identity in church and state, new communities of discourse, like the scholarly republic of letters, and new forms of mass communication, like the broad dissemination of print, shape new kinds of discussion and debate? And what was the cultural and political outcome of all this new speech and writing?

This study has explored the transformations of various kinds of public discourse in one small place. Historians of Europe counterpose the new, evolving eighteenth-century publics against the old absolutist regimes, where the king was the public body and the court visually displayed his power. In Puritan Connecticut, there were few displays of the king's body as a public representation of state power. The corporate body was defined by the covenant, and state and church power was legitimated by reference to the ultimate Sovereign through his Word. The shift from "covenant" to "conscience" in the language used to discuss the basis of society's moral order discloses a symbolic movement from public to private authority. Corporatism was not suddenly replaced by individualism, for, after the stress upon the rights of conscience following the Awakening, New Englanders could still talk about themselves as a single people, a single body rewarded and punished by God. The arguments for private judgment and the rights of conscience, however, did help erode the legitimacy of the church's and state's claims to police moral behavior. The shift of emphasis in moral and religious responsibility away from the state might have actually empowered (private) patriarchal family government more than the (personal) self-government of individuals following their consciences. Yet, although the locus of power shifted, self-control, family government, and magisterial rule were still thought to be organically related. If that organic community swelled to include all of America in the flush of Revolutionary patriotism, late in the century Federalist clergymen tried to reawaken the sense of New England's distinctive corporate identity.

The tension between public and private authority and identity was also central to the religious debates about visible sainthood and the nature of the church. Proponents of inclusive church membership wanted people to come forward and declare their faith before the worshiping community but would leave the question of the candidate's actual spiritual fitness, and even the specific meaning of the words of the public profession, to the individual's private conscience. Others argued for a closer correlation between public and private identity, public and private meaning. The identity of the church as a public institution, too, was in question. A state church, which divided the territory of the commonwealth into parishes and ministered to the whole population, might consider itself coextensive with society at large. This idea became much more difficult to sustain for the Standing Order descendants of the Puritans, who had to tolerate competing denominations in a far more pluralistic religious environment. The ecumenically inclined might still imagine that different sects and churches could form a public community of Christians united by the mere fact of their "public worship" on the Sabbath, even though they worshiped in different ways and with different interpretations of religious truth. Many dissenters resolutely maintained, however, that even the rhetorical vestige of the state church tradition was an anti-Christian abomination and considered their congregations to be private, voluntary communions of the faithful called out from the rest of world.

The often ambiguous boundaries of the public and private frequently became the subject of legal disputes. The midcentury debates over Yale were about whether Connecticut's single institution of higher learning was a public entity subject to the General Assembly's oversight and control or a private corporation defined by the designs of its clerical founders. Arguments about this question in turn highlighted broader legal uncertainties in the colonial period. The law had to be determined and applied by a legitimate public authority, but which one? To what extent, and in what circumstances, were the colonists to look to the customary practices of local communities, scholarly jurists, protesting crowds, colonial assemblies, or the crown? The men who stepped forward to sort out such questions quickly became the dominant intellectuals of the Revolutionary period. Yet, lawyers were also harshly criticized for pursuing private interests by manipulating public institutions (assemblies and the courts) with an arcane legal language that was intelligible only to a cadre of professional experts.

Some historians of the Enlightenment have stressed that the new public culture of the late eighteenth century that rose to oppose authoritarian tyranny had its roots in an earlier scholarly or literary republic of letters, a private cosmopolitan community of intellectuals predicated upon the unrestricted communication of ideas and the wide application of critical reason. Private enlightenment, though, did not necessarily, or even usually, lead to radical politics. One of the earliest public applications of enlightened criticism and experimental science was the effort toward agricultural improvement. Improvers appealed to both private interest and the public good in their efforts to enlist common people in a program of social and economic (and not just agricultural) progress. Learned men who supported the effort to increase the general fund of practical knowledge, though, could still be leery about making the republic of letters ideal of free communication and criticism the model for public discourse as such. Much as they praised the diffusion of knowledge through the entire social order, they worried—especially after the French Revolution—about dangerous ideas falling into the wrong hands.

The elite men who did most of the public speaking and writing did not simply monitor the content of the orations and publications intended for broad consumption. They also paid attention to how different forms of communication linked public expression and private experience in different ways. We should not refer to separate print and oral cultures, at least not for eighteenth-century New England, where speech, print, and handwritten messages were interwoven in complex webs of communication. We should also be careful not to overgeneralize about the connection between form (print, speech) and function (rhetorical appeals to the head or heart). It is not that print is *essentially* a "cooler," more impersonal medium that promotes, by its very nature as a sequence of regularized typographic marks in space, objective analysis and rational reflection in a solitary reader; nor is it that speech is *naturally* "hotter," a personal and social encounter between a speaker and a listener demanding a more immediate emotional response. The question is how people *understood* the effects of print and speech. Revivalists could certainly link too much book learning to spiritual deadness and passionate oratory to gracious affections. Newspaper writers championed anonymous print as a form best suited to an impersonal, disinterested, and rational exchange of ideas, and they hailed literacy and the broad dissemination of publications as a triumph of reason. But eighteenth-century New Englanders could also construe the effects of speech and print upon individual listeners and readers in the opposite way. Late in the century, clergymen argued that cheap, anonymous publications were the infidel's primary weapon; they were subversive texts aimed at seducing the emotions of a reader and could do so more effectively than speech because the printed page could so easily screen the author's real character and motives.

Other voices suggested that face-to-face dialogues with trusted speakers were more conducive to reasonable communication and rational persuasion.

Formal speeches and tavern harangues, newspapers, pamphlets, and broadsides, committee correspondence and circulating manuscripts—all shaped the new politics of the Revolutionary age. Speakers and writers condemned private (selfish) interests and extolled public (selfless) virtue. The enlightened elite hailed the "public mind" of the new sovereign people yet expected that they, the educated gentlemen, would both tutor their fellow citizens and shape expressions of public opinion. Federalist clergymen like Dwight stressed the tutelary role; Republican politicians like Bishop wanted to be perceived as spokesmen for "the people," opposing an aristocratic elite.

Should we focus upon the emancipatory power—the positive connection to intellectual freedom and democratic revolution—of the new, enlightened, more secular public discourse that emerged in the eighteenth century and the new forms of communication and association that sustained it? Or did this torrent of words simply reformulate patriarchal power, floating universalistic language about enlightenment and freedom while in fact empowering the usual suspects to exclude and control everyone else? Is the transformation of public discourse in eighteenth-century New England a story about democratization or the reconstitution of elite hegemony? As we look back upon the 1700s, we can emphasize the potential for liberation lodged in new language and social practices. Or, as we stop the story with Timothy Dwight and Abraham Bishop in 1800, we can contrast rhetorical ideals to the realities of political participation and cultural power. The moral and political judgment we pass upon the eighteenth century, however, may ultimately have less to do with that century than with our own.

Connecticut Imprints

Figure 19 depicts the number of American imprints from 1700 to 1800; Figure 20 shows eighteenth-century Connecticut imprints. The year-by-year development of Connecticut printing, however, is better illustrated by Figures 21 and 22, which record the number of imprints in four categories through the second half of the century. Figures 21 and 22 were tabulated from 3,575 Connecticut titles in the bibliography of Early American Imprints, 1st Series. I sorted imprints into the following categories: *Government* (including state laws, town bylaws, the governor's proclamations, and circulars on taxation), *Civic* (including orations, addresses, nonreligious essays, pamphlets, and memorials), *Literary* (poetry, fiction, music, and juvenile literature), *Educational* (including almanacs, textbooks, primers, and dictionaries), *Religious* (including, besides sermons and other clerical writing, hymnals and devotional tracts), *Other* (including travel accounts, news publications, and scientific or medical publications). For the purposes of the figures, *Civic* has been combined with *Government,* and *Literary* with *Educational.*[1]

The category labeled *Civic* includes publications about politics and government as well as publications by the government. The sharp increase in civic publications in the early 1770s registers the great increase in government activity as much as the expansion of a public sphere of discussion and debate. But there is no doubt about the increase in public political discourse during the Revolutionary period, much of it carried by newspapers rather than individual pamphlets. Indeed, the graph's apparent post-Revolutionary decline in civic print is misleading; although government publications did drop with the end of the war, political discussion and debate continued (and, in the 1790s, greatly increased) in the growing number of newspapers.

The record of religious print is also revealing. Connecticut's single press in the 1740s did produce some sermons and declarations in response to the Awakening, but Boston presses issued the vast majority of the publications relating to that period of revivalism and religious turmoil in New England. The number of religious imprints in Connecticut increased in the late 1750s and then spiked upward in the late 1760s and early 1770s, as clerics and laymen alike argued about church membership, religious orthodoxy, the religious nature of Yale College, and the colony's ecclesiastical constitution. The recovery and growth of religious

---

1. The bulk of this research was completed before the revised edition of Early American Imprints became available on CD-ROM. I have checked my information against the revised list, using a printout of Connecticut imprints graciously provided by John B. Hench of the American Antiquarian Society in Worcester, Mass., and am convinced that, despite some additions and revisions, the pattern depicted here remains accurate. I am also convinced that my research could not be quickly duplicated by searching by subject on CD-ROM. Sorting the imprints into the broad subject categories listed below required more than a reliance upon a key word someone else might have entered into a subject field; it required a close examination of the full bibliographic record of every imprint and a personal familiarity with many, if not most, of the documents themselves.

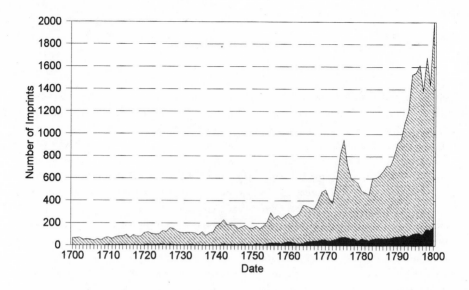

Figure 19. American imprints, 1700–1800

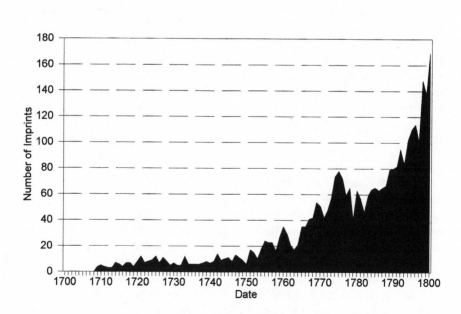

Figure 20. Connecticut Imprints, 1700–1800

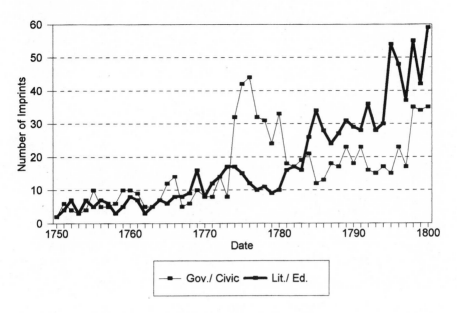

Figure 21. Connecticut Imprints, 1750–1800: *Government/Civic* and *Literary/Educational*

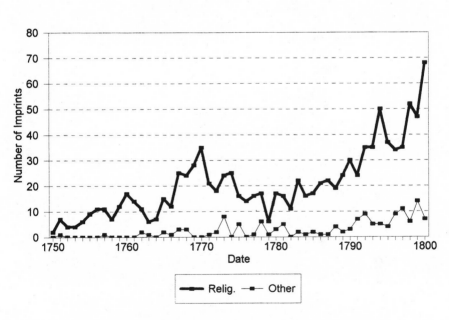

Figure 22. Connecticut Imprints, 1750–1800: *Religious* and *Other*

print in the 1780s and 1790s indicates that, despite the heightened interest in politics and government, we should not exaggerate the secularization of post-Revolutionary society. The increasing number of almanacs, textbooks, and collections of poems, grouped in the *Literary/Educational* category, also contains significant religious content.

APPENDIX 2
Connecticut Election Sermons

1732   Edwards, Timothy. *All the Living Must Surely Die, and Go to Judgment*. New London, 1732.

1733   Adams, Eliphalet. *A Discourse Shewing That So Long as There Is Any Prospect of a Sinful People's Yielding Good Fruit Hereafter, There Is Hope That They May Be Spared*. . . . New London, 1734.

1734   Chauncey, Nathanael. *The Faithful Ruler Described and Excited*. . . . New London, 1734.

1735   Mix, Stephen. [Not published].

1736   Marsh, Jonathan. *God's Fatherly Care of His Covenant Children*. . . . New London, 1737.

1737   Colton, Benjamin. *The Danger of Apostasie*. . . . New London, 1738.

1738   Eliot, Jared. *Give Cesar His Due; or, The Obligations That Subjects Are Under to Their Civil Rulers*. . . . New London, 1738.

1739   Woodbridge, Timothy. [Not published].

1740   Heminway, Jacob. *The Favour of God the Best Security of a People and a Concern to Please Him Urged*. . . . New London, 1740.

1741   Williams, Solomon. *A Firm and Immovable Courage to Obey God, and an Inflexible Observation of the Laws of Religion, the Highest Wisdom and Certain Happiness of Rulers*. New London, 1741.

1742   Stiles, Isaac. *A Prospect of the City of Jerusalem, in It's Spiritual Building, Beauty, and Glory*. New London, 1742.

1743   Steel, Stephen. [Not published].

1744   Worthington, William. *The Duty of Rulers and Teachers in Unitedly Leading God's People*. . . . New London, 1744.

1745   Whitman, Elnathan. *The Character and Qualifications of Good Rulers and the Happiness of Their Administration*. . . . New London, 1745.

1746   Hall, Samuel. *The Legislatures Right, Charge, and Duty in Respect of Religion*. . . . New London, 1746.

1747   Hunn, Nathanael. *The Welfare of a Government Considered*. . . . New London, 1747.

1748   Eells, Nathanael. *The Wise Ruler a Loyal Subject*. New London, 1748.

1749   Todd, Jonathan. *Civil Rulers the Ministers of God, for the Good of Men; or, The Divine Original and Authority of Civil Government Asserted*. . . . New London, 1749.

1750   Hobart, Noah. *Civil Government the Foundation of Social Happiness*. . . . New London, 1751.

1751   Lord, Benjamin. *Religion and Government Subsisting Together in Society, Necessary to Their Compleat Happiness and Safety*. . . . New London, 1752.

1752   Woodbridge, Ashbel. *A Sermon Delivered before the General Assembly of the Colony of Connecticut, on the Anniversary Election in Hartford, May 14, 1752*. New London, 1753.

1753   Devotion, Ebenezer. *The Civil Ruler, a Dignify'd Servant of the Lord*. . . . New London, 1753.

1754   Lockwood, James. *Religion the Highest Interest of a Civil Community, and the Surest Means of Its Prosperity*. . . . New London, 1754.

1755   Dickinson, Moses. *A Sermon Preached before the General Assembly of the Colony of Connecticut*. . . . New London, 1755.

1756   Beckwith, George. *That People a Safe and Happy People, Who Have God for, and among Them....* New London, 1756.

1757   Raynolds, Peter. *The Kingdom Is the Lord's; or, God the Supreme Ruler and Governour of the World....* New London, 1757.

1758   Throop, Benjamin. *Religion and Loyalty, the Duty and Glory of a People....* New London, 1758.

1759   Lockwood, James. *The Worth and Excellence of Civil Freedom and Liberty Illustrated, and a Public Spirit and the Love of Our Country Recommended....* New London, 1759.

1760   Fish, Joseph. *Christ Jesus the Physician, and His Blood the Balm, Recommended for the Healing of a Diseased People....* New London, 1760.

1761   Ingersoll, Jonathan. *A Sermon Preached before the General Assembly of the Colony of Connecticut.* New London, 1761.

1762   Bellamy, Joseph. *A Sermon Delivered before the General Assembly of the Colony of Connecticut.* New London, [1762].

1763   White, Stephen. *Civil Rulers Gods by Office, and the Duties of Such Considered and Enforced....* New London, 1763.

1764   Welles, Noah. *Patriotism Described and Recommended....* New London, 1764.

1765   Dorr, Edward. *The Duty of Civil Rulers, to Be Nursing Fathers to the Church of Christ.* Hartford, [1765].

1766   Lee, Jonathan. *A Sermon Delivered before the General Assembly of the Colony of Connecticut....* New London, 1766.

1767   Eells, Edward. *Christ, the Foundation of the Salvation of Sinners, and of Civil and Ecclesiastical Government.* New London, 1767.

1768   Salter, Richard. *A Sermon Preached before the General Assembly of the Colony of Connecticut....* New London, 1768.

1769   Williams, Eliphalet. *A Sermon Preached in the Audience of the General Assembly of the Colony of Connecticut.* New London, 1769.

1770   Johnson, Stephen. *Integrity and Piety the Best Principles of a Good Administration of Government....* New London, 1770.

1771   Cogswell, James. *A Sermon, Preached before the General Assembly of the Colony of Connecticut....* New London, 1771.

1772   Leavenworth, Mark. *Charity Illustrated and Recommended to All Orders of Men....* New London, 1772.

1773   Wetmore, Izrahiah. *A Sermon Preached before the Honourable General Assembly of the Colony of Connecticut....* New London, 1773.

1774   Lockwood, Samuel. *Civil Rulers an Ordinance of God, for Good to Mankind....* New London, 1774.

1775   Perry, Joseph. *A Sermon, Preached before the General Assembly of the Colony of Connecticut....* Hartford, 1775.

1776   Champion, Judah. *Christian and Civil Liberty and Freedom Considered and Recommended.* Hartford, 1776.

1777   Devotion, John. *The Duty and Interest of a People to Sanctify the Lord of Hosts....* Hartford, 1777.

1778   Whittelsey, Chauncey. *The Importance of Religion in the Civil Ruler Considered....* New Haven, 1778.

1779 Dana, James. *A Sermon Preached before the General Assembly of the State of Connecticut.* . . . Hartford, 1779.

1780 Williams, Nathan. *A Sermon Preached in the Audience of the General Assembly of the State of Connecticut.* . . . Hartford, 1780.

1781 Mather, Moses. *Sermon, Preached in the Audience of the General Assembly of the State of Connecticut.* . . . New London, 1781.

1782 Trumbull, John. [Not published].

1783 Stiles, Ezra. *The United States Elevated to Glory and Honor.* . . . New Haven, 1783.

1784 Huntington, Joseph. *God Ruling the Nations for the Most Glorious End.* . . . Hartford, 1784.

1785 Wales, Samuel. *The Dangers of Our National Prosperity; and the Way to Avoid Them.* . . . Hartford, 1785.

1786 Hart, Levi. *The Description of a Good Character.* . . . Hartford, [1786].

1787 Goodrich, Elizur. *The Principles of Civil Union and Happiness.* . . . Hartford, 1787.

1788 Whitney, Josiah. *The Essential Requisites to Form the Good Ruler's Character.* . . . Hartford, 1788.

1789 Robbins, Ammi R. *The Empires and Dominions of This World Made Subservient to the Kingdom of Christ* . . . Hartford, 1789.

1790 Strong, Nathan. *A Sermon, Delivered in Presence of His Excellency Samuel Huntington.* . . . Hartford, 1790.

1791 Dwight, Timothy. *Virtuous Rulers a National Blessing.* Hartford, 1791.

1792 Stone, Timothy. *A Sermon, Preached before His Excellency Samuel Huntington.* . . . Hartford, 1792.

1793 Backus, Charles. *A Sermon, Preached before His Excellency Samuel Huntington.* . . . Hartford, 1793.

1794 Edwards, Jonathan, [Jr.]. *The Necessity of the Belief of Christianity by the Citizens of the State, in Order to Our Political Prosperity.* . . . Hartford, 1794.

1795 Lee, Andrew. *The Origin and Ends of Civil Government; with Reflections on the Distinguishing Happiness of the United States.* Hartford, 1795.

1796 Marsh, John. *A Sermon, Preached before His Honor Oliver Wolcott.* . . . Hartford, 1796.

1797 Lewis, Isaac. *The Political Advantages of Godliness.* Hartford, 1797.

1798 Backus, Azel. *Absalom's Conspiracy.* . . . Hartford, 1798.

1799 Strong, Cyprian. *The Kingdom Is the Lord's.* . . . Hartford, 1799.

1800 Smalley, John. *On the Evils of a Weak Government.* . . . Hartford, 1800.

A Note on the Historiography of the Great Awakening

Modern historians have been too eager to interpret the "Great Awakening" as a massive, transformative event in American history. The modern historiography of the Awakening is marked by strained efforts to characterize it as both a short-lived dramatic event and a long-term evolutionary process in American cultural development. The Awakening is at once described as stretching from the late seventeenth century to the present, yet peaking or cresting or centered (the metaphors vary) in the early 1740s. This coupling of the ephemeral event with the longue durée has allowed historians to incorporate theological shifts, revival traditions, and social changes as extended prologues and epilogues to a central drama focused on George Whitefield, Jonathan Edwards, and the awakened multitudes. However anticipated before 1740 and complicated by other events after 1745, the Awakening becomes a watershed in American history, an intellectual paradigm shift, an inner revolution that leads toward 1776, a profound revitalization of culture, or a new birth of evangelicalism and democracy.[1]

The stories historians have told about American religious history, therefore, often resemble the revival preacher's morphology of spiritual conversion. The Awakening is America's conversion experience. Beneath life's complications and contradictions lies the essential spiritual fact of regeneration, the sudden infusion of grace that transforms the sinner into a saint. The pilgrim's halting progress through the world may be rendered in shades of gray, but underlying it is the soul's new birth, the quick passage from darkness to light. The historian, of course, refers, not to the soul, but to similarly mystified notions of a public "mind" or American "culture." The transformation described is, not from sinner to saint, but from Puritanism to evangelicalism or from colonial to American society. Yet, the historian's gaze pierces to the heart of the matter, to the deep structures of history, to the fundamental transformation lying beneath the surface of the Awakening's transient existence. That most of the revivals had petered out by the 1750s does not hinder those who argue for the Awakening's profound impact upon the Revolution and beyond. America at midcentury is like the backsliding saint. The convert's return to a sinful life does not necessarily invalidate the conversion experience; grace in this new creature may be temporarily latent rather than manifest. In America, too, fervor ebbed, and attention shifted from the next world to this one, but the Awakening, it is claimed, had left embers that continued to "smolder and flare" or a "sediment or residue [that] permanently altered the American spiritual landscape."[2]

1. J. M. Bumsted and John E. Van de Wetering, *What Must I Do to Be Saved? The Great Awakening in Colonial America* (Hinsdale, Ill., 1976), iv.

2. Cedric B. Cowing, *The Great Awakening and the American Revolution: Colonial Thought in the Eighteenth Century* (Chicago, 1971), 178; Martin E. Marty, *Religion, Awakening, and Revolution* (n.p., 1977), 93. H. Richard Niebuhr, in *The Kingdom of God in America* (New York, 1937), 126, wrote that the Awakening was "our national conversion"; the analogy is implicit in many other works. For a critique of the way that invocations of a hazy, totalizing, abstract concept of "culture" have come to pervade the humanities and social sciences, see

In the 1960s and 1970s, such metaphorical explanations of the Awakening's eighteenth-century impact were paired with exaggerated estimates of its broader historical significance. An introduction to a collection of documents, for example, described the Awakening as being more powerful than "the civil rights demonstrations, the campus disturbances, and the urban riots of the 1960s combined." The editor of another collection of documents called the Awakening "a 'crisis' in the history of American civilization," "the 'birth pangs' of a new epoch in the history of American Protestantism," and the awakening of "the spirit of American democracy." By the 1980s, scholars continued to disagree about the causes, nature, and specific consequences of the Awakening, but almost all agreed that, somehow, the stirrings in the 1740s were extremely important to the coming of the American Revolution and the future of American religious life.[3]

Revisionists have effectively deflated the more extravagant claims and have even charged that the notion of a "Great Awakening" is a misleading historical fiction. Jon Butler, in a powerful critique, argued that "the label 'the Great Awakening' distorts the extent, nature, and cohesion of the revivals that did exist in the eighteenth-century colonies, encourages unwarranted claims of their effects on colonial society, and exaggerates their influence on the coming and character of the American Revolution." According to Butler, the term itself (and, implicitly, the tendency to homogenize eighteenth-century revivalism into a single transformative episode) was created by the historian Joseph Tracy, who titled his 1841 book *The Great Awakening.* Tracy's "Great Awakening" was subsequently adopted by historians later in the nineteenth century. Another commentator, Joseph Conforti, followed Butler's lead and described the "invention" of the Great Awakening. But Conforti argued that "it originated as a cultural production of the Second Great Awakening, not as a historiographical development of the late nineteenth and twentieth centuries." Beginning in the 1790s, Edwardsean Calvinists shaped a usable past while promoting a "Second" Awakening in New England. For Conforti, Tracy's volume "culminated rather than launched" the historical reification of the colonial revivals.[4]

The flaws in interpretations that place the Great Awakening at the vital center of eighteenth-century American culture, however, should not be blamed upon old Yankee fil-

---

Daniel Cottom, *Text and Culture: The Politics of Interpretation,* Theory and History of Literature, LXII (Minneapolis, Minn., 1989), chap. 2.

3. Richard L. Bushman, "Introduction," in Bushman, ed., *The Great Awakening: Documents on the Revival of Religion, 1740–1745* (New York, 1970), xi; Alan Heimert, "Introduction," in Heimert and Perry Miller, eds., *The Great Awakening: Documents Illustrating the Crisis and Its Consequences* (Indianapolis, Ind., 1967), xv, xxv, lxi. See also Stephen A. Marini, "The Great Awakening," in Charles H. Lippy and Peter W. Williams, eds., *Encyclopedia of the American Religious Experience: Studies of Traditions and Movements* (New York, 1988), 775–776; Leonard I. Sweet, "The Evangelical Tradition in America," in Sweet, ed., *The Evangelical Tradition in America* (Macon, Ga., 1984), 1–14, a comprehensive review of the historiography through the early 1980s.

4. Jon Butler, "Enthusiasm Described and Decried: The Great Awakening as Interpretative Fiction," *Journal of American History,* LXIX (1982–1983), 305–325 (quotation on 308); Joseph Tracy, *The Great Awakening: A History of the Revival of Religion in the Time of Edwards and Whitefield* (Boston, 1841); Joseph A. Conforti, "The Invention of the Great Awakening, 1795–1842," *Early American Literature,* XXVI (1991), 99–118 (quotation on 114).

iopietists. Writers from different eras have construed the revivals in various ways and have constructed narratives to suit their own purposes. *The Christian History* (1743–1745), by Thomas Prince, Jr., linked New England's revivals to a great, general, world-historical transformation even as they were occurring, although his focus was on a decidedly transatlantic outpouring of God's grace rather than on a peculiarly American revitalization. Benjamin Trumbull's *History of Connecticut* (1818) and Tracy's *Great Awakening* twenty-three years later might indeed have reified the Awakening, but, focused on the gathering of souls to Christ, they placed little emphasis on any specific long-term political or sociological impact. In Tracy's "classic" study, the link between the Awakening and the Revolution, the modern historian's fixation, merited only a brief dismissal. "It would be saying too much," Tracy concluded, "to ascribe to the revival any appreciable influence in producing the independence of the United States."[5]

Problems with twentieth-century interpretations of the Awakening have arisen from an accretion of rhetorical excess and hasty generalization within modern historiography. Preoccupied by the formation of "the American character," overgeneralizing from local studies, and prone to language representing the Awakening as a hurricane, firestorm, or earthquake, historians have leaped too quickly from descriptions of dramatic action to assumptions about historical significance. Indeed, the strength of Butler's critique lies, not in locating the historiographical origins of the interpretive model, but in exposing its failures. Descriptions of the Calvinist roots of the revivals ignore the eclectic theological currents contributing to religious stirrings south of Connecticut. Discussions of the Awakening as a pancolonial phenomenon glaze over inconvenient facts of chronology and geography: revivalism in Virginia did not emerge until the 1750s or become a significant force until the 1760s, long after things had quieted in New England; New Hampshire, Maryland, Georgia, New York, Delaware, North Carolina, and South Carolina were hardly touched at all. Sweeping claims about the Awakening's impact upon America arise from the old habit of seeing the mainland colonies as New England writ large.[6]

Even if confined to New England, historical interpretations that translate eighteenth-century religious terminology into the language of modern psychology, sociology, and anthropology often reveal more about our own concerns than help us understand the past. Modern historians have in effect created a secular image or shadow of the things eighteenth-century divines discussed. They have created a Great Awakening whose greatness is almost necessarily defined by the relationship of the revivals to the breakdown of colonial social order and the emergence of Revolutionary politics because they are interested in modernization and 1776, not in a Calvinist God's harvest of souls.

Newer studies have responded to the revisionist critique in two ways. First, as Marilyn Westerkamp put it, they have turned the causal model on its side, seeing both the Awakening and the Revolution emerging from broader and more diffuse social, cultural, and economic developments. Two reinterpretations of Whitefield's ministry, for example, show how the Grand Itinerant borrowed merchandising techniques from the marketplace and

---

5. Thomas Prince, Jr., *The Christian History, Containing Accounts of the Revival and Propagation of Religion in Great Britain, America . . .* , 2 vols. (Boston, 1744–1745); Benjamin Trumbull, *A Complete History of Connecticut, Civil and Ecclesiastical . . .* (1818; reprint, New London, Conn., 1898); Tracy, *The Great Awakening*, 420.

6. Butler, "Enthusiasm Described and Decried," *JAH*, LXIX (1982–1983), 309–310.

adapted the language of consumption for religious purposes in a rapidly commercializing society. Second, some works have approached the events of the early 1740s with an entirely different sense of context. They are careful not to slight the regional diversity of colonial America, the heterogeneous theological origins of colonial revivalism, or the continuing importance of Old World religiousness. A study of Scots-Irish Presbyterians and a fresh look at New England describes the Awakening as an evolving movement or as part of a slowly developing tradition rather than as a dramatic event. Both books argue that the Awakening's significance is primarily religious rather than intellectual or social, and both place it within narratives about transatlantic Protestantism, not the formation of American character.[7]

If previous studies overplayed the drama of the early 1740s, these histories underplay it: Whitefield did not innovate or initiate, they say, he just reinforced tradition; Edwards did not inaugurate a whole new understanding, he merely refined and standardized evangelical terminology. In a sense, these studies resemble evangelical redemptive history rather than a personal conversion narrative. Edwards's *History of the Work of Redemption* described the ebbs and flows of grace within history as the church moved through periods of revival and declension toward inevitable millennial glory. These newer studies of colonial revivalism similarly focus upon long traditions, where religious fervor waxes and wanes, and the stirrings of the 1740s are just another step toward the emergence of modern evangelicalism. We gain a more nuanced understanding of the Awakening's place in the sweep of religious history but lose a sense of the contingency of events and the surprise and hesitancy of the people who tried to interpret and respond to them. The first half of Chapter 2 in this book is an attempt to discuss the religious excitement, ideological divisiveness, and institutional shake-ups in the 1740s without either slighting the Awakening's dramatic power or exaggerating and simplifying its impact.[8]

7. Marilyn J. Westerkamp, *The Triumph of the Laity: Scots-Irish Piety and the Great Awakening, 1625–1760* (New York, 1988), 4; Harry S. Stout, *The Divine Dramatist: George Whitefield and the Rise of Modern Evangelicalism* (Grand Rapids, Mich., 1991); Frank Lambert, "'Pedlar in Divinity': George Whitefield and the Great Awakening, 1737–1745," *JAH*, LXXVII (1990–1991), 812–837. See also Lambert, *"Pedlar in Divinity": George Whitefield and the Transatlantic Revivals, 1737–1770* (Princeton, N.J., 1994); Michael J. Crawford, *Seasons of Grace: Colonial New England's Revival Tradition in Its British Context* (New York, 1991); W. R. Ward, *The Protestant Evangelical Awakening* (Cambridge, 1992), which describes Protestant revival movements from a European (not just Anglo-American) perspective.

8. Jonathan Edwards, *A History of the Work of Redemption,* ed. John F. Wilson, in Perry Miller et al., eds., *The Works of Jonathan Edwards,* IX (New Haven, Conn., 1989). This sermon series was first preached in 1739 and published after Edwards's death in 1774.

Astronomy, 240–244, 248–250, 266–267, 269–270, 276–277, 294

Awakening (concept), 89, 91–96; of individuals, 89, 91–93, 133; and conversion, 92–98

Awakening (1740s), 86-108, 142; preaching and, 3, 89–92, 246–247, 480; and authority, 3, 246–247; historiography of, 4, 48, 73, 86–88, 104–107, 495-498; and millennialism, 31, 105; and Saybrook Platform, 44, 49; obedience and, 47–48; and church membership, 48, 104; Elisha Williams and, 53; Jonathan Edwards and, 86, 102, 114, 120, 129–130; and enthusiasm, 89, 96–98, 415; Joseph Bellamy on, 102; and church schism, 104, 462–463; Thomas Clap and, 150–152; Ezra Stiles and, 231, 238–239, 245–247; and disestablishment, 342

Baptists, 57, 78, 87, 102, 103, 107, 341–344, 349–350, 463

Barlow, Joel, 288, 292, 297, 324, 336, 392, 411

Bee (New London, Conn.), 2, 340, 392–393, 454–458, 469, 471, 474, 478–479. *See also* Holt, Charles

Beecher, Lyman, 380, 382

Bellamy, Joseph, 102, 110–111, 128, 134, 136–143, 243, 253, 269, 306–308

Belles lettres, 278, 285–290, 293–294, 298–299, 323–326

Benevolence, 80, 223, 305, 357–358, 362, 368–371, 410

Bishop, Abraham, 14–15, 399–401, 406–407, 448, 461–462, 464–465, 469–475, 478–479, 481, 485

Boston, Mass., 19, 100, 169, 193, 214–216, 310–311, 462

Brewster, Walter, 14–15, 416–418, 429, 435

Calvinism: in Connecticut, 38, 61, 106–107, 464–465, 469; and Arminianism, 45–46, 106; Elisha Williams and, 46–47; as party label, 76; and Awakening, 101–102, 106; Thomas Clap and, 144–148, 153, 157, 171, 184; Ezra Stiles and, 189, 234–238,

243, 262, 277–278; Edwardsean, 223, 231, 269–271, 367–369; John Trumbull and, 305; Timothy Dwight and, 338–339; and Enlightenment, 444; Zephaniah Swift and, 445–446

Catholics, 78, 254, 463

Certificate law, 341–344, 348, 378

Character: American, 28, 319, 447; of rulers, 46–47, 79–80, 84, 439, 444–445; Puritan and Yankee, 61–62; private, 64, 392, 432, 459; public, 64, 387–389, 431–432, 443, 446–447, 457; clerical, 138, 444; types of, 276, 295; New England, 283, 384–385; political, 283–284, 355–357, 389, 433–434, 446–448, 478–479; author's, 309, 325–326, 355, 484; speaker's, 355; corporate, 359, 366, 374–375, 461; Washington's, 363, 431; citizen's, 363, 370–371; Christian, 371, 461; real, 387, 431–432, 448, 457, 459; false, 389, 431, 459; assassination of, 392, 447; of learned man, 403–404; lawyer's, 435–436, 438–439, 444–445; rhetorical, 439; of ideal editor, 449

Charters: Connecticut, 19, 25, 35, 51, 74, 162, 168, 221, 281, 359, 423, 464; New England, 35, 78; gospel, 64; colonial, 74, 76, 146–147; Yale, 147, 150, 168–169, 171, 173, 177–179, 324, 346

Chauncy, Charles, 57–58, 63, 90–92, 95, 99, 102, 104–106, 217–218, 338

Chesterfield, Lord (Philip Dormer Stanhope), 340, 357

Church: schism in, 2, 13, 87, 104–105, 463; discipline of, 25, 40–45, 83, 147–151, 178, 445; as gathered communion, 66, 110, 139, 142

Church of England, 38, 68, 107, 167, 188, 191, 251, 256, 260. *See also* Anglicans; Episcopalians

Clap, Thomas: and moral order, 22–23, 148; as Old Light and New Light, 106; and law, 144–184, 480; and orthodoxy, 147–148, 152–154, 156–160; and Calvinism, 147–153, 157; and New England founders, 147–148, 171–173, 177–178; and church discipline, 148–151; and Awakening, 150–152; and George Whitefield, 150–151, 178–179; and Jonathan Edwards, 152; and Wallingford controversy, 154–162; and interpretation, 158–160; and moral philosophy, 175, 178; resignation of, 175, 182–183, 288, 290; as Yale historian, 176–177; and college unrest, 181–182; and Jared Eliot, 198, 212; and Ezra Stiles, 237, 243, 252–253, 271; and Timothy Dwight, 283, 377; and Yale curriculum, 402

Clergy: as aristocracy, 1, 12–13, 22, 88, 139–142, 346, 378–379, 481; and authority, 2–4, 12–13, 22–23, 107–111, 120, 137–138, 246–247, 375, 380–381; and lawyers, 4, 6–7, 183–184, 442–448; New Divinity and, 22–23, 88, 111, 137–143; and discipline, 22–23, 108–109; Jonathan Edwards on, 112–113; character of, 138–139, 444–445; John Trumbull on, 305–307; and knowledge, 339–340, 346–347, 445–446; as Federalists, 358, 368, 377–381, 399, 483, 485; Timothy Dwight on, 378–381. *See also* Anticlericalism

Clubs, 294–295, 298, 324–326, 396–399, 410
Cogswell, James, 6–7, 350
Cole, Nathan, 90, 103
Commerce: Elisha Williams and, 62–64; and Anglicization, 188; Jared Eliot and, 191, 208, 218, 222–224; in Connecticut, 220, 463; and publications, 287, 300, 322–323; and progress, 332–333; Timothy Dwight and, 332–333, 366, 383; and New England character, 383

Committees of Correspondence, 229, 296, 425–427, 485
Committees of Inspection, 390–392
Common sense: Walter Brewster and, 14; and politics, 84; Solomon Williams and, 127; Thomas Clap and, 174–175; Jared Eliot and, 193, 205; John Trumbull and, 306; Timothy Dwight and, 353, 355, 365; Middletown Convention and, 414–415; gentlemen and, 423; rhetorical appeals to, 481. *See also* Sentimentalism
Communion controversy, 108–143

Confessions, 40, 151, 154–160, 237, 252, 341
Congregationalists: and Federalists, 4, 15, 357–358; New England, 38; and Anglicans, 38, 45, 68, 107, 188–189, 462–463; and Presbyterians, 40, 239, 260; and church polity, 41–44; and Saybrook Platform, 41–42, 44–45; and Arminianism, 45; tax support for, 88, 274–275; growth of, 105, 248, 275, 349, 462–463; and moral order, 107–108; Jared Eliot and, 187–188, 191; Ezra Stiles and, 187–188, 230–231, 238, 248, 260, 261, 273; establishment of, 343–344, 358; criticism of, 345–346, 378; missions and, 382; in 1800, 463

Congress, U.S.: oratory in, 407, 439; debates of, 413, 451–452, 456; petitions to, 426; qualifications for, 431; voting for, 433, 475–477; lawyers and, 437; candidates for, 440, 471, 474, 479; Zephaniah Swift and, 447; Griswold-Lyon brawl in, 457–459

Connecticut: settlement of, 19; economy of, 19, 187–188, 220–222, 281, 300, 424–425, 463–465; population of, 19, 281; growth of, 19, 461; Revolution in, 281; religious denominations in, 349. *See also* Charters; Saybrook Platform; Town meetings; Voting

Connecticut Courant (Hartford), 2, 299–302, 318–323, 390, 452, 454–456, 468–469, 473–474

Conscience: Puritans and, 40; and moral order, 48, 50–51, 55–57, 80, 108, 159–160, 181–182, 482; Elisha Williams on, 50–65, 77–79, 111, 126–127; liberty of, 51–65, 68, 78, 154–182, 239, 260, 342–344, 445, 482; Thomas Paine on, 82; and common sense, 84, 159–160; and church membership, 111–112, 123, 126, 133, 142; Thomas Clap on, 159, 182; rhetorical appeal to, 217; Ezra Stiles on, 238, 253, 260; and Middletown Convention, 387, 414–415; and gentlemen, 414–415, 423; Zephaniah Swift on, 445; and public profession, 482–483

Constitutions: British, 22, 31, 53, 68, 142,

147, 160, 180–181, 223, 225; ecclesiastical, 24, 49, 83, 151, 153–156, 160–162, 167, 173; interpretation of, 66, 74, 146, 153–156, 160–162, 174, 180, 181, 470–471; design of, 66, 356–359; rights and, 76, 78, 142, 174, 181–182, 416; Yale, 169; collegiate, 173; Stiles family, 256, 261, 276; U.S., 321, 340–343, 360–363, 430, 467–468, 470–472; Connecticut, 329, 358–359, 426–427; Massachusetts (1780), 341; state, 356–360; and stability, 362–363; and virtue, 360–364; of fraternal societies, 399; duties and, 426, 428

Conversation: religious, 7, 91, 157–159, 283; and Northampton controversy, 114–115, 136–137; style of, 137–138, 201, 204, 207–208, 303–304; educational, 240–241; polite, 286, 293–294, 298, 303–304, 309–310, 419–421; private, 309–310, 390–392; in clubs, 324; sociable, 340, 389, 465–466, 475; and Federalist clergy, 378; and character, 387; political, 418, 466, 479; women and, 419–420

Conversion: Elisha Williams and, 46; and awakening, 91–95; Jonathan Edwards and, 92, 94, 96–97, 118, 125–126; in 1740s, 93–97, 104; and Separatists, 125; and Stoddardean church, 125–126; Ezra Stiles on, 247–248; Timothy Dwight on, 370–371

Correspondence: private, 8, 113, 392–393; and Awakening, 87; Jonathan Edwards and, 113, 114; Jared Eliot and, 193, 205, 210–212, 224; Ezra Stiles and, 236, 276; polite, 286; poetic and literary, 294, 298; of women, 294, 296–297; form of, 303–304; of gentlemen, 392

Covenant discourse: historiography of, 5, 28; national and public, 5, 22–143, 148, 367; and corporate identity, 22, 24–25, 30–31, 482; interpretation of, 22–23, 28–30; and order, 22–23, 42–45; and church-state authority, 22–23, 30–31, 41–44, 49–50, 482; and Bible, 24–25, 27–28, 65–66; Elisha Williams and, 27–28, 36–37, 41–44, 51–54, 64–66; and

covenant of grace, 27–28, 43–45, 64, 112, 119, 122, 123, 128, 130, 132, 134, 137–138, 141; and church, 28, 71–72, 108–111, 115–123, 136–143, 294, 372, 374; and New England election, 30, 34–35, 38–39, 128, 255; in Revolutionary era, 31, 71–73, 76–77, 83–85; Deuteronomic, 34, 36–50, 73, 128; and Providence, 37–39, 75–76; and Solomon Stoddard, 42–43, 130–131; and Solomon Williams, 64–65, 69–71, 122–128, 130–133; and French wars, 68–69; and William Vinal, 68–69; and Benjamin Trumbull, 72; and Jonathan Edwards, 109–113, 115–117, 119–123, 128–136; and New Divinity, 128–129; and Christian union, 129–130; and Joseph Bellamy, 136–143; Ezra Stiles and, 253–255; Timothy Dwight and, 372–373; and contracts, 445

Cutler, Timothy, 37–38, 45, 188

Daggett, David: on Connecticut, 1–2, 12–13, 15; on agricultural improvers, 227, 480; on sumptuary laws, 405; and oratory, 406–407, 411; and politics in 1790, 440–443, 448; and Abraham Bishop, 475; and John Adams, 478

Dana, James, 154, 156, 160, 262, 307

Dana, Samuel Whittelsey, 176–178, 183–184

Davenport, James, 53, 90, 96, 98–100, 150–151, 156

Day, Jeremiah, 79, 81–82

Deference, 14, 20n. 2, 141, 151, 164n. 35, 225, 271, 307, 378–379, 428, 448, 479

Deism, 234–235, 241–245, 251, 271, 274, 348, 350, 446–447

Democratic-Republicans: and Federalists, 4, 14–15, 284, 325, 392–393, 440–441, 447–450, 465–480, 485; and Timothy Dwight, 377–378; societies of, 399; and press, 450–456, 458–459, 474, 480

Determinism, 250–251, 261–262

Devotion, Ebenezer, 138–141

Devotion, John, 77, 262–263, 266

Dialogue, 110, 136–141, 303, 306, 314, 389, 400–401

Dionysius the Areopagite, 231, 266–269, 277

Discourse, 6–8

Dissent: religious, 4, 40, 51, 104–105, 249, 256, 260, 329, 340–344, 348–350, 378; political, 4, 249, 260, 320–321, 454–455, 471–473, 475

Dwight, Timothy: Ezra Stiles and, 271; and Thomas Clap, 283; and John Trumbull, 285, 288, 292, 294, 297, 299; historiography of, 327–328; and myth of America, 329–338, 372–374; youth of, 330; and rhetoric, 331–332, 334–335, 338, 345–346, 374; and infidelity, 338–339, 348–355, 377–379, 381–385, 399, 442, 461–465; and newspapers, 339–340; and church and state, 344, 346–350; and public worship, 356–367; and virtue, 356–374; and constitutions, 358–366; and Jonathan Edwards, 368–371; and national covenant, 372; and New England, 373–376, 382–385; criticism of, 377–378, 419, 454; and clerical authority, 379–381, 480–481, 485; after 1800, 381–385; and race, 384; and women, 419; and lawyers, 437; on eighteenth century, 461–462, 464–465

Earthquakes, 214–218

Edwards, Jonathan: on public discourse, 2–3, 7, 127–128; on church membership, 22–23, 88, 108–136; and Elisha Williams, 51, 55; and New Light dissent, 51, 152; on free will, 55, 250–251, 261–262, 307; on Awakening, 86, 94, 102; and individual awakening, 92–94; on conversion, 96–97, 371; on partisan division, 97–99; and Separatists, 102, 124–125; and historiography, 105–107, 109, 128–129; and religious discourse, 108–112, 142–143; and Northampton controversy, 108–128, 136; and clerical authority, 112–113; preaching of, 115–123, 128–129, 134–136; on visible sainthood, 123–125; on signification, 126–128, 131, 139; and covenant discourse, 128–136, 141; and Israel, 131–132; and post-Awakening rhetoric, 133–134;

Ezra Stiles on, 250, 262, 266–270; on true virtue, 368–371

Edwards, Jonathan, Jr., 269, 270, 368, 408, 463

Edwards, Pierpont, 440–442, 448, 474, 478, 479

Edwardseans. *See* New Divinity

Eells, Nathanael, 61, 99

Election day, 45, 82–83, 91, 370, 380, 407–409, 418–419, 471, 475–476, 478–480

Electioneering, 441, 465, 474–479

Elect nation, 30, 34–36, 66, 71–72, 128–129, 135, 255, 367, 373

Eliot, Jared: on state of nature, 54, 224; and Enlightenment, 187–188; and Anglicanism, 188; and Ezra Stiles, 188–189, 215, 222; and agricultural reform, 190–229; style of, 192–193, 201, 207–213; and Jethro Tull, 193–200; and Thomas Clap, 198, 212; readers' response to, 199–200, 210–212; and experimental philosophy, 203–205; on New England, 208–209, 220, 223–225; and astrology, 209; communications network of, 212; on earthquakes, 214–215; on providence, 217–220; on sublime and pastoral, 218; on future settlement, 222–223; on forms of government, 223–225; legacy of, 225–229

Emmons, Nathanael, 134, 381

Enlightenment: and knowledge, 2, 4; and progress, 4, 359–360; and optimism, 14; English, 38, 247; and Pietism, 106; moderate, 187–188; Ezra Stiles and, 189, 231–234, 240–242; pagan, 241–242; Scottish, 289–290, 299; radical, 338, 352–353; and Calvinism, 444–447; and science, 480; culture of, 483–484

Enthusiasm: religious, 1, 50, 53, 57, 98–102, 106–108, 118, 125, 153, 204–205, 241, 308, 316, 353–354, 432; political, 1–2, 78–79, 353–354, 387, 415, 432, 459; and authority, 461

Episcopalians, 11, 78, 349, 377, 463. *See also* Anglicans; Church of England

Essay: newspaper, 14, 278, 285, 299–311, 321, 329, 416–418, 451; style of, 84, 192–193,

199–208, 301–394, 424, 433; and sermon, 84, 201–202

Establishment, religious, 41, 49, 59–60, 68, 105, 154–155, 160, 178, 340–346

Experimental philosophy, 201–205, 214, 217–218, 222, 228–229, 252

Faith: and covenants, 27–28, 43–44, 72; and morality, 43–44, 51, 54; and patriotism, 80–81; common and saving, 112, 123; codification of, 157; power of, 204–205; and science, 213–214; and freedom of thought, 213–214; and skepticism, 235–236, 252–253; and knowledge, 242–243

Family: and social authority, 3, 164, 441, 447; and moral order, 62–65, 225, 482; as New England institution, 220–221, 329–330, 337, 364, 383; and farming, 220–222, 383; and government, 225; Ezra Stiles's fantasy of, 256–261, 276

Farmington, Conn., 425, 427–428

Federalists: power of, 4, 15, 325, 329, 380–381, 471–473, 476–479; and partisan division, 284, 447–448, 450, 457–459, 474–480; clergy as, 358, 368, 378, 399, 483, 485; criticism of, 378, 471, 473; newspapers and, 391–393, 430, 452–459, 473; and voluntary associations, 399; oratory of, 405, 473; satire of, 430, 473; as label, 430–431; rhetoric of, 467–478

Fitch, Thomas, 156–157, 169, 301

France: wars with, 22, 31, 35, 68–69, 70, 73, 78, 107, 135–136, 191, 218, 221, 332, 384, 466–467; attitudes toward, 107, 297, 321, 329, 351–354, 384, 399, 454–469, 473–474, 484

Franklin, Benjamin, 192, 202, 206, 212–213, 222, 252, 259, 299, 304

Freemasons, 11, 398, 409, 410, 440, 464, 482

Free will, 55, 63, 250, 307

French Revolution, 321, 329, 351, 456, 466, 468, 484

Frontier, 34, 70, 106, 135, 327, 382–383

Frothingham, Ebenezer, 58, 110, 123–125, 142, 155

Gale, Benjamin, 157, 163–164, 167–169, 174–175, 179, 182, 226, 392, 427, 430

Goodwin, George. *See* Hudson and Goodwin

Government: civil, 1, 14, 19, 34–43, 47–54, 61, 64, 147, 162, 224–225, 341, 445; moral, 34, 36, 38–39, 48–49, 61, 64–67, 74–77, 134, 253–255, 275, 357–360, 366–373; church, 41–42, 48–49, 61; nature of, 51–54, 58–61, 66, 74–76, 147, 149–150, 223–225, 341–345, 357–362, 413, 469; family, 64–65, 225, 364, 482; college, 149–150, 176; separation of powers in, 164; of colonies, 169, 225, 281; legitimacy of, 180, 429; patriarchal, 224–225, 482; republican, 345, 351, 354–367; and society, 358–367, 382; popular, 378–379, 405, 423–424, 428–429, 479; oppressive, 424–425, 428–429, 469–471

Grace: saving (inner, infused), 27–28, 45–46, 92, 96–97, 125–126, 130–132, 137–138, 142, 239–240, 245, 371; and Christ, 63; outpouring of, 78, 89, 93, 376; seasons of, 89; and enthusiasm, 99; and awakening, 99–100; and nature, 110, 133–134; sanctifying, 123–124; knowledge of, in others, 124, 142; experience of, 124–125, 148, 240, 276–277; common, 133; and rights, 142; free, 234; doctrines of, 239–240; growth in, 239–240; irresistible, 247–248, 369–371; and knowledge, 247, 268; search for, 270, 371; dispensations of, 335–336; and benevolence, 358, 363

Granger, Gideon, 468, 471, 475, 478–479

Great Britain: covenants and, 31, 36, 48, 130; revivals and, 89; and colonial prosperity, 188–189, 191–193, 229; and husbandry, 201, 205, 208, 222, 229; and Israel, 255; John Trumbull and, 287, 289; literary criticism in, 292–293, 299; Timothy Dwight and, 332, 357–358, 384–385; tyranny of, 357–358, 428; and infidelity, 384; Jay's Treaty with, 466; Republicans and, 468–469; electioneering and, 475

252–253, 337. *See also* Common sense; Sentimentalism

Moral sense. *See* Common sense

Morse, Jedidiah, 322, 352, 379, 381, 405, 440

Mysticism, 231, 266–269

Myth, 28–30, 34, 66, 71, 111, 329–336

Nature, state of, 51–54, 58, 224, 469

Neoplatonism, 231, 265–268

New Divinity: and church membership, 22, 88, 136–143, 463; and clerical authority, 23, 88, 111, 137–143, 147; and religious factions, 105–107; and Jonathan Edwards, 111, 269–270; and covenants, 128, 133–135; and politics, 128, 368–369; rhetoric of, 133; and economics, 223; Ezra Stiles and, 231, 253, 261–262, 269–272, 277; John Trumbull and, 307; and virtue, 357; Timothy Dwight and, 368–369; Jonathan Edwards, Jr., and, 463, 498

New Haven, Conn.: commerce in, 19; revivalists in, 90, 150–151; politics in (1750s), 156–157; Stamp Act protests in, 182; printing in, 184, 281–282, 464–465; churches in, 269, 462–463; and Yale commencement, 271, 408; British attack on, 281; newspapers in, 300, 440–441; and literature, 302; oratory in, 409; and lawyers, 440–441; in 1704, 461–462; in 1800, 461–464, 475, 478–479; July Fourth in, 472

New Lights: as label, 1–2, 5, 76, 87, 106, 147, 236–237; criticism of, 1–2, 95–98; and church, 58, 87, 154; and liberty, 68, 106, 153–154; and Old Lights, 87–88, 101, 105–107, 147; variations of, 87–88, 124, 142; and Thomas Clap, 106, 152–154, 156; and covenants, 129, 130; and Christian union, 129–130; and legalism, 154; Ezra Stiles and, 236–238, 247, 270; John Trumbull on, 290. *See also* Old Lights

New London, Conn., 19, 90, 98–99, 151, 220, 281–282, 410, 454–455, 466, 474

Newspaper editors, 339, 390, 392–393, 419–421, 449–457, 468–469, 471, 474

Newspapers: and partisanship, 2, 281, 283, 324–325, 389–391, 433–434, 440, 454–455, 457, 471–472, 475, 480; growth of, 4, 281–282, 286, 299–300; and Awakening, 87, 89; and Stamp Act, 180; and agriculture, 210, 274; and public mind, 278; and literature, 281–282, 286, 318, 323–325; and public discourse, 282–283, 286, 302–304, 323–324, 329, 339, 345, 415–416, 424, 449–452, 464–466, 471–472, 484–485; evolution of, 302, 323; and Revolution, 311–314, 389–391; and religion, 339–340, 345; infidelity in, 354; and women, 419–420; and impartiality, 449, 453–454; legislative reports in, 450–451; on July Fourth, 473

Newton, Isaac, 37, 187, 232, 240, 243, 252–253, 265, 289, 480

New York, 19, 166, 169, 318, 329, 373–374, 382, 384, 468

Northampton, Mass., 108–132

Novels, 11, 286, 295–298, 406, 419, 464

Noyes, Joseph, 150–162

Ogden, John C., 377–379

Old Lights: as label, 2, 5, 76, 87, 106–107, 147, 236; and authority, 49, 106; and rights, 58, 68; and liberty, 68, 106, 153–154; and New Lights, 87–88, 101, 105–107, 147; and awakening, 92; Thomas Clap and, 106, 152–153; Ezra Stiles and, 230, 236, 271; and enthusiasm, 415. *See also* New Lights

Oliver, Peter, 194, 198–199, 211–212

Oratory: July Fourth, 1, 411–413; Phi Beta Kappa, 13; Republican, 14–15, 461, 478; and Awakening, 99; in Revolutionary era, 281; lawyers and, 284, 438; study of, 299, 394–396, 405–407; and town meetings, 314–316; prophetic, 323; Timothy Dwight and, 327–328, 330, 355; and character, 355, 431; student, 395–396, 401, 405, 431, 473; Federalist, 405, 473; courtroom, 405–407, 413, 440; Congressional, 407; and institutions, 407–408; and politics, 433; and clergy, 445–446; and passions, 484–485

Prophecy, 76, 242, 265, 312, 323, 331–336, 351, 373, 378

Providence, 30–40, 48, 61, 65–67, 72–77, 81, 85, 218

Pseudonymity, 301, 303, 325, 339, 386–387, 433, 440. *See also* Anonymity

Public sphere: and democracy, 13; and elite, 15; and private judgment, 64; and republic of letters, 277; transformation of, 282, 419; republican, 286–288, 302, 353; kinds of, 286–288, 323; and debate, 309; and anonymity, 320, 355; liberal, 322–323; boundaries of, 364; participation in, 364–365; and private life, 365, 482–485

Public worship, 43, 124, 130, 341–348, 367, 375, 483

Puritans: and jeremiads, 21, 24–25, 128–129, 328–329; covenant discourse and, 24–25, 31, 73, 128–129, 367, 372, 482; and conscience, 56; and Yankees, 61–62; and magistracy, 83–84, 162; Ezra Stiles and, 188–189, 231–236, 247–248, 259–260, 270–276

Refinement, 188, 207, 219–220, 282, 290–294, 298–299, 320, 366, 462. *See also* Politeness

Republicanism: classical, 31, 80–81, 222–223, 357–358, 360–361, 370, 401, 409; and virtue, 81–82, 357–359, 370, 405; tenets of, 302–303; and liberalism, 368; and secrecy, 393

Republicans. *See* Democratic-Republicans

Republic of Letters, 184, 187, 191, 208–209, 276–277, 287, 326, 352, 482, 484

Revivals: and preaching, 2–3, 61, 234, 246, 484; and Revolution, 78; in 1740s, 86–108, 114, 128–129, 350; in Northampton, 114, 118, 128–129; at Yale, 153, 376; in 1790s, 277, 349, 367, 376, 384–385

Rhetoric: and logic, 45, 65–66, 68–71, 130, 136; and head and heart, 105–106, 217, 234, 238–239, 336–337, 484; classical, 336, 395–396; and education, 345, 394–396, 406

Rights: religious, 43, 50–62, 107–108, 111–112, 121, 137, 141–142, 253, 341–344, 347–348; natural, 51–58, 74, 170, 174, 182, 225, 341, 405, 415–416; of conscience, 53–62, 78, 107–108, 111–112, 157, 181–182, 342–344, 445, 482; civil, 57, 142, 263, 381, 387, 414–418, 421, 425–426, 428, 468–469; property, 58, 225, 282, 318–319, 332–334, 405; human, 461, 466–467; and written documents, 470–471

Saints: visible, 41, 110, 116, 123–125, 128, 483; and sinners, 43, 370–371; experience of, 63, 240, 247, 268, 371; in church, 66, 110, 142, 291; and revivals, 93; and covenants, 130

Saltonstall, Gurdon, 24–25, 40–41, 47, 49, 61, 83–85

Satire: in verse, 4, 11–12, 209, 338, 450, 464, 473, 486; David Daggett and, 227, 411, 480; John Trumbull and, 282, 287, 291, 295, 298, 302, 307–327; political, 310–319, 321, 427, 430, 442, 450, 451, 473, 480; Timothy Dwight and, 338, 354, 377; of women, 421

Saybrook Platform: passage of, 24, 39–41; abrogation of, 25, 83, 341, 367, 444; nature of, 39–40, 83, 85, 178; support for, 40–41, 44; in 1740s, 48–49, 51, 68, 154–155; and ecclesiastical organizations, 95, 151; in 1750s, 156; interpretation of, 160

Sedition Act, 404, 453–454, 468, 473–474

Sentimentalism, 239–240, 290–293, 396–397

Separatists: in New England, 7, 51, 87, 104–106, 342, 349–350, 463; Ebenezer Frothingham and, 58, 110, 123–126, 142, 155; Jonathan Edwards and, 102, 113, 123–126, 142; Thomas Clap and, 152–153

Sermons. *See* Preaching

Sherman, Roger, 165, 430, 439–441

Sherwood, Samuel, 74–76, 78

Signification: Jonathan Edwards on, 110, 120–127, 131–133, 139; John Locke on, 126–127; Thomas Clap on, 178; Timothy Dwight on, 353, 365